91
Michelin
2013

THEGREENGUIDE
Switzerland

Winter in Grindelwald with the Wetterhorn just beyond © Grindelwald Tourismus/Switzerland Tourism

MICHELIN

THEGREENGUIDE **SWITZERLAND**

Editorial Director	Cynthia Clayton Ochterbeck
Book Packager	Jonathan Gilbert, Azalay Media
Contributing Writer	John Malathronas
Production Manager	Natasha G. George
Cartography	Alain Baldet, Michèle Cana, John Dear, Peter Wrenn
Photo Editor	Sean Sachon
Interior Design	Chris Bell
Cover Design	Chris Bell, Christelle Le Déan
Layout	Michelin Travel Partner, Jonathan Gilbert, Azalay Media
Cover Layout	Natasha G. George

Contact Us

Michelin Travel and Lifestyle North America
One Parkway South
Greenville, SC 29615
USA
travel.lifestyle@us.michelin.com
www.michelintravel.com

Michelin Travel Partner
Hannay House
39 Clarendon Road
Watford, Herts WD17 1JA
UK
℘01923 205240
travelpubsales@uk.michelin.com
www.ViaMichelin.com

Special Sales

For information regarding bulk sales, customized editions and premium sales, please contact us at:
travel.lifestyle@us.michelin.com
www.michelintravel.com

HOW TO USE THIS GUIDE

PLANNING YOUR TRIP

The blue-tabbed PLANNING YOUR TRIP section gives you **ideas for your trip** and **practical information** to help you organize it. You'll find tours, practical information, a host of outdoor activities, a calendar of events, information on shopping, sightseeing, kids' activities and more.

INTRODUCTION

The orange-tabbed INTRODUCTION section explores **Switzerland Today**, including food and wine, while the **History** section spans from Roman rule to Swiss-EU relations in the early 21C. **Architecture** and **Art** are covered, as well as Switzerland's **Nature,** geology and climate.

DISCOVERING

The green-tabbed DISCOVERING section features Principal Sights by region, featuring the most interesting local **Sights**, **Walking Tours**, nearby **Excursions**, and detailed **Driving Tours**. Admission prices shown are normally for a single adult.

ADDRESSES

We've selected the best hotels, restaurants, cafes, shops, nightlife and entertainment to fit all budgets. See the Legend on the cover flap for an explanation of the price categories. See the back of the guide for an index of hotels and restaurants.

Sidebars

Throughout the guide you will find blue, orange and green-colored text boxes with lively anecdotes, detailed history and background information.

A Bit of Advice

Green advice boxes found in this guide contain practical tips and handy information relevant to your visit or a sight in the Discovering section.

STAR RATINGS★★★

Michelin has given star ratings for more than 100 years. If you're pressed for time, we recommend you visit the ★★★ or ★★ sights first:

★★★ **Highly recommended**

★★ **Recommended**

★ **Interesting**

MAPS

Regional Driving Tours map, Places to Stay map and Sights map.

Region maps.

Maps for major cities and villages.

Local tour maps.

All maps in this guide are oriented north, unless otherwise indicated by a directional arrow. The term "Local Map" refers to a map within the chapter or Tourism Region. A complete list of the maps found in the guide appears at the back of this book.

PLANNING YOUR TRIP

INTRODUCTION TO SWITZERLAND

CONTENTS

© Robert Boesch/Switzerland Tourism

DISCOVERING SWITZERLAND

Welcome to Switzerland

Switzerland, perhaps the most culturally, linguistically and geographically diverse country in western Europe, is located right at its centre, bordered by Germany in the north, Austria in the east, Italy in the south and France in the west. The country is divided into 26 cantons that have been organised into seven regions for the purposes of this Guide and which comprise French-speaking Suisse Romande, bilingual Valais, the mostly German-speaking Bern and Jura, Graubünden, North and Centre, and Italian-speaking Ticino.

SUISSE ROMANDE *(pp84–183)*

This, the most French of the Swiss regions, is often referred to by French speakers as Romandie. It shares a border with France, and the cosmopolitan city of Geneva – home to the monumental Jet d'Eau and the headquarters of many of the world's international organisations – is almost totally surrounded by France. With two of Switzerland's largest lakes, Lakes Geneva (Lac Léman) and Neuchâtel, the region offers much for the visitor to explore, from the mountainous cheese-producing Gruyères region to the medieval city of Fribourg, and Lausanne, world capital of the Olympic Movement.

BERN AND JURA CANTONS
(pp184–239)

Until 1979 the Jura was part of the ancient canton of Bern but opted to leave mainly for linguistic and religious reasons. With no large towns, the Jura is characterised by mountains and valleys and is a major winter sports destination. The Swiss capital, Bern, has a beautiful old town with street after street of arcades and shops to keep even the most enthusiastic shopper happy. The crowning glory of the region is the Bernese Oberland where the iconic mountains of the Eiger, Monch and Jungfrau stand above Brienzer See and Thuner See lakes, and the resort of Interlaken.

THE VALAIS *(pp240–287)*

The French- and German-speaking Valais covers southwest Switzerland and boasts three world-famous ski resorts – Verbier, Crans-Montana and Zermatt – where a full range of winter sports for any ability is available.

Skiiing in Zermatt, Valais

Simon Stankl/Valais Tourism/Switzerland Tourism

Martigny has a fine Roman heritage with a 2C amphitheatre still used for events such as the quirky "Queen of Queens" cow contest. Named after the valley along which the River Rhône flows, the Valais is Switzerland's third largest canton and has 14 mountains over 4 000m/13 123ft, including the iconic Matterhorn.

TICINO *(pp288–317)*

Italian-speaking Ticino, the southernmost canton of the Confederation, combines Latin flair with legendary Swiss orderliness. A mountainous area with the Lepontine Alps in the north, the canton is divided

Gandria by Lake Lugano, Ticino

© Lugano Turismo

by three river systems. The barrier formed by the massif shelters the shores of Lake Maggiore and Lake Lugano, gracing their resorts with a pleasant Mediterranean climate. Bellinzona with its three castles and well deserved UNESCO World Heritage status is an essential city to visit, while for sheer excitement try the *Goldeneye* bungee jump from the Verzasca Dam near Locarno. This southernmost part of the Alps can be fully appreciated when taking the St Gotthard or Lukmanier Pass roads on one of our driving tours.

CENTRAL SWITZERLAND
(pp318–353)

Central Switzerland comprises the cantons of Lucerne, Zug, Schwyz, Uri, Unter-walden and Nidwalden. Apart from Zug, these cantons are all adjacent to scenic Lake Lucerne or, as it is known to most Swiss, the Vierwaldstätter See. The bustling university town of Lucerne, with its fascinating covered wooden bridges, is also the place to embark on the many wonderful boat trips offered on historic vessels such as the *Schwyz* and the *William Tell*. Nearby Mounts Pilatus and Rigi can be accessed by cogwheel railway from Alpnachstad or Vitznau respectively.

GRAUBÜNDEN *(pp354–385)*

This canton is bordered by Austria, Italy and the tiny state of Liechtenstein. Though the majority of the population speak German or Italian, Graubünden is the only canton where the ancient Romansh language continues to be spoken. Several unforgettable train journeys can be taken here, including the amazing Glacier Express. The capital is the fascinating city of Chur, located close to the mighty river Rhine which has its source in the high Alps in the west of the region. Graubünden also boasts the world-renowned and ritzy resorts of St Moritz, Davos and Klosters.

THE NORTH *(pp386–447)*

The North consists of the Cantons of Basle-Land and Basel-Stadt, Aargau, Zürich, Schaffhausen, Thurgau, St Gallen and Appenzell, most of which share a border with Germany or Austria and are therefore German-speaking. Zürich, the financial centre of Switzerland and of the Reformation in German-speaking Switzerland has a fantastic arts scene, world-class museums and great nightlife. The surrounding lush grasslands are epitomised by the green hills of the Emmenthal, traditional dairy-farming country.

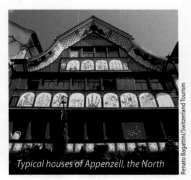
Typical houses of Appenzell, the North

Renato Bagattini/Switzerland Tourism

Cable car from Stechelberg to the Schilthorn
© Jost von Allmen/Schilthornbahn AG/Switzerland Tourism

Michelin Driving Tours

GRAND TOURS

These tours are highlighted on the map on the inside front cover.

SUISSE JURA AND LAKE GENEVA

(650km/400mi)

This tour takes in four splendid lakes (including two of the three largest in Switzerland), the undulating central Swiss Plateau and, for good measure, a few magnificent mountains.

Starting from Geneva and heading north along the shores of Lake Geneva with mountain ranges on either side, you come to the walled town of Nyon. Continuing around the Lake leads to Lausanne and the beautifully situated Montreux. From here the route heads north onto the plateau of the Mittelland past Murten See and on up to the old town of Solothurn. The drive then goes north over the last ridge of the Jura, the Weissenstein, and onto Basel and the River Rhine. The return trip goes into the Jura Mountains before dropping down into Neuchâtel and its vineyard-fringed lake. After leaving the Lake the tour proceeds through the Vallée de Joux, the jewel of the Vaud Jura, and back down to Geneva via Nyon and the tranquil waters of Lac Geneva.

VALAIS AND BERNER OBERLAND

(950km - 590 miles)

The Valais and Berner Oberland drive includes offers a taste of Swiss scenery at its best. It includes some of the most well-known mountains, two or possibly three spectacular mountain passes, a couple of small lakes and a 188km/117.5mi journey along the banks of one of Europe's major rivers, the Rhône.

Beginning at the Swiss capital city of Bern the drive heads south to Thun where there is the option of heading up to the resort of Kandersberg via the beautiful lakeside town of Spiez. Return to the main route and onto Interlaken where again a spur leads to Grindelwald and Murren which both have to views of the magnificent Jungfrau, Monch and Eiger, not to mention most of the Bernese Oberland. Retuning to Interlaken, the route heads to the Susten Pass and the resort of Andermatt which lies at the junction of the St Gotthard and Furka Passes. Here the tour joins the course of the Rhône and follows it along the Furkastrasse all the way to Brig at the foot of the road to the breathtaking Simplon Pass. As the drive continues through the Valais there are various other side routes to barrages and resorts until eventually the wine town of Aigle is reached. The drive turns east here passing over the Alps

Postal bus at the Furka Pass with a view to Grimsel Pass and Finsteraarhorn, Valais

© Christof Sonderegger/Switzerland Tourism

Vaudoises to the resort of Gstaad and then travels through the renowned Gruyères region up to the medieval city of Fribourg before returning to Bern.

GRAUBÜNDEN
(700km/435mi)

The Alpine canton of Graubünden is the country's largest. This driving tour is the best way to enjoy its dramatic and varied landscapes, as well as to reach the little-known Italian-speaking canton of Ticino to its south. Departing from dynamic Davos, head east along the lateral valleys of the Flüela in to the Engandin and stop off at the pretty village of Guarda, before following the Inn river to the spa town of Schuls, set dramatically amid rocky slopes and scattered forests. The route along the lower plateau of the Upper Engandin takes you to the high-altitude resort of Zuoz before you reach sunny St Moritz, "Top of the World" and beloved by winter sports enthusiasts. There's a stunning panorama in almost every direction, especially at the Bernina Massif, right at the edge of Graubünden. Next, head south and west on the historic transalpine San Bernadino Pass to Bellinzona in the sunny Lower Ticino Valley. Lugano, Morcote and Locarno look and feel entirely different from their northern neighbours, and it's easy to linger in any of Ticino's warm and welcoming lakeside resorts. Head north along the St Gotthard Pass road to Andermatt and then east along the thickly wooded Valley of the Vorderrhein, popular with biking, hiking and swimming enthusiasts. Finish at Chur, historical, administrative and religious capital of Graubünden for more than 500 years.

LAKES AND APPENZELLERLAND
(600km/375mi)

Gently rolling hills, flowery meadows and rugged mountains typify Appenzellerland, in the northeast corner of the country, while the lovers of classic lake views will enjoy driving along the shores of some Switzerland's most pristine bodies of water.

Head north from Zürich to Roman Winterthur and then Renaissance Schaffhausen, stopping off at Europe's most powerful waterfalls, Rheinfall. Follow the Sitter Valley next to tranquil Lake Constance to the UNESCO World Heritage Site of St Gallen and then drive south in to the heart of Appenzellerland, before reaching the tiny principality of Liechtenstein. The route skirts the south of Walensee and then takes in Glarus at the foot of the Vorder Glärnisch and numerous lakeshore towns, such as exclusive Seelisberg, pretty Zug and up the Ibergeregg Road to the pilgrimage site of Einsiedeln, in pine-clad, rugged hills. Return to Zürich by driving along the south side of Lake Zürich, the chain of Albis hills stretching up to your left.

LOCAL DRIVES

Use the Discovering section to explore Switzerland's hidden routes in:

- **LES ALPES VAUDOISES**
- **ALTO TICINO**
- **VAL D'ANNIVIERS**
- **LA CHASSERAL**
- **ENGELBERG**
- **ROUTE DE LA FORCLAZ**
- **FURKASTRASSE**
- **INTERLAKEN**
- **VALLÉE DE JOUX**
- **KANDERSTEG**
- **LAKE GENEVA**
- **LOCARNO**
- **LUGANO**
- **MONTREUX**
- **VAL DE MORGINS**
- **SACHSELNER STRASSE**
- **SAN BERNARDINO-STRASSE**
- **ST GALLEN**
- **ST MORITZ**
- **LE VALAIS**
- **LAKE LUCERNE**
- **ZÜRICH**

When and Where to Go

WHEN TO GO

Switzerland's dramatic Alpine peaks, rolling meadows and sparkling lakes change with each season, adding new facets to this natural playground with every visit. This sense of movement is reflected in Switzerland's cosmopolitan cities, which buzz with culture and nightlife, while the rural villages still prefer a timeless, traditional lifestyle.

Europeans have sought Switzerland's snow-covered Alps in **winter** ever since skiing was first invented. Today, skiers and snowboarders alike delight in the country's world-famous resorts (*see WHAT TO SEE AND DO)*; Zermatt is the iconic destination, lounging at the foot of the iconic Matterhorn; exclusive St Moritz is considered to be the oldest ski resort in the world and has hosted the winter Olympics twice (1928 and 1948); while celebrity-studded Gstaad is known for luxurious hotels, shopping and high-society nightlife. The skiing hard core tend to seek out the quieter, but more challenging slopes of Titlis and the glacier plateau of Les Diablerets. Winter is also a magical time to visit Ticino, where a downhill piste can end with palm trees and flowering bushes in this surprisingly temperate Alpine micro-climate. Here on the Italian border, the warmth of Italian *brio* (vigor) tempers legendary Swiss efficiency.

Switzerland's network of hiking and biking trails is open throughout **spring**, **summer** and **autumn**. The routes take in monumental glaciers, churning rivers swelled by glacial meltwater (excellent for white-water rafting) and serene boating and fishing lakes that polka-dot the countryside. Let us not forget golf; one of the highest courses in the world is in Arosa, where golfers often share the 18-hole course with grazing cows. Warmer weather is ideal, too, for a relaxing lake cruise, especially

at sunset; or take a cable car or cog railway to the top of a mountain such as Rigi or Pilatus, and marvel at the unfurling panorama of Alpine peaks.

Festivals abound year-round (*see WHAT TO SEE AND DO)*, celebrating the culture and history of Switzerland and the world at large. The Montreux Jazz Festival each July attracts the world's top musicians; while Christmas markets in numerous cities and villages focus on traditional crafts.

Switzerland's turbulent history has created a chain of **historic castles**, while the historic districts of many major cities, such as Basel, Zürich, Lucerne and Bern, have survived the test of time unscathed. Today, the sandstone city centre arcades house modern shops and boutiques, while the lofty turrets of castles such as Chillon, immortalized by Lord Byron's poem, can be explored for a small fee.

CLIMATE

The climate is temperate, with temperatures rarely higher than 86F/30C in summer, and rarely colder than 41F/-5C in winter, except high in the mountains. The warmest regions are Ticino (Lucarno and Lugano claim 298 sunny days a year), and Valais, south of Lake Geneva. Even so, capricious wind patterns can turn a bright, sunny day into a rainy or snowy one in minutes.

There is no excessive heat or humidity, so the air is always crisp. Southern Switzerland has subtropical vegetation and enjoys year-round mild temperatures.
Weather Reports - 162.

IDEAS FOR YOUR VISIT
SHORT BREAKS (2 DAYS)

Bern

Begin your visit to Bern (*see BERN)* at the **Bear Park** with a 20-minute multimedia tour of the city and a stop at the **Tourist Center** for the audio tour package (2hr) or tickets to the **Old Town Tour** (1hr30min). Follow this with a relaxing river tour of the

View over the Old Town, Bern

© Terence du Fresne/Bern Tourismus/Switzerland Tourism

city by **dinghy**, and then make your way to the **Clock Tower** for a narrated show (1hr). Don't miss the **Botanical Gardens** (1–2hr), as well as the city tours by **horse-drawn carriage** and **tram** (to the summit of the Brienz Rothorn, 1-3hr). The **Postbus** system offers a full day ride through four passes (Grimsel, Nufenen, Gotthard, and Susten) departing from and returning to Bern. Information and tickets are available through the Tourist Office (℘(0)31 328 12 12; www.bern.com).

Geneva

Don't miss out on Geneva's (see GENEVA) **boat tours**, with your choice of paddle wheeler or steamer, and durations of 1hr to one day, many including meals (℘0848 811 848; www.cgn.ch). **Minitrains** offer short (35-55min) trips past the lakefront and rose gardens and parks with the option to stop off at various sites and rejoin the tour at your own pace (**Pâquis Express & Vielle Ville** departing from Rotonde du Mont-Blanc; ℘(0)22 781 04 04; **Trans Eaux-Viviens** deparing from Jardin Anglais ℘(0)22 310 53 00). Geneva also offers a multitude of **cable-car rides** (leave at least 1 hour for round trip with sightseeing) to surrounding peaks and spectacular views (℘(0)22 909 70 00; www.geneve-tourisme.ch).

Lucerne

A visit to Lucerne (see LUCERNE) should begin at the **Chapel Bridge** (30min), followed by a leisurely walk along the stunning shores of **Lake Lucerne**, or a guided tour of the city either by foot (2hr) or by **horse drawn carriage** (1hr; www.Lucerne.org). A trip on the world's steepest cogwheel train to the peak of **Pilatus** (4-5hr) may be combined with boat and cable car rides for the ultimate tour of the region (℘(0)41 329 11 11; www.pilatus. ch). Visit the summit of **Mount Titlis** by train and cable car (5hr total) to explore its glacial caves (www.titlis.ch).

Neuchâtel

A visit to Neuchâtel (see NEUCHÂTEL) is well begun with the **city tour by train** (45min). A guided walking tour provided by the Tourist Office includes a visit to the Old Town's stunning **castle**, which houses the Cantonal Government (1-2hr) and a panoramic view of the town from the **Prison Tower**. The **Laténium Museum** covers 50 000 years of the region (1-2hr), while the **Papilliorama-Nocturama** in nearby Kerzers is home to exotic butterflies and animals. No visit is complete without a cruise on **Lake Neuchâtel**, with options to explore two other lakes in the same trip (2-4hr). For more information: www.juratroislacs.ch.

ONE WEEK

While Switzerland is not a large country it is probably best to concentrate on one region or even one city and its immediate locality if you only have a week at your disposal. With such cultural and linguistic diversity things differ considerably from region to region and there is much to see in each. Most regions are relatively compact and most cities have plenty of interesting sights and attractions either in the centre or nearby. There is also a good selection of local drives at the beginning of the Planning Your Trip chapter (see p13) which are described in detail in the relevant part of the Discovering Section. By selecting one of the cities which is also beside a lake the possibilities are almost endless! Not only that, but Swiss train and bus services are legendary in terms of their service and reliability so it's possible to explore without your own vehicle. Some suggestions are given below:

The Suisse Romande

Geneva is the obvious choice of destination here. Right at the southern end of the Romandie, the city, canton and nearby Vaud have it all. Lake Geneva comes right to the edge of the City centre where it turns into the River Rhône. The magnificent Jet d'Eau can be viewed at fairly close quarters by joining one of the organised walking tours of the harbour and lake shores. There is much of interest in the old city which clusters around the cathedral and will be forever associated with the Reformation.

Ticino

The Ticino in the far southeastern corner of Switzerland provides a little Italian flair combined with legendary Swiss organisation. Both Lugano and Locarno combine beautiful lakeside settings with interesting sights and attractions while the stronghold of Bellinzona offers three amazing castles as well as being a good base for touring the canton.

TWO WEEKS

In two weeks it should be possible to explore parts of at least two regions especially if you have access to a car. A Swiss Rail Pass (see p35) which allows unlimited access to trains, boats and buses throughout the country should enable you to see quite a lot of Switzerland if you wish in this time. it is also possible to include any, or even two or three, of the four driving tours suggested at the beginning of Planning Your Trip (see p12). Further suggestions are:

Jura and Berne

The Jura is one of the more relaxed parts of Switzerland and its green mountain scenery combined with

Excursion boats travel the Lac des Brenets, the Suisse Romande

© Christof Sonderegger/Switzerland Tourism

the absence of large towns make it the ideal place for relaxing walks in summer and skiing in the winter. The Berne canton further south offers the fascinating Swiss capital city of Bern with the UNESCO World Heritage Site of its medieval old town together with first-class shopping. To the south east, however, is what most people associate the Canton with: the Bernese Oberland above Interlaken, which makes a fine base from which to access the legendary mountains of the Jungfrau, Monch and Eiger.

Central Switzerland
The city of Lucerne and the Lake of the same name are at the centre of arguably the most typically Swiss region of all. The old city with its amazing flower decked covered wooden bridges and medieval buildings and squares provides a good base from which to tour the surrounding region. Boat trips around the lake should not be missed.

Valais
The appropriately named Valais in the southeast is an unspoiled region with the fascinating cities of Sion and Martigny to explore as well having the world famous mountain resorts of Zermatt and Crans-Montana to enjoy.

What to See and Do

WINTER SPORTS
Thanks to its mountainous landscape, Switzerland has always been *the* ideal place for a winter holiday. It is, in fact, the first country where winter sports were developed on a large scale. Villages such as St Moritz started to welcome British tourists for the winter season from the early 19C.

In most Swiss resorts, the winter season is from just before Christmas through to early April with the best conditions usually between mid-January and mid-March, depending on the altitude. The latter part of the season offers the advantages of longer days, mild temperatures and far fewer people. In the higher resorts (Zermatt, Saas Fee, St Moritz), snow coverage is generally satisfactory until Easter, even early May in locations above 2 500m/8 202ft. Spring snow is ideal for off-piste skiing.

Most Swiss ski resorts are above the tree line, giving even inexperienced skiers access to summits reaching some 4 000m/13 123ft, and frequently commanding panoramic views. Many resorts have winter hiking trails for long treks along gentle slopes.

If you would rather just bask in the winter sun, you can pull up a chair as a spectator at any of the numerous competitions and events that take place throughout the winter season.

ALPINE SKIING
Switzerland simply has some of the world's best skiing and the world's best known resorts. The largest are the duo of **Davos** (248km/154mi of prepared pistes) and **Klosters** (170km/105.6mi), followed by the ensemble of the Four Valleys (**Verbier** as the main resort with 400km/248.5mi of pistes and the Jungfrau region of **Interlaken, Wengen, Murren,** with 220km/136.7mi of pistes). Some individual resorts are equally as expansive, such as **St Moritz** (230km/143mi of pistes in the Engadin Valley) and **Zermatt** (313km/194.5mi of pistes, including on the Klein Matterhorn glacier). Each resort has impressive modern networks of mountain railways, funiculars, cable cars and drag lifts (t-bars on the glaciers), while the terrain suits all levels of skiers and

Snowshoe excursion in the Chablais region, Valais, Dents-du-Midi in the background

© Christian Perret/Valais Tourism/Switzerland Tourism

snowboarders. Even resorts that are smaller by comparison, such as **Engelberg-Titlis** (82km/51mi of pistes) and **Aletsch** glacier (99km/61.5mi of pistes) have enough terrain to satisfy a ski holiday. Because of their proximity, it is possible to stay in one resort and visit another by train or bus for a day.

Some border resorts have teamed up with their French, Italian or Austrian counterparts, such as the Franco-Swiss resort of **Les Portes du Soleil**, offering 600km/372.8mi of pistes lying mainly in the French resorts of Avoriaz and Morzine Châtel. **Zermatt**'s partnership with Breuil-Cervinia In Italy requires purchase of a separate ski pass for each country. Lastly, there is **Samnaun**, linked to the Austrian resort of Ischgl.

Many Swiss resorts are sought for their charming **architecture**, inspired by local tradition. Some developed from existing villages (Klosters, Arosa, Saas Fee, Zermatt, Adelboden). The chalet style has been preserved in larger resorts like Verbier, which can provide accommodation for up to 25 000 visitors. However, a boom in the popularity of winter holidays spurred the construction of vast, impersonal developments lacking traditional Swiss charm. This is the case with Davos, St Moritz-Bad, Thyon and even Crans-Montana.

SNOWBOARDING

All Swiss resorts welcome snowboarders and many have snowparks with facilities such as half-pipes, boardercross and high jumps, as well as competitive events. The best equipped are Les Diablerets, Saas Fee and Laax, where World Cup events are held every year. Snowboarding was introduced as an official skiing event at the 1998 Winter Olympic Games held in Nagano, Japan.

CROSS-COUNTRY SKIING

Cross-country skiing is one of the most popular sports after downhill skiing. The prettiest sites are in Graubünden (150km/94mi of pistes near St Moritz, 75km/47mi in Davos), at Laax-Flims and in the Gstaad region.

OTHER SNOWSPORTS

Ski touring is a combination of cross-country and alpine skiing. The boots are fastened to the heel for downhill skiing but left free for upward walking. The Swiss Alps offer countless opportunities for this sport, especially between Chamonix and Zermatt and at Engadin. Always use the trails in the company of an experienced mountain guide.

Skijoring, in which one is towed behind a galloping horse, requires the skier to be of moderate skill or better.

St Moritz is one of the resorts that regularly organizes skijoring races.
Walking: All resorts feature signposted packed snow trails near the villages and much higher up (*access by chairlifts*). Some of these trails are more suitable to walking with **snowshoes**. If you are going off the beaten track, it is advisable to go with a guide, especially to avoid areas prone to avalanches.

Many resorts set aside gentle slopes for **snow-tubing**, in which you sit in an inflated donut-like tube. Also, many villages offer **dogsledding**.

Ice-rink sports are a popular feature of Swiss resorts, with many natural or artificial **skating rinks**, both indoors and outdoors. The Swiss are also fond of **ice hockey** and **curling**.

Switzerland is a great place for **sledding**. Many resorts offer kilometres of signposted trails where the snow has been carefully packed. Grindelwald and Saas Fee boast outstanding facilities, with reserved hillsides. Bobsled runs are available for those in search of high-speed excitement , such as the descent (with a pilot) at St Moritz.

OUTDOOR FUN
HIKING AND WALKING

Switzerland's network of public footpaths is one of the world's longest with 68 000km/42 500mi of marked paths. Signs give the length and duration to various stops on the walk. Some footpaths are suitable for children and for wheelchairs. The most attractive of these include the walk around the Tomlishorn on Mount Pilatus, the "cheese circuit" (Käserstatt) on the Halisberg, and the panoramic walk around Aletsch Glacier.

Trail Markings

Signposts with **black on a yellow background** and a yellow lozenge indicate footpaths suitable for children and inexperienced walkers. Mountain hikes for experienced walkers in good physical condition are marked by **yellow signs with a white arrow and red line** and a red lozenge. Difficult footpaths across glaciers, scree or snowfields, which require experience in rock-climbing, are indicated by **blue signs with a white arrow and a thin blue line**; tricky sections are specifically marked and have safety rails and ropes. Signs with **white text on a brown background** highlight cultural sights of interest.

The Swiss Path

Built to celebrate the 700th anniversary of the Swiss Confederation in 1991, this 35km/21.7mi trail edges the fjord-like Lake Uri, the southernmost end of Lake Lucern. Marble markers bearing the

Nordic walking in the Engelberg valley, Central Switzerland

coats of arms of each canton and other information mark different sections of the route, with boat, bus or train connections at each destination. Visit www.weg-der-schweiz.ch for more information.

Information

The **Swiss National Hiking Association** publishes maps and guides, many of which can be bought at bookshops in the country.

A selection of walks is listed at **www.myswitzerland.com**, as well as information on hiking safety and links to organisations such as the Swiss Alpine Club and Wandersite.

If you are interested in a serious hiking holiday, it would be worth contacting the **Swiss National Hiking Association** (ASTP) (Im Hirshalm 49, 4125 Riehen, &(0)61 606 93 40).

HIKES AND WALKS

Bassins Du Doubs

The hikes in this region explore the River Doubs, Lake Brenets, and Chatelot Dam, which form a section of the border with France. A wooded path (2hr15min) leads from the small town of Les Brenets to Brenets Lake's overflow at Doubs Fall (27m/88.6ft). The hike from Les Brenets to Les Roches de Mauron has pleasant views and is quite short (45min). *See p182.*

Val d'Hérens

Alpe Bricola is easily ascended for spectacular views of glaciers and the valleys below (5hr); allow at least 5hr to explore the Cabane des Aiguilles Rouges. *See p263.*

Zermatt

Allow a half day to explore Schwarzsee to Zermatt (*see ZERMATT*) on foot, while experiencing views of the Matterhorn as well as the Zmutt and Arben Glaciers; alternate views are on the hike to Grünsee, Grindjisee and Leisee (beginning with a rack railway ride). Allow at least half a day.

BOAT TOURS

Explore the main Swiss lakes and parts of some major rivers on the large white boats that can be seen cruising up and down. A few of these boats still feature the original paddle wheels.

Mountain bikers near St Moritz, Graubünden

© Markus Greber/ENGADIN St. Moritz/Switzerland Tourism

CYCLING

Swiss Federal Railways (SBB/CFF) and most private railway companies accept bicycles as **accompanied baggage**. Bicycles can be rented in over 100 railway stations and returned to a different station.

The **train + bike** formula includes transport, bicycle hire, and civil liability insurance in case of an accident. Contact the Rail Service ℘0900 300 300; www.rail.ch.

Cycle Routes and Paths

There are nine national cycle routes (3 300km/2 050mi), each starts near a railway station and follows a clearly marked route with signs indicating distances, destinations and altitude differentials. One of the most challenging is the "Alpine Panorama" (480km/298mi); it crosses a dozen mountain passes and finishes at the Klausenpass (alt 1 948m/6 391ft). Switzerland also has over 3 000km/1 864mi of cycle paths. **La Suisse à vélo** publishes detailed guides and a list of hotels specifically recommended for cyclists, with covered bike shelters and repair kits. (P.O. Box 8275, CH 3001 Berne; ℘(0)31 307 47 40. www.suisse-a-velo.ch).

MOUNTAINEERING

Climbing routes pop up throughout Switzerland. The largest is the **Via Ferrata Tälli** in the Bernese Oberland, open to all experience levels, including beginners: the route has 78m/256ft of ladders and 550 steel pitons embedded into the wall of the imposing Gadmerflue, at the Susten Pass. In Liechtenstein, the steep walls of the Eggstöcke, above Braunwald, are also suitable for serious climbing enthusiasts. The www.myswitzerland.com website lists suggested climbs. Most major resorts have their own **climbing school** plus expeditions with trained guides and instructors.

BEACHES

Some of the country's most attractive lakeside beaches are at Lenzerheide on the Heidsee, on Lake Cauma (whose waters are heated by underground streams), and Estavayer-le-Lac, the country's largest natural sandy beach.

Sailing, Windsurfing and Water-skiing

Most larger lakes have their own sailing school. Visit www.myswitzerland.com for further information.

WATER SPORTS

Switzerland's wild Alpine rivers provide some of the best white-water **rafting** in Europe. For more information contact **Swissraft** ℘081 911 5250; www.swissraft.ch. The Rotsee near Lucerne is a particular favorite for **rowing**. **Canoeing and kayaking** are available on many lakes and rivers. **Water parks** are extremely popular and often feature wave machines, huge water slides and swimming pools. Two of the largest are the Säntispark at Abwill, near St Gallen, and the Alpamare at Pfäffikon, near Zürich.

FISHING

Switzerland's 32 000km/19 883mi of rivers and 135 000ha/333 592 acres of lakes are a paradise for anglers. For further information on seasons, regulations and licences, apply to local Tourist Information Centers or **Schweizerischer Fischerei-Verband** (Swiss Fishing Federation), Wankdorffeldstrasse 102, Postfach 261, CH-3000 Bern, ℘(0)31 330 28 02; www.sfv-fsp.ch.

HANG-GLIDING AND PARAGLIDING

Hang-gliding and paragliding competitions are frequently held in Villeneuve in the Lake Geneva region. For information, contact:

Paragliding over Lake Thun

© Markus Zimmermann/Interlaken Tourismus/Switzerland Tourism

Office de Tourisme, *15* Grand-Rue, 1844 Villeneuve; ℘(0)21 960 22 86; http://www.redbull.ch.

ACTIVITIES FOR KIDS

In this guide, sights of particular interest to children are indicated with a symbol. Some attractions may offer discount fees for children. In Switzerland, children can enjoy;

Aigle Adventure Park Vaud
see p142

Appenzell Museum Inner Rhoden
see p442

Basel Zoo *see p411*

Adventure Playground Parco Civico Lugano Ticino *see p292*

Verkehrshaus Transport Museum Lucerne *see p328*

St Bernard Dog Museum Martigny
see p248

Tierpark Peter und Paul St Gallen
see p439

Naturhistorisches Museum Bern
see p193

SPAS

Switzerland has a wealth of thermal spas fed by natural hot springs, often accompanied by luxurious man-made swimming pools, Jacuzzis and saunas. Spas are open to visitors of all ages and are particularly suitable for families. The baths at Saillon and Leukerbad, in the Valais mountains, are popular in summer. **Schweizer Heilbäder**, Avenue des Bains 22, 1400

Yverdon-les-Bains; ℘(0)24 420 15 21; http://www.swissthermalspa.ch.

SHOPPING
OPENING TIMES

Most shops open from 9am–noon and 2–6.30pm (Sat 4pm or 5pm) although in large towns they may not close for lunch. Most towns have a late opening evening often until 9pm. All shops close on Sunday. Some cafés open early and close when the shops close. Others open at lunchtime or later and become bars in the evening, often closing at midnight or even 1am in some cities. Restaurants serve meals only at normal mealtimes and close in between.

TIMEPIECES & JEWELLERY

Bucherer produces timepieces and jewellery, famous for their exceptional craftsmanship (*www.bucherer.com*). Smaller shops operated by fine goldsmiths and watchmakers can be found throughout Switzerland.

SWISS ARMY KNIVES

Victorinox is the country's leading producer of pocket knives and multi-tools, whose line also inlcudes apparel, luggage and other products celebrating the highest quality of the Swiss-made tradition. (Schmiedgasse 57, CH-6438 Ibach-Schwyz; ℘(0)41 818 12 11; www.victorinox.com).

The Swiss Army Knife

The Swiss penknife, an essential part of any Boy Scout's kit, is recognizable by its red handle, white cross logo and rounded corners (accept no imitations). This gem of the miniature cutlery industry was originally created over a century ago as a Swiss army field knife. Within a short time, the **"Schweizer Militärmesser"**, or Swiss Army Knife, became world famous and was adopted by outdoor and do-it-yourself enthusiasts worldwide. Today there are over 400 different models, ranging from the most basic to extremely sophisticated, including models specifically for left-handed users. Designs can include an altimeter, a barometer, a computer USB memory card, and a range of fashionable colours. It deserves its nickname as the world's smallest toolbox, one which can cut, slice, file, carve, sharpen, remove bottle tops, tighten, loosen, measure, download and more.

The Swiss Army Knife is made by Victorinox, whose factory is in Schwyz (*See Shopping*).

GOURMET FOODS

Swiss Chocolate

Switzerland is home to some of the world's finest chocolatiers. Internationally recognised brands, such as Lindt and Frey, can be found in most grocery and speciality shops.

Cheese

Over 450 cheese makers produce local varieties as well as the popular Emmental (Swiss Cheese), Appenzeller, Gruyère, Sbrinz, and Tête de Moine. For traditional national recipes and information on specific dairies (often open for visits and tours) contact **Switzerland Cheese Marketing AG**, Brunnmattstrasse 21 Postfach, 3001 Bern; ℘(0)31 385 26 26; www.switzerland-cheese.ch.

VAT REFUND

With the **Global Refund** system, any non-resident can get back the 7.6% VAT on any purchase of CHF400 or more as long as it is exported within the thirty days. Vouchers received at the time of the purchase are stamped by customs officials, and then turned in with several payment options. **Global Blue Schweiz** *AG, Zürichstrasse 38, 8306 Brüttisellen; ℘0800 32 111 111; www.global-blue.com/destinations/switzerland.*

Swiss chocolate

© Francois Bertin/Switzerland Tourism

Markets

Adelboden – Adelboden traditional autumn market; early Oct. Culinary specialities and arts and crafts produced locally and nationally are offered for sale in the bustling main street.

Les Mosses – The country's highest grocer's market and flea market Jun–Sept, Sun; www.lesmosses.ch.

Vevey – Vevey Folk Market, 2nd week July until end August. Known locally as *Marchés Folkloriques*, these markets attract at least 2 000 visitors who come to buy and listen to brass bands and folk music.

DUTY-FREE

The **Zürich Airport** offers one of the largest duty-free malls available. ℘(0)43 816 22 11; www.flughafen-zuerich.ch.

SIGHTSEEING
ALPINE TRAINS

Swiss Pre-Alps

The **Voralpen-Express** running between Romanshorn and Lucerne provides a link between Lake Constance and Lake Lucerne. This 2hr30min trip affords delightful views of the pre-Alpine ranges and lakeside country; www.voralpen-express.ch.

The **GoldenPass Line** offers panoramic views between Lucerne and Montreux via the Brünig Pass, Lake Brienz to Interlaken (6hr). You can stop at Interlaken for the excursion to Jungfraujoch (3 454m/11 332ft), on the highest railway in Europe. The Golden pass line also offers trips (🕐*all year; www.goldenpass.ch*) on the **Train du Chocolat** that runs between Montreux, on the Swiss Riviera, and Gruyères, home of the famous cheese and milk chocolate. The trip includes coffee and croissants, entrance to the château and cheese factory at Gruyères, and a visit to the **Cailler-Nestlé** chocolate factory, including a tasting (🕐 *daily Jul–Oct, Mon, Wed and Thu May –June, Sep-Oct).*

The **Train du Vignoble** (*13km/8mi; www.lavauxexpress.ch*) operates in the Lavaux, along the shores of Lake Geneva, passing through wine-growing countryside with vineyard, wine cellar and museum stops

Graubünden (Grisons)

The **Bernina-Express** links Chur to St Moritz and the Bernina Pass (2 253m/7 392ft) in 4hr, with an onward bus connection to Tirano (Italy) and Lugano.

The **Heidi-Express** travels between Landquart and Tirano (Italy) via Davos and the Bernina Pass (4hr).

The famous **Glacier-Express** links Zermatt and Chur to St Moritz or Davos (7hr 30min), passing through the majestic Alps, crossing 291 bridges, and negotiating 91 tunnels. The route crosses the Oberalp Pass (2 033m/6 670ft) by rack railway from Andermatt; www.glacierexpress.ch.

The **Engadin Star** links Landquart to St Moritz (9hr), passing through the new Vereinatunnel and crossing the Engadin; www.rhb.ch.

Valais

The **Saint Bernard Express** runs from Martigny to Orsières (30min) through the Vallée de la Dranse. In summer (Jun–late Sept), there is a bus connection to Champex-Lac, La Fouly and the Great Saint Bernard hospice (55min); www.momc.ch

The **Mont Blanc Express** runs through the Trient and Vallorcine valleys, linking France and Switzerland between Martigny and Le Fayet, stopping at Argentière, Chamonix and Les Houches.

The **Allalin-Express** leaves from Bern or Interlaken to Brig; continue by bus to Saas Fee, a charming village closed to road traffic. You then have the option of taking the **Alpin-Express** (45min) to a huge glacial cave hollowed out of the landscape at an altitude of 3 500m/11 483ft.

Heidi-Express on Alp Grüm, Graubünden

© Peter Donatsch/Rhaetische Bahn/Switzerland Tourism

Ticino

The **William Tell Express** links central Switzerland to the Ticino area, taking passengers by paddle boat from Lucerne to Lugano or Locarno on Lake Maggiore. The journey (6hr) then continues by train. The trip only runs from north to south from May–Oct. The **Centovalli Railway** connects Berne to Locarno through the Simplon Tunnel to Domodossola in Italy (4hr); www.centovalli.ch.

STEAM TRAINS

Steam trains operate mostly during the summer, especially weekends.

Vaud canton:
- Blonay-Chamby ☎(0)21 943 21 21
- Le Pont-Le Brassus ☎(0)21 845 17 77
- Lausanne-Échallens-Bercher nicknamed "La Brouette" (The Wheelbarrow) ☎(0)21 886 20 00

Neuchâtel canton:
- St Sulplice-Travers ☎(0)32 751 38 07.

Bernese Mittelland:
- Ballenberg steam train www.ballenberg-dampfbahn.

Valais:
- Rhone Glacier steam train www.furka-bergstrecke.ch

Lucerne canton:
- Sursee-Triengen www.dampfzug.ch.

Steam train of Dampfbahn Furka-Bergstrecke AG at the Rhone glacier, Valais

© Christof Sonderegger/Switzerland Tourism

Boat cruise on the Lake Geneva

© Regis Colombo/Lausanne Tourisme/Switzerland Tourism

BUS TOURS

The **Palm-Express** links St Moritz with Lugano by post bus, crossing the Upper Engadin region before heading to Val Bregaglia and Lake Como.

The **Romantic Route Express** leaves Andermatt by the Furka Pass (2 431m/7 973ft) and follows the Rhône Glacier as far as Gletsch. The tour passes over the Grimsel Pass (2 165m/7 101ft), through the Hasli Valley, to Meiringen and Grindelwald, at the foot of the north face of the Eiger; www.post.ch.

LAKE BOATS

The steamer is another familiar site. Many serve meals. On Greifensee, Lake Brienz, Lake Constance, Lake Geneva, Lake Lucerne, Lake Maggiore, Lake Thun, and Lake Zürich, traditional steamboats also provide regular ferry services. The Swiss Boat Pass (*www.vssu.ch*) costs only CHF 80 and is valid for one year. It entitles you to unlimited travel at half fare throughout Switzerland on the network of the 16 ASNC-member companies.

MUSEUM PASS

The **Swiss Museums Passport** provides entry to 400 museums, including temporary exhibitions. The pass can be purchased at major Tourist Offices or participating museums.

(Hornbachstrasse 50, Zürich ✆(0)44 389 84 56; hosting.museumspass.ch).

BOOKS
SWITZERLAND / REFERENCE

The Early Mountaineers by Francis Gribble (1899). Accounts of pre-19C Alpine exploration and engineering.

Winter in the Alps: Food by the Fireside by Manuela Darling-Gansser (2008). Exploration of Swiss culture through its cuisine; includes cookbook section.

Turner in the Alps by David Hill (1992). Accounts of travels in France & Switzerland in 1802.

Historical Dictionary of Switzerland by Leo Schelbert (2007). Swiss history, part of the Historical Dictionaries of Europe series.

Target Switzerland: Swiss Armed Neutrality in World War II by Edward Whymper (1998). Discusses the controversy around WWII and Swiss neutrality during and after the Nazi threat

Swiss Watching: Inside Europe's Landlocked Island. by *Diccon Bewes (2010).* An Englishman in Switzerland observes the country and its people with a sharp eye and plenty of humour.

BIOGRAPHY

François de Bonivard and his Captivity —The Prisoner of Chillon by Lord Byron (2004).

FICTION

Swiss Family Robinson by Johann David Wyss,(1812). Chidren's story about a family stranded on an island.

Heidi by Johanna Spyri (1880). Enchanting story of a girl's youth in the Swiss Alps.

Dr Fischer of Geneva or The Bomb Party by Graham Greene (1980). A satire on capitalism and how greed can corrupt, Set in Geneva and around Lake Geneva.

The Cow by Beat Sterchi (2000). A first novel about a Spanish guest worker in Switzerland who works on a dairy farm and later an abattoir, experiences which finally destroy him.

FILMS
FILMED IN SWITZERLAND

Star Wars III: Revenge of the Sith (2005). Continuation of the Star Wars saga. Grindelwald Mountains appear as a backdrop.

Syriana (2005). A political thriller starring George Clooney, Matt Damon (as an analyst based in Geneva), and Jeffrey Wright.

GoldenEye (1995). Modern adventures of the classic James Bond tales, starring Pierce Brosnan. Verzasca Dam base jump.

Frankenstein (1994). Oscar-nominated performance by Robert DeNiro of Mary Shelley's classic horror tale. Scenes shot in the Swiss Alps.

A View to a Kill (1985). More action from Ian Fleming's James Bond series, starring Roger Moore and Christopher Walken. Various Swiss Alps locations.

On Her Majesty's Secret Service (1969). Starring George Lazenby, this James Bond thriller was nominated for a Golden Globe. Scenes shot on Piz Gloria and in Bern.

Goldfinger (1964). The adventures of Ian Fleming's James Bond, starring Sean Connery who won an Oscar for his role in this film. Located outside Geneva.

Heidi (1954). The classic book brought to life, starring Elsbeth Sigmund. Various Swiss locations.

The Bourne identity (2002). A spy film based on a novel of the same name by Robert Ludlum starring Matt Damon and set partially in Zürich.

Five Days One Summer (1982). A romance directed by Fred Ziinemann starring Sean Connery who plays a middle-aged Scottish doctor on holiday in the Alps.

Heidi (1954)

© UPPA/Photoshot

Calendar of Events

The Swiss find something to celebrate all year round and many regional Tourist Offices publish brochures listing local festivals, fairs, carnivals and other events. Forthcoming events can also be found on their websites. The National Day on 1 Aug (⌂ *see p29*) is celebrated around the country. From regionally celebrated Swiss home-cooking to Switzerland's popular haute cuisine, there are myriad festivals that make the best of the country's ingredients and rich culinary heritage.

JANUARY

Solothurn — Swiss Film Festival
Davos — World Economic Forum
Château D'Oex — International Hot Air Balloon Week
Basel — Vogel Gryff - Festival of the Griffin (in Kleinbasel)

FIRST MONDAY IN LENT

Basel — Carnival (3 days)

Carnival, Basel
© Philipp Giegel / Switzerland Tourism

FEBRUARY

Dorf Lenk, Gadmen — International Sled Dog Races
Scuol, Engandine — Burning of Hom Strom (First weekend of February)

Engadin — International Free-Ride Competition
late Feb:
Ticino — Traveling carnival with risotto served outdoors

MARCH
early Mar:
Fribourg — International Film Festival
Bellinzona — Rabadan Carnival
Geneva — International Motor Show
Basel — European Watch, Clock and Jewellery Fair

APRIL

Geneva — Chocolate Festival
Caprices — Caprices Festival (Music)
Zürich — Sechseläuten: a spring festival to mark the end of winter; including burning of "Böögg" (Old Man Winter)
late Apr:
Aarberg — Second-hand market
Appenzell — Landsgemeinde: open-air assembly
mid-Apr–mid-May:
Morges — Tulip Festival
late Apr–early May:
Montreux — International "Golden Rose" Television Festival
late Apr–early May:
Zürich — 2nd International Bach Days

MAY
first Sun in May:
Glarus — Landsgemeinde
Berne — International Jazz Festival
late May–early Jun: l
Beromünster — Ascencion Day
May or Jun:
Appenzell, Fribourg, Saas-Fee Lötschental: Kippel, Ferden, Wiler, Blatten — Corpus Christi Thursday processions

JUNE

Basel — International Art Fair (modern and contemporary art)
Boverasse — Absinthe Festival (mid-June)
Sierre — International Comic Book Festiva

Jazz Festival on the Piazza della Riforma, Lugano

© Lugano Turismo

late Jun–early Jul:
Ascona — New Orleans Jazz Festival
late Jun–Sept:
Interlaken — Open-air performances
    of Schiller's *William Tell* in German

JULY
Fribourg (even years) — International
    Jazz Festival
Lausanne — Athlétissima:
    International Athletics Meeting
Lugano — Jazz Festival
Montreux — International
    Jazz Festival
Nyon — Paléo Festival: International
    Open-Air Rock and Folk Music

LATE JULY/EARLY AUGUST
Montreux, Vevey, La Tour-de-Peilz
    — Léman Tradition Festival

LATE JULY/EARLY SEPTEMBER
Gstaad/Saanen — Classical
    Music Festival

AUGUST
Geneva — Genevese festivities;
    floral floats and fireworks
Locarno — International Film Festival
Saignelégier — National horse show,
    fair and horse racing (second
    weekend in August)
Montreux — Comedy Festival
mid-Aug–early Sep:
Lucerne — International Music Weeks
late Aug:

Fribourg — International
    Folk Festival
Vevey — Street Theatre Festival
Aarberg — Second-hand
    Antique Market
late Aug–early Oct:
Ascona — International Classical
    Music Festival
Brunnen—More than 25 private
    providers turn the village into a
    huge restaurant (late Aug).
    www.brunnentourismus.ch.

SEPTEMBER
Saas-Fee — Pilgrimage to the
    Hohen Stiege Chapel — Early Sept

The National Festival

Throughout Switzerland the
anniversary of the alliance
sworn on 1 August 1291 by the
representatives of Uri, Schwyz and
Unterwalden, is commemorated
with patriotic demonstrations,
fireworks displays and spectacular
mountaintop bonfires. It has
been held every year since and is
thought to be the first national
day to be celebrated anywhere
in the world. The historic sites of
Lake Uri, especially the Rütli Field
where a vow of brotherhood was
taken, and the Axenstrasse, are
floodlit for the occasion.

Christmas Market at Klosterplatz Square, Einsiedeln

© Christof Sonderegger/Switzerland Tourism

Christmas Markets and Fairs

Brunnen – The city's former wine cellars are turned into the venue for over 50 Christmas stalls.

Einsiedeln – Held in the Klosterplatz Square; over 140 themed wooden huts.

Lucerne – Christkindlimarkts at both the railway station and Löwenplatz

Ticino – Local townships and villages celebrate with markets and fairs. Markets at Airolo and Bellinzona mid Dec; Biasca and Locarno just before Christmas.

Pilatus – At 2 132m/6 995ft and held in the restaurant during mid-November, this is probably the highest Christmas Market of all.

Zürich – Zürich Christkindlimarkt, the largest indoor Christmas Market in Europe claiming to have over 15,000 visitors per day. Late Nov–Christmas Eve.

Zürich (Albisgütli) —
Knabenschiessen (Shooting Contest): a competition for Zürich schoolchildren

mid-Sept:

Locarno—Festival of Grapes (mid-Sept)

Lausanne — Swiss Trade Fair (Late Sept)

Neuchâtel —
Grape Harvest Festival

Charmey — Fête de la Désalpe

Martigny — Valais Fair

Vevey — Festival Images (photography, cinema, multimedia)

Pratz—Wine Festival (late Sept)

OCTOBER

St Gallen — National Show for the Dairy and Farming Industry

Lugano — Autumn Festival

Châtel-St-Denis — Bénichon (Benediction or harvest) festival

Bulle— Gruyère gastronomic fair (late Oct–early Nov

Basle —Basel Wine Fair (late Oct-Nov)

NOVEMBER

Bern — Zibelemärit (4th Monday)

DECEMBER

Geneva — Feast of the Escalade

Fribourg — St Nicholas parade and fair

Zibelemärit, Bern

© Christof Sonderegger/Switzerland Tourism

Know Before You Go

USEFUL WEBSITES

www.myswitzerland.com
The Swiss National Tourist Office (SNTO) website is full of practical information on destinations, accommodations, weather, events and festivals. Another section provides suggestions for specific types of holiday experiences, including family, golf, wellness spas and, of course, skiing. There are links to each region, within which there are links to individual destinations.

www.alpseurope.com
The Alpine Tourist Commission is a marketing organization for the five Alpine countries of Austria, France, Germany, Italy and Switzerland, with links to tour operators, airlines and special travel package offers.

www.visiteurope.com
The European Travel Commission provides useful travel information for 27 countries, plus links to rail schedules, car rental agencies, weather reports and more.

www.swissinfo.org
This website has comprehensive information about Swiss business, industry, education and politics. There also are links to developments in the arts, science and technology that involve Switzerland.

www.switzerland.tv
A guide to Swiss products and services, including chocolate, watches, cheese, private medical clinics and spas, plus banks and business centres. There also are links to shopping by city or category of product.

www.swisstravelsystem.ch
Comprehensive information about the various Swiss Pass options for train, bus, boat, cable car and other public transport.

TOURIST OFFICES
SWISS NATIONAL TOURIST OFFICES (SNTO)

For information, brochures, maps and assistance in planning your trip, contact the relevant national office. (www.myswitzerland.com)

♦ **Headquarters**
Switzerland Tourism, PO Box 695, 8027 Zürich, ☎ international toll free 00 800 100 200 29.

♦ **United Kingdom**
Switzerland Tourist Board, 30 Bedford St, London WC2E 9ED, ☎(0)20 7420 4900.

♦ **United States**
Swiss Center, 608 Fifth Avenue, New York City, NY 10020-2303, ☎International toll free 011 800 100 200 29.

Other Locations
There are also SNTO locations in the following cities: Amsterdam, Brussels, Frankfurt, Madrid, Milan, Paris, Rome, Stockholm, Tokyo and Vienna.

TOURIST INFORMATION

Information Centres
Look for the 🅸 *on town maps.*
Tourist Information Centres (Verkehrsbüro; office de tourisme; ente turistico) can be found in most large towns and tourist resorts. Their contact details are shown after the introduction to each principal sight, where applicable.

Information Association
A total of 23 towns from several different cantons have joined to form an organisation providing information to visitors. The towns involved are Appenzell, Baden, Basel, Bellinzona, Bern, Biel/Bienne, Chur, Fribourg, La Chaux-de-Fonds, Geneva, Lausanne, Lugano, Montreux, Neuchâtel, St Gallen, Schaffhausen, Sierre, Sion, Solothurn, Winterthur, Thun, Zug and Zürich.

For further information, contact:
Information and Reservation Center, Chur Tourismus, Grabenstrasse 5, CH-7002 Chur; ℘(0)81 252 18 18;

Hotel Association
Swiss Hotel Association
(Schweizer Hotelier-Verein) – Monbijoustrasse 130, CH 3007 Bern; ℘(0)31 370 41 11; Fax (0)31 370 44 44; www.swisshotels.ch.

INTERNATIONAL VISITORS
SWISS EMBASSIES AND CONSULATES ABROAD

United Kingdom
Swiss Embassy, 16-18 Montagu Place, London W1H 2BQ; ℘020 7616 6000; www.eda.admin.ch/london.

Republic of Ireland
Swiss Embassy, 6 Ailesbury Road, Ballsbridge, Dublin 4; ℘353 1 218 63 82/83; www.eda.admin.ch/dublin.

United States
Swiss Embassy, 2900 Cathedral Avenue NW, Washington DC 20008, ℘202 745 7900; www.eda.admin.ch/washington (with consulates in 26 major cities and Puerto Rico).

Canada
Swiss Embassy, 5 Marlborough Avenue, Ottawa ON K1N 8E6, ℘613 235 1837; www.eda.admin.ch/canada (plus seven provincial consulates).

FOREIGN EMBASSIES AND CONSULATES IN SWITZERLAND

United Kingdom
♦ **Embassy**, Thunstrasse 50, CH-3000 Bern 15; ℘(0)31 359 77 00; www.ukinswitzerland.fco.gov.uk.
♦ **Consulate General**, rue de Vermont 37-39, Geneva; ℘(0)22 918 2400.
♦ **Vice-Consulate**, Hegibachstrasse 47, CH-8032 Zürich; ℘(0)44 383 65 60.

Republic of Ireland
♦ **Embassy**, Kirchenfeldstrasse 68, CH-3005 Bern; ℘(0)31 352 14 42.
♦ **Consulate General**, Claridenstrasse 25, Postfach 562, 8027 Zürich; ℘(0)41 289 25 15.

United States
♦ **Embassy**, Jubiläumstrasse 93, 3001 Bern; ℘(0)31 357 70 11; http://bern.usembassy.gov.
♦ **Consulate General**, rue Versonnex 7 Geneva; ℘(0)22 840 51 60.
♦ **Consulate**, Dufourstrasse 101, c/o Zürich America Center, 8008 Zürich; ℘(0)43 499 29 60.

Canada
♦ **Embassy**, Kirchenfeldstrasse 88, 3000 Bern 6, ℘(0)31 357 32 00; www.canada-ambassade.ch.
♦ **Consulate** , 5 avenue de l'Ariana, 1202 Geneva; ℘(0)22 919 92 00.

ENTRY REQUIREMENTS

Visitors travelling to Switzerland must have a valid national passport, including citizens of European Union countries (in case of loss or theft, report to the embassy or consulate and the local police). Entry visas are required for Australian, European, New Zealand, Canadian, and US citizens if the intended stay exceeds 90 days. The nearest Swiss consulate or embassy will help if there is any doubt. US citizens may find the booklet **Safe Trip Abroad** useful for information on visa requirements, customs regulations, medical care, etc. when travelling in Europe. Contact the Superintendent of Documents, *PO Box* 371954, Pittsburgh, PA 15250-7954; ℘(202) 512 1800; www.access.gpo.gov; www.bfm.admin.ch.

CUSTOMS REGULATIONS

There are no restrictions concerning the import, export and exchange of Swiss francs. Switzerland is not a member of the EU and has stricter conditions for the import and export of goods; contact the Swiss Tourist Office (&see Tourist Offices) for more information. Tourists under the age of 17 are not allowed to import or export alcohol or tobacco.

Pets brought into Switzerland require a veterinary certificate stating that the animal has been vaccinated against rabies in your home country, except for puppies and kittens aged under-3 months, which simply require a health certificate issued by a veterinary surgeon. For further information, contact: **Swiss Federal Veterinary Office (FVO)**, Schwarzenburgstr. 155 Bern; &(0)31 323 30 33; www.bvet.admin.ch.

HEALTH

Visitors are strongly advised to have medical or travel insurance to cover personal accident and sickness. There is no state health service in Switzerland and patients are required to pay for all medical treatment (keep any receipts). Special winter sports policies should be arranged where required.

For more information contact the **International Association for Medical Assistance to Travellers** (www.iamat.org).

ACCESSIBILITY

Many of the sights described in this guide are accessible to those with special needs. Sights marked with the & symbol offer wheelchair access. However, it is always advisable to check beforehand by telephone. More than 170 Swiss railway stations have wheelchair ramps. Trains that do not have lifts may be accessed by notifying the **SBB Call Center** (&0800 00 71 02) at least one hour prior to boarding. Those travelling from abroad should call for assistance 3 days ahead of arriving &41 51 225 71 50. Some cog railways and mountain cable cars also are wheelchair accessible, but the volunteer system **Compagna** will respond to any request for help accessing sites not already equipped

&41 71 220 16 09. Local Tourist Offices can also give information on accessibility options.

Larger lake steamers are wheelchair-accessible, but it is best to avoid purchasing a first-class ticket, which requires climbing steep stairs.

An **International Wheelchair Badge** on the dashboard of your vehicle is required to park in designated spots. Large modern and renovated hotels and holiday apartments usually have special disabled facilities such as wide-door bathrooms and roll-in showers; inns and pensions may have only cramped elevators. Larger cities and towns have wheelchair-accessible public toilets, most often unisex facilities, marked with the & wheelchair symbol.

Mobility International Switzerland (MIS) publishes a guide for wheelchair users. Froburgstrasse 4, CH-4600 Olten, &(0)62 212 67 40. www.mis-ch.ch.

Access-Able (http://access-able.com) provides a multitude of resources for the disabled and elderly.

SwissTrac wheelchair power unit attaches to your existing or rented chair, and enables ease of movement over all terrains including curbs, grass, and nature paths &(0)41 854 80 20, www.swisstrac.ch.

Mobility assistance at Zürich Airport

© Careport AG

Getting There and Getting Around

BY PLANE

The world's top airlines, including the Swiss National Airline, Swiss, operate scheduled flights to Basel, Geneva and Zürich, plus budget airlines such as easyJet (www.easyjet.com). There is also a domestic service to Lugano.

CONNECTIONS WITH AIRPORTS

Geneva and Zürich airports both have rail stations with regular services to all major cities and to their own city centres; shuttle buses also operate from Basel, Bern and Lugano airports (between 15min and 20min). Taxis are available at each airport.

Fly-Rail

This service allows visitors flying into Zürich or Geneva to have their luggage transported directly to the railway station nearest to their destination. It also operates for out-going flights from 50 railway stations in Switzerland to the passenger's final destination. **Swiss Federal Railways** ℘0900 300 300; www.rail.ch.

BY TRAIN
INTERNATIONAL RAIL

For travellers coming from the UK, **Eurostar** (℘08705 186 186; www.eurostar.com) operates high-speed passenger trains (**TGV**) to Paris from London St Pancras International. From Paris, the high-speed trains run to a number of cities in Switzerland, including Geneva, Lausanne (with some trains calling at Montreux, Aigle, Bex, Martigny, Sion, Sierre, Visp and Brigue) and Zürich (with stops at Neuchâtel and Berne). All trains leave from the Gare de Lyon, with the exception of the train to Basel, which operates from the Gare de l'Est. Direct TGV trains also run to Neuchâtel and Bern from Dijon.

Switzerland's Main Railway Bridges
Sitterviadukt (St Gallen): 97m/319ft
Wiesenviadukt (Graubünden): 92m/302ft
Solisbrücke (Graubünden): 85m/278ft
Viaduc de Grandfey (Fribourg): 82m/269ft
Reussbrücke (Uri): 77m/252ft
Meienreussbrücke (Uri): 71m/232ft
Langwiesviadukt (Graubünden): 66m/216ft
Landwasserviadukt (Graubünden): 65m/214ft

NATIONAL RAIL

Within Switzerland, the extensive Swiss railway system operates a frequent and efficient service. For tickets, prices and discounts apply to:

- ◆ **Rail Europe**, 178 Piccadilly, London W1; ℘08448 484 064; www.raileurope.co.uk.
- ◆ **Swiss Federal Railways** (SBB/CFF); ℘0900 300 300 (within Switzerland); www.sbb.ch.
- ◆ **Railaway** Zentralstrasse 7, Lucerne ℘(0)51 227 36 40; www.railaway.ch.

The Swiss rail network covers about 4 989km/3 100mi. Swiss trains are famous worldwide for running on time. All major cities and large towns have excellent connections and regular services. Trains include fast intercity trains (IC); regular direct trains; regional trains serving destinations normally considered to be off the beaten track; rack railways

Switzerland's Longest Railway Tunnels
Lötschber base Tunnel (Bern, Zermatt): 34.6km/21.5mi (2007)
Simplon (Valais): 19.8km/12mi (1906)
Furka (Valais, Uri): 15.4km/9.5mi (1982)
St Gotthard (Uri, Ticino): 15km/9.3mi (1882)
Ricken (St Gallen): 8.6km/5.4mi
Grenchenberg (Solothurn, Berne): 8.6km/5.4mi
Hauenstein (Solothurn, Basel): 8.1km/5mi

in the mountains; scenic railways and steam railways; not forgetting funicular railways, cable-cars, chairlifts and underground trains. Motorail services also operate between Kandersteg and Goppenstein (Lötschberg), Brig and Iselle di Trasquera in Italy (Simplon), Thusis and Samedan (Albula), Oberwald and Realp (Furka) and Andermatt and Sedrun (Oberalp).

SWITZERLAND'S LONGEST ROAD TUNNELS	
St Gotthard (Uri, Ticino): 16.3km/10.2mi (1980)	
Seelisberg (Nidwalden, Uri): 9.3km/5.8mi (1981)	
San Bernardino: 6.6km/4mi (1967)	
Gr St Bernhard (Graubünden): 5.9km/3.6mi (1964)	
Belchen (Solothurn, Bern): 3.2km/1.9mi	
Landwasser (Graubünden): 2.8km/1.7mi	
Isla Bella (Ticino): 2.4km/1.4mi	
Binn (Valais): 1.9km/1.1mi	

SWISS TRAVEL SYSTEM

The Swiss public transport system is second to none, especially in large cities where buses, trams and trolleycars operate a highly efficient service. Automatic **ticket machines** are available at each stop (exact change often required). **Swiss Pass** holders are entitled to free, unlimited travel.

TRAVEL PASSES

The **Swiss Travel System** (STS) offers several different 1st and 2nd class passes. These can be purchased from Swiss National Tourist Offices, local travel agents or railway stations upon presenting a passport or identity card. The **Swiss Pass** allows visitors unlimited travel on a network of 16 000km/12 000mi of trains, boats, postal buses, tramways and urban bus services in 35 Swiss cities and towns. Discounts are also offered on many mountain and panoramic railways and a 15% reduction is available for two people or more. The Swiss pass is valid for 4, 8, 15, 22 days or one month, and also serves as a discount card for many museums and sightseeing tours.

The **Swiss Flexipass** allows 3, 4, 5, or 6 days unlimited travel in a one month period, with a 15% discount for two people or more, also serving as a discount card.

The **Swiss Youth Pass** is a discounted version of the Flexipass for those under 26 years of age; children up to the age of 16 traveling with at least one parent with a valid STS ticket travel free of charge on the entire network.

The **Swiss Card** entitles visitors to a 50% discount on trains, postal buses and mountain railways in one area. For groups of 2 to 5 , the **SaverPass** provides unlimited travel on the Swiss Travel System including trains, buses and boats . Passes are available for 4, 8, 15, or 22 days and one month and include the discount benefits on local attractions and tours as well.

The **Swiss Transfer Ticket** includes two transfers by rail between any Swiss airport or border town plus any one destination in Switzerland plus a 50% discount on all further train, bus or boat travel in between. Each transfer must be completed in one day.

The **Swiss Museum Passport** provides free entry to more than 420 museums and exhibits. Family and plus passes available for those traveling with children ℘(0)44 389 84 56, www.museumspass.ch.

POSTAL BUSES

The famous **postal buses** (*postauto*) usually leave from train stations or post offices and for many visitors provide a leisurely, inexpensive and scenic way to visit remote villages. There is currently a plan to fit 70 per cent of them with free wi-fi, so check when you board. **PostBus Switzerland Ltd**. Aareckstrasse 6, CH-3800 Interlaken, ℘(0)33 828 88 28, www.postbus.ch.

BY CAR
MAIN ROUTES

Visitors traveling by road from one of the Channel ports can choose one of two main routes: via **Calais** and the French motorway system through **France** (A 26 to Troyes, A 5 to Langres, A 31 to Beaune, A 6 to Mâcon and A 40 to Geneva—about 800km/500mi); or via **Ostende** and then through **Belgium, Luxembourg, France** and **Germany** (along E 40 to Liège, E 25 to Luxembourg, A 31 to just north of Metz, and the A 4 to Strasbourg, where you cross the Rhine and the German border to pick up the E 35 (A 5) to Basel—about 700km/450mi).

PLANNING YOUR ROUTE

Michelin's national Swiss map 729 covers all of Switzerland, including a list of towns and enlarged maps of the main cities. More detailed orange maps covering the North (551), South-West (552) and South-East (553) indicate very narrow roads (single track, where overtaking is difficult or impossible), gradients, difficult or dangerous roads, tunnels and the altitudes of passes.

The itineraries described in this guide often follow local roads that may intimidate drivers unfamiliar with mountain driving. All of these roads are accessible, at least in summer. The Michelin maps mentioned above highlight **snowbound roads** (with their opening and closing dates) as well as the location of emergency telephones.

Michelin offers a computerised route-finding system integrating information about roads, tourist sights, hotels and restaurants available on the **internet** at www. ViaMichelin.com. For route planning, specify your point of departure and destination, stipulate your preference for motorways or local roads and it will do the rest. The website also gives information on campsites and interesting sights en route.

DOCUMENTS

A valid driving licence or international driving permit, car registration papers (log-book) and a nationality licence plate are required. An International Insurance Certificate (Green Card) is available from your insurance company and is the most effective proof of insurance coverage, recognised by all Swiss police and other officials.

ROAD TAX

Instead of tolls, an annual road tax called a **vignette** is levied on cars and motorbikes using Swiss motorways. The *vignette* is valid from 1 December until 31 January of the following year; it must be displayed on the windscreen. The *vignette* costs 40CHF (trailers an additional 40CHF) and is available at border posts, post offices, petrol stations, garages and cantonal car registration offices. To avoid delays at the border, purchase the *vignette* in advance from the Swiss National Tourist Office (*see Tourist Offices*).

ROAD REGULATIONS

Laws are strictly enforced and police are authorised to collect on-the-spot fines. Drivers must be at least 18 years old. **Seat belts** are compulsory; children under-12 are required to sit in the back. **Dipped headlights** are compulsory in tunnels. A red **warning triangle** or **hazard warning lights** are obligatory in case of a breakdown. Use of the **horn** is discouraged except on mountain roads with blind turns. **Studded tires** are forbidden on motorways; on other roads, they are permitted only between 1 November and 30 April. **STOP signs** at crossings should be strictly obeyed. **Tram and light railway systems** are modern and run at high speed; take great care at unguarded crossings, where the warning is generally three red blinking lights, arranged in a triangle and connected with a bell. **Pedestrians** getting on or off buses and trams have priority over motorists.

It is strictly prohibited to overtake on the right, even on motorways. On **mountain roads**, if you want to pass another vehicle and meet an on-coming vehicle, it is the responsibility of the car coming down to pull over and if necessary reverse back to a suitable stopping place. **Post buses**—easy to recognise by their yellow colour and distinctive three-note horn (the first notes of Rossini's overture to *William Tell*)—always have priority.

Trailers are restricted to 2.5m/8.2ft in width and 12m/39.37ft in length. Owners of larger trailers registered outside the country can apply to the Customs Office for authorisation to drive them in the country (20CHF tax). The Klausen, Nufenen, Schelten and Weissenstein Passes are closed to these cars; access is permitted to Bürgenstock and Diemtigtal.

SPEED LIMITS

Maximum speed on motorways is 120kph/75mph; on other roads 80kph/50mph and in towns and villages 50kph/31mph. Police radar speed trap detectors are forbidden. The speed limit for cars towing trailers is 80kph/50mph (up to 1t) or 60kph/37mph (over 1t) on all roads, including motorways.

PARKING

There is a charge for most city-centre parking; areas (marked by a blue sign) permit parking up to 90min. Visitors should buy a **parking disc** from the local police station or Tourist Office.

ROAD SIGNS

Motorways are indicated by signs in white on a green background. There are priority roads, numbered and marked by arrows in white on a blue ground. Secondary roads are marked and numbered in black on a white ground. These green signs are not to be mistaken for those used for indicating diversions, known as *itinéraires bis*.

CAR RENTAL

There are car rental agencies at airports, railway stations and downtown locations in most larger cities. Except at airports, rental agencies are closed Sundays; most non-airport locations close before 6pm weekdays and Saturdays. Smaller vehicles have manual transmissions; automatics require advance reservations. Drivers must be over 21 years of age (**SIXT-Eurorent** will rent mini-cars to drivers 18 to 21); drivers must be at least 25 for some luxury vehicles and large SUVs. Avis does not charge for an additional driver. Fly-drive packages are generally less expensive than renting separately. For longer stays, 17 days to six months, **Renault EuroDrive** offers a short-term lease that can be less costly than renting. ✆1-888-532-1221 (in USA); www.renaultusa.com.

Car rental companies
Avis: www.avis.ch
Kemwel: www.kemwel.com
AutoEurope: www.autoeurope.com
SIXT-Eurorent: www.esixt.com
Rhino Cars: www.rhinocarhire.com

PETROL (GASOLINE)

Most petrol stations are closed at night, even on motorways; self-service petrol pumps remain open (10CHF or 20CHF notes). Four-star and unleaded petrol are cheaper than the European average, whereas diesel is more expensive. Unleaded petrol is widely available.

EMERGENCIES

Emergency telephones are available on motorways, larger roads and in the mountains; motorist help calls can also be made from any telephone 24hr a day by dialling ✆140. Automobile associations include the **Touring Club of Switzerland** (TCS) (4 Chemin de Blandonnet, 1214 Vernier, ✆0844 888 111; www.tcs.ch) and the **Swiss Automobile Club** (ACS) (Wasserwerkgasse 39, CH-3000 Bern 13, ✆(0)31 328 31 11; www.acs.ch).

Where to Stay and Eat

Hotel and Restaurant recommendations are located in the Address Books throughout the Discovering Switzerland section of this guide. For coin ranges and for a description of the symbols used in the Address Books see the legend on the cover flap.

WHERE TO STAY
USEFUL WEBSITES

www.switzerlanddirect.ch
The Switzerland direct site (also www.suissedirect.ch) allows internet searching and booking of hotels by region. Also special offers.

www.switzerlandhotels.ch
Direct links to many hotels and apartments in the large cities and some resorts. Also links to descriptions by the Switzerland Hotel Association.

www.rooms.ch
Direct links to 200 Swiss budget hotels in all regions. Budget holidays are also available where your entire stay can be organised for you.

www.myswitzerland.com
The Swiss National Tourist Office offers a list of child-friendly accommodations on its website, arranged by region with complete contact details.

FINDING A HOTEL
For an exhaustive list of hotels consult the *Michelin Red Guide Switzerland*. The **Swiss Guide to Hotels** (Guide Suisse des Hôtels), published by the Swiss National Board of Hotel Owners, classifies hotels by region or canton and is available from **Schweizer Hotelier-Verein Hotel-Boutique**, Monbijoustrasse 130 Postfach CH-3001 Bern; ℘(0)31 370 41 11. www.swisshotels.ch.

VELOTELS, APARTMENTS, BED AND BREAKFAST

Velohotels, distinguishable by their sign, cater specifically to cyclists. (℘01 680 22 23) (*see Outdoor Fun*). The publication **Vacances à la Campagne** lists furnished flats, bed and breakfasts, lodgings with full- or half-board, communal accommodation, mainly for German-speaking Switzerland; it is available from **Caisse Suisse de Voyage Reka** (Neuengasse 15, 3001 Bern, ℘(0)31 329 66 33; www.reka.ch). Charming bed and breakfast accommodations throughout Switzerland can be recognised by signs along the road. **Bed and Breakfast Switzerland** has over 100 members (www.bnb.ch). Highly recommended B & B accommodation all checked regularly can be selected by canton or by a simple alphabetical search. A 504 page book, Guide to Swiss B & Bs, is available and also vouchers valid for 2 years to give to friends and family.

STAYING ON A FARM
Bauernhof Ferien (Holiday Farms) provides information on stays at over 250 farms. Participating farms must

---

Hospitality Industry Terms

Bündnerstube – Traditional sitting room from Graubünden, furnished and decorated in accordance with the local custom.
Café – Tea room (in German-speaking Switzerland).
Carnotzet – In hotels of the Vaud and the Valais, a room where local cheese and wines are served.
Gasthaus – Inn.
Kurhaus – Spa. There are also thermal and mountain *Kurhäuser*.
Restaurant – Establishment serving lunch and dinner. In some German-Swiss towns, "restaurants" may provide only drinks, as in cafés, unless there is a notice saying *Speise-Restaurant*.
Wirtschaft – Very modest inn or pub, used mainly by local people.

meet criteria, including quality of rooms and a range of animals; some offer extra facilities such as horse riding. **Swiss Holiday Farms**, Reka, Neuengasse 15, 3000 Bern, ℘(0)31 329 66 99; www.agrotourismus.ch.

YOUTH HOSTELS

Switzerland has 67 youth hostels, open to visitors of all ages who belong to a youth hostel association. Hostels are popular with families, especially during school holidays. To join in the UK, contact the **Youth Hostels Association**, Trevelyan House, Dimple Road, Matlock, Derbyshire DE4 3YH, UK. ℘0870 770 8868 or 01629 592 700; www.yha.org.uk; or **Hostelling International-American Youth Hostels**, 8401 Colesville Road, Suite 600, Silver Spring, MD, ℘(301) 495-1240; www.hiayh.org. A full list of Swiss youth hostels is available at www.youthhostel.ch.

CAMPING AND CARAVANNING

Camping is only permitted on authorised sites. Maps and lists of sites with prices and facilities are published by the **Swiss Camping and Caravanning Federation** (www.swisscamps.ch) and the **Swiss Touring Club** (CP 820, CH-1214-Vernier, ℘(0)22 417 22 20). A full list of Swiss camping associations and information is available from the Swiss National Tourist Office (ⓘ see Tourist Offices).

MOUNTAIN HUTS

The **Swiss Alpine Club** (Club Alpin Suisse) manages numerous mountain huts. Contact SNTO or the Swiss Alpine Club (Schweizer Alpenclub – SAC), Monbijoustrasse 61, CH-3000 Bern 23, ℘(0)31 370 18 18; www.sac-cas.ch. SAC members have priority over other applicants. The **Swiss Backpackers Association** offers mountain and family-friendly accommodations (Alpenstrasse 16, CH-3800 Interlaken; ℘(0)33 823 46 46; www.swissbackpackers.ch).

Lidernen hut of the Swiss Alpine Club in the Riemenstaldner Valley, Schwyz

© Schweizer Alpenclub (SAC)/Switzerland Tourism

WHERE TO EAT

Addresses in the sight descriptions have dining suggestions and their prices (see the Legend on the cover flap for coin ranges). An exhaustive list can be found in the Michelin Red Guide Switzerland.

USEFUL WEBSITES

www.viamichelin.co.uk
Click on 'Restaurants' and enter the location you require in order to find a selection of eating places some of which are also in the Michelin Red Guide.

www.foodeu.com
By selecting Switzerland on the drop down menu you can browse and select restaurants, bistros, brasseries, cafés and bar in all cities and regions.

EATING OUT

Some **restaurants** levy a cover charge, which may include bread *(pain et couvert)*. At lunch, the *plat du jour,* or dish of the day, usually represents good value.

REGIONAL SPECIALTIES

Be sure to try **perch fillet**, caught in Lake Geneva, with a glass of Fendant or Perlan; a cheese **fondue** with Gruyère or Vacherin with a dry white wine; a tasty **raclette**, cheese melted under a grill and served with pickles and potatoes; or **tripe à la neuchâteloise** with an Oeil de Perdrix rosé. Meat specialties include **game** from the Valais with a Cornalin wine, dried and smoked **beef** from Graubünden enhanced by a velvety Pinot Noir, or Zürich-style **veal slices** *(geschnetzeltes Kalbfleisch)*. Other specialities include the Bernese dish of **assorted cold meats**, spicy meat balls *(polpettone)* from the Ticino region, **papet vaudois**, a winter dish of sausages with cabbage, leeks and potatoes, **Rösti** (delicious diced potatoes, fried then baked); and traditional **veal sausage**, a nationwide specialty.
Desserts favour cream pastries, and the mouth-watering chocolates for which the country is world famous.

DRINKS

Wine – Switzerland produces some 200 million bottles of wine a year.

Whites: Fendant (Valais), Perlan (Geneva), Chasselas (Neuchâtel, Vaud) and Johannisberg (Valais).
Reds: Gamay (Geneva), Pinot Noir (Graubünden, Neuchâtel), Dôle (Pinot Noir and Gamay; blend, Valais).
Rosé: Oeil de Perdrix (Neuchâtel), Merlot Rosato (Ticino).

Wines are served in two- to five-decilitre carafes or may be sampled by the glass in a **weinstube** (wine bar).

Beer – Draught and bottled beer (Adler, Cardinal, Egger, Eichhof, Feldschlösschen, etc) are popular. In German-speaking areas, the **bierstube** is similar in atmosphere to a *weinstube*.

Mineral water – Most Swiss order bottled water in restaurants, either still or sparkling mineral water. Swiss brands are Henniez and Passuger.

Coffee – This is often served with a small pot of cream *(Kaffeesahne)*.

Raclette

© Valais Tourism/Switzerland Tourism

Useful Words and Phrases

GERMAN	ENGLISH	FRENCH
Bahnhof	Railway station	Gare
Brücke	Bridge	Pont
Burg	Feudal castle	Château
Denkmal	Monument or memorial	Monument
Fähre	Ferry	Ferry
Fall	Waterfall	Cascade
Garten	Garden	Jardin
Gasse	Street, alley	Ruelle
Gletscher	Glacier	Glacier
Hafen	Port, harbor	Port
Haupt...	As a prefix: main, chief, head	Principal...
Kirche	Church	Église
Kleintaxi	Small taxi	Minicab
Kloster	Monastery, convent, abbey	Monastère
Kursaal	Casino	Casino
Markt	Market	Marché
Münster	Important church (cathedral)	Cathédrale
Ober...	High, upper	Haut...
Rathaus	Town hall	Mairie
Schloss	Castle, château	Château
Schlucht	Gorge	Gorge
Schwimmbad	Swimming pool	Piscine
See	Lake	Lac
Spielplatz	Sports ground	Aire de jeu
Strandbad	Bathing beach	Plage
Strasse	Street	Rue
Tal	Valley	Vallée
Talsperre	Dam	Barage
Tobel	Ravine	Ravine
Tor	Gate (of a town)	Porte
Unter...	Under, lower	Bas...
Verboten	Forbidden, prohibited	Interdit
Wald	Forest, wood	Forêt
Zeughaus	Arsenal	Arsenal

VOCABULARY FOR SKIERS

GERMAN	ENGLISH	FRENCH
Skischule	Ski school	École de ski
Abfahrt	Ski run	Départ, piste
Schi, Ski (Bergski, Talski)	Top ski, bottom ski	Ski (amont, aval)
Kanten	Ski edges	Carres
Bindung	Ski bindings	Fixation
Skistock	Ski stick	Bâton
Skiwachs	Ski wax	Fart
Schussfahrt	Straight run	Descente directe
Schneepflug, Stemmen	Snow-plough position	Position de chasse-neige

GERMAN	ENGLISH	FRENCH
Abrutschen	Side slipping	Dérapage
Kurvenschwung,	Curve, swing, turn	Bogen Virage
Wedeln	Wedling	"Godille"
Riesenslalom	Giant slalom	Slalom géant
Abfahrtslauf	Clear run	Descente libre
Kombination	All-round test	Combiné
Langstreckenlauf	Long-distance race	Course de fond
Sprungschanze	Ski jumping	Tremplin de saut
Skilift	Ski lift	Téléski, remonte-pente
Sessellift	Chairlift	Télésiège
Kabinenbahn	Cable car	Télécabine
Schwebebahn	Cable car	Téléphérique
Drahtseilbahn	Funicular	Funiculaire
Lawine	Avalanche	Avalanche
Schutzhütte	Refuge	Refuge
Skiwerkstatt	Ski-repair shop	Atelier de réparation de skis
Rodelbahn	Sledge run	Piste de luge
Eisbahn	Skating rink	Patinoire

Basic Information

BUSINESS HOURS

Shops are usually open Mon–Fri 8am–6.30pm; Sat 8am–4pm or 5pm. Banks are open Mon–Fri 8.30am–4.30pm. Shops generally close at 4pm on Saturday afternoons. In large towns, department stores are closed on Monday mornings, but have late-night shopping until 9pm once a week.

LAST ADMISSION TIMES

In the Discovering section of the guide the times we generally give are opening hours: 10am–6pm means the site *closes* at 6pm. In practise many places have a last admission time of 30mins to an hour before closing time. If the last admission time is more than an hour before closing time (normally only larger attractions stipulate this) or the attraction specifically states last admission time (as opposed to closing time) we also state this.
In general however it is always best to arrive at least 90min before an attraction closes.

COMMUNICATIONS

Credit cards are accepted in many phone boxes. Telephone cards, called **Taxcards**, are available from post offices, railway kiosks and hotel reception desks for 10 or 20 CHF. The minimum cost of a call is 0.60 CHF. Calls are cheaper after 7pm and on weekends.
For calls within Switzerland, the number is formed by a three-figure code starting with 0, given in brackets, followed by another group of five, six or seven figures. When calling within the same telephone district, do not dial the area code.

For **international calls** dial 00 plus the following country codes:
Australia: ☎61
Canada: ☎1
New Zealand: ☎64
UK: ☎44
USA: ☎1

If calling from outside the country, the international code for **Switzerland** is 41. Dial the international access code,

USEFUL TELEPHONE NUMBERS	
1181:	Directory enquiries for Switzerland
117:	Police in case of an emergency
118:	Fire brigade
187:	In winter, snow reports and avalanche bulletins; in summer, tourist information provided by the Swiss National Tourist Office
140:	Car breakdown service (open 24 hours)
144:	Emergency doctor; ambulance
161:	Talking clock
162:	Weather forecast
163:	Information on snow-bound roads, traffic conditions
187:	Avalanche bulletin
1141:	International numbers and information on calling abroad

followed by 41, then the area code without the first 0, followed by the correspondent's number; for example, when calling Bern from the UK, dial 00 41 31, followed by the correspondent's number.

The international dialling code for the **Principality of Liechtenstein** is 423. There is a 24hr **English-speaking** information and help line called Anglo-Phone: ✆157-5014, which costs 2.13 CHF per minute. The operators speak French, German and Italian depending on the region; English in main cities and major resorts.

The Swisscom Mobile network covers 99% of Switzerland; for additional information contact www.swisscom-mobile.ch.

EMERGENCIES
Police: ✆17
Fire Brigade: ✆118
Ambulances: ✆144

ELECTRICITY
220 volts (AC) is the usual voltage; most power sockets are designed for three-pin round plugs. Adaptors for two pin plugs are available in most hotels.

MAIL/POST
All letters to Switzerland should have the international abbreviation CH and the post code number before the name of the town, e.g. CH-3000 Bern. In the cities, post offices often have a café serving sandwiches and pastries, and a stationery store selling anything from paper clips to DVDs. Offices are closed on Saturdays from noon onwards. Stamps are sold at two rates: priority mailing and standard (usually arriving within three days).

♦ Airmail postcards and letters to the USA and Canada: 1.90CHF.
♦ Airmail postcards and letters to the UK (up to 20g): 1.40CHF.
♦ Postcards and letters within Switzerland: 1CHF.

Additional information is available online at www.post.ch.

MONEY
CURRENCY
The currency is the Swiss Franc. The abbreviation, CHF is the official financial ISO code, which stands for Confederation Helvetica France, Switzerland's formal Latin name. Advertisers and stores tend to prefer Fr. Denominations in circulation are: 5, 10, 20 and 50 *centimes* (*rappen* in German-speaking areas) and 1, 2 and 5 francs (coins), 10, 20, 50, 100, 200, 500 and 1 000 francs (notes).

BANKS
Traveller's cheques and foreign currency can be exchanged in banks and official exchange offices. Your passport is necessary as identification when cashing checks. Commission charges vary, with hotels charging more than banks. Generally, banks are open from 8am–4.30pm (Mon–Fri).

Money can also be withdrawn from cash dispensers by using your credit or debit card. Always check with your bank whether your debit or credit card will be accepted. You may have more difficulty when trying to use your debit card to pay for items at a till.

CREDIT CARDS

Major **credit cards** (American Express, Diners Club, Eurocard/MasterCard, Visa, EC-Maestro, EC-Cirrus, Japan Card Bank, etc) are accepted in shops, hotels, restaurants and ATMs, although perhaps not in the smallest villages where cash is preferred. The **euro** is accepted by some establishments on the borders of Germany, France, Italy and Austria. Geneva and Basel in particular have been keen to accommodate the European single currency.

PUBLIC HOLIDAYS

Various general holidays are observed throughout the country. Public offices, banks, and major companies will be closed on public holidays.

January 1 and 2—New Year
March—Good Friday
March—Easter Sunday and Monday
May—Ascension Day
May—Whitsunday and Monday
August 1—Swiss National Day
December 25—Christmas Day
December 26—Boxing Day

Other holidays tend to vary from canton to canton. Thanksgiving (*Jeûne Fédéral* in French; *Buß- und Bettag* in German), not to be confused with the American holiday, is observed in all the cantons, except Geneva, on

the third Sunday in September. The *Jeûne Fédéral* is a period of fasting and penitence, accompanied by processions and pilgrimages. The Geneva canton observes Thanksgiving on the second Thursday in September. Some cantons observe local and regional holidays as well, including Labor Day (May 1) and Corpus Christi (June 7).

REDUCED RATES

Discounts on admissions and fares are available for children and groups traveling together at most major sites, including all-inclusive passes such as the Museum Pass and Swiss Pass. ⓒ*See GETTING THERE AND GETTING AROUND for travel discounts.*

TAXES & TIPPING
TAXES

8% VAT is included in the retail price of most goods. Foreign tourists who shop in stores with the sign "Tax Free" and whose purchases equal or exceed 400CHF can claim back the VAT on their purchase when they leave the country. Ask the store for the form.

TIPPING

A service charge is included on all restaurant, hotel, hairdresser, and taxi bills, so you are not usually expected to leave anything extra.

SMOKING

Smoking restrictions have finally been introduced in Switzerland but they vary from canton to canton. Restaurants and trains all have at least one non-smoking room.

TIME

Switzerland is 1hr ahead of GMT, 6hr ahead of EST (USA/Canada) and 9hr ahead of PST.

In summer, the country operates a daylight-saving scheme when clocks are advanced by an hour. The actual dates are announced annually but always occur over weekends in March and October.

Christmas time in St Moritz
© Christof Sonderegger/Switzerland Tourism

CONVERSION TABLES

Weights and Measures

EU	US	UK	
1 kilogram (kg) 6.35 kilograms 0.45 kilograms	**2.2 pounds (lb)** 14 pounds 16 ounces (oz)	**2.2 pounds** 1 stone (st) 16 ounces	*To convert kilograms to pounds, multiply by 2.2*
1 metric ton (tn)	**1.1 tons**	**1.1 tons**	
1 litre (l) 3.79 litres 4.55 litres	**2.11 pints (pt)** 1 gallon (gal) 1.20 gallon	**1.76 pints** 0.83 gallon 1 gallon	*To convert litres to gallons, multiply by 0.26 (US) or 0.22 (UK)*
1 hectare (ha) **1 sq kilometre (km²)**	**2.47 acres** 0.38 sq. miles (sq mi)	**2.47 acres** 0.38 sq. miles	*To convert hectares to acres, multiply by 2.4*
1 centimetre (cm) **1 metre (m)**	**0.39 inches (in)** **3.28 feet (ft) or 39.37 inches** **or 1.09 yards (yd)**	**0.39 inches**	*To convert metres to feet, multiply by 3.28; for kilometres to miles, multiply by 0.6*
1 kilometre (km)	**0.62 miles (mi)**	**0.62 miles**	

Clothing

Women	EU	US	UK
Shoes	35	4	2½
	36	5	3½
	37	6	4½
	38	7	5½
	39	8	6½
	40	9	7½
	41	10	8½
Dresses & suits	36	6	8
	38	8	10
	40	10	12
	42	12	14
	44	14	16
	46	16	18
Blouses & sweaters	36	6	30
	38	8	32
	40	10	34
	42	12	36
	44	14	38
	46	16	40

Men	EU	US	UK
Shoes	40	7½	7
	41	8½	8
	42	9½	9
	43	10½	10
	44	11½	11
	45	12½	12
	46	13½	13
Suits	46	36	36
	48	38	38
	50	40	40
	52	42	42
	54	44	44
	56	46	48
Shirts	37	14½	14½
	38	15	15
	39	15½	15½
	40	15¾	15¾
	41	16	16
	42	16½	16½

Sizes often vary depending on the designer. These equivalents are given for guidance only.

Speed

KPH	10	30	50	70	80	90	100	110	120	130
MPH	6	19	31	43	50	56	62	68	75	81

Temperature

Celsius (°C)	0°	5°	10°	15°	20°	25°	30°	40°	60°	80°	100°
Fahrenheit (°F)	32°	41°	50°	59°	68°	77°	86°	104°	140°	176°	212°

To convert Celsius into Fahrenheit, multiply °C by 9, divide by 5, and add 32.
To convert Fahrenheit into Celsius, subtract 32 from °F, multiply by 5, and divide by 9.
NB: Conversion factors on this page are approximate.

*Hiking trails in the vineyards between
Lausanne and Montreux by the
Lake Geneva, Vaud*
Urs Achermann/Lausanne Tourisme/Switzerland Tourism

The Country Today

Switzerland remains a fascinating mix of traditional and modern, pastoral and cosmopolitan. No other nation has a greater density of museums, a more efficient transport network, or as well-educated a population more skilled in welcoming tourists. The Swiss enjoy one of the best standards of living in the world, with a strong currency, driven in part by the country's political stability and international neutrality. Beyond Alpine panoramas, cheese, chocolate and trains that run on time, the country is a scenic, gastronomic and cultural delight.

21ST CENTURY SWITZERLAND
POPULATION

Switzerland's population stands at 7 701 856 with a large foreign contingent (21.7%). Of the latter, about 37% originate from the big surrounding countries of Germany, Italy and France and about two-thirds from all EU states. Although it is relatively easy for EU citizens to live and work in Switzerland, naturalisation is extremely difficult and costly. This explains why 40% of those still claissified as foreign have lived in Switzerland for more than 10 years and 20% have actually been born in the country. The population is not spread out evenly, as most people tend to live in the central plateau stretching from Lake Geneva to Lake Constance and in the Rhône Valley, while the mountains in the south are almost empty.

LIFESTYLE

As one might expect from their history of banding together against their neighbours, the Swiss are a conservative and reserved people whose primary commitment is to their family and their local community. Despite this, they are remarkably liberal in social matters: same-sex registered partnerships were adopted through a referendum in 2005, and two euthanasia charities operate lawfully. Although espousing neutrality, they are also well prepared for war, via nuclear shelters for the whole population (prescribed in building regulations) and a citizen's militia: every able male between 18 and 34 does three weeks of military service per year and keeps his personal weapons at home.

LANGUAGE AND RELIGION

One of the successes of the Swiss Confederation is the coexistence of four languages and several religions in a single community.

Languages

German-speaking Swiss represent 64% of the Helvetian people. **Schwyzerdütsch** (Swiss German) is a dialect of the Alemannic group, with many local variations. It can be difficult to follow at first, even for native Germans and Austrians. It is used in daily conversation, while classical German (*Hochdeutsch*)

Landsgemeinde in Appenzell

© Stephan Engler/Switzerland Tourism

Traditions and Folklore

Swiss folklore can always point to a rich collection of local costumes, and it is in the mountains that visitors have the best chance of seeing people who wear their traditional costumes every day, especially in Gruyères and the Valais.

Escalade festival in Geneva

© Christof Sonderegger/Switzerland Tourism

The *armailli* (herdsman) of Gruyères still wears the *bredzon*, a short cloth or canvas jacket with puffed sleeves which dates back to the Empire period, embroidered with thorn-points and with edelweiss on the lapels. The straw toque edged with velvet is called a *capette*. Similar costumes are found in the pastoral districts of the Bernese Oberland, although less often, but the man's jacket from this area is often made of velvet.

At Evolène the women's working dress includes a simple frock, with a red and white neckerchief, and a straw hat with a brim edged with velvet and turned down over the ears; the crown is encircled by crochet-work ribbons arranged in bands. On high feast days the women of Evolène put on a rustling silk apron and the *mandzon* (a sort of jacket with long sleeves), and a very flat, round felt hat on top of a white lace bonnet.

Pastoral traditions are still very much alive in mountain districts like the Val d'Anniviers, where life is governed by the movements of cattle from the villages to the *mayens* and the high Alpine pastures *(alpe)*. The trek to summer pastures creates joyful and picturesque parades *(late May, early June)*. Scores of beasts with beribboned and flower-decked horns move along the roads with cowbells tolling, escorted by herdsmen carrying necessities for living in the chalets, including a huge cheese-boiler on a yoke. In the Valais the end of the journey is marked by **cow competitions**, after which the "queen" of the herd may wear the giant bell reserved for her.

Midsummer festivals lessen the loneliness of the *armaillis* by bringing a crowd of friends and relatives up from the valleys. The return from the alp, referred to as the *désalpe*, is equally spectacular and lively. The open-air performances of *William Tell* at Interlaken begin with a procession of this kind.

Urban traditions – These are generally patriotic and civic, like the commemoration of the Escalade in Geneva or the *Knabenschiessen* in Zürich (*see Calendar of Events*). In quite a different spirit, more like the Rhenish customs, Basel Carnival, in which there are masked dances and processions preceding Lent, brings a touch of frivolity to the city of Erasmus. From behind the mask of some grotesque figure the merrymaker is free to taunt and tease friends and acquaintants.

Traditional rustic sports survive only at certain village fêtes in German Switzerland, where you might see games like wrestling on the grass, stone throwing, flag throwing and, most inscrutable of all, *Hornussen*, a team sport in which defenders with paddles try to deflect a puck which is hit, like a golf tee shot, as far as possible up the field. A summer festival in the Emmental is also the place to hear the cavernous tones of the great trumpet, the Alpenhorn.

Sport in Switzerland

The Swiss take full advantage of the outdoor opportunities their country offers, with one in four being a member of a sports club. Summers are spent **sailing** in the lakes or **hiking** on the mountains, with several prestigious alpine marathons on offer. The most spectacular is the **Zermatt Run** on the lower slopes of the Matterhorn, starting at an altitude of 1 600m/5 249 ft and ending in 2 585m/8 481ft. However, winter sports predominate with everyone capable of **skiing**, **ice skating** and **tobogganing** from a young age, a fact reflected in recurring Swiss successes in the Winter Olympics (nine medals in 2010). **Ice hockey** is extremely popular and teams from smaller towns compete in the professional league alongside metropolitan giants. This is not possible in **football** where money plays an important role and where, unsurprisingly, teams from Zürich and Basel predominate. The national team has been improving recently and made the headlines in the **2010 World Cup** with a memorable win over Spain.

is reserved for official business and the written word. On the other hand, the French-speaking group (18%) have seen their dialect fall more and more into disuse. Italian (11%) is spoken almost entirely throughout the Ticino and in part of Graubünden.

Romansh was recognised as a fourth national language in 1938. The Romansh League has done all it can to preserve and even spread its use in schools and in the press. Of Latin origin, Romansch is used by 7% of the Swiss in Graubünden canton, especially in the Engadin and Graubünden Oberland.

German, French and Italian are the official languages of the Confederation and are used by the authorities and the federal civil service. At least two languages are taught compulsorily in schools.

Religion

Until the middle of the 19C, the religious question seemed an obstacle to unity in the Confederation. This was proved by the Sonderbund War of 1847, but since 1848 complete tolerance is the rule. Today Protestants represent only 35% of the population, the Roman Catholics 42%, while 11% claim no religious affiliation.

The Swiss Protestant temperament, in its fundamentally democratic and patriotic aspects, owes more to the forceful personality of a man like Zwingli than to the strict doctrine of Calvin, whose influence was felt chiefly in Geneva. The flexible organization of Protestant churches reflects the federalist structure of the country and allows subsidised state churches to exist alongside free churches supported by donations.

Roman Catholics are attached to their dioceses: Basel (&see SOLOTHURN), Lausanne-Geneva-Fribourg (&see FRIBOURG), Sion, Chur, St Gallen and Lugano. Clergy are distributed among some large abbeys like those of St Maurice, Einsiedeln and Engelberg. The small Jewish population lives mostly in large cities such as Basel and Zürich.

THE SWISS CANTONS

Under the shield: The name of the canton and its official abbreviation (used for car registration).

On the map: The boundaries of the cantons and their capitals. Cantons are listed alphabetically by their local names with their English version and/or alternative name. Area, population, language, and religious majorities follow.

ABBREVIATIONS:

F: *French*, **G**: *German*, **I**: *Italian*, **P**: *Protestant*, **RC**: *Roman Catholic*.

AARGAU (Argovia)

◆ 1 404sq km/542sq mi
◆ population 591 632 (**G-P**).

The name means "the country of the Aare" and the river is represented by wavy lines. The three stars represent the three districts which together form the canton.

APPENNZELL

Innerrhoden (AI):
- 172sq km/66sq mi
- population 15 549 (**G-RC**).

Ausserrhoden (AR):
- 243sq km/94sq mi
- population 53 504 (**G-P**).

The bear, which represents the Abbey of St Gallen, adorns the shield of the canton. (AR includes the letters VR.)

BASEL (Bâle)

Basel District (BL):
- 482sq km/165sq mi
- population 271 214 (**G-P**).

Basel Town (BS):
- 52sq km/20sq mi
- population 186 672 (**G-P**).

Coat of arms include a bishop's crosier (red for Basel District, black for Basel Town).

BERN (Berne)

- 6 050sq km/2 659sq mi
- population 969 299 (**G-P**).

🔎 For the origin of the coat of arms see BERN.

FRIBOURG

- 1 670sq km/645sq mi
- population 268 537 (**F-RC**).

The shield of Fribourg is black and white, the colours of the dukes of Zähringen.

GENEVA (Genève, Genf)

- 282sq km/109sq mi
- population 446 106(**F-P**).

🔎 For the origin of the coat of arms see GENEVA.

GLARUS

- 684sq km/2 654sq mi
- population 38 370 (**G-P**).

Its coat of arms represents St Fridolin, the patron saint of the district.

GRAUBÜNDEN (Grisons)

- 7 106sq km/2 744sq mi
- population 190 459 (**G-P**).

The modern history of Graubünden, also referred to as Les Grisons (French), Grigioni (Italian), Grischun (Romansh) and *Rhaetia* in ancient times, begins with the alliance of the three Leagues in the 14C and 15C. The Gray League (shield half sable, half argent, black and white), which means Graubünden, ruled the upper Rhine Basin. The banner of the Ten Jurisdictions League (a cross of gold and blue quartering) flew in the Prättigau, the district of Davos and Arosa.

JURA

- 837sq km/323sq mi
- population 69 822 (**F-RC**).

The canton was formed 24 September 1978 by popular vote ratifying a Federal decree of 9 March 1978. Its three districts, Delémont (the capital), Porrentruy and Les Franches Montagnes were formerly part of the canton of Berne.

LUCERNE (Lucerne, Luzern)

- 1 492sq km/576sq mi
- population 368 742(**G-RC**).

NEUCHÂTEL

- 797sq km/308sq mi
- population 170 924 (**F-P**).

The present coat of arms dates from the proclamation (1848) of the Republic of Neuchâtel. The white cross on a red background commemorates its adhesion to the Confederation.

ST GALLEN

- 2 014sq km/778sq mi
- population 471 152 (**G-RC**).

The fascine on the shield recalls the union of the various districts which were joined in 1803, when the canton was formed.

SCHAFFHAUSEN

- 298sq km/115sq mi
- population 75 303 (**G-P**).

SCHWYZ

- 908sq km/350sq mi
- population 143 719 (**G-RC**).

The shield of Schwyz used to be plain red. Later, it was charged with a white

APPENZELL (AR/AI)

AARGAU (AG)

BASEL-LAND (BL)

BASEL-STADT (BS)

BERN (BE)

FRIBOURG (FR)   GENÈVE (GE)   GLARUS (GL)   GRAUBÜNDEN (GR)   JURA (JU)   LUZERN (LU)   NEUCHÂTEL (NE

cross and became the emblem of the entire Swiss Confederation.

SOLOTHURN

* 791sq km/305sq mi
* population 251 830 (**G-RC**).

TICINO (Tessin)

* 2 811sq km/1 085sq mi
* population 332 736 (**I-RC**).

THURGAU

* 1 013sq km/391sq mi
* population 241 811 (**GP**).

The two lions pictured on the coat of arms were borrowed from the arms of the counts of Kyburg.

UNTERWALDEN

Nidwalden (NW):

* 276sq km/107sq mi
* population 40 737 (**G-RC**).

Obwalden (OW):

* 491sq km/190sq mi
* population 34 429 (**G-RC**).

The arms bear the keys of St Peter: Those of Nidwalden are on a red background; those of Obwalden on a red and white background.

URI

* 1 076sq km/415sq mi
* population 35 162 (**G-RC**).

VALAIS (Wallis)

- 5 226sq km/2 018sq mi
- population 303 241 (**F-RC**).

The shield is red and white to commemorate the episcopal banner of Sion. It bears 13 stars representing the 13 *dizains* (districts) of the canton.

VAUD (Waadt)

- 3 219sq km/1 243sq mi
- population 688 245 (**F-P**).

The green flag was adopted when the Lemanic Republic was founded in 1798. The white flag with the motto "Liberté et Patrie", or "Freedom and Homeland", was adopted when Vaud joined the Confederation in 1803.

ZUG

- 239sq km/92sq mi
- population 110 384 (**G-RC**).

ZÜRICH

- 1 729sq km/667sq mi
- population 1 332 727 (**G-P**).

GOVERNMENT

The Constitution of 1848, revised in 1874 and more recently in 1999, set up a modern federal state in place of the former Confederation of Cantons. Each canton had its own coinage, postal services, and customs.

53

THE COMMUNITIES

Liberty of the individual, liberty of faith and conscience, liberty of the press and of association are recognised by the Constitution, which gives every Swiss citizen over the age of 18 the right to vote and to be elected. Women, at last, obtained the vote in federal elections in 1971 but still do not always have a say in cantonal and community affairs. The whole regime, however, rests upon the principle of the sovereignty of citizens living in 2 905 free communities and forming the basis of the national will.

In all matters the community is competent to decide in the first instance. The canton intervenes only on appeal. So powerful is the citizenry that foreigners must first be admitted to the "corps of citizens" of a given community in order to acquire Swiss nationality.

CANTONAL AUTHORITY

Each canton has political sovereignty, with its own constitution and legislative body. In each of the 23 cantons (26 including the half-cantons—ⓘ see Welcome to Switzerland) executive power belongs to the State Council and legislative power to the Grand Council.

The practice of direct democracy survives in a few mountain cantons like Appenzell, Glarus and Unterwalden. Here, each spring, citizens vote by a show of hands on questions affecting the community. These highly ceremonial meetings are called the **Landsgemeinden** (ⓘ see Calendar of Events).

THE FEDERAL AUTHORITIES

Legislative power is exercised by two assemblies, the National Council and the Council of States; executive power by a collegial of seven members called the Federal Council. The two assemblies, when sitting jointly, form the Federal Assembly. The National Council represents the people, with one deputy being elected for more than 30 000 inhabitants (200 members); each canton or half-canton is represented by at least one seat. The Council of States, which represents the cantons, has 46 members: two per canton and one per half-canton, regardless of the size of the population.

This bicameral system, similar to American and parliamentary institutions, protects the interests of the small communities.

Executive power resides with the Federal Council. Its seven members are elected for a four-year term by the Federal Assembly, and each administers a department, or ministry. The annual election of the President—whose official title is President of the Confederation—and of the Vice-President, appears to be a mere formality: The Vice-President invariably succeeds the President and his successor is chosen from a roster drawn up by agreement.

THE SOVEREIGN PEOPLE

Decisions by the Federal Assembly can be taken only after a favourable vote by both chambers. Here again, however, popular sovereignty has a role to play. If, within 90 days after a decision by the Assembly, signatures can be obtained from 50 000 citizens, the entire population is then called upon to decide whether a law should finally be accepted or rejected. This is the **right of referendum**, which in practice has a conservative influence. Citizens of Vaud, according to tradition, are fond of saying: "The referendum is our right to say No when Bern has said Yes." During a referendum in December 1992, the Swiss nation answered no to joining the EEE (Espace Économique Européen).

The Swiss also have the right to **initiate legislation**. Thus, 100 000 citizens may demand an amendment of the articles of the Constitution or the adoption of new articles. Therefore, the popular will finds expression at every level of political activity and exercises permanent control over the country's institutions.

NATIONAL SERVICE

Although Switzerland is known to be a neutral country, military service plays a prominent part in the life of its citizens, though there is a provision for performing civilian service instead of military service since 1996. The **Swiss Army** is a militia without "regular" units. "Active" service begins only at general mobilisation. The Army has a general only in time of war or general mobilisation, the last being General Guisan, in 1939–1945. In 2003, voters approved a major military reform, *Army XXI*, reducing the size of the army by half to 220 000 conscripts and reducing mandatory service to 260 days. Service is required for able-bodied men; for women, it is voluntary.

The Swiss soldier keeps all his equipment at home: Uniform, rifle, ammunition, and gas mask against nuclear, biological, or chemical weapons.

While landlocked Switzerland does not have a navy, **military boats** patrol Swiss border lakes Lake Geneva, Lake Maggiore and Lake Constance. There is also a Swiss **Air Force**, which defended national air space from Allied and Axis incursion in the Second World War.

Electoral Duty

Communal, cantonal and federal elections occur with a frequency that may seem surprising to outsiders. In cantons like Bern and Zürich, which are very much attached to strict control of their budgets, it is a common joke that voting is as frequent as *Jass*, the Swiss game of poker. As a result, many elections, which are usually scheduled on a Sunday, have low turn-outs (35–50% participation); with cantonal voting, attendance can be as low as 30%.

ECONOMY

Switzerland enjoys one of the highest standards of living in the world. Its economic success relies on a thriving services sector, a highly skilled and motivated workforce, strong currency and stable political situation. Swiss industry, known to be both traditional and innovative, is efficient, but depends heavily on exporting its goods. A mountainous country where only 10% of the land is arable, it is also highly dependent on the import of raw materials to meet the needs of its population. Even so, the overall mentality remains protectionist and immigration is subject to strict regulation.

Swiss voters decided in 1992 not to join the European Community (now the European Union), but in 1995, Switzerland became a member of the International Trade Organization (ITO). In the 21C, bilateral treaties with EU countries and entry into the Schengen area in December 2008 have made it an EU member in all but name.

The country remains a **"haven of peace"** and a refuge for many foreigners. Geneva is the seat of many international organizations, including GATT and specialised agencies of the United Nations, including the High Commission for Refugees.

WORLD FINANCE

Zürich is the country's economic capital, where most banks have their headquarters. Swiss neutrality has done much to attract foreign capital, thanks to a strong, steady currency and its famous bank confidentiality: 40% of the world's personal savings are concentrated in Switzerland. However, in 2009, banking spats with Germany and most notoriously with the US forced Switzerland to co-operate in lifting elements of the banking secrecy to help in cases of suspected tax evasion.

The banking system also supports important insurance and shipping industries; vasts amounts of international financial trade passes through Switzerland. Life insurance is a prosperous sector, and it is said that Swiss citizens enjoy the best and most comprehensive insurance in the world. Rentenanstalt/Swiss Life, Winterthur and Zürich dominate.

AGRICULTURE

Agriculture enjoys a privileged status. Strongly protected, heavily subsidized by the state, and closely integrated into rural life and the Swiss landscape, it is simultaneously an integral part of Swiss culture and a major tourist attraction. Livestock farming accounts for 75% of the agricultural production.

Since the Swiss farming industry can grow only enough to satisfy 60% of the country's needs, everything grown

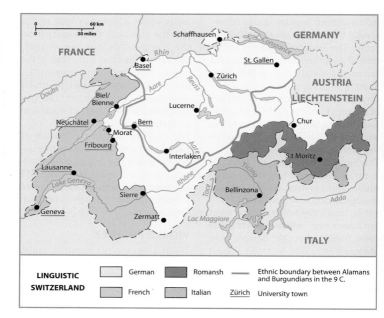

| LINGUISTIC SWITZERLAND | German | Romansh | —— Ethnic boundary between Alamans and Burgundians in the 9 C. |
| | French | Italian | Zürich University town |

is consumed in the home country; the remainder is imported.

Cereals, heavily subsidised by the government, remain expensive, although the use of chemical fertilisers has increased yield. Such farming methods, thought to damage the environment, are not well accepted by the population. Organic farming is very much en vogue, but is still too costly to be applied on a large scale.

Half the cheese made in Switzerland (25% of dairy production) is exported. The country is famous worldwide for its Gruyère (from the Gruyères region) and Emmental (from the Emmen valley). **Forestry** has been carefully regulated since 1993. Forests cover about one-third of the land and contribute to the prevention of natural disasters such as avalanches and landslides. For these reasons, deforestation is strictly forbidden.

INDUSTRY AND TRADE

Swiss industry is characterised by extremely high standards of quality—an attitude which has earned it a worldwide reputation of excellence. The most prosperous sectors are those of machinery (machine tools, farming and printing equipment) and electro-mechanics, representing 45% of Swiss exports. Zürich, Baden, and Winterthur are the major industrial centres.

The chemical and pharmaceutical industries, largely concentrated in the Basel area, are flourishing; research and development are extremely active. Swiss pharmaceutical groups are among the world's most powerful: Roche and Novartis (resulting from the merger of Ciba and Sandoz), two of the world's largest, are headquartered here; others have major offices here.

Watchmaking has also come to symbolise Switzerland. Renowned as the "international custodian of time," Switzerland boasts artisans that specialise in luxury timepieces, producing high-quality products that utilise classic hand-crafting and modern techniques. Swiss clocks and watches are universally appreciated and the "Made in Switzerland" label enjoys worldwide esteem; indeed 95% of the national production is exported.

The **food-processing industry** is booming. Swiss **chocolate** enjoys an excellent reputation abroad; just over half the annual production is exported.

2012 display from the Hall of Innovations BASELWORLD—World Watch and Jewellery Show

© BASELWORLD

The rest is consumed by the Swiss at an estimated 11.7 kg per person per year. The designation "Swiss chocolate" is carefully controlled; it must be made entirely in Switzerland out of cocoa beans, cocoa paste, cocoa butter, sugar, and sometimes milk. Swiss chocolate pioneers include François-Louis Cailler, Philippe Suchard, Rodolphe Sprungli, Rudolf Lindt and Henri Nestlé.

The Swiss **textile industry** has had the same problems as other nations with comparably high labour costs against the onslaught of low-cost Asian products. However, its embroidery still has a niche in haut-couture, and was recently given a strong impetus by Michelle Obama's presidential inauguration yellow dress made by textiles from St Gallen.

Protecting the Environment

Preserving nature is equally important to private firms, public authorities and the population. The Swiss show great awareness of ecological issues and are careful to recycle their rubbish individually, with 78% of currently recyclable items being recycled.

FINANCIAL

Services are the backbone of the Swiss economy: They employ 70% of the working population and account for 70% of the GDP. The national currency attracts many foreign investments.

TOURISM

Picturesque chalets, beautiful landscapes, and a tradition of hospitality have made Switzerland an ideal holiday destination for generations. Switzerland also benefits from its reputation as one of the safest destinations in Europe.

After metalworking and pharmaceuticals, tourism is the country's main industry, attracting an international clientele. German tourists account for the highest number of visitors, followed by the British and the Dutch. Destinations such as Zermatt and Grindelwald also attract Japanese and American tourists.

More recently, the use of the Alps in Bollywood films (instead of the Himalayas) and high-tech immigration has led to a slew of Indian visitors.

Where winter and summer seasons were once distinct, increasing tourism has created a year-round season as visitors take advantage of discounts and offers in non-peak times, especially for wellness retreats at Swiss spas and resorts. Switzerland is renowned for the excellence of its hotel industry, with some establishments over 100 years old.

Many multinational companies are headquartered or have subsidiaries here, boosting business-related tourism. International organizations, such as the United Nations in Geneva, and the International Olympic Committee in Lausanne, also perform this role.

FOOD AND WINE
SWISS SPECIALTIES

Swiss cuisine combines the culinary traditions of France, Germany, and Italy. **Cheese dishes** – The great hard cheeses, Gruyère and Emmental, which carry the fame of the Swiss dairy industry abroad, are the basis of **fondue**, which is a national institution among the French Swiss. Every canton, especially Vaud, Neuchâtel and Fribourg, claims the perfect mix of Gruyère, Emmental, Vacherin, and other ingredients.

Raclette, a Valais specialty, is prepared by toasting one side of a slice of Valais cheese (the soft cheese of Bagnes or Conches – Goms) at a fire. The melted cheese is scraped directly onto the plate with a knife or a wooden blade. *Raclette* is eaten with gherkins and bread or potatoes cooked in their jackets.

Beef, Pork and Fish – The most original Swiss specialty is the dried meat of Graubünden, **Bündnerfleisch**. This is raw beef smoked and air-dried, served in thin slices. The most frequent meat dishes are fillet of veal *(Schnitzel)* and pork chop. A popular Zürich dish is minced veal or calf's liver with cream *(geschnetzeltes Kalbsfleisch)* and *Leberspiessli* (calf's liver cooked on a spit, with bacon). There is an extraordinary variety of *Wurst* (sausage). *Gnagi* (knuckle of pork, much enjoyed in Berne for an afternoon snack), *Klöpfer* (saveloy) in Basel, *Schüblig* (long pork sausage) in St Gallen, *Kalbsbratwurst* (veal sausage) in Zürich and *Salsiz* (small salamis) in the Engadin. The national dish of German Switzerland is **Rösti**: Potatoes boiled, diced, fried and finally baked with fried onion rings and bacon bits).

The French Swiss prefer smoked sausages with a stronger taste *(boutefas* in Payerne, *longeole* in Geneva). The monumental **Berner Platte** (Bernese platter) combines bacon, sausages, ham, sometimes boiled beef, pickled cabbage *(Sauerkraut)* and potatoes.

Swiss rivers and lakes produce a wide variety of fish such as trout, pike, tench, carp, and perch (a specialty from Lake Geneva). All are seasoned according to local tradition.

Sweets and desserts – Fresh cream is used in many sweets and desserts, such as meringues and *Schaffhauserzungen* (baked biscuits with fresh cream). The *kirschtorte* of Zug and the *Leckerli* of Basel—spiced bread with honey and almonds—are also enjoyed. Swiss chocolate, of time-honored reputation, is used to make delicious cakes and sweets.

SWISS WINES

Switzerland's vineyards produce only 36% of the wine consumed nationally. Vaud's best-known white-wine vintages are Lavaux, Dézaley, Aigle, and Yvorne. Fendant is the best known of the Valais white wines. Dôle, the most popular Valais red is a fragrant, fruity blend of Pinot and Gamay grapes.

The Geneva canton produces whites for fish dishes: Perlan; Aligoté; Pinot Gris. Oeil de Perdrix, the rosé version of Pinot Noir, is best served chilled. Although Cortaillod is a heavy red wine, most wines from Neuchâtel, such as Auvernier, Boudry, and Colombier, are lighter whites drawn from a noble vine, the Chasselas, grown in chalky soil. Ticino vines yield highly alcoholic wines, such as Mezzana and Nostrano, which are pleasant with dessert. The red, white and rosé wines *(Süssdruck)* from the eastern region and the Alpine Valley of the Rhine are most appreciated for their light and subtle quality.

Fondue

© Andy Mettler/Switzerland Tourism

History

Unlike the popular perception, Switzerland's history is full of bloody wars and internecine strife, as one might expect for a country right in the middle of Europe. Its famed neutrality has been mostly a product of the late 19C and early 20C.

TIMELINE
EARLY HELVETIA

BC	Cro-Magnon man is believed to have lived about 12000 BC, an estimate reinforced by a Cro-Magnon skull discovered in the Jura.
200 BC	The **Helvetii** cross the Rhine. This powerful Celtic, semi-nomadic tribe settles on a territory stretching from Lake Constance to Geneva, from the Alps to the Jura.
100 BC	The Helvetii are driven out by the Germanic Alemanni. Their exodus into Gaul is hindered by the Romans, led by Julius Caesar; the battle of Bibracte (Autun) takes place in 58 BC. This leads to the foundation of several settlements extending into the heart of the Alps, including those of Nyon and Augusta Raurica.
AD 1C	Helvetia becomes a province of the Roman Empire, with Vindonissa as its capital.
2C	Helvetia's geographical location compels the Romans into large-scale construction of roads and fortifications. The golden age of Aventicum (Avenches), founded by Augustus.
3C–5C	The **Burgundians**, originally a northern tribe, settle in the western part of Helvetia which becomes part of the Kingdom of Burgundy. The **Alamans** occupy Aventicum and colonise central and eastern Helvetia.
6C–9C	In 530 Franks invade the country. Their supremacy over the Merovingians and Carolingians extends to western Helvetia until 888. Irish monks, led by Columba, arrive in Helvetia to preach to the population and help build several monasteries. St Gallen, founded by Gallus, becomes a major seat of learning in Europe.

THE MIDDLE AGES

1032	Death of Rudolph III of Burgundy. The country passes to the rulers of Germany.
11C–13C	Feudal lords and their free cities are given the power to rule over Helvetia, although they are officially accountable to the kings and subsequently the emperors of Germany.
1191	The city of Bern is founded.
1291	**Rudolph of Habsburg** bequeaths Helvetia to his sons, the dukes of Austria.
1 Aug 1291	The three original forest cantons (Waldstätten) of Uri, Schwyz and Unterwalden, refuse to submit to the Habsburgs and the bailiffs and conclude a pact of mutual assistance and take the **Oath of the Everlasting League** at Rütli. This pact is the founding document of the **Helvetic Confederation** (named Switzerland in 1350). The legend of archer **William Tell**, stems from this time and he eventually becomes a national hero.
1315	The Confederates defeat Duke Leopold of Hapsburg at **Morgarten**.
1386	The cantons (eight by now) are again victorious at **Sempach**.
15C	The **St Gotthard issue**: in order to gain possession of this strategic route, the Swiss occupy part of the Ticino, Aargau, Thurgau, St Gallen and Graubünden regions. Encouraged by the King of

France, Louis XI, they invade the Pays de Vaud.

BURGUNDIAN WARS AND ITALIAN WARS

1476 Charles the Bold, **Duke of Burgundy**, is defeated by the Swiss at **Grandson (VD)**, then at **Murten (FR)**. Burgundy ceases to exist as a state.

1513 The number of cantons is extended from eight to 13.

1515 Allied with the Pope and the Milanese, the Swiss are defeated at Marignano by the King of France, **Francis I**, with whom they then sign a treaty of alliance.

1525 The crushing Franco-Swiss defeat at Pavia, where the Swiss are wiped out by Emperor Charles V, marks the end of Switzerland's political and military history outside its own borders.

REFORMATION TO THE 18C

16C The **Reformation** preached by Zwingli and Calvin is spread throughout Romansh Switzerland and heavily influences the 13 cantons.

1536 Bern regains possession of the Pays de Vaud from the Duke of Savoy.

1648 Swiss independence and neutrality is officially acknowledged with the **Peace of Westphalia** after the Thirty Years War which Switzerland escaped unscathed.

18C A united country where several languages and religions coexist, Switzerland is influenced by theories of the **Age of Enlightenment**, supported by such philosophers as **Jean-Jacques Rousseau**; revolutionary ideas spread.

1798 The French Republican army marches into Bern and occupies the city.

A centralised Helvetic Republic is founded.

19TH CENTURY

1803 Disputes between conservative and progressive forces lead Bonaparte to introduce a new Federal constitution and annex Geneva and the Valais to Switzerland.

1804–15 Switzerland becomes a battlefield of Napoleon's troops.

1815 The **Congress of Vienna** reaffirms Switzerland's neutrality. The number of cantons is extended to 22. Part of the French Jura is annexed to the Bern canton.

1846 Deep religious divisions lead to a separatist League of Roman Catholic cantons, known as the **Sonderbund**. It is soon disbanded by the Diet, reunited in Bern. General Dufour, Commander of the Confederate Army, ends hostilities and paves the way for a general reconciliation.

1848 A new constitution introduces centralised, secular rule.

1863 **Henri Dunant** from Geneva founds the Red Cross.

THE 20TH CENTURY

1914–18 Switzerland guards its frontiers and extends hospitality to those exiled by war.

1919 Tribute is paid to Swiss neutrality by making Geneva the seat of the **League of Nations**.

1939–45 During the Second World War, Swiss troops are sent to their frontiers under the command of **General Guisan**. In the post-war years, Geneva, site of European UN headquarters, undertakes diplomatic conferences.

1954 The first disarmament talks bring together Eisenhower,

Famous Swiss

Despite its small size, Switzerland boasts many world-famous citizens, and many more have decided to make their homes there during their careers. The greatest problem the Swiss seem to have is that of recognition since their famous offspring is often mistaken as French (Le Corbusier), German (Max Frisch) or Italian (Alberto Giacommetti).

14C – The mythical William **Tell**; Arnold von **Winkelried**.

15C to 17C – St Nicholas of **Flüe**, Cardinal Matthew **Schiner**; Ulrich **Zwingli**; Joachim von Watt, known as **Vadian**; Theophrastus Bombastus von Hohenheim, known as **Paracelsus**, natural scientist and alchemist; François de **Bonivard**; Domenico **Fontana**, architect, and his student Carlo **Maderno**; Kaspar Jodok von **Stockalper**.

18C – Mathematicians Jakob, Johann and Daniel **Bernoulli**, Leonhard **Euler**; painters Jean-Étienne **Liotard** and Salomon **Gessner**; philosopher Jean-Jacques **Rousseau**; Albrecht von **Haller** anatomist; and physicist Horace Bénédict de **Saussure**.

19C – Jacques **Necker**, financier and statesman; Johann Kaspar **Lavater**, poet and physiognomist; Johann David **Wyss**, writer; Johann Heinrich **Pestalozzi**, educator; General Frédéric de **Laharpe**, politician; Guillaume-Henri **Dufour**, Swiss army general; Léopold **Robert**, painter; Albert Bitzius, known as Jeremias **Gotthelf**, writer; artist Rodolphe **Toepffer**; Louis **Agassiz**, geologist; Nikolaus **Riggenbach**, engineer; Jacob **Burckhardt**, philosopher; Gottfried **Keller**, poet; Henri Frédéric **Amiel**, writer; Conrad Ferdinand **Meyer**, author and poet.

20C – Arnold **Böcklin**, painter; Henri **Dunant**, founder of the Red Cross; César **Ritz**, hotelier; Carl **Spitteler**, poet; Ferdinand **Hodler**, painter; Ferdinand **de Saussure**, linguist; Félix **Vallotton**, painter; Carl Gustav **Jung**, psychoanalyst; Charles Ferdinand **Ramuz**, writer; Ernest **Ansermet**, orchestra conductor; Frédéric Sauser, known as Blaise **Cendrars**, writer; Édouard Jeanneret-Gris, known as **Le Corbusier**, architect; Frank Martin and Arthur **Honegger**, musicians; Michel **Simon**, actor; Alberto **Giacometti**, painter and sculptor; Mario **Botta**, architect; Hans **Erni**, painter; Jean **Tinguely**, sculptor; Max **Frisch**, writer; Friedrich **Dürrenmatt**, writer; Ursula **Andress**, actress and sex symbol; Clay **Regazzoni**, racing driver; **H.R.Giger**, sculptor, painter and most famously set designer for the **Alien** films.

21C – Roger **Federer**, tennis player; Martina **Hingis** tennis player (naturalised).

Famous Swiss Residents

Other famous residents are foreigners, including painters **Konrad Witz** and **Holbein** the Younger; **Richard Wagner** who lived in Triebschen near Lucerne for six creative years; Visual artists **Paul Klee** and **Daniel Spoerri**; author **Hermann Hesse**; film director/actor **Charlie Chaplin**; **Vladimir Ilyich Lenin** who spent 18 months in Zürich, where in 1916 he wrote **Imperialism, the Highest Stage of Capitalism**; writer **Georges Simenon**; father of artist Commissaire Maigret; writer **James Joyce** who visited and lived in Zürich several times and who is buried there; singer/composer Charles **Aznavour**; actress Audrey **Hepburn**; fashion designer Coco **Chanel**; author Frédéric **Dard**; writer **Graham Greene** who is also buried in Vevey; and Albert **Einstein**, who did much of his work on the Theory of Relativity while living in Bern. Currently, many famous people, such as singers **Tina Turner** and **Céline Dion**, director **Roman Polanski** and British actor **Roger Moore** have made their homes in Switzerland.

The National Flag

All the boats gliding along Swiss lakes and rivers can be seen proudly sporting their national banner—a white cross on a red background. It was on 21 July 1840 that the Diet officially adopted this national emblem. Formerly, each contingent serving in the federal army fought under the colours of their own canton. As early as 1815, General Dufour, who was colonel at the time, had advocated the creation of a single flag in order to reinforce national unity and foster feelings of patriotism and comradeship. The flag is inspired from the white cross featured on the banner belonging to the mercenaries of the canton of Schwyz, which had been bestowed by Emperor Frederick II as a token of his appreciation.

Dulles, Eden and Faure from the West and Bulganin and Molotov from Russia.

1971 The **World Economic Forum** is held for the first time in Davos, where it will become an annual summit of the world's political and economic leaders.

1978 The Jura canton is created. Cantons now number 23.

1986 76% of the electorate votes not to become a member of the United Nations. However, the country continues to be active in UN-specialised agencies and programmes.

1989 The Swiss vote to maintain their federal army.

1991 The voting age drops from 20 to 18.

1992 Switzerland decides not to join the European Community but becomes a member of the International Monetary Fund and the World Bank.

1995 The International Trade Organisation (ITO), replaces the GATT (General Agreement on Tariffs and Trade). Headquarters are in Geneva.

1999 Ruth Dreifuss becomes the first woman elected President of the Swiss Confederation.

1999 Swiss scientist Bertrand Piccard and British co-pilot Brian Jones befome the first balloonists to circumnavigate the globe with a non-stop, non-refuelled flight. It takes 19 days, 21 hours.

THE NEW MILLENNIUM

2000 67% of the electorate votes for bilateral agreements to strengthen economic ties with the European Union.

2002 54.6% of the electorate votes to join the United Nations. Switzerland becomes the UN's 190th member state.

2003 Roger Federer, the tennis star, becomes Swiss of the Year.

2007 Lavaux Vineyard Region was named a UNESCO World Heritage Site.

2008 European Championships in Bern, Basel, Geneva and Zürich. Switzerland joins the Schengen area.

2009 After pressure from the G20, Switzerland abandons its banking secrecy and agrees to co-operate in matters of tax evasion.

2010 A drilling machine completes the world's longest tunnel beneath the Alps.

Art and Architecture

Its position at the crossroads of three important civilizations—French, Italian and German—has made Switzerland a melting pot combining the cultural characteristics of its neighbours, drawing on their cultural and artistic heritage, and adapting them to suit its own traditions. Swiss art did not acquire its own identity until the late 19C, but it soon influenced the Continent's cultural history rapidly, carving a niche in the international avant-garde art scene.

UNDER ROMAN RULE

Roman customs and traditions exerted a strong influence over early Swiss cultural heritage: Vestiges of the Roman period bear the signs of Imperial art, but with strong regional and popular characteristics. Some sites contain many remains dating back to this period. One of the most famous, the site of **Augusta Raurica** (Augst) near Basel, provides a fascinating insight into daily life under the Romans and some of their remarkable technological achievements, such as villas fitted with sewers and central heating.

Mosaics and frescoes also reflect the high degree of sophistication and taste for refinement of this civilization. The **Roman Villa** at **Orbe** features magnificent mosaics depicting mythological scenes; the **Villa Commugny** near **Nyon** boasts vivid murals with gold leaf, still brightly coloured when excavated in 1904.

EARLY MIDDLE AGES

The collapse of the Roman Empire in the 5C led to a slackening of artistic activity. Eventually, a new aesthetic—inspired by Christianity—revived artistic life as the Church played a key role in art throughout Europe. The early Middle Ages were characterised by the development of religious mural paintings.

The only remaining example, the **ceiling of Zillis church**, has scenes illustrating the Life of Christ, featuring angels, allegorical figures and mythological beasts. Evangelisation spread throughout the country from the 7C, evidenced by the construction of many convents, which became bastions of artistic activity and were seen as temples of cultural life.

The **Abbey of St Gallen** exerted considerable influence within Europe between the 8C and 10C. This flourishing of the arts was reflected in the superb illuminations and manuscripts from the 9C that have been carefully preserved in the library.

ROMANESQUE AND CLUNY

Switzerland underwent a variety of influences, illustrated by its churches, which imbibed the artistic movements

Ceiling of Saint Martin Church in Zillis, Graubünden

© Roland Gerth/Switzerland Tourism

of surrounding countries and then moulded them to suit the Swiss national character. The stamp of Lombard art can be observed in most churches in the Ticino area, such as the **Chiesa di San Nicolao** in **Giornico**, with its doorway columns resting on crouching beasts. Likewise, in the **Chiesa dei Santi Pietro e Paolo** in **Biasca**, the basilica, displaying three naves and a single apse closing off the chancel, is typical of Lombard architecture. Lastly, in Zürich, the north doorway of the Grossmünster cathedral is shaped like a triumphal arch, a common occurence in Italy.

Burgundian influence is best observed in **Basel Cathedral**, whose original late Romanesque figure was destroyed by an earthquake in 1356 and rebuilt in part-Gothic style, with a three-tier elevation, lancet arches, and the polygonal chancel. The carved tympanum on the famous "**St-Gallen Doorway**," on the east side, is the best example of Romanesque carving in the whole of Switzerland. Inside the cathedral, the **Apostle panel** and the **St Vincent panel** are masterpieces of late Romanesque sculpture that sit side to side with the remarkable late Gothic **pulpit**. Lastly, Germanic Romanesque art is very well illustrated by the **Münster zu Allerheiligen in Schaffhausen**, distinguished by stark geometry surrounding a square and pure architectural lines.

The influence of Provence is especially evident in the sculpture of Romandie. The four statue-columns depicting the Apostles in **Chur Cathedral** bear a strong resemblance to earlier sculptures in Saint-Trophime at Arles with the tight folds of their robes falling stiffly over their legs. However, the capitals in **Geneva Cathedral** are more reminiscent of those found in Lyon or Vienne.

The foundation of **Cluny Abbey Church** in 910 led to the creation of several hundred convents over the next two centuries. Cluny left its mark on many of these buildings, which featured the same tall, slender proportions. The abbey churches in Romainmôtiers and Payerne in the Vaud canton were early examples of Romanesque architecture influenced by Cluny Abbey. Romainmôtiers' abbey is a replica of the Cluny Abbey Church. The abbey in **Payerne**, with its double elevation, chapels, apsidioles, and its narthex at the entrance, represents pure Cluniac tradition.

The 12C saw the golden age of Romanesque art in Romandie with the emergence of a new Christian community, the Cistercian Order. Simplicity, austerity and formal perfection were its dominant traits. **Bonmont Abbey** near Nyon is a fine example of Cistercian architecture, with its plan designed in the shape of a Roman cross.

Bonmont Abbey, Vaud

© Abdul Sami Haqqani/Dreamstime.com

SCULPTURE

The various figures and motifs represented in sculpture tended to reflect their architectural environment; they did not seek to depict reality but to express the supernatural. Imagery was extremely rich and punctuated by references to the Old and New Testaments. The capitals of the **Église St-Jean-Baptiste de Grandson** are among the most minutely executed in Switzerland, including the "Eagle with Spread Wings" and "St Michael Slaying the Dragon."

GOTHIC PERIOD

Gothic art and the ribbed arch were introduced to Switzerland in the 13C by Cistercian monks. In architecture, the Gothic style was conveyed by systematic use of lancet arches and flying buttresses to support the imposing nave and high clerestory windows enhanced by stained glass. In sculpture, it led to the creation of statues carved out of the same block of stone as the column. This new movement paved the way for many great construction projects, including **Geneva Cathedral**. In the 13C and the 14C, the Franciscan and Dominican religious orders developed an unadorned style of their own.

The **abbey** at **Königsfelden**, founded in 1308 by the Franciscans, reflects such austerity, with its flat, wooden ceiling crowning the bare nave.

PAINTING

Economic recovery was instrumental in allowing art to expand throughout Europe. From the 14C onward, foreign artists were often called upon for projects in Switzerland, bringing with them many styles and techniques. Byzantine influence was evident in paintings such as the frescoes adorning the narthex of the 13C **Payerne Abbey Church**, devoted to the theme of the Apocalypse. Paintings often associated religious and secular elements: In Romainmôtiers, episodes from Genesis were depicted alongside scenes of musicians. In Gothic art, paintings were often replaced by stained glass.

Gothic painting flourished under such artists as **Konrad Witz** (1400–1446), who worked in Basel and Geneva. His most famous canvas, *The Miraculous Draught of Fishes* (1444), represents Lake Geneva and its shores and displays both astounding realism and minute attention to detail. The religious subject is presented, perhaps for the first time, in a recognisable, rather than an idealised, landscape. However, in this he appears to have been an exception, since most of his contemporaries remained closer to the symbolic, more iconic representation associated with the Gothic tradition. Up to 1536, painting prospered with a fair amount of creativity. On the eve of the Reformation, fewer works were commissioned as reformers turned against visual imagery, and ended the last remaining vestiges of medieval art.

SCULPTURE

Gothic sculpture displays a far freer approach, shedding Romanesque aesthetics for a more humane, graceful representation. Burgundian, Germanic and Lombard influences were still felt in projects involving artists working elsewhere, such as the German sculptor **Johann Parler**, member of the famous Parler family, who executed the chancels in the cathedrals of Fribourg and Basel around 1350. In the late 14C, an international style spread to all of Europe. Works of art became smaller so they could be transported more easily and foster cultural exchanges among countries. The Marian cult and the worshipping of saints became widespread and many sumptuous altarpieces were commissioned; the one designed for **Chur Cathedral** is an outstanding example. Sculpted doorways also drew inspiration from Gothic art; the celebrated **painted doorway in Lausanne Cathedral** is a telling example. Remarkably well-preserved, the polychrome panel illustrates the *Dormition of the Blessed Virgin* and is clearly based on the one in Senlis Cathedral. This religious imagery was exceptional for the Gothic period. Such works were seen as decorative as well as intended to enlighten the faithful.

Last Judgement on the doorway of Bern Cathedral

The ultimate expression of Flamboyant Gothic is the doorway of **Bern Cathedral**, portraying the *Last Judgement*. The graphics are said to be the most detailed in Europe and every episode is conveyed by a sculpture.

Sculpted furniture also was key to the development of Gothic art and exemplified the artistic changes occurring between the 13C and the Reformation.

THE RENAISSANCE

The late 15C and the early 16C were characterised by flourishing arts and political upheavals. Large altarpieces were replaced by painted panels and canvases. The Renaissance also added a touch of humanism.

ARCHITECTURE

Arcades, considered to be typically Renaissance, were becoming more widespread in Switzerland; the **Hôtel de Ville de Palud** in Lausanne is the most representative building of this period. Architects from Bern, including Abraham **Düntz** and Samuel **Jenner**, displayed a novel approach to their art from 1667, advocating a plain, sober style devoid of Baroque embellishments. It was in this spirit that the oval became a popular feature of many buildings. This simple geometrical figure allowed the faithful to be reunited in an area that was both simple and aes-

thetically pleasing, as is evidenced by the **Temple de Chêne-Paquer** (1667) in the Vaud canton.

Although the Reformation gave a new lease of life to civil architecture, the building of religious sanctuaries slowed down during the 16C, with reformers appropriating those Catholic churches which already existed.

In German-speaking Switzerland, Late Gothic architecture, influenced by Germanic art, coexisted with Renaissance tradition in good harmony. The city of **Schaffhausen** is a perfect example of this trend with its richly sculpted "olliers." These Gothic towers, originally placed at the corners of houses, were subsequently moved to the centre of the façade above the main entrance. Italian influence gradually spread to the Ticino canton. This was reflected in the frescoes adorning **Santa Maria degli Angeli** in Lugano or those displayed in the former town hall of Lucerne. These two different manifestations of Renaissance art, associated with the north and the south respectively, are indicative of distinct cultural traditions.

PAINTING AND ENGRAVING

Artists such as the Bern painter **Niklaus Manuel Deutsch** (1484-1530) successfully negotiated the transition between Gothic and the more modern approach of the Renaissance. **Hans Holbein the Younger**, a German who settled in Basel, not only produced the portrait of his patron Erasmus (displayed in the city's Museum of Fine Arts), but undertook many influential façades and frescoes. The Reformation seriously jeopardised his career and painting at large. Although reformers objected to religious images, they tolerated decoration with foliated scrolls, such as those in the **Temple of Lutry** (1577).

This period was marked by the invention of printing, which spread the views advocated by the Reformation. Printing was first introduced into Basel in 1468, and from then onwards, books replaced manuscripts. The new medium made it possible to popularise ideas more quickly and effectively. **Urs Graf** (1485-

1527), a famous engraver, depicted macabre, erotic and military scenes, which carried strong dramatic impact.

SCULPTURE

The stiffness that characterised this period was to replace the ornamental profusion of Late Gothic. The decline in commissions from the clergy led to the construction of fountains to enhance urban landscapes, a feature typical of Renaissance art in Switzerland. The centre of the basin was taken up by a tall sculpted and gilded column, frequently surmounted by an allegorical figure such as Justice. A monument of this type can be found in Lausanne: it portrays a woman with her eyes blindfolded holding a pair of scales and a sword.

18C

Society became more refined, elegant and sophisticated. Literary salons and musical societies flourished. Geneva and Lausanne dazzled the rest of Europe and attracted foreign artists and intellectuals. The period was symbolised by a taste for the extravagant and a strong spirit of imagination, fantasy, and freedom.

ARCHITECTURE

Up to 1770, Switzerland was mainly dominated by Baroque architecture, sculpture, painting, and applied arts.

To serve the views of the Counter-Reformation, Baroque was applied to religious buildings, becoming Rococo. The **abbey church** in **Einsiedeln** built by **Kasper Moosbrugger** (1656–1723) between 1674 and 1745 is a perfect example, as is the **abbey church** and **library of St-Gallen** designed by **Peter Thumb** (1681–1766) and **Johann Michael Beer**. Jesuits and Franciscans encouraged construction of Baroque chuches in **Lucerne**, **Fribourg** and **Solothurn**.

This grand era produced sumptuous creations featuring scrolls, painted ceilings, and lavish ornamentation. The **abbey church** in **Disentis/Mustér** (1695–1712) shows the influence of Austrian Baroque.

The association of painting and sculpture with architecture is a typical feature of Baroque art. *Trompe-l'œil* motifs extended architectural plans, as do the paintings in St Gallen by **Johann Christian Wentzinger** (1710–1797).

In the 18C, French architects such as Saussure came to work in Switzerland, strongly influencing local artists. In Bern, the Swiss adapted Mansard's principles to their own country's traditions. The most outstanding architectural achievements derived from the French model are to be found in Geneva—**Hôtel Buisson**, **Hôtel de Saussure**—and in Solothurn—**Hôtel de la Couronne**.

Abbey church in Einsiedeln, Schwyz at Christmastime

© Christof Sonderegger/Switzerland Tourism

PAINTING

The art of the portrait, much en vogue during the 18C, marked the revival of painting with the Geneva-born artist **Jean-Étienne Liotard** (1702–1789), with realistic style, and a light, confident hand featuring bold colour contrasts and finely observed details. At the end of the 18C, it became fashionable to give free rein to one's feelings; in his portraits **Anton Graff** (1736–1813) depicts his subjects with a modish Romantic sensibility.

After 1750, historical painting returned to fashion with the emergence of Neoclassical style. Events of national importance were commemorated and the country began to develop a patriotic consciousness and sense of national identity; the Geneva artist **Jean-Pierre Saint-Ours** (1752–1809) worked on the Allegory of the Republic of Geneva in 1794. These portrayals of Swiss history remained popular until the mid-20C.

At the end of the 18C, a new genre appeared: Landscape painting.

Celebrating Mother Nature in lush landscapes became a feature of Swiss painting and, for the rest of Europe, defined Switzerland in the popular imagination. The two forerunners of this movement were **Wolf** (1735–1783) and **Johann Heinrich Wüest** (1741–1821), The most famous English exponent was **JMW Turner**, whose views of Lake Geneva, Lucerne and Montreux fired a growing British enthusiasm for the Alps and helped launch the Swiss tourism industry.

Around this period, many Swiss artists travelled abroad (Rome, Paris, or Munich) to complete their training, and some settled in those countries. **Heinrich Füssli** (1741–1825), anglicised as Henry Fuseli, became well known in London. His tortured, obsessive visions often draw on literary works and are thought, in turn, to have been one source of inspiration for Mary Shelley's *Frankenstein*.

Dismissed as a sensationalist by some critics, his weird, nightmarish canvases exerted considerable influence on his peers and on following generations.

19C

Republican ideals and nationalistic values found natural expression in the Neoclassicism that permeated official art and academic works. With this return to themes taken from Antiquity, new genres emerged, characterised by strong emphasis on emotion and feelings.

ARCHITECTURE

The gradual fading of Baroque led to sober Neoclassicism, which embodied the republican ideal. In Lausanne, the edifice housing the Great Council, is a perfect example. Designed by the architect **Alexandre Perregaux** in 1803–1806, it became a symbol for the Vaud canton. In Avenches, the Casino, a private club, was conceived as a small temple of antiquity. The masterpiece of Palladian architecture remains the **Gordanne** in **Féchy**; with its cupola and its portico flanked by Ionic columns it seems to date back to Antiquity.

After 1840, the trend turned toward classical landscaped gardens and mock ruins. The **Château de l'Aile** in **Vevey**, conceived by **Philippe Framel** and **Jean-Louis Brocher** in 1840–1842, is an excellent representation of this lighter, neo-Gothic current.

PAINTING

Alongside academic Neoclassicism, new genres caused a revival of the pictorial art form, namely Romanticism, Symbolism, poster art and satire.

Nostalgia and sentimentality reflected the romantic spirit of the century, aptly conveyed by the works of **Charles Gleyre**, whose tender, graceful characters are bathed in a soft light. **Landscape painting** also took on a sentimental dimension, with light playing an essential part of the composition.

Alexandre Calame (1810–1864) paid tribute to Alpine landscapes by revealing their grandiose, mysterious nature. **Arnold Böcklin** (1827–1901) adopted a similar approach; his *Isle of the Dead* (1880–1886) is an eerie landscape shrouded in silence and mystery, said to have inspired the famous symphonic poem by Rachmaninoff.

Detail of Verdun, tableau de guerre interprete *(1917) by Félix Vallotton*

© akg-images/Alamy

At the end of the 19C, painting explored a new form of expression under the influence of Symbolism, which offered a spiritual or even mystical explanation for reality. **Ferdinand Hodler** (1853–1918) is seen as a Symbolist for his symmetry that reveals a sense of unity inherent in the world (*Truth*, 1903). **Félix Vallotton** (1865–1925), a member of the Nabis movement, contributed to Symbolism by describing the social mores of his time in accordance with the theoretical principles of a pure and symbolic art form.

Lastly, **poster art** and **satire** developed considerably throughout the 19C thanks to Vallotton, **Théophile-Alexandre Steinlen** (1859–1923) and **Eugène Grasset** (1845–1917).

Their role was to expose injustice, to defend the oppressed, and to describe daily life in a simple manner, making art accessible to a wide cross-section of the population.

SCULPTURE

Sculpture saw a tremendous revival during the 19C. Salons in particular were instrumental in popularising small sculptures among private collectors, especially those belonging to the bourgeoisie. In the public sector, this art form was expressed through the decoration of theatres, casinos, banks and rail stations. It accompanied the other changes affecting Swiss urban landscapes and fostered deep feelings of patriotism and national identity.

The exuberance of Rococo was replaced by the grandiose dignity of Neo classicism. The early 19C was also marked by a return to the styles and qualities of the Middle Ages, particularly in painting and architecture. Nostalgia for the past and for bygone feudal traditions can be felt in the creations dating from this period, resulting in a neo-Gothic trend.

To counter this Neoclassical movement, **Vincenzo Vela** (1820–1891) produced naturalistic sculptures and developed the concept of *Vérisme*. He was much appreciated in France, where, in 1866, he painted *The Last Days of Napoleon I*, which portrays the emperor as an ageing, disillusioned man. Vela was known for speaking out in favour of the oppressed and his political commitment took shape in *Memorial to the Victims of Work* in 1883. In the latter part of the 19C, sculpture flourished with a new freedom of expression. The Symbolist movement and Art Nouveau both gave a new lease of life to sculpture. **Auguste de Niederhäusern**, known as Rodo, drew on Rodin's Symbolist theories and produced sculptures from which matter projected, like his *Jet of Water* from 1910–11. The different arts were skillfully combined under the influence of **Art Nouveau**. This approach was successfully explored by **Hermann Obrist**, who strove to achieve the merging of art, spirit and nature through his utopian reflection on the spiral—the ultimate expression of vital energy.

Rural Architecture

Valais house
(Évolène)

Central Switzerland house
(Lucerne area)

Appenzell house
(Trogen area)

Bernese Country house
(Évolène)

Bernese Oberland house
(Jungfrau region)

R. Corbel/Michelin

Rural Architecture

Carefully adorned with flowers, the Swiss peasant house shows, especially in German Switzerland, a remarkable care for comfort and propriety as well as a highly developed practical sense.

The Bernese Oberland House

The Swiss chalet style features a low-pitched roof, with wide eaves on all sides; in the high valleys, it is still covered with shingles weighted down by large stones. The ornamentation is profuse: The beams are carved with facets and the props of the roof are elaborately finished.

The Central Switzerland House

A highly distinctive style of building, recognisable by its steep roof and separate weatherboards sheltering the row of windows on each storey. The ground floor is high above the ground.

The Appenzell House

In this rainy district, farm buildings are grouped together to form a single block and wooden shingles cover the roof and sometimes part of the façade. The gable invariably faces the valley, and the windows of the cellar are located at "ground level" to aid in an even temperature.

The Bernese Country House

A huge roof extending down to the first floor at the sides also covers a large barn. The wealthier country dwellers, imitating townspeople, often choose to remove the triangular roof surmounting the gable and replace it with an imposing timber arch with wood paneling.

The Ticino House

A stone building of a somewhat primitive design with outdoor stairs and wooden galleries. Because of the uneven shape and size of the stones used in its construction, the Ticino house has very thick walls (up to 0.9m/3ft) and is roofed with stone slabs.

The Valais House

Living quarters (wooden section) are joined by open-side galleries to the kitchen area (masonry section). Nearby stands a **raccard** (🕭 *for illustration see The VALAIS*), a small wooden barn perched on piles and used as a granary or storehouse. These are known as a *torba* in the Ticino area.

The Engadin House

The typical Engadin house, a massive grey structure, has plenty of room under a broad gable crowning a façade. Floral, geometrical or heraldic designs frequently adorn the white walls. These may be decorated by a technique known as **sgraffito**, obtained by applying a layer of rough gray plaster, covering with a coat of limewash, and scraping the surface into designs such as rosettes and foliated scrolls.

Wonderful examples of local furnishings are at the Engadin Museum at St Moritz. The most typical room is the **sulèr**, a covered court common to the barn and living quarters, which serves both as a study and a meeting room. This cool, dark room, featuring carefully kept stone flags, a low, whitewashed vault and coffered ceiling, is lit only by an opening in the carriage gate.

20C AND EARLY 21C

Switzerland was part of the cultural wave that swept through Europe, most notably after 1930. The country was the recipient of artistic trends from abroad and began playing an active role in the international art scene.

ARCHITECTURE

During the 1920s, Swiss architecture was heavily influenced by the Bauhaus movement of Walter Gropius. Artistic creation was seen as a means of associating all art forms to create a new architectural identity. The notion of "order" was abandoned and buildings were stripped of their ornamentation. **Robert Maillard** (1872-1940) specialised in designing bridges with "aesthetic perfection." **Charles Édouard Jeanneret** (1887–1965), alias **Le Corbusier**, opted for functional architecture and became known as the "builder of radiant cities." Most of his work was carried out abroad, as his unusual views on architecture were not always well received at home. **Karl Moser** developed a new art form using modern materials such as reinforced concrete to design huge areas where light played an essential role. **St Antonius Kirche** in Basel is his most typical work.

In Lucerne, his work was continued by his pupils Fritz Metzger (St Charles' Church) and Otto Dreyer (St Joseph's Church).

Post-war architecture developed mainly in the Ticino area, Basel, Baden and French-speaking Switzerland, as economic growth required building up areas which, hitherto, had remained unexploited. Switzerland's national road network was the main achievement of this period.

In this utilitarian atmosphere, **Christian Menn** and **Rino Tami** produced outstanding creations, such as the south entrance to the St Gotthard tunnel at Airolo (Ticino), designed by Tami.

With the decline of industry, disused warehouses and factories were converted into arts centres, a trend which became a distinguishing feature of the period. Contemporary architecture became linked to the prestigious image of firms which offered their patronage and for which it acted as a showcase. Since the mid-1970s, environmental concern has spurred an ecological approach to architecture.

In the 1960s, **Aldo Rossi** reacted against the "radiant cities" of Le Corbusier and advocated a universal vision of townscapes. Each building is designed for a particular purpose but nonetheless remains open to change if the situation requires it. His example was followed by architects **Luigi Snozzi**, **Aurelio Galfetti**, and **Mario Botta**, known for his pure, geometrical proportions. Botta conceived the **Tinguely Museum** in Basel, the **Cappella di Santa Maria**

Chiesa di Santa Maria degli Angeli on Monte Tamaro

© Lugano Turismo

Jean Tinguely

Born in Freiburg on 22 May 1925 but raised in Basel where he went to school, worked as a youth and finally studied in the town's Fine Arts Academy (1941–45), Jean Tinguely is the most interesting plastic artist to emerge from Switzerland—some would say, Europe—in the 20C. His assemblages already appear strange to the eye, looking like three-dimensional versions of Dali canvases, but what makes them even weirder is that most of them have been designed for movement, having parts that interlock, turn and shift in the most unexpected manner. Her made his name with self destroying sculptures (**Homage to New York, End of the World Part 2**) although his most popular works are the gigantic **Meta-Harmonie** a crazy hotchpotch of musical instruments welded together making a mighty noise when switched on, and his playful, public fountains in Basel and by the Pompidou Center in Paris. He died in Bern on 20 August 1991.

degli Angeli on Monte Tamaro and what is considered its masterpiece, the Church of **San Giovanni Battista** in the village of **Mogno**, Ticino. Post-Modernism explored the history of architecture, focusing on its structure, materials and motifs. **Bruno Reichlin** and **Fabio Reinhart** drew inspiration from past masters such as Andrea Palladio in the 16C and Francesco Borromini in the 17C. **Jacques Herzog** and **Pierre de Meuron** developed an aesthetic based on surprising and unexpected juxtapositions of materials.

In the second half of the 20C, modern architecture returned to fashion as buildings originally designed in the 1920s and 1930s needed restoration and the designs of **Karl Moser**, **Rudolf Gaberel**, and **Maurice Braillard** were updated. The talent of Swiss architects did not pass unnoticed abroad: **Bernard Tschumi** took part in the Parc de la Villette project in Paris, and **Mario Botta**, as Switzerland's most celebrated architect, was commissioned to design buildings in Tokyo, San Francisco and Paris.

PAINTING AND SCULPTURE

The Modernist movements which spread to Europe at the end of the First World War were represented in Switzerland only through temporary exhibitions. Swiss painting became isolated as ideas from abroad were perceived as a threat. Themes of isolation and escape became common in the work of Alberto Giacometti and **Meret Oppenheim**. However, from 1915–20, Zürich and Geneva became the center of opposition to conventional art.

This was Dadaism, which abolished logic, concentrating on absurd and irrational aspects of everyday life. In this period of World War I, the barbaric products of civilisation were denounced through collages, photomontages and poetry. It was abroad that avant-garde Swiss sculpture truly blossomed, with **Hans Arp**, **Sophie Taeuber-Arp**, and **Alberto Giacometti**. In the 1920s, **Hermann Scherer** and his highly Expressionist wooden sculptures introduced a touch of novelty.

The inter-war period saw a revival of Swiss sculpture. **Alberto Giacometti** (1901–1966) renewed the representation of human figures with his symbolic creations, inspired by tribal art. His spindly, elongated sculptures present a rough texture bearing the imprint of his thumbs and the blade of a knife, and convey the fleeting, elusive nature of man. **Max Bill** was a staunch defender of Concrete Art, which advocated order and rationality. Both his paintings and smooth, aesthetic sculptures (*Endless Ribbon*, 1935) are governed by rigorous mathematical considerations.

Simultaneously, a form of national art emerged, with many public buildings commissioned by the State. The government wanted to maintain calm and order and encouraged art aimed

Beautifully painted Haus zum Ritter, Schaffhausen

© Schaffhausen Tourismus/Switzerland Tourism

Urban Architecture

Swiss villages and cities generally have an old quarter still unchanged from medieval times. The best examples are in **Stein-am-Rhein**, **Schaffhausen**, **St Gallen** and **Chur**.

Fountains – Always charmingly decked with flowers, fountains are a welcoming note to the lively squares and streets of Swiss cities.

Arcades – Originating beyond the Alps, arcades (*Laufen* in German) became popular from the 14C onwards, when they were adopted by Bern.

Painted Façades –Such painting (not to be confused with *sgraffito*, *"The Engadin house"*) has been popular since the Renaissance, especially in German Switzerland. Throughout Switzerland, the shutters of historic monuments and public buildings are painted with chevrons in the colours of the canton's coat of arms.

Covered Bridges – These are especially popular in German Switzerland. In addition to providing towns like Lucerne with pleasant sheltered walks, the roof protects the walkway, reducing maintenance on a structure made wholly of timber. The latest covered bridge built in Switzerland was in 1943 (Hohe Brücke, on the road from Flüeli to Kerns – *See p333*).

Oriel Windows – These corbelled loggias (*Erker* in German), sometimes built over two storeys, are to be seen in northeastern towns and the Engadin region where they are often elaborate works of art decorated with carving and painting.

Official Buildings – Public buildings testify to the quality of civil architecture in the Gothic, Renaissance and Classical periods. Their rooms are richly ornamented and furnished with stucco, woodwork, glazed cabinets, and magnificent porcelain stoves. Important buildings, like the great Gothic cathedrals, are Swiss specimens of foreign styles.

Covered bridge of Baden

© Christof Sonderegger/Switzerland Tourism

at achieving a state of well-being. Any doctrine straying from this vision of happiness and seeking to combine different art forms was deemed degenerate and was systematically rejected (Meret Oppenheim, Sophie Taeuber-Arp).

During the Second World War, Switzerland became a refuge for many European artists, for example **Germaine Richier**, who expressed the war's traumas through highly imaginative sculptures, with strange mutilated surfaces featuring human, vegetable and animal motifs. Some Swiss artists returned to their home country, such as **Paul Klee** (1879–1940), who explored the inner world of dreams and imagination, creating a new style halfway between Abstract and Figurative art, based on colour and perspective.

Sculpture returned to vogue after the Second World War, and Zürich artist **Hans Äschbacher** (1906–1980) created precariously superimposed blocks of marble or granite that seem to defy the laws of gravity. **Walter M Förderer** (b. 1928), designed St Nicholas Church in Hérémence as a huge concrete sculpture. **Walter Bodmer**, a forerunner with his experimental wire paintings,

undertook research in monumental iron works, focusing on lightness and transparency. The iron sculptures of **Bernard Luginbühl** (b. 1929) and **Jean Tinguely** (1925–1991) were far more imposing, overpowering, and excessive: The former showed nostalgia for the bygone era of the Industrial Revolution, while the latter expressed his contempt for history and the art trade through ephemeral, self-destructive machines. His sculpture, *Eureka*, exhibited at the 1988 World Fair in Brisbane (Australia) was crafted with the precision that has earned the Swiss their worldwide reputation.

During the 1960s, **André Thomkins**, **Daniel Spoerri**, **Dieter Roth**, and **Karl Gerstner** spearheaded the Fluxus movement. Thomkins worked on the notion of changing identity and function while Spoerri paid tribute to objects with his ironical booby-trapped paintings.

Since the 1980s, **Samuel Buri** and **Markus Raetz** have worked on the concept of metamorphosis. **Buri** is perhaps best known for his life-size polyester cows which he exhibits at shows and fairs, while **Raetz** studies the changes occurring in the human body and head, the effect of shade and movement.

Art Lovers

Art lovers will enjoy admiring works typifying the following famous painters and artistic movements:

Paul Klee in the Zentrum Paul Klee in Bern

Jean Tinguely in the Musée Jean-Tinguely in Basel

Arnold Böcklin and Konrad Witz in the Musée des Beaux-Arts in Basel

Félix Vallotton in the Musée des Beaux-Arts in Lausanne

Impressionism in the Fondation Collection EG Bührie in Zürich and the Stiftung "Langmatt" Sidney und Jenny Brown in Baden

Post-Impressionism in the Villa Flora in Winterthur and the Fondation Beyeler in Riehen

© Stephan Engler/Switzerland Tourism

Sculptures by Alberto Giacometti, Fondation Beyeler, Basel

Contemporary art in the Kunsthaus in Zürich and the Kunstmuseum in Basel.

Nature

Switzerland consists of a lowland area (the Mittelland or Middle Country) between two mountain barriers: the Alps and the Jura. Both of these highlands arose in the Tertiary Era, 65 million years ago.

THE SWISS ALPS

The Alps cover three-fifths of Swiss territory, making Switzerland the second most Alpine country in Europe after Austria. Apart from the part of Graubünden to the east of the Hinterrhein Valley—a high valley like the Engadin, which, with its extra continental climate, is more typical of central Europe—the Swiss Alps, like the French ones, belong to the western Alpine group: the steepest and most contorted chain, and therefore, the most affected by erosion.

The pinnacle of this world of lakes and glaciers is the Dufour Peak at Mount Rosa 4 634m/15 203ft), although the St Gotthard Massif (highest point: Pizzo Rotondo: 3 192m/10 473ft), which represents the cornerstone of the whole structure. Any motorist crossing a pass like the St Gotthard is made aware of the sharp contrast between the relatively gentle slopes of the north face and the sudden descent which occurs on the south. In the longitudinal direction, the remarkable depression which slashes through the mountains from Martigny to Chur and is drained in opposite directions by the Rhône and the Vorderrhein, forms a great strategic and tourist thoroughfare.

GLACIERS

The Swiss Alps comprise about 2 000sq km/772sq mi of glaciers. Most typical are the valley glaciers, of which the Aletsch Glacier (&see GOMS) is the most extensive in Europe (169sq km/65sq mi). Moving downstream, a **névé** (*Firn* in German), or snowfield, in which snow accumulates and is compacted into ice, is succeeded by a slowly moving **glacier** (*Gletscher* in German) traversed by a close network of crevasses. Breaks or 'steps' in the downward slope, which in the case of a torrent would form cascades or rapids, are marked by unstable masses of ice (*séracs*).

Moraines are accumulations of rocky debris brought down by the glacier. They often soil the whiteness of its tongue of ice and sometimes mask it completely, as at the Steingletscher. Once they halt they form characteristic embankments, known as lateral moraines.

About 1 000 years ago, the predecessors of present glaciers completely filled in the depression between the Jura and the Alps, reaching gigantic proportions. The Rhône Glacier, in what is now the Valais, was at least 1 500m/5 000ft thick. As glaciers withdrew, they created the rocky bars or **bolts** obstructing certain valley floors, as well as tributary **hanging valleys**, described as **scoops** because of their U-shaped cross-sections. When the ice disappeared, the new river flow began to soften these contrasts. **Connecting gorges** then made deeper cuts through the bolts, as in the Aareschlucht, or connected valleys, as in the Trient Gorges.

Alpine torrents were not only destructive, they also built up obstacles in the form of **cones of rubble**. The largest example in Switzerland is the cone of Illgraben as seen from Leuk.

ALPINE VEGETATION

Vegetation is closely bound to climatic and soil conditions as well as altitude and the degree of exposure to prevailing winds and sun. Above the agricultural land, which extends to about 1 500m/4 921ft, is the zone dominated by coniferous forest.

At 2 200m/7 218ft this makes way for mountain pasture (*alpe*) where sturdy, short-stemmed species, bilberry and Alpine flowers grow. At 3 000m/9 842ft, the mineral zone, moss and lichen cling to the rock faces of an otherwise desolate landscape.

Forests

These are the most familiar types of conifers in the Swiss Alps.

Alpine flax

©Alberto Nardi/Tips Images

Purple Columbine

Giorgio Perbellini/iStockphoto

Alpine Clover

Arco Images/Tips Images

Alpine Squill

Arco Images/Tips Images

Edelweiss

Chromorange/Tips Images

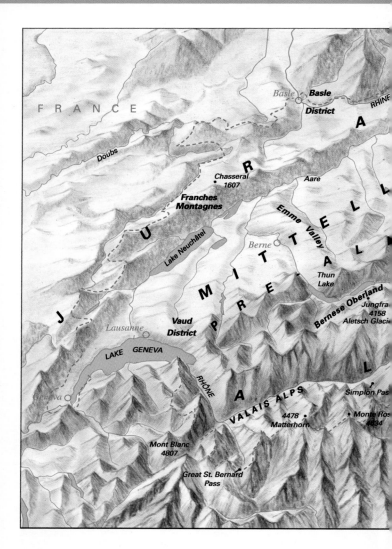

The map shows: FRANCE, RHINE, Basle, Basle District, Doubs, JURA, Chasseral 1607, Franches Montagnes, Aare, Emme Valley, Lake Neuchâtel, Berne, MITTELLAND, Thun Lake, PREALPS, Lausanne, Vaud District, Bernese Oberland, Jungfrau 4158, Aletsch Glacier, LAKE GENEVA, RHONE, Geneva, ALPS, VALAIS ALPS, Simplon Pass, 4478 Matterhorn, Monte Rosa 4634, Mont Blanc 4807, Great St. Bernard Pass

Norway spruce

In French: *épicéa*; in German: *Fichte*; in Italian: *abete rosso*. Found on north-facing slopes, it has a slim, pointed crest and a generally "hairy" appearance, with branches curled like a spaniel's tail. The reddish bark becomes very wrinkled as it grows old, and it bears prickly needles.

Spruce or fir

In French: *sapin*; in German: *Tanne*; in Italian: *abete bianco*. The tree has a broad head, flat on the top, like a stork's nest in older specimens. The bark covers various shades of gray. Cones stand up like candles and, when ripe, disintegrate on the branch, dropping their scales.

Larch

In French: *mélèze*; in German: *Lärche*; in Italian: *larice*. This is the only conifer in the Swiss Alps that sheds its needles in winter.
The tree is found on sunny slopes in the high mountains, especially in the Valais and Graubünden. Cones are very small.

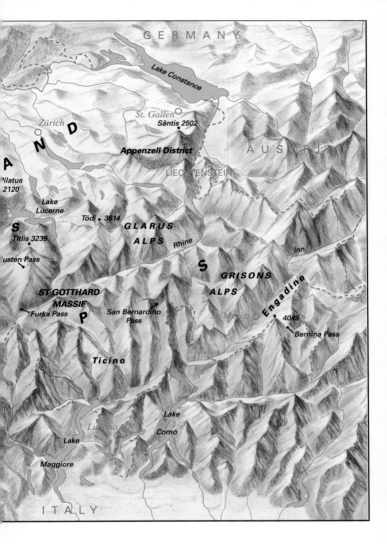

Arolla pine

In French: *pin arolle*; in German: *Arve*; in Italian: *pino cembro*. A characteristic feature of the many species of pine is the arrangement of their needles in tufts of two to five, held together by a scaly sheath. Their cones have hard, tough scales.

The arolla pine can be recognised by the shape of its branches, which are deeply curved, like those of a candelabrum. The tree is often damaged by the wind.

Flora

The term "Alpine plants" is reserved for those which grow above the upper limits of the forests. The early flowering of these species, which are usually small and strong, reflects the brevity of the growing season (June to August).

Disproportionately large blossoms, compared with the plants as a whole, and bright colouring, are directly related to the high ultraviolet content of the light at high altitude.

Protection of Alpine flora

The picking of certain Alpine flowers that are particularly threatened, including cyclamen, Alpine aster, primrose, and edelweiss, is strictly prohibited.

ALPINE CLIMATE

Differences in altitude, mountain formation, and exposure create many variables. During the warm season, daily temperature variations produce winds called *brises*, similar to sea and land breezes elsewhere. Toward noon, the warm, expanding air rises and causes clouds to form around the mountain tops—a sign of steady, fine weather. Walkers should head for viewpoints early, since the valley breeze dies away at about 5pm, and the air suddenly turns cold, especially in the shade.

The Föhn – This relatively warm wind, most keenly felt on the north side of the Alps in the upper Aare and Reuss valleys, unleashes torrential rainstorms and causes thundering avalanches. The arrival of the *Föhn* first sheds its moisture on the Italian side of the Alps, then pours violently over the crest-line, finally growing warmer and becoming dry. Increased risk of disastrous forest fires prompts some communities to apply strict rules, often posted in cafés.

The Majestic Peaks

Swiss mountains over 4 000m/ 13 123ft include:

- ◆ **Monte Rosa** (Valais): 4 634m/15 203ft
- ◆ **Dom** (Mischabel; Valais): 4 545m/14 911ft
- ◆ **Weisshorn** (Valais): 4 505m/14 780ft
- ◆ **Matterhorn** (Valais): 4 478m/14 692ft
- ◆ **Dent Blanche** (Valais): 4 357m/14 295ft
- ◆ **Grand Combin** (Valais): 4 314m/14 153.5ft
- ◆ **Finsteraarhorn** (Valais): 4 274m/14 022ft

Some go so far as to forbid smoking completely. But the Föhn also melts the snow, enabling earlier crops and extended grazing time for animals.

THE SWISS JURA

The Jura massif in Switzerland curves for 200km/125mi between the Dôle (alt 1 677m/5 502ft) and the Lägern (alt 859m/2 819ft above Baden) and ends at the Crête de la Neige (alt 1 723m/5 653ft) in France. The last ridges of the Jura mountains rise above the Mittelland to more than 1 000m/3 280ft to face the Bernese Alps and the Mont Blanc Massif. This mountain chain was created in the Tertiary Era (65 million years ago). Beside this "fixed swell" of valleys and hills there are high, almost level plateaux such as the Franches Montagnes (&see Les FRANCHES MONTAGNES).

Erosion has developed lush valleys and laid bare dramatic rock escarpments. The slashes made by erosion on the hills form the **ruz**.

The **cross-valley** cuts across the hill, connecting two valleys. The **coomb** runs longitudinally along the top of a hill; its escarped edges are called **crests**.

MITTELLAND OR MIDDLE COUNTRY

From Lake Geneva to the Bodensee, between the Alps and the Jura, stretches a gently sloping plateau. All the drainage from here feeds the Rhine through a furrow running along the foot of the last ridge of the Jura. Before the Ice Age, the Rhône itself flowed through this depression, in which a string of lakes (those of Biel and Neuchâtel) and marshy areas now lie.

WILDLIFE

The Alpine slopes are naturally rich in wildlife. Like the flora, fauna has adapted to a hostile environment: protection against cold (dark colour for better heat retention, hibernation), or against predators (white colour to blend with the snow). Of these, man has been the worst. **Chamois** has been greatly hunted and the species, which now numbers 90 000 individuals, has only

Conquest of the Heights

The victories of the 19C over the supposedly inaccessible peaks gradually destroyed the superstitious dread with which they were regarded (♦ see PILATUS). Switzerland, with many of its summits exceeding 4 000m/13 123ft (♦ see left), is a paradise for climbers. One of the first mountains to be climbed here was glacier-covered Titlis in 1744, by four friars from Engelberg. In 1792, Spescha, a monk from Disentis, conquered Oberalpstock. In 1811, the **Meyer brothers**, rich merchants from Aarau, reached the Valais via Grimsel and, starting from Lötschental, climbed the **Jungfrau** (4 158m/13 642ft).

At the same time, Frenchmen and Austrians were attacking the highest alpine peaks. In 1786 French guide **Jacques Balmat** reached the **Mont Blanc** summit and repeated his expedition in 1787 with the Swiss physicist De Saussure (♦ see Michelin Green Guide French Alps). Austrians summited **Grossglockner** (3 797m/12 457ft) in 1800. Breithorn (4 165m/13 665ft) was conquered in 1813, Tödi in 1824, and Piz Bernina (4 049m/13 284ft) in 1850.

The British also recorded some famous first ascents, including **Stockhorn** in 1842 and **Wasenhorn** in 1844, by **JD Forbes**; **Pic Dufour** (4 634m/15 204ft) in 1855 by the three **Smyth brothers**; **Eiger** in 1858 by **Charles Barrington**; and, above all, in 1865, **Matterhorn** (Mont Cervin 4 478m/14 692ft) by **Edward Whymper**. These achievements, with those of the French and Italians, make the 19C the golden age of mountaineering.

survived thanks to draconian regulations. The **Ibex** was not so lucky and was exterminated in the mid-19C. They were reintroduced in 1920 and their current number is 15 000 individuals in Graubünden, Valais and Oberland.
Lynx spontaneously colonised the central and southern Alps since its reintroduction in the 1960s. **Gray Wolves**—extinct for 100 years—are also slowly returning to Switzerland from Italy, where strong protection measures led to an increase in their population. The **Marmot**, which hibernates for nearly six months, is common in the Alps and in some parts of the Jura. The **Golden Eagle**, a protected species since 1953, spends its life in an altitude of 1 500–3 000m, which covers around 100sq km in the Alps. The **Bearded Vulture** disappeared from the Alps in the late 19C, but was successfully reintroduced in 1986 and gradually resumed possession of its original habitats.
The Swiss Biodiversity Monitoring (BDM), established in 2001 by the Federal Office of Environment, monitors biodiversity. Although such diversity is surprisingly well-developed on the alpine slopes thanks to the variety of

climate, elevation and relief, it is much reduced on the overpopulated Central Plateau. Of the 2 729 species recorded in the country, 132 have disappeared and 969 are threatened; of the 195 recorded species of birds, 77 are endangered or extinct.

Marmot in Valais

© Max Schmid/Switzerland Tourism

Skiers on the Corvatsch in Graubünden
© Robert Boesch/Switzerland Tourism

SUISSE ROMANDE

The Suisse Romande (Romandie) is the most westerly region of Switzerland, sharing its border with France in the northwest and the west, and with the canton of Bern to the east. It boasts a wide variety of landscapes ranging from two of the country's largest lakes, Lake Geneva (Léman) and Neuchâtel, to world-renowned mountain summits such as the Matterhorn and the Dent Blanche. The central Swiss Plateau (Mittelland) between the Jura mountains and the Swiss Alps covers a third of the country and is the most densely populated region. While the countryside offers a wide range of activities—from hiking arond La Chaux-de-Fonds to lazing on the beach beside Lake Geneva—the cities of Suisse Romande could keep you busy for weeks.

Highlights

1 Vineyard tour of **Lake Geneva** (p108)
2 **Lausanne**'s Olympic Museum (p128)
3 Attending a festival in chic **Montreux** (p137)
4 Cable car to **Scex Rouge** (p142)
5 Musée International d'Horlogerie at **La Chaux de Fonds** (p180)

A Bit of History

The Suisse Romande actually refers to French Switzerland and is synonymous with the French-speaking area of the country adjacent to France. It consists of six cantons: Jura, Neuchâtel, Vaud, Fribourg, Geneva and Valais, although for the purposes of this Guide, Jura and Valais are treated separately. The cantons of Romandie came relatively recently into the Swiss Confederation as their histori-

cal and linguistic connections tended to be with the Latin world, rather than with their Germanic neighbours, despite being part of the German Holy Roman Empire for a time. Fribourg was the first to join in 1481 but the others came later: Vaud in 1803; Valais, Neuchâtel and Geneva in 1815; and Jura in 1979.

The Canton of Geneva

Geneva is the westernmost canton and as such is almost surrounded by France, with the cosmopolitan city of Geneva at its centre and isolated from all the other cantons except Vaud. Before 1798 Geneva was actually an independent republic although it had been allied to the Swiss Confederation since the late 16C. During the Napoleonic Wars it was annexed to France until liberation in 1813, before finally joining the Swiss Confederation two years later.

Geneva is a very important financial and trading centre with many Swiss banks and international corporations having their headquarters in the city. It is one of

Creux du Van, Val de Travers, the Canton of Neuchâtel

© Roland Gerth/Switzerland Tourism

the centres of the renowned Swiss watch industry with several famous manufacturers based in the canton. There are also numerous international organisations based here, from the Red Cross to the World Trade Organisation, not to mention the European headquarters of the United Nations.

The Canton of Vaud

Vaud, pronounced "*Voh*" in English, is situated in the southwest of Switzerland and shares its borders with Geneva in the south, Neuchâtel in the north and Valais, Bern and Fribourg in the east. In the west lie the Ain, Jura and Doubs *départements* of France.

The Romans, under Julius Caesar, defeated the Celtic Hevetia tribe and founded Lausanne, the modern capital of the Vaud. They were followed by Alemans, Burgundians, Franks, Germans and the Counts of Savoy before the neighbouring Bernese took control. Invading French troops were welcomed by the population in 1798 and by 1803 the Vaud had joined the Swiss Confederation as a canton.

Today Vaud has a flourishing service sector based around finance, tourism and telecommunications, plus a strong manufacturing sector mostly concentrated around Lausanne producing watches and pharmaceuticals. Agricululture remains important too and white wine is produced, mostly in the vineyards above Lake Geneva. Lausanne houses the headquarters of the International Olympic Committee.

The Canton of Fribourg

Fribourg, the first canton in the Suisse Romande to join the Swiss Confederation in 1481, lies at the eastern edge of the Suisse Romande surrounded by Bern in the north and east and by Vaud in the south and west. The Lac de Neuchâtel forms the northwestern frontier and the city of Fribourg is the capital. Although undoubtedly French, there are many German speakers in the east and both Fribourg and Murten are bilingual towns. The west of the canton is part of the Mittelland Plateau, but towards the southeast the land rises to the Pre-Alps with peaks over 2 000m/6 560ft—these pastures make up the Gruyère region renowned for its cheese.

The Romans were here but left few traces, most of which can be found around Fribourg which became a city state in 1157 under the Zähringrens from Germany. It passed to the Habsburgs at the end of the 13C and began to expand before being passed to the Dukes of Savoy. As the power of the Dukes waned, Fribourg became a Free Imperial City in 1478, paving the way for entry to the Swiss Confederation.

The economy of the canton relies heavily on its agricultural sector with cattle breeding, dairy farming, cereal, fruit and tobacco production all being significant. Manufacturing mostly takes place around Fribourg while tourism is becoming very important, especially around the lakes and in the mountains.

The Canton of Neuchâtel

Neuchâtel is sandwiched between France in the west and the lake of the same name in the east. It stretches from Bern canton in the north to Vaud in the south and occupies the eastern slopes of the Jura mountains. There are three regions: the Vignoble on the lake shores, Les Vallées (Val de Travers and Val de Ruz) and the Neuchâtelais mountains above the Val de Travers.

The name of the canton goes back to the Roman designation Novum Castellum (new castle). Following their withdrawal, the area was subjected to alternating claims of Franks, Burgundians and Germans. In 1707 the lands eventually came under the control of the Hohenzollerns who ruled until 1848. Despite not being a Republic, Neuchâtel became part of the Swiss Confederation in 1815 and in 1848 a revolution removed the Hohenzollerns for good.

Neuchâtel is one of the main centres of Swiss watch-making and it is famous for the wines produced on the shore of the lake. Also important are dairy farming, horse and cattle breeding and, of course, the notorious beverage of Absinthe is concocted in the Val de Travers.

SUISSE ROMANDE

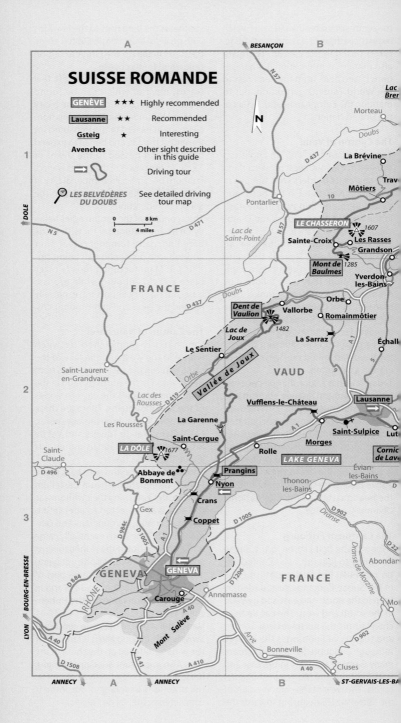

SUISSE ROMANDE

GENÈVE	★★★	Highly recommended
Lausanne	★★	Recommended
Gsteig	★	Interesting
Avenches		Other sight described in this guide
⟶		Driving tour
🔍 LES BELVÉDÈRES DU DOUBS		See detailed driving tour map

0 ___ 8 km
0 ___ 4 miles

FRANCE

VAUD

LAKE GENEVA

GENEVA

FRANCE

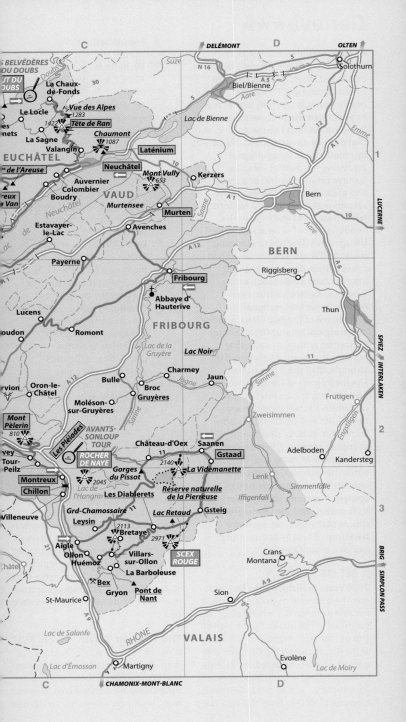

Geneva★★★

An exceptional location makes Geneva one of Switzerland's most privileged cities; it is blessed with a mild climate and its natural environment is carefully protected to guarantee the best possible living conditions. The result is that despite its cosmopolitan and international atmosphere and sprawling residential suburbs, Geneva retains the feel of a small and pleasant town. Geneva is the second seat of the United Nations (after New York) and houses the headquarters of several specialised UN agencies devoted to economic issues and social and humanitarian causes (disarmament, etc.), and international bodies such as the European Centre for Nuclear Research, the International Committee of the Red Cross, and the International Labour Organization. Clustering around its cathedral remains the town of Calvin and the stronghold of the Reformation. The metropolis of French-speaking Switzerland, it is an intellectual city which has welcomed many naturalists and teachers. It is also known for its busy streets and shopping centers. A very Helvetian atmosphere of order and discipline binds these three Genevas into one. Visitors will be charmed by the opulent mansions, the harbour and its fountain, and the shimmering shores of the lake, set against a backdrop of lush vegetation and wooded mountains.

A BIT OF HISTORY

2000 Years of History – The first settlement here dates from around 3000 BC. It became a Roman city when Julius Caesar drove off an attack by the Helveti and its strategic location on the banks of the Rhône caused the city to be conquered and reconquered repeatedly, by Burgundians, Francs, Merovingians, Carolingians, and in 1032, Germanic emperors; all this time the city was

▶ **Population:** Geneva 183 287.

◉ **Michelin Map:** National 729: C7. Includes Town Plan.

▤ **Info:** Rue du Mont-Blanc 18, ℘(0)22 909 70 00. www.geneva-tourism.ch.

▷ **Location:** The city sits around the southwest corner of Lake Geneva, much of which is bordered by pedestrian walkways. Alt. 375m/1 227ft.

ℙ **Parking:** There is a handy park-and-ride system as well as metered parking.

◉ **Don't Miss:** The *Jet d'Eau* (Water Fountain), a man-made geyser that sends up a 122m/400ft fountain over the lake, the city's symbol.

◑ **Timing:** At least 3 days for the city and its museums. To explore more, go on excursions to nearby vineyards and summits, and take a lake cruise.

▲ **Kids:** The Science and History Museum, with dinosaurs, reptiles, and minerals.

ruled by its bishops. Geneva developed into an important commercial center in the Middle Ages, but its independence was threatened by Savoy, whose princes tried unsuccessfully from the 13C–15C to control it. The city's autonomy was saved in the early 16C by the intervention of the Swiss cantons of Fribourg and Bern, and Geneva became a republic in 1535. Geneva's coat of arms reflects its status until then as an Imperial town (half-eagle) and a bishopric (symbolised by a golden key).

The Town of Calvin – From 1532 onward reform was preached successfully in Geneva by French humanists. Shortly after Calvin settled in the town (1536), he dictated laws, decreed laws, built new ramparts, welcomed

Geneva and the Jet d'Eau

© Lucia Degonda / Switzerland Tourism

Marot, Theodore Beza and others, and sentenced the Spanish doctor Miguel Serveto to be burnt at the stake for his religious opinions. Meanwhile, the dukes of Savoy could not resign themselves to the loss of their state's leading city, and in 1602, Charles-Emmanuel delivered an unexpected night attack on Geneva. This was the famous unsuccessful attempt at scaling the rampart walls (*L'Escalade*), which the Genevese still commemorate annually (& *see Calendar of Events*). The first flood of Protestant refugees to Geneva in the mid-16C followed by second wave at the end of the 17C fleeing Louis XIV's persecution of Protestants in France turned the city into a beacon of faith and learning.

GETTING THERE
PUBLIC TRANSPORT

The public transport company Transports Publics Genevois (TPG) operates the city's tram, bus, and trolleybus network. The city is divided into zones (zone 10 is the city center, while zones 82, 84, 87 and 81 are in France). The lines serving zone 10 are numbered (1, 2, 3, etc.), those serving zones 21, 31, 41, 61 and 71 are identified by letters (A, B, C, etc.), and line 51 is operated by Transports Annemassiens Collectifs (TAC). Information and tickets are available from TPG agents at Cornavin Railway Station, Rond-Point de Rive and Bachet de Pesay. The main ticket office can be contacted at &*(0)22 308 34 34* (Mon–Fri). Tickets and day passes can also be purchased from automatic ticket machines at bus stops in zone 10, as well as from licensed vendors. Geneva Transport Cards are provided at no extra cost when you check in at your hotel or hostel. The card provides free access to public transportation for the duration of your stay. *www.unireso.com*.

BOATS – The two banks of the lake are connected by boat, with departures every 10min from 9am–7pm. Line M1 operates between Pâquis and Molard, and M2 from Pâquis to Eaux-Vives. (**CGN** – &*(0)84 881 18 48; www.cgn.ch*). Boat trips are available to visitors, from a trip round the harbour to a grand tour of the lake.
& *See Lake Geneva.*

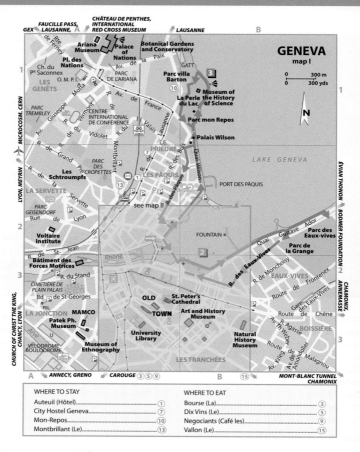

GENEVA
map I

0   300 m
0   300 yds

N

FAUCILLE PASS,
GEX, LAUSANNE, A

CHÂTEAU DE PENTHES,
INTERNATIONAL
RED CROSS MUSEUM

LAUSANNE   B

Ariana
Museum

Palace
of
Nations

Botanical Gardens
and Conservatory

Pl. des
Nations

Ch. du
Pt Saconnex

LES
GENÊTS

O.M.P.I.

PARC
DE L'ARIANA

Parc villa
Barton

Museum of
La Perle the History
du Lac of Science

PARC
TREMBLEY

CENTRE
INTERNATIONAL
DE CONFÉRENCE

Parc mon Repos

Palais Wilson

LE
PRIEURÉ

LAKE GENEVA

Parc
des
Croquettes

LES PÂQUIS

Les
Schtroumpfs

PORT DES PÂQUIS

LA SERVETTE

see map II

PARC
GEISENDORF

FOUNTAIN

Parc des
Eaux-vives

Voltaire
Institute

Parc de
la Grange

Bâtiment des
Forces Motrices

Rhône

R. des Eaux-Vives

EAUX-VIVES

CIMETIÈRE DE
PLAIN PALAIS

R. du Stand

LA JONCTION

MAMCO

Patek Ph.
Museum

Museum of
Ethnography

VÉLODROME
BOULODROME

OLD
TOWN

St. Peter's
Cathedral

Art and History
Museum

University
Library

Natural
History
Museum

BOISSIÈRE

LES TRANCHÉES

ANNECY, GRENO   CAROUGE ③⑤⑨   MONT-BLANC TUNNEL
CHAMONIX

WHERE TO STAY		WHERE TO EAT	
Auteuil (Hôtel)	①	Bourse (La)	③
City Hostel Geneva	⑦	Dix Vins (Le)	⑤
Mon-Repos	⑩	Negociants (Café les)	⑨
Montbrillant (Le)	⑬	Vallon (Le)	⑮

Geneva, Capital of the Mind – Intellectual life flourished in the 18C: Jean-Jacques Rousseau, Mme d'Epinay, the banker Necker and his daughter Germaine (the future Mme de Staël), Dr Tronchin, the mountaineer and scientist, De Saussure, the painter Liotard, and Voltaire were citizens of Geneva by birth or by adoption. Diderot and D'Alembert had several volumes of their controversial 18C French encyclopaedia, *L'Encyclopédie*, printed here from 1777 to 1779. The city was annexed by France in 1798 and for 16 years the town was the capital of the French *département* of Léman. It joined the Swiss Confederation, after the collapse of the Napoleonic Empire, in 1815, when the unification treaty was signed. In 1846, a revolution led by James Fazy overthrew the government of the Reforation and established the constitution that is still in force today. Geneva's tradition of intellectual and religious freedom set the stage for its becoming an international city: Henri Dunant (1828–1910) had governments sign the Geneva Convention in 1863, limiting the effects of war, which led to the creation of the International Red Cross and cemented the city's reputation of a centre of peace and humanism and commerce, including watchmaking.

WALKING TOURS

① **OLD TOWN**★★
1hr 30min.
With its narrow cobbled streets, the old town is a labyrinth of architectural gems spanning the 12C–18C, and is dotted with fine restaurants and vibrant bistros and cafés.

Place Neuve

This large square is surrounded by several majestic buildings dating from the 19C: the Music Conservatory, the work of Jean-François Bartholoni, and the Grand Theatre and the Rath museum, housed in a Greek architecture-inspired building which acts as a exhibition venue, are the focal point for culture in Geneva. In the middle of the square there is a bronze statue of the 19C Swiss hero General Dufour, on horseback.

Musée Rath (Rath Museum)

Place Neuve. ◷*Open 10am–6pm, Wed 10am–8pm.*◷*Closed Mon.* ↻*10CHF, free for under-18s.* ✆*(0)22 418 33 40. www.ville-ge.ch/mah.*

This museum, fronted by a portico, was built in the 19C in Greek classic style. It features temporary exhibits organised by the Art and History Museum. Special emphasis is placed on archeology and ancient art and on contemporary and modern art.

Promenade des Bastions

These public gardens, located at the foot of the city's ramparts, date from the eighteenth century. In the middle of the gardens, on the left hand side, you will find the vast mural (100m/109yds long) the **Monument de la Réformation**⋆ (Protestant Reformation), built against a 16C rampart and kept deliberately plain. The great statues of the four Genevese reformers Farel, Calvin, Beza, and Knox stand in the centre underneath the motto *Post Tenebras Lux.* The memorial (erected 1917) and its other statues and low reliefs with explanatory texts recall the origins of the Reformed Church and its repercussions in Europe. In front of it the arms of Geneva—bishop's key and imperial eagle—appear on the pavement between the Bear of Bern and the Lion of Scotland. On the other side, the boundary of the park is the University Library.

▷ *Leave the promenade des Bastions, opposite the Place Neuve, by rue St-Léger, turn left, pass under the bridge.*

Place du Bourg-de-Four

Fairs used to take place during the Middle Ages on this quaint square in the heart of old Geneva. It is flanked by old houses, some of which have kept their former inn signs. Antiques shops, art galleries and cafés surround the flower bedecked fountain.

▷ *Walk along rue des Chaudronniers and then down rue Charles-Galland.*

Musée d'Art et d'Histoire⋆⋆ (Art and History Museum)

◷*Open Tue–Sun, 10am–6pm.* ◷*Closed 1 Jan and 25 Dec.* ↻*5CHF (no charge for the permanent collection).* ✆*(0)22 418 26 00. www.ville-ge.ch/mah.*

General Dufour, a National Hero

Guillaume-Henri Dufour was born in 1787 in Germany to Swiss parents in exile. He attended military studies in Paris and became an officer in Napoleon's Grand Army, resigning his commission in 1817 to return to Switzerland, where he was appointed captain in the federal forces and *chef du génie genevois*. He helped to found the **Military Academy** at Thun in 1819 and was a military instructor until 1830; soldiers he trained included Prince Louis **Napoleon Bonaparte**, the future Emperor Napoleon III. Dufour reorganised the armed forces and was appointed Chief of Staff, commanding the Swiss Army against the rebels of separatist Catholic cantons in the Sonderbund War (1847). Between 1832-64 he surveyed Switzerland, publishing a series of topographical maps on a scale of 1:100 000, known as the **Dufour Map**. Perhaps his most enduring legacy was **the national flag**, officially recognised by the Diet on 21 July 1840. When he died on his estate at Contamines in 1875, he was honored with a hero's funeral. The highest point of Mount Rosa, Pointe Dufour (alt. 4 634m/15 202ft), was named in his honour.

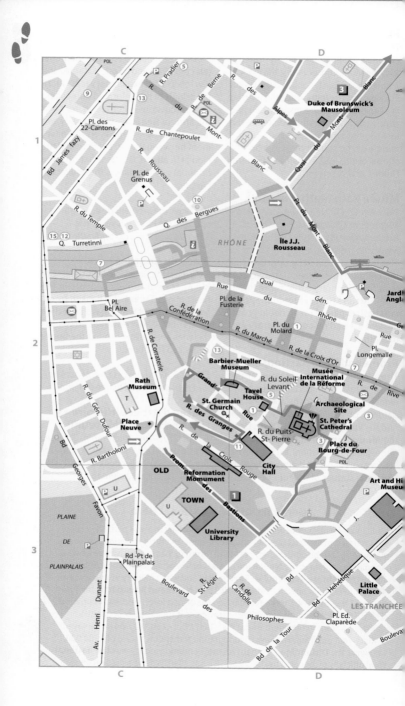

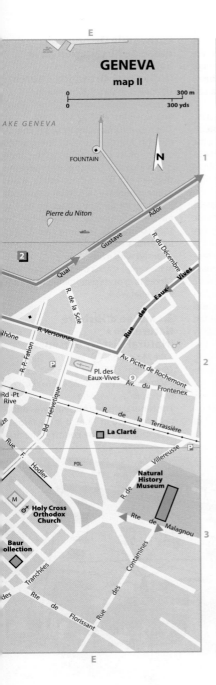

GENEVA
map II

0 ————————— 300 m
0 ————————— 300 yds

LAKE GENEVA

FOUNTAIN

Pierre du Niton

Ador

Gustave

Quai

R. du Décembre

Vives

Rue des Eaux

R. de la Scie

R. Versonnex

Rhône

R. P. Fatton

Av. Pictet de Rochemont

P

Pl. des
Eaux-Vives

Av. du Frontenex

Rd-Pt
Rive

Bd Helvétique

R. de la Terrassière

Rue

F.

Hodler

La Clarté

POL

Villereusse

P

R. de

Natural
History
Museum

M

Holy Cross
Orthodox
Church

Rte de Malagnou

Baur
Collection

Contamines

Tranchées

Rte de des

des

Rue des Florissant

N

1

2

3

E

E

WHERE TO STAY

WHERE TO EAT

The Art and History Museum collections present an outline of the history of civilisation, from prehistoric times up to the 21C. The largest sections are devoted to archaeology and painting. Several rooms of a castle have been reconstructed, complete with raised panelling and 17C furniture.

Archeology – Several rooms in succession are devoted to prehistory (objects of local origin), Egypt, Mesopotamia, the Near East, Greece, Rome and the Etruscans. The Numismatic Room contains a wide range of ancient monetary weights and coins.

Painting – The celebrated altarpiece by **Konrad Witz** (1444), one of whose panels shows the New Testament story of the miraculous draught of fishes, is generally held to be the first exact representation of landscape in European painting: Geneva and Le Môle can be glimpsed in the background. Other rooms pay tribute to the Italian and Dutch Schools. These are succeeded by pictures of the 17C and especially the 18C. There are a number of masterpieces by Quentin de la Tour, including *Abbot*. Tribute is paid to the Impressionist movement, with works by Pissarro (*The Harbor in Rouen*), Monet (*Peonies*), Cézanne (*The House in Bellevue*), Renoir (*Summertime*) and Sisley (*The Lock at Moret-sur-Loing*).

▷ *Continue along rue Charles-Galland.*

Cathédrale Orthodoxe Russe de l'Exaltation de la Sainte-Croix (Holy Cross Orthodox Church)

🕐*Open Tue–Sun, 9.30am–noon, 2.30pm–5pm in summer; 2.30pm–5pm only in winter.* 📞*(0)22 346 47 09.*

This beautiful Russian Orthodox church dates from the late 19C. The golden domes of its cupolas are in the style of old Moscow churches, reproducing the plan of a Greek cross. Inside, walls, vaulting and pillars are ornamented with paintings inspired by Byzantine art. The nave is separated from the chancel by the iconostasis, forming five arches in Carrara marble, finely carved and adorned with icons.

In the center stands the sacred doorway, carved in cypress pine, gilded with intricate relief work.

🧍🧍Musée d'Histoire Naturelle★★ (Natural History Museum)

1 Rte Malagnou. 🕐*Open Tue–Sun, 10am–5pm.* 🕐*Closed 1 Jan and 25 Dec.* 💶*No charge.* ♿ 📞*(0)22 418 63 00. www.ville-ge.ch/mhng.*

The Natural History Museum was originally founded in 1820. It is the largest such museum in the country. The first

Courtyard, Musée d'Art et d'Histoire

The Geneva Escalade

This traditional festival commemorates the successful defence of the town against the Savoyards who attemped to scale *(escalader)* the walls. Celebrations include a torchlit procession with the Genevese in period costume through the narrow streets of the town and along the banks of the Rhône. The procession stops along the way when a herald on horseback reads out the official proclamation claiming victory over Savoy. Local confectioners make chocolate cauldrons, symbolising the heroic deed of one semi-mythical Genevese housewife who put the enemy to flight by pouring the boiling contents of a cauldron over their heads. Fireworks and a religious service in the Cathédrale St-Pierre complete the day's festivities.

floor, set aside for tropical birds and mammals, takes visitors from the African savannah to the South and North Poles, as well as Asia and Latin America. You can see several species of tiger, some of which have become extinct, as well as the dodo, a bird which used to inhabit the Mauritius and Réunion Islands. The second floor shows reptiles and amphibians from around the world.

The third floor focuses on paleontology, geology and mineralogy, giving a chronological account of the history of the earth, other planets, and meteorites. Note the dinosaur display with its huge triptych in the background, explaining three prehistoric ages. Another fascinating exhibit is the fossil of a *Xiphactinus audax*, a predatory fish from the Cretaceous period (96 to 75 million years ago). The section devoted to the *Hominidae* is illustrated by Lucy, who was discovered in Ethiopia in 1974 and whose origins are thought to go back some 3.5 million years.

The fourth floor focuses on the geology of Switzerland.

▷ *Retrace your steps along rte. de Malagnou and go left up blvd. des Tranchées. Take the second road on the right (rue Charles Sturm) and then turn immediately left on to rue du Mont de Sion.*

Collections Baur★

8 rue Munier-Romilly. ⏱*Open Tue–Sun, 2pm–6pm (8pm Wed).* ↻*Guided tour first Wed of the month.* ⏱*Closed 1 Jan and 25 Dec.* ⊜*10CHF.* ℘*(0)22 704 32 82; www.fondation-baur.ch.*

This museum, housed in a 19C mansion, is devoted to art from the Far East amassed over a half-century by Swiss collector Alfred Baur (1865–1951) plus temporary exhibitions. The permanent collection features porcelain, stoneware, celadon jade, and other items from China and Japan.

▷ *Walk down rue Munier-Romilly, left on to rue François-le-Fort and right down rue St Victor. Return to Place duBourg-de-Fer, then take promenade de Pin and then rue Étienne-Dumont. Pass the Mortimer café, at number 2, to access the stairs which lead to the cathedral.*

Cathédrale St-Pierre★★ (St Peter's Cathedral)

⏱*Open Jun–Sept, Mon–Sat 9.30am– 6.30pm, Sun noon–6.30pm; Oct–May, Mon–Sat, 10am–5.30pm, Sun and public holidays, noon–5.30pm.* ℘*(0)22 311 75 75. www.saintpierre-geneve.ch.*

This vast cathedral, erected 12C-13C, partly rebuilt during the 15C, has been a Protestant church since 1536. It was given a surprising neo-Grecian façade in the 18C. The interior is plain but impressive. It was here that John Calvin preached his fierce, protesting sermons; you may see Calvin's seat, 15C stalls and the tomb of the Duke de Rohan, who was the head of the Reformed Church in France during the reigns of Henri IV of Navarre and Louis XIII.

The Chapelle St-Pierre or Chapelle des Macchabées opens out of the first bay in the south aisle. It is an elegant structure in the Flamboyant Gothic style, built by Cardinal de Brogny at the beginning of the 15C and heavily restored in the 19C in the neo-Gothic tradition after designs by the famous architect Viollet-le-Duc.

North Tower

🕐*Same opening times as the cathedral (last admission 30min before closing time).* ➼*4CHF.*

The top of the tower commands a superb **panorama**★★ of Geneva, the lake, the Jura, and the Alps.

▷ *Once out of the cathedral you come to the Cour St-Pierre.*

Site Archéologique★

🕐*Open Tue–Sun 10am–5pm. Last admission 30min before closing time.* 🕐*Closed Mon except Easter, Whitsun and Jeûne federal holiday.* ➼*8CHF.* ℘*(0)22 311 75 74. www.site-archeologique.ch.*

In front of the west face of the Chapelle des Macchabées a staircase leads down to the archeological site found under the present cathedral. A chronological itinerary leads the visitor through the excavations, some of which date back over 2 000 years.

Cross Cour St-Pierre and turn right into rue du Soleil-Levant.

On the corner of the street stands a bronze statue of the Prophet Jeremiah, executed by Rodo.

▷ *Turn right as you leave the crypt.*

Musée International de la Réforme★

4 rue du Cloître. 🕐*Daily Tue–Fri 10am–5pm.* 🕐*Closed Mon, except Pentecost and Jeune Fédéral.* ➼*10 CHF (-16 years, 5 CHF).* ♿ ℘ *(0)22 310 24 31. www.musee-reforme.ch.*

This museum which was opened in 2005, presents the history of the Reformation in an attractive and engaging style. The movement turned Geneva life on its head in the 16C with thousands of refugees escaping to the city from France, Italy, the Netherlands and Scotland. Pictures, drawings, Calvin's

manuscripts, unusual works of art and other rare objects are displayed in 12 rooms, each having a different theme (Calvin and Geneva, the religious wars, the 19C Reformation and so forth). In the fine central room, decorated in 18C style, a 15min informative audiovisual film is shown every hour (at quarter past). In another room, a virtual banquet has been laid out, and there you can listen to Rousseau and Calvin exchanging views on the issue of predestination.

▷ *Turn left along the Rue du Cloître, bear right and head along the Rue de l'Evêche to the Rue du Puits.*

Maison Tavel★ (Tavel House)

6 Rue du Puits-St-Pierre. ℘*(0)22 310 37 00.* 🕐*Open Tue–Sun 10am–6pm.* 🕐*Closed 25 Dec and 1 Jan.* ➼*Temporary exhibitions 3CHF.* ♿ *For guided tours, call* ℘*(0)22 418 25 00. www. ville-ge-ch/mah.*

This house is the oldest in Geneva. After the great fire of 1334—which ravaged more than half the town—it was rebuilt and gradually acquired its present appearance. Its elegant stone façade features amusing stone effigies representing heads of animals and human beings. A niche above one of the windows on the first floor carries the sculpted coat of arms of the Tavel family. Displays focus on the history of Geneva between the 14C and 19C. The town's ramparts, architecture, religious and political activities, and day-to-day life are vividly evoked through a collections of coins, early photographs, locks, door panels, and roof ornaments.

▷ *Turn left from the Maison Tavel and left again at Rue Jean Calvin.*

Musée Barbier-Mueller★ (Barbier-Mueller Museum)

10 r. Jean-Calvin. 🕐*Open daily 11am–5pm.* ♿*(ground floor only).* ➼*8 CHF (-12 years free of charge).* ℘*(0)22 312 02 70. www.barbier-mueller.ch.*

Drawing its riches from a family collection, amounting to more than 7000 items, this museum has a rotating exhibition of ancient works of art, plus sculptures, masks, ceramic pieces, jewellery and material from "primitive" civilisations throughout the world. Creative use of lighting adds to the appreciation of the works.

▷ *Follow rue Calvin, turn left to join the Grand'Rue.*

Grand'Rue

This picturesque street, one of the best preserved in the old city, offers visitors a remarkable choice of bookstores, art galleries, and antique shops. Several buildings are associated with famous people: number 40 is where **Jean-Jacques Rousseau** was born; the great actor **Michel Simon** (1895–1975) was born at number 27.

▷ *When you reach the place du Grand-Mézel, ornamented with a flower-decked fountain, turn left.*

Rue des Granges

Lined with large, comfortable residences in the style of French 18C architecture. The Hôtel de Sellon at number 2 houses the **Musée-Fondation Zoubov** (✎*guided tours (50min) mid-Jun–late Sept, Mon–Fri 3.45pm; Oct–mid-Jun, Thu at 5pm, Sat at 2.30pm and 3.30pm; ⊚5CHF; unguided visits Mon–Fri 2.30pm–5pm; ⊚no charge; ⏱closed two weeks at Easter and three weeks at Christmas; ℘(0)22 312 16 97. www.ge.ch/zoubof*) made up of Countess Zoubov's personal mementoes and brought back from her many trips abroad, including *cloisonné* enamels from Peking and painted enamels from Russia (imperial palaces of St Petersburg).

Furniture pieces signed by the greatest 18C French cabinetmakers, portraits executed by court painters such as Vigée-Lebrun, the Baron Gérard, Lampi the Elder and Lampi the Younger, as well as sumptuous carpets and tapestries decorate the various rooms of the Hôtel: the private entrance, the dining hall, the vast lounge, the bedrooms, and the boudoir of Catherine II. At number 7

stands the house where **Albert Gallatin** (1761–1849) was born, who emigrated to America and became an American statesman, including as peace commissioner to Ghent in 1814.

Église St-Germain – *Call ahead on ℘(0)22 311 41 30 to organise a visit to this church.*

Rebuilt in the 15C, this church as a bell tower which dates from the 13C. Christian relics, dating back to the 5C, including the remains of a primitive altar are also evident. Modern stained glass allows light to illuminate the interior of the church. One of the most interesting features is a fountain and sundial work.

The church hosts regular concerts of chamber music on Sundays and Mondays during the summer starting at 6.30pm. They are free on a first-come, first-served basis with the doors opening at 6pm.

▷ *At the end of rue des Granges, you come out on rue Henri-Fazy and the Hôtel de Ville.*

Hôtel de ville (City Hall)

This building dates mainly from the 16C and 17C with an older (1455) tower, the Baudet. Go into the courtyard to see an unusual spiral ramp, paved with pebbles, which allowed visitors to gain access to higher floors without having to get off their horses or climb out of their sedan chairs.

On the ground floor, visit the Alabama room where the first Red Cross agreement (named the Geneva agreement) was signed on 22 August 1864.

In the summer (July and August) the Hôtel de Ville acts as a stage for a variety of concerts from jazz to classical. Entry to the **Summer Musical Festival** (*℘(0)22 418 36 18; www.ville-ge.ch/culture/mus_ete/infos.html*) is by ticket only.

▷ *At the bottom of rue Henri-Fazy, head down towards the Place Neuve via the promenade and the Treille ramp.*

A Monumental Jet of Water

Most big cities boast a recognisable landmark which identify it: The Eiffel Tower in Paris, London's Big Ben, New York's Statue of Liberty, Rome's Colosseum, Athens has the Acropolis and Geneva has its monumental jet of water. It gushes not from the earth but from the lake at a speed of around 200kph/125mph to a height of 140m/460ft. This gigantic white column, on which the Genevese pride themselves and which tourists flock to admire, is operated by a powerful pumping system driven by electrical engines which draw in lake water and shoot it into the air at a rate of 500l a second. The water falls in a fine spray which, if a strong wind is blowing, can take tourists by surprise! To avoid any problems, particularly with boats crossing the lake, the jet is subject to strict wind and weather regulations. A meteorological center inside the machine room and a team of technicians are on duty to monitor the city's symbol. The *Jet d'Eau* is traditionally turned on on the first day of the Salon de l'automobile in March, and operates until 31 October.

② THE LEFT BANK

3hrs. Start from Pont du Mont-Blanc.
The quays along the south of the lake are flanked by lawns planted with trees and flower beds.

Jardin Anglais

A floral clock dominates the part of the English garden which looks out onto Quai Général-Guisan. The clock consists of 6 500 different flowers and symbolises the expertise of Geneva's clock-making industry. The terrace affords an interesting panorama of the harbour and, farther back, the Jura mountain range. One of the most famous landmarks of Geneva is the harbour and its magnificent **Jet d'Eau,** whose great white plume marks the city from afar. It is now the emblem of Geneva and for a good, close-up view of the fountain, situated at the end of the Jetée des Eaux-Vives, take a walk along Quai Gustave-Ador. There, an impressive collection of sailing boats are moored to an artificial marina, confirming Geneva's reputation as an important yachting harbour.

The lake itself, teeming with many boats, including paddle steamers and the famous mouettes, is a memorable sight.

Parc de la Grange★

It features the finest rose garden in Switzerland (flowering season mid-June) and, in the centre of the grounds, an elegant 18C residence. Next to it lies the charming **Parc des Eaux-Vives★**.

③ THE RIGHT BANK

Take a walk along **Quai du Mont-Blanc**, which runs parallel to the north bank of the lake and which features stately mansions decked with flags. The route offers distant **views★★★** of the surrounding mountains (Voirons, Môle, Salève, Mont Blanc on a clear day).

▷ *Start from the junction formed by the bridge, the street and Quai du Mont-Blanc.*

The prow of the **Île Jean-Jacques Rousseau** juts out downstream from the bridge. On it stands a statue of the famous writer.
The Quai du Mont-Blanc is a bustling centre of activity, frequented by both local residents and tourists, who enjoy strolling along the lake shores and visiting the cafés and souvenir shops.

Mausolée du Duc de Brunswick (Mausoleum)

The mausoleum of Charles II of Brunswick (b. 1804, d. in Geneva 1873), a distinguished benefactor of the town, was built in 1879 in the style of the Scaliger tombs in Verona.

▷ *Proceed along Quai Wilson, the continuation of Quai du Mont-Blanc, or go to the Débarcadère des Pâquis and use the "Mouettes Genevoises", a regular shuttle service linking several points of the harbour.*

Parc Villa Barton, La Perle du Lac, and Parc Mon Repos★★

These three connected parks form the finest landscaped area in Geneva. There are elegant mansions within the gardens and around its perimeter.

Farther on there is a good view of the **Little Lake** towards Lausanne.

👥Musée d'Histoire des Sciences (Museum of the History of Science)

🕐*Open Wed–Mon, 8.30am–5pm.* 🕐*Closed 1 Jan and 25 Dec.* 🚫*No charge.* 📞*(0)22 418 50 68; www.ville-ge.ch/mhs.*

In La Perle du Lac stands the stately Bartholoni Villa (1825), lavishly decorated with mural paintings, now a museum devoted to scientific equipment from the 18C and 19C. One room pays tribute to the Genevese physicist De Saussure (inventions, personal instruments, and mementoes); others display exhibits relating to astronomy (sundials, planetaries), navigation (sextants, compasses) and surveying (theodolites).

Other historical medical artifacts include stethoscopes, portable first-aid kits), electricity and electromagnetism, meteorology (thermometers, barometers), and physics (models of steam engines, various measuring devices, including an acoustic spoon used for calculating the speed of sound crossing water).

THE INTERNATIONAL DISTRICT

Musée Ariana★★

Avenue de la Paix 10 🕐*Open Tue–Sun 10am–6pm.* 🕐*Closed 1 Jan and 25 Dec.* 🚫*free; temporary exhibitions 5CHF.* 📞*(0)22 418 54 50; www.ville-ge.ch/ariana.*

The museum, founded by Gustave Revilliod (1817–1890), was built by Émile Grobety between 1879 and 1884 in the style of an Italian palace. The collections provide a riveting illustration of 1 000 years of ceramics in Europe, Asia and the Middle East, from the first earthenware pieces (a 9C bowl from Mesopotamia) to Italian Renaissance maljolica and Delft earthenware up to early Meissen pottery at the beginning of the 18C. The building also houses the headquarters of the International Academy of Ceramics.

Palais des Nations★★ (Palace of Nations)

Entrance at 14 avenue de la Paix, Portail de Pregny. 👣*Guided tours (1hr) daily in Jul and Aug, 10am–4pm; Sept–Mar Mon–Fri, 10am–noon, 2–4pm; Apr-June daily 10am–noon, 2–4pm. ID required.* 🕐*Closed Nov to Mar, Sat–Sun and two weeks before Christmas.* 🚫*12CHF.* 📞*(0)22 917 48 96. www.unog.ch.*

The palace in Ariana Park was built between 1929 and 1936 as the headquarters of the League of Nations. Since 1946 it has been the second centre of the United Nations, the seat of which is located in New York City. A new wing added in 1973 is said to be one of the most active conference centres in the world. The **Salle des Pas-Perdus**, adorned with various kinds of marble donated by UN member countries, leads into the great **Salle des Assemblées**

The Last Days of Sissi

Elisabeth, Empress of Austria and Queen of Hungary, wife to Emperor Franz-Joseph, died in Geneva in 1898. Just as she was stepping onto a boat, Sissi, as she was affectionately known by the population, was stabbed in the heart by Italian anarchist Luigi Lucheni. She staggered on board and collapsed. Rushed to the private suite which she occupied at the Hôtel Beau-Rivage, on Quai du Mont-Blanc, she died of her wounds soon afterwards. To mark the centenary of her death, the Hôtel Beau-Rivage organised an exhibition devoted to the sovereign including her poems, which she had bequeathed to Switzerland.

A bust in her memory stands on the lake opposite the hotel.

Palais des Nations

Heinz Schwab/Switzerland Tourism

(capacity 2 000 people) where plenary meetings are held. Pass along a gallery onto which several meeting rooms open, to reach the **Salle du Conseil** where the most important conferences take place. It is also known as the Spanish Room in honour of Francisco de Vitoria, who is considered by many to be the founder of international law. The Spanish artist José Maria Sert decorated this room with huge frescoes depicting the technical, social and scientific achievements of mankind. The visit ends with a film explaining the role of the UN and its famous peacekeeping forces.

Musée International de la Croix-Rouge et du Croissant-Rouge★ (Red Cross Museum)

Access to the museum is through the Avenue de la Paix.
🕒*Closed until 2013* ♿ ℘*(0)22 748 95 25. www.micr.org.*
In the entrance hall, a bronze by US sculptor George Segal entitled *The Petrified* symbolises the violation of human rights.

Genevese businessman **Henri Dunant** witnessed the Battle of Solférino, during which 40 000 men were killed or wounded in one day. He decided to launch a movement to aid the wounded. Four years later, he founded the Red Cross. Eleven exhibition areas describe the activities of the Red Cross and the Red Crescent throughout the world. Also on display is the uniform worn by Napoleon III during the battle. The museum provides a moving insight into the history of mankind, inviting both respect and contemplation.

Conservatoire et Jardin Botanique★ (Botanical Gardens and Conservatory)

🕒*Open Apr–Sept, daily 8am–7.30pm; Oct–Mar, daily, 9.30am–5pm. Greenhouses open all year 9.30–4.30pm.* 🚶*Guided tour Nov–Apr, Tue at 12.30pm; May–Oct, by appointment.* 🎫*No charge.* ℘*(0)22 418 51 00. www.ville-ge.ch/cjb.*

This 17ha/42-acre garden is both a pleasant recreational spot and a living museum of the plant kingdom.

It features a **rock garden★★**, where the different plants are divided into geographical groups, a deer pen and aviary, and a series of hothouses with a superb winter garden, containing many luxuriant species from both equatorial and tropical countries. Noticeboards direct visitors to the most interesting flower varieties. There are more than 16 000 plant species from around the world and the herbarium of 5.5 million samples makes it one of the five largest in the world.

PLAINPALAIS DISTRICT

From Cornavin station take number 13 or 15 tram to Cirque station on boulevard Georges-Favon.

The three museums below are located on the other side of the Plainpalais plain. This enormous piece of land seems to be nondescript at first site, but has markets on several days of the week (*see p107*) and on the north side an area is dedicated to enthusiasts of skateboards and rollerskates.

Patek Philippe Museum★★

Open Tue–Fri, 2pm–6pm; Sat, 10am–6pm. Guided tours by appointment. Closed public holidays. 10CHF. (0)22 807 09 10. www.patekmuseum.com.

The history of Patek Philippe began in 1839, when Antoine Norbert de Patek founded a watch and clock manufacturers with his compatriot, François Czapek. Czapek retired in 1845 and the French watchmaker Adrien Philippe, inventor of the keyless watch, joined the company, which soon built an international reputation for unparalleled technical expertise and aesthetic style. A beautifully restored factory now houses the Patek Philippe Museum, which exhibits a collection of magnificent timepieces collected over a period of 30 years. Each floor focuses on a particular aspect of watchmaking and history.

Musée d'Ethnographie - Ports Francs (Museum of Ethnography)

Open Tue–Sun, 10am–5pm. 5CHF for temporary exhibitions, no charge for permanent collections and 1st Sun of month. (0)22 418 45 50. www.ville-ge.ch/meg.

The Museum of Ethnography presents miscellaneous collections from all over the world, featuring both works of art and simple objects for everyday use. It also hosts temporary exhibitions, each focusing on a specific theme or ethnic group.

MAMCO

Open Tue–Fri, noon–6pm; Sat-Sun, 11am–6pm. Closed 1 and 2 Jan, Good Fri, 1 May, 1 Aug, first Thu of Sept (Jeûne Genevois), 25 and 26 Dec. 8CHF. (0)22 320 61 22. www.mamco.ch.

This Museum of Modern and Contemporary Art, housed in an old factory, displays recent avant garde works (post-1960), taken from over 40 private and public collections, both in Switzerland and abroad. Relying for the most part on unusual or relatively unknown artists, the museum's aim is to surprise and provoke visitors, whether they be seasoned critics or simply amateur art lovers.

ADDITIONAL SIGHTS

Bibliothèque Universitaire (University Library)

1 Promenade des Bastions. Open Mon –Fri 9am–noon, 2pm–6pm, Sat 9am– noon only. Closed public holidays. (0)22 418 28 00. www.ville-ge.ch/bge.

The Ami-Lullin library room is reserved for a permanent display of manuscripts, books and archives relating to the history of the Reformation and literary life in Geneva. The room named after **Jean-Jacques Rousseau** contains personal mementoes belonging to the writer (manuscripts, prints, and a bust by Houdon).

Fondation Bodmer★★ (Bodmer Foundation)

19-21 rte du Guignard (from Rive, take bus A, to Cologny-Temple stop or bus 33, Croisée de Cologny stop). Every day except Mondays and Hols. 2pm–6pm. 15 CHF. (0)22 707 44 36. www.fondationbodmer.org.

The Bodmer foundation has drawn together the most notable of the documents written by scholar, collector and bibliophile Martin Bodmer (1899-1971). In 2003 a new underground museum, designed by Swiss architect Mario Botta was opened. This has a lovely above ground terrace with a lake view. The foundation has an enviable collection of works from the dawn of time up to modern day, including ancient tablets, Greek and Coptic papyrus documents, among which figure manuscripts written by John the Baptist. Under muted lights there are also works from leading philosophers, writers and well known people over the centuries—among the Dante, Napoleon I, Zola, Kierkegaard and Tolstoy.

Microcosm

CERN, route de Meyrin. From Geneva, follow the signs for the airport, Lyons or Meyrin. From Meyrin, continue to St-Genis. The CERN is on the left, just after the French border. 🕐*Microcosm Mon-Fri 8.30am-5.30pm Sat 9am-5pm* 🕐*Universe of particles Mon-Sat 10am-5pm Sat 9am-5pm* ✆*(0)22 767 76 76. http://public.web.cern.ch/public.*

The European Organisation for Nuclear Research explains wider issues of the universe as well as the work of scientists in this field. A combination of audiovisual and multimedia presentations, games and hands-on exhibits allow visitors to get to grips with complex issues such as the forces of nature and how a particle accelerator functions.

Domaine de Penthes

18 chemin de l'Impératrice, Pregny-Chambésy. Access via Avenue de la Paix to the N and then the road to Pregny. Located within grounds of 12 hectares/29.6 acres of beech groves, the Penthes château is rich with history, having been built during the 14C and then often remodelled until the 1800s. Among notable visits was that, in the 1850s, of the Duchess of Orléans and her sons, the Count of Paris and the Duke of Chartres.

Musée des Suisses dans le Monde★

🕐*Open Tue–Sun, 10am–noon, 1–5pm.* 🕐*Closed Mon, Christmas and New Year.* 🚫*5CHF free during the first Sunday of each month.* ✆*(0)22 734 90 21. www.penthes.ch.*

This museum devoted to Switzerland's relations with the rest of the world from the Middle Ages to today, focuses on economic, military, diplomatic, scientific, cultural and literary aspects of Swiss

society. Emphasis is on the Franco-Swiss alliances from 1444 to 1830, and on the armed forces or famous Swiss personalities who served the European powers. In the Le Fort Room, enhanced by delicate wainscoting, are several portraits worth noting and an oval embossed silver platter depicting the oath of alliance taken by Louis XIV and the Swiss cantons after a tapestry by Le Brun.

The first floor captures the French Revolution and its tragic result for Louis XVI's Swiss Guards, the French Occupation, and the role of the Swiss regiments during the Empire, as well as traditions followed by the Papal Guard, founded during the 16C). Mementoes of Beatus von Fischer, Switzerland's first postmaster, and of the national postal system, are presented in the Salon des Dieux, decorated with lovely **woodwork**★, seven gilded and painted panels representing the Gods of Olympus, taken from Reichenbach Château near Bern. The exhibition rooms on the second floor are devoted to Swiss celebrities who acquired a worldwide reputation: archeologists (Burckhardt), leading figures in industry and aeronautics (Breguet), forerunners of the modern banking system (Necker), diplomats (Gallatin) and statesmen (Haldimand), writers (Blaise Cendrars), scientists and physicians (De Haller), artists (JH Füssli), and famous women (Sybille Merian).

Musée Militaire Genevois

🕐*Open Tue–Sat 2pm–5pm, Sun 10am–noon, 2pm–5pm.* 🕐*Closed Mon and Christmas to February.* 🚫*No charge.* ✆*(0)22 734 48 75. www.museemiltaire-ge.com*

The former stables of Penthes Château presently house a small museum which explains the history of the Genevese troops from 1814 to 1815, when Geneva joined the Confederation, up to the present day. The landmarks in Geneva's military history are illustrated through collections of arms, equipment, documents, and around 30 figures in uniform.

Musée International de l'Automobile★

Voie des Tray 40 (Palexpo), halle 7, along the bypass on the road to Ferney. Ⓟ*Leave your car in car park P26.* Ⓞ*Open Wed–Fri 1.30pm–6.30pm, Sat–Sun 10am–6pm.* ☞*12CHF.* ♿ ✆*(0)22 788 84 84.*

Laid out over two 7 000sq m/8 300sq yd exhibition areas, the Automobile Museum presents around 400 vehicles in chronological order, grouped together by make and country of manufacture. All the cars are in perfect condition. General Patton's Jeep, Mussolini's Fiat, General Guisan's Buick, Stalin's Zis, as well as a Cadillac and a Ferrari which belonged respectively to Elvis Presley and Sophia Loren, are the star attractions. Of particular note are the Swiss models (Ajax, Felber, Monteverdi, etc.) and the superb Italian machines, such as Ferrari, Lamborghini and Maserati, to name but a few.

Finally, a number of exceptional automobiles will not fail to seduce even the most hardened professionals: three Bugatti T35 models (1926, 1927 and 1929), Voisin C14 (1930), Auburn Speedster (1932), Hispano-Suiza (1934), Alfa-Romeo 2500 (1939), Allard 81M (1945), Facel-Vega HK500 (1959) Austin Healy MKIII (1967), and a gull-wing Mercedes-Benz SLR McClaren (2005).

Les Schtroumpfs

North bank, rue Louis-Favre and rue I.-Eberhardt.

These modern housing blocks (1982–89) in the Grottes district near Cornavin Station bring to mind the work of the Spanish architect Gaudí.

Institut et Musée Voltaire★

25 rue des Délices, 1203 Geneva. Ⓞ*Open Mon–Sat, 2pm–5pm; Ascension, Whit Mon and Jeûne Genevois, 2pm–6pm.* Ⓞ*Closed 2 Jan, Good Fri, Easter Mon, 24, 26 and 31 Dec.* ☞*No charge.* ✆*(0)22 418 95 60.* *www.ville-ge.ch/bge/imv.*

"Les Délices"—Voltaire's residence in Geneva (1755-65) has become a centre for research into his life and the period in which he lived. The Institute, which published the very first edition of the author's vast correspondence and which houses an impressive library, presents a series of exhibits retracing the career of **François-Marie Arouet**, the famous author better known as Voltaire. Displays contain an original edition of *Candide*, and handwritten documents, mainly letters signed by or addressed to Voltaire. Another curiosity is the collection of 199 wax seals bearing his heraldic insignia he used in his correspondence. Among the portraits of the author, note the painting by Largillière, representing him at the age of 24 (*ground floor*) and a terracotta replica of Houdon's famous statue *Voltaire Seated* (*first floor*). An audio-visual presentation (*45min*) enlightens visitors on Voltaire's stay in Geneva.

EXCURSIONS

Carouge★

▶ *2km/1.25mi S of Geneva City Centre.*

Founded in the late 18C by Victor-Amadeus III, Duke of Savoy and King of Sardinia, the town has often been in conflict with its neighbour, Geneva. Many left puritan Geneva to enjoy themselves in the cabarets and inns of Carouge. The town was annexed to the Geneva canton in 1816 by the Treaty of Turin. The old district still has streets which were laid out in the 17C.

Mont Salève

Alt. 1 380m/4 525ft. 7km/4.4mi from Geneva. A lift is located at the frontier at Veyrier (accessible by the number 8 bus. Get off at the Veyrier terminus, cross the border in to France, from where the lift is 500m/1 640ft away). From Switzerland ✆*00 33 450 39 86 86.* Ⓞ*Lift open Apr and Oct daily except Mon 9.30am–6pm, May–Sept daily 9.30am–6pm.* ☞*10.80 CHF (children 6CHF).*

Known as the "Mountain of Genevese" le Salève in France is the playground for walkers, as well as mountain bikers, rock climbers, paragliders and handgliders.

ADDRESSES

🏠STAY

City Hostel Geneva – *2 rue Ferrier.* ✆ *(0)22 901 15 00. www.cityhostel.ch. 54 rooms (dormitory style and private).* This hostel is in a good location, just a 5min walk from Cornavin railway station. Each room has a washbasin; toilets and showers are on the landing. Kitchen available for guest use. Good place for those on a tight budget.

Bel'Espérance – *1 rue de la Vallée.* ✆ *(0)22 818 37 37. www.hotel-bel-esperance.ch. 40 rooms.* Traditional establishment with an interesting location halfway between the old city and the shores of Lake Geneva.

Best Western Strasbourg & Univers – *10 rue Pradier.* ✆ *(0)22 906 58 00. http://www.hotelstrasbourg.ch. 51 rooms.* Comfortable hotel at the top of rue du Mont-Blanc near the railway station but away from the bustling Place Cornavin and rue des Alpes, a one-way street which channels traffic from the lake shores towards the station.

Les Tourelles – *2 boulevard James-Fazy.* ✆ *(0)22 732 44 23. www.destourelles.ch. 22 rooms.* Excellent value given its location on the banks of the Rhône. Simple rooms which are refurbished regularly.

Hôtel Auteuil – *33 r. de Lausanne.* ✆ *(0)22 544 22 22. www.manotel.com. 104 rooms.* One of the six hotels in the Manotel Froup in Geneva, which each have their own particular design—Swiss, Feng Shui, Colonial etc.). The rooms are designer inspired and comfortable, with quality furnishings in dark wood.

Mon Repos – *131 rue de Lausanne.* ✆ *(0)22 909 39 09. www.hmrge.ch. 80 rooms.* Cosy, traditional hotel near Lake Geneva, opposite the Mon Repos park. Convenient location near UN head-quarters and other international organisations.

The Neu Midi – *4 place Chevelu.* ✆ *(0)22 544 15 00. www.hotel-du-midi.ch. 78 rooms.* ⌷ *24CHF.* Just off Quai des Bergues, surrounded by lively narrow streets, this is an ideal starting-point for visiting the old quarter and the right bank of the city.

Suisse – *10 place Cornavin.* ✆ *(0)22 732 66 30. www.hotel-suisse.ch. 62 rooms.* Facing the station, on the corner of rue du Mont-Blanc and its pedestrian zone. At the end of this main street lie the harbour, the landing-stages and, on the left bank, the old city. Restaurant with flower-decked terrace.

Les Armures – *1 rue du Puits-Saint-Pierre.* ✆ *(0)22 310 91 72. www.hotel-les-armures.ch. 32 rooms.* Sophisticated 17C hotel with great charm close to the Cathédrale Saint-Pierre. An unforgettable experience.

La Cigogne – *17 place Longemalle.* ✆ *(0)22 818 40 40. www.cigogne.ch. Restaurant* ⌷⌷. *52 apartment-style rooms.* Luxury hotel at the heart of the old city offering excellent service with a personal touch. Quality furnishings and quiet, peaceful atmosphere.

Le Montbrillant – *2 rue de Montbrillant.* ✆ *(0)22 733 77 84. www.montbrillant.ch. 82 rooms.* A comfortable hotel in a 19C building directly behind Cornavin station. The rooms are soundproofed; those on the top floor decorated with wood paneling. No parking facilities.

Cornavin – *23 boulevard James-Fazy.* ✆ *(0)22 716 12 12. www.fassbindhotels.com. 169 rooms.* A modernised establishment, the upper floors have beautiful views of the lake. Rooms are spacious and soundproofed, with cherry-wood furniture and light, airy bathrooms. Note the unusual 30m/98ft-high clock, whose clockface is on the 8th floor. The panoramic breakfast room is on the same floor.

🍽EAT

At lunchtime, many restaurants offer reasonably priced menus or plats du jour (dishes of the day), which include a main dish and a salad, for around 20CHF. À la carte dinner with good wine can easily cost around 70-80CHF.

Chez ma Cousine – *6 pl. du Bourg-de-Four.* *(0)22 310 96 96. Open daily.* Near the cathedral, this colourful restaurant (yellow walls, green tables) serves chicken in all its forms.

La Romantica – *3 place des Trois-Perdrix* *(0)22 311 41 10. Closed Sun lunchtime.* A pizzeria located at the bottom of the Old Town. Simple fare but well prepared. Friendly welcome.

Café du Centre – *5 place du Molard* *((0)22 311 85 86. www.cafeducentre.ch. Mon–Fri 6am–1am (midnight on Mondays), Sat 9am–1am, Sun 9am–midnight.* Well located restaurant in an area populated with smart shops, coffee houses and good restaurants. Excellent fish.

Aux Halles de l'Île – *1 place de l'Île.* *((0)22 311 52 21. www.brasseriedes hallesdelile.ch.* Situated on an island in the middle of the River Rhône. Very popular at lunchtime, with its magnificent panoramic dining room overlooking the river. The restaurant serves simple, traditional cuisine and offers a number of different menus. Jazz some nights of the week.

Café Papon – *Old town. 1 rue Henry-Fazy.* *(0)22 311 54 28. www.cafe-papon.com. Closed Sat lunchtime in winter, and Sun.* In part of the historical building housing the town hall and gives onto a pretty, shaded square. Rustic dining hall with bare stone walls and undeniable charm. The clientele includes local politicians.

La Favola – *Old town. 15 rue Jean-Calvin.* *(0)22 311 74 37. www.lafavola.com. Mon–Sat noon–2pm , noon–2pm, 7pm-10pm. Closed Sat lunchtime and Sun. Booking recommended.* This attractive restaurant is in a 17C building with a wooden façade. One dining room is on on the ground floor and one on the first floor, linked by a narrow spiral staircase. The restaurant serves well-presented, inventive cuisine from Ticino.

Opéra Bouffe – *5 avenue de Frontenex* *(0)22 736 63 00. www.opera bouffe.ch. Tue–Fri noon–3pm, 7pm–midnight, Sat 7pm–midnight, closed Sun and Mon.* Romantic atmosphere in the evenings with candle-lit tables and interior design along the opera theme. The menu changes frequently and there are often special offers at lunchtime.

Le Vallon – *182 route de Florissant.* *(0)22 347 11 04. www.chateauvieux.ch.* A small restaurant with informal décor situated in Conches 5km/3mi southeast of Geneva. Excellent wine selection.

CAROUGE

Café Les Négociants – *29 rue de la Filature.* *(0)22 300 31 30. www.negociants.ch. Closed Tue.* Good food at reasonable prices. Customers can select wine directly from the wine cellar, or order by the glass.

L'Ange du Dix Vins – *31 rue Jacques-Dalphin.* *(0)22 342 03 18. Closed 29 Jul–20 Aug, Christmas and New Year.* Two dining rooms, one of which is bistro-style. Good service and fine cuisine, including some delicious desserts.

La Bourse – *7 place du Marché.* *(0)22 342 04 66. www.resto.ch/labourse. Closed Sun, Mon.* A brasserie in the Parisian style. The menu is broad and inviting with seafood, sausage and a variety of meat, including a tartare of seabass and a horse steak. Traditional cuisine is served on the ground floor, and pizzas and meat pierrades in the more informal vaulted basement.

NIGHTLIFE

At night, the neighbourhood between Cornavin station and Les Pâquis is always bustling with people on account of the many cinemas, bars, pubs and restaurants, mainly serving exotic food.

The **Les Brasseurs** *(20 Place Cornavin;* *(0)22 731 02 06; www.les-brasseurs.ch)* micro-brewery produces its own beer on the premises, and has a brewing room and fermentation vats. If there are several of you and you get a seat, it's worth ordering a *colonne* of beer, which comes in either 3l/0.8gal or 5l/1.3gal measures. Three types of beer are on offer: *blonde, blanche* and *ambrée.*

The **Casino de Paris** on Quai du Mont-Blanc attracts a lively crowd. If you prefer the tango, cha-cha, or the waltz, visit to the **Palais Mascotte** (*rue de Bern*) after 10pm.

In the old district, centred around Place du Bourg-de-Four, the **Mortimer** is an unusual place with its collection of advertising posters, early gadgets and splendid zinc counter. In summer, enjoy a drink on the terrace of the **Clémence** (fountain and huge chessboard).

For Irish beer and ambience, try the busy **Flanagan's Irish Pub** (*4 rue du Cheval Blanc*), which often hosts live music. The fashionable **Demi-Lune** café (*3 rue Étienne-Dumont*) attracts an international clientele, especially late in the evening. Décor is traditional, in keeping with its location in the old town, and the atmosphere jazz-inspired. A range of snacks, including tapas, salads, and hamburgers, are served until 11.30pm.

There are also several smart cinemas and establishments around place du Molard, popular at aperitif time or later in the evening. These include the **Brasserie Lipp** (*8 rue de la Confédération; ✆(0)22 318 80 30; www.brasserie-lipp.com*) the antechamber of world finance and trade.

Many of the stylish cafés in the Eaux-Vives quarter are patronised by foreign dignitaries or executives. **La Coupole** (*116 rue du Rhône*) features two types of atmosphere, depending on your mood. For an aperitif or after-dinner drink, the comfortable **Café or American Bar** has a large choice of alcoholic and non-alcoholic cocktails, and a wide selection of fine whiskies. If you feel like dancing, climb the stairs to the café's nightclub, **Le Dancing**. **L'Opéra Bouffe**, in avenue de Frontenex, is a favorite haunt among artists, journalists and intellectuals, with opera music playing in the background.

OUTSIDE GENEVA

Head out on the Thonon road to Vésenaz, where you can't miss **Le Trois-Huit** café on the side of the road. With their leather armchairs and sofas, the **Night Café** and **Bibliothèque** (*open 7pm–5am*) have a cosy, almost British ambience. From 10pm, the Night Café alternates as a piano-bar and disco-bar with a live DJ; on Sunday afternoons it holds tea dances. The **Bibliothèque**

(lined with bookshelves, as the name suggests), is quieter and more suited to a drink and a chat. The café has a good choice of drinks, with over 70 different types of blended and pure malt whiskies.

In France, in **St-Julien-en-Genevois** (going southbound along the A 40 motorway then the N 201 towards Annecy), the **Macumba** is a the largest nightclub complex in Europe, with 17 themed club rooms and 7 restaurants (*✆33 4 5049 2350; www.macumba.net*). The nightclub is very popular on Saturdays, with people coming here from miles around. **Le Gk** is for lovers of electronic music, while **La Villa** attracts Latin aficionados with its classic Spanish theme and a full Tapas bar. Each of the city's diverse clubs has its own unique niche. For a romantic night out, try **Les Mille et Une Nuits** with its Arabian Nights gossamer, or **la Mere** for a more traditional night out.

🛍 SHOPPING

The main shopping areas, with a huge range of stores to suit all tastes and budgets, are in the following streets:

North bank – Quai des Bergues, quai du Mont-Blanc and rue du Mont-Blanc. **Manor** department store (*6 rue Cornavin*).

South bank – Rue du Rhône, rue de la Confédération, rue du Marché, galerie Jean-Malbuisson, rue Neuve du Molard,

Rues des Basses - main thoroughfare of the South Bank

Samuel Mizrachi/Switzerland Tourism

rue de la Croix-d'Or (which includes the Confédération Centre shopping mall), rue de Rive, cours de Rive and rue de la Corraterie.

Globus department store (48 rue du Rhône and rue de la Confédération).

MARKETS

Geneva has several colourful local markets, offering visitors the chance to soak up the atmosphere of the city.

NORTH BANK

Place de la Navigation – Tue and Fri, 8am–1pm: fruit and vegetables.

Place de Grenus – Sat, 8am–1.30pm: fruit and vegetables.

SOUTH BANK

Plaine de Plainpalais – Geneva's largest markets are held in this square. Tue and Fri, 8am–1pm; Sun, 8am–6pm: fruit and vegetables. Wed and Sat, 8am–5pm: flea market; wide selection of antique and second-hand goods.

Boulevard Helvétique – Wed and Sat, 8am–1pm. Fruit and vegetables.

Place de la Fusterie – Wed and Sat, 8am–6pm: fruit and vegetables. Thu, 8am–6.45pm: handicrafts. Fri, 8am–6.45pm: second-hand books.

THEATRE AND MUSIC

Grand Théâtre – 5 place Neuve. ℘ (0)22 418 31 30. www.genevaopera.com. Modeled after the Paris Opera, this well-known theatre hosts performances of opera, ballet and music.

Bâtiment des Forces Motrices – 2 place des Volontaires. ℘ (0)22 322 12 20. www.bfm.ch. An annex of the Grand Théâtre, this is a venue for plays, opera, and conferences. Excellent acoustics.

Comédie de Genève – 6 boulevard des Philosophes. ℘ (0)22 320 50 01. www.comedie.ch. Contemporary and classical drama.

Les Salons – 6 rue Bartholoni. ℘ (0)22 807 06 30. www.les-salons.ch. Musical performances and plays by modern authors.

Théâtre le Poche – 7 rue du Cheval-Blanc. ℘ (0)22 310 37 59. www.lepoche.ch. This small theatre in the old town has developed a reputation for its contemporary works, with a focus on experimental drama.

Casino-Théâtre – 42 rue de Carouge. ℘ (0)22 418 44 00. www.ville-ge.ch/culture/casinotheatre. Satirical reviews, operetta, and variety shows.

Forum Meyrin – 1 place des Cinq-Continents, Meyrin. ℘ (0)22 989 34 34. www.forum-meyrin.ch. The theatre's varied program includes drama, dance, and classical and modern music.

Théâtre de Carouge – 57 rue Ancienne, Carouge. ℘ (0)22 343 43 43. www.tcag.ch/. This renowned theatre offers a varied international programme of drama, with works by classical and modern playwrights, including Racine, Molière, André Roussin, Chekhov and Pirandello.

Victoria Hall – 14 rue du Général-Dufour. ℘ (0)22 418 35 00. www.ville-ge.ch/vh. For over a century this impressive auditorium with its superb acoustics has hosted classical concerts by the Orchestre de la Suisse Romande and visiting orchestras.

Conservatoire de Musique – 12, Rue de l'Arquebuse ℘ (0)22 319 60 60. www.cmusge.ch. Classical music concerts performed by renowned soloists.

FOR KIDS

Les Marionnettes de Genève – 3 rue Rodo. ℘ (0)22 807 31 07. www.marionnettes.ch. This puppet-theatre group presents works by the Grimm Brothers, Russian fairy tales and contemporary stories. For children of any age.

Am Stram Gram – 56 route de Frontenex. ℘ (0)22 735 79 24. www.amstramgram.ch. Traditional favourites for children and parents alike. The repertoire includes Beauty and the Beast, Peter Pan and Robinson Crusoe.

Lake Geneva ★★★

Known to the French as Lac Léman, the area spreads its great arc fringed with vineyards successively along the last slopes of the Jura, the ridges of the Swiss Plateau, and the foothills of the Vaud Alps. This shore, especially in the Vevey-Montreux section, became, after Jean-Jacques Rousseau had stayed there, the refuge of the Romantics. The pilgrimages which became more and more frequent among nature lovers started a great tourist industry.

- **Michelin Map:** National 729: C7.
- **Info:** Rue du Mont-Blanc 18. ☎(0)22 909 70 00, www.geneve-tourisme.ch.
- **Location:** The Swiss shore of Lake Geneva.
- **Parking:** Public transportation is most sensible for most parts of this region.
- **Don't Miss:** The vineyard tour.
- **Timing:** Allow one day to complete both tours.

🚗 DRIVING TOURS

In addition to the following itineraries, the corniche section of the main road connecting Vevey and Rennaz affords wonderful views of the Upper Lake.

① VINEYARD TOUR★
70km/43mi. About 3hr.

▷ *Leave Geneva by the shore road to Lausanne (which does not leave Geneva's built-up area until after Versoix).*

Coppet
This little town 9.7km/6mi southwest of Nyon is crossed from end to end by a main street lined with arcaded houses built after the invasion by Bernese troops in the 16C.

Château★
🎧 *Guided tours (35min) Easter–Oct 2pm–6pm (last admission 5.30pm). ⊜8CHF. ☎(0)22 776 10 28.*
Rebuilt in the 18C, the château overlooks Lake Geneva. It once belonged to Jacques Necker, a banker from Geneva who was Minister of Finance to Louis XVI. His dismissal by the king in 1789 was one of the decisive moments which drove France to revolution. His daughter, Mme de Staël, spoke out against Napoleon's regime and was sent into exile; she fled to Coppet, where she remained until the Restoration. Here she wrote *Corinne, Ten Years in Exile, Literature Seen in Relation to Social Institutions* and her often cultural critique, *On Germany.* Coppet soon became a sort of literary principality, frequented by celebrities such as Benjamin Constant, Lord Byron, Schlegel, Chateaubriand and Mme Récamier.

The château has remained in the same family ever since. The interior is lavishly decorated. The rooms remain unchanged since the Revolution.

Visitors are shown round the library, Mme de Staël's bedroom, Mme Récamier's suite and, on the first floor, the Great Salon embellished with Aubusson tapestries and a Portrait Gallery displaying works by Duplessis, Gérard, Carmontelle and Mazot. In the park, in a grove near a shaded path, lie the remains of Mme de Staël and other members of her family.

▷ *Continue along the Route de Suisse (shore road) for 6km/3.75mi until Crans and turn left into the Route du Port.*

Crans
The château, which boasts good lines and proportions, is a fine example of the Louis XV period. The small church nearby offers a nice view of the vineyard, the lake, and in the far distance, the French Mountain range.

▷ *Return to the Route de Suisse and turn left towards Nyon.*

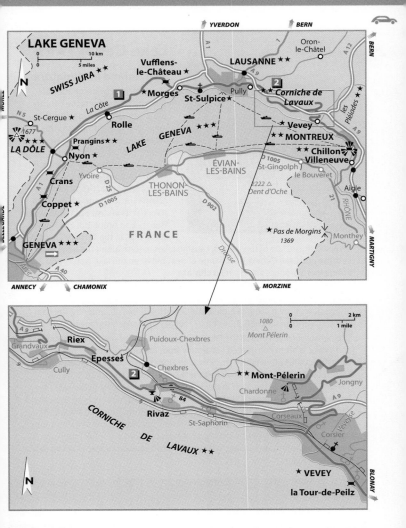

Nyon★ – ⚐See NYON.

⚐ *Leave Nyon by the Route de Lausanne and in 2km/1.25mi turn left to Prangins.*

Château de Prangins★★
2km/1mi NE by the road to Lausanne.
⏰*Open Tue–Sun 10am–5pm.*
⏰*Closed 1 and 2 Jan and 25 Dec.*
💰*10CHF.* ♿. ☏*(0)22 994 88 90.*
www.musee-suisse.ch/e/prangins.
In a landscaped garden dominating Lake Geneva, the Château de Prangins, which successively fulfilled the role of seigneu-

rial manor, prince's residence, school and private house, currently houses a branch of the **Swiss National Museum** of Zürich. It presents the history of 18C and 19C Switzerland, focusing on its political, economic and cultural background.

Ceremonial rooms on the **ground floor** explore the theme of *The Dream of the Enlightenment*.

Note the beautiful music box in the shape of a bird's cage in the living room. In room 7 farther along, the optical instrument in the shape of a house (1781), known as "the television of the

Great Lake with a view to the Dents du Midi

© Christof Sonderegger/Switzerland Tourism

Lake Geneva★★★

Switzerland in Miniature

Characterised by geographical diversity that reflects the country as a whole, the region around Lake Geneva encompasses the peaceful shoreline, gentle wooded slopes, lush green fields and snow-capped mountain peaks. It is 310m/1 018ft deep with a surface area of 58 000ha/143 323 acres, 72km/45mi long and 13km/7.5mi across at its widest point, between Morges and Amphion. The folding of the Alps in the Tertiary Era reversed the incline of the valleys, causing lakes to form along the edge (Lake Lucerne and Lake Geneva). Exchange of heat between the lake waters and the atmosphere produces a very mild **climate**.

Crescent-shaped Lake Geneva is Switzerland's largest lake (the southern shore belongs to neighbouring France). It is the body of water into which the River Rhône flows from its source high in the St Gotthard Massiff, entering the near Montreux and exiting at Geneva on its journey to the Mediterranean.

The narrow western end of the lake, known as the Little Lake, between Geneva and Yvoire is often considered separately from the Great Lake. The latter is the widest section, within which the so-called Upper Lake can be seen off Vevey-Montreux. Since the line of Swiss altimetry was fixed at the Niton Rock (alt. 374m/1 227ft above the level of the Mediterranean), the level of the lake may be regarded as the general standard of altitude in Switzerland. Lake Geneva has been a study centre for naturalists since the Reformation and during the 1960s it was found that the it had become very polluted. A massive clean-up operation restored Lake Geneva to its former condition and a full range of activities including swimming, sailing, wind surfing and scuba diving can safely take place again.

Aerial view of Lake Geneva region

© Regis Colombo/Switzerland Tourism

Ancien Régime", was an object of entertainment.

The **first floor** is dedicated to the period from the Revolution to the Federal State (1750–1920), a period of great upheaval. Note the **hat of liberty**, which symbolised the Swiss Republic in 1798 and took the form of William Tell's hat in the 17C. Switzerland became an urban society in the 19C; middle-class life in this period is depicted by the reconstruction of a living room (1850) and the development of transport portrayed through a collection of old bicycles and motorcycles, including several dandy-horses for children. An unusual circular shower is one of the exhibits devoted to health and hygiene. In the first-floor corridor, a striking painting by the pastor Jean-Élie Dautan entitled *Famous Swiss* appeals for unity and tolerance. Note also the small carriage known as a *char de côté*, very popular at the time, where passengers sat on the side of the carriage.

On the **top floor**, Switzerland's immigration, emigration, import and export, is explored, as is development of the country's tourist industry. The reconstruction of a storehouse for colonial foodstuffs near Seewen station (1883) is particularly worthy of note. The **cellars** are devoted to the history of the château, wine and cereals, energy, heating and light. Note the hail-cannon, much in vogue around 1900; blank shots were fired to disperse hail. The **vegetable garden** laid out in an old moat was planted in accordance with designs of the period; fruit and vegetables are grown here as they would have been in the 18C. From the garden, there are splendid views of Mont Dôle, with the Jura Mountains in the distance.

▷ *Take the Route de l'Étraz, direction Lausanne, via Luins and Bursins to Rolle.*

After Luins and the church standing in a clump of cypresses, it is a fast trip to Bursins and then on to Mont-sur-Rolle. Besides the Savoy shore of the lake—with Thonon—and the summits of the Haut-Chablais, you see the Vaud shore from Rolle Bay to the Naye Rocks with Lausanne in between. The south-facing hills which slope down to the lake are one of the great wine-growing areas of Switzerland.

Rolle

This town lies on the north shore of Lake Geneva halfway between Geneva and Lausanne. The triangular 13C **castle** was built by a Prince of Savoy. On a small artificial island is an obelisk erected to the memory of **General Frédéric de Laharpe** (1754–1838).

The road from Mont-sur-Rolle to Aubonne reveals typical villages surrounded by vineyards such as Féchy. The **views**★★ open out toward the Little Lake as far as Geneva and the Salève. Immediately after leaving Aubonne, toward Lavigny, the crossing of the Aubonne Ravine offers an attractive general view of the town.

▷ *Drive to the A1 autoroute and head towards Lausanne. After 14km/8.75mi take exit 15 towards Vufflens.*

Vufflens-le-Château★

Vufflens Castle stands on a plateau overlooking the ravine of the Morges, with a view of the Jura, Lake Geneva and the Alps. The castle was entirely rebuilt with brick in the 15C in the Italian tradition and extensively restored in the 19C.

▷ *Drive S along the Route du Village and Route de Morge for 4km/2.5mi.*

Morges★

Alt. 378m/1 240ft. Rue du Château 1110.
𝄞(0)21 801 32 33. www.morges.ch.
The little town of Morges is an important wine-growing centre on the Vaud hillside. It has a pleasant site on the shore of Lake Geneva, facing the Savoy Alps. The port, built from 1691 to 1696, was busy with trade between the Vaud district and Geneva until the development of the railway system. Now, it is a **pleasure-boat harbor**. From the quay, near the castle (a former residence of the Bernese bailiffs) is an excellent **view**★ of Lake Geneva at its widest point and beyond it of the Alps, from Mount Salève

to the Fribourg Alps, including the Savoy Alps, among which the Dent d'Oche and the Mont Blanc are prominent.

Musée Alexis-Forel★★

54 Grand'Rue. ◑*Open mid-Mar–Nov, Wed–Sun 2pm–6pm.* ◑*Closed Dec–mid-Mar.* ◉*10CHF.* ✆*(0)21 801 26 47. www.museeforel.ch.*

Founded by the engraver **Alexis Forel** and his wife, the museum is housed in part of the Blanchenay Mansion, a handsome residence from the 15C, 17C and 18C. Note the panelled ceilings (15C and 16C), the 17C carved Burgundian doors and the two monumental fireplaces. Each exhibition room pays tribute to a particular period in history: 15C–19C French and Swiss furniture, most of which Forel collected himself; mementoes (17C and 18C salons), porcelain from Nyon and the East India Company; 16C–19C glasswork, 18C and 19C silverware. An exhibition of dolls occupies two floors, displaying numerous 18C–20C pieces together with their accessories.

Castle

◑*Open Mar–Nov, Tue–Sun 10am–noon, 1.30pm–5pm, Sat–Sun and public holidays 1.30pm–5pm, Jul and Aug daily 10am–5pm.* ◑*Closed Easter Mon, Whit Mon and mid-Dec–31 Jan.* ◉*10CHF.* ✆*(0)21 316 09 90. www.chateau-morges.ch.*

Built on a strategic location west of the town, this massive 13C fortress, flanked by four circular corner towers defining four bulwarks arranged around a central courtyard, houses the collections belonging to three museums.

The **Swiss Figurine Museum** (*ground floor*) presents a series of dioramas with lead or tin soldiers which illustrate major historical events from Antiquity to the 19C, including Babylon, the Aztec rebellion against Spanish settlers, the Field of the Cloth of Gold and the Berezina Crossing on Napoleons's retreat from Russia. Each figurine has been painstakingly reconstructed with minute attention to detail.

The **Vaud Military Museum** (*ground floor and first floor*) presents an exhaustive collection of the weapons, uniforms and types of headdress associated with the Swiss Army from Napoleonic times to the present day, including the Pope's famous Swiss guard. A succession of rooms recreate particular periods of history: the Tower of Justice or the Tower of Torture, the Davel Room, devoted to Major Jean-Daniel Abraham Davel, a Vaud patriot executed in 1723 for having fought against the Bernese authorities, or the room paying tribute to General Guisan, Commander-in-Chief of the Swiss army between 1939 and 1945 (military record, personal belongings). The **Artillery Museum**, set up in a series of fine cellars enhanced by barrel vaulting, displays around 40 real exhibits along with miniature models which explain the development of this weapon: early artillery pieces from the 16C, mountain artillery carried by beasts of burden, 75mm/3in field canon and carriage; an unusual boule-shaped 12mm/0.5in mortar able to revolve around its axis, adjustable on slopes, with a range of 3km/1.8mi.

▷ *Between Morges and Lausanne leave road no. 1 to make a detour through St Sulpice.*

St Sulpice★

The little **St-Sulpice Church**★ is a pure specimen of Romanesque within sight of Lake Geneva and the Savoy Alps. The interior is austere and simple but tempered by multicoloured decoration.

▷ *Return to road no. 1 for the drive to Lausanne.*

② LAVAUX CORNICHE★★ FROM LAUSANNE TO VILLENEUVE

39km/24mi. About 1hr 30min.

The road described here, which crosses the motorway after the La Croix crossroads, is the same road that is sandwiched between the motorway and the coastal road (no. 9) as far as the outskirts of Vevey. If traffic is too heavy, take the small road from Chexbres to the Puidoux railway station (5km/3mi), which then links up to the road described. It, too, borders and overlooks the motorway. You can catch splendid views from this road, though they are often interrupted by the many tunnels.

▷ *Leaving from Ouchy, you can join up with the tour at Grandvaux by taking coastal road no. 9. After leaving Lutry, turn left into the "Route de la Petite Corniche", then follow directions to Riex.*

Lausanne★★
See LAUSANNE.

▷ *Leave Lausanne by avenue de Béthusy going toward La Rosiaz.*

After this the road runs through a residential suburb and wooded ravines and emerges on a slope planted with fruit trees within view of the Upper Lake and its Savoy shore. This is marked from left to right by the Meillerie Cliffs, the green undulations of the Gavot Plateau (behind Évian) and the Drance Delta.
After the crossroads at La Croix, the whole of the Great Lake (Grand Lac) can be seen: the curves of the Vaud shore make a bend at the foot of the Jura, beyond the houses of Lausanne. The Yvoire Point juts out from the far shore.

▷ *After a steep descent you will cross the motorway and railway.*

The road then enters the **Lavaux vineyard**, where its slopes plunge down into the Upper Lake opposite the shores of Savoy. Then come the wine-growing villages of Riex and Epesses enclosed by terraces of vines. The slope steepens and you enter the Le Dézaley district. Where the road skirts a sharp little spur, a **viewpoint**★★ offers the Valais Rhône Valley through a gap in which the snowy Grand Combin summit appears in the distance. Beyond are the towns of Vevey and Montreux. They cover every bend in the shore at the foot of the characteristic Dent de Jaman and the cliffs of the Naye Rocks.
The Vinorama at Rivaz *(2 rte. du Lac;* ◷ *open Wed–Sun 10.30am–9.30pm;* ◎*free;* ℘*(0)21 946 31 31; www.lavaux-vinorama.ch)* has an informative film and an opportunity to buy local wines. From this area, you can visit **Vevey**★, **Mont-Pélerin**★★ (*see VEVEY*) and **Montreux**★★ (*see MONTREUX*).

▷ *Drive S along the Avenue de Chillon for 2.5km/1.6mi.*

Terraced vineyards of Lavaux

© Stephan Engler/Switzerland Tourism

The Prisoner of Chillon

The castle and its dungeons have been used as a state prison more than once, but **François de Bonivard** remains its most famous prisoner. Bonivard attempted to introduce the Reformation when he was Prior of St Victor at Geneva. His theories displeased the Duke of Savoy, a staunch supporter of Catholicism. Bonivard was arrested and cast into the castle dungeons which have borne his name ever since. He lived chained to one of the pillars and it is said that his footprints can still be traced in the rock. He remained there for four years until he was freed by the Bernese in 1536. When **Lord Byron** visited Chillon in 1816, he commemorated the captivity of Bonivard in a poem, *The Prisoner of Chillon*, which contributed to making the castle Switzerland's most popular monument.

Château de Chillon★★

🕐*Open daily Apr–Sept 9am –7pm, March & Oct 9am–6pm, Nov–Feb 10am –5pm* 🕐*Closed Christmas, 1 Jan*⮐*12CHF.* ✆*(0)21 966 89 10. www.chillon.ch.*

Vaud/Chillon Castle is built on a rocky islet; its towers are reflected in the waters of Lake Geneva. The picturesque **site★★** lies at the centre of the lake, within sight of Montreux, the French shore and the Alps: the Dents du Midi are clearly visible. The first fortress was built in the 9C to guard the road from Avenches to Italy, which crossed the Great St Bernard after skirting Lake Geneva. The castle became the property of the bishops of Sion, who enlarged it, and then of the counts of Savoy from 1150. It took on its present appearance in the middle of the 13C.

The drawbridge which once spanned the moat has been replaced by an 18C bridge. The dungeons, used as magazines for the Bernese fleet in the 17C and 18C, have fine ogive vaulting and are hewn from the rock. While he was visiting the prison, Byron carved his name on the third pillar in Bonivard's cell.

The Great Hall of the Bailiffs, which bears the coat of arms of Savoy, has an imposing 15C fireplace. The former

Chillon Castle by the Lake Geneva, the Dents du Midi in the background

Banqueting Hall (Aula Nova) houses the **museum**; the collections comprise pewter, armour, furniture and weapons. The visit ends with a section of the wall-walk and two fortified towers, converted into a prison during the 17C.

▷ *Continue S along the Avenue de Chillon for 2km/1.25mi.*

Villeneuve

Located at the east end of the lake, this small town has a pleasant lake front. The Grand'Rue has kept its old narrow houses fronted by wooden gates. Several shops have façades decorated with quaint wrought-iron signs. Near the Place du Temple and its pretty fountain stands **St Paul's Church** (12C), noted for its stained-glass windows. Not far from the station, an unusual town hall has been set up in the former chapel of the hospital. Many world celebrities fell in love with the town and decided to make it their home. Among those whose name will forever remain associated with Villeneuve were writers like **Byron** (one hotel is named after him), Victor Hugo, and Romain Rolland.

ADDRESSES

🏨 STAY

🍴🛏 **Auberge du Chasseur** – *10 rte. d'Yverdon, 1028 Préverenges.* ℘*(0)21 811 50 80. 12 rooms.* 🚭. This charming hotel is only a 5-minute drive away from Morges and a 10-minute drive from Lausanne and offers comfortable rooms including free Wi-Fi. The restaurant serves local and international cuisine. Buffet breakfast is included in the room rate. The beach on Lake Geneva is only 600m away; free car park.

🍴🛏 **Pré Fleuri** – *1 rue du Centre – St. Sulpice.* ℘*(0)21 691 20 21. Fax (0)21 697 40 40. http://pfen.hotelprefleuri.ch/. 17 rooms.* Rooms overlook a charming garden with pool. Meals (arrange beforehand) can be served in a pretty dining room or on the terrace.

🍴🛏🛏 **Romantik Hotel Mont Blanc au Lac** – *Quai du Mont-Blanc, 1110 Morges.* ℘*(0)21 804 87 87. www.hotel-mont-blanc.ch.* 🚭. *45 rooms.* Built in 1857 on the lakeside of Morges opposite the majestic Mont Blanc, this legendary hotel offers elegant rooms, most with superb lake views. During the summer season you can enjoy the beautiful shaded terrace. The proximity of the water and the serenity of the place provide ideal conditions for relaxing after a long day.

🍴 EAT

🍴🛏 **Rive-Bleue** – *La Lagune, route de la Plage, La Bouveret.* ℘*(0)24 482 42 82.* A welcoming dining hall extended by a terrace facing Lake Geneva. Traditional cuisine with by a wide choice of dishes.

🍴🛏 **La Plage** – *5 ave de la Plage, Préveranges.* ℘*(0)21 803 07 93. www.hotel-laplage.ch. Closed Sun–Mon.* On a walk around the lake, discover this café, fine restaurant and terrace serving modern cuisine. Neat, clean, tidy rooms also available. Pretty garden for relaxation at the rear.

🍴🛏🛏 **L'Ermitage** – *26 route du Vilage, Vufflens-le-Château.* ℘*(0)21 804 68 68. www.ravet.ch. Closed 23 Dec–15 Jan, 1–19 Aug, Sun and Mon.* An entire family looks after diners in this charming old residence featuring a garden with lakes. Classical yet creative delicacies and spit-roasted specialities from the father and son. Personalised rooms and junior suites for extending your stay.

SIGHTSEEING

THE LAKE BY BOAT

The steamers of the Compagnie Générale de Navigation *(www.cgn.ch)* offer many trips including the Tour of the **Little Lake** (Petit Lac—starting from Geneva) and the more interesting Tour of the **Upper Lake** (Haut Lac—starting from Ouchy-Lausanne).

A round trip of the lake takes 11hr-12hr.

Nyon★

A pleasant town above Lake Geneva, Nyon was founded by Caesar under the name Colonia Julia Equestris (succeeding the Helvetian burg of Noviodunum). In the 16C Nyon was occupied by the Bernese. Examples of their style of architecture can be seen in the castle and the arcaded houses on Place du Marché. Today Nyon is at the centre of the vineyards on the southeast facing hillsides above the Lake and the wine cellar at the château is well known to wine lovers.

▶ **Population:** Vaud 18 269.

Michelin Map: National 729: C6.

Info: Av. Viollier 8. ☎(0)22 365 66 00. www.geneva-tourism.ch.

Location: On the north-western shore of Lake Geneva. Alt. 410m/1 345ft.

P Parking: Park in designated areas; many streets restricted.

Don't Miss: A walk around the city walls.

Timing: Allow the better part of a day to visit the sights and go on an excursion to the summit of La Dôle.

OLD TOWN

Walk around the Town Walls★

The walk skirts the ivy-covered walls (19C) and widens onto the Esplanade des Marronniers from where there is a pretty view of the town, the Little Lake as far as Geneva, the Salève and Mont Blanc. Roman columns add a romantic touch to the scene.

Castle★

Open daily exc Mon and public hols Apr–Oct, 10am–5pm; Nov–Mar 2pm–5pm. ☎8CHF. ☎(0)22 363 83 51. www.chateaudenyon.ch.

Heavily altered in the 16C, the feudal castle has five different towers, all crowned with pepper-pot roofs. From the terrace there is a nice **view** of the Rive quarter and the Little Lake (*viewing table*).

This château, which was re-opened in 2006 after six years of restoration, houses the History and Porcelain Museum. It was much altered during the fifteenth century during the Bern Period, is of fuedal origin and was owned by the town of Nyon from 1804. It has five towers of differing design but all finished with a "pepper pot" cap. From the terrace, which has an orientaton table, there is a fine view over the Rive district and the Petit Lac.

The entrance to the museum is from the basement. The ground floor is dedicated to temporary exhibitions.

On every floor there are pictures of the people of Nyon over the centuries, some of which are very moving.

First floor – divided into several rooms which house the finest collection of Nyon porcelain from between 1781 and 1813. The original use of the rooms is indicated, including the "Coat of Arms Room". You can also see a large outside gallery, decorated with murals which date from 1690.

Second floor – a floor used for ceremonial purposes in the sixteenth century, until 1836 when it was used as a town court and the local council. It has been redecorated using wallpaper based on original styles. The rooms contains ceramics from the 19C and furniture ordered for the château before it was repurchased by the town of Nyon.

Third floor – the top floor served as storage space and a torture chamber in the 17C, and was converted in 1832 to provide a prison, plus a flat for the gaoler and his family.

The cells were still used until 1979 and have been preserved in their original state. Graffiti scrawled on the walls by prisoners can be seen.

Paléo Festival

For more than 20 years, Nyon has hosted a lively international music festival. Concerts are held in a large meadow near the shores of Lake Geneva, where several stages are set up for performances. All styles of music are represented: Rock, jazz, blues, reggae, salsa, rap, country, techno, and even classical music. Performers have included Johnny Clegg, Joe Cocker, Eddy Mitchell, Noa, Al Jarreau, Placebo, Patricia Kaas, Mc Solaar and Alan Stivell. The event attracts large crowds of locals

© Philippe Dutoit/Switzerland Tourism

and visitors from abroad and the atmosphere is noisy and convivial. The Prix de la Scène is a prize awarded to a young singer or group from Switzerland by an international panel made up of professional performers. During the Paléo Festival, the town of Nyon becomes a living stage, with improvised shows taking place in the streets: theatre, dance, mime, circus and magic (*www.paleo.ch*).

Musée Romain

Open Apr–Oct, Tue–Sun 10am–5pm. Closed Mon except on public holidays. 8CHF (ticket gives admission to the other museums. Free every first Sunday of the month. Guided tours available). (0)22 361 75 91. www.mrn.ch.

This underground museum is marked above ground by a statue of Caesar. On the façade of the neighbouring house there is a drawing of how the Forum must have looked during the Roman era. The excavated part of this vast 1C public building (more than a third of its foundations) is the centrepiece of the museum.

Around it are artefacts excavated from digs at Nyon and its environs: fragments of mosaics with simple geometric patterns or foliage motifs (including the famous Artemis mural), stone debris (capitals, military milestones), domestic objects (lamps, ceramics, crockery, coins) and a host of **amphorae** of different origins.

Quartier de Rive

A park and quays with attractive flower beds border the small sheltered yachting harbour and provide views of Lake Geneva and France on the far side. Farther

along on Quai des Alpes stands the 11C Tour César. Note, high up, the Roman masque of the god Attis, consort of the Great Mother of the gods (Cybele).

Musée du Léman

Same opening times as the Musée Romain. 8CHF (ticket gives admission to the other museums). (0)22 361 09 49.

The museum is housed in an 18C hospital overlooking the harbour. The origins of Switzerland's largest lake and its flora and fauna (aquariums are home to several species of fish) are the themes of the first exhibition.

The next section illustrates the various activities associated with the lake: fishing (boats, nets, and tools), forestry and timber-working (barges used to transport the logs prior to the advent of the railway) as well as the history of shipping (from the early lateen-sail fishing boats, so typical of the lake, to machinery from the steamer *Helvétie II*).

The first floor is dedicated to artists, both Swiss and non-Swiss, who have been drawn to Lake Geneva in the past; an area devoted to the Swiss General Navigation Company contains a collection of models, including one of the first steamboats ever used on the lake (1823).

EXCURSIONS

Abbaye de Bonmont

▶ *10km/6.2mi W by the road to Divonne. Then take the narrow road on the right.* ⊙*Open 1pm–5pm; Apr–Jun Sat–Sun, Jul–Aug Tue –Sun, Sept–Oct Sat–Sun.* ⊙*Closed most public holidays and during concerts and other events.* ⊚*8CHF.* ✆*(0)22 369 23 68. www.bonmont.ch*

At the foot of the Vaud Jura, a few buildings remain from the former Bonmont Abbey, which became Cistercian during its construction (1131). Over the centuries, it was used as a cheese dairy and even as a garage, and consequently has not suffered too much damage. Built in the same Burgundian style as the Abbaye de Clairvaux—designed like a Latin cross, with a tripartite nave and a flat east end flanked by oblong chapels—and recently restored, the austere church nonetheless has elegant lines and boasts a fine porch enhanced by capitals with floral motifs.

La Dôle★★★

Alt. 1 677m/5 500ft.

La Dôle can be reached by car via two routes. From Nyon go to the La Barrillette parking ground (about 20km/12.5mi). From St-Cergue go to the St-Cergue parking ground (about 21km/13.1mi) The travelling time is 1h10mins from La Barillette and 1h35mins from St-Cergue. Walking boots required.

Leave the car at the foot of La Dôle and continue on foot. Follow the path on the left, marked out in yellow. It leads to the summit, where a navigation beacon and radar station have been constructed.

A **panorama**★★★ extends over the Alps right up to the peaks of the Valais (Matterhorn) and the Oisans (Meije). Mont Blanc looms between the two, with Lake Geneva in the foreground. You can see the Jura including Mount Tendre and the Chasseron on one side and the Valserine as far as the Reculet, on the other.

Saint-Cergue★

Alt. 1 044m/3 480ft. 15km/9.4mi.

▶ *Leave Nyon and drive NE by Route Signy and Route Blanche. Place Sy-Vieuxville.* ✆*(0)22 360 13 14. www.st-cergue.ch.*

The high-altitude resort of Saint-Cergue has long been known to the Genevese and the French for its bracing mountain climate. St-Cergue stands at the point where the corridor of the Girvine Pass opens out within sight of the Mont-Blanc Massif and Lake Geneva. There are many belvederes near the resort, from which there are good views of the forest-clad foreground and the giant of the Alps.

Borsattaz Meadow

Those interested in botanical phenomena should go to the Borsattaz meadow, where giant pine trees, known locally as *gogants*, prosper; they are to be found only in the Jura. You reach the meadow from the Lausanne road; after 1.5km/1mi turn left into a tarred road (Route de la Prangine et du Plumet); 1.5km/1mi farther on bear right at the Carrefour des Fruitières. St-Cergue offers more than 50km/31mi of trails for **cross-country skiing** and a variety of training grounds and fairly difficult ski runs for **downhill skiing.**

Belvédère du Vieux Château★★

30min on foot there and back by a path signposted Le Vieux Château. Splendid view of Lake Geneva and Mont Blanc.

Parc Jurassien Vaudois★★★

Rte du Marchuairuz 2. ✆*(0)22 366 51 70 www.parc-jurassien.ch.*

In 1973, 13 communities and a number of private landowners combined to create this regional natural park to preserve the mountain sides of the Jura for future generations, Now comprising more than 100sq km/38.6mi in 23 towns on the Jura highlands above the northern shores of Lake Geneva, the park includes not only woodlands but pasture lands lined with dry masonry stone walls as well. The pastures are home to the cattle that provide the milk for the region's famed Gruyère cheese. Throughout the

Parc Jurassien Vaudois with a view to Lake Geneva to Savoyen and Mont Blanc

© Roland Gerth/Switzerland Tourism/BAFU

year the lands are available for public uses and the park administration has a number of programmes available to the public explaining the natural and human history of the region. Saint Cergue is at the southwest end of the park.

🚗 DRIVING TOUR

1 VALLÉE DE JOUX★★

From Nyon to Vallorbe. 90km/56mi – allow approx 2hrs. ⊖The Marchairuz road (Le Brassus to St-George) is usually blocked by snow from November to April.

The jewel of the Vaud Jura, the Joux Valley and its lake, presents an agreeable stop on an otherwise hilly road linking Lake Geneva to the French border. Thanks to its lake, pastures, pine forests and the mountains which surround it, the Joux valley is the jewel in the crown of the Jura in the Vaud area.

Zoo de la Garenne

🕓*Open daily, 9am–6pm (5.30pm Dec–Feb). ⊜10CHF. ℘(0) 22 366 11 14. www.lagarenne.ch.*
This small zoo presents mostly European species (wolf, lynx, eagle etc). The hairpin section between Burtigny and Begnins offers particularly open **views**★★ of the Savoy shore of Lake Geneva.

▷ *Return to Marchissy and continue to St-George.*

From St-George, the panorama from Sapin to Siméon provides a lovely view over the Mont Blanc massif, the Aravis chain of mountians, plus the plateau and ranges of the Glières and the Grand Salève.

▷ *Continue to Brassus.*

The road crosses the Amburneux valley at the heart of the Vaud's Jurassic Park, one of Switzerland's largest parks. The countryside is distinctive due to its dry stone walls which were built between the end of the 19C and the beginning of the 20C. They were built to divide the pastures and to fence in animals.

▷ *At Brassus, turn right to return to the village.*

Vallée de Joux★★

Rue de l'Orbe. ℘(0)21 845 17 770. www.myvalleedejoux.ch.
The road then leads into the Joux Valley, gently hollowed out between the minor ranges around Mont Risoux and Mont Tendre. After the small Lake Brenets and the villas and hotels of Le Pont (facilities) scattered around it, Lake Joux, the largest of the Jura lakes, appears.
Its calm waters are frozen during the long harsh winter. Until a few years after the World War I this ice, cut into regular blocks, was stored at Le Pont in underground ice-houses before being sent to Paris by rail.

View of Lake Joux from the Dent de Vaulion

© Roland Gerth/Switzerland Tourism/BAFU

Follow the south shore, bordered by wooded hills, wide pastures and hospitable villages, which are both pleasant country resorts and small industrial centres employed in watch and clock-making. The **Espace Horloger de la Vallée de Joux** (🕐*closed until summer 2012; www.espacehorloger.ch*) at **Le Sentier** introduces visitors to a display of splendid clocks and watches dating from the 16C–19C and a reconstruction of a typical watchmaker's workshop.

The climb from Le Brassus (facilities) to the Marchairuz Pass affords pleasant views of Lake Joux and its valley, closed by the bold spur of the Dent de Vaulion.

▷ *Take the south bank from Joux lake (l'Orient, les Bioux). After Abbaye village, take the road to Lausanne-Cossonnay. At Petra Felix, turn left towards Vaulion. Several kilometres further on turn left again towards the Dent de Vaulion chalet.*

Dent De Vaulion★★

Alt. 1 482m/4 865ft.

Dent de Vaulion, one of the steepest summits in the Swiss Jura, offers a sweeping panorama of the Alps, from the Jungfrau to the Meije and the Joux Valley.

Climb to the Dent

From the road from Romainmôtier to L'Abbaye, 5km/3mi – allow 45min.

The access road, tarred as far as the chalet on Dent de Vaulion, branches off from the main road on the ridge between the Vaulion Valley and the Joux Valley. It soon becomes very narrow (*passing only possible at certain points*). From the chalet you can see your way to a signpost marking the summit (*viewing table*).

Panorama★★★

The great glory of this view is the Mont-Blanc Massif beyond the mists of Lake Geneva; the first ridges of the Jura towards the Joux Valley and its lakes are also a majestic sight. Beware the alarming precipice: a sheer drop of over 200m/600ft.

Vallorbe

Alt. 769m/2 523ft. 11 Grandes-Forges. 𝄞 *(0)21 843 25 83.*

www.vallorbe-tourisme.ch.

The town of Vallorbe owes its activity to its varied industries (light engineering, plastic products) and especially to its frontier station, well-known to users of the Simplon line.

Musée du Fer et du Chemin de Fer

The Carte Trèfle (⊜30CHF) is a ticket valid from Palm Sunday to All Saints giving access to the caves, the Iron and Railway Museum, the Parc du Mont-d'Orzaires, and the Vallorbe fort. Contact the sights for further information. 🕐*Open Apr–Oct, Tue–Sun 10am–6pm, Mon 2pm–6pm; Nov–Mar, Tue–Fri 2pm–6pm. ⊜12CHF. 𝄞 (0)21*

843 25 83. www.museedufer.ch.
Access to the Iron and Railway Museum is through the Tourist Information Centre.

On the former site of the Grandes Forges, the **Iron Museum** celebrates the history of the region's iron industry. In addition to early forges, displays include anvils, grinding-stones, and other tools manufactured on site, as well as modern products made through precision engineering.

Vallorbe's golden age as one of the stops on the Simplon line is vividly evoked at the **Railway Museum**. There is a maquette of the station in 1908: plus historic railway tools and equipment, tickets, old posters, and an inspector's uniform. On the second floor, visitors can follow the adventures of their favorite train on a miniature toy circuit: *micheline*, high-speed *TGV*, regional Swiss trains.

Grottes de Vallorbe★

Open Mar 1.30pm–4pm; Apr, May, Sept, Oct , 9.30am–4.30pm (5.30pm Jun, Jul and Aug). 15CHF, 7CHF children). (0)21 843 22 74. www.grottesdevallorbe.ch.

The Orbe rivier has created underground chambers which are among the most spectacular in Switzerland. The grottos hadn't been explored much before the 1960s. Having passed through a large artificial gallery, there is a succession of lakes and grottos rich with stalactites, stalagmites and concretions (masses formed of solid particles). Just before the exit, it is worth visiting the Trésor des Fées (Fairies' Treasure) where 250 examples of minerals from around the world, are displayed.

Fort de Vallorbe

Guided tours (1hr30min) Jul and Aug, daily 10.30am–5pm; Mar–Oct, Sat–Sun 11am–4.30pm. 13CHF. (0)32 843 25 83.

This stronghold, carved out of rock and facing the French border, was built shortly before the Second World War. It consists of three small forts and six heavily guarded blockhouses and watchtowers, connected by a maze of underground galleries. 30m/98.4ft below ground level sits a machine room, ammunition dump, telephone exchange, barracks, dormitory, kitchen, mess, canteen, infirmary, dental surgery, and operating theatre. Figurines, weapons, documents, and sound effects complete this evocation of military life in the Fort de Pré-Giroud, which could house around 100 men.

Source of the Orbe

3km/1.8mi—plus 30min on foot there and back. Leave Vallorbe by the road to the Joux Valley, and then take the road to the left marked Source-Grottes, sloping gently downhill. Leave your car near the power station.

Walk along a shady path and you will reach the end of the little rocky hollow where the Orbe rises: a reappearance of the waters of the Joux and Brenet lakes.

ADDRESSES

STAY

Hostellerie du 16e siècle –
Pl. du Marché. (0)22 994 88 00. www.16eme.com. 19 rooms.
In the centre of Nyon next to the château, this hotel housed in a lovely old building offers light and pleasant rooms together with a restaurant which offers very good value for money considering the quality of the cuisine.

Hôtel Ambassador –
26 r. St-Jean. (0)22 994 48 60 - www.hotel-ambassador-nyon.ch. 20 rooms. Comfortable spacious rooms with traditional muted decor. Several of the rooms have a large terrace overlooking the lake.

EAT

Le Rive – *15 r. de Rive. (0)22 362 34 46. www.lerive.ch. Non-stop meals available every day.* Simple but good fare in this brasserie on the lake. The menu includes crêpes. Friendly welcome and terrace.

Lausanne★★

Lausanne is a welcoming, cosmopolitan city, much loved by its university students and its high society, who enjoy the scenic views of the lake and the surrounding Alps. The city is built on uneven ground. After being confined to the promontory of the present city for several centuries, Lausanne spread southward to the delightful shores of Ouchy, a former fisherman's hamlet. Its new quarters contrast sharply with the old, steep, narrow streets that lead to the cathedral.

A BIT OF HISTORY

The life of the city is concentrated within Place de la Riponne, rue du Bourg, Place Saint-François, rue du Grand-Chêne and Place Bel-Air. These are joined by the Grand Pont, spanning the valley where the Flon torrent once flowed.

An important centre for both art and entertainment, Lausanne has acquired a worldwide reputation for the famous ballet troupe directed by Maurice Béjart and the classical concerts performed by the French Swiss Orchestra and the Chamber Orchestra of Lausanne. The Palais de Beaulieu and the Théâtre Municipal are frequently used to host dance performances and musical shows. The municipality of **Vidy**, part of Lausanne, enjoys Olympic status since it houses the International Olympic Committee (IOC), which was founded in 1894 by Baron Pierre de Coubertin.

The Olympic Museum, opened in Ouchy in 1993, has made Lausanne the world capital of the **Olympic movement**.

Early days – Recent excavations show Lausanne was originally built on the site of the present city, perched on the promontory where Neolithic skeletons have been uncovered. Southwest (at **Vidy**), part of the former Roman Lousonna has been excavated. Of particular interest is a section of Roman road, located exactly where the Geneva-Lausanne road is today.

▷ **Population:** Vaud 114 518.

Michelin Map: National Map 729: D6. Includes Town Plan.

Info: 9 Place de la Gare – 1000. ℰ(0)21 613 73 73. www.lausanne-tourisme.ch.

Location: 62km/36mi northeast of Geneva, on the lakeshore. Alt. 455m/1 493ft.

P **Parking:** Leave the car; use the rapid subway between lakefront and city centre.

Don't Miss: The Olympic Museum in a beautiful park on the lake, where the Olympic flame has burnt uninterrupted since opening.

Timing: Allow at least two days for the museums and a lake excursion.

Cathedral City – At the end of the 6C Bishop St Marius came to live in Lausanne; the first cathedral was built two centuries later. In the Middle Ages, religious leadership combined with economic and political expansion: the quarters of Place de la Palud, the Bourg, St Pierre, St Laurent and St François were added to the town. In the 13C many religious orders settled here and the Prince-Bishop Guillaume de Champvent consecrated the new cathedral; later Pope Gregory X dedicated it in the presence of Emperor Rudolf I of Habsburg. The city or upper town was the religious and intellectual centre; commercial activities flourished in adjoining districts.

From the Reformation to Bernese domination – The Reformation scored a sweeping success at Lausanne; it was preached there by Guillaume Farel. In 1536 the town and all of the Vaud Country were occupied by the Bernese. All of Lausanne's churches except for the cathedral and the Church of St Francis disappeared. In 1723 the Bernese

View of Old Town

© Regis Colombo/Lausanne Tourisme/Switzerland Tourism

harshly suppressed an attempt by the Vaud people to regain their independence; Davel, the instigator of the revolt, was beheaded at Vidy. It was not until 1803 that the Vaud region attained political autonomy, with Lausanne as its capital. In 1874 it became the seat of the Federal Court of Justice.

The Age of Enlightenment – The 18C was an era of prosperity. Lausanne came under French influence; Voltaire stayed in the city, where his play *Zadig* was performed. Byron and Shelley visited Lausanne in 1816, as did Wordsworth in 1790 and 1820; Dickens resided here twice: in 1846, where he was visited by, among others, Thackeray and Tennyson; and again in 1853. It was during his stay in Lausanne (1921–22) that **TS Eliot** wrote *The Waste Land*, which secured his international reputation. Literary salons flourished. The best known local figures, however, were Dr Tissot, who lived in the 18C and was known as the "Healer of the Sick of Europe", Dr Jules Gonin, an eye surgeon who specialised in operating on detached retinas, and Maurice Lugeon (d. 1953), an outstanding geologist and an authority on the Alps.

Today, the city hosts festivals throughout the year, including cultural Festival de la Cité, Athlestissima at Olympic stadium, and a marathon in the autumn.

⚑ WALKING TOUR

OLD TOWN
1hr. ⚑ *Longer guided tours from May–Oct every Tue and Fri at 3pm; ☞40CHF. For further information, contact Lausanne Tourist Office. Depart from place St François.*

Place de la Palud
Lined by old houses and by the Renaissance façade of the town hall, which proudly bears the arms of the city of Lausanne, this square is adorned with the Fountain of Justice (16C–18C). Nearby, an animated clock strikes the hours of the day, exhibiting a gallery of historical figures. The curious covered **staircase** beyond the fountain leads through to the cathedral.

Cathedral★★
🕐*Open 7am–7pm, Sat–Sun 8am–7pm (Sept–Mar 5.30 pm).* 📞*(0)21 316 71 61.*
This is the finest Gothic building in Switzerland. Its construction began during the episcopate of St Amadeus (1145–59) and was completed in the mid-13C; it was consecrated in 1275 and entirely restored in the late 19C. The east end abuts two picturesque square towers, dominated by the lantern-tower at the transept crossing. Both it and the bell tower are reminiscent of Anglo-Norman

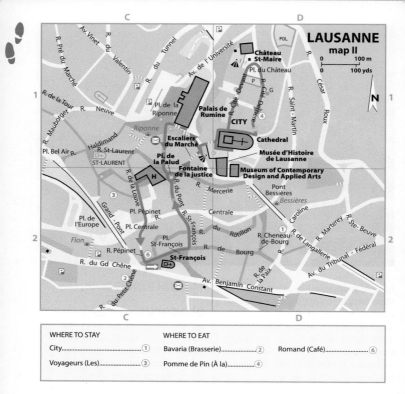

WHERE TO STAY

City...................................... ①

Voyageurs (Les)........................ ③

WHERE TO EAT

Bavaria (Brasserie)...................... ②

Pomme de Pin (À la)................. ④

Romand (Café)........................... ⑥

architecture, clearly marking the transition from Romanesque to Gothic.

The **south door**, known as the Painted Doorway, is adorned with a fine group of 13C sculptures. The pillars supporting the roof bear figures of the Prophets. The lintel is carved with low reliefs. The Montfalcon Doorway is named for the bishops Aymon and Sébastien de Montfalcon (1517, restored in the early 20C). In a chapel on the right, murals (1505) portray the life of the Virgin Mary.

Other features are influenced by the English Gothic style: note the original arrangement of sturdy columns, alternating with pairs of slender pillars. The rare and unusual 13C **stalls** feature exceptionally fine figures on the cheek pieces. Other stalls, in the Flamboyant style (16C), are in the St-Maurice chapel. In the south arm of the transept a 13C rose window, *Imago Mundi* (elements, seasons, months, and signs of the Zodiac), is remarkably harmonious. In the chancel rests the tomb of Othon I

of Grandson. In the ambulatory note the tomb of the 13C bishop-builder Roger de Vico-Pisano.

Lausanne is one of the last towns to maintain a nightwatch. From the top of the cathedral tower the nightwatchman cries the hour between 10pm and 2am.

Tower

Access to the stairway (224 steps) at the end of the south aisle. ◐*Ascent Mon–Fri 8am–6.30pm (6pm in winter); Sat 8.30am–6pm (5pm in winter); Sun 2pm–7pm (5.30pm in winter).* ◐*Closed 1 and 2 Jan and 25 Dec.* ◉*4CHF.* ℘*(0)21 316 71 61.*

From the top of the tower there is a fine **view**★ of the town, Lake Geneva, and the Alps. The parvis of the cathedral affords bird's-eye views of the town and the lake.

Go round the cathedral to the left of the east end, rue Cité-Derrière, a small medieval street decorated with wrought-iron signs.

▷ *Two museums are located just to the right of the cathedral.*

Musée de Design et d'Arts Appliqués Contemporains (Museum of Contemporary Design and Applied Arts)

🕐*Open 11am–6pm.* 🕐*Closed Mon (except Jul and Aug), 1 Jan, and 25 Dec.* ⚫*10CHF (combined ticket with Musée Historique* ⚫*15CHF). Free entry 1st Sat of month.* ♿ 📞*(0)21 315 25 30. www.mudac.ch.*

This museum devoted to design and contemporary art includes early exhibits coming from Egypt and China along with glass sculptures made by contemporary artists.

Musée Historique de Lausanne

🕐*Open Tue, Wed, Thu 11am–6pm; Fri, Sat–Sun 11am–5pm.* 🕐*Closed Mon (except in Jul and Aug, open 11am–6pm) and religious holidays.* ⚫*8CHF.* 📞*(0)21 315 41 01. www.lausanne.ch/mhl.*

Rooms of the former bishop's palace have been restored to house these collections, which recall the town's history from prehistoric times to today. The first section features a vast miniature model of the city as it was in 1638. Several 19C displays include a general store, grocery shop, printing house and photogra-

pher's studio. Note the safe which once belonged to the Kohler House (1828) with its original and elaborate ironwork.

Château St-Marie

This 15C brick and stone castle was originally the residence of the bishops of Lausanne and then the Bernese bailiffs. The cantonal government sits there today. The terrace affords a sweeping **view** of Lausanne and Lake Geneva.

▷ *Continue along rue Cité-Derrière. Then turn left into avenue de l'Université, which leads to Place de la Riponne, situated at the foot of the promontory.*

PALAIS DE RUMINE

Built in the early 20C it houses the library and these five museums:

Musée des Beaux-Arts★

🕐*Open Tue, Wed 10am–6pm; Thu 10am–8pm, Fri–Sun and public holidays, 11am–5pm.* 🕐*Closed Mon, 1 Jan and 25 Dec.* ⚫*10CHF.* ♿. 📞*(0)21 316 34 45.*

Most of the paintings in this Museum of Fine Arts in the first three rooms are the work of Swiss nationals, many of whom were born in the region. There are many works by Lausanne artist Félix Vallotton, of whom the museum possesses the largest **state collection**★.

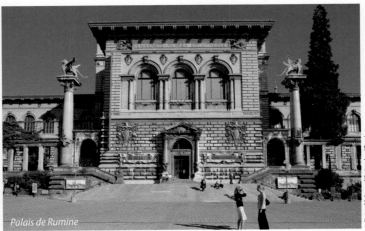

Palais de Rumine

© Christof Schuerpf/Switzerland Tourism

This section ends with French painters, namely Largillière, Géricault, Courbet, Cézanne, Bonnard, Renoir, Degas, Matisse, Marquet, Vlaminck, Vuillard, and Utrillo. Also, sculptures of Rodin and Giacometti are exhibited alongside more recent works by Nauman and Boltanski.

Musée de Géologie

First floor, on the left. Open Tue–Thu 11am–6pm (5pm Fri and Sat–Sun). Closed 1 Jan and 25 Dec. 6CHF, no charge first Sat in the month. *(0)21 316 33 90. www.unil.ch/mcg.*
The Geological Museum contains rock specimens from the country plus relief models and a skeleton of a mammoth.

Musée de Paléontologie

Opposite the Musée de Géologie; same hours; use the same ticket.
A collection of plant and animal fossils and skeletons.

Musée de Zoologie

Second floor. Same hours as the Musée de Géologie; use the same ticket.
The Zoology Museum houses specimens of flora from countries all over the world. Displays include a comparative anatomy between Man and the animal race, a living Mexican ant colony, and a gallery of mineralogy.

Salle d'Archéologie et d'Histoire

Sixth floor. Same hours as the Musée de Géologie. ; use the same ticket.
The History and Archaeology Museum displays artefacts discovered during excavations of local sites.

PROMENADE DE SAUVABELIN

1h30mins. Take the number 16 bus from Place St-François or Lausanne-Flon and get off at the Lac de Sauvabelin stop.
A pleasant walk for the family, this pretty rural route heads to the Sauvabelin Lake, to the north of the town, to Château St-Maire, near to the cathedral. From time to time the paths crosses the route of St-Jacques-de-Compostelle.

On Sundays, families from Lausanne come here to relax in the countryside, just a stone's throw from the town.
It is possible to cross the lake in a boat or to take a walk around the perimeter. There's also a restaurant, childrens' playgrounds and animals (sheep, pigs and goats). Take the path beside the Pinte à Fromage restaurant.

Sauvabelin Tower

Summer 9am–9pm, winter 9am–5pm. No charge. *(0)21 315 42 74. www.tour-de-sauvabelin-lausanne.ch.*
This 35m wooden tower was erected in 2003 and has ever since been the major attraction of the park. After the climb of 151 steps visitors can enjoy a 360 degree view over Lausanne, Lake Geneva, the Alps, the back country and the Jura.
At the base of the tower, take the gently inclining path and then turn left.
At the crossroads, go straight ahead (following the yellow tourist markers) until reaching a road bordered with a stand of trees. Go past the Chalet Suisse restaurant.

Vue du Signal★★

Alt. 643m/2 109ft.
This belvedere *(viewing table, telescope)* affords a pleasant **view** of Lake Geneva, the Savoy, Fribourg and the Vaud Alps and, in the foreground, the historic centre of Lausanne.

Fondation de l'Hermitage (Hermitage Foundation)

2 route du Signal. Exhibitions from 25 Jan–28 May and 21 Jun–28 Oct. Every day except Mon, 10am–6pm (Thu 9pm). Closed between the exhibitions. Guided visits (1hr) 16CHF (children free). *(0)21 320 50 01. www.fondation-hermitage.ch.*
This former abode of the Vaud Family, the Bugnion was built in 1841 and is surrounded by gardens with rare plants. It hosts temporary art and history exhibitions. From the lawns there is a good view of Château St-Maire, the cathedral and the lake.
Follow the yellow markers to return to the town. The path which goes through

Collection de l'Art Brut

© Christof Schuerpf/Switzerland Tourism

woodland, leads to the Place de la Barre which has a pretty fountain, close to Château St-Maire.

ADDITIONAL SIGHTS
Collection de l'Art Brut★

🕐*Open Tue–Sun 11am–6pm.*
10CHF. Free 1st Sat of each month.
(0)21 315 25 70. www.artbrut.ch.
The four floors of this unique museum—housed in the former stables of Beaulieu Château (18C)—present 1 000 objects (out of some 5 000) collected by the painter Jean Dubuffet since 1945 and donated to the city.

The paintings, drawings, sculptures, modeling, and embroidery are the work of schizophrenics, inmates confined to prison cells or psychiatric hospitals, spiritualist mediums, and others.

Montriond Park

On this spot where, in 1037, the first Truce of God was proclaimed in the district, there is a great esplanade reached by a ramp and a staircase.

The **view**★★ extends southward over Ouchy, the shores of Lake Geneva and to the Alps. One section of the park is by a **botanical garden** (🕐*open May–Sept, daily 10am–6.30pm; Mar–Apr and Oct, daily 10am–5.30pm; no charge; museum open by appointment; (0)21 316 99 88).*

It consists of an arboretum, an alpine garden with mountain flora, flowers,

succulents, and a variety of medicinal, carnivorous, and aquatic species.

Parc Mon Repos

This pleasant garden is also the site of the Empire style villa where Voltaire used to live. To the north of the park the Federal Court of Switzerland is housed in a huge building.

Musée Romain de Lausanne-Vidy

24 chemin du Bois-de-Vaux (from Lausanne, follow signs to Geneva)
🕐*Open every day except Mon, 11am–6pm. Daily July – Aug. Closed 24, 25, 31 Dec and 1 Jan. 8 CHF, No charge 1st Sat of month. (0)21 315 41 85. www.lausanne.ch/mrv.*
This museum was built in 1993 on the remains of Gallo-Roman site called Lousonna which lasted until the fourth century. The settlement which lies on the banks of the lake had a population of between 1 500 and 2 000 people. From the house a well and a room decorated with frescoes has been preserved. The room also displays items of furniture from the time and relics from everyday life, as well as temporary exhibitions.

Pully

The old village of Pully has become a residential suburb of Lausanne.
From the terrace of the Church of St Germain a charming **view**★ opens out onto

the eastern part of Lake Geneva to the French side of the lake from Évian to Meillerie.
In the church precincts stand a museum and the remains of a Roman villa.

Musée de Pully

⏰*Open Wed–Sun 2pm–6pm.* ⏰*Closed Easter, Christmas and according to temp. exhibitions.* 🎫*7CHF.* ♿ ☎*(0)21 729 38 00. www.museedepully.ch.*
The museum is located near the house where **Charles-Ferdinand Ramuz** (1878–1947) lived until his death. The museum displays souvenirs of Ramuz together with paintings by contemporary artists from Pully. Visitors may also admire clay sculptures by Derain and precious objects (writing desk, model of royal barge) that belonged to the King of Siam, a resident of Pully between 1925 and 1945.

OUCHY★★

Ouchy is linked to Lausanne by its *métro,* an electrically-driven funicular once known as the "rope" (cable-driven) and later as the "tire" (mounted on wheels). Ouchy—a famous hotel resort and popular spot for Sunday strollers—is also one of the liveliest navigation centres on the lake, now that its time as a fishing port has passed. The large sailing port adjoining Place de la Naviga-

tion has been refurbished and is now reserved for pedestrians, who can enjoy its charming fountains and four giant chess games. Many leisure boats are also available for cruises. The shaded quays, adorned with tropical plants and flowers, stretch for over 1km/0.6mi and are prolonged eastward by the lakeside path. This charming route offers lovely **views**★★ of the harbour, Lake Geneva and the Chablais mountains.

Musée Olympique★★ (Olympic Museum)

⏰*Closed for renovation until the end of 2013.*
This museum sits on the shores of Lake Geneva, with a public garden enhanced by statues, fountains, and pavilions.
The **park** extends across terraced slopes, offering nice views. All along the path to the museum entrance (420m/1 378ft, the length of an Olympic stadium), a series of statues symbolises the marriage of sport and culture.
The modern ensemble, inspired by a Greek temple, is the work of architects Pedro Ramirez Vázquez and Lausanne native Jean-Pierre Cahen. In front of the white marble façade (the stone is from the Greek island of Thassos), two rows of four columns carry the names of the towns which have hosted the Olympic Games and the names of the Olympic

Musée Olympique

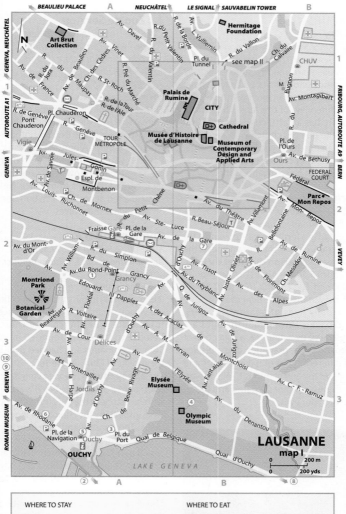

LAUSANNE
map I

| 0 | | | 200 m |
| 0 | | | 200 yds |

LAKE GENEVA

WHERE TO STAY		WHERE TO EAT	
Agora	①	Lacustre (Le)	②
Angleterre & Résidence	③	Olympique (Restaurant du musée)	④
Aulac	⑤	Pêcherie (La)	⑥
Mirabeau	⑦	Port de Pully	⑧
Pierrettes (Les)	⑨		
Pré Fleuri	⑩		

Committee presidents. In a granite bowl, decorated with allegorical motifs illustrating the myth of Prometheus, the Olympic flame burns forever.

Ground Floor – Largely devoted to the history of the Games, with particular emphasis on ancient Greece. Terracotta figures, marble and bronze sculptures, vases decorated with figures of athletes, gold laurel wreaths, and *strigils* are exhibited.

Also on display: all the torches that have carried the Olympic flame, from the Berlin Games of 1936 to the present. Note two fine bronze statues—*The American Athlete* by Rodin and *The Archer* by Bourdelle.

EXCURSIONS

Lutry

▶ *4 km/2.5mi E of the town, via Avenue de l'Élysée, then road number 9.*

This village with narrow streets is worthy of a short stop. It sits on Lake Geneva with its own small marina and the plus of a fine view of the Alps. The central square has an attractive fountain and a white painted church with an ornate Roman porch. As you leave the village, an imposing château (now a medical centre) can be seen among the vines.

Échallens

▶ *15km/9mi by avenue d'Échallens then take road number 5.*

Located in a fertile cereal-growing agricultural area, this small town boasts the fascinating **Maison du Blé et du Pain** (◯ *open 8.30am–6pm;* ◯ *closed Mon 25 cDec and 1 Jan ;* ☞*10CHF*✆*(0)21 881 50 71; www.maison-ble-pain.com).*

The daily lives of peasants, millers, and bakers throughout the ages are illustrated by a diorama, a collection of farming tools, granaries, and a display of different types of baking ovens and mills. At the end of the visit, rolls, loaves, and croissants are prepared and baked before your eyes.

St-Pierre-le-Viex, Romainmôtier

© Stephan Engler/Switzerland Tourism

👥 Zoo de Servion

▶ *18km/11mi by the road to Bern.*

◯*Open 9am–7pm (6pm in winter). Last admission 1hr before closing.*

☞*10CHF, children 5CHF.*

&. ✆*(0)21 903 16 71.*

www.zoo-servion.ch.

This estate is home to a wide range of animal species. After the Monkey Pavilion, visitors enter the tropical hothouse with exotic birds. Alongside the Ostrich Pavilion you will find Chilean flamingoes, as well as crowned cranes and pink-backed pelicans from Africa. Next come the red deer, American buffaloes, brown bears, and wolves.

Romainmôtier★

Alt. 676m/2 163ft. 44km/27.5mi N on the Pontarlier road. 323 Romainmôtier. ✆*(0)24 453 14 79.*

www.romainmotier.ch.

It is impossible to miss the charm of this old village encircling a plain but graceful Romanesque church. The church belongs to the abbey founded in the 5C by St Romanus and handed over to the monks of Cluny in the 10C.

The **abbey church** (◯ *open daily 8am–6pm,* ☞ *free* ✆*(0)24 453 14 65)* was built with Jura stone in the 11C and later modified, inspired by the church St-Pierre-le-Vieux. The transept and nave date from the 11C. A large, early-12C narthex is preceded by a 13C Gothic porch. Inside are 13C murals; pointed arches (13C) have replaced the original timbering; aisles have semicircular vaulting.

The chancel contains priors' tombs of the 7C. The church has been Protestant since 1536. To the right of the façade, stands the former prior's house (now a tea room) dated 1605—but going back to the 13C—with a pepper-pot roofed turret and an embossed doorway.

Château de la Sarraz

▶ *27km/16.9mi N via road number 9. Guided visits available Jun–Aug.*

◯*Jun–Aug open every day except Mon 1pm–5pm; Apr–May, Sept and Oct, weekends 1pm–5pm.* ☞*9 CHF.*

✆*(0)21 866 66 64*

www.chateau-lasarraz.ch.

This château is just outside the village. Built in the 11C and re-built in the 15C and 16C. The château sits in its own grounds as an unusually shaped building, dominated in the centre by two square towers. A guided visit really allows the visitor the chance to appreciate the wealth of fine furniture in its rooms, plus silverware, china items and chandeliers dating from between the 17C and 19C, paintings and precious antiques. In an old chapel close to the château there is an amazing 14C carved cenotaph of François de la Sarra.

Mosaïques d'Urba

▶ *2km/1m N of Orbe on the road to Yverdon.*

Alongside the road, four separate pavilions house **Roman mosaics** dating back to the early 3C (○*open Easter–Oct, 9am–noon, 1.30pm–5pm, Sat–Sun and public holidays 1.30pm–5.30pm; ○closed 1 Nov and Easter; ☞3CHF. ✆(0)24 441 52 66; www.orbe.ch).* Starting from the farm nearby, the themes are: Calendar of Divinities, the loveliest, consisting of polychrome medallions; pastoral scene with chariots, the most evocative; maze with lion and birds; geometric mosaic in black and white.

ADDRESSES

🛏STAY

🛏 **Les Pierrettes** – *In Saint-Sulpice, on the route Cantonale 19. 22 rooms. ✆(0)21 691 25 25.* Conveniently situated at the western entrance to Lausanne. Each room has a private terrace with a table and garden chairs. Relax on the lawn or by the outdoor pool in summer.

🛏🛏 **Les Voyageurs** –*19 rue Grand-St-Jean. ✆(0)21 319 91 11. www.voyageurs.ch. 33 rooms.* This hotel, nestling in the old part of Lausanne, is an ideal starting-point to discover the city on foot.

🛏🛏 **Agora Swiss Night** – *9 avenue du Rond-Point. ✆(0)21 555 59 55. www.fhotels.ch. 82 rooms.* Modern hotel decorated in bold colours: blue, pink and silver. Large rooms. The lobby features a sculpture of white marble.

🛏🛏 **Aulac** – *In Ouchy, 4 place de la Navigation. ✆(0)21 612 15 00. www.aulac.ch. 84 rooms.* Hotel situated just opposite the lake, near the landing stage for excursions to Évian (trip there and back overnight).

🛏🛏 **City** – *5 rue Caroline. ✆(0)21 320 21 41. www.fhotels.ch. 51 rooms.* Located near the Pont Bessière (no restaurant).

🛏🛏 **Pré Fleuri** – *1 r. du Centre, St-Sulpice ✆(0)21 697 40 40. www.hotelprefleuri.ch. 21 rooms.* 🛏. A pleasant hotel with rooms overlooking a garden and swimming pool.

🛏🛏🛏 **Angleterre et Résidence** – *In Ouchy, 11 place du Port. ✆(0)21 613 34 34. www.laresidence.ch. 75 rooms.* Three imposing pavilions exuding great charm, including an 18C hôtel particulier, located just off the lakeshore. Outdoor pool and ornamental garden. Complete the experience with delicious meal at the gourmet restaurant.

🛏🛏🛏 **Best Western Hotel Mirabeau** – *31 Avenue de la gare. ✆(0)21 341 42 43. www.mirabeau.ch. 72 rooms.* An attractive hotel close to the station and the centre of town. The style is art deco, with every comfort offered in its rooms. Half of the rooms have a balcony, a third of them a lake view.

🍴EAT

🍴🍴 **Brasserie Bavaria** – *10 rue du Petit-Chêne. ✆(0)21 323 39 13. www.labavaria.ch. Closed Sun & Mon.* On the boundaries of the old city, an old-fashioned restaurant with a nostalgic décor serves sauerkraut and cold meats made from pork. Remarkable choice of beers.

🍴🍴 **Le Lacustre** – *In Ouchy, on the landing stage, quai Dapples. ✆(0)21 617 42 00. Closed mid-Dec–mid-Feb.* The Brasserie offers nice views of the lake, while the Café Français offers views of the park.

🍴🍴 **Port de Pully** – *rue du Port 7, In the port of Pully, skirting the lake to the E. ✆(0)21 728 78 78. www.pullyport. ch. Open Tue-Sat 11.30am–2pm, 11.30am–2pm,6.30pm-10pm. Closed Sun night & Mon.* Charming establishment facing the marina. Dining choices are brasserie, traditional restaurant or rotisserie.

Café Romand – *2 place St-François. (0)21 312 63 75. www.caferomand.com. Closed Sun and public holidays.* Typical old Lausanne brasserie gathers a local crowd. Specialties such as cheese fondue and *tête de veau* (head of veal).

Mövenpick – *In Ouchy, 4 avenue de Rhodanie. (0)21 612 76 12. La Pêcherie restaurant closed in Jul and Sat lunch.* Pleasant location facing the lake and its marina. **La Pêcherie** is one of several restaurants where meals are served in a pleasant setting. Large choice of dishes. In the restaurant Le Général, where prices are more affordable, the life of General Guisan is illustrated with paintings and panels displayed on the walls.

À la Pomme de Pin – *11 rue Cité-Derrière. (0)21 323 46 56. Closed Sat at lunchtime, Sun, public holidays.* A friendly establishment in a narrow street lying behind the cathedral. Clients can choose between two dining rooms: simple fare in the café or a more elaborate and more expensive meal in the restaurant.

NIGHTLIFE

Lausanne has the best nightlife in the Romandie. Nestling in its superb setting on the shores of the lake, the **Ouchy** district is extremely lively, both during the day and at night. On a fine day, you can enjoy the many pavement cafés and their sunny terraces. Those yearning for an English atmosphere can go to **Sherlock's Pub** in Avenue de Rhodanie, where a disc jockey will liven up the evening. For beer drinkers, the **Bavaria** (rue du Petit-Chêne), one of the oldest cafés in town (1872), offers a selection of 22 different beers.

Finally, for those who appreciate jazz, the **Pianissimo** (rue des Deux-Marchés) with its outstanding pianist is definitely the place to go; live concerts of jazz-soul and occasionally rock are held at the **V.O.** (Place du Tunnel). The old vaults of a 14C cellar are the hallmark of the unusual **Disco Zille** (Rue Cite-Devant 10).

Ouchy district at night

© Regis Colombo/Switzerland Tourism

SHOPPING

Most main shopping streets are located in the old district and include: place St-François, rue des Terreaux, rue de l'Ale, rue Mauborget, rue Chaucrau, rue St-Laurent, rue de Bourg, rue St-Jean and rue St-François. **Department store:** Innovation (rue Centrale).

THEATRE AND MUSIC

Théâtre Arsenic – *57 rue de Genève. (0)21 625 11 36. www.theatre-arsenic.ch.* Centre of Contemporary Drama.

Théâtre Vidy-Lausanne – *5 avenue E.-Jacques-Dalcroze. (0)21 619 45 45. www.vidy.ch.* Stage performances.

L'Octogone – *41 avenue de Lavaux-Pully. (0)21 721 36 20. www.theatre-octogon.ch.* Theatre, concerts, dance.

Le Petit Théâtre – *12 place de la Cathédrale. (0)21 323 62 13. www.lepetittheatre.ch.* Theatre, plays for children.

Vevey★

Vevey occupies a beautiful site★★ facing the Savoy Alps at the mouth of the Veveyse Valley and the foot of Mount Pèlerin, with the blue sheet of Lake Geneva and the Alps making a splendid backdrop.

A BIT OF HISTORY

Already capital of the Lavaux vineyards, in the 19C Vevey became the cradle of the Swiss industry of milk and dietetic products, and also chocolate. The powerful Nestlé group has its headquarters here, together with its central laboratory and an experimental factory. Picturesque traditional markets (*Saturday mornings*) are held on place du Marché in July and August.

> ▶ **Population:** Vaud 17 676.
> ⏱ **Michelin Map:** National 728: E6.
> 🅸 **Info:** rue de Théatre ✆ (0) 848 86 84 84. www.montreux-vevey.com.
> ▶ **Location:** Between Lausanne and Montreux. Alt. 400m/1 312ft.
> ✎ **Don't Miss:** The Alimentarium at Nestlé's former headquarters.
> 🕐 **Timing:** Allow two days for museums and a lake excursion.
> 👥 **Kids:** The antique carousel along the lake front.

Nestlé

This world food-processing giant was founded by **Heinrich Nestlé**, who was born in Frankfurt am Main in 1814 and settled in Vevey in 1843, having first worked as a pharmacist. He had inherited a small business that manufactured fertiliser and mustard, and later developed an interest in baby food. Nestlé's baby cereal, introduced in 1867 and made from milk, wheat flour and sugar, became a great success. In the previous year, the Americans George and Charles Page had turned Cham into the leading European manufacturer of condensed milk. In 1905, Nestlé and Cham merged under the name of Nestlé and Anglo-Swiss Condensed Milk Company. Other companies were later purchased by the group turning Nestlé into one of the world's leading companies.

A Distinguished Resident

Charles Spencer Chaplin was born in London in 1889 to a family of impoverished music-hall artistes. Charles and brother Sydney began performing at an early age in pantomime shows, which enabled them to travel abroad. During a tour of the United States in 1913,

Vevey

© Stephan Engler/Switzerland Tourism

young Charles made the acquaintance of Mack Sennett, who directed and produced burlesque movies in Hollywood. Sennett immediately offered the young man a job, which led to the birth of the **The Little Tramp** character and his legendary silhouette. With his moustache, derby hat, baggy trousers falling onto out-sized shoes, tight frock coat and cane, distinctive shuffling gait and pale features, Chaplin became highly popular and gained international acclaim.

During the 1920s, his tumultuous private life was strongly criticised by the American press; after his second divorce, authorities requested that he be expelled from the country. In 1952, during McCarthy's anti-Communist campaigns, Chaplin left America with his family and settled in Corsier-sur-Vevey. In 1975, he was knighted by Queen Elizabeth II, and on 25 December 1977, he passed away in his Swiss home.

A statue of Chaplin has been erected by the city of Vevey on the shores of Lake Geneva, in front of the Alimentarium; his former home is to become the Chaplin Museum in 2012.

SIGHTS
Église St-Martin
The present church (1530) stands on a site originally occupied by an 11C sanctuary whose walls were discovered during excavation work.

The church is dominated by a large, square tower and four corner turrets. The terrace (viewing table) affords a sweeping **view**★ of the town, the Alps and Lake Geneva.

Musée Jenisch
Closed until summer 2012. Check website for opening dates. ♿ ℘(0)21 925 35 20. www.museejenisch.ch.
Inside this 19C neoclassical building are two museums. The ground floor houses the **Cantonal Prints Gallery**, presenting engravings by great masters of the past (Dürer, Rembrandt, Lorrain, Belletto, Corot) and by modern Swiss artists, which are shown in rotation. The **Fine Arts Museum** on the first floor displays temporary exhibitions of works by Swiss and foreign artists from the 19C and 20C.

Musée Historique du Vieux-Vevey
🕐Open Apr–Oct, Tue–Sun 11am–5pm; Nov–Mar 2pm–5pm only. Open Mon during public holidays. 🕐Closed 1 Jan and 25 Dec. 🎫 Free. ℘(0)21 921 07 22. www.museehistoriquevevey.ch.
This museum is housed in the castle which was once the residence of the Bernese bailiffs. It relates the history of the area and contains a fine collection of furniture from the Gothic period to the 17C, small wrought-iron objects and caskets, costumes and local mementoes. On the first floor, visit the **Museum of the Wine-Growers Fraternity** (Confrérie des Vignerons), where models of the costumes worn at wine-growers' festivals (since 1791) are kept, together with prints, records and banners used during these festivities.

Musée Suisse de l'Appareil Photographique★
99 Grande-Place. 🕐Open Tue–Sun, 11am–5.30pm. 🕐Closed 25 Dec. 🎫8CHF. ♿ ℘(0)21 925 34 80. www.cameramuseum.ch.
The five floors of this **Swiss Camera Museum** present the history of photography, its famous inventors, and its techniques through a remarkable collection of cameras dating from early models to the most recent and sophisticated devices including digital imaging. One floor is devoted to photographic equipment made in Switzerland.

The camera obscura in the entrance hall provides an insight into the birth of photography. Magic lanterns illustrate the theory of projection; the importance of photography in the army is explained via spy cameras that can be hidden in everyday objects. Another section includes the first small cameras, first flashes, early Swiss cameras (Alpa, Escopette de Darier), famous names such as Kodak and Leica (1930–40), multi-image cameras, miniature cameras, image transmission and projection, and tracing the development of photography

Alimentarium

© Andy Mettler/Switzerland Tourism

and film industries. 👥 The "**clic-clac**" studio introduces children to the art of photography.

Alimentarium★★

Quai Perdonnet. ⏱*Open Tue–Fri 10am–5pm; Sat, Sun until 6pm.* ⏱*Closed Mon exc Easter Mon and Pentecost, 1 Jan, 24, 25 and 31 Dec.* ✎*12CHF, children 8CHF.* ✆*(0)21 924 41 11. www.alimentarium.ch.*

Since 1985 this neoclassical mansion, formerly headquarters of Nestlé, has housed a food museum. Exhibits are arranged by themes. *Cuisiner* (Cooking) illustrates cooking methods found around the world at different periods in history and in various ethnic and social environments, as well as various utensils. *Manger* (Eating) illustrates the importance of pleasure and communication in eating, as does the art of laying a table. This section highlights plants and animals eaten by humans, celebratory and everyday meals, and how the act of eating differs by culture. The New York push-cart and snack trolley men can be considered to be the precursors of the fast-food industry, also explored here. *Acheter* (Buying) resembles a supermarket and explores agricultural and production methods, food safety, and our eating habits. *Digérer* (Digestion) is portrayed through biology, including the importance of sports. The Nestlé Room traces the history and importance of the now-global company, including advertisements and packaging dating back to 1867. There is also, of course, chocolate! There are cooking classes for adults and children (*in French only*) and a garden planted with herbs and vegetables, interspersed with picnic areas.

EXCURSIONS

Mont-Pèlerin Resort★★

Alt. 810m/2 657ft. ▶ *Round trip of 25km/15.5mi about 30min.*

⛅*Consult the local maps under LAKE GENEVA. Leave Vevey by the Châtel-St-Denis-Fribourg road 2.5km/1.5mi after having passed the road to Chardonne on your left, turn left toward Attalens, then sharp left again toward the Pèlerin or Pilgrim Mountain.*

Several of these roads run corniche fashion among the vines. From a point near the arrival station of the funicular, there is a fabulous wide open **view**★★ of Lake Geneva and the crest of the Vaud Alps (Dent de Jaman, Rochers de Naye, Aï Tower). The drive back through Chardonne and Chexbres is along roads with magnificent views of the Dents du Midi and the summits of the Haut-Chablais in Savoy.

La Tour-de-Peilz

▶ *2km/1.2mi by road number 9 heading towards Montreux.*

The castle was commissioned by the Comtes de Savoie (13C, altered in the

18C). The ramparts, moats, and two corner turrets still stand. Inside the former keep is the **Musée Suisse du Jeu** (🕙open Tue–Sun 11am–5.30pm and Mon during public holidays; 🕙closed 1 Jan and 25 Dec; 🎫9CHF; ✆(0)21 977 23 00. www.museedujeu.com), a collection of games from all countries and all epochs.

These are split into five groups: educational games, strategic games, simulation games, games of skill, and games of chance. Each section stresses the qualities required for playing and is illustrated by a series of examples. Visitors may test their own natural ability by playing, learning, and even creating new games.

If you bypass the castle on the left, you will come to the yachting harbour; from there you can take a pleasant walk along the shores of the lake. Opposite stands the Grammont, dominating the landscape from a height of 2 172m/6 800ft.

Oron-Le-Châtel

Alt. 720m/2 362ft. 25km/15.6mi.
▶ *Take the motorway from Vevey (direction Lausanne) and exit at J15 following Bern and then Oron.*

This little medieval village is dominated by the imposing mass of its fortified castle (👁🔍guided tours Apr–Sept, Sat, Sun 2pm, 3pm, 4pm(also 5pm on Sun); 🎫9CHF; children 5CHF; ✆(0)21 907 90 51, ✆(0)21 907 88 14; oron-le-chatel.ch; www.swisscastles.ch/vaud/oron). This forbidding citade on a rocky promontory was built in the late 12C and early 13C. An impressive display of various families' coats of arms is in the main hall. For 241 years the castle was the official residence of the Bernese bailiffs. The rooms on the first floor give a good idea of French middle-class life The dining hall houses some superb collections of Sèvres and Limoges porcelain, as well as pieces of Wedgwood. The library is believed to contain around 18 000 books dating from the 16C to the 19C. The visit ends with a series of tastefully decorated rooms: music room, smoking salon decorated with wallpaper printed with hunting scenes, playroom and study for the children, tea parlor (Louis XV commode in rosewood), prior's bedroom, etc.

ADDRESSES

🛏STAY

⊜⊜ **Hôtel des Négociants** – *27 r. du Conseil.* ✆(0)21 922 70 11. www.hotelnegociants.ch. 23 rooms. ⬜. A hotel located in the pedestrian zone, conveniently located near to the lake, the station and the town's cinemas. Airy plain rooms decorated with jolly colours.

⊜⊜ **Hostellerie de Genève** – *11 Pl. du Marché* ✆(0)21 921 45 77. www.hotelgeneve.ch. 23 rooms. ⬜. A small but well located hotel on the liveliest of the squares in Vevey, next to the markets. Comfortable rooms with a shaded terrace; ideal for the summer months

⊜⊜⊜⊜ **Hôtel du Lac** – *1 rue d'Italie.* ✆(0)21 921 06 06. www.hoteldulac-vevey.ch. 50 rooms. A stone's throw from the harbour and the lake, this venerable hotel features comfortable rooms and a lovely terrace with a private pool.

🍽EAT

⊜⊜ **La Terrasse** – *Corseaux, 8 chemin du Basset.* ✆(0)21 921 31 88. Closed Mon and 23 Dec–22 Jan. Good food and reasonable prices, whether you choose the set menu or go à la carte. In summer, meals are served on the terrace.

⊜⊜⊜ **Hostellerie chez Chibrac** – *Mont-Pèlerin.* ✆(0)21 922 61 61. www.chezchibrac.ch. Closed Sun eve, Mon and mid-Oct–1 Mar. A simple establishment with a congenial atmosphere.

⊜⊜⊜⊜ **Á la Montagne** – *Chardonne, 21 rue du Village* ✆(0)21 921 29 30. Closed Mon, Sun, 23 Dec–7 Jan and 30 Jun–15 Jul. A small, unassuming family inn offering tasty dishes, and affordable prices.

⊜⊜⊜⊜ **Restaurant Denis Martin "Le Château"** – *2 Rue du Château.* ✆(0)21 921 12 10. Open eve only. Closed Sun, Mon and 23 Dec–15 Jan. Located in a baronial villa with creative cuisine to match. Fixed price menus include one with 15 mini courses.

Montreux★★

Thanks to its beautiful **site**★★ and pleasant surroundings—which have won literary fame since **Jean-Jacques Rousseau** chose the village of Clarens, now a suburb, as the setting for *La Nouvelle Héloïse*—Montreux is the most frequented resort on Lake Geneva and has acquired an international reputation. It stretches along the shores of a large bay facing south and rises in tiers to heights covered with woods and vineyards which shelter it from winds. Its sumptuous palaces and Edwardian hotels are reminiscent of the French Riviera. It is an important cultural city, hosting many festivals and major world events such as the International Choral Festival (the week following Easter), the Golden Rose Television Festival (spring), a jazz festival (July) and the September Musical Concert (&see Calendar of Events).

▶ **Population:** Vaud 24 520.
  Michelin Map: National Map 729: E6.
  Info: 5 rue du Théâtre. (0)848 86 84 84. www.montreux-vevey.com.
  Location: Montreux is on the eastern edge of Lake Geneva. Alt. 398m/1 305ft.
  Don't Miss: The panorama from Les Pléiades on the Avants-Sonloup driving tour.
  Timing: Allow two or three days for the city and nearby excursions; longer if you are attending the world-famous Montreux Jazz Festival (July).
  Kids: The Museum of Food at former Nestlé headquaraters in nearby Vevey, easily reached by public transport.

SIGHTS

Many local trains leave Montreux station for the nearby summits, offering panoramic views of Geneva, the Mont Blanc, the Matterhorn: the two most famous are the Montreux-Oberland Bernois (MOB) and the Montreux Crystal Panoramic Express (&reservations necessary).

Steamboat cruises are available for tours of the Upper Lake.

Walk up through old Montreux to the terrace of the church for a lovely **view**★★ of Clarens-Montreux-Territet and the lake with the Château de Chillon, the mountains of the Savoy Chablais and the sparkling Dents du Midi.

Montreux

© Adam Glinski/Montreux-Vevey Tourisme

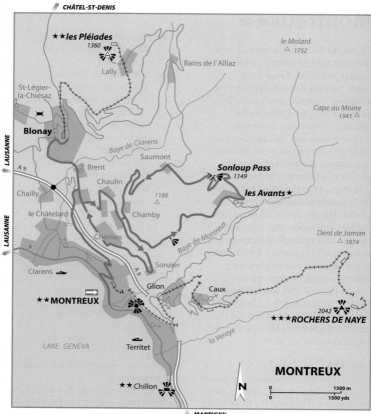

CHÂTEL-ST-DENIS

★★les Pléiades
1360

le Molard
△ 1752

Bains de l`Alliaz

Lally

St-Légier-
la-Chiésaz

Cape au Moine
1941 △

Blonay

Baye de Clarens

Saumont

Brent

Sonloup Pass
1149

les Avants ★

LAUSANNE

A 9

Chaulin

1188
△

Chailly

le Châtelard

Chamby

Dent de Jaman
△ 1874

LAUSANNE

9

Chernex

Baye de Montreux

Clarens

Sonzier

A 9

Glion

Caux

★★MONTREUX

2042
★★★ROCHERS DE NAYE

LAKE GENEVA

Territet

la Veraye

★★ Chillon

MONTREUX

N

0   1500 m
0   1500 yds

MARTIGNY

The Vaud Riviera

The mild climate (average annual temperature 10°C/50°F) and lake shore earns it the name of Vaud Riviera. This exceptional climate produces varied and luxuriant vegetation: vines grow at an altitude of nearly 600m/1 968.5ft, walnut trees up to 700m/2 296.5ft and fruit trees up to 1 000m/3 281ft.

Fig, bay, almond and mulberry trees and even cypresses, magnolias and palm trees flourish on the lake shores at truly Mediterranean temperatures. In spring, the fields overlooking the town are covered with narcissi.

Musée Montreux

40 rue de la Gare. ⏰*Open Apr– first week of Nov, daily 10am–noon, 2pm–5pm.* 🎫*6CHF.* ✆*(0)21 963 13 53.*
In the heart of the old quarter, the museum presents a lively account of the region's eventful history. Prehistoric times, Roman era, Middle Ages, reconstruction of interiors from different centuries, the expansion of tourism, technology, coins, architecture and town planning are some of the themes presented on three levels, explaining the development of the city of Montreux throughout the ages.

EXCURSIONS

Rochers de Naye★★★

2 042m/6 699ft. About 3hr there and back, including 2hr by rack railway. In summer, an old-fashioned steam train departs every hour, except at noon, from 9.05am–5.05pm. In winter, last departure at 3.05pm. 🎫*Fare there and back 59CHF. Other tourist train— Montreux, Bernese Oberland—MOB: 12 panoramic-express trains per day in summer, Sat–Sun all year round.*

View from Rochers de Naye

© Stephan Engler/Switzerland Tourism

From the summit of Rochers de Naye you will enjoy a bird's-eye view east of Lake Geneva and a splendid panorama of the Bernese, Valais and Savoy Alps and the Jura.

🚗 DRIVING TOUR

AVANTS-SONLOUP TOUR★★

27km/16mi. Allow approx 1hr.

See map p138.

▷ *Leave Montreux by the route signed "Les Avants".*

On the left, the **Château du Châtelard**, with its large rectangular 15C crenellated tower stands out.

▷ *4km/2.5mi from Montreux turn left towards Chernex-Les-Avants, then left 200m/220yd farther on before Chamby (two bends) and cross the railway line, and another right turn for Les Avants.*

Blonay

4km/2.5mi E. 29 Grande-Place, Vevey – 1800. ℘(0)21 922 20 20.

The **Chemin de Fer-Musée Blonay-Chamby** (*Musée Blonay-Chamby;* 🕐 *operates May–Oct, Sat–Sun 10am–6pm; Jul–Aug, Thu and Fri 2pm–6pm;* 🎫*14CHF;* ♿ *℘(0)21) 943 21 21*) has given new life to a railway section which opened in 1902 and closed down in 1966. Electric trams and early steam-driven trains take travellers along a steep, winding route covering a distance of 2.95km/1.8mi. Halfway up the hill stands the former shed. It has been converted into a museum displaying early vehicles, including a 1914 postal van, a 1904 tram from the Fribourg area, and a steam engine which once linked Le Locle to Les Brenets.

Les Pléiades★★

From Lally 30min on foot there and back.

From the Les Pléiades summit (alt. 1 360m/4 462ft) there is a **panorama**★★ of Lake Geneva, the Molard, the Dent de Jaman, the Rochers de Naye, the Savoy Alps, and the Mont Blanc Range.

Return by the Blonay road which and reveals, to the right, **Château de Blonay**, dating back to the 11C.

Les Avants★

Alt. 968m/3 176ft.

This is a small resort overlooked on the southeast by the Dent de Jaman and the Naye Rocks.

Col de Sonloup

Alt. 1 149m/3 769.5ft.

A fine **view**★ of the Rochers de Naye, the Dents du Midi and the Savoy Alps.

▷ *The return to Montreux is via the villages of Saumont, Chamby and Chernex. Narrow at first, this road reveals new glimpses of the lake and of the Vevey-Blonay region.*

ADDRESSES

🛏 STAY

🍽🍷🛏 **Auberge des Planches** – *2 rue du Temple. ☎(0)21 963 49 73. 36 rooms. Closed Jan.* Located on a steep street on the outskirts of town. Rooms tend to be large and decorated in rustic style. The Don Chico Restaurant has Mexican-style décor and serves typical Mexican dishes.

🍷🛏 **Hôtel du Pont** – *12 rue du Pont. ☎(0)21 963 22 49. 10 rooms.* Congenial establishment in the old district, at the foot of the funicular. Restaurant offers traditional cuisine, and Italian specialties.

🍷🛏 **Eden Palace au Lac** – *11 rue du Théâtre. ☎(0)21 966 08 00. www.eden montreux.ch. 100 rooms. Closed Jan.* Who hasn't dreamed of spending the night in a sumptuous, turn-of-the-century palace? The rates may seem outrageously high but they are definitely worth it. The Victorian architecture, period furniture, lofty rooms, gastronomic cuisine, and romantic atmosphere will transport you back in time, while offering all the advantages of modern sophistication!

🍷🛏 **Eurotel Riviera** – *81 Grand-Rue. ☎(0)21 966 22 22. 152 rooms.* Centrally located hotel with a pontoon for mooring boats and the choice between two restaurants: the Bel-Horizon and the Matara.

🍷🛏 **Golf-Hôtel René Capt** – *35 rue de Bon-Port. ☎(0)21 966 25 25. www.golf-hotel-montreux.ch. Closed 22 Dec–mid-Jan. 75 rooms.* Away from the bustling town centre, this hotel has a pretty garden overlooking the lake shores.

🍷🛏 **Masson** – *In Veytaux, 5 rue Bonivard. ☎(0)21 966 00 44. www.hotel masson.ch. Closed 18 Oct–25 Mar. 31 rooms.* The oldest hotel in Montreux (1829) has undeniable charm, evoking the splendor of bygone times. The small garden is perfect for long, relaxing afternoons in the shade.

🍴 EAT

🍷🛏 **Restaurant du Montagnard** – *In Villard-sur-Chamby, 7km/4.3mi N. ☎(0)21 964 36 84. Closed Mon, Tue.*

A genuine 17C mountain farmhouse serving traditional fare. Lively evenings with folk music.

🍷🍷🛏 **Auberge de la Cergniaulaz** – *In Les Avants, 8km/5mi N by the Col de Sonloup and the road to Orgevaux. ☎(0)21 964 42 76. Closed Mon, Tue, and Jan–Mar.* Traditional Swiss specialties served on a lovely terrace.

🍷🛏 **Caveau des Vignerons** – *30 bis rue Industrielle. Open daily to midnight. ☎(0)21 963 25 70. www.caveau desvignerons.ch.* Décor focuses on grapes and the art of oenology (display of tools used during grape harvesting). The restaurant serves fondue, raclette, and meat on hot slates, and local wines.

🍷🛏 **Le Museum** – *40 rue de la Gare. ☎(0)21 963 16 62. www.museum-montreux.ch. Closed Sun and Mon.* This former convent house dating back to the 13C features three fine dining halls with vaulted ceilings. Fondue, raclette, and grilled meat are served in a rustic décor with an open fireplace.

🌙 NIGHTLIFE

The Grand-Rue has live music: the **Sunset Bar and Piano Bar,** located in the Hôtel Royal Plaza (97) and **Harry's New York Bar** (Raffles Le Montreux Palace Hotel, 100) offers hundreds of cocktail varieties.

At night, a lively, bustling crowd can be found in rue du Théâtre, where the **Casino de Montreux** complex (9 rue du Théâtre) caters for all tastes. **Le Piano Bar** (*in the hotel Mirador Kempinski, Mont-Pelerin*) is a stylish bar with fireplace, breathtaking view of Lake Geneva, and more than 70 varieties of champagne.

🛍 SHOPPING

Many shops and boutiques are on avenue des Alpes, Grande-Rue, avenue du Casino, and rue de la Paix. **Department store:** Innovation (*avenue du Casino*).

🎭 THEATRE AND MUSIC

Théâtre Montreux-Riviera – *32 Rue du Pont. ☎(0)21 961 11 31. www.theatre-montreux-riviera.ch.* **Auditorium Stravinski** – *95 Grand-Rue. ☎(0)21 962 21 19.*

The Alps★★

The Vaud Alps owe their strong individuality to their landscape of wide green valleys and limestone escarpments, forming majestic snowy summits. Their mountain people speak French, are Protestant, and build houses like those of the Bernese Oberland. A striking feature of the local landscape is the extraordinary scattering of these chalets over the slopes above the Grande Eau and the Sarine.

GEOGRAPHY

The Ormonts and Enhaut district valleys around Lake Geneva and the Bernese Oberland are dotted with holiday resorts such as Château-d'Oex or Les Diablerets. Higher up, on terraced sites 1 000m/3 280ft above the Rhône Valley and facing the Dents du Midi, Leysin and Villars-Chesières draw the world of sport and fashion. This is ideal walking country with well signposted trails and beautiful panoramas with high peaks, green valleys and mountain lakes.

🚗 DRIVING TOURS

① VALLÉE DES ORMONTS★★

From Aigle to Saanen 45km/28mi. Allow approx 1hr30min. ⊗The Col du Pillon is usually blocked by snow from November to April.

Aigle

Alt. 417m/1 369ft. 5 Rue Colomb, 1860. ℘(0)24 466 30 00. www.aigle.ch.
A wine and industrial centre, Aigle is a small, pleasant town surrounded by famous vineyards. Stroll along the shaded Gustave-Doré Avenue (beside the torrent of the Grande Eau) and into the town centre by the unusual Jerusalem Alley (Ruelle de Jérusalem), with its covered wooden galleries decked with flowers.

Castle

⊙Open Apr–31 Oct, Tue–Sun 11am–6pm and Mon public holidays. ⊙Closed Nov–

Michelin Map: 729 F6-F7.
Info: Les Diablerets rue de la Gare. ℘(0)24 492 00 10. www.diablerets.ch.
Leysin Place Large ℘(0)24 493 33 00. www.leysin.ch.
Gstaad Haus des Gastes ℘(0)33 748 81 81. www.gstaad.ch.
Location: The Vaud Alps are divided between the Rhône and Aare basins (Upper Sarine Valley).
Don't Miss: A cable car ride to Scex Rouge.
Time: Leave at least a full day for tour itineraries and visiting sites.

Mar⊗11CHF, children 5CHF. ℘(0)24 466 21 30. www.chateauaigle.ch.
This 13C feudal fortress originally belonged to the House of Savoy but was captured and rebuilt by the Bernese in the 15C. It now houses the **Musée de la Vigne et du Vin**.

👫Aigle Adventure Park

⊙Open Apr–Oct, Jul–Aug daily 9am–7pm; other months see website. ⊗36CHF; discounts for a family group. ℘(0)24 466 30 30. www.parc-aventure.ch.
Offers over 100 outdoor adventures including five skill levels, welcoming ages 4 and up.

Leysin★

From the touring route, 4km/2.5mi by a road on the left before reaching Le Sépey.
The splendid terraced **site★★** of Leysin, overlooking the Rhône Valley and facing the Dents du Midi, enjoys a mild climate and strong sun: An ideal location for either summer holidays or winter skiing.

Les Diablerets❋

Chief town of the Ormonts Valley. The resort is spread over a widening basin of meadows dotted with ash trees and maples. The **site★★** is both delightful and impressive, with very fine chalets,

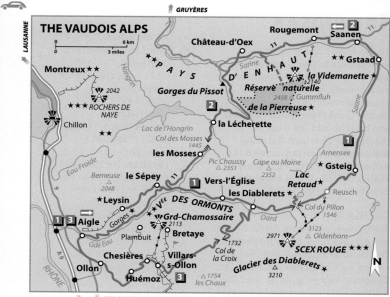

built and decorated in the traditional style of the Bernese Oberland. Here the wall of the Les Diablerets Mountain curves deeply to form a cirque (Creux de Champ) between the Scex Rouge spur and the Culan. Between Les Diablerets and the Pillon Pass, a bend in the ravine crossed by the Bourquin Bridge affords glimpses, between the trees, of white monoliths, formed by the dissolution of gypsum. On the opposite slope the Dard Torrent escapes in thin cascades from two overlapping rock **cirques**★.

The Ski Area

The Diablerets resort is renowned for its snowfields, spread out over three massifs: Le Meilleret (1 949m/6394ft), which can be reached by skiing from **Villars-sur-Ollon**★ (see VILLARS-SUR-OLLON), Isenau (2 120m/6 955ft at Le Floriettaz) and the **Scex Rouge Glacier** (2 979m/9 774ft). In spite of its small size (50km/31mi of slopes) and somewhat impractical equipment, the resort offers several splendid slopes. Intermediate skiers will appreciate the Isenau area, the long forested pistes around Le Meilleret and especially the red trail between Cabane and Oldenegg.

Seasoned skiers can swoop along the **Combe d'Audon**★★, starting from Scex Rouge, which features high-quality snow and breathtaking vistas. Snowboarders will find snowparks laid out along the Isenau in winter and Scex Rouge in summer. The **Forfait Intégral des Alpes Vaudoises** ski pass grants visitors unlimited access to 220km/137mi of slopes and 77 cable cars covering Villars, Leysin and Les Mosses. Cross-country skiers have at their disposal 31km/20mi of pistes at high altitude as well as lower down in the valleys.

Scex Rouge★★★

Access: 35min by cable car from the Pillon Pass (Col du Pillon) or by cable car leaving from Reusch.

During the ascent, marmots and chamois goats take a backseat to the dramatic view of the Les Diablerets Basin and the splendid escarpment immediately before you reach the upper station. From here, a staircase (open only in summer) leads to the Scex Rouge Peak (alt. 2 971m/9 747ft) where there is a magnificent **panorama**★★★: Southward from the Swiss Alps (Matterhorn) and French Alps (Mont Blanc) to the

"*Breitling Orbiter 3 over the Alps following its launch from Château d'Oex 1 March 1999*

© EPA/Photoshot

Round the World in a Hot-Air Balloon

On 28 January 1998, French navigator Olivier de Kersauzon lit the burners of *Breitling Orbiter 2* with the Olympic flame, which had been specially brought from Lausanne for the occasion. At precisely 9.56am, the Swiss hang-gliding specialist Bertrand Piccard (whose grandfather Auguste Piccard invented the bathyscaph), Belgian Wim Verstraeten and Andy Elson from Great Britain slowly rose into the air in a pear-shaped Rozier balloon made of aluminium and filled with helium. This non-stop flight around the world, which seemed to spring from the pages of a Jules Verne novel, would last three weeks and follow a specific flight path—Italy, Greece, Cyprus, Israel, Saudi Arabia, India, China, the Pacific Ocean, California, Florida, Bermuda Islands, Canary Islands and North Africa—achieving an unprecedented feat in the history of aviation.

The mission suffered a serious setback when Chinese authorities denied them access for national security, despite strong diplomatic pressure from the International Olympic Committee, and the *Breitling Orbiter 2* team was forced to abandon the operation. Then, China changed its mind and gave permission for the balloon to fly over the country, but it was too late. The delays incurred by China's indecision slowed the flight so the balloon could no longer reach the jet stream, a narrow belt of high-altitude, fast-moving winds which would have propelled *Breitling Orbiter 2* over the Pacific Ocean at around 200kph/124.3mph. The team nonetheless continued their flight and eventually landed in Burma after 9 days, 17 hours and 51 minutes, having covered a distance of 8 473km/5 265mi. Although they failed to complete their full orbit, the team did succeed in establishing a new world record for living in a hot-air balloon.

A little over a year later on 21 March 1999, Swiss balloonist Bertrand Piccard and British pilot Brian Jones finally achieved their world record round-the-world flight in *Breitling Orbiter 3*. Sponsored by the renowned Swiss watchmaker, they took off from the Swiss resort of Château d'Oex at 8.05am on 1 March and eventually landed in the Eygyptian dessert 19 days, 21 hours and 55 minutes later. The distance they travelled was 40 814km/25 361mi (the circumference of the Earth is 40 075km/24 901mi at the equator) climbing to altitudes of 11 735m/38 500ft, a world record for this type of balloon. Amongst the first people to congratulate Picard and Jones were rival balloonist and entrepreneur Richard Branson who had made earlier unsuccessful attempts with Per Lindstrand and the late Steve Fossett.

nearby peaks of Les Diablerets and the superb **Les Diablerets Glacier**★★ (an extension to the north of the Tsafleuron Glacier). Northward the view extends to the Tornette and Palette peaks, which rise behind the Ormonts Valley.

Lac Retaud★

1.5km/1mi by a narrow mountain road from the Pillon Pass (Col du Pillon).
This pretty sheet of green water fills a hollow opposite the double cirque of the Dard, dominated on the left by the Oldenhorn and on the right by the Scex Rouge. A third cirque lies between the spurs of the Oldenhorn (in the Oldenbach Valley) from Col du Pillon to Gsteig, ending in sight of the solidly buttressed Spitzhorn pyramid.

Gsteig★

The rocky hanging valley farther upstream between the escarpments of the Spitzhorn and the Mittaghorn, and from which a powerful cascade flows, leads to the Sanetsch Pass, which used to be a well-traveled link between the Oberland and the Valais.

Gstaad✳✳

Alt. 1 080m/3 543ft. Haus des Gastes. ℰ(0)33 748 81 81. www.gstaad.ch.
Gstaad lies on the boundary between the Bernese and Vaud Alps at the junction of four gently sloping valleys: The Upper Sarine Valley, the Lauenen Valley, the Turbach Valley and the Saanenmöser Depression.
The resort at Gstaad, with its carefully restored old chalets and many luxury boutiques, is pleasing for its restful setting and the variety of its sporting and social facilities. Popular with celebrities in winter, Gstaad offers a number of pleasant walks in summer: explore the **Eggli** (alt. 1 557m/5 108ft) and the nearby plateau, accessible by cable car. Helicopter rides of the area are available from Gstaad-Grund heliport.

The Skiing Area

Thanks to the blue trains of the local railways, the resort shares with Saanenmöser (alt. 1 272m/4 173ft—facilities) and even with Zweisimmen (equipped with a large cable car for ascents to the Rinderberg) a magnificent ski area served by about 60 ski lifts. There are more than 85km/53mi of groomed local runs and more than 250km/155mi in the region, which encompasses six ski resorts with inteconnected lifts. The Eggli (alt. 1 671m/5 483ft) has good, long intermediate runs and connects with nearby Rougemont. Wassergrat (alt. 1 942m/6 372ft) is for intermediates and experts, offering both open snowfields and piste routes through the trees. Cross-country skiers can enjoy 100km/62mi of classic tracks and 40km/25mi of skating tracks.

Saanen

The road from Lausanne to Interlaken (via Bulle or the Mosses col) leaves the Sarine Valley (Saane in German) en route to the Saanenmöser by the Simme valley. Saanen is a charming and peaceful place in contrast to its neighbour Gstaad. Even in winter the area preserves its individual style, and has an extensive network of chair lifts - Kalberhöni-Vorder Eggli.
The sun kissed wooden chalets of the area often have large overhanging traditional roofs bedecked with hanging baskets. Some of the chalets date from the sixteenth century (note the dates) Visitors can see the fine bell tower from afar. Inside the church, the chancel is decorated with wall paintings dating from the fifteenth century. The paintings portray biblical scenes, events during the life of the Virgin Mary and the martyr St Maurice, the patron of the sanctuary. Information is provided by the pulpit.

② PAYS D'ENHAUT★★

From Saanen to Aigle. 45km/28mi – allow 1hr (excluding visits).

Lying between Saanen and Château-d'Oex, the short **Défilé des Allamans** marks the boundary between the cantons of Bern and Vaud as well as the switch from French to German. The slim, rocky point aptly named Rubli (carrot), continually catches the eye.

Pays d'Enhaut

© Marcus Gyger/Switzerland Tourism

Rougemont

This charming village was the site of a Cluniac priory between the 11C and the Reformation. The church is typical of early Swiss Romanesque structures. Note the crane mascot in the stained-glass windows.

La Videmanette★

Alt. 2 140m/7 021ft. Access by cable car in 18min leaving from Rougemont. The upper station is on top of the Videmanette Mountain, situated between the Rubli and Rocher Plat summits. From the restaurant's roof terrace, the **vista**★ encompasses (*right to left*): The three summits of La Tornette, Les Diablerets, Lake Arnensee, and Lake Retaud; behind, the Gummfluh, the Oldenhorn Range, the Jungfrau Mountain range in the distance; to the far left, the Eiger.

Réserve de la Pierreuse★

On foot: allow half a day.
At Les Granges bear left (*hairpin bend*) onto the downhill road from Gérignoz, which goes through a tunnel and crosses a bridge over the Sarine. Before a large sawmill bear right and take the road up the opposite side of the valley.

Leave the car before the Les Leyssalets Bridge and proceed on foot.

This nature reserve, at the foot of the rocky north face of the Gummfluh, lies at an altitude of between 1 300m/4 264ft and 2 460m/8 068ft, a hilly **site**★ covering approximately 880ha/2 174 acres. The flora and fauna (spruce trees, ibexes, marmots) are protected. The twin Gummfluh peaks can be glimpsed through a gap formed by the tributary valley of Gérignoz.

Château-D'Oex

Alt. 1 000m/3 281ft.
Low season: open Mon–Fri, 8am–noon and 2pm–6pm; Sat 9.30am–3.30pm. High season (from Christmas) Mon–Fri, 8am–6pm; Sat and Sun 9am–5pm. (0)26 924 25 25. www.chateau-doex.ch.
Château-d'Oex (pronounced Château Day) is a little pre-Alpine mountain centre which has long lived apart, spreading its chalets and hotels at the foot of the last wooded slopes of the Gummfluh and the Vanils. This is a typical Vaud Alps family resort, highly popular because of the many water sports facilities it offers.

The Balloon Festival

Château d'Oex is the self-styled "world capital of ballooning" and it organises an international hot-air ballooning event each year in late January. More than 80 balloons from 20 different countries take part over ten days. Look out for the special event for unconventionally shaped balloons (bagpipes, roosters, tortoises etc). The venue is at the junction of the Saanen road and the one to Col des Mosses. Staying elsewhere in the valley will help you to avoid paying higher accommodation costs. An entry fee of 10CHF is payable if you wish to enter the venue. *www.festivaldeballons.ch.*

Musée d'Art Populaire du Vieux Pays d'Enhaut★

Open Tue–Sun, 2pm–5pm. Closed Nov, 1 Jan, Easter and 25 Dec. 8CHF children 4 CHF. (0)26 924 65 20. www.musee-chateau-doex.ch.
Located in a three-storey building, the museum illustrates the region's rich historical past (12C–19C). Exhibits include parchment, engravings, drawings, photographs, popular or religious works of art, weapons, beautifully carved tools, old-fashioned utensils and other objects, painted or inlaid furniture, and reconstructed interiors: blacksmith's forge, peasant's kitchen, bourgeois kitchen, and bedrooms belonging to a herdsman and a weaver.

Stained glass, a fine collection of 19C paper cuttings, and black bobbin pillow lace are also worth noting. Reconstituted in two separate pavilions are a chalet which housed herders up in the mountain pastures: note the cheese room with its gigantic copper cauldron (800l/211gal), and the carpenter's workshop. Also part of the museum, but located at the end of the town, is the **Étambeau Chalet**, which houses artifacts of regional architecture. Visitors are also shown the cheese cellar and the barn, which houses an exhibition on Alpine transport.

Winter sports in Château d'Oex

Downhill and cross-country skiing and winter hiking are also available in Château d'Oex (*open mid-Dec–3 Jan/ 31 Jan–28 Feb 9am–1.30pm and 3.30pm-6pm; low season: 9am-10.30 and 3.30-6pm; (0)26 924 68 48; www.ess-chax.ch).*

Gorges du Pissot

A **viewpoint**★ on a curve allows you to appreciate the steepness of this rocky cleft, through which the Torneresse flows. After passing through the Pissot Gorges, the road curves to the Etivaz Valley, you will then come to the extensive lowland of Mosses with its woods and fields.

At La Lécherette you reach the upper valley of the Hongrin. On the Ormonts slope the view extends along the Comballaz to Les Diablerets; on the left, the Scex Rouge and the Oldenhorn.

Looking down the Grande Eau Valley, you can pick out the spa and large hotels of Leysin and, on the horizon, the Dents du Midi.

Between Le Sépey and Aigle the road runs along a ledge above the wooded **Grande Eau Gorges**★, and after a few hairpin bends, goes down to the floor of the Rhône Valley. The town of Aigle, dominated by its castle, nestles in a vineyard setting.

3 CROIX PASS ROAD★★

From Aigle to Les Diablerets via Villars. 29km/18mi. Allow 1hr. The Croix Pass is only open in summer.

Aigle – See p142.

Ollon

This is a charming wine-growers' village. The road climbs, tortuous but excellent, along a *corniche*. 3km/1.8mi after Ollon a superb **view**★★ opens onto the Grand Muveran and Les Diablerets, the Pas de Cheville Valley between.

Villars-Sur-Ollon✳, Chesières and Arveyes

Alt. 1 253m/4 111ft. Rue Centrale,
℘(0)24 495 32 32. www.villars.ch.
Together Villars, Chesières, and Arveyes form a resort perched 800m/2 625ft above the Lower Valais. It is the most highly developed mountain resort in French Switzerland and offers a panorama of the French Alps, the Dents du Midi, and the Muverans Range with Mont Blanc, the Trient Glacier, and the peaks of Les Diablerets in the distance. These resorts are recommended to residents who are looking for peace and quiet rather than fashionable society. The panorama from Chesières includes the Mont-Blanc Massif, between the Trient Glacier and the Aiguille Verte.

Villars

The town lies along an esplanade of parkland in an attractive rural setting dotted with low mountains. Villar's summer facilities include a golf course, swimming pool, 300km/186.4mi of hiking trails, and 150km/93mi of mountain-bike tracks. In winter, the skating rink and sledge piste attract large crowds. Villars hosts many cultural events, including classical music concerts.

Skiing Area

The Villars-sur-Ollon skiing area is smaller than some neighboring resorts (220km/136.7mi of ski slopes), a definite plus for families and others looking for a leisurely resort pace and a variety of novice and intermediate terrain on sunny slopes. The two main peaks (Grand Chamossaire and Croix des Chaux) are perfect for intermediates. Try the Combe d'Orsay, with its **views**✶ of Leysin, and one of the many forest trails. Seasoned skiers can tackle slopes running from Croix des Chaux to La Rasse or Les Fracherets. A skiing pass now enables you to go skiing all over the Vaud Alps including Les Diablerets and its glacier (50km/31mi of challenging slopes, accessible by the Conches chairlift) as well as Leysin (60km/37mi of pistes) and Les Mosses (40km/25mi), which can only be reached by car. There

are also 44km/27mi of cross-country trails around the resort.

Bretaye

Alt. 1 806m/5 925ft. ▭Rack railway.
Pretty route crossing the forest. After reaching Col de Soud, there are stunning views of Croix des Chaux and the impressive Diablerets peaks.

Grand Chamossaire

Alt. 2 120m/6 955ft. ⛷ Access to skiers by chairlift starting from Bretaye.
Sweeping panorama of the Vaud Alps mountain range (Leysin, Gryon, Les Diablerets) with the Valais, Mont Blanc and Dents du Midi nestling in the background.

AROUND VILLARS
Gryon

Alt. 1 114m/3 655ft.
Old terraced village overlooking the Avançon Valley. The road dips rapidly, winding between fir and larch. Bear left toward Les Plans 2km/1mi before Bex. At Frenières note on the left the perched village of Gryon. After Les Plans the road climbs through woodland, running parallel to a stream.

Bex Salt Mines (Mines de Sel de Bex)★

Route des Mines de Sel, Les Dévens.
🕐 *Guided tours Apr–Oct, Tue-Sun; daily Jun–Aug; 9.45am–3.45pm. ▭19CHF.*
℘(0)24 463 03 30. www.mines.ch.
The two-hour tour begins with an audiovisual show and a long underground narrow-gauge train ride, continuing on foot through passageways carved deep into the mountain. Wear sturdy shoes and a warm jacket.

This 300-year-old **salt mine** is still fully operational (the only one in Switzerland) producing 150 tons of salt daily and has been worked since the 15C. The salt is obtained through traditional means: A stream of fresh water is injected into the salt rock, flooding every crevice, until the brine shows a salt content of 30%. This technique is known as leaching. Water is then evaporated through boiling, leaving a salt deposit at the bottom of the container. The mine consists of 40km/25mi of shafts, passageways and steps, originally hollowed out by chisels and sledgehammers.

Part of the mine has been made into a **museum** which can be visited on foot and in a small train. Exhibits include tools and machinery which have served the mining industry over the past centuries.

La Barboleusaz
Alt. 1 211m/3 973ft.

This winter sports resort is located in a lovely site overlooked by Les Diablerets. From here you can get to the ski fields of **Les Chaux**★ (5km/3mi by a narrow, winding road; in winter access by cable car) or to the **Solalex Refuge**★ (alt. 1 466m/4 809ft)—via a small picturesque road (6km/3.5mi) following the Avançon torrent—in a cirque of Alpine pastures at the foot of Les Diablerets.

Pont de Nant★
A lovely cirque at the base of the Grand Muveran Glaciers. An Alpine rock garden can be visited (water lily pond; more than 2 000 kinds of Alpine or medicinal plants from all over the world).

ADDRESSES

🛏 STAY
LES DIABLERETS
🍽🍷 **Hôtel des Diablerets** – *Chemin des Ormonts.* ℘*(0)24 492 09 09. www.diablerets.com. Closed May and Oct–Nov. 59 rooms.* Treat yourself to one of the higher-priced rooms with sumptuous views of the glacier. Covered pool.

🍽🍷 **L'Ours** – *Towards l'Église (hamlet 2km/1.25mi from Diablerets)* ℘*(0)24 492 44 00. www.aubergedelours.ch. 6 rooms. Closed Nov and Apr.* Plain wood lined rooms, but pleasant and airy.

🍽🍷🍴 **Du Golf** – *r. Centrale, Villars-sur-Ollon.* ℘*(0)24 496 38 38. www.hotel-golf.ch. 70 rms.* A hotel just 100m/109yds from the charilifts. Spacious rooms.

🍽🍷🍴 **La Renardière** – *rte des Layeux, Villars-sur-Ollon.* ℘*(0)24 495 28 02. www.la-renardiere.ch. 20 rooms. Open mid-Dec–mid-Apr and mid-Jun–mid-Nov.* Attractive rooms in a peaceful setting. Three large chalets linked by walkways, near to a forest. Prices for each of the chalets vary considerably. The rooms in the annexe are less expensive.

🍽🍷🍴 **Hostellerie Les Sources** – *Chemin du Vernex.* ℘*(0)24 492 01 00. www.hotel-les-sources.ch. Closed May and mid-Oct–Nov. 48 rooms.* A family friendly hotel with the finest of modern amenities. Pleasantly situated near the village centre, overlooking the Diablerets Massif.

🍴 EAT
LES DIABLERETS
🍽 **Café de la Couronne** – ℘*(0)24 492 31 75. Closed Wed in low season.* Delicious homemade charcuterie.

🍽🍷 **Les Lilas** – ℘*(0)24 492 31 34. www.hotelleslilas.ch. Closed 22 May–8 Jun, Sun evenings and Mon in low season.* This charming chalet converted into a guesthouse serves regional cuisine.

🍽🍷 **Miroir d'Argentine** – *Solalex. 9km/5.6mi E of Villars-sur-Ollon.* ℘*(0)24 498 14 46. www.solalex.ch. Open mid- May–end Oct, daily exc Mon and Tue.* A restaurant, beautifully positioned, surrounded by mountains. Friendly welcome with excellent traditional cuisine. Well recommended.

🍽🍷🍴 **Restaurant de Plambuit** – *Plambuit. 6km/3.75mi N of Villars-sur-Ollon.* ℘*(0)24 499 33 44. www.plambuit.com. Open 1 May–31 Oct, Wed lunchtime–Sun lunchtime.* A rustic dining room offering food which is created from local market produce. As places are limited, it is best to reserve in advance. Terrace with a wide ranging view.

Gruyères★

This little fortified town is perched on a hill in a harmonious landscape. It charms visitors to Romansh Switzerland by its friendly atmosphere, derived from the time when the whole Sarine Valley lay under the benevolent rule of the counts of Gruyères (12C–16C).

SIGHTS

Visitors will immediately be charmed by the locality of Gruyères, which they approach by its main street. It is lined with old houses with twin windows and wide eaves, and slopes down to the town fountain before rising again toward the castle.

Go up to the castle on foot, noticing on the right the old grain measures hollowed out of a stone block, and then, on the left, the house with delicately carved 16C window frames of the jester Chalamala, who became famous at the court of the counts of Gruyères.

Castle★

🦆Guided tour (1hr) Apr–Oct, 9am–6pm; Nov–Mar, 10am–4.30pm. Last admission 30min before closing time. 🕐Closed 1 Jan and at Christmas. 🎟10CHF combined with Giger Museum 17CHF. 📞(0)26 921 21 02. www.chateau-gruyeres.ch.

▶ **Population:** Fribourg 1 753.
🦆 **Michelin Map:** National Map 729: F6.
🅸 **Info:** 1663 Gruyères. 📞(0)24 424 424. www.gruyeres.ch.
▶ **Location:** In the Fribourg region of western Switzerland. Alt. 830m/ 2 657ft.
🅿 **Parking:** Cars should be parked outside the town (car park).
👁 **Don't Miss:** The HR Giger Museum, as well as Historial Suisse, a wax museum located in the La Locanda restaurant in Moléson village.
🕐 **Timing:** Allow at least a full day.

Most of the former castle of the counts of Gruyères dates from the late 15C (façades on the courtyard of the main dwelling). The internal arrangement recalls both the feudal period (kitchen and guardroom) and 18C refinements. Their decoration, more or less tasteful, is largely the work of the Bovy family, a dynasty of artists who saved the castle from destruction in the 20C and welcomed many foreign artists (namely

Château de Gruyères

© OT Moleson/Switzerland Tourism

Corot). The heraldic crane of the counts of Gruyères can be seen in many places, over doors, in stained-glass windows and on firebacks. The most valuable pieces assembled here are the three mourning **copes**★ of the Order of the Golden Fleece, used by almoners of Charles the Bold to celebrate masses for the repose of knights who died in the campaign of 1476. These sumptuous vestments became, for the people of Fribourg, their most glorious trophy of the Battle of Murten. Four 16C Flanders tapestries depicting scenes from the Old Testament are displayed in the count's bedroom, whose ceiling is typical of the Savoyard period. In the Baroque Salle des Baillis, note the impressive sculpted wood furniture. The Salle des Chevaliers, notable for its size and decoration, has a coffered ceiling with hanging keystones and walls painted with scenes illustrating the history of the counts' lands.

The 15C **Chapelle St-Jean** stands on a pleasant terrace within view of the Lower Gruyères (Bulle-Broc district), partly drowned by the reservoir of the Rossens Dam, and of the two graceful Dent de Broc peaks. Near the chapel, on the ramparts, is a splendid view of the surrounding area, including the Moléson and the Jura chain (viewing table).

Musée HR Giger

◔*Apr–Oct, daily 10am–6pm; Nov–Mar, Tue–Fri 1pm–5pm, Sat–Sun 10am–6pm.* ▦*12 CHF, children 5CHF. Some rooms are for adults only.* ℘*(0)26 921 22 00. www.hrgiger.info.*

This museum is a must-see destination for art and science-fiction film fans. Housed in Château St-Germain, the museum is dedicated to Swiss sculptor HR Giger, who created the *Alien* life forms. The *Birth Machine* sculpture at the entrance sets the tone for a visit, which includes a room dedicated to the movie, with various sketches used for the film, paintings, sculptures, and unique pieces of furniture made from glass, plexiglass, polyester, metal and rubber and artifacts from the artist's other major works, *Species, The Spelll-IV* and *Harkonnen*.

Tibet Museum

4 Rue du Château. ◔*Open daily Apr–Oct 11am–6pm (Nov–Mar Fri 1pm–5pm, Sat–Sun 11am–6pm).* ▦*12CHF (5CHF)* ℘*(0)26 921 30 10. www.tibetmuseum.ch.*

Adjacent to the Musée HR Giger is this recently opened collection of Buddhist and Himalayan art.

◔ *Follow the main street, which offers a view of the Moléson (see below), the most typical Gruyères peak. Turn right in front of the fountain.*

Maison du Gruyère

1km/0.6mi away, at the entrance to Pringy. ◔*Open 9am–7pm (6pm Oct–Mar).* ▦*7CHF* ⌗ ℘*(0)26 921 84 00. www.lamaisondugruyere.ch.*

This former industrial cheesemaking factory houses a demonstration cheese dairy. The ground floor contains the cellars where the cheeses are stored. The first floor features the ripening area, an exhibition on local customs, a videotape explaining cheesemaking techniques and galleries overlooking the demonstration area where Gruyère is made in wheels of 35kg/77lb.

EXCURSIONS
Moléson-sur-Gruyères

◔*6km/3.7mi to the SW. 6 Place de l'Aigle, 1663.* ℘*(0)26 921 85 00.*

This pretty village features a **Fromagerie d'Alpage** (◔*open mid-May–end Sept; 9am-7pm; tour at 10am only, 50 people max; else by prior appointment* ▦*5CHF;* ℘*(0)26 921 10 44; www.fromagerie-alpage.ch)*, an Alpine cheese dairy set up in a 17C chalet, with a roof made up of 90 000 shingles. After an audio-visual presentation (in French) of regional specialities, visitors are shown the humble sleeping quarters of a local cowherd (*armailli*). Then they can watch a cowherd prepare Gruyère cheese according to traditional methods, baking it in an old-fashioned stove fuelled by firewood. Fresh products are kept in the milk room and the more mature cheeses are stored in the salting house, a small square building located near the farm.

A cable car will take you up to the **Observatoire de Moléson** (alt. 2 002m/6 568ft) (⌖*cable car leaving from Moléson-Village every 20min;* 🕐*May–Oct daily 9am–6pm, Jun–Oct (to 11pm Fri, Sat), Dec–Apr Mon – Fri 9am–4.30pm (from 8.30am Sat, Sun);* 🚡*41-29CHF;* ✆*(0)26 921 29 96*) which commands a panoramic view of the Gruyères area and the Swiss plateau. The observatory organizes evening classes on the subject of astronomy (telescopes). During the winter season 35km/20mi of carefully marked-out ski runs are available to tourists.

Bulle

Alt. 769m/2 523ft. 4 Avenue de la Gare, 1630. ✆*(0)26 912 80 22.*
Bulle is the capital of the "green Gruyères", one of the most attractive districts in Switzerland with its peaceful scenery and quaint folklore. The market town deals in timber and cheese, and the black-and-white Fribourg cattle.

Musée Gruérien★★

🕐*Open mid-Jun–Sept Tue–Fri 10am–noon, 1.30pm–5pm; Sat 10am–5pm; Sun and public holidays, 1.30pm–5pm.* 🕐*Closed 1 Jan and 25 Dec.* 🚡*8CHF.* ♿ ✆*(0)26 916 10 10.*
www.musee-gruerien.ch.
Founded by the writer **Victor Tissot**, the Museum of the Gruyères Region is in the basement of a modern building at the foot of the castle. Exhibits are superbly arranged and include some 10 000 pieces of rural furniture, craft objects and documents illustrating the cycle of the seasons. The first section contains several reconstructed peasant interiors, including a cheese room and a typical Fribourg house. Note the pyramid-shaped fireplace in one of the kitchens and painted scenes of the life of the prophet Elijah in one of the bedrooms.
Myriad objects highlight the **folklore of the Gruyère region**. Large paintings (19C) known as "poyas" (from the verb *poyî*," to move up the mountain") show the herds being led up to mountain pastures. One of these is by a master of the

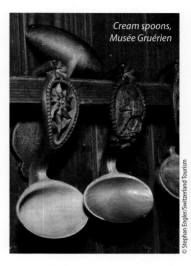

Cream spoons, Musée Gruérien

© Stephan Engler/Switzerland Tourism

genre, Sylvestre Pidoux. The *armaillis* (cowherds) are depicted in their *bredzon* (short jacket with puffed sleeves), with their *loyi* (bag of salt) slung over their shoulder. Also admire the large variety of fine **old furniture**: Tables, beds, chests, wardrobes, sideboards, decorated cribs, and chairs, such as the 16C bench from Fribourg. The 18C Gruyères **regional costumes** are also worth noting as well as the wax crèches from the same period. Also on display are 18C–19C medallions on cut-out paper, religious statues, church plate (gold monstrance dated 1752), cowbells and horns from the Alps, and a diorama of the local fauna.
The second section contains 16C–17C engravings and paintings from the Italian School. Also represented are the French School, with works by Corot and Courbet, including a lovely portrait of a young Bulle girl, and the Swiss School (Vallotton, Alexis Grimou), and the painted cupboard by Netton Bosson.

Castle

⌖*Not open to the public.*
The castle is an imposing 13C building, built for Bishop Boniface of Lausanne in the style of Burgundy and Savoy.

Cailler, Suchard, Kohler, Nestlé, Lindt, Tobler...

Attractive presentations and mouth-watering contents characterize the high-quality confectionery of Swiss chocolate-makers, many of whom have been making chocolate since the 19C. As in the case of a good wine, one should savor the aroma and taste. Dark, white or milk chocolate comes in many forms—cakes, mini-slabs, figurines, sweets, and in a variety of shapes—and is often combined with various other ingredients such as nuts, raisins, or ginger.

Jaunpassstrasse

Jaun Pass Road. 381 Hauptstrasse.
℘*26 929 81 81. www.jaun.ch.*
The **Jaun Pass Road** is the most mountainous in the Fribourg Alps. For the sightseer it combines lakes, rocky crests and stretches of pasture.

Broc

From the garden in front of the town hall, you will enjoy a lovely **view**★ of the Gruyères area with Vanil Blanc, Vudalla and Moléson summits as a backdrop. The **Nestlé-Callier chocolate factory** (◷*open daily Apr–Oct 10am–6pm, Nov–Mar to 5pm* ◷*Closed 1 Jan and 25 Dec;* ✆*10CHF;* ℘*(0)26 921 51 51; www.cailler.ch*) is open to the public (short film and tasting).
Electrobroc (◷ *guided-only visit upon appointment* ✆*no charge;* ℘*0840 40 40 30*), next to the factory, is run by the Fribourg electricity company and introduces visitors to the world of electricity, with information on consumption, distribution and production, as well as explaining how a hydroelectric plant works. The tour finishes with an impressive audio-visual display of the effects of lightning.

Charmey

The **Musée du Pays et Val de Charmey** in the Tourist Office (℘*(0)26 927 55 87; www.musee-charmey.ch*) houses a collection of objects relating to life in the region.

Jaun

This little town, quite close to the dividing line between Romansh and German Switzerland, still features several fine old chalets and a church with a traditional shingle roof.

ADDRESSES

🛏 STAY

Those wishing to sample local specialities should taste these dishes: The traditional fondue and raclette, jambon (ham) and meringue à la crème de la Gruyère (sweet topped with cream).

🍴 **Fleur de Lys** – ℘*(0)26 921 82 82. ww.hotelfleurdelys.ch. Closed Feb and Nov–Easter. 10 rooms.* Rooms decorated with pretty wainscoting. Large, rustic dining hall where traditional meals are served.

🍴 **Hostellerie de St-Georges** – ℘*(0)26 921 83 00. www.st-georges-gruyeres.ch. 14 rooms.* Old inn dating back to the 16C. Peace and quiet guaranteed. Lovely views of the ramparts and surrounding mountains.

🍽/EAT

🍴 **Le Chalet** – ℘*(0)26 921 21 54. www.chalet-gruyeres.ch. Closed 25 Dec.* A country chalet serving local cuisine in the heart of the town centre.

🍴 **Auberge de la Halle** – ℘*(0)26 921 21 78. www.lahalle-gruyeres.ch.* Restaurant with a rustic setting offering regional dishes and a charming atmosphere.

🍴 **Hôtel de Ville** – ℘*(0)26 921 24 24. www.hoteldeville.ch. Closed Wed low season, 1–20 Dec and 3–17 Jan. 8 rooms.* Located in the main street, this old-fashioned, rustic hotel has a restaurant which serves regional cuisine.

Fribourg★★

Fribourg is a remarkable site★★ on a rocky spur circled by a bend of the Sarine. The old quarters extend from the river to the upper town; bristling with church towers and monasteries, they still bear the appearance of a medieval city. Fribourg boasts many **sculpted fountains** gracing the squares and along the streets, built during the Middle Ages as outlets for the many springs which supplied the town with water. Later, in the 15C, they were adorned with elegantly chiselled basins and stone columns, the work of renowned artists such as Hans Geiler, Hans Gieng and Stephan Ammann.

A BIT OF HISTORY

From its foundations to the Reformation – In 1157 **Berchtold IV of Zähringen** founded Fribourg at a ford on the Sarine and made it a stronghold to command this important thoroughfare. After the Zähringen family died out, the town changed hands several times. It passed to the Kyburgs and then to the Habsburgs, but finally to the rule of Savoy. Fribourg joined the Confederation in 1481 after having acquired extensive lands in the Vaud Country. Here the Reformation had no decisive influence and the Catholic Restoration inspired by Father Canisius reaffirmed the Catholic

▶ **Population:** Fribourg 34 084.

⏱ **Michelin Map:** Map: F5.

ℹ **Info:** 1 avenue de la Gare – 1700. ℘(0)26 350 11 11. www.fribourgtourisme.ch.

▷ **Location:** Fribourg is located 29km/18.2mi east of Estavayer-Le-Lac. Alt. 640m/2 100ft.

Ⓟ **Parking:** Use public parking areas and explore by foot or public transport

⟳ **Don't Miss:** A tour of the Old Town on foot.

⏱ **Timing:** Allow at least half a day to explore the city and its sights; a full day to include an excursion.

feelings of the town, which became the seat of the Bishopric of Lausanne, Geneva, and Fribourg.

A bastion of Catholicism – In the 17C many religious orders were added to those already settled in Fribourg during the 13C: Franciscans, Jesuits, and other communities made it the Catholic capital of Switzerland. Among the most famous and brilliant establishments were the College of St Michael, founded by the Jesuits, the Capuchin Church and Monastery, the Franciscan Monastery,

View of Fribourg

© Franck Auberson/Switzerland Tourism

and the Monastery of Maigrauge, built by the Cistercians in the 13C.

The university – In 1889 the foundation of a Catholic state university gave a new impulse to the crucial role played by religious instruction in modern times. Fribourg University, one of the most prestigious seats of learning, still enjoys an excellent reputation in Switzerland and abroad. Its five faculties (theology, law, social and economic sciences, languages, and natural sciences) and 15 independent institutes (computer technology, journalism, and more) welcome students from all over the world.

↝ WALKING TOUR

This route explores the history of Fribourg. Visitors can appreciate the modern areas of the town and then immerse themselves into the medieval streets, having taken in the town's museums and the cathedral. Allow 1h30 for the walk, not including a museum visit. Start from the Place de la Gare and then follow the Rue de Romont, pass place Georges-Python and go down rue Lausanne to place Nova-Friburgo. Go down rue Pierre Aeby and the Murtengasse.

Art and History Museum★

🕓 Open Tue–Sun 11am–6pm (8pm Thu).
🕓 Closed 24, 26, 31 Dec, 1 Jan. ⸻8CHF.
♿ ✆ (0)26 305 51 40. www.mahf.ch
The collections displayed in the Hôtel Ratzé, an elegant Renaissance building (16C), and in a former slaughterhouse converted in 1981, illustrate the art and history of Fribourg from its origins to the present day. Many exhibits date back to the Middle Ages, a period rich in artistic events.

Note the Late Gothic collections of remarkable works of art executed by local artists such as Martin Gramp, Hans Fries, Hans Gieng and Hans Geiler. Fries—the city's official poet from 1501 through 1510—exerted a strong influence over his contemporaries and several of his works are on display. The 17C is present with works by Pierre Wuilleret and Jean-François Reyff, the 18C with paintings attributed to Got-

tfried Locher. In the room devoted to regional guilds and associations, a series of engravings and watercolours present the city of Fribourg and its canton. The artifacts displayed in the archeological section can be traced back to prehistoric times, ancient Rome and the early Middle Ages.

The stone museum, set up in the former slaughterhouse, features a fascinating collection of fourteen **15C stone statues**★ taken from the Cathedral of St Nicholas, depicting the Annunciation and the Apostles. Visitors may also admire a splendid 11C Crucifixion scene from Villars-les-Moines and a group of 16C sculptures attributed to Hans Gieng, contrasting sharply with the monumental compositions of Jean Tinguely. The rest of the exhibition consists of a rare collection of objects in silver and gold (14C–18C), some stunning pieces of Burgundian jewellery (7C–8C) and works by Marcello (the pseudonym of the native artist the Duchess Castiglione Colonna, née Adèle d'Affry), extremely popular during the 20C. A number of 19C and 20C works, including several by Eugène Delacroix, Félix Vallotton and Ferdinand Hodler, are in the attic room above the former slaughterhouse.

▷ Continue down Murtengasse.

Franciscan Church

A Franciscan community settled in Fribourg in 1256. The monastery buildings were completed about the end of the 13C and remodelled in the 18C. The monastery, which then had a superb bookbinding workshop and the richest library in town, received the most influential people passing through Fribourg.

The first chapel on the right contains a gilded and carved wood **triptych**★ made in about 1513 for Jean de Furno, which shows Alsatian influence. The central panel depicts the Crucifixion, with Mary Magdalene at the foot of the Cross; the panel on the left shows the Adoration of the Shepherds, and that on the right, the Adoration of the Magi. The folding shutters on the left illustrate the

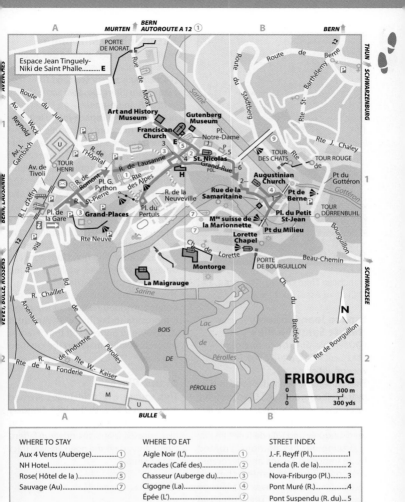

BERN
MURTEN BERN AUTOROUTE A 12 ①

Espace Jean Tinguely-
Niki de Saint Phalle...........**E**

Art and History
Museum
Franciscan
Church
Gutenberg
Museum
St. Nicolas
Augustinian
Church
Rue de la
Samaritaine
Mᵉᵉ suisse de
la Marionnette
Lorette
Chapel
Montorge
Grand-Places
La Maigrauge

FRIBOURG

	300 m
0	
0	300 yds

BULLE

WHERE TO STAY		WHERE TO EAT		STREET INDEX	
Aux 4 Vents (Auberge)	①	Aigle Noir (L')	①	J.-F. Reyff (Pl.)	1
NH Hotel	③	Arcades (Café des)	②	Lenda (R. de la)	2
Rose(Hôtel de la)	⑤	Chasseur (Auberge du)	③	Nova-Friburgo (Pl.)	3
Sauvage (Au)	⑦	Cigogne (La)	④	Pont Muré (R.)	4
		Épée (L')	⑦	Pont Suspendu (R. du)	5
		Grand Pont "La Tour Rouge"	⑨	Zaehringen (R.)	6

Annunciation; those on the right present
a pretty Coronation of the Virgin.
The **chancel** is a good example of
13C Franciscan architecture, with four
keystones in the vaulting bearing the
symbols of the Evangelists. It contains
oak **stalls**★ dating from c.1280. On the
left of the chancel is the altarpiece of
St Anthony, known as *The Death of the
Usurer*, painted in 1506 by the Fribourg
artist Hans Fries. The picture illustrates
the words of the Gospel: "Where a man's
treasure is, there will his heart be too."
Over the high altar stands the magnificent **altarpiece**★★ by the Masters of

the Carnation, painted at Solothurn and
Basel in 1480. The picture is very large
(8 x 2.7m/26 x 8.5ft) and was installed
during the restoration of 1936, replac-
ing a 1692 Baroque altarpiece. The central scene represents a Crucifixion; it is
flanked by four Franciscan saints: St Ber-
nardine of Siena, St Anthony of Padua,
St Francis of Assisi, and St Louis, Bishop
of Toulouse. The Adoration of the Shepherds is on the left shutter, that of the
Magi on the right; the background suggests the Fribourg Alps. Folding shutters
feature an Annunciation in their centre,
St Elizabeth of Hungary, patroness of the

La fointaine de Jo Siffert' by Jean Tinguely at Grand-Places

© Hans-Peter Siffert/Switzerland Tourism

Franciscan Third Order, on the right, and St Clara of Assisi on the left.

Espace Jean Tinguely – Niki de Saint-Phalle★

🕐Open Tue–Sun, 11am–6pm (8pm Thu). ⊚6CHF. ♿ ℘(0)26 305 51 40. www.mahf.ch .

The former tram depot designed in 1900 by the Fribourg architect Léon Hertling, has been converted into a gallery displaying the works of the famous artists Jean Tinguely and Niki de Saint-Phalle; and temporary exhibitions. Fronted by an imposing façade and decorated with neo-Baroque gables, the gallery permanently houses the Niki de Saint-Phalle donation. The artist (Jean Tinguely's wife, who died in 2002) conceived her *Monumental Relief* especially for this new cultural venue: A series of 22 brightly coloured tableaux evoking Jean Tinguely's stay in Fribourg (left-hand wall as you enter). In the middle of the room, the central sculpture, *Retable to Western Opulence and Totalitarian Mercantilism*, is one of the many large altarpieces that Tinguely started making in 1981. This huge machine, which grinds into motion at regular intervals, is decorated with toys and various objects symbolizing the wealth of Western society.

▷ *Go along the road to the left of the square.*

♟♟Gutenberg Museum★★

16 pl. Notre-Dame. ℘ *(0)26 347 38 28. www.gutenbergmuseum.ch.* ♿
🕐*Open daily except Mon and Tue 11am–6pm (8pm Thu, 5pm Sun),* ⊚*10 CHF. Audio-guide.*

Just behind the Espace Jean Tinguely, the Swiss museum of Graphic Art and Communication is located in a building which was built in 1527, and served its purpose as a customs office, among other roles. The museum explores the history of the written word and the printing process across the centuries, from Gutenberg to the technology driven world today. The exhibitions are educational and appeal to children as well as adults. The first floor concentrates on former times, while the second floor covers the industrial era.

The third floor contains both very old books and video footage of the printing process today. In the basement it is possible to understand the different processes which make up the creation of a book

Grand-Place

This square which includes lawned areas, is graced with the Jean-Tinguely fountain, dedicated by the Swiss artist to his deceased friend, the driver Jo Siffert. On summer days the open areas attract lots of people.

▷ *Walk up rue des Alpes and turn left on to the little square.*

Hôtel de Ville★ (H)

The town hall stands near a square famed for its lime tree, planted, it is said, on 22 June 1476 to celebrate the victory of the Confederates over **Charles the Bold** (♿*see INTRODUCTION: History*) in Murten.

This fine, early-16C building, and its canopy and double staircase (17C) is dominated by a large roof of brown tiles. The belfry and its Jack-o'-the-clock figure are crowned with pinnacle turrets. On the square stands the Fountain of St George (1525), featuring a group of sculptures by Hans Geiler.

▷ *Go along the Grand Rue and take the first pedestrianised street on the right.*

Cathédrale St-Nicolas★

🕐*Open Mon–Sat 7.30am–7pm, Sun 8.30am–9.30pm. www.stnicolas.ch.*

The cathedral rears its fine Gothic tower above the roofs of the old town. The first stone was laid in 1283; the cathedral was intended to take the place of the church built a century earlier by the founder of the town, Berchtold IV of Zähringen. The far end of the church was altered in the 17C by the rebuilding of an apse with three walls and five bays to replace the flat east end. The tower, 76m/250ft high, was built in the 14C, on the octagon completed c.1490 with a crown of pinnacles in the style of the period.

The **tympanum**★★ of the main porch, surmounted by a rose window, is devoted to the Last Judgement: Heaven and Hell are shown on either side of the Weighing of Souls; the archivolts portray the Angels, Prophets and Patriarchs; the doorway, the Apostles. The sculptures in the south porch date back to the 14C. Inside, a square vestibule is formed by the lower part of the tower, with side walls adorned with fine arcades, precedes the ogive-vaulted nave. Pictures from the 17C adorn the corner-pieces of the great arcades, which is surmounted by clerestory windows (the work of Alfred Manessier in 1983). The aisles, which also feature ogive vaulting, are lit by windows designed by the Polish painter Mehoffer.

The side chapels (16C and 17C) received Baroque altars in the mid-18C. The chancel, with a Gothic wrought-iron screen, is adorned with 15C **stalls**★ representing the Prophets and Apostles. A beam supports a large Calvary carved in the first half of the 15C. To the right, the Chapel of the Holy Sepulchre contains a fine **Entombment** (433) and more stained glass by Alfred Manessier.

The late-15C font on the south side of the chancel is made of finely carved stone. Its wooden cover is 17C. The organ, one of the glories of 19C Fribourg, was built in 1834.

Tower of Cathédrale St-Nicolas and the belfry of Hôtel de Ville

© Stephan Engler/Switzerland Tourism

▷ *Descend towards the Vieille Ville by rue du Pont-Suspendu, turn right into rue de Zaehringen, follow by Stalden, then turn left along rue de la Lenda.*

Augustinian Church

The interior of the church, commissioned by the mendicant orders, presents a large nave divided into four bays, separated by Gothic arches resting on spherical pillars. The furnishings are characteristic of the Baroque period. The wooden retable surmounting the high altar—gilded and painted to resemble marble—is the work of Peter and Jacob Spring: Three levels, two of which feature niches flanked by columns, portray religious scenes, mostly taken from the Life of the Virgin.

The two retables placed at the entrance to the chancel were made at the Ryeff workshops. The one on the right features an elegant polychrome composition, *Virgin and Child*. On the square is an annex to the church: A gallery with six arcades, supporting a first floor reinforced by half-timbering.

▷ *Go down rue des Agustins and then turn left on to rue d'Or.*

Pont de Berne

A charming wooden bridge with oak supports spans the River Sarine.

▷ *Take the road opposite the bridge.*

Place du Petit-St-Jean

This square, located south of the Auge district, extends up to the Pont de Berne and owes its name to St-Jean-de-Jérusalem, a former Knights' Chapel built in the 13C and demolished in the 19C.

The Fontaine de Ste-Anne (1560), a tribute to the city's patron saint of tanners, is the work of Hans Gieng; note the lovely façade at number 29.

▷ *Take the road uphill.*

Rue de la Samaritaine

This steep, paved street will return you to **place du Petit St-Jean**. The Samaritans' Fountain (1551), yet another token of Hans Gieng's talent, represents Jesus and the Samaritan at Jacob's well. Level with the fountain, note the impressive Late Gothic façade, punctuated by eight picture windows embellished with Flamboyant tracery.

At number 34 the **Musée Suisse de la Marionnette** (*⃝open Wed–Sun, 10am–5pm, guided visits only Mon–Tues; ⃝closed 25, 26 Dec; ⚏5CHF, children 4CHF; ℘(0)26 322 85 13; www.marionette.ch*) will whisk you away to the magical world of dolls, puppets, paper or chiffon figurines, shadow pantomimes, masks, and similar games from countries all over the world. Performances can be arranged on a regular basis.

▷ *By going back up route des Alpes and on to rue St-Pierre you can reach the Grand Place, which has a Tinguely fountain dedicated to his late racing driver friend, Jo Siffert. Rejoin avenue de la Gare.*

SIGHTS
Musée d'Histoire Naturelle

In the Faculty of Science on the route de Marly (not on the map) via the boulevard de Pérolles. ⃝Open daily 2pm–6pm. ⃝Closed 1 Jan, Good Fri and 25 Dec. ⚏No charge. ♿ ℘(0)26 305 89 00. www.fr.ch/mhn.

The Natural Science Museum occupies seven rooms on the first floor. The first rooms display fossils (geological and paleontological sections), a relief model of the Aletsch Glacier and its region, and a splendid collection of minerals, along with a reconstruction of a crystal cave. The other rooms are devoted to zoology. Stuffed specimens of local fauna are presented in their natural setting and a diorama shows a variety of bird species, complete with their recorded songs. Other displays include animals from the five continents. The fascinating world of insects is given special attention: Morphology, reproduction, evolu-

Schwarzsee

© Franck Auberson/Switzerland Tourism

tion of the species, recorded stridulations of the grasshopper and cricket, and studies conducted under a microscope.

EXCURSIONS
Schwarzsee★
27km/17mi. About 1hr.
◗ *Leave Fribourg across the Zaehringen Bridge on the road to Bourguillon and then road N 74.*
When you reach Tafers, turn right on to a picturesque road offering charming views towards the Berra on the right and towards the Guggershorn on the left.
After Plaffeien, a pretty village of varnished wooden chalets, the road climbs through the Sence Valley to end at the **Black Lake** (Schwarzee—*angling*) in a pretty mountain **setting**★. A pleasant resort has grown up beside the lake.

Barrage de Rossens★
Round tour of 55km/34mi.
◗ *Leave Fribourg by road number 12. After 13km/8mi take the Rossens road on the left.*
A large dam was built across the Sarine in 1948, upstream from the village of Rossens. The dam is arched, 320m/1 049ft long and 83m/272ft high. The 14km/8.5mi-long reservoir, forming a magnificent pool in a pretty, steep-sided setting, is known as **Lake Gruyères**. To enjoy a good view, follow the road on the right towards Pont-la-Ville. At La Roche take road 77 on the right and cross the lake at Corbières. At Riaz you rejoin road number 12 to Fribourg.

Abbaye de Hauterive
7km/4.3mi SW of Fribourg by the road to Bulle. ◗ *After 4.5km/3mi take the Marly-le-Grand exit and turn right.*
◗ *Guided tour (1hr), Mon–Sat 9.45–11.30am, 2.15pm–5pm, Sun and public holidays, 11.00–11.30am, 3pm–4pm.*
℘ *(0)26 409 71 00.*
www.abbaye-hauterive.ch.
After Chesalles, a road on the left leads to the abbey, which stands in a loop of the Sarine. The Cistercian abbey, founded in 1138 by 12 French monks, was secularised in 1848 but resumed the life of prayer and work in 1939. It is the oldest remaining Cistercian abbey in Switzerland. Situated on the route to St-Jacques-de-Compostela, it extends hospitality to pilgrims or other travellers wishing to go into retreat.

The church, built in 1160, has undergone many alterations, especially in the 14C and 18C. It was furnished with stained-glass windows (14C and 15C) in the chancel with fine stalls with panels carved with human figures and crowned with open-work canopies, a 16C mural painting and in the north side aisle the recumbent figure of a knight whose feet rest on a lion. The monastery buildings were rebuilt in the 18C, with a Baroque façade. Inside, the main staircase is adorned with elegant wrought-iron balustrades. The Gothic **cloisters**, entirely remodeled in the 14C, are roofed with painted groined vaulting featuring finely carved keystones.

🚗 DRIVING TOUR

LE PLATEAU VAUDOIS

Avenches
4km/2mi S of Lake Murten – Alt. 473m/1 574ft. 3 place de l'Église – 1580.
℘ *(0)26 676 99 22. www.avenches.ch.*
Avenches is built on the site of the former capital of the Helvetii. The Roman city of Aventicum, founded by the Emperor Augustus and expanded into a colony by Vespasian, had some 20 000 inhabitants and flourished throughout the 2C AD and destroyed in AD 259. The château, with the Renaissance façade which stands in the centre of the town, dates from the late 13C. It was commissioned by the bishops of Lausanne. In the 16C, the château was enlarged by the authorities in Bern into a residence for their bailiffs.

Roman legions – The town was defended by a ring of fortifications about 6km/3.7mi round, with walls over 7m/23ft high, crowned with battlements; semicircular towers were used as observation posts; one of them, the Tornallaz, is still standing but it has been badly restored. Visitors are allowed to visit the remains of the amphitheatre, the Roman arena (on the Fribourg road) and a large sanctuary known as the "storkery", of which only one pilaster has survived. Recent excavations have revealed the ruins of a portico and temple podium.

Amphitheatre – The amphitheater is thought to date from the end of the 1C AD. Duels between gladiators and fights against wild animals were staged in this elliptical arena, which, in its heyday, was able to seat up to 16 000.

Today – The modern town is much smaller than the Ancient city, whose size can be judged from the excavated ruins. These became the property of the town in 1804. General Guisan, commander-in-chief of the Swiss army from 1939–45, was born here; his bust stands in the plaza in front of the post office.

Musée Romain d'Avenches★

○ Open Apr–Sept, Tue–Sun, 10am–5pm; Oct–Mar, 2pm–5pm. Open Mondays on public holidays. ○ Closed 1 and 2 Jan, 25, 26 and 31 Dec; Tue, Nov–Jan. ☞ 4CHF Combined ticket with Vallon museum 8CHF. ℘ (0)26 557 33 00. www.aventicum.org.

The museum is housed in a square tower, built in the Middle Ages over the main entrance to the amphitheatre. It contains objects discovered during the excavations. On the ground floor are displayed a very fine statue of a wolf suckling Romulus and Remus, several inscriptions, mural paintings, and mosaics; an audio-visual presentation explains the history of Avenches.

On the first floor, admire the copy of a golden bust of the Emperor Marcus Aurelius (the original is in the Musée des Beaux-Arts in Lausanne), along with some bronze pieces (Bacchus, Silenus, votive hand, Gaul divinity), marble sculptures (Minerva, Mercury, funerary art) and a collection of coins minted at Aventicum.

The second floor displays old tools and pottery pieces recreating Roman daily life in Switzerland in a lively and evocative manner.

▷ 6km/3.75mi W . Take the road in the direction of Estavayer-le-Lac.

Musée Romain de Vallon

○ Open Jun–Sept Wed–Sun, 2–6pm, 1 Oct–31 May, Wed–Sun 2–5pm. ○ Closed Mon, Sun, 1 & 2 Jan, 24–26 & 31 Dec. ☞ 6 CHF. ℘ (0)26 667 97 97. www.museevallon.ch.

A Gallo-Roman villa has been uncovered at the base of Caringan's rocky outcrop, where a water course had been planned. A museum has subsequently been created. The findings confirm that several large domaines existed in the countryside around Aventicum. Here there is evidence of three large buildings with a total of some 40 rooms. The rooms of note boast a superb mosaic depicting Bacchus and Ariadne, as well as hunting scenes—the latter of 97sq m/116sq yds being the largest in the Northern Alps area.

Among the exhibits in the museum are a collection of small bronze statues of Lares—deities believed to protect the household.

▷ Continue in the direction of Estavayer-le-Lac and after 1km/0.6mi turn left to Payerne.

Payerne★

Alt. 450m/1 476ft 1 place Général Guisan – 1530. ℘ (0)26 660 61 61.

Payerne boasts a remarkable abbey church, once attached to a Benedictine abbey. This abbey is believed to have been founded in the 10C by Empress Adelaide, wife of Otto the Great, first of the Holy Roman Emperors and daughter of the legendary Queen Bertha, nicknamed Bertha the Spinner, the widow of Rudolph II, King of Trans-Jura Burgundy.

Abbey Church★★

○ Open Tue–Sun 10am–noon, 2pm–6pm (5pm Oct–Apr). ○ Closed Good Fri. ☞ 6CHF. ℘ (0)26 662 67 04.

The 11C church is virtually all that remains of this once large Cluniac abbey. The church fell into disuse when the Bernese introduced the Reformation into the Vaud district. It was converted into a storehouse and barracks and suffered considerable damage. Large-scale renovation has restored this Romanesque church to its former glory.

Interior – The plain nave is lit by tall windows and crowned with barrel vaulting; harmony of proportion conveys an impression of grandeur but also of severity, emphasised by sparse decoration. Remarkable capitals adorn tall windows of the chancel and transept pillars. Their crude but expressive design dates them back to the abbey's founding. Beautiful 13C frescoes can be seen in the choir, transept and narthex, including Christ at the Last Judgement, with the 24 Elders of the Apocalypse seated before him.

Adjoining the church, the elegant **chapterhouse** with groined vaulting houses an exhibition on the history of the church. Note the two original bronze knockers (10C).

Museum – The museum is reached through the right arm of the transept. Permanent collections are devoted to two famous natives of the area.

Aimée Rapin (1868–1956) was an artist born without arms who painted with her toes. Her work was presented at the Paris World Fair in 1888, when she gained widespread recognition. Her wide-ranging talent is clearly expressed in her still life works (*Fruit, The Hunt*), portraits (*Young Girl at the Lake, Man with Pipe*), and drawings in charcoal and crayon (*Portrait of Monsieur Pierre Libaud, Woman Sitting*).

General **Antoine-Henri Jomini** (1779–1869) served under Napoleon I, becoming aide-de-camp to Marshall Ney and subsequently his Chief of Staff. After a misunderstanding with the marshall, Jomini left the French army and served under the Tsar of Russia, Alexander II. He died in Passy, near Paris, in 1869.

Lucens

This small town is associated with Sherlock Holmes, since the famous detective's author, Sir Arthur Conan Doyle, once owned a château here and founded a museum. The **Musée Sherlock Holmes** (👥👤🕐*open Wed, Sat–Sun 2pm–5pm;* 🎫*4CHF;* 📞*(0)21 906 73 33)* is dedicated to Sir Conan Doyle and his well-known, fictitious hero, and is worth a visit.

Moudon
Alt. 522m/1 713ft. Place de la Douane – 1510. 📞*(0)21 905 88 66. www.moudon.ch.*

Moudon enjoyed great prosperity under the counts of Savoy (14C): most of the buildings which give the town its medieval air date from that time. From the bridge over which the N 1 secondary road crosses the Broye, there is a pleasing view of the old quarter with its 15C-17C houses.

Église St-Étienne

This church, built in the 13C and early 14C, has an imposing fortified belfry, once part of the town walls. The Gothic nave, roofed with vaulting, bearing coats of arms, has lovely stained-glass windows and an organ (1764). The chancel contains fine stalls (early 16C and early 17C). Original 16C frescoes, which have undergone extensive restoration, are noteworthy.

Rue du Château
Start from Place de la Grenette.

This is the main street of the old quarter, beginning with a fountain depicting Justice. Farther along, the 12C Broye Tower (in ruins) stands on the right of the street, which is lined on either side by houses dating from the 15C, 16C and 17C; note the Bernese-style house at number 34. Midway to the left the view overlooks the river, spanned by a covered bridge; at the end of the street are the museums (on the right) and a second fountain (1557) called Moses.

Musée du Vieux-Moudon
🕐*Apr–Nov, Wed, Sat–Sun 2–6pm.* 🎫*6CHF, 9CHF (combined ticket with Musée Eugène-Burnand).* 📞*(0)21 905 27 05. www.vieux-moudon.ch.*

Housed in the 13C Maison de Rochefort in the upper town, this museum is

View of Romont

© Stephan Engler/Switzerland Tourism

dedicated to local and regional history, including documents, weapons, and a period kitchen. Additional sections are dedicated to the town (old wrought-iron signs that once hung outside cafés in Moudon, finials and paintings) and rural areas (tools, ploughing instruments and cow bells). A spiral staircase leads to the first floor, where a model of the town as it was in 1415 is displayed.

Musée Eugène-Burnand

🕙*Open Apr–Nov, Wed, Sat–Sun 2pm–6.30pm.* 🎫*6CHF, 9CHF (combined ticket with Musée du Vieux-Moudon), (-16 years, no charge). Visit by appointment 10 days in advance to the Tourist Office on* 𝄢*(0)21 905 88 66.*
The Bâtiment du Grand'Air houses works by Eugène Burnand, who was born in Moudon in 1850 and died in Paris in 1921.

Romont

Alt. 760m/2 736ft. 112Rue du Château.
𝄢*(0)26 651 90 55. www.romont.ch.*
The little town of Romont was built by Peter II of Savoy in the 13C, and is still encircled by some of its ramparts. It occupies a picturesque **site**★ on a crest overlooking the valleys of the Glâne.

Collégiale Notre-Dame-de-l'Assomption

🕙*Open Apr–Oct, 9am–7.30pm; Nov–Mar, 9am–6.30pm.* 👥*Guided tour, contact the Tourist Office for further information* 𝄢*(0)26 651 90 55.*
This collegiate church is one of the finest Gothic churches in Romansh country.

Don't miss the 15C **chancel**★ (adorned with carved stalls) and 14C and 15C stained-glass windows.

Castle

The castle dates from the 13C, as can be seen from the keep of Peter II of Savoy, but has been remodelled several times. The main gateway (16C) is surmounted by several coats of arms of Fribourg and Romont. Since 1981, the castle has housed the **Musée Suisse du Vitrail** (🕙*open daily Apr–Oct, Tue–Sun 10am–1pm, 2pm–5pm; Nov–Mar Thu–Sun, 10am–1pm, 2pm–5pm.* 🕙*Closed 25 Dec, 1 Jan* 🎫*10CHF.* 𝄢*(0)26) 652 10 95. www.vitromusee.ch).* The museum collections include medieval stained glass and Swiss heraldic glass as well as works by non-Swiss glass-makers.

ADDRESSES

🏨STAY
🛏️ **Auberge Aux 4 Vents** – *2km/1.25mi N of Fribourg, exit N. 124 route de Grandfey.* 𝄢*(0)26 347 36 00. www.auberge.aux4vents.ch. Closed 3 weeks Jan. 8 rooms.* A well renowned hotel, worth a detour. Easy to find despite its rural location, the hotel's rooms are a real experience. In the Blue Room, which is the best known, the bath is half suspended outside the window which gives the impression of being in the water and above the garden. The Angel room is truely romantic and the luxury of the Babylon

room is exceptional. Anyone on a lesser budget can opt for the Dormitory room which has four beds. Outdoor swimming pool and good restaurant.

🍽 **Best Western Hôtel de la Rose** – *1 rue de Morat.* ☎*(0)26 351 01 01. www.hoteldelarose.ch. 40 rooms.* Located a stone's throw from the Cathédrale Notre-Dame and the Église des Cordeliers.

🍽 **NH Hotel** – *14 Grand-Places.* ☎*(0)26 351 91 91. www.nh-hotels.com. 122 rooms.* Just 300m/328yds from the station, a modern hotel with comfortable rooms.

🍽 **Hôtel du Sauvage** – *12 Planche-Supérieure.* ☎*(0)26 347 30 60. www.hotel-sauvage.ch. 16 rooms.* This hotel in the heart of the old city is easy to spot because of its sign. It offers a choice of different rooms, each with its own personality and charm.

❢/EAT

🍽 **Café des Arcades** – *1 place des Ormeaux.* ☎*(0)26 321 48 40. www.cafe desarcades.ch. Closed Mon.* A good choice for lunch, located just next to the cathedral. Service can be slow at busy times.

🍽 **L'Épée** – *39 Planche-Supérieure.* ☎*(0)26 322 34 07. Closed mid-Jul–mid-Aug, Mon evenings and Sun.* Carefully prepared dishes at reasonable prices.

🍽 **L'Aigle Noir** – *10 rue des Alpes.* ☎*(0)26 322 49 77. www.aiglenoir.ch. Closed 25 Dec–12 Jan, Sun and Mon.* Choose to dine in a traditional room, one opulently furnished with antiques to evoke old-fashioned Switzerland, or on the terrace with a lovely view of the old city and the mountains.

🍽 **Auberge du Chasseur** – *10 rue de Lausanne.* ☎*(0)26 322 56 98. Open daily exc Mon. Closed 1–15 Jun.* In the town centre. Fondues and raclettes are the speciality of the house.

🍽 **Grand Pont "La Tour Rouge"** – *2 route de Bourguillon.* ☎*(0)26 481 32 48. Closed Tue, Wed and Sun evenings.* Traditional restaurant and brasserie (La Galerie). Terrace commanding pretty views of the Sarine River and the old city.

🍽 **La Cigogne** – *24 rue d'Or.* ☎*(0)26 322 68 34. www.la-cigogne.ch. Closed Sun and Mon, and last two weeks Feb.* Bistro near Pont de Berne in the old district providing good, affordable cuisine.

🛒 SHOPPING

The main shopping streets are **boulevard de Pérolles**, from the train station to the Jardin des Pérolles, **rue de Romont**, **rue St-Pierre**, and **rue de Lausanne.** There is a **vegetable and flower market** on place Georges-Python every Wednesday morning and on place de l'Hôtel-de-Ville on Saturdays.

🎭 THEATRE AND MUSIC

Club Fris-on, 13 route de la Fonderie: Rock music.
Le Nouveau Monde, 12A Arsenaux 1Jazz, rock, salsa, reggae etc.

🎭 NIGHTLIFE

The **Rock Café** features rock 'n' roll music and décor: Gold and platinum records and instruments which belonged to famous performers. Near pont de Zaehringen, in the street bearing the same name, the **Golden Gate** (enter through the Auberge de Zaehringen) offers a pleasant 13C setting (rough walls with pebble masonry, sturdy wooden beams and pillars). In the vicinity of place de Notre-Dame: The **Gothard** (typical fondue from the Fribourg area) with its young, trendy crowd; **Les Arcades**, a more relaxed restaurant and bar; **La Cave** (basement dance hall situated below the Hôtel de la Rose) has a fine vaulted cellar with thick stone walls and opens its doors at 10pm, although the place livens up later in the night. **Banshee's**, a pub offering a remarkable choice of beers and live folk music on weekends, is the place to go, especially on St Patrick's Day, when the atmosphere is at its wildest. The **Baccara** nightclub in the **Hôtel au Parc** has a DJ.

Murten★★

Murten has a yachting marina which attracts visitors. This former fortified city, which has kept most of its ramparts and towers, exudes picturesque charm.

✎WALKING TOUR
Hauptgasse
The main street runs through the heart of the **old town** with arcaded houses, fountains and the Bern Gateway, surmounted by a graceful pinnacle.

◯ *Take Deutschekirchgasse which starts just before the Berntor, go around the German Protestant church, behind which a wooden stairway leads to the walls.*

Stadtmauer★
Take the wall-walk, covered with an attractive timber roof, to the right. It affords pretty views over the old town, the castle and the lake. Mount Vully and the Jura foothills rise on the horizon. At the end of the wall-walk, climb the tower for views of the castle and the lake in the distance.

◯ *Retrace your steps and leave the wall-walk by the square tower.*

Schloss
Built in the 13C by Duke Peter of Savoy, this is a grim, imposing castle.

Historisches Museum
◷*Open Tue–Sat 2pm–5pm, Sun 10am–5pm and Mondays on public holidays.* ≋*6CHF, children 2CHF.* ✆*026 670 31 00. www.museummurten.ch.*
The historical museum is located in the town's restored 18C watermill. Exhibits include prehistoric and Gallo-Roman relics, local historical objects from the Middle Ages to the 18C, Burgundian treasures, and exhibits on the crucial Battle of Murten.

▶ **Population:** Fribourg 6 024.
⌖ **Michelin Map:** National Map 729: F5
▤ **Info:** Französische Kirchgasse 6 – 3280. ✆026 670 51 12. www.murten tourismus.ch.
◖ **Location:** On the eastern shore of Lake Murten. Alt. 458m/1 503ft.
◉ **Don't Miss:** The wall-walk on Stadtmauer.
◷ **Timing:** Allow at least two hours to visit the sights.
♙♙ **Kids:** Papiliorama— tropical forest environment.

Rathausgasse
This street leads to the small **French church**, with its single nave and ogival-vaulted choir.The balcony has views of the lakes and the foothills of the Jura mountains in the distance.

◯ *Französischegasse leads to the Berntor and back to the main street.*

NEARBY
Murtensee (Morat Lake)
The Murtensee runs parallel to the northern part of Lake Neuchâtel and is linked to it by the Broye Canal. Lake Murten has a bird sanctuary on its north shore and a beach on its south shore.

♙♙ Papiliorama-Nocturama
At Kerzers(Chiètres), 13km/7.5mi NE of Morat. ◷*Open summer, 9am–6pm; winter, 10am–5pm.* ≋*18CHF.* ✆*(0)31 756 04 61. www.papiliorama.ch.*
The **Papiliorama** and **Nocturama,** housed in two enormous bubbles, give visitors a chance to experience tropical forests. The Papiliorama exhibits very humid tropical heat, and the cooler Nocturama introduces animals from South America in a moonlit atmosphere. Unusual creatures here include the spectacled owl, the paca, the nine-striped armadillo, the night monkey and the ocelot.

Neuchâtel★★

Neuchâtel enjoys a charming site between its lake, with 4km/2.5mi of quays, and Chaumont Hill. The pleasant, attractive town stands in the middle of vineyards; its pale ochre houses prompted Alexandre Dumas to say it was carved out of a pat of butter. The silhouettes of the collegiate church and the castle dominate the scene.

OLD TOWN
Lake Neuchâtel

This is the largest wholly Swiss lake, being nearly 38km/23.6mi long and 8km/5mi wide. Canals used by pleasure boats join it with Lake Biel and Lake Murten. Its iridescent waters and hilly, vine-clad shores are favorite subjects for painters and writers; André Gide is one of many to have been inspired in the past.

A BIT OF HISTORY

Middle Ages – The name Neuchâtel is derived from a structure built as a stronghold during Burgundian rule (1011). Later, the town became the property of the French Orléans-Longueville family. It is said that in order to celebrate his entry into the town during a 1657 visit, Henri II of Orléans had 6 000l/1 585 gal of the local red wine poured into the Griffin Fountain, which still stands in rue du Château. Neuchâtel became the personal property of the King of Prussia after 1707.

Struggle for independence – After being placed under the rule of Marshal Berthier (Chief of Staff of Napoleon I) as a principality (1806-14), Neuchâtel joined the Swiss Confederation in 1815 and was then in a peculiar political position as a Swiss canton bound to the King of Prussia.

An independence effort in 1831 failed, but succeeded in 1848, and the Republic was proclaimed. The King of Prussia finally recognised the canton's independence in 1857 but kept the courtesy title of Prince of Neuchâtel. The French

▶ **Population:** Neuchâtel 32 592.
Michelin Map: National Map 729: E5
Info: Hôtel des Postes. ℰ(0)32 889 68 90. www.juradreiseenland.ch.
Location: At the feet of the Jura hills in western Switzerland. Alt. 440m/ 1 444ft.
Parking: It is easiest to use public or hotel car parks.
Don't Miss: The old town or an excursion to the observation tower at Chaumont.
Timing: A stay of at least two days is recommended in order to enjoy the most important sights.

spoken at Neuchâtel is considered by many to be the purest in Switzerland. Neuchâtel today is an important watch and clock research centre, whose observatory gives the official time to all of Switzerland. It is also a wine market— a great wine harvest procession takes place here in September.

SIGHTS
Old Town★

Guided tours on request only 130CHF for 25 people. Contact the Tourist Office ℰ(0)32 889 68 90.

A picturesque quarter (rue du Château, rue du Trésor, rue du Seyon, rue du Pommier, rue des Moulins) with old houses, 16C and 17C fountains (Fontaine de la Justice, Grand-Rue; Fontaine du Banneret, on the corner of rue du Château and rue du Trésor; Fontaine du Lion, on the corner of rue du Temple-Neuf and rue du Bassin) and defensive towers, extends between the town hall (1788), a classical building by the architect and painter Paris (1747–1819), from Besançon, and the group formed by the collegiate church and the castle. On the oblong Place des Halles (Market Square)

are 17C houses, and, at the far end, the Renaissance house Maison des Halles.

Collegiate Church and Château★

Open daily. Guided tours Apr–Sept, Mon–Sat hourly 10am–noon, 2pm–4pm, Sun and public holidays at 2pm, 3pm, 4pm. No charge. ℘(0)32 889 60 00. www.collegiale.ch.

The **collegiate church** is a fine 12C and 13C construction with multicoloured glazed tiles, and was heavily restored during the 19C. A statue of the protestant reformer **Guillaume Farel** (1489–1565) faces the main church entrance. Under an arcade in the chancel, the cenotaph of the counts of Neuchâtel (14C) is a striking example of medieval sculpture: This superb stone composition comprises 14 stiff, impressive polychrome statues depicting knights and noblewomen at prayer. The south portal, Romanesque, decorated with archivolts and carved capitals, is flanked by the statues of St Peter and St Paul.

The **Castle** (15C and 16C, restored) is the seat of the cantonal government. The main entrance gate is flanked by two crowned towers and embellished with broken arches. Under the passageway, the arms of Philippe de Hochberg, Lord of Neuchâtel, can be seen. In the northern wing, you may visit the former kitchen area, the antechamber, the semicircular Great Council Hall, seat of the cantonal government (note the stained-glass windows by Georges Froidevaux, representing municipal coats of arms), and the Knights' Hall, the largest room in the castle, used for receptions.

In the south wing, visitors are shown the room named after Mary of Savoy, niece of Louis XI and wife to Count Philippe de Hochberg (the count's arms hang above the stone fireplace), the Philippe de Hochberg Gallery, and the States' Room or Tribunal Room, whose walls recount the history of the Neuchâtel district. The wall-walk offers lovely views of the town.

Prisons Tower

Open Apr–30 Sept, 8am–6pm. 2CHF. ℘(0)32 717 75 00.

The Prison Tower sits at the foot of the hill on which the castle stands, in rue Jehanne-de-Hochberg. The interior contains two wooden dungeons used until 1848 and two maquettes of Neuchâtel from the late 15C and late 18C. The viewpoint affords a fine **panorama** of the town and the lake.

Art and History Museum★★

Start from the Fine Arts section. Open Tue–Sun 11am–6pm. Closed 26 Sept, 1 Jan, 24, 25 and 31 Dec. 8CHF. No charge Wed. ℘(0)32 717 79 25. www.mahn.ch.

Fine Arts (*Upper floor*) – A staircase decorated with frescoes by Paul Robert and stained glass by Clement Heaton leads to this part of the museum, which houses a retrospective of Swiss painting occupies five halls, presenting works by Léopold Robert (*Weeping Woman at the Water's Edge*), Ferdinand Hodler (*Autumn Evening*) and Albert Anker (*Bernese Peasant Reading his Newspaper*). Another room is largely devoted to French Impressionism (*The Boat-Workshop* by Monet).

History and Decorative Arts (*Ground floor and mezzanine*) – A series of large and small galleries display regional crafts and the history and lifestyle of the

Art and History Museum is noted for three 18th century "automata"

canton via collections of gold and silver plate, coins and porcelain. Gallery 4 includes timepieces from Neuchâtel and three delightful **automata**★★, made in the 18C by Jaquet-Droz and Sons as well as by Jean-Frédéric Leschot: they are the Musician, the Writer and the Draughtsman. Do not miss the admirable **Strübin Collection**★, presenting weapons, armour, and uniforms from the French Revolution, the First Napoleonic Empire, the Restoration and the Second Empire.

Museum of Ethnography★

🕐 *Open Tue–Sun 10am–5pm.* 🕐 *Closed Mon, 1 Jan, 24, 25 and 31 Dec.* 🎫 *8CHF. No charge Wed.* 📞 *(0)32 718 85 60. www.men.ch.*

The **Museum of Ethnography**'s modern annex is used exclusively for themed temporary exhibits. The northern façade has a huge mural, *The Conquests of Man,* by the Swiss painter **Hans Erni**.

Ground floor rooms are dedicated to Ancient Egypt, with collections of *shabti* statuettes and funerary boats, wooden sculptures dating from the 6th and 10th Dynasties, and exhibits explaining the ritual of mummification. Another room displays artifacts from the Himalayas, including Tibetan statues and a collection from Bhutan. On the first floor is the private study of the traveller and collector Charles-Daniel de Meuron (1738–1806), containing his collections. This floor also houses traditional ethnographical collections, with exhibits that include a Tuareg tent, spears, Angolan musical instruments, masks from New Caledonia, Nigeria and Angola, a reliquary head from Gabon and an androgynous "Uli" statue from New Ireland, near Papua New Guinea.

Quai Osterwald

Viewing table. Superb **view**★★ of the lake and the Alpine range.

👥 Natural History Museum

🕐 *Open Tue–Sun, 10am–6pm.* 🕐 *Closed 25 Dec and 1 Jan.* 🎫 *8CHF.* ♿ 📞 *(0)32 717 79 60. www.museum-neuchatel.ch.*

The Natural History Museum houses exhibitions of mammals, as well as several species of aquatic and sylvan birds, displayed in dioramas which reproduce their natural setting.

Hôtel Du Peyrou

An elegant building in the style of Louis 16th which was built in the eighteenth century by the financier DuPeyrou; a friend of Jean-Jacques Rousseau.

The entrance allows visitors to appreciate the clean lines of the outside of the building and leads to a French style garden. The centre piece within a water feature is a statue, the Bather, by A. Ramseyer.

Red Church★

The Église Notre-Dame de Neuchâtel is a neo-gothic structure, built between 1897 and 1906, which was classified as a national monument in 1986. Fourteen years of restoration then took place. The style of the church is certainly original, from its artificial stone walls and vaulted ceilings, to which coloured cement (reminiscent of Alsatian work) was added, to its British Victorian Gothic and even Portuguese influences.

There is also an unusual gallery as well as a ceiling adorned with 10 000 stars. Above the main altar is a splendid depiction of Christ created by the Swiss sculptor Marcel Feuillat in the early twentieth century. The stained glass windows, installed in 1903 are also notable.

Dürrenmatt Centre

74 Chemin du Pertuis-du-Sault. The centre is located a little farther out of town than the Jardin Botanique. Bus number 9, alighting at the Chapelle de l'Ermitage. 🕐 *Open Wed–Sun 11am–5pm.* 🎫 *8CHF.* 📞 *(0)32 720 20 60. www.cdn.ch.*

Although Swiss author Friedrich Dürrenmatt is best known as a novelist and playwright, he was also an avid artist who wanted his paintings and drawings to be accessible to the public after his death. His widow donated the villa and garden he had purchased in 1952 to the Swiss Confederation and commissioned the Ticino architect Mario Botta to design an exhibition and research

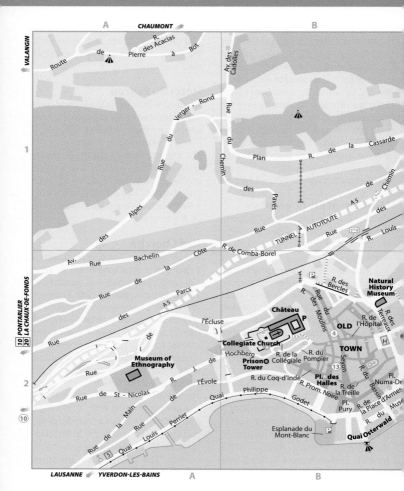

centre, which involved adding an unusual slate-covered building. *The Sistine Chapel* on the same floor as the cafeteria is one of the museum's outstanding works.

EXCURSIONS
Laténium★★ (at Hauterive)

▶ *4km/2.5mi E along the Bern road.*
⏱ *Museum open Tue–Sun 10am–5pm.*
⏱ *Closed 1 Jan, 31 Dec.* ∞*9CHF. First Sun of month no charge. Free access to the gardens.* ♿ *℘ (0)32 889 69 17. www.latenium.ch.*

The Laténium retraces 50 000 years of regional history via artifacts found during archaeological digs in the canton of Neuchâtel and on the site.

Visitors may wander through the lakeside **Parc de la Découverte** before or after the museum visit; exhibits include a lake house, piles symbolising a 6 000-year-old village, a Gallo-Roman barge, a Celtic bridge, and a pool showing the level of the lake in the distant past.

The modern **Musée d'Archéologie** features a permanent exhibition entitled *Yesterday… between the Mediterranean and the North Sea.*

The Gallo-Roman barge from Bevaix (copy) is the showpiece in the navigation section (*Room 4*); dating back to AD 182. Other exhibits cover the environment, daily life of the Celts, and the weapons, tools and jewellery from the site of **La**

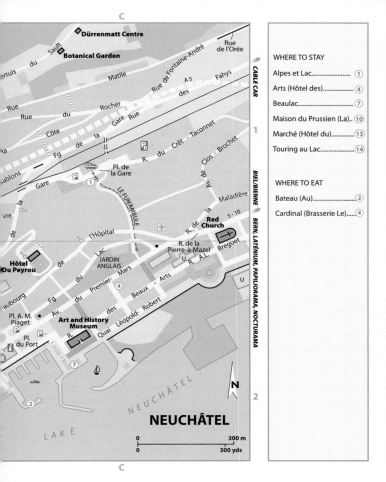

WHERE TO STAY

Alpes et Lac.................... ①
Arts (Hôtel des)................ ④
Beaulac............................ ⑦
Maison du Prussien (La).. ⑩
Marché (Hôtel du)........... ⑬
Touring au Lac................ ⑭

WHERE TO EAT

Bateau (Au)...................... ②
Cardinal (Brasserie Le)......④

NEUCHÂTEL

Tène (*Room 5*), which gave its name to the second phase of the Iron Age. Room 6, dedicated to lake dwellings, has a fine exhibition of everyday objects and a statue-menhir from Bevaix-Treytel, discovered in 1997.

Le Landeron

▷ *16km/10mi E of Neuchâtel, heading for the Bel/Bienne motorway.*
Not far from the Bel/Bienne lake, this well preserved medieval town is an ideal spot to wander between antique shops, art galleries and restaurants. The Town Hall, dating from the fifteenth century, is split between its civil duties and the Dix-Mille Martyrs Chapel. Of note is a museum of local history.

Chaumont★★

▷ *8km/5mi E. Take the road to Chaumont on the right.*
🅿 Leave your car at the upper Neuchâtel-Chaumont funicular station (alt. 1 087m/3 576ft). To the left of and behind the station is an **observation tower** (🚪*turnstile: 2.20CHF; 🖋(0)32 720 06 00*). An immense **panorama** of the Bernese Alps and the Mont Blanc Massif unfolds.

▷ *It can also be reached by the **funicular** (departures from La Coudre about once an hour, 9.30am–7.30pm; 🚪fare there and back: 9.20CHF; 🖋032 720 06 00; www.tn-neuchatel.ch) from La Coudre,*

3km/1.8mi from the centre of Neuchâtel, allow 12min.

Château de Valangin

▶ *4km/2.5mi N along the La Chaux-de-Fonds road.* ◐ *Open Mar–Oct, Wed–Sun 11am–5pm.* ☞ *7CHF.* ✆ *(0)32 857 23 83. www.chateau-de-valangin.ch.*

This castle dates to the 12C and was considerably extended under the Lords of Valangin in the 14C and 15C. Used as a prison in the 17C, it then became the property of the Neuchâtel Canton History Society at the end of the 19C. Rooms open to the public include the Salle Louis XVI (Louis XVI-style furniture); the Salle d'Armes (a fine collection of swords and sabres from the 17C–19C); the Salle des Chevalier (sideboards, beautiful sculpted wedding chests, Neuchâtel clocks and watches); the Salle René de Challant, named after the Lord of Valangin; the Salle de Guillemette de Vergy (lace cushions and *abigans*, globe-shaped objects used by lacemakers); and the oratory (Neuchâtel lace, an important industry in the 18C, along with exhibits of clock- and watchmaking and painted canvases, also known as Indian canvases).

Visitors may also tour the guardroom and the prison cell known as Farel's cell, where the French reformer is said to have been imprisoned.

🚗 DRIVING TOURS

1 LAKE NEUCHÂTEL

From Neuchâtel to Estavayer. 65km/40.6mi. 45mins without visits.

This drive, as the name indicates, is a tour of the Lake passing through villages and pleasant small towns giving a choice of regional roads or motorways if you are pressed for time.

Auvernier

This charming village which is both a centre for wine production and a residential haven, is centred around its fountains, a church dating from the 15C and a pretty château from the 16C.

▶ *Leave Auvernier by rue de la Bâla and continue 1.5km/0.9mi.*

Colombier

This village near Lake Neuchâtel is renowned for its white wines. It is dominated by its imposing castle, built in the 15C in Late Gothic style and enlarged during the two following centuries. In 1762 the philosopher **Jean-Jacques Rousseau** stayed at the castle, which remained the property of the counts of Neuchâtel for many years. Today the building is a barracks and military museum.

Military Museum

◐ *Open late Feb– 23 Dec, Tue–Sun 10am–noon, 2pm–5pm; otherwise by request.* ☞ *Guided tours upon request.* ☞ *9CHF.* ✆ *(0)32 889 54 99. www.chateau-de-colombier-ne.ch*

Patriotic frescoes adorn the walls of the Knights' Hall on the first floor and, on the second floor, important historical events in medieval Switzerland are highlighted. Also displayed are hundreds of arms (14C–20C), either cutting and thrusting weapons or firearms, armour, flags and regimental memorabilia (portraits, uniforms, etc). A large gallery on the third floor exhibits cannons. There is also a display of textiles made in the area in the 18C and 19C.

▶ *Drive SW on the same road for 3km/1.9mi.*

Boudry

10km/6.2mi S along the Yverdon road or by tramway, starting from Esplanade du Mont-Blanc.

This small medieval-looking town was the birthplace of the French revolutionary leader **Jean-Paul Marat**, editor of *L'Ami du Peuple*, murdered in his bath by Charlotte Corday in 1793. A sculpture called *Marat-L'œil* has been erected in his honor near the house where he was born. This 14m/46ft-high structure in painted steel slowly revolves, creating dazzling effects of light. The renowned chocolate manufacturer **Philippe Suchard** was born at 7 rue Louis-Favre in 1797 and spent many childhood years in the house at number 37, which is now the town hall.

The 13C–16C castle, which served alternately as a counts' residence and a prison, houses the **Musée de la Vigne et du Vin** (○open Wed–Sun 2pm–6pm; ○closed for 3 weeks after Christmas; ☎7CHF, children 5CHF; ℘(0)32 842 10 98; www.chateaudeboudry.ch) founded by the Compagnie des Vignolants. The wines of Neuchâtel are made with grapes grown on a vineyard extending between Neuchâtel Lake and the Jura. The visit begins with a history of the wine bottle, ranging from the amphora to the wine box, and provides a review of regional wine-making from the 18C through today. The exhibition explains the work of the wine-grower, defined by the seasons and the equipment used, diseases of the vine, harvesting techniques, and the process right up to bottling.

⊙ Follow the A5 towards Lausanne and take exit 3.

Grandson★
Alt. 440m/1 442ft.
Maison des Terroirs. ℘(0)24 445 60 60. www.grandson-tourisme.ch .
Situated near the southern end of peaceful Lake Neuchâtel, not far from the foothills of the Jura, the little town of Grandson was the backdrop to a major historical event: the humiliating defeat suffered by Charles the Bold, Duke of Burgundy, in 1476.

Castle★★
○Open Apr–Oct, 8.15am–6pm; Nov–Mar, 8.15am–5pm. ○Closed 1 Jan and 25 Dec. ☎12CHF. ℘(0)24 445 29 26. www.chateau-grandson.ch.

The first stronghold was built at the beginning of the 11C by the lords of Grandson, but the castle as we know it today dates from the 13C. After 1476 Grandson became the property of the town of Bern and Fribourg; the castle became the bailiffs' residence and was rearranged inside. Its high walls, large round towers and a covered watch-path, occupy a remarkable **site**★★ on the shore of the lake. There are rooms of historic interest and collections of ancient arms. The wall-walk particularly should be seen, also the Knights' Hall (fine Renaissance stalls), a museum devoted to the Burgundian wars (dioramas) and to Charles the Bold, the great armoury, the fortresses' museum, the dungeons and the chapel as well as a museum devoted to the Grandson District. An **Automobile Museum** occupies the basement. The collection includes an 1898 Delahaye as well as the 1927 white Rolls-Royce Phantom which once belonged to Greta Garbo.

Église St-Jean-Baptiste
The church is half-Romanesque, half-Gothic, with a striking contrast between the very simple nave and the chancel, which is lit by many stained-glass windows. A fine fresco depicting the Entombment is in the chapel on the south side of the chancel. The acoustic

---

The Battle of Grandson

Charles the Bold, Duke of Burgundy and rival of the King of France Louis XI, longed to recreate former Lotharingia, which extended from the Alps to the North Sea including the Swiss Confederation. In 1476, the duke's troops besieged the city of Grandson and its castle and the garrison was forced to surrender. Charles the Bold ordered his enemies hanged. The Confederates raised an army of around 18 000 men and marched on Grandson. It was a cruel, bloody battle. The Confederates defeated the Burgundians, who only survived by fleeing. Charles abandoned the whole of his camp: horses, artillery, and his precious treasure, which accompanied him on all his campaigns. This bitter Battle of Grandson is a famous landmark in Swiss history and has inspired many authors, novelists, and playwrights.

drums are also noteworthy. Leave the church, go around to the east end and the fountain (1637); then, to the right of the church, note the former Bailiff's House, which has a sun with a human face supported by savages, wearing loincloths and brandishing clubs, carved on its pediment.

▷ *Follow the road along the Lake shore for 4.5km/2.8mi.*

Yverdon-les-Bains

Alt. 439m/1 440ft.
2, avenue de la Gare. ☎(0)24 423 61 01.
www.yverdonlesbains-tourisme.ch.
Yverdon-les-Bains is a well-known spa because of the healing properties of its waters, which feature a high content of sulphur and magnesium, and which for many centuries have sprung from a depth of 500m/1 640ft. A pleasant lake side beach also adds to the town's attractions. A group of menhirs, known as the Promenade des Anglais are the remains of a Celtic settlement. The only Roman remains are a *castrum* (fortified citadel), located near the graveyard. The town hall (Louis XV façade) is worthy of attention.

Castle

This castle dates from the 13C, built by Peter II of Savoy, who captured the town in 1259 and erected this imposing fortress with its four round towers. After extensive restoration, the castle has become an important arts centre, housing the **Museé d'Yverdon et région** (☉open Jun–Sept, Tue–Sun 11am–5pm; Oct–May, Tue–Sun 2pm–5pm; ☉closed 1 Jan and 25 Dec. ▭8CHF; ☎(0)24 425 93 10. http://www.musee-yverdon-region.ch). The collections recall the history of the area since prehistoric times. Regional fauna is also represented. One room in the northeast tower presents an exhibition on the famous teacher Pestalozzi (ⓖsee TROGEN).

Maison d'Ailleurs

☉Open Tue–Fri, 2pm–6pm, Sat–Sun, 11am–6pm. Public holidays 2pm–6pm ▭12CHF, children 8 CHF. ☎(0)24 425 64 38. www.ailleurs.ch.
This unique museum dedicated to science fiction, utopia, and extraordinary journeys hosts temporary exhibitions of sculpture, art, and design. The amusing and often disturbing exhibits are displayed on three floors.

▷ *Follow the road along the Lake shore for 19km/11.9mi or the A1.*

Estavayer-Le-Lac

Alt. 454m/1 489ft.
 Place du Midi. ☎(026) 663 12 37.
www.estavayer-le-lac.ch.
The little town of Estavayer is built on a hill overlooking the south shore of Lake Neuchâtel. It has preserved its

---

A Brilliant Educator

Born in Zürich in 1746, **Johann Heinrich Pestalozzi**, the son of an Italian-born surgeon and the grandson of a priest, was influenced from an early age by the educational principles of Jean-Jacques Rousseau's *Émile*, to such an extent that he devoted most of his life to educating poor children, mainly in rural areas. His theories about education are clearly presented in *Léonard et Gertrud* (1781-87). In 1804, he accepted the invitation extended by the city of Yverdon to teach deprived children. The following year, he founded an institution on the castle premises, which gained a Europe-wide reputation. In 1806, he opened an institute for girls next to the town hall, in which the teaching standards were the same as those for boys. After twenty years in Yverdon, Pestalozzi returned to the Maison de Neuhof. He died in Brugg in 1827.

His philosophy and his achievements are neatly summed up in the words which he had inscribed on the pedestal of his statue: "I myself chose to live like a beggar, so that beggars might learn to live like men."

medieval city look (ramparts, towers, old houses). Its pleasure-boat harbor makes it a popular resort among water sports enthusiasts.

Église St-Laurent

A Late Gothic church crowned with a large square tower. Inside, the **chancel** is embellished with fine 16C stalls and a painted and gilded high altar in the Baroque style, enclosed by an elaborate wrought-iron screen.

Museum

⏱ *Open daily Mar–Oct, 10am–noon, 2pm–5pm; also Mon in Jul–Aug; Nov–Feb Sat, Sun only 2pm–5pm.* ⏱ *Closed public holiday and two weeks over Christmas and new Year.* 📞 *5CHF.* ✆ *(0)26 664 80 85. www.museedesgrenouilles.ch.*
This yellow sandstone mansion (1435) features tiered bay windows. It houses a Regional History Museum with a remarkable collection of stuffed frogs parodying human scenes (a card game, a political gathering), impressive collections of weapons and early engravings, a reconstruction of an old kitchen and utensils, and an exhibition room devoted to railway transport (Swiss trains, lanterns).

② LE VAL DE TRAVERS★

From Neuchâtel to Sainte Croix. 52km/ 32.5mi. Allow 1hr20mins without visits. 15 Clos-Pury. ✆ *(0)32 889 68 96. www.neuchateltourisme.ch.*

The River Areuse winds through this wide lush valley where fields of crops are interspersed with attractive towns, and slopes are blanketed with firs. This valley, one of the main crossover points between France and Switzerland (the road from Pontarlier to Neuchâtel passes through) offers two pleasant walks: the Areuse Gorges and the Creux du Van Nature Reserve.

Gorges de l'Areuse
© Christof Sonderegger/Switzerland Tourism

Gorges de l'Areuse★★

Tourisme Neuchâtelois – Val-de-Travers. ✆ *(0)32 889 68 96. www.neuchatel tourisme.ch.*
Located in the Val de Travers, which stretches from Lake Neuenburg across the Jura.

Hiking

🚶 *About 1hr on foot from Noiraigue railway station, where there is a car park.*
Beyond the Plan-de-l'Eau hydroelectric power station the path descends to follow the Areuse. Steep limestone sides of this gorge rise to jagged crests. A viewpoint halfway offers a plunging view of the narrowest part of the gorge where the torrent gushes over cascades. An old humpbacked bridge adds a romantic touch to this attractive **beauty spot**★.

Champ-du-Moulin

A surfaced path leads through the woods to this hamlet.
Champ-du-Moulin stands at the southern end of the gorge, don't miss the house where the famous French philosopher **Jean-Jacques Rousseau** lived in exile in 1764. Climb back up to Champ-du-Moulin railway station *(30min on foot)* for another good view of the southern end of the gorge. Take one of the many trains back to Noiraigue, or walk back.

Creux du Van★★

From the Ferme Robert allow 2hr30min there and back to walk up to the Soliat by a path to Dos d'Ane, 1km/0.6mi E of the Soliat.

This nature reserve (flora and fauna, protected chamois, ibexes) covering 11sq km/4sq mi, includes a typical example of a Jura blind valley crowned by a superb cirque of cliffs which open in a U-shape toward the Areuse Gorges and look down on rocks blanketed by fir trees. From its highest point, the Soliat (alt. 1 463m/4 800ft), there is a **view**★★ to the south onto Neuchâtel Lake and the of the Alps beyond.

From paths along the cliffs are views onto the hills of the nature reserve and onto the Jura heights.

▷ *From Noiraigues drive SW along the Valley towards Couvet 8.5km/5.9mi. The Mines are on the left before Couvet.*

Mines d'Asphalte

Guided tours (1hr30min) Apr–Oct at 10.30am and 2.30pm (Jul and Aug, additional tours 12.30pm and 4.30pm); Nov–Mar, daily at 2.30pm and Sun only at 12.30pm. Booking required before 11am. 16CHF. Temperature around 8°C and 1 km/0.6mi walk; wear warm clothes and good shoes. (0)32 964 90 64. www.gout-region.ch.

The first deposit of asphalt here was discovered in 1711 by Eirini d'Eyrinys. Two million tons were exported between 1830 and 1986. Visitors are first shown the **Mining Museum** (geological cross-sections, diagrams explaining asphalt extraction and exploitation, photographs of miners, of early mining equipment, lumps of asphalt etc), from where you continue on foot through several galleries (*helmets and electric torches are provided*) with stops for commentary on the various aspects of mining, bringing to life an important chapter in the industrial and social history of the Val de Travers.

▷ *From Couvet follow the signs for Môtiers 2.5km/1.6mi.*

Môtiers★

This village has well preserved 17C and 18C houses and a church, a former Gothic abbey rebuilt in 1679.

Its two small **museums** are worthy of attention: the **Rousseau Museum** (*guided tours (1hr) May to mid-Oct, Tue, Thu, Sat-Sun 2.30pm–4.30pm; 7CHF; (0)32 725 84 74*), located in the house Rousseau lived in from 1762 to 1765; and the local museum set up in an 18C home, known locally as the Maison des Mascarons.

Sainte-Croix/Les Rasses★

Alt. 1 069m/3 507ft.
Balcon du Jura Vaudois Tourisme.
Rue Neuve 10. (0)24 455 41 42.
www.sainte-croix.ch.

The twin townships of Sainte-Croix and Les Rasses lie on a sunny shoulder of the Chasseron, facing the Alps, approxi-

---

The Village of Sound

The history of Sainte Croix since the mid-19C is a good example of the adaptability of Swiss industry to international economic changes. Around 1850, like most small towns in the Jura, the village was making watches. The establishment in the United States of great watch and clock making factories with sophisticated machine tools caused a grave crisis at Sainte Croix, which turned to the musical-box industry. But when Edison developed the phonograph, the public lost interest in little musical boxes with their tinkling notes, considered childish. Sainte Croix moved with the times and switched to making gramophones. Since then the popularity of radio has required more changes in the workshops, but today musical boxes again play an important part in local industry and Sainte Croix is still "the village of sound".

mately 9.5km/6mi west of lake Geneva. They deserve a special place among Swiss Jura resorts for their commanding situation and their excellent tourist organization.

In winter, Sainte-Croix-les-Rasses is recommended for beginners or intermediate skiers who want to enjoy themselves rather than break records. Where cross-country skiing—the specialty of the Jura—is concerned, the resort offers more than 80km/50mi of marked trails.

Resorts

Sainte-Croix lies in a pastoral basin well protected from the winds at the mouth of the wooded pass of the Covatannaz Gorges, through which a wide section of the Bernese Alps can be seen.

Les Rasses★ is an annexe of Sainte-Croix with several hotels and scattered chalets enjoying a magnificent terraced **site**★★ within view of the Alps.

For those interested in hiking, there are more than 200km/124mi of paths.

⚄ Centre International de la Mécanique d'Art

☙⚄Guided tours (1hr15min) Apr–Sept 2pm, 3.30pm and 5pm; Jun-Aug extra tour at 10.30am; Oct–Mar 3pm. ⚅*Closed Mon, Christmas.* ⚆*14CHF.* ♫*(0)24 454 44 77. www.musees.ch.*
Step into this old music-box factory (display of disused machinery) and be transported into a wonderful, magical world where you discover the vibrant melodies coming from beautiful handmade instruments, masterpieces of acoustics and cabinetmaking.

This **music box museum** gives a new lease on life to musical boxes operated by discs or cylinders (the first model dates from 1796), radio sets, phonographs, pianos, street organs, automata (clowns, acrobats, Pierrot writing to Colombine), barrel organs and bird-organs. The **Salle Guido Reuge**, named after the famous industrialist from the Jura, contains a remarkable collection of exhibits donated by his widow, presented in a superb setting portraying a magic forest.

Musée Baud

☙⚄Guided tours (1hr) all year round on Sun and public holidays, 10am–noon, 2pm–6pm; Jul–Sept, daily 2pm–5pm. ⚅*Closed at Christmas.* ⚆*10CHF.* ♿ ♫*(0)24 454 24 84. www.museebaud.ch.*
This small museum displays and keeps in working order an exceptional **collection of old musical instruments**★ (Utrecht organ, barrel organ, player organ) and phonographs (note especially the ones dating from 1900, 1912 and 1920). Also exhibited and functioning are automata and animated scenes. In display cases, music boxes, mechanisms, bonbonnières, etc. can be admired.

▷ *Follow the same road to Sainte Croix and turn left to Les Rasses.*

Le Chasseron★★★

Alt. 1 607m/5 272ft. From Les Rasses, 3km/1.8mi – 1hr15min by a small, winding, tarred road (there is also a chairlift ending at Les Avattes, about 1hr walk from the summit).
Follow the road from Sainte-Croix to Les Rasses, 0.5km/0.3mi beyond the Grand Hôtel des Rasses. Turn left on the Chasseron road. At the Avattes crossroads, bear right toward the Hôtel du Chasseron. On emerging from the woods, leave the car at the hotel car park.

Walk to the Hôtel du Chasseron and the summit *(signpost)* where you will see a sweeping panorama of the Alps, the Jura and Lake Neuchâtel.

▷ *Take the Route du Château from Bullet and return to the main road. Turn left to Vuiteboeuf and right to Baulmes.*

Mont de Baulmes

Alt. 1 285m/4 216ft. From Sainte-Croix 4.5km/2.8mi – about 30min by a narrow mountain road, steep toward the end but wholly paved, plus 15min on foot there and back.
Leave Sainte-Croix by the level-crossing at the railway station and continue through the hamlets of La Sagne and Culliairy. Leave the car at the Chalet-Restaurant of Mount Baulmes, and go along an avenue to the viewing table, on the

edge of the precipice, for a **bird's-eye view** of the Swiss plateau, its lakes (in particular Lake Neuchâtel), and the Alps.

③ VUE DES ALPES ROAD★★

From Valangin near Neuchâtel to the Vue des Alps. 10km/6mi. Allow 45min to 1 hour excluding the walk up to the Tête de Ran.

Valangin

Between Neuchâtel and Valangin the road follows the wooded Seyon Gorges. This picturesque little town nestles at the foot of an attractive 12C and 15C castle protected by an imposing curtain wall with towers (levelled).
The 16C Gothic collegiate church (inside, interesting tombs and funerary plaques), the town gate with a clock tower and 16C to 17C houses make a nice, old-fashioned picture.

> *Drive N on the road to La Chaux de Fonds for 10km/6mi to the Vue des Alpes.*

Vue des Alpes★

Alt. 1 283m/4 209ft.
The viewing table will enable the visitor to fit names to the peaks in this tremendous **panorama**★: Finsteraarhorn, Jungfrau, Weisshorn, Dent Blanche, and Mont Blanc. The best light is in the late afternoon.

Tête de Ran★★

Alt. 1 422m/4 655ft. From the Vue des Alpes, 2.5km/1.5mi to the Tête de Ran Hotel, plus 30min on foot there and back to reach the summit, climbing straight up the steep ridge overlooking this hotel on the right.
Lovers of panoramic views may prefer this view (*steep stony path*) to that of the Vue des Alpes: Tête de Ran is better placed for a wide view of the Jura ridges in the foreground (Val de Ruz, Chasseral and Chaumont Chains), even though fir trees hide the view to the northwest; most of Lake Neuchâtel can be seen. On the way down through the fir trees of the southern slope are interesting views of the **Ruz Valley** depression. This immense "ship's hold" has struck geographers with the regularity of its

features: *ruz* has, therefore, become a scientific term to describe the first stages of erosion on the side of a mountain (*see INTRODUCTION*).

> *Take route number 20 to La Chaux-de-Fonds.*

La Chaux-de-Fonds –
See La Chaux-de-Fonds.

ADDRESSES

🛏 STAY

Hôtel du Marché – *4 place du Marché. ℰ(0)32 723 23 30. www.hotel-dumarche.com. 10 rooms.* Very pleasant hotel in the heart of the village. Rooms with toilets and showers on first floor.
Restaurant closed Sun.

Hôtel des Arts – *3 rue Pourtalès. ℰ(0)32 727 61 61. www.hotel-des-arts.ch. 46 rooms.* This friendly, recently renovated, modern hotel enjoys a good location near the lake and the town centre; suites & apartments available.

Alpes et Lac – *2 place de la Gare. ℰ(0)32 723 19 19. www.alpesetlac.ch. 30 rooms.* This hotel is located away from the centre but is conveniently close to the station. Views of town and lake.

Touring au Lac – *1 place Numa-Droz. ℰ(0)32 725 55 01. touringaulac.ch. 30 rooms. ⊿15.5CHF.* Conveniently located next to the harbour, a stone's throw from the bustling town centre with its pedestrian streets. Try to book a room with views of the lake.

Beaulac – *2 esplanade Léopold-Robert. ℰ(0)32 723 11 11. www.beaulac.ch. 94 rooms. Restaurant and Sushi Bar.* Splendid location on the lake shore, near the marina. Forget about price and reserve a room overlooking the lake.

La Maison du Prussien – *Gor du Vauseyon by rue de St-Nicolas. ℰ(0)32 730 54 54. www.hotel-prussien.ch. 10 rooms. Restaurant 11.30am –2pm 6.30pm midnight. Closed Sat afternoons and Sundays.* For a change of scene, take a room at this 18C former brewery nestled among trees, offering large, rustic-style bedrooms named after local people. The Chambre Jean Chambrier is most unusual.

♀/ EAT

One of the region's specialities is a cheese fondue known as "moitié-moitié", literally meaning half Gruyère, half Vacherin. Leave Neuchâtel and drive a few miles towards the Jura. Stop at one of the many inns dotting the countryside around Valangin, Dombresson or Vallon de St-Imier, settle down on the terrace and sample the fondue with a glass of white wine.

Brasserie Le Cardinal – *9 rue du Seyon. ℘(0)32 725 12 86. www.lecardinal-brasserie.ch. Closed Sun and last week Jul and first week of Aug.* The interior of this traditional brasserie is decorated with a mixture of brightly coloured tiles. The food is non-pretentious, delicious and not too expensive. Fish is a speciality and the menu is changed regularly. A "must".

Au Bateau – *Neuchâtel Harbour. ℘(0)32 724 88 00. www.aubateau.ch. Closed Mon.* If you dream of gliding along the water, then step aboard this old steamboat moored along the quays. Reasonable prices, delicious meat and fish dishes and an original setting.

⬚ SHOPPING

The main shopping area is concentrated in the largely pedestrianised old town, bordered by rue du Coq-d'Inde, rue de la Place-d'Armes, rue de l'Hôtel-de-ville and rue de l'Écluse.

The two main department stores, **Migros** (*12 rue de l'Hôpital*) and **Globus** (*14 rue du Temple-Neuf*) are also located here. On Saturdays, the **Place de Halles** market brims with regional produce, cheese, and olives.

BOAT TRIPS

Boat trips on the lake run through the year, although visitors will have a greater choice of excursions between May and October. For further information, contact the Société de Navigation sur les Lacs de Neuchâtel et Morat at the port. ℘(0)32 729 96 00.

⬚ THEATRE AND MUSIC

Théâtre du Passage – *Passage Max-Meuron. ℘(0)32 717 79 07. www.theatre dupassage.ch.* This theatre hosts comedies and dramas by both Swiss and non-Swiss playwrights.

Maison du Concert – *Rue de l'Hôtel-de-Ville. ℘(0)32 724 21 22. www.maison-du-concert.ch.*

Temple du Bas – *Rue du Temple-Neuf. ℘(0)32 717 79 08.* Classical and choral music.

⬚ NIGHTLIFE

The **Amiral Bar** of the Hôtel Beaulac features a lovely terrace looking out onto the sailing harbor. Themed evenings can be arranged and a wine exhibition is open to customers. The bar of the **Hôtel Beau-Rivage** attracts a friendly crowd and commands lovely views of the lake; there is a nightclub in the basement.

Train enthusiasts or those looking for an elegant but unique experience will love the **Orient Express**, located at the main station; cocktails, light food.

Visitors looking for good beer and a pub-like atmosphere should try the Highlander (*rue de l'Hôpital*) or **Sherlock's** (*rue du Faubourg-de-l'Hôpital*). The **Bleu Café** (*faubourg du Lac 27*), popular with students, is next to the Bio cinema and offers an all-inclusive café-cinema option, which includes a snack. The **King** café (*rue du Seyon 38*) has live jazz several nights a week.

Night-owls should make for the **B Fly** nightclub (*ruelle du Port, in the basement*), which has a dynamic DJ and is particularly lively on a Thursday night.

La Chaux-de-Fonds

La Chaux-de-Fonds is the biggest watch and clockmaking centre in Switzerland as well as being one of the most important towns for the Swiss farming industry. The town was almost entirely destroyed by fire in 1794 and afterwards rebuilt to a geometrical plan. The cradle of the clockmaking industry since the early 18C, this city also plays an important part in the production of microtechnology, electronics and mechanics, as well as in the tertiary sector.

▶ **Population:** Neuchâtel 37 240.

Michelin Map: National Map 729: E4.

Info: Tour Espacité, Place Le Corbusier. ℘(03)2 919 68 95. www.neuchatel tourisme.ch or www.chaux-de-fonds.ch (in French only).

▶ **Location:** The main town of the Neuchâtel mountains, La Chaux-de-Fonds lies in an upper valley of the Jura. Alt. 992m/3 254ft.

Don't Miss: The Musée International d'Horlogerie.

Timing: The watchmaking, history, and art museums are grouped together conveniently (allow at least half a day).

A BIT OF HISTORY
Local Celebrities

La Chaux-de-Fonds is the native town of the automaton maker **Pierre Jaquet-Droz** (1721–1790), the painter Léopold Robert (1794–1835), automobile designer **Louis Chevrolet** (1870–1941) ,and writer Frédéric Sauser, better known as **Blaise Cendrars** (1887–1961), who, with Guillaume Apollinaire, heralded the age of Surrealism. Like his literary work, his personal life was governed by his overriding passion for travel, both across land and in his own mind.

The Cradle of Clockmaking

From Geneva to the Jura – In the 16C, the reformer Calvin compelled the goldsmiths to turn their attention to making watches, forbidding them to make "crosses, chalices and other instruments of popery and idolatry." The development of this industry was spurred on by the arrival of French Huguenots driven from their country. Clockmaking soon spread from Geneva to the Neuchâtel Jura.

Daniel Jean Richard and the Horse Dealer – In 1679 a horse dealer returning to the Neuchâtel mountains from London brought back a watch which was admired by everyone until, one day, it stopped. The people of Sagne, a village near La Chaux-de-Fonds, advised him to have his watch exam-ined by Daniel Jean Richard, who was said to be highly skilled. He managed to repair the watch, studied its mechanism and decided to make watches himself. This he did, using tools of his own design, and subsequently settled at Le Locle, where he trained many others. The watch industry gradually spread throughout the Jura.

A World-Famous Industry – Most of the watchmaking industry today is concentrated in French-speaking Switzerland, and especially in the Jura. Many firms are located in La Chaux-de-Fonds, Le Locle, Biel, Neuchâtel, Solothurn, and Granges. They employ about 32 000 white-collar employees and manual workers. Workshops have sophisticated technical equipment which enables them to produce a quantity of high-quality watches. However, perfection has always been very important to Swiss watchmakers. At present the precision tolerance for the industry's working parts is of the order of 1/400th of a millimetre—1/10 000th of an inch. In certain workshops, the daily production of 1 000 workers could be carried

Villa Turque

© Christof Schuerpf/Switzerland Tourism

Le Corbusier Villas

Charles-Édouard Jeanneret was born on 6 October 1887. After studying painting and architecture at the local art school, he embarked upon a European tour. In 1918 he gained recognition as a painter and published the *Purist Manifesto* with Amédée Ozenfant. "After Cubism" advocated formal simplicity, economy of means and mathematical precision without denying emotion. The same principles were to guide his work as an architect. In 1920 he changed his name and became known as Le Corbusier. The same year, together with Ozenfant and the poet Paul Dermé, he founded the literary magazine *L'Art Nouveau*, which remained in circulation until 1925.

Le Corbusier was an inventive man who believed in structuring man's habitat along vertical lines. He invented the "living machine," which illustrated his views on the relationship between society and technology. His accomplishments in the field of community housing stand out on account of their revolutionary conception; he established an artful balance between the different elements, combining a variety of building materials and using light to enhance the cement blocks and exploit their full potential. His work was by no means limited to Europe and many examples of his creative genius can be seen in Russia, Brazil, Japan and India. Strongly criticised or highly praised, Le Corbusier remains one of the undisputed masters of 20C architecture and his impact on modern urbanism was considerable. He died in 1965.

There are three Le Corbusier house which can be visited at La Chaux de Fonds.

Villa Turque – *167 r. du Doubs. ℘(0)32 912 31 23. 1st and 3rd Sat of each month, 11am–4pm. Visit 1 hour of which 20 min for film. No charge.* Built in 1916–17 for a clockmaker, Anatole Schwob, this house is the best known Le Corbusier creation in the town. The name of the house is thanks to its neo-Greek style, flat roof and terra cotta brick cladding. However, the project finally drove Le Corbusier to move to Paris and later it was bought by Ebel.

Maison Blanche – *12, ch. de Pouillerel. ℘(0)32 910 90 30. www.maisonblanche. ch. Fri–Sun, 10am–5pm. Visit 30min–1 hour. ⌾10 CHF.* Le Corbusier built this home for his parents in 1912, after a trip to the Orient. It was his first private project, built in a neo-Classic style, at odds from the Art Nouveau influences of the time.

Villa Fallet – *1 ch. de Pouillerel.* A young Le Corbusier was involved with the creation of this villa in 1906, thanks to Charles L'Eplattenier. The result is an Art Nouveau style with local influence.

away in a jacket pocket. Precision has improved with the introduction of computer technology. Together with chemical products and machinery, clockmaking is one of the country's largest export industries. It plays a major role in the economy, and in spite of fierce competition from Japan and Southeast Asia, it remains a key factor in the stability of Switzerland's balance of trade.

SIGHTS
Musée International d'Horlogerie★★

29, Rue des Musées ○*Open Tue–Sun, 10am–5pm* ○*Closed Dec 24, 25, 31, Jan 1.* ∞*15CHF.* ♿ *℘(0)32 967 68 61. www.mih.ch.*

Founded in 1902, this fascinating **International Watchmaking Museum** has been housed since 1974 in a concrete bunker. The museum illustrates the ways time has been measured throughout history, with more than 3 000 items from all over the world. The museum also has a centre for the restoration of antique clocks and watches; be sure to stop at the glassed-in workshops to watch craftsmen working. The main gallery displays instruments for measuring time and Renaissance, 17C (exquisite enamel watches) and 18C instruments. Marine chronometers, watches from the Neuchâtel region and other countries, as well as unusual astronomical instruments, musical clocks, and amusing 19C automata are also displayed.

UNESCO Recognition

La Chaux-de-Fonds and neighbouring Le Locale were recognised in 2009 by UNESCO for their exceptional universal value as examples of mono-industrial manufacturing towns. Successful urban planning has accommodated the transition from a cottage industry to 21C factory production, evident on a walk through the town centres, which reveal how residential housing and workshops stand side by side.

Continue on to the centre of scientific clocks and watches (astronomical, atomic and quartz-crystal clocks). The belfry offers a pleasant view of the museum's park; proceed into a raised gallery which introduces modern clockmaking techniques. Outside is the imposing **Carillon**, a 15t tubular steel structure made by the sculptor Onelio Vignando erected in 1980. Every quarter hour it chimes (the tune varies according to the season) and at night it offers a captivating light show.

Musée des Beaux-Arts★ (Fine Arts Museum)

33, Rue des Musées. ○*Open Tue–Sun, 10am–5pm.* ○*Closed Dec 24, 25, 31, Jan 1.* ∞*8CHF.* ♿ *℘(0)32 967 60 76. cdf-mba.ne.ch.*

Built in the 1920s in the Neoclassical style, the Fine Arts Museum is devoted to regional art in Switzerland and abroad. Beyond the entrance hall with mosaic tiling, rooms display works by artists Charles L'Eplattenier (*Springtime, The Doubs River*), François Barraud (*Self-Portrait*), Charles Humbert (*Friends*) and Charles-Édouard Jeanneret, later known as Le Corbusier (*Woman in Bathrobe, The Musicians*). Elsewhere, daily lives and working conditions of the local population are vividly illustrated by such artists as Édouard Kaiser (*Engraver's Workshop, Box Maker's Workshop*), Albert Anker (*The Grandparents*), and Édouard Jeanmaire (*Leaving the Stables*). Swiss painting is represented by the work of Félix Vallotton (*Nude with Green Scarf*) and Ferdinand Hodler (*Marignan Warriors*). The prestigious **René and Madeleine Junod Collection** features masterpieces of Modern Art, in particular from France: Delacroix (*St Sebastian Released by the Saintly Women*), Renoir (*The Colettes*), Derain (*L'Estaque*), Matisse (*Young Girls in a Garden*). It also includes pictures by Liotard (*Marie Favart*), Constable (*Dedham from Langham*) and Van Gogh (*Young Girl with Tousled Hair*). Abstract art is present with painters belonging to various movements that blossomed after 1950: Manessier (*The Passion of Our Lord Jesus Christ*), Bissière (*The Angel in* the Cathedral) and Graeser, Christen and Glattfelder for Concrete Art in Switzerland.

Musée d'Histoire Naturelle
On the 2nd floor (lift) of the main post office. ○*Open Tue–Sat, 2pm–5pm, Sun and public holidays 10am–5pm.* ○*Closed Dec 24, 25, 31, Jan 1.* ∞*6CHF.* ℘*(0)32 967 60 71. www.mhnc.ch.*

The **Museum of Natural History** houses a wonderful collection of stuffed animals. Various Swiss and exotic species (of African origin, particularly from Angola) of mammals, birds, and reptiles are exhibited in dioramas of their natural setting. A room devoted to marine fauna displays several hundred types of seashells.

Musée d'Histoire
○*Closed until spring 2013.* ℘*(0)32 967 60 88. http://cdf-mh.ne.ch.*

The **Local History Museum** is housed in a former mansion used for the meetings of the town council. A collection of 17C to 19C Neuchâtel interiors are on show on the first floor: Bedrooms with sculpted ceilings, kitchens complete with cooking utensils, etc. The Medal Room presents collections of local and foreign coins, along with medals bearing the effigy of famous personalities from Switzerland (Calvin, General Dufour, Le Corbusier) and abroad (Abraham Lincoln, Louis XVI, Queen Victoria).

Musée Paysan
SW of the town, at 148 Rue des Crêtets. ○*Open Apr–Oct, Tue–Sun, 2pm–5pm; Nov–Mar, Wed, Sat-Sun, 2pm–5pm.* ○*Closed 1 Jan, Mar and 25 Dec.* ∞*6CHF.* ♿*summer only.* ℘*(0)32 926 71 89. http://cdf-mpa.ne.ch.*

The **Peasant Museum** is located in an old Jura farmhouse (1612). Although restored, the farmhouse has preserved some Gothic elements (mullioned windows on the ground floor) of the original 1507 building. It is an imposing shingled structure with its triangular gable and discreet, carved decoration. The interior has a pine framework with a large central fireplace. The life of a wealthy 17C farmer is re-created. There is a clockmaker's workshop, a cheese room, a still, as well as furniture, utensils, tools, and porcelain stoves. Local lacemakers can be seen at work on the first Sunday of every month. The life of peasants is illustrated by temporary exhibitions held every year.

EXCURSIONS
La Sagne
▶ *10km/6.2mi S and after 4km/2.5mi by a road on the right which runs along the railway line.*

Fine 16C–18C Jurassian farms are interspersed along the road. Daniel Jean Richard was born in this village in the 17C. The church (15C and 16C) was partially restored in 1891 and more thoroughly in 1952 and 1983. The nave features ogive vaulting. Modern windows are glazed in plain glass in pale shades of green, yellow, gray, and violet.

Le Locle
▶ *9km/5.6mi from La Chaux de Fonds via Rue de Locle and Rue Girardet.*
31 rue Daniel-Jean Richard – 2400. ℘*(0)32) 931 43 30.*

Le Locle is in the Jura Valley, linked to Franche-Comté by the Rock Pass (Col-des-Roches). This small town owes its prosperity to **Daniel Jean-Richard**, a young goldsmith who introduced the art of clockmaking into the area during the 18C.

Musée d'Horlogerie★
○*Open May–Oct, Tue–Sun,10am–5pm; Nov–Apr, Tue–Sun, 2pm–5pm.* ○*Closed Mon (except on public holidays), 1 Jan and 25 Dec.* ∞*10CHF.* ℘*(0)32 931 16 80. www.mhl-monts.ch.*

The **Château des Monts** is an elegant 18C mansion on the heights of Le Locle, surrounded by a lovely park. The site houses a museum containing many superb artifacts from many countries and is seen as the indispensable complement to the Horology Museum of La-Chaux-de-Fonds. The ground floor is a showcase for 18C interior decoration: a large drawing room, an antechamber, a panelled dining hall, a library—all tastefully furnished and decorated—provide the charming setting for a splendid collection of clocks delicately worked in silver and gold. The AL Perrelet Room illustrates the history of clockmaking from the very first timepiece with automatic rewinding to the tiniest digital watch. The Maurice-Yves Sandoz Room presents clocks with miniature automatons, like the Carabosse fairy, a gilt copper figure portraying an old woman walking with great difficulty. The second floor explains the science of horology (old instruments, clocks, watches, chronometers, precision tools etc). Look around the workshop of a local clockmaker, faithfully reconstructed.

Musée des Beaux-Arts

☛ Closed to the public; check the website for re-opening date. ✆8CHF. ℘(0)32 931 13 33. www.mbal.ch.
In addition to rooms devoted to Swiss painting and sculpture in the 19C and 20C (Girardet, Koller, Kaiser, Mathey) the Fine Arts Museum features an interesting display of work by foreign artists.

Moulins Souterrains du Col-des-Roches

✎ Guided tours (1hr) May–Oct, daily 10am–5pm; Nov–Apr, Tue–Fri 2pm–5pm & Sat–Sun (guided visits only) 2.30pm & 4pm. ⏱Closed 24 Dec – 2 Jan. ✆14CHF. ℘(0)32 931 89 89. www.lesmoulins.ch. ☺Temperature is 7°C, so wear warm clothes.
Built in the 16C to use the waters of the Le Locle Valley as a new energy source, these underground mills expanded rapidly from the mid-17C to the late 19C: the gushing waters of the river activated huge wheels, which in turn operated beaters, baking ovens, and sawmills.
In the early 20C the mills were turned into slaughterhouses, subsequently abandoned, and then restored to their former glory. Exhibitions explain different types of mills, their roles and mechanisms. The downstairs grotto is certainly worth a visit, featuring numerous wells and galleries that the men had to dig with their bare hands. The grotto also contains several remarkable pieces

of machinery (gear mechanisms, flour mills, saws, superimposed wheels).

La Brévine

▶ 24km/15mi SW of La Chaux de Fonds.
This small plateau has received the nickname "Swiss Siberia" because of its bitter winters: it registers the lowest temperatures in Switzerland. The plateau is sprinkled with chalets and has as its centre La Brévine (alt. 1 043m/3 422ft) at the edge of an immense combe of high pastures.

🚶 HIKING
LE SAUT DU DOUBS

🚶 16km/10mi to the S, in the direction of Le Locle by car, then on foot (by a forest path bordering the E bank) 2hr15min there and back or 1hr plus return trip by boat. By boat: 1hr there and back plus 20min there and back on foot. ⏱Summer service May–Sept, departures every 45min starting at 10am. ✆Fare there and back 12.50CHF. ℘(0)32 932 14 14. www.nlb.ch.

Les Brenets

A small border town pleasantly terraced on the slopes which plunge into **Lac des Brenets**★. This lake was a bend in the Doubs transformed into a reservoir following a series of landslides. It is 3.5km/2mi long and averages a width of 200m/656ft. At one point its sides become extremely narrow, forming two basins: the first (average depth 10m/32.8ft) spreads over an area between gentle slopes; the second (average depth 30m/98ft) flows between abrupt limestone cliffs—crowned with fir, Norway spruce and beech trees—the crests of which, here and there, are said to resemble famous people in profile (Louis-Philippe, Calvin and others).
The federal cross painted onto the rock face in 1853 and the so-called Grotto of the King of Prussia can be seen on the Swiss side.

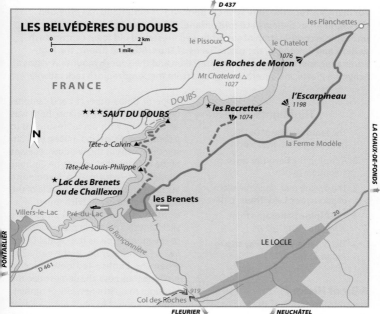

Saut du Doubs★★★

The waterfall can be reached by the landing stage which marks the end of the lake, via a forest path.

This famous waterfall, the overfall of Brenets Lake, 27m/89ft high, is far more spectacular when it is seen from the French side. The site is heavily wooded.

LES BELVÉDÈRES DU DOUBS

14km/8.75mi by car, towards Biaufond, then les Planchettes, leads to the hamlet of Recrettes. A further 2hrs (the circuit) on foot following a signposted route and you reach the three look out areas mentioned below.

After leaving Les Brenets in the direction of Le Locle, bear left at the crossroads onto the road towards Les Planchettes. The road passes through woods, climbs to the plateau, and arrives near the hamlet of Les Recrettes.

Les Recrettes viewpoint★

Alt. 1 074m/3 524ft. 30min on foot there and back.

From the belvedere there is a good **view**★ onto the loop of the Doubs made

by Châtelard Mountain on the French side and the hinterland covered with fir trees and pastures.

Just before the farm *(Ferme Modèle)* bear left onto a path *(private: close the gates after you)* and continue along it for about 700m/765yds until you are right by the cliff.

Point de vue de l'Escarpineau

Alt. 1 198m/3930ft.

From this wonderfully located view point it is possible to see the dam, the area around Chatelot, as well as the peaks over in France.

▷ *Turn left in front of the model farm. Before the village of Plancettes, take a tree lined road to the left.*

Les Roches de Moron

Alt. 1 076m/3 530ft.

Walk to the viewpoint near the restaurant, from where there is a plunging view onto the Doubs, hemmed in by the Châtelard Promontory and the Chatelot Dam.

BERN AND JURA CANTONS

For many visitors, the time spent in Bern and its hinterland has provided the highlight of their visit to Switzerland. No wonder, since it offers the unbeatable combination of superbly well preserved old town centres such as Bern and Solothurn, the glacial lakes of Thun, Biel and Brienz, the high-adrenaline sports playground of Interlaken and the superb mountain vistas at Schynige Platte, in Lauterbrunnen and from the Jungfraujoch rack railway.

Highlights

1 The **famous view** of Old Bern from the Rosengarten (p191)
2 A stroll in the **Baroque town** of Solothurn (p210)
3 The driving tour along the shore of photogenic **Lake Thun** (p214)
4 The **Alpine panorama** from Schynige Platte (p222)
5 The magnificent **railway trip** to Jungfrau (p224)

A Bit of History

The transformation of the belligerent, patrician society that used to characterise Bern to a tourist paradise could form a parable for the whole of Switzerland. It's difficult to conceive today the power of the city during the late Middle Ages up until the Napoleonic Wars, yet a glimpse of the grand throne of the town's mayor in the Historical Museum of Bern is enough to convince any doubters, for this was a seat fit for a king or an emperor. Unlike other city and cantonal democracies in Switzerland, Bern was an oligarchy with power restricted to a handful of patrician families: you can see their arms in the window recesses of the Münster that used to be Catholic chapels pre-Reformation. Napoleon's invasion ended abruptly the rule of the *ancien régime* along with much of its territory, and with typical diplomatic skill Bern succeeded in presenting and re-inventing itself as the capital of the Swiss Confederation. In the early 20C when the English-led new craze of Alpinism took hold, the Bernese had the foresight to build a network of tunnels, cable cars and railways to reach villages and mountain tops that transformed the landscape and catapulted the canton into the forefront of the tourism industry. Finally, in the 1960s and 1970s when the political cracks threatened Swiss unity with the troubles in the Jura, Bern defused the explosive situation via peaceful and constitutional means, as if final proof was needed of its political maturity.

Solothurn on the bank of the Aare

© Roland Gerth/Switzerland Tourism

La Neuveville— a town in the canton of Jura

Stefan Boegli/Jura Bernois Tourism/Switzerland Tourism

Jura: Switzerland's Newest Canton

In 1815 the Congress of Vienna, granted the Jura (largely French-speaking and Catholic) to Bern (largely German-speaking and Protestant) in compensation for the loss of the territory of Vaud. In 1947 a Jura independence initiative was born and by the 1960s a secession struggle had began involving riots, arson attacks and embassy occupations by the separatist *Béliers* (Battering Rams) movement. There was a whiff of Northern Irish politics in the air for a while, as the southern part of the Jura (French-speaking but Protestant) wanted to remain under Bern and formed its own anti-independence group the *Sangliers* (wild boars). A series of constitutional referendums defused the situation and northern Jura achieved canton status in 1979. Still, the question never really went away: a *Béliers* member, Christophe Bader, died in Bern in 1993 when his explosive device detonated early; in 1994 the German-speaking district of Laufental seceded from Jura and joined Basel-Land; and in 2004 a Federal Commission proposed the unification of the two Francophone Jura sections as two half-cantons.

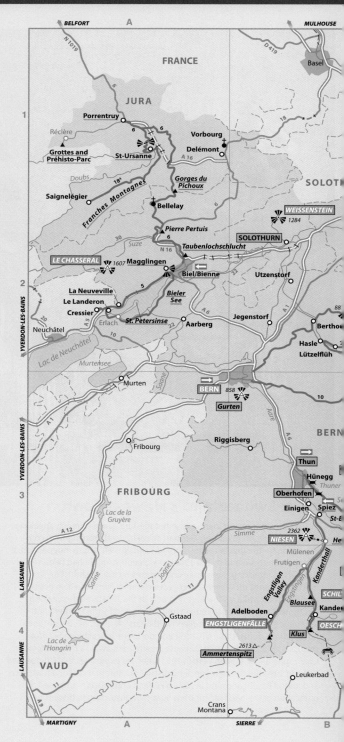

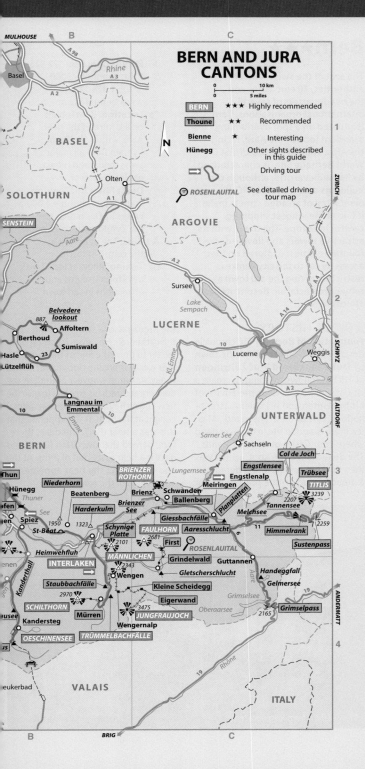

BERN AND JURA CANTONS

BERN	★★★	Highly recommended
Thoune	★★	Recommended
Bienne	★	Interesting
Hünegg		Other sights described in this guide
		Driving tour
ROSENLAUITAL		See detailed driving tour map

0   10 km
0   5 miles

N

MULHOUSE

Basel

BASEL

SOLOTHURN

...SENSTEIN

Olten

ARGOVIE

Aare

Rhine

A 98
A 3
A 2
A 1
A 2

Sursee

Lake Sempach

LUCERNE

887
Belvedere lookout
Affoltern
Berthoud
Sumiswald
Hasle
Lützelflüh
23

Langnau im Emmental

Emme

Kl. Emme

Lucerne

Weggis

ZURICH
SCHWYZ
ALTDORF

A 2
A 14
A 4

BERN

Thun

Hünegg
Niederhorn
Beatenberg
...ofen
...en   Spiez
St-Béat
Thuner   See
1950   1323

Harderkulm

Heimwehfluh

INTERLAKEN

Staubbachfälle
2970
SCHILTHORN
...usee
Kandersteg
OESCHINENSEE
...us

Mürren
3475
JUNGFRAUJOCH
TRÜMMELBACHFÄLLE

MÄNNLICHEN
2343
Wengen

Schynige Platte
2101

FAULHORN
2681

First
ROSENLAUITAL

Grindelwald
Gletscherschlucht
Kleine Scheidegg
Eigerwand
Wengernalp

Guttannen

BRIENZER ROTHORN
Schwanden
Ballenberg
Brienz
Brienzer See
Giessbachfälle
Aareschlucht

Meiringen

Engstlenalp
Engstlensee

Planplatten

Melchsee
Tannensee
2207

Col de Joch
Trübsee
TITLIS
3239

UNTERWALD

Sarner See
Sachseln
Lungernsee

11
Himmelrank
2259
Sustenpass

6

Aare

Handeggfall
Gelmersee
Grimselsee
Oberaarsee
2165
Grimselpass

19

ANDERMATT

VALAIS

...eukerbad

Kandersee

Rhône

19

BRIG

ITALY

187

Bern★★★

The seat of the Swiss federal authorities, 70 embassies and the headquarters of several international organisations, Bern is situated on a spur overlooking a verdant loop of the Aare, facing the Alps. The old town, a UNESCO World Heritage Site, is characterised by its medieval grid, although the buildings date from the 19C. Its 6km/3.7mi of arcaded streets make it one of the longest shopping centres in Europe. The town, with its attractive towers and flower-decked fountains, is best explored on foot: access by car to the city centre is restricted, giving the old town a rather provincial air, despite its lively atmosphere.

> ▶ **Population:** Bern 122 925.
> 🛈 **Info:** Bahnhof – 3000.
> 📞(0)31 328 12 12.
> www.berninfo.com.
> ▶ **Location:** Bern is built on a U-turn of the river Aare, within 1hr30min by train from all major swiss towns and is best explored on foot.
> 😊 **Don't Miss:** The Zentrum Paul Klee, with some 4 000 works by this native son; the Zytgloggeturm at noon.
> 👪 **Kids:** The Bear Park in the centre of town.
> 🕐 **Timing:** Allow at least two days for museums and attractions in Old town.

A BIT OF HISTORY

Foundation of Bern – A 15C chronicle describes the foundation of the town by **Duke Berchtold V of Zähringen** in 1191 as follows: Wishing to create a city, the duke asked for the advice of his huntsmen and his chief master of hounds. One of them answered, "Master, there is a good site in the river bend where your Castle of Nydegg stands." The duke visited the spot, which was then thickly wooded, and ordered that a moat be dug on the present site of the Kreuzgasse (a street running up to the cathedral). However, it was thought better to draw the line of the moat farther west, where the clock tower stands today. As game was very abundant the duke agreed with his advisers to give the new town the name of the first animal caught at the hunt. It so happened that this was a bear (*Bär*). The duke, therefore, named the town Bärn (Bern) and gave it a bear as its coat of arms. At the end of the 15C, the bear appeared in engravings of the town.

View of Bern from Rosengarten

GETTING AROUND

As much of the city centre is closed to cars, visitors are advised to explore Bern on foot, by **tram** or by **bus**. Passes (for 1, 2 or 3 days) can be bought at the Tourist Office or at hotels. A night bus operates from the railway station until 3.15am on Fri, Sat, and Sun (not included in passes). **Bicycles** can be rented from the rail station or Hirschengraben for free by producing a passport (20CHF deposit).

VISITOR'S CARD

This card, available from the Tourist Office, grants you free access to all forms of local transport except the night buses. (12CHF).

GUIDED TOURS

Tour of the town by bus (2hr) Apr–Oct, 2pm daily; Nov–Mar, Sat only. 24CHF. Tour of the old town on foot (1hr30min) Jun–Sept, 11am daily. 16CHF. Contact the Tourist Office for further information. *(0)31 328 12 12.*

Expansion – From the 14C to the 16C, Bern followed a clever policy of expansion and played a dominant part in the Confederation. Many annexations, such as those of Burgdorf and Thun after the struggle with the Kyburgs, secured its hegemony on both banks of the River Aare. In the 15C, the conquest of Aargau enabled it to extend to the Lower Reuss, and its resolute attitude in the Burgundian wars placed it in the front rank of Swiss cantons. In the 16C, by annexing the Gruyères and Vaud districts, Bern ruled over all the country between the Lower Reuss and Lake Geneva.

Bern in the Confederation – When the Constitution of 1848 was drafted after the defeat of the Sonderbund, Bern was chosen by common consent as the seat for the federal authority. The choice was amply justified on account of the leading political part the city had played for several centuries and its privileged position at the heart of the Confederation and at the dividing line between the Latin and Germanic cultures. Though the city became the seat of the Federal Chambers, the civil service and the federal postal and railway services, this did not make it the administrative centre of its country in the manner of London and Washington. The federal system prevented any one town from enjoying political supremacy.

Ferdinand Hodler

One of the most important Swiss painters of the 20C, Hodler was born in Bern in 1853 (d 1918 in Geneva). Orphaned at the age of 12, he was apprenticed to Ferdinand Sommer, a painter of Swiss landscapes for tourists in Thun. At 19 he went to Geneva to copy the romantic landscapes by Calame. With the help of his professor Barthélemy Menn (1815–1893), a student of Ingres and friend of Corot, Hodler broke with conventional painting. A trip to Spain (1878–79) enabled Hodler to admire the technique of Velázquez. During this period Hodler painted many landscapes: The Alps and Thun Lake were his preferred subjects.

Although the major artistic currents (Realism, Symbolism, Art Nouveau) of the time are echoed in his works, from 1885 Hodler branched off to adopt Parallelism. This style can be found in his allegorical works (*Night*, 1889–90; *Day*, 1899–1900), as well as his historical canvases (*The Defeat at Marignano*), which earned Hodler first prize in an 1897 competition organised by the Swiss National Museum in Zürich. At the end of his life, Hodler was painting what he called "planetary landscapes," curious compositions consisting only of lines and space, with no trace of life or death.

WALKING TOUR
OLD BERN★★

Allow 2hr30min.

The old town, rebuilt in yellow-green sandstone after the terrible fire of 1405, is full of winding streets and terraced gardens overlooking the river. From Easter to the end of October the main monuments are floodlit until midnight. In the summer, the sound of horse-drawn carriages echoes through the streets.

Holy Spirit Church

The Baroque Heiliggeistkirche was built between 1726 and 1729. Spitalgasse is a bustling street lined with arcades which boasts many shops. A Piper's Fountain (16C and 19C) stands in the centre.

Bärenplatz

In former days, this square was occupied by a large bear pit. Today it is a vast esplanade, a lively meeting place surrounded by pavement cafés.

Marktgasse★

The smart and lively Marktgasse, with luxury shops and many florists' windows, is the main street of the old town. Fine mid-19C houses present a series of arcades, lending remarkable unity to the whole. The 16C–17C fountain (Seilerbrunnen) is dedicated to Anna Seiler, who in 1354 provided the town with its first hospital. Farther on, the Marksman's Fountain (Schützenbrunnen, 1543) depicts a standard-bearer with, between his knees, a small bear wearing armour and firing a gun.

On **Kornhausplatz**, to the left, the Ogre Fountain (Kindlifresserbrunnen) represents an ogre devouring a small boy and holding other children in reserve under his left arm.

Zytgloggeturm★ (Clock Tower)

Guided tour May–Oct, daily 2.30pm. ⊜15CHF. ℘(0)31 328 12 12.

This famous Bern landmark acts as the reference point from which all distances from the city are measured. Built between 1191 and 1250, the clock

Old Bern towards Zytgloggeturm

tower once marked the western limits of the city. Note the 15C Jack (on the Kramgasse side of the gate) and the two ducal crowns above the gilded clockface. Chimes strike at four minutes to the hour, and the many painted **figurines** (15C–17C) then start to move: the cockerel crows, flapping his wings, a procession of bear cubs march to the sound of pealing bells, followed by a second cock crow. The god Chronos turns his apron upside down and the large bell sounds the hour, struck by Hans von Thann, a knight made of lime wood and dressed in gilded armor. At the same time, Chronos counts the strikes and waves his sceptre, while the lion turns his head. The show ends with a third cock crow. A tour inside the **clock** enables visitors to admire its elaborate, sophisticated mechanism.

Kramgasse★

Kramgasse is a more crowded extension of Marktgasse. Along Kramgasse notice the Zähringen Fountain (16C) with its bear wearing armour and holding the Zähringen coat of arms in his paw, and the Samson Fountain (16C), surmounted by a statue of the giant prising apart the jaws of a lion.

At nnumber 49 stands **Einsteinhaus** (⊙open Apr–Nov, Mon–Sat 10am–5pm; Oct–Dec, Tue–Fri 10am–4pm; ⊙closed public holidays, Jan, Feb; ⊜6CHF; ℘(0)31 312 00 91; www.einstein-bern.ch). It was here, on the second floor, that the great scientist Albert Einstein wrote his Theory of Relativity in 1905. Einstein spent seven years in Bern (1902–09). Visitors are able to view his study and bedroom, as well as a collection of portraits and photos. In 1909 Einstein was appointed Professor of Physics at Zürich University.

▷ *At the end of Kramgasse, turn left into Kreuzgasse leading to Rathausplatz.*

Rathausplatz is decorated with a fountain bearing a banneret (Vennerbrunnen) by Hans Gieng (1542).

City Hall

The Rathaus is the seat of the Bern Municipal Council (legislative assembly of the city of Bern) and the Grand Council (legislative assembly of the canton). It was erected between 1406 and 1417 and has been heavily restored, although its double staircase and covered porch make it one of the most typical buildings in the city.

Return to Kreuzgasse which leads to Gerechtigkeitsgasse, where the **Justice Fountain** stands. Its shaft is crowned by a Corinthian capital (1543).

Nydeggasse, which is a continuation of Gerechtigkeitsgasse, contains the Church of the Nydegg (*Nydeggkirche*) built in the 14C on the foundations of a 13C fortress.

Nydeggbrücke

The bridge spans the Aare and affords an attractive **view**★ of the quarters huddled in the meanderings of the river and the wooded slopes which overlook it.

⚌ Bear Park★

🕐*Open 8am–5pm (4.30pm in winter).* 🚫*No charge.* ℘*(0)31 357 15 15.*

The old bear pit has closed and a new larger and more animal-friendly bärenpark opened in October 2009. The bears of Bern have been local celebrities. They receive many visits, not only from tourists but also from the Bernese, who are particularly fond of them. Near the bear park, the **Bern Show** uses video and an animated model to recount the history of the town.

▷ *At the number 12 bus stop take the steepest path up signed Rosengarten.*

Rosengarten (Rose Garden)

From here, you have the best view of the **old city**★★★. The garden contains 200 varieties of roses, all kinds of irises and many rhododendrons.

▷ *Turn round. At the entrance to Gerechtigkeitsgasse turn left into Junkerngasse.*

Junkerngasse★

This street is lined with old houses. Note the **Erlacher Hof** at number 47, a fine Baroque dwelling influenced by French architectural style, now home to the city hall.

Approaching the cathedral from the east, there is a general view of the tall tower, the nave and flying buttresses, and the pinnacles surmounting the buttresses. Skirt the building to the left until you come to a fine terrace planted with trees and flowers. From the terrace there is a bird's-eye **view**★ of the Aare locks and, to the right, the Kirchenfeldbrücke, which spans the river over a distance of 40m/135ft.

St Vincent's Cathedral★

🕐*Hours vary significantly; 10am–5pm in summer.* 🕐*Closed Mon.* 🚫*No charge.* ℘*(0)31 312 04 62. www.bernermuenster.ch.*

One of the last great Gothic churches in Switzerland, the Münster St Vinzenz dates from 1421. Construction continued until 1573, and the bell tower, over 100m/328ft high, the highest in Switzerland, was only completed in 1893.

The splendid **tympanum**★★ of the main portal, by the Master Erhard Küng, was spared the destruction of the Reformation. It illustrates the Last Judgement (1495) with 234 figures, some of which are still painted. *The Damned* and the *Elect* are very realistically treated. There are statues of Prophets on the recessed arches, *Wise and Foolish Virgins* in the embrasures (*left and right respectively*) and *grisaille* frescoes dating from the early 16C on either side of the portal. The nave is a vast structure with reticulated vaulting and 87 painted keystones adorned with coats of arms. Note the Bern Bear Keystone over the choir. The chancel has great 15C stained-glass windows by Hans Acker, depicting the *Passion* and the *Crucifixion*; other windows depict the Victory of the 10 000 Knights, and the Magi. Stalls, which date from the Renaissance (1523), are richly sculpted with scenes from everyday life. Visitors who do not mind a climb can take the spiral staircase of 254 steps to the tower platform (⏰*open summer Tue–Sun, 10am–4.30pm (11.30am Sun); winter Tue–Sat, 10am–11.30am, 2pm–3.30pm (4.30pm Sat), Sun 11.30am–1.30pm;* ⏰*closes 30min before the cathedral;* ✆*4CHF;* ✆*(0)31 312 04 62/3)* for a **panorama**★★ encompassing, in the foreground, the various quarters of the town, with their fine reddish-brown tiled roofs, many turrets and belfries, the bridges over the Aare and, in the background, the majestically spreading chain of the Bernese Alps.

▷ *On leaving the cathedral, cross Münsterplatz and turn left into Münstergasse (several narrow covered passages leading to Kramgasse) to Casinoplatz. Just before reaching the bridge (Kirchenfeldbrücke) take Bundesterrasse on the right.*

Federal Palace
✎*Guided tours (45min) daily except Sat–Sun, at 9am, 10am, 11am, 2pm, 3pm and 4pm, preferably at 11am, 4pm for individual visitors. Book a day in advance.* ⏰*Closed public holidays and during parliamentary sessions (access to the public galleries only during this period).* ✆*No charge.* ✆*(0)31 322 85 22. www.bundeshaus.ch.*
The **Swiss Government** (Federal Council) and **Swiss Parliament** (National Council and Council of the States) are housed in the Bundeshaus, a heavy, domed building (1902), whose design was inspired by the Florentine Renais-

sance. A guided tour describes the workings of Swiss democracy (✆*see INTRODUCTION).* The view from the terrace encompasses the Aare, the town and, in the background, the Bernese Alps.

▷ *After the Bundesplatz, rejoin Bärenplatz and cross Kirchenfeldbrücke to Helvetiaplatz where you can find many museums.*

Note the Kunsthalle on your left—this is where Paul Klee's first exhibition was panned and where Christo's first wrapping installation in 1968 made him a household name. It is worth checking what is on show when you are around.

MUSEUMS
The following three museums are all on or around Helvetiaplatz.

Bern Historical Museum/ Einstein Museum★★
⏰*Open Tue–Sun 10am–5pm.*
⏰*Closed 26 Nov, 25 Dec.* ✆*18CHF (additional charge for special exhibits).*
✆*(0)31 350 77 11. www.bhm.ch.*
This French château-like building, constructed in 1881, contains a vast, historic, prehistoric, ethnographic and numismatic collection on the ground floor and basement and on the top floors it is devoted to the life and times of Albert Einstein who spent so much of his life in Switzerland.
The bottom two floors are divided in five sections: **Medieval concept of the world**: here are bronzes and gilded ornaments and sarcophagi from the Alemanni and Burgundian period as well as the originals from the Münster's Last Judgement Portal; **City of Bern**: the focus here is on the painting cycle from the Rathaus depicting the city's legendary foundation by Humbert Mareschet, a Huguenot refugee and the Dance of Death from the Dominical Convent in Bern painted by Niklaus Manuel; **War and Public Life**: here you will find mediaeval armour and weapons from chainmail to cannon balls; **Private Life**: domestic exhibits from the old patrician families of Bern; and **Glory and Decline**

of Ancien Regime: here there is almost a complete reconstruction of the old Council Hall in Bern (check out the Mayor's throne, fit for a King) as well as paintings and furniture that shows the power of the city's patriciate.

The first floor led through a sci-fi glass construction is an excellent multi-media exhibition of **Einstein's life**, from his birth in Ulm and his Jewish roots to his childhood in Munich, schooldays in Aarau, study in Zürich and life in Bern where he published the first relativity paper (the originals are all displayed) that changed science forever. It continues to his life in Berlin and escape to America up to his death in 1955. All this plus "special relativity in four easy lessons". Unbeatable.

Swiss Alpine Museum★★

○Open Tue–Sun 10am–5pm (Thu until 8pm) ○Closed 1 Jan, 1 Aug, 24, 25 and 31 Dec. ⊜12CHF. ℰ(0)31 350 0440. www.alpinesmuseum.ch.

Soon to be renovated and expanded, the Schweizerisches Alpines Museum is dedicated to the Alps, which cover 60% of the country's total area. Visitors view an audio-visual presentation called "A Mountainous Country." Several relief maps—the early ones date back to 1750—connect the famous summits and their valleys: Bietschhorn, the Matterhorn, Dents-du-Midi, Jungfrau, Säntis, Bernina, etc.

A series of interactive booths focus on specific aspects of the exhibition (history, geology, transportation and industry, tourism, climate, flora and fauna); all the commentaries are in German, French, English, and Italian. On the first floor "Mountains seen through Maps" covers the 16C–18C and is followed by presentations on art, popular traditions and regional lore, as well as habitat.

The last room is the raison d'être for any visit: it is decorated with seven huge canvases by Ferdinand Hodler, *The Climb and the Fall*, inspired by the conquest of the Matterhorn. It also presents the evolution of climbing gear and life-saving equipment in the Alps. In the centre there is a huge raised map of the Bernese Oberland. The top floor has been earmarked for exhibitions on Alpine photography since the 19C.

Natural History Museum★★

○Open Mon 2pm–5pm, Tue–Fri 9am–5pm (6pm Wed), Sat–Sun 10am–5pm. ○Closed most public holidays. ⊜8CHF. ℰ(0)31 350 71 11. www.nmbe.ch.

The museum is surprisingly child-friendly: no wonder when the first thing you see when you enter is Barry, the stuffed St Bernard dog (1800–1814) who saved 40 lost souls in his brief life. On the ground floor there is a fossil of an ichthyosaurus to be admired in the hall. In the basement, dioramas display Asian fauna as well as minerals (reconstructions of all famous diamonds among them). The ground floor contains Alpine and African fauna while the first floor contains, amphibians, fish and snakes as well as the skeletons of several whales. The second floor has the must-see skeleton of a Plateosaurus found in Frick (1983) while the top floor is devoted to insects and includes a completely closed anthill ecosystem.

Communication Museum★

○Open Tue–Sun, 10am–5pm. ○Closed 1 Jan, 24, 25 and 31 Dec. ⊜12CHF. ℰ(0)31 357 55 55. www.mfk.ch.

This museum explains the history of communications from early smoke signals through the transmission of highly sophisticated digital systems. Special coverage is given to the history of postal institutions (founded in 1849) and philately (more than 500 000 stamps displayed).

Art Museum★★

Hodlerstrasse 8-12 ○Open Tue–Sun, 10am–5pm (9pm Tue). ○Closed most public holidays. ⊜7 CHF (price varies for temporary exhibitions). ℰ(0)31 328 09 44. www.kunstmuseumbern.ch.

This Fine Arts Museum contains a splendid collection of 13C–20C paintings. Its renowned collection of works by **Paul Klee** has been moved to the new Zentrum Paul Klee (*see Zentrum*

BERN

0   200 m
0   200 yds

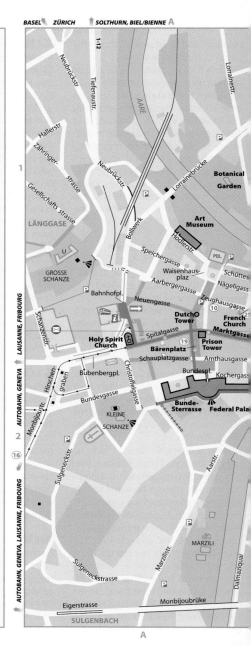

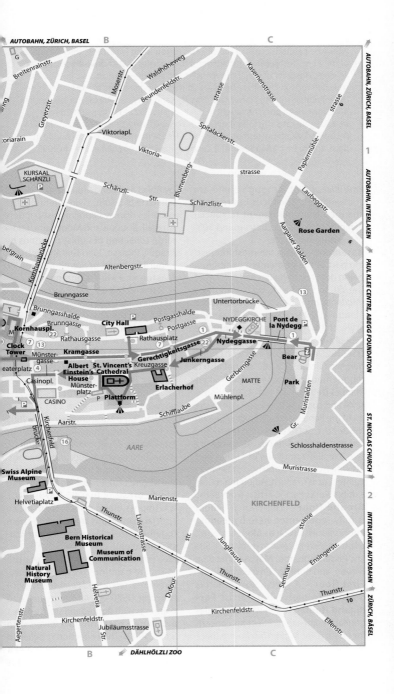

AUTOBAHN, ZÜRICH, BASEL

B

C

AUTOBAHN, ZÜRICH, BASEL

AUTOBAHN, INTERLAKEN

PAUL KLEE CENTRE, ABEGG FOUNDATION

ST. NICOLAS CHURCH

INTERLAKEN, AUTOBAHN

ZÜRICH, BASEL

Breitenrainstr.

Waldhöheweg

Moserstr.

Greyerzstr.

oriarain

ing

G

Viktoriapl.

Viktoria-

Spitalackerstr.

Beundenfeldstr.

strasse

Kasernenstrasse

strasse

KURSAAL SCHÄNZLI

Schänzli-

Schänzlistr.

Str.

Blumenberg-

strasse

Papiermühle-

strasse

Laubeggstr.

Aargauer Stalden

Rose Garden

bergrain

Kornhausbrücke

Altenbergstr.

Brunngasse

Brunngasshalde

Brunngasse

Kornhauspl.

City Hall

Postgasshalde

Postgasse

Rathausplatz

Untertorbrücke

NYDEGGKIRCHE

Pont de la Nydegg

13

T

M

Clock Tower

7

13

22

Rathausgasse

Kramgasse

Münster-gasse

4

Casinopl.

eaterplatz

Nydeggasse

Gerechtigkeitsgasse

22

Kreuzgasse

Junkerngasse

Bear

Gerberngasse

Park

Muristalden

Albert Einstein's House

St. Vincent's Cathedral

Erlacherhof

MATTE

Münster-platz

Plattform

Mühlenpl.

CASINO

Aarstr.

Schifflaube

Kirchenfeld brücke

16

AARE

Gr.

Schlosshaldenstrasse

Muristrasse

Swiss Alpine Museum

Helvetiaplatz

Marienstr.

KIRCHENFELD

Thunstr.

Luisenstrasse

str.

Jungfraustr.

strasse

Ensingerstr.

Seminar-

Bern Historical Museum

Museum of Communication

Natural History Museum

Helvetia

Dufour-

Thunstr.

Thunstr.

10

Aegertenstr.

Kirchenfeldstr.

Jubiläumsstrasse

Kirchenfeldstr.

Elfenstr.

B

DÄHLHÖLZLI ZOO

C

Paul Klee

Paul Klee was born in 1879 at Münchenbuchsee and spent his youth in Bern, where he painted scenes of the city and surrounding landscape: the meanders of the Aare, the Niesen mountains and the quarries at Ostermundigen. He was an ironic observer of social conventions and also drew caricatures. In 1906, he travelled to Munich, where he made contact with members of the Blauer Reiter movement, including Franz Marc, Wassily Kandinsky and Alexej von Jawlensky. A violinist and a poet, he taught in the Bauhaus (1921–33). Considered to be a "degenerate artist" by the Nazis, Klee saw his teaching contract at the Dusseldorf Academy terminated in 1933. He spent the latter part of his life in Bern, where he died in 1940. The Zentrum Paul Klee opened in Bern in 2005.

Paul Klee, p196) although some are still exhibited. The focus has recently changed from permanent to special exhibitions which occupy around 50% of the museum space.

Basement – This is the most interesting part of the permanent exhibition, being devoted to Italian early artists of the 13C to 15C, including Fra Angelico (*Madonna and Child*) and Duccio, whose *Maestà* (c.1290) reflects the Byzantine style characteristic of the Siennese School and works by the Swiss Primitives (15C–16C), especially *Master with Carnation from Berne*. The 16C school also is represented by Bernese painter Niklaus Manuel Deutsch (c.1484–1530), whose style and composition were akin to the art of the Renaissance: *Triptych of St John the Baptist, St Luke Painting the Virgin, Temptation of St Anthony*. Also note the two excellent portraits of Luther and his wife from the workshop of German painter Lucas Cranach. Adjoining rooms exhibit works by 17C artists from Bern.

Ground floor – The French School is fully represented here by leading Impressionists such as Monet, Manet, Cézanne (*Self-portrait in a Felt Hat*), Sisley, Pissarro, Renoir, Matisse (*The Blue Blouse*), and Bonnard (*In a Garden*).

First floor – A special exhibition is devoted to native-born artist **Ferdinand Hodler**. Along with large allegorical frescoes that reflect his concern for death (*Day, Night, The chosen*),there are his portraits (*Young Girl with a Poppy*) and self-portraits (he depicts himself with wild, menacing features in *The Madman*). There are also many works by Anker and Cuno Amiet who favoured a palette of bright, vivid colours. Other galleries display Expressionist painters Chagall, Soutine and Modigliani, and a large collection of Cubist paintings by Braque, Picasso, Juan Gris and Fernand Léger (*Contrasts of Form*), Kandinsky, Masson and Mirò. Contemporary art is represented by Swiss artists Meret Oppenheim, Franz Gertsch and Markus Raetz, and the Americans Jackson Pollock and Mark Rothko.

Zentrum Paul Klee ★★★
Take bus 12 or 5 to the final stop.
🕐*Open Tues–Sun 10am–5pm.*
🚃*20CHF.* ♿ ✆*(0)31 359 01 01.*
www.paulkleezentrum.ch.
The Paul Klee Museum opened in 2005 to house more than 4 000 paintings (*Steinbruch, Monument in Fruchtland*), gouaches, watercolours and drawings, plus archives and biographical material of one of the most significant and prolific artists of the 20C (1879–1940). It is impossible to exhibit them all, so special exhibitions try to group them together (*Klee in Morocco, Klee and Picasso* and so on).

Klee's striving for colour effects gave rise to square paintings (*Pictorial Architecture in Red, Yellow and Blue*), to Divisionist works (1930–32, *Ad Parnassum*) and paintings with figures and signs against a coloured background (*Flowers with Stone*, 1940). The collection is believed to be the largest single collection of a major artist in the world. The artwork is housed in a dramatic building designed by award-winning Italian architect

Zentrum Paul Klee

© Dominique Uldry/Zentrum Paul Klee

Renzo Piano; three soaring hills of steel and glass offer natural light to showcase Klee's colourful creations, which seem to blend primitive art, surrealism and cubism with gentle humor and allusion to dreams. The main exhibits are in the centre section; the other sections contain restaurants, shops, galleries, and a performance theatre. There is also a separate children's museum within the complex. Temporary exhibits focus on the connection between Klee and other artists, such as Kandinsky and Max Beckmann. The site includes a sculpture park. **Wege zu Klee** (Theme Path) from the city centre to the museum is punctuated by additional information about the artist and his works.

During the excavation, boulders buried by the retreating Aare Glacier more than 10 000 years ago were unearthed; these now form a natural landscape around ponds on the park-like site, which includes the 19C Villa Schöngrün, summer home of one of Bern's patrician families.

ADDITIONAL SIGHTS
Botanical Garden★
This vast botanical garden, with its fountains and pools, descends to the banks of the Aare in terraces. Some 6 000 plants, including a wide variety of Alpine species, grow in the garden, which covers an area of 2ha/5 acres. The seven greenhouses contain a collection of tropical plants, such as ferns, grasses, and orchids.

👪👤 Dählhölzli Zoo★
Entrance in Jubiläumstrasse.
Vivarium open summer 8.30am–7pm; winter 9am–5pm. 10CHF children 6CHF. (0)31 357 15 15.
www.tierpark-bern.ch.
The 13ha/32-acre Tierpark Dählhölzli, overlooking the Aare, is home to a number of European and Nordic animal species, including otters, musk ox, lynx, wolves, bison, elk, reindeer, and black grouse. The aviary contains hundreds of tropical birds, butterflies, rare specimens of local fauna, a termites' nest, and an ant hill. There is also a children's playground and a picnic area.

EXCURSIONS
Gurten★★
Alt. 858m/2 815ft – 2.5km/1.5mi .
About 30min including 10min by funicular. Take tram 9 direction Wabern until stop Gurtenbahn. Operates all year round. 5CHF one-way; 10 CHF there and back. (0)31 961 23 23.
www.gurtenpark.ch.
The Gurten, a magnificent belvedere with a **panorama**★★ of Bern and the Bernese Oberland, is a pleasant place in which to stroll; it also has a good sit-down and self-service restaurant and a fun-filled 👪👤children's playground.

Abegg-Stiftung★★

Open May–mid-Nov Tues–Sun 2pm–5.30pm. 10CHF. (0)31 808 12 01. www.abegg-stiftung.ch.

As you enter **Riggisberg** town from the north (Bern road), bear right onto the road to the Abegg Foundation; the modern buildings of this prestigious cultural venue are located on the mountainside in a verdant and peaceful setting.

The Foundation was established in 1961 by **Werner and Margaret Abegg** for conducting scientific research in applied arts, especially textiles, and their preservation. Collections include exhibits from Europe and the Middle East dating from Antiquity to the Renaissance. In addition to its vast library boasting around 160 000 titles, there are displays of Neolithic pottery, marble pieces from the Cyclades, Iranian ceramics and gold, bronzes from Luristan, Pharoic Egyptian pieces, ivory plaquettes from the pre-Achaemenid Era, and Byzantine ceramics.

The foundation runs a university-level degree course on the conservation and restoration of textiles, and maintains a related research library (open to the public), and an online catalogue. It also issues regular publications on subjects such as applied arts, textile art, and other applicable subjects.

Jegenstorf

16km/10mi N of Bern via route 12.

The houses in this cheerful, flowered town cluster around a Late Gothic church, with a saddleback roof and a shingled bell tower. The interior is decorated with woodwork; the stained-glass windows are 16C–18C. The town's **château** (*open mid-May–mid-Oct, Tue–Sun 10am–noon, 2pm–5pm; 7CHF; (0)31 761 01 59*), an 18C town house added to a feudal tower, stands in a small wooded park and presents temporary exhibitions in lovely 18C period rooms.

🚗 DRIVING TOUR

EMMENTAL★

100km/62mi. Leave aside one whole day.

▷ *Leave Bern from the N/NE via the route to Bolligen Burgdorf.*

The Emmental (The Emmen Dale) whose name immediately brings to mind the well-known Swiss cheese, is cut across by the River Emme, a tributary of the Aare, into which it flows east of Solothurn. Originating in the Hohgant Massif north of Lake Brienz, the River Emme crosses first a mountainous area, and then runs through an area of forests and fields dotted with flower-decked chalets. The area's wealth comes from forestry, crop farming, and cattle raising.

Burgdorf

Poststrasse 10 – 3400. (0)34 422 24 45. www.burgdorf.ch.

At the entrance to the Emmental, Burgdorf is a busy little town in the canton of Bern. The modern district, with its large textile works, is overlooked by the old quarter, crowned by its **castle**, built by the dukes of Zähringen at the end of the 12C. There are three museums in the castle: the main **Castle Museum**, plus the smaller **Swiss Gold Museum** and the **World Culture Museum** (*open Apr–Oct, daily 2pm–5pm (11am Sun); Nov–Mar, Sun only 11am–5pm; 7CHF. (0)34 423 02 14. www.kulturschloss.ch*).

Castle Museum

The museum occupies three floors in the tower. Visit the Knights' Hall, with fine furniture, Emmental costumes, porcelain, an instrument collection, and mementoes of **Johann Heinrich Pestalozzi**, who worked here (1799–1804). From the top floor there is a **view** of Burgdorf and the Bernese Alps.

Leave Burgdorf by the road to Wynigen.

▷ *On leaving town you will cross two ferro-concrete bridges over the Emme. After 1.5km/1mi take a narrow, winding road to the right which passes through Gutisberg. Leave a byroad to Wynigen on your left and park the car after the Lueg restaurant.*

Belvedere Lookout★
Alt. 887m/2 910ft. ⚑ 8.5km/5.3mi – about 30min.

You reach the top of the bluff along a very steep path among fir trees. A monument commemorating the Bernese cavalry (1914–18) has been erected on the open space; from here the semicircular **panorama**★ includes the Jura and the Bernese Alps on the horizon.

🚶 Affoltern Show Dairy
🕐*Open Apr–Oct 9am–6.30pm, Nov–Mar, 9am–5pm.* 🎫 *Free.*
✆ *(0)34 435 16 11. www.showdairy.ch.*

A trip to the Emmen valley is not complete without a visit to this modern cheese dairy, the only one in the region open to the public. Equipped with an audio guide, visitors can attend several times a day and watch behind windows the famous regional cheese being made. Butter-making takes place every Tuesday and Friday morning. Demonstration of the old-fashioned cheese production is made in the small cottage dated from 1741 and located next to the modern cheese factory. A shop and restaurant offering fondue and raclette bring the gastronomic visit to the end.

▷ *Head E and join the B 23, driving S to Sumiswald.*

Sumiswald
This pretty Bernese village has fine wooden houses characteristic of the region: A large façade carries one or two tiers of windows close together; the overhanging roof is immense; the gable is often painted and decorated with designs in bright colours. The **Kramerhaus** and the **Zum Kreuz Inn** are quite remarkable.

Lützelflüh
This lovely village on the Emme has a church that was built in 1494 (modernised). Inside the church are six old stained-glass windows and an organ loft

---

Emmental Cheese

Emmental cheese is to German Switzerland what Gruyère cheese is to the French cantons. It is the most widely exported of all Swiss cheeses: its enormous wheels, hard interior with large irregular holes (Gruyère is more compact and has fewer and smaller holes) and hazelnut taste are known throughout the world. Indeed, Emmenthaler Switzerland Premier Cru, which is aged for 14 months, beat more than 1 400 other competitors to be named World Champion at the 2006 Cheese World Championships.

(1785). Outside the door is the tomb of Albert Bitzius (pseudonym of Jeremias Gotthelf), pastor and writer during the 19C, whose unsentimental depictions of Emmenthal village life were based on his time as a curate here.

Hasle
On the west bank of the River Emme, this village is linked to the Rüegsauschachen (east bank) by a remarkable **covered bridge** (1838). Built entirely of wood, the bridge crosses the river in one span. The Protestant church, a former chapel rebuilt in the 17C, is worth noting. Inside are small 17C stained-glass windows, heraldic bearings and 15C frescoes showing the *Last Judgment* and the *Crucifixion*.

▷ *Retrace your steps and take the direction to Langnau-im-Emmental.*

Langnau-im-Emmental★
Schlossstrasse 3 – 3550.
✆ *(0)34 402 42 52.*

The picturesque town of Langnau lies on the banks of the Ilfis (spanned by a covered bridge), a tributary of the River Emme. Its commerce is based on forestry and Emmental cheese (main exporting centre for the latter).

ADDRESSES

🛏 STAY

Hotel Glocke – *Rathausgasse 75. ℰ(0)31 311 37 71. www.bernback packers.com. 12 rooms.* Those on a limited budget will like this hotel, located in the heart of old Bern. Shared rooms are simple and clean. Those on the top floor overlook the rooftops and cathedral.

Zum Goldener Schlüssel – *Rathausgasse 72. ℰ(0)31 311 02 16. www.goldener-schluessel.ch. 48 rooms.* This reasonably priced and friendly hotel is situated in a picturesque street in the old town. A good restaurant on the ground floor, under the arcades, serves a range of meat (especially game) and vegetarian dishes.

Landhaus – *Altenbergstrasse 4/6. ℰ(0)31 331 41 66. www.landhausbern.ch. 🅿 32 beds (dormitory or room).* A short walk from the bear enclosure, this old house has been brilliantly converted into a hotel for backpackers. Hygienic conditions in the dorms *(from 30CHF)*, and beautiful views of the Gurten in the attic rooms. Affordable restaurant on the ground floor.

Kreuz – *Zeughausgasse 41 - ℰ(0)31 329 95 95. www.kreuzbern.ch. 100 rooms.* Almost all the rooms in this three star hotel have been tastefully renovated. Its central location, set back from the street, makes it a good base for exploring the city on foot. Avoid the rooms at the front, which can be rather noisy, especially on weekends. Nice view of the city and the Bernese Alps from the rooftop terrace.

La Pergola – *Belpstrasse 43. ℰ(0)31 343 43 43. www.hotel-lapergola.ch. 🅿 55 rooms.* Three stops away from the train station on bus number 3, this hotel scores in that it provides parking space. But rooms are small, there are no cupboards (just shelves) and the Internet reception is unreliable.

Bern – *Zeughausgasse 9. ℰ(0)31 329 22 22. www.hotelbern.ch. 95 rooms.* Cosy hotel a stone's throw from the lively shopping district and its picturesque arcades. Piano bar in a sophisticated setting.

Belle Époque – *Gerechtigkeit 18. ℰ(0)31 311 43 36. www.belle-epoque.ch. 17 rooms.* As soon as you cross the threshold, you are transported back to the turn of the last century. "Toulouse Lautrec" bar and Art Nouveau furniture, decoration, vases and paintings. This elegant establishment could almost qualify as an art museum.

🍴 EAT

On menus in Bern, Gschnätzeltes are thin slices of veal (or émincé), Suurchabis is Sauerkraut and Gschwellti are potatoes boiled in their skins.

Klötzlikeller – *Gerechtigkeitsgasse 62. ℰ(0)31 311 74 56. www.kloetzlikeller.ch. Closed Sun in winter, Sun and Mon in summer.* A typical Bernese wine bar which has traditionally been run by women for over 100 years: in 1635, there were more than 230 of these establishments in the city. The Klötzlikeller also serves light meals.

Vatter – *Bärenplatz 2. ℰ(0)31 313 11 21. Closed Sun. www.vatter.ch.* Above the shop of organic products of the same name, this is an organic restaurant for those on tight budgets. Use the extensive buffet (salads, pasta), then pay by weight. For an exotic touch, taste Indian and vegetarian specialties. Pleasant terrace balcony on Bärenplatz.

Verdi – *Gerechtigkeitsgasse 5. ℰ(0)31 312 63 68. Closed 24 & 25 Dec.* The famous composer himself would not turn up his nose at gnocchi with truffles or spaghetti alla scapara in this fine Italian diner in old Bern. The decor pays tribute to the maestro: old scores, red velvet curtains, candles at night—romantico!

Zum Äusseren Stand – *Zeughausgasse 17. ℰ(0)31 311 32 05. www.aeussererstand.ch. Closed Sun.* This restaurant is housed in the former town hall where the Constitution of the Bern canton was first drawn up in 1831. In this building, representatives of 22 countries gathered in 1874 to found the Universal Postal Union. The huge dining hall upstairs, decorated in the Empire style, is reserved for formal banquets.

Punkt – *Rathausgasse 73.* *(0)31 318 18 88. www.restaurant-punkt.ch. Closed Sun.* For a change from Bern staples sausages and fried potato, try this excellent Asian place. The Thai, Chinese, Japanese and Indian flavours and convivial décor make for a charming atmosphere. Those of a suspicious demeanour can monitor the chefs at work via a camera placed in the kitchen.

Kornhauskeller – *Kornhausplatz 18.* *(0)31 327 72 72. www.bindella.ch. Closed Mon lunchtime in summer.* In the early 18C, a warehouse used for storing wheat and wine was dug out beneath the old covered market. Converted into a village hall in 1896, it currently houses this restaurant. The paintings dating from that period are the work of the Bernese artist Rudolf Mänger. The huge barrel set up in the main dining hall can contain up to 41 055 litres. An unusual yet welcoming place where diners can sample traditional Bernese cuisine.

Harmonie – *Hotelgasse 3.* *(0)31 313 11 41. www.harmonie.ch. Closed Sat evenings, Sun and Mon lunchtime.* Old-fashioned café, whose décor has remained exactly the same since 1915. Famous for its fondues.

Brasserie Bärengraben – *Muristalden 1.* *(0)31 331 42 18.* Situated at the end of Nydeggbrücke, towards Bärengraben. Small, congenial restaurant with mouthwatering homemade desserts.

Schwellenmaetteli – *Dalmaziquai II.* *(0)31 350 50 01.* www.schwellenmaetteli.ch. Closed Mon.* Salmon and perch are popular with the Bernese in this restaurant-bar conveniently located down by the main Aare lock. The old city spreads out on the other side of the river. There is also a snack bar on stilts over the water and a romantic cocktail bar. Reached via a staircase on the side of the Helvetiaplatz or, better by car, as the way up afterwards is steep.

NIGHTLIFE

It is true that Bern lags behind Zürich and Lausanne in nightlife, but it is by no means a cemetery

town. Try walking the streets behind the railway station, in particular Neuengasse, Aarbergergasse and Speichergasse, and you will find that there are many busy clubs and bars under the arcades.

At number 35, there is a gay bar, **Samurai** (*www.samurai-bar.ch*). Outside this area you can find **Club Viente Sur** (*Lerchenweg 33*) for dancehall and reggae, the **ISC** (*Neuenbrueckestrasse 10, isc-club.ch*) which offers nights for every taste (rock to hiphop and goth), and next door the Reitschule Bern (*Neubrückstrasse 8, www.reitschule.ch*), an alternative cultural centre with live music.

You can enjoy some good jazz at **Marian's Jazzroom** in the basement of the Hotel Innere Enge (*Engerstrasse 54 www.mariansjazzroom.ch*). Very popular among connoisseurs.

🛒 SHOPPING

The main **shopping streets** are Spitalgasse, Marktgasse, Kramgasse and Gerechtigkeitsgasse. Note the late shopping on Thursdays until 9pm. The new pride of Bern is the recently opened **Westside** shopping centre designed by **Daniel Libeskind.** Containing hundreds of shops, it is just eight minutes from Bern main railway station by S-bahn nos. S5, S51 and S52. www.westside.ch.

There are **markets** selling fruit, flowers, vegetables and, various other articles every Tuesday and Saturday morning on the Bundesplatz. The traditional **onion market (Zwiebelmarkt)** is the fourth Monday in November at various locations around the city. .

🎭 THEATRE AND MUSIC

Stadttheater – *Kornhausplatz 20.* *(0)31 329 51 11. www.stadttheaterbern.ch.*

Puppentheater (*Puppet Theater*) – *Gerechtigkeitsgasse 31.* *(0)31 311 95 85. www.berner-puppentheater.ch.*

Kursaal – *Kornhausstrasse 3.* *(0)31 339 55 00.* A complex featuring restaurants, a casino, a hotel, a piano bar, a nightclub and a cabaret (international variety shows).

Biel/Bienne★

Biel is a good excursion centre and its beach, not far from Nidau, is much appreciated. The city marks the linguistic frontier between French and German: one third of the inhabitants speak French. The ugly modern town contrasts with the quaint old quarters of the upper city.

▶ **Population:** Biel/Bienne 50 455.

🏢 **Info:** Zentralstrasse 60. ✆(0)32 329 84 84. www.biel-seeland.net.

◑ **Location:** Biel/Bienne lies at the foot of the last spurs of the Jura and on the shore of the lake that bears its name; approx 30 min form Bern. Alt. 438m/1 437ft.

A BIT OF HISTORY

The population of Biel (Bienne in French) has increased ten-fold within a century, thanks to the watch and clock industry, which still employs about 6 000 people. The first Omega watch factory was set up here in 1879. Other industries have been established to ward off possible economic crises (precision machine-tool works, wire-mills and graphic art workshops).

Biel is also a shining example of successful bilingualism, even by Swiss standards: German and French are official languages on an equal footing, with street signs in both languages. It is not unusual to come across two locals conversing without difficulty, each in his own language. In summer, the place to see and be seen is **Strandboden**, the park on the lake.

OLD TOWN★

This area of town is very picturesque, with many fountains and façades decorated with remarkable wrought-iron

Watch Mecca

Since the mid-19C, Biel/Bienne has seen itself as the capital of the watch industry: the first factory—Omega—was founded here in 1879; it is the home of Swatch, the biggest company in the watch industry; and is an important site for Rolex, too. Thanks to the watch industry, the city has seen its population increase tenfold in a century.

signs, often painted in bright colours. On the main street, **Burggasse**, stand the town hall, notable for its stepped gable and façade adorned by windows with red sandstone mullions, and a Fountain of Justice dating from 1744. **Obergasse** is lined with houses influenced by both Bernese and French architectural styles. To the right, the houses are arcaded and accessible directly from street level; to the left, short flights of steps lead to the entrances.

Ring

This charming square was the centre of old Biel when the town was governed by the prince-bishops of Basel, from the 11C to the Revolution.

Justice was rendered here; the accused appeared before members of the Council seated in a semicircle, and it was from this arrangement that the Ring drew its name. In the middle of the Ring is the curious **Banneret Fountain** (1546), symbolizing the militia and war. The houses, with their arcades and turrets, form a fine architectural group.

Note the massive tower of the Gothic Church of St Benedict and the frescoes to the left as you enter. The highly decorated corner house with a turret is particularly attractive. Now home to the local registry office, it was once the forest workers' house.

Obergasse leads to **Juraplatz**, another picturesque square surrounded by arcaded houses. Note the beautiful Angel's Fountain (1480), decorated with an angel holding a lamb in its arms, which it is protecting from the devil.

Center PasquArt★★

71-75 Faubourg du Lac. ⏰*Mon–Fri 2pm –6pm, Sat–Sun and holidays 11am– 6pm* ◉ *11 CHF.* ☏*(0)32 322 55 86. www.pasquart.ch.*

A place to visit as much for its works on display as for its architecture. This centre of contemporary art with a programme of innovative exhibitions is distributed in two buildings: a former hospital, and since 2000, an absolutely modern vast cube by the firm of Diener & Diener. The artists exhibit large volumes of works and the brightness of rooms provides a dream space for expression. The first floor houses the Foto Forum, dedicated to photography. Temporary exhibitions occupy the 2nd and 3rd floors.

Neuhaus Museum

26 Promenade de la Suze . ⏰*Tue–Sun 11am–5pm (11am–7pm Wed.)* ◉ *7CHF (children free).* ☞⌐*Guided tours on Wed (free).* ☏*(0)32 328 70 30/31. www.mn-biel.ch.*

Located in one of the city's oldest fabric-printing factories to contribute to Biel's prosperity, this museum brings together several regional exhibitions devoted to the industrial history of Biel: local bourgeois life in the 19C, animal and plant watercolours from the Robert family, collection, artefacts from brothers Robert (a writer) and Karl (a painter) Walser, and numerous pieces of equipment, such as old and new projectors to ilustrate the history of cinema.

Museum Schwab★

⏰*Open from Oct 2012, Tue–Sun 2pm–6pm, Sun and public holidays, 11am–6pm.* ⏰*Closed 1 Jan, 24 and 31 Dec.* ◉*5CHF.* ☏*(0)32 322 76 03. www.muschwab.ch.*

Housed here are the discoveries of Colonel Schwab (1803–1869), a pioneer in the research of the prehistoric epoch in Romansh Switzerland. The museum contains the best-known examples of the lake-dwellers' era. Artefacts uncovered in the lakes of Biel, Neuchâtel and Murten are displayed alongside those from the Gallo-Roman settlement at Petinesca and La Tène.

A Bilingual City

Written sources trace the town's bilingualism to the Middle Ages, but it was most certainly revived in the late 19C by the arrival en masse of Jurassien watchmakers. Today, both German and French are official languages, placed on an equal footing (the street names are also written in both languages). It is not uncommon to hear two Biennese talk, without embarrassment, each in his language. In schools, they teach both French and German.

EXCURSIONS

Magglingen★

8km/5mi. About 30min.

▶ *Leave Biel by the road to Delémont and 200m/220yd after going under a bridge between two bends, turn left onto the byroad to Evilard.*

At Magglingen, also known as Macolin, you will find an extensive **panorama**★ of the Swiss plateau, the lakes at the foot of the Jura and the Alps. Magglingen is known for its Federal School of Gymnastics. ⌐*Accessible by funicular from Biel (W on the town plan).*

Aarberg

▶ *11km/6.8mi S (road number 22).*

A canal links this small yet prosperous town to Biel Lake. The upper town, joined to the lower town by a covered bridge (16C) spanning the River Aare, is well worth a visit. Its main square, **Stadtplatz**★, oblong in shape and paved, is embellished with two flower-decked fountains and lined with classical façades and a small 15C church (restored). A picturesque second-hand fair is held annually on the last weekend in April.

Le Chasseral ★★★

▶ *Drive 30km/18.5mi to the W by Highway 5 to La Neuveville, then towards Nods (signposted). After the toll, go to the hotel Chasseral where you can park your car.* ⌐*Caution: the road is narrow and is usually blocked by snow* from December to April. Jura Bernois Tourisme, 4 Rue du Marché. ℘(0)32 751 49 49. www.jurabernois.ch.

The highest point of the northern Jura (alt. 1 607m/5 272ft), Le Chasseral has a famous panorama of the Swiss Alps.

Panorama★★★

The Hotel Chasseral, situated just below the route's highest point, marks the end of the public thoroughfare. The nearby viewing table allows visitors to take their bearings on the main peaks of the Bernese and Valais Alps and the Mont Blanc Massif. This wonderful backcloth extends for some 250km/156mi.

Walk to the Chasseral beacon (1hr there and back by a wide, gently sloping path) near a Swiss postal service's telecommunications relay station. From the beacon you get a **circular view**★★★ of the horizon, extending from the Swiss Alps to the northern Jura, the Vosges and the Black Forest.

Motorists can return to Biel via **St-Imier**. This bustling watch and clock-making centre is located on the south face of Mount Soleil. St-Imier's past is recalled by the Tower of St Martin (or Queen Bertha), all that remains of an 11C church, and its 12C former **Collegiate Church** (now a Reformed Church). The interior features a narthex with archaic capitals (heads on the right), an apse with oven vaulting and a chancel with ogive vaulting and mural paintings.

🚗 DRIVING TOURS

BIELER SEE★

55km/34mi. Allow 1hr15min.
www.bielersee.ch.

▷ Leave Biel/Bienne via Route 5, W.

Lake Biel (Lac de Bienne) is of glacial origin. It was once larger; when the water level dropped about 2m/6.5ft in 1878, it uncovered a score of lake-dwellings on the south shore. At the same time some of the waters of the Aare were deflected from the lake. "The shores of Lake Biel are wilder and more romantic than those

of Lake Geneva... but they are not less smiling," wrote French philosopher Jean-Jacques Rousseau.

The north shore, with charming French-speaking villages such as La Neuveville nestling amid vineyards, is more picturesque.

La Neuveville

4 rue du Marché – 2520. ℘(0)32 751 49 49. www.jurabernois.ch.

The town's economic activity includes wine-producing, precision engineering, and tourism. An old-world feeling lingers about the town with its paved streets, lanterns and five towers (remains of the fortifications), and it is an excellent base for excursions to Île St-Pierre, the three lakes (Biel, Neuchâtel, and Murten) and Le Chasseral.

Two hours is ample for exploring this pleasant area, including Tour de Rive (1312–18), the entrance to the town, whose heavy oak door is adorned with the arms of the town. From the place de la Liberté, take a look at the houses on the left on **Rue de l'Hôpital**, whose top floor, protected by a roof overhang, is equipped with a winch that was used to bring goods up the attic.

Rue du Marché★, a long street, with two old gates at either end (Tour de Rive and Tour Rouge), pretty Renaissance fountains in-between and flower-decked houses (two of which dated from 1647 and 1697) in between.

The Old Town Hall houses the **Museum of History of Neuveville**, which contains the trophies of the Burgundy wars, antiques and paintings. It also hosts temporary art exhibitions (Apr–Oct, Sun afternoon; ☞admission free).

Blanche Église

E of town towards Biel/Bienne, on the left. To visit, contact the Tourist Office, 4 rue du Marché in La Neuveville.
℘(0)32 751 49 49.

This Carolingian building remodelled in the Gothic period and restored in 1915 is surrounded by 17C and 18C tombstones. Inside are a painted wooden pulpit (1536) and remains of 14C frescoes on the right of the chancel: Temptation of

Christ, Christ Reviled, Entrance to Jerusalem, Adam and Eve.

St Petersinsel★★
*By boat from Biel or la Neuveville.
Allow half a day for the whole excursion.*
⏱*Departure from Biel Apr–mid-Oct,
9.45am–4.45pm (times vary according
to the season).* ⛴*Fare there and back
30.40CHF.* ☎*(0)32 329 88 11. Departure
from La Neuveville Apr–mid-Oct,
10.30am–5.15pm (times vary according
to the season: Weekends only in winter).*
⛴*Fare there and back 18.40CHF from
La Neuveville.* ☎*(0)32 329 88 11.*
St Peter's Island, at the extreme southwest end of the lake, effectively became
a peninsula when the lake's water level
was lowered, but it has retained its former name of island. In the autumn of
1765 it was visited by **Jean-Jacques
Rousseau**, who recalls his idyllic stay
there in *The Confessions* and in *Musings
of the Solitary Walker.*
The visitor can walk round the north
side of the island easily and enjoy pretty
glimpses of the lake, especially toward
the village of Ligerz (Gléresse). After
seeing the small landing stage used by
Rousseau, you will come to the house
in which he lived. St Peter's Island and
its neighbour, the small **Rabbits Island**
(joined to the shore by a strip of marshy
land since the waters of the lake were
lowered), are nature reserves, providing
a delightful haven of peace for migra-
tory birds, as well as hare, and deer.

Cressier
Set back from the lake, this wine-growing village has preserved some of its old
buildings; on Rue des St-Martin there
is a house (1576) with an oriel window
and the Vallier Château (1610) with its
pointed turrets lies nearby.

Le Landeron
Nearer to the lake, this small hamlet is
hemmed in by vegetable gardens and
orchards. The charm of this village lies in
its unique, long shaded square adorned
with two fountains with bannerets. It
is defended at each end by a fortified
gate (1659 north side, 1596 south side)

and lined with old houses. The town hall
(15C) is built onto the Martyrs Chapel. At
36 note a house dating from 1550.

GORGES DU PICHOUX★
*From Biel to Porrentruy 61km/38mi –
Allow 2hr30mins (not including visits).*
From Lake Biel to the Ajoie region (area
around Porrentruy), deep gorges, pastures, fir or deciduous forests follow the
road which, in the Sorne Valley, runs
between the Franches Montagnes and
the Delémont region.

▷ *Leave Biel by Madretschstasse and
the road to Solothurn and Zürich, and
at Bözingen take a path just before the
Suze Bridge, near a wire-mill.*

From Biel to Sonceboz the road climbs
quickly above the suburbs of Biel and
halfway up the slope threads its way
through the Taubenloch Gorges.

Taubenlochschlucht★
🚶 *Allow about 1hr30min.*
These gorges, often wild and mysterious, are served by an excellent tourist
path.
The road goes up the industrialised Suze
Valley. Between Sonceboz and Tavannes,
the **Pierre-Pertuis** section resembles
a small Alpine pass. This corridor has
been used since the beginning of the
3C by the Roman road from Aventicum
(Avenches) to Augusta Raurica (Augst)
and takes its name from the arch under
which the former road passed on the
Tavannes slope.

Tavannes
This town, situated in the Upper Birse
Valley, at the foot of the rock of Pierre-
Pertuis, is known for its clock-making
industry. The modern Roman Catholic
church was decorated by artists of its
Société St-Luc, a school of sacred art
well known in Romansh Switzerland.
The mosaic on the façade, represent-
ing the Ascension is by Gino Severini.

▷ *Turn left after the church in the
direction of Delémont.*

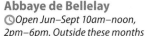

Abbaye de Bellelay

Open Jun–Sept 10am–noon, 2pm–6pm. Outside these months request the key from the Services Psychiatriques building next door. 7CHF guided tour minimum 12 persons. (0)32 494 53 43.

The **abbey church** (buit 1710–14) features an imposing array of Baroque architecture in the interior, which art lovers may compare to that of St Urban and Rheinau. The **interior**★ is remarkably impressive. The Fathers of Bellelay hold the secret of making Tête-de-Moine, a semi-hard cheese. After winding through wooded pastureland, the road glides into the depths of the gorges cut by the Sorne.

Gorges du Pichoux★

This cutting is the deepest of the *cluses,* or transverse valleys, hollowed out by the Sorne between Le Pichoux and Berlincourt. The gorges have limestone cliffs to which cling forests of fir trees. The **climb**★ from Boécourt to the Les Rangiers Pass at first crosses the flank of an open slope planted with birch and oak. The Doubs slope is reached when the road joins the itinerary called the Jura Corniche.

Porrentruy★

Porrentruy, a small town in the northeast of the Bernese Jura and the 16C residence of the prince-bishops of Basel, has many tourist attractions. Its pedestrianised old town is full of colourful façades and wrought-iron signs. Many museums tell the history and geology of this region that was annexed by revolutionary France in 1793. The city of Porrentruy became the capital of the Mont-Terrible *département,* **which included the present Jura canton and Bernese Jura as far as Biel/Bienne.**

ADDRESSES

⌂ STAY

⊖ **Villa Lindenegg** – *Lindenegg 5.* ☎ *(0)32 322 94 66. www.lindenegg.ch.* ⊞. *8 rooms.* Restaurant in the evening (except Sat) and weekend lunchtimes. Closed Tues . A taste of la dolce vita in this elegant 19C building, carefully restored and surrounded by a beautiful garden. Enough to want to stay on after a drink on the terrace and dine in the excellent Bistro.

⊉/ EAT

⊖ **Restaurant Pfauen** – *Ring 7, Altstadt. Closed Wed.* ☎ *(0)32 322 49 13.* Spectacular views of the beautiful fountain and watchtowers of the Ring from the tables on the terrace of this restaurant. In the cosy room, with its parquet floor and light walls, let yourself be tempted by the seasonal dishes on offer.

⊖⊖ **Elite** – *Bahnhofstr. 14. Closed Sat lunch, Sun and mid Jun–mid Aug.* ☎ *(0)32 328 77 77. www.hotelelite.ch.* In a 1930s Art Deco atmosphere, this brasserie serves traditional, quality fare.

▸ **Population:** 6 637.
🛈 **Info:** 5 Grand-Rue – 2900. ☎ (032) 466 59 59.
▶ **Location:** In the centre of the Ajoie region in the Jura. Alt. 445m/1 460ft.
🄿 **Parking:** There is no parking in the old town; use car parks and walk in.
☺ **Don't Miss:** The château, or the Grottes de Réclère.
♟ **Kids:** Exploring the Grottes de Réclère.
🕐 **Timing:** This town is not on many tourists' radar, making weekend visits easier for the casual visitor.

OLD TOWN

The **Porte de France**, marks the entrance to the old town. The town centre features many wealthy residential mansions with inner courtyards and turrets worthy of note (22 Grand-Rue) magnificent 16C fountains that are the work of Laurent Perroud: The Banneret Fountain (rue des Malvoisins), the Samaritan Fountain (Grand-Rue, in front of a corner house with oriel windows) and the Gilded Sphere Fountain (rue des Annonciades).

Musée de l'Hôtel-Dieu

🕐Open Tue–Sun, 2pm–5pm. ✎6CHF. ♿ 𝒫(0)32 466 72 72. mhdp.ch.

Devoted to local history, this museum features an exhibit about the hospital's **pharmacy**, a fine example of 19C cabinet-making and presents an interesting display of pots and phials made of glass and porcelain.

The other exhibit is the treasury of St Peter's Church, which contains precious objects, some dating back to the Gothic period: A 1487 crucifix used in processions and a large monstrance known as Ostensoir de Morat (1488).

Château

Perched on a rocky spur, the castle's silhouette rises above the Allaine Valley. Only the Tour Réfous (45m/148ft, pretty views from the top) remains of this medieval stronghold, a round tower standing near a group of buildings now housing administrative offices. One corridor inside the Law Courts displays portraits representing prince-bishops (1575–1737) including Jacques-Christophe Blarer from Wartensee, a charismatic figure whose strong personality was to mark the history of the town.

Botanical Garden

🕐Garden Mon–Fri 8am–5pm, greenhouses 8am–11.45am, 2pm–5pm; Sat–Sun 10am–5pm. greenhouses 2pm–5pm. ✎Free. 𝒫(0)32 466 30 15.

The gardens border the former bishop's residence whose front yard is home to an impressive Foucault pendulum, which demonstrates the rotation of the Earth. The tropical greenhouses hold a

Jurassic Era

In 1795 the German naturalist Alexander von Humboldt was on a scientific expedition in the Swiss Jura mountains when he realised that the limestone deposits which make up these mountains were a new, unknown strata which he called "Calcaire de Jura". Although he originally dated the deposits wrongly, he had discovered a complete geologic era in the Earth's history (between c.200 and 145 million years ago), which was characterised by the prevalence of dinosaurs on land (and sea) and wide conifer forest cover.

fine collection of tropical plants including carnivorous plants and orchids.

Jurassic Museum of Natural Sciences

Within the botanical garden.

🕐Tue–Sun 2pm–5pm. 🕐Closed Dec 25 & 1–3 Jan. ✎5CHF (-16 years free). 𝒫(0)32 467 37 10. www.mjsn.ch.

While this museum traces the history of the universe, two rooms are devoted to the natural heritage of Jura such as fauna and fossils (this is where the word Jurassic and the corresponding era originate).

EXCURSIONS

Préhisto-Parc Réclère & caves

▶ 15km/9.5mi by the road to Besançon. 🐾Guided caves tour, Easter–Nov, 11.30am & 2.30 pm; Sun also 4.30pm. 🕐Closed Dec–Easter. ✎9CHF (15CHF caves and park). www.prehisto.ch.

These caves, located 100m/328ft underground, were discovered in 1886. Admire the fine array of stalactitites and stalagmites; the latter feature "the great dome", said to be the largest in the country (13m/43ft high for 250 000 years of age). The tour may be combined with that of **Préhisto-Parc** (🕐Easter–Nov, 10am–noon, 1pm–5pm (9.30am–6pm Jul–Aug). 🕐Closed Dec–Easter; ✎8CHF (15CHF caves and park); ♿ 𝒫(032) 467

61 55), an area of the forest filled with life-size replicas of prehistoric creatures.

Delémont

▶ *30km/18mi E via the A 16, exit Delémont. 12 place de la Gare – 2800.* ℰ *(0)32 422 97 78.*

Until 1792 Delémont was the summer residence of the prince-bishops of Basel, whose crosier appears in the arms of the town. Today it owes its importance to its watch and precision-instrument factories. Since 1978 it has been the capital of the new canton of Jura.

The **old town** or high town, on either side of rue du 23 Juin, has kept its monumental gates, 16C Renaissance fountains and noble 18C classical buildings.

Musée Jurassien d'Art et d'Histoire

◉ *Open Tue–Fri, 2pm–5pm; Sat, Sun 11am–6pm.* 🎫 *6CHF.* ℰ *(0)32 422 80 77. www.mjah.ch.*

The regional Art and History Museum contains archeological finds from the prehistoric to the Merovingian Era discovered in the area, ancient religious objects, mementoes of Napoleon, and examples of local crafts and furniture. Also included are works by artists from the Jura.

Chapelle du Vorbourg

▶ *2km/1.2mi NE of Delémont.*

This pilgrimage shrine is reached by a shady road offering beautiful views of Delémont. The chapel with its Baroque altars and walls adorned with votive offerings of the 18C and 19C, stands in a wild and woody site over a deep valley.

🚗 DRIVING TOURS

LES FRANCHES MONTAGNES★

41km/25.5mi from Porrentruy to Saignelégnier. Allow 2hrs (not including visits).

▶ *Exit Porrentruy SE by Highway 6 in the direction of Delémont. At Courgenay, just after the church towards Courtemautruy, take a right and then the panoramic de la Croix pass. After a steep incline (18%) is Saint Ursanne.*

Saint-Ursanne★

Alt. 494m/1 621ft. 18, rue du Quartierl. ℰ *(0)32 461 37 16. www.juratroislacs.ch.*

Lying away from the main roads deep in the Doubs Valley, Saint Ursanne, a quaint old town that has remained unchanged since the beginning of the 19C, makes

Saint-Ursanne

© Christof Sonderegger/Switzerland Tourism

a charming place to stop when cross-ing the Swiss Jura. It originated with the hermitage that Ursicinus, a disciple of Columba set up in the 7C.

You enter this medieval town through fortified gates surmounted by a bear carrying the symbolic crosier of the prince-bishops of Basel. The town is littered with medieval architecture, including collégiales, a church, a cloister, ruins of a 14C castle, and a hermitage. There is a good **view★** from the bridge over the Doubs River. The town roofs are dominated by the church tower and the castle.

Collegiate Church

○ *Open daily except Sun am, 7.30am–7pm (8pm Jun–Oct).*
℘*(0)32 461 31 74.*
The east end and apse are Roman-esque and comprise a single-arched **doorway★** adorned with statues. The Romanesque chancel has a Baroque canopied altar; the nave is early Gothic (13C).

▶ *From Saint Ursanne, rejoin road 18A at the place called Les Manettesheading towards Delémont.*

The high plateau of the Franches Mon-tagnes (average altitude 1 000m/3 281ft) between the Doubs Valley and Mount Soleil Chain is known as the "Watch Valley." Its low houses, pastures dotted with fir trees and natural parks where bay horses and milk cows graze, are most attractive.

Tourism flourishes in winter because of the popularity of cross-country skiing, and in summer thanks to the temperate climate and abundance of natural sites.

Saignelégier

The chief town of the district, it is well-known throughout the Jura for its **August Horse Fair** (○*see Calendar of Events*).

While visiting, you may also want to take a tour through **Gruère pond**, where signs along the log path explain the fascinating 20 000-year history of this 40ha/98.8-acre peat bog.

ADDRESSES

☞STAY

○○ **Hôtel Bellevue** – *46 route de Belfort.* ℘*(0)32 466 55 44. www.bellevue-porrentruy.ch. 10 rooms. Restaurant.*
At the gates of the town, a low building where the rooms offer the usual level of comfort. The Brasserie offers simple but good meals of pizza, pasta, fish and meat (○○◎menus, ○dish of the day).

○○ **De la Gare** – *2, rue de la Petite-Gilberte, Courgenay (3km/1.8mi to the SE).* ℘*(0)32 471 22 22. Closed 4–8 Jan. 6 rooms.* Opposite the station, an establishment with individually designed and named rooms, some with antique furniture. Reserve the one called Gilberte, which is also the name of the hotel brasserie (○○◎*; closed Sun & Mon*). Beautiful quiet patio at the back.

⏓/EAT

○○ **Les Grottes** – *2912 Réclère.* ℘*(0)32 476 61 55.* Restaurant near the Réclère caves and the Prehistoric Park. It allows for a nice break between visiting the two. There is a possibility of accommodation in small cabins and Mongolian yurts which can take a families up to 5 persons.

○○ **Hôtel du Bœuf** – *7 rue de l'Eglise, Courgenay (3km/1.8mi to the SE).* ℘*(0)32 471 11 21. www.boeuf-courgenay.ch. Closed Mon and Tue.* This restaurant offers "*effet bœuf*", the signature dish of this family business whose pink facade stands in the middle of the village. Meals for every taste, carefully chosen menus.

August Horse Fair, Saignelégier

© G. Dubois/Switzerland Tourism

Solothurn★★

Solothurn lies at the foot of the last ridge of the Jura (Weissenstein) and today extends to both banks of the Aare. On the north bank of the river the old nucleus of the town, still encircled by its 17C walls, has justifiably acquired the reputation of being the most beautiful Baroque town in Switzerland.
The Krummturm (Crooked Tower) is the most striking feature of this fortified group.

▶ **Population:** 15 623.

🛈 **Info:** Hauptgasse 69 – 4500. ℘(0)32 626 46 46. www.solothurn-city.ch.

◗ **Location:** The town of Solothurn is in Solothurn canton, and lies at the foot of the Jura (Weissenstein). Alt. 436m/1 430ft.

👁 **Don't Miss:** St Ursenkathedrale.

🕐 **Timing:** Allow at least a day to enjoy the sights properly.

A BIT OF HISTORY

Solothurn remained Catholic until 1792 and was chosen as a residence by the French ambassadors to the Swiss Diet. Intellectual and artistic exchanges flourished between the two countries; Bourbon court fashions were adopted and the town's fortifications were built (1667) according to principles of the French military engineer Vauban.

OLD TOWN★

The Basel Gate (**Baseltor**) and the Biel Gate (**Bieltor**) access the old quarter, with picturesque streets lined with houses featuring brightly painted shutters, wrought-iron signs, half-timbered facades with window boxes overflowing in colourful flowers, and overhanging roofs. **Hauptgasse**, **St-Urbangasse**, and **Schmiedengasse** are noteworthy. **Marktplatz**, the heart of the old town, is adorned with a fountain with 16C painted figures (St Ursen Brunnen). This is one of eleven painted wooden fountains for which the town is famous. It is dominated by the 12C clock tower (Zeitglockenturm) whose astronomical clock face is surmounted by three figures (the King between Death and Saint Ursus, patron saint of the town).

St Urs Cathedral★

This imposing Baroque building was designed in the Italian style (18C) by two Ticino architects, dedicated to St Ursus and St Victor, martyrs from the Theban Legion who, having escaped the massacre of Aguane (🔖 see ST MAURICE),

were beheaded at Solothurn. The vast nave is supported by piers with engaged pilasters and capitals embellished with floral motifs. This decoration continues along the false gallery under the clerestory. The carved pink marble pulpit and the paintings in the chancel and at the transept crossing are the main ornamental features. Pleasant gardens are laid out behind the east end of the St Ursenkathedrale.

Jesuits Church

The Jesuitenkirche (end of the 17C) features a **nave**★ consisting of three bays decorated with frescoes and stucco work. A gallery runs along the first two bays, so that the third one appears to form a transept. The gigantic high altar is adorned with a great painting representing the Assumption, framed between two large green marble pillars. The organ-loft is delicately decorated.

Old Arsenal Museum

🕐*Open Tue–Sat 1pm–5pm; Sun 10am–5pm.* 🕐*Closed Easter, Christmas and 1 Jan.* 🎟*6CHF.* ℘*(0)32 624 60 70. www.museum-alteszeughaus.ch.*
The **Museum Altes Zeughaus** contains a large collection of weapons and uniforms dating from the Middle Ages up to the 20C. The second floor boasts 400 breastplates and suits of armor; the ground floor displays a German tank used in the World War II and a collection of cannons, both old-fashioned and modern.

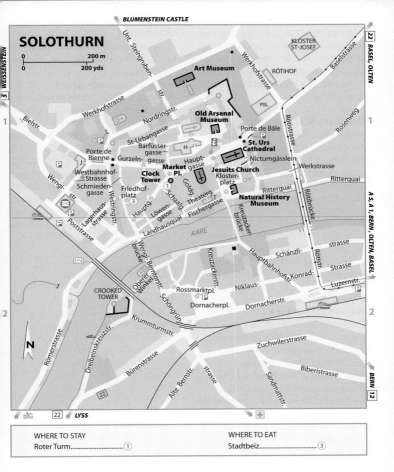

SOLOTHURN

0 200 m
0 200 yds

BLUMENSTEIN CASTLE

Art Museum

KLOSTER ST-JOSEF

RÖTIHOF

Old Arsenal Museum

Porte de Bâle

St. Urs Cathedral

Nictumgässlein

Porte de Bienne

Clock Tower

Market Pl.

Jeuits Church

Klosterplatz

Natural History Museum

Ritterquai

AARE

CROOKED TOWER

Rossmarktpl.

Dornacherpl.

N

WHERE TO STAY		WHERE TO EAT	
Roter Turm	①	Stadtbeiz	③

Kunstmuseum Solothurn★

⊙Open Tue–Sun, 11am–5pm, Sat-Sun 10am–5pm. ⊙Closed 1 Jan, Good Fri, Easter, Whitsun and Christmas. ⊜Donation. ℘(0)32 622 23 07. www.kunstmuseum-so.ch.
This is maybe the best small Fine Arts museum in Switzerland with an excellent collection mostly of Swiss art from 1850 onwards—and it's free! The most interesting collections are on the first floor. Alongside some of the best works by Ferdinand Hodler (his *William Tell* is here ⓑ p318) and many known works by Félix Vallotton and Cuno Amiet, both contemporary painters of his. Take note of two stunning portraits executed by bygone masters: **Virgin with Strawberries**★ is a painting on wood from

the Rhenish School (c.1425), remarkable for its strong, vivid colours (blue, green, gold, crimson, ruby) and the graceful attitude of the two characters. As for the **Madonna of Solothurn**★—the work of Holbein the Younger—it is full of majesty and shows strict composition in which gold, red and blue predominate. Visitors may also admire works by Klimt, Van Gogh, Renoir, Matisse, Leger and Degas.

Natural History Museum

⊙Open Tue–Sun, 2pm–5pm, Sun 10am –5pm. ⊙Closed 1 Jan, Easter, Whitsun and Christmas. ⊜Free ⓑ ℘(0)32 622 70 21. www.naturmuseum-so.ch.
The Naturmuseum enlightens the visitor on the human race and regional fauna

(alive and fossilised). The second floor contains displays on Swiss geology and mineralogy. Of interest are the fossilised tortoises, starfish and dinosaur footprints. The basement houses temporary exhibitions.

Museum Schloss Blumenstein

Access NW of the town centre (follow directions for Schloss Blumenstein)
○Open Tue–Sat 2pm–5pm, Sun 10am –5pm. ◎Free. ℘(032) 622 54 70. www.museumblumenstein.ch.
This large 18C building, surrounded by a small park, exhibits furniture, tapestries, sculpture (religious and cult objects), costumes, ceramics and musical instruments. On the ground floor veranda, note the lovely 16C stained-glass windows.

EXCURSIONS
Weissenstein★★★

○ *10km/6.2mi from Solothurn.*
The most difficult section of mountain road can be avoided by taking the chairlift from Oberdorf station (4km/2.5mi N of Solothurn) to Kurhaus Weissenstein (16min). Allow 2hrs.
The crests of Weissenstein, standing like a rampart above the Solothurn lowland, offer one of the most impressive panoramas in the Jura. There is a chairlift from Oberdorf to the spa hotel at the summit.

Panorama★★★

⛷○Operates Apr–Oct, 8.30am–6pm (8am Sun), Nov–Mar, 9am–5pm (8am Sun). ○Closed three weeks in spring and autumn. ◎Return fare 19CHF. ℘(0)84 884 15 25. www.seilbahnweissenstein.ch.
When driving from Solothurn or Gänsbrunnen, the summit is marked by a pastoral coomb. Turn into the road to the Kurhaus, which stands on the crest. Walk down the path (7km/4.3mi) on the road to Gänsbrunnen.
Park at the restaurant; here views of the great barrier of the Alps can be seen, from the Säntis on the left to the Mont Blanc on the right.

Utzenstorf

This lovely shaded and flowered village has a small church with 16C stained-glass windows.
North of Utzenstorf stands the 17C and 18C white turreted **Schloss Landshut★**, the residence of the bailiffs of Bern until 1798 (○open mid-May–mid-Oct, Tues–Sat 2pm–5pm, Sun 10–5; ○closed public holidays; ◎7CHF; ℘(0)32 665 40 27; www.schlosslandshut.ch). Interior decor includes heavy period furnishings and huge porcelain stoves. It houses the **Swiss Hunting Museum** with trophies, decoys, and a remarkable collection of seignorial hunting arms from the 16C–20C.

ADDRESSES

⌂STAY

◎◎◎ **Roter Turm** – *Hauptgasse 42.* ℘(0)32 622 96 21. www.roterturm.ch. *36 rooms.* Next to the clock tower, this family hotel is located in the historic district of the city. All rooms with modern conveniences. Great view of the tower from the fifth floor.

♈EAT

◎◎ **Stadtbeiz** – *Friedhofplatz 10.* ℘(0)32 622 11 09. www.alterstephan.ch. *Tue–Sum 11am–2pm, 6pm–10pm. Closed 1–5 Apr, 1–9 Aug, 17–31 Oct, 24 Dec–4 Jan.* On the ground floor of the chic restaurant **Zum Alten Stephan, Stadbeiz** has nothing to envy in terms of the quality of the food it serves—and at better prices. Excellent traditional and regional dishes.

⛵BOAT TRIPS

From Biel/Bienne, four daily boats travel eastward on a 2hr30min trip along the River Aare to Solothurn. ℘(0)32 622 33 22. www.bielersee.ch
The scenery is pastoral with reedy banks, farmhouses and birds along the glacial blue-green river. Half-timbered towns along the shore add interest, especially in **Büren**, where a covered bridge crosses the river. **Altreu** is a popular stop for its stork colony where the nests can be seen from the river.

Thun★★

Thun is one of the most typical Swiss towns, occupying an admirable site★★ within view of the Bernese Alps. The city, which has been populated since the Stone Age, was first established on an islet in the Aare where the river flows out of Lake Thun (Thunersee), and it gradually spread over the neighbouring shores at the foot of the Schlossberg, while passing from the hands of the Zähringens (*see BERN*) to those of the Kyburgs (1218). The second dynasty having become extinct in its turn, Thun came under the control of the Patriciate of Bern in 1384. The old quarters lie on the right bank of the Aare but the modern town with its ironworks has spread westward over the left bank.

- ▶ **Population:** 42 129.
- ⚙ **Michelin Map:** Town plan in Michelin Red Guide Switzerland.
- ℹ **Info:** Seestrasse 2/Bahnhof. ℘(0)33 225 90 00. www.thun.ch.
- ▶ **Location:** Thun is located where the river Aar flows out of Lake Thun. Alt. 560m/1 837ft.
- ✦ **Don't Miss:** A cruise on Lake Thun, past castles and palaces and sun-blackened wooden chalets; excursion boats stop directly at the train station.
- ◷ **Timing:** This town can be very busy on weekends and holidays so plan accordingly.

THE OLD TOWN

The bustling **Obere Hauptgasse**★ has an amusing feature: the flower-decked terraces of the houses serve as foot-paths, so that one walks on the roofs of the shops installed in the arcades at ground level. From the upper part of this street with its broad overhanging roofs a curious covered staircase (Kirchtreppe) to the church and the Zähringen Castle. Look for the city's narrowest house, only 2m/6.6ft wide, at No 61.

The **Rathausplatz**★ is surrounded by arcaded houses and adorned with a flower-decked fountain. Dominated by its castle, the Rathausplatz makes a fine picture. A covered wooden bridge (Obere Schleuse), crosses the Aare.

Schloss

Reached by the covered staircase (Kirchtreppe) mentioned above.

The castle is is a massive Romanesque construction—flanked by four towers—which now houses the Schlossmuseum, at the north end of the Schlossberg.

Schlossmuseum★

◷*Open Jun–Sept 10am–5pm, Feb and Mar, 1pm–4pm, Nov–Jan, Sun 1pm–4pm.* ☞*8CHF; guided tours available.*

℘*(0)33 225 90 00. www.schlossthun.ch.* The magnificent Knights' Hall contains beautiful tapestries—one from the tent of Charles the Bold, seized by the Confederates after the Battle of Grandson in 1476—together with standards, breast-plates, chests, ceramics (a fine collection of old "Heimberg" pieces), archeological artefacts, items relating to local folklore, instruments, furniture and popular art-work evoking Thun in the 18C.

Above the Knights' Hall are special exhibits, such as Swiss Army firearms and uniforms. From the top floor of the tower you can reach the four corner turrets for a **panorama**★★ of the town, the Aare, Lake Thun and the Bernese Alps from the Stockhorn in the west to the Niesen in the south, embracing the Jungfrau, the Eiger and the Mönch.

Stadtkirche

At the opposite end of the Schlossberg stands the parish church, its large octagonal tower and the steeple covered with small round tiles, dominating a porch decorated with frescoes.

From the terrace of the church, there is a beautiful **view**★★ of the city, the lake and the Alps.

THE LAKE SHORE
Jakobshübeli★★

From this hill equipped as a belvedere *(viewing table)*, there is a semicircular **panorama★★** toward the Stockhorn and the Jungfrau.

Schadau Park and Castle★

Access by bus number 1 from the station. www.schloss-schadau.ch.

Set on the lake shore, this pleasant garden surrounding **Schadau Castle** offers a fine **view★★** *(viewing table)* of the summits of the Bernese Alps, particularly the Finsteraarhorn (alt. 4 274m/14 022ft), which is the highest point of this mountain group. The Castle houses the Arts Restaurant and the **Swiss Gastronomy Museum** (◷*Tue–Thu 2pm–5pm;* ◉*5 CHF; www.gastronomiemuseum-thun.ch)* which displays books, menus and old utensils. The library is unique in its kind, bringing together more than 5 000 cookbooks in several languages, including some rare copies of 16C first editions. Just at the left of the entrance to the park, do not miss the Scherzligen church with its 9C Romanesque nave where modern furniture (altar, benches) rubs shoulders with ancient frescoes painted in the nave, the apse and the porch (13C–16C).

Wocher Panorama★

◷*Open Apr–Oct, Tue–Sun, 11am–5pm.* ◉*6CHF.* ☎*(0)33 225 84 20.*

Schadau park is also the setting for the rotunda housing Marquard Wocher's panorama portraying Thun and its environs from 1814. It is the oldest circular painting in existence.

EXCURSION
Einigen

▷ *11km/6.5mi S by Frutigenstrasse.*

Halfway between Thun and Spiez, the charming village of Einigen is located on the south bank of Lake Thun, across from a lovely mountain landscape. The small Romanesque church, with a brilliant roughcast façade and 15C and 16C stained-glass windows, is topped by a pinnacle turret. With the tiny cemetery surrounding it, and sloping down in terraces to the lake, the church forms a picturesque **scene★**.

🚗 DRIVING TOUR

Thunersee★★ (Lake Thun)

From Thun to Interlaken 23km/14.3mi. Allow about 1hr. www.bls.ch.

Lake Thun 18km/11mi long, almost 4km/2.5mi wide and 217m/712ft deep, is one of the loveliest and largest sheets of water in Switzerland. Countless tourists have been captivated by its location amid green mountains and the snow-capped summit of the Jungfrau.

▷ *After the pretty residential suburbs of Thun, the road to Oberhofen remains within view of the summits of the Bernese Alps (Eiger-Mönch-Jungfrau and, more to the right, the three characteristic snowy ridges of the Blümlisalp). In the foreground, on the opposite shore, the Niesen pyramid and the rocky Stockhorn are prominent.*

Schloss Hünegg★★

◷*Open daily mid–May to mid–Oct, 2pm–5pm, Sun 11am–5pm.* ◉*9CHF.* ☎*(0)33 243 19 82.*

Located in a wooded park that slopes down to the lake, this large edifice (1863), in spite of its size, cannot be seen from the road. The apartments (1900) have been arranged into a museum of *Jugendstil (Art Nouveau)*. One room evokes the life of the Swiss student at the time (uniforms, duelling weapons etc.); works by the Bernese painter Martin Lauterburg (d. 1960) are exhibited on the second floor.

Oberhofen

This 12C **castle★★** (◷*open mid–May– mid–Oct, Tue–Sun 11am–5pm, Mon 2pm– 5pm;* ◉ *free, museum 10CHF;* ☎*(0)33 243 12 35. www.schlossoberhofen.ch)* jutting into the waters of the lake, forms an enchanting fairytale picture (*illuminated at night*), opposite the summits of the Bernese Alps. Enlarged and restored (17C to 19C), is now a branch of the Ber-

Oberhofen Castle by Thunersee

© Max Schmid/Switzerland Tourism

nisches Historisches Museum displaying period furniture (Louis XIV, Louis XV, Empire) and collections of popular art illustrating life in the Bernese Oberland. The landscape park on the shores of the lake is one of the most pleasant features of the visit.

Before leaving Oberhofen, visit the **Museum of Timepieces and Mechanical Music Instruments** (⏰*open mid-May–mid-Oct, daily 2pm–5pm; ⊚10 CHF; ℘(0)33 243 43 77; www.uhrenmusem.ch*), housed in a 16C building in a large park by the lake. The museum displays a splendid collection of watches and musical instruments spanning seven centuries.

Between Oberhofen and Merligen, there is a superb **run along the quays**★★, facing Spiez and the mouth of the Kander Valley, the best side of the lake for sun and flowers. The Blümlisalp Massif, clearly visible through this gap, now draws near.

Merligen

At the end of a deeply cut valley, the village lies between green hillsides and the lake. It is known for its music, with frequent concerts, and for its 250-year cheese-making tradition, celebrated each September in a fair.

After Merligen, the road becomes a corniche along the steep slopes of the Nase (Nose) promontory over the eastern basin of the lake, whose lonely shores form a contrast with the little Riviera you have just come through.

Niederhorn ★★

Alt. 1 950m/6 397ft 🚶*1–2hrs round trip, including the funicular ride from Beatenbucht to Beatenberg. Operates Jun–early Nov, daily 8am–5pm. ⊚50CHF. ℘(0)33 841 08 41.*

A gondola lift carries hikers and sightseers to the top of the Niederhorn, where views stretch across the Bernese Alps, including the three summits of the Eiger, Mönch, and Jungfrau and down across Thuner See. A short trail leads to a viewing platform with a telescope and map. During the descent through several tunnels, beginning 1km/0.6mi after Beatenbucht (the starting-point of the Beatenberg funicular), the view opens over the Bödeli Plain, between the wooded chains of the Harder (on the left) and the Rugen (on the right, dominated in the background by the rocky points of the Schynige Platte). Before Unterseen, the road passes at the foot of the St Beatus Caves with a cascade tumbling down.

Beatenberg ★
(St Beatus Caves)

Allow 1hr15min, including 1hr for the guided tour. Remember to dress warmly since the temperature is between 8°C/45°F and 12°C/55°F. 🚶Guided tour (50min) every half hour late May–

Oct, 9.30am–5pm. ✆18CHF. ☎(0)33
841 16 43. www.beatushoehlen.ch.
It is in these caves, according to legend,
that the 6C Hermit St Beatus spent his
life in prayer (and slew a dragon while he
was at it). In the 18C the only access was
along the picturesque pilgrims' path
which can also be traversed today starting from **Beatenbucht** (60–70 mins) or
from Interlaken itself (2hr30min). This
was an important pilgrimage centre and
the ruins of an old Pilgrim's inn can be
seen after the entrance on the right.
Of the 14km/8.8mi of galleries which
have been excavated, only 900m/985yd
are open to the public. They are reached
by a steep path (10min) running alongside a pretty **waterfall**★.
First you will come across a series of
caves evoking man's life in prehistoric
times. Then you enter the actual grot-
toes, of which the most notable features
are the Domed Grotto (11m/36ft high),
the Mirror Grotto (note the stalactites'
reflection in the sheet of water), the
Witches' Cauldron and the Snake's
Grotto. You can also visit a small **Cave
Museum** (Tue–Sun 11.30am–5.30pm)
devoted to geology and speleology,
which displays several panels explaining the history of Swiss Caving.

Unterseen

This peaceful village, contiguous to
Interlaken has a church, whose rustic
steeple with a steep sloping gabled roof
provides a very photogenic composition with the Mönch (left) and Jungfrau
(right) in the background.
Just steps away, the small **Jungfrau
Region Touristikmuseum**★ (Jungfrau
tourist region museum, Obere Gasse 28;
⏰open May to mid–Oct, Tue–Sun 2pm–
5pm; ✆5CHF, children 2CHF; ☎033 822 98
39; www.touristmuseum.ch) traces the
increase in tourism in the region since
the early 19C. Exhibits illustrate a century of road transport in the Oberland:
the Habkern postal carriage, models of
other postal vehicles and the first bicycle to have been used in Interlaken. The
milestone (studenstein) indicated the
distance and length of time required
for those on foot to reach Bern. Other

displays illustrate the expansion of the
hotel industry (accommodation in private homes, inns and hotels) and development of the railway network (model
of a locomotive from the Brünig Pass's
rack railway). Nautical instruments and
furnishings are grouped together in
the boat section. The most interesting exhibit is undoubtedly a miniature
model of the Bellevue, the very first boat
to sail on Lake Thun. There are additional
displays on winter sports, with a section
on development of skis and sledges, the
growth of mountain railways such
as those on the Giessbach, Wetterhorn
and Jungfrau, and the sport of mountaineering. The top floor is reserved for
temporary exhibitions.

Interlaken★★★
👁See INTERLAKEN.

ADDRESSES

🛏STAY

🍽**Pension-Restaurant zum Lärch** –
3988 Obergesteln. ☎(0)27 973 10 01.
www.laerch.ch. Cosy guesthouse with
restaurant.

🍽🏦🏦 **Krone** – Rathausplatz 2.
☎(0)33 227 88 88. www.krone-thun.ch.
27 rooms. Located in the heart of the
old town, with recently renovated and
refurbished, elegant rooms.

🍴EAT

🍽🏦🏦🏦 **Arts Schloss Schadau** –
Seestrasse 45. ☎(0)33 222 25 00. www.
schloss-schadau.ch. Open 10am–9.30pm.
Closed Mon and Tue Nov–Apr; Mon only
M ay–Oct. This 19C chateau in the
sumptuous setting of a leafy park on
a lake, has a restaurant and a bistro for
different budgets.

🎷NIGHTLIFE

Dancing and socializing on five levels at
Musikpark (Scheibenstrasse 49-51).

Spiez★

This charming little town at the foot of the Niesen enjoys a beautiful **site**★, best seen from a terrace at the exit from the town beside the road to Interlaken. Spiez is a pleasant summer resort and a good excursion centre.

SIGHTS

Schloss

The medieval **castle**, crowned with several massive towers, stands on a spur of the Spiezberg overlooking the lake and the bay. It was built in the 12C and 13C and has since been enlarged and restored several times.

From the public garden on the esplanade in front of the castle entrance, you overlook the harbour containing sailing and pleasure boats. Many chalets nestle among the greenery on the far shore. The Castle Museum (◯open Easter–mid-Oct, Mon 2pm–5pm; Tue–Sun 10am–5pm (6pm Jul–mid-Sept); ⌘5CHF; ℘(0)33 654 15 06) contains mementos of the former owners of the castle, the Erlachs and Bubenbergs, and some fine Gothic, Renaissance and Baroque inlaid furniture. The rooms are adorned with ornate woodwork and stained-glass windows.

From the top of the great tower you can admire a fine **panoramic view**★★ of the lovely sites of Spiez, Lake Thun, the Niesen in the south and the Beatenberg in the east.

Schlosskirche

This Romanesque church (late 10C, now disused) near the castle was designed as a basilica with three aisles and semicircular apses (fine frescoes). Especially remarkable are, to the left of the chancel, the Baroque tomb of Sigismond of Erlach (1700) and the grave of Jeanne de la Sararz , second wife of Adrian von Budenberg (15C)

▶ **Population:** 12 453.
▪ **Info:** Info-Centre – 3700 Spiez. ℘(0)33 654 20 20. www.spiez.ch. Hauptstrasse, Kanderthal. ℘(0)33 675 80 80. www.kandersteg.ch.
◖ **Location:** On the south shore of Lake Thun. Alt. 628m/2 060ft.
◈ **Don't Miss:** The castle museum.

🚗DRIVING TOURS

KANDERTAL★

From Spiez to Kandersteg 26km/16mi – about 2hr30min. ⊙This excursion ends in a cul-de-sac at Kandersteg, but the railway is fitted out to take cars through the Lötschberg Tunnel to the Valais.

This valley is divided into two sections orientated differently: firstly the Frutigtal which goes southwest as far as Frutigen; then the Kandertal which goes south to Kandersteg.

◖ *Leave Spiez SW by the Kandersteg road and stop in Mülenen.*

Crossing the spur which separates Spiez from the Kander, the road drops towards the valley floor and begins to encircle the huge Niesen Pyramid.

Climb to the Niesen★★★

Alt. 2 362m/7 749ft. ⌁From Mülenen station, about 2hr round trip, including 1hr by funicular. ⊙Operates May–mid-Nov. Departure every 30min (15min if busy), 8am–5pm (enquire in advance). ⌘Return fare 53CHF. ℘(0)33 676 77 11. The funicular rides above the Frutigtal and stops at Schwandegg (alt. 1 669m/5 474ft), before continuing to Niesen Kulm, from where there is a magnificent **panorama**★★★ of the Berner Oberland. A footpath leads to the summit *(allow half a day)*, where visitors will find a hotel-restaurant.

Frutigen

15min on foot there and back to go up to the church (following the Adelboden road for a moment and then turning up the first ramp to the right).

This large village at the confluence of the Kander and the Engstligen, is the best-equipped medium altitude resort in the Lötschberg district. The church is built high up within view of the Balmhorn and the Altels.

Crossing the Kander at the foot of the Tellenburg ruins your approach to the Bühlstutz ridge. This separates the Kandergrund shelf from the Kandersteg Basin and compels the Lötschberg railway to make a hairpin loop around the Felsenburg ruins, which stand out clearly on their rocky spur.

Blausee★

About 45min walk and trip by boat.
🕒*Nature reserve open from Apr–Oct, 9am–5pm; Nov–Mar 10am–5pm.*
🎟*Admission 5CHF, only in summer.*
📞*(0)33 672 33 33. www.blausee.ch*

This site comprises not only a little lake with incredibly clear, blue water, lying deep in the forest within view of the snowy Doldenhorn summit, but also a mass of rocks among the woods, a trout farm, and a restaurant. The road now takes on the Bühlstutz ridge in a more austere landscape of fields and woods dotted with rocks. At last you emerge into the Kandersteg Basin with steep slopes laced with waterfalls.

Kandersteg★

Alt. 1 176m/3 858ft. Hauptstrasse.
📞*(0)33 675 80 80. www.kandersteg.ch.*

Lying at the foot of rugged escarpments, which frame the snow-peaks of the Blümlisalp to the east and dip into a green Alpine basin, Kandersteg is best known today for its position at the north end of the **Lötschberg Tunnel**.

This railway tunnel, 14.6km/9mi long (Kandersteg–Goppenstein), has created, since 1913, a direct link between Bern and the Rhône Valley and can also convey cars.

As a mark of the close co-operation between Eurotunnel and the Swiss railway system, one locomotive of the Bern-Lötschberg-Simplon train has been given the name *Eurotunnel*. Likewise, one of the engines which carries passengers across the Channel is called *Lötschberg*. *(For information on how to transport your car through the tunnel, ask at Tourist Information Centres or railway stations.)* The life of the locality is kept going in summer by the proximity of natural wonders like Lake Oeschinen and, in winter, by facilities for skiers.

◗ *Follow the main road towards the floor of the valley and leave your car at the lower cable-car station at Stock.*

Klus★★

1hr on foot there and back.

Climb, on foot, a little road that goes into a tunnel over the Klus. Go on to the bridge over the Kander after a second tunnel. Sure-footed tourists will prefer to descend by the steep path, sometimes wet with spray, which leaves the road between the two tunnels.

ENGSTLIGENGRAT VALLEY

30km/18.5mi from Spiez to Adelboden – Allow 2hrs. www.engstligenalp.ch.

This tour follows the same route as above, then branches off to turn right to Frutigen to Adelboden.

Adelboden

Alt. 1 356m/4 446ft. Dorfstrasse 23, 3715.
📞*(0)33 673 80 80. www.adelboden.ch.*

Adelboden lies in the wide, sunny **basin**★ at the upper end of the Engstligen Valley. It is one of the highest of the fashionable resorts in the Bernese Oberland both in summer and in winter, and is known for its healthy and agreeable climate. The village clusters halfway up the slope, facing a majestic skyline of limestone mountains. The most striking feature is the snow-covered, flat top of the Wildstrubel (alt. 3 243m/10 640ft), completing the great mountain circle of the Engstligenalp, from which the powerful Engstligenfälle bursts forth, leaping from a rocky shelf to form an impressive spectacle.

⛷ The Skiing Area

Adelboden skiing area, linked to that of Lenk, comprises 160km/99.5mi of pistes and some 50 lifts. Its highest point is Luegli (alt. 2 138m/7 014ft); it is particularly suitable for intermediate skiers.

Engstligenfälle★★★

4km/2.5mi along the Adelboden road, 🚡then access by cable car (ascent 5min). ⊘Bring warm, waterproof clothes and sturdy shoes.

From the top, the **view**★ of Adelboden is dominated by Gsür (2 708m/8 884ft), the Gross Lohner Massif, and the upper part of the Engstligen Falls. To the south extend the Engstligenalp pastures.

🏔 Hikers can choose several **itineraries**, including those leading to Ammerten Pass (*2hr climb*, 2 443m/8 015ft) and the **Ammertenspitz** summit (*2hr30min climb*, 2 613m/8 573ft), for a splendid **panorama** of Steghorn, Tierhorn, Les Diablerets and the Walliser Alpen. The most spectacular excursion leads down past the falls, featuring a vertical drop of 476m/1 562m (*1hr30min on foot*). From Engstligenalp, follow directions for "Unter dem Berg" and continue towards "Wasserfall."

After 30min, you will discover a breathtaking **view**★★★ as you approach the bridge spanning the falls. Follow directions for "Engstligenfall," within sight of the cable-car terminal. A steep, narrow path leads to Alpine columbine, a rare mountain species. Finally you reach the **belvedere**★★ overlooking the lower falls, which are equally spectacular. Return to the car park by following directions for "Unter dem Berg" (*10min*).

🏔 HIKES DEPARTING FROM KANDERSTEG

Oeschinensee★★★

🚡*About 1hr30min there and back, including 7min by chairlift, plus a 20min walk.* 🕐 *Jun–Sept 9am–5.45pm; May & Oct 9.30am–4.30pm. Departure every 30min.* 🚡*Return fare 24CHF. Toboggan run 4CHF* 📞*(0)33 675 11 18. www.oeschinensee.ch.*

The road leading to the lower chairlift station branches off the main road from Kandersteg directly after the bridge over the Oeschinenbach, on the left. From the upper station a road leads down to the lake shore (*bear to the right at a fork after a 5min walk*) encircled by a vast amphitheatre of cliffs, crowned by the snowy Blümlisalp Peaks. After reaching Lake Oeschinen, good walkers can continue to Kandersterg by the direct road, others can return to the upper chairlift station.

Oberbergli★★★

Allow at least 3hr15min or even a whole day if you plan to climb up towards the Blüemlisalp refuge. ⊘*Not to be attempted in wet weather. Sturdy mountain shoes are necessary.*

A path (*good condition*) skirts Lake Oeschinen and reveals splendid **views**★★★ of the steep surrounding summits: Doldenhorn, Fründenhorn, Oeschinenhorn, and Blüemlisalphorn. At the far end of the lake, a steep path leads to Oberbergli. To enjoy a sweeping panorama of the glacier, continue climbing for 1hr (⊘*very steep slope*) toward the Blüemlisalp refuge until you reach a small lake.

ADDRESSES

🛏STAY

⊜⊜**Seerose** – *Interlakenstrasse 87 Faulensee. 2km/1.2mi SE of Spiez.* 📞*(0)33 654 10 25. www.seerose-faulensee.ch.* 🅿🛏. *13 rooms. Closed Jan & Feb.* ⊜⊜*Restaurant open daily for lunch and dinner, closed Mon & Tue Mar–Apr, Oct–Dec.* This house overlooks Lake Thun in a small village.

🍴/EAT

⊜⊜⊜**Restaurant Im Schloss** – *Schlossstrasse 16.* 📞*(0)33 654 94 74.* 🅿 *www.im-schloss.ch. Open May–Oct Thu–Sat evenings and by appointment.* A gastronomic stop to enjoy the atmosphere of Spiez castle. Original local cuisine from chef Bruno Wüthrich.

Interlaken★★★

Interlaken is the tourist centre of the Berner Oberland. It is renowned for its superb view of the Jungfrau Massif, which is home to the highest railway station in Europe. Framed between the small wooded ranges of the Rügen and the Harder, the town extends over the low plain of the Bödeli, formed by deposits from the Lombach in the north and the Lütschine in the south. These finally divided the single lake (into which the Aare used to flow between Meiringen and Thun) into two distinct sheets of water, Lake Thun and Lake Brienz (Thunersee and Brienzersee).

A BIT OF HISTORY

The Latin sound of the name Interlaken recalls the clerical origin of the town; it grew up between the lakes from the 12C onwards, around an Augustinian monastery of which traces, such as the cloister gallery, can still be found in the block of buildings formed by the castle and the Protestant church. The resort is extremely popular in the summer months, when its many souvenir shops are busy with tourists.

▶ **Population:** 5 319.

◔ **Michelin Map:** Town plan in The Michelin Red Guide Switzerland.

▯ **Info:** Höheweg 37 – 3800. ✆(0)33 826 53 00. www.interlakentourism.ch.

▶ **Location:** Interlaken has two train stations, West and Ost. West station goes to the city centre; take Ost station for excursions to nearby villages and peaks such as Grindelwald and Jungfraujoch.

◉ **Don't Miss:** An excursion to one, if not all, of the majestic summits: Schilthorn, Jungfrau, Eiger.

SIGHTS
Höheweg★★

This famous avenue is bordered on one side by the lawns and flower beds of the Höhematte, on the other by a row of grand hotels and behind them, the casino (Kursaal). The promenade links the urban centre of Interlaken West with the much more scattered township of Interlaken East. It offers dazzling

Interlaken with a view to Eiger, Mönch and Jungfrau

© Jost von Allmen/Interlaken Tourismus/Switzerland Tourism

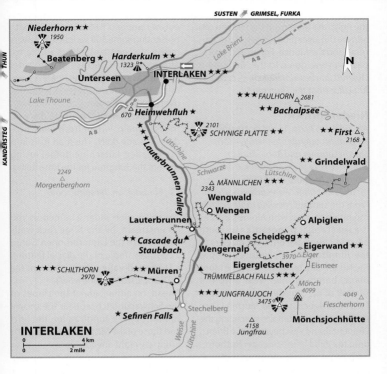

SUSTEN GRIMSEL, FURKA

Niederhorn ★★
1950

Beatenberg ★   **Harderkulm ★★**
1323
Unterseen   **INTERLAKEN ★★★**

Lake Thoune

★★★ FAULHORN 2681
★★ Bachalpsee

670 **Heimwehfluh ★**
2101
SCHYNIGE PLATTE ★★
★★ First 2168

★★ Grindelwald

2249
Morgenberghorn

★★ MÄNNLICHEN ★★★
2343
Wengwald
Wengen

Alpiglen

Lauterbrunnen
★★ Cascade du Staubbach
Kleine Scheidegg ★★
Wengernalp
★★ Eigerwand ★★
3970 *Eiger*
Eigergletscher
Eismeer

★★★ SCHILTHORN 2970
★★ Mürren
TRÜMMELBACH FALLS ★★★
Mönch 4099
4049
Fiescherhorn
★★★ JUNGFRAUJOCH 3475

★ Sefinen Falls
Stechelberg
4158
Jungfrau
Mönchsjochhütte

INTERLAKEN
0   4 km
0   2 mile

Lake Brienz
Lütschine
Lauterbrunnen Valley
Schwarze Lütschine
Weisse Lütschine

views★★★ of the Jungfrau, through the opening of the lower Lütschine Valley. It is pleasant to stroll beneath the trees, glancing at the pavilion of meteorological instruments or the well-known floral clock in the casino gardens. A second attraction on the opposite bank of the River Aare is the open-air swimming pool and miniature golf course. These are both popular weekend activities during the summer season.

EXCURSIONS
Harderkulm ★★
Alt. 1 323m/4 341ft. About 1hr there and back, including 10min by funicular from Interlaken East. Operates daily, Apr–Oct, 8.10am–5.45pm. Departures every 20 or 30min. Fare there and back 27CHF. (0)33 828 72 33.
A small park near the lower funicular station is home to a variety of animals typically found in the Alps. From the panoramic restaurant at the summit, there is a clear view of the two Interlaken lakes and the Jungfrau Massif.

Heimwehfluh ★
Alt. 670m/2 218ft. 1–2hr round trip, including 5min by funicular.
Operates mid-Apr–Nov 10am–5pm. Departures every 15min. All attractions combi ticket 23CHF. (0)33 822 34 53. www.heimwehfluh.ch.
A cool, shady hill overlooking Lake Thun and Lake Brienz. Don't miss the unique toboggan run for both children and adults, as well as a model railway display and playground.
There are many shaded walks, especially on the slopes of the Rügen or the Harder.

Beatenberg ★
Alt. 1 150m/3 773ft.
The winding but excellent road (connecting to Scheidgasse in Unterseen), climbs amid fir trees, offering good glimpses of Interlaken, the Jungfrau and Lake Thun. Beatenberg, a terraced resort, extending along more than 7km/4.5mi, consists mainly of hotels and holiday chalets nestling in the trees. It overlooks Lake Thun and, farther to

the right, the Niesen; on the left you can admire the sweeping ranges of the Jungfrau and the Mönch. For an all-encompassing view, go up to the Niederhorn *(10km/6.2mi from Interlaken; ⛰ access by funicular from the Thun road).*

Niederhorn★★

Alt. 1950m/6397ft. Access by chairlift.
⛰*Chairlift operates (generally) 8am–5pm in summer and 8am–6pm in winter.* 🚢*Fare there and back from Interlaken incl boat trip 65CHF.*
☎*(0)33 841 0841. www.niederhorn.ch.*
From the summit *(viewing tables)* of this mountain covered with Alpine pastures is a spectacular **panorama★★**: south beyond Thun Lake onto the glaciers of the Jungfrau Massif; southwest onto the Niesen and far in the distance Mont Blanc, barely visible; west onto the summit of the Stockhorn; northwest as far as the Neuchâtel and Murten lakes; north onto the mountains preceding the Emmental; and east beyond Lake Brienz, onto the cliffs of the Brienzer Rothorn.

🚗 DRIVING TOUR

LAUTERBRUNNENTAL★★★

23km/14mi from Interlaken to Stechelberg. About 3hr including 2hr 45min cable-car and sightseeing.

▷ *Leave Interlaken south on the Lauterbrunnen road; stop at Wilderswil.*

Schynige Platte★★

Alt. 2 101m/6 891ft. About 4hr there and back, including 2hr by rack railway starting from Wilderswil station.
🕐*Operates Jun–Oct. Departure every 50min, 8am–6.30pm.* 🚢*Fare there and back 66.80CHF.* ☎*(0)33 828 72 33. www.jungfrau.ch.*
This climb is especially suited to tourists who have no time to venture farther into the Jungfrau Massif. Schynige Platte is one of the most popular destinations for vacationers staying in Grindelwald (🌿*see GRINDELWALD.*)
Near the upper station, an Alpine garden and a botanical section have been laid

out over an area of 8 000sq m/9 570sq yds, presenting some 500 varieties of flowers (edelweiss, gentian), plants and ferns. The panoramic terrace of the hotel affords easy access to the nearest summit (alt. 2 076m/6 812ft—viewpoint overlooking the Jungfrau, Interlaken and its lakes). Note the Alpine dairy on the Iseltenalp, where fresh dairy produce is made daily. The road runs into the wooded Lütschine defile, losing sight of the Jungfrau for the time being.

▷ *Continue on the same road.*

The valley soon widens, framed, as you go upstream, by the huge rock walls which make the Lauterbrunnen Gorge a classic example of the glacial feature: a U-shaped valley (🌿*illustration, see INTRODUCTION: Alpine relief*).
Ahead, on either side of the slopes of the Schwarzmönch, appear the snowy summits of the Jungfrau (on the left) and those of the Mittaghorn-Grosshorn group (straight ahead).

Lauterbrunnen

This village has heavy through traffic.
🅿 *Motorists who wish to go to Wengen must leave their cars in the car park.*
Here the **Staubbachfall★**, which Byron compared with the "tail of the pale horse ridden by Death in the Apocalypse," plunges 300m/1 000ft from the terrace at Mürren, dissolving almost entirely into fine spray. In line with the valley you will see the Breithorn summit, clearly detached to the right of the Grosshorn.

Wengen✳✳

Alt. 1 275m/4 183ft.
Wengen is situated on a sunny and wind-sheltered mountain terrace at the foot of the Jungfrau massif, dominated by the Jungfrau and the Eiger. One of the most fashionable and best equipped mountain resorts in the Bernese Oberland, it is popular year-round for its picturesque old-fashioned charm and car-free streets.
The **site★★★** is a perfect starting point for walks, which follow well-maintained paths, even in winter with

Wengen at the foot of Eiger, Mönch and Jungfrau

© Wengen-Muerren-Lauterbrunnental Tourismus AG/Switzerland Tourism

500km/310.6mi of posted hiking trails. The **ski resort** has 44 lifts leading to more than 200km/124mi of pistes; beginner areas are ideal for families. Kleine Scheidegg (alt. 2 061m/6 762ft) is reached by the mountain railway from the centre of town. From here, you can ski the famous Lauberhorn, site of the men's downhill World Cup **Lauberhorn race**, which takes place in early January; the railway also accesses the Eigergletscher. There are 50km/32mi of groomed toboggan runs, some are illuminated at night.

▷ _At the exit from Lauterbrunnen, turn to the direction of Stechelberg._

Trümmelbachfälle★★★
3hr to 4hr on foot there and back.
🕐_Open Jul and Aug, 8am–6pm; Apr, May, Sept and Oct, 9am–5pm._
🚶_11CHF._ 🅿️_Leave your car in the Trümmelbachfälle car park. Take waterproof clothes._ 🖉_(0)33 855 32 32._
A lift passing through the rock leads to the beginning of the galleries. These are well sited over the winding fissure where the Trümmelbach leaps and boils, forcing its way through a series of great eroded potholes. On returning to the lower entrance of the funicular, be sure to walk up the path to the left (to the right when facing the mountain) to see the incredible gush of water coming

from the second last falls of the Trümmelbachfälle.
Return to your car and drive up the valley to Stechelberg, the Mürren-Schilthorn cable-car station and the place from where you can see, to the south _(1km/0.6mi)_ the lovely, almost vertical **Sefinenfall★**.

Mürren★
Alt. 1 650m/5 413ft. 🚠_Access: 10min by cable car. Mürren Tourismus._
🖉_(0)33 856 86 86. www.muerren.ch._
Perched on a shelf of Alpine pasture forming a balcony overlooking the steep cleft of the Lauterbrunnen Valley, Mür-

Trümmelbachfälle

© Marcus Gyger/Switzerland Tourism

ren faces a series of giant peaks carved out of rock or ice: from left to right, the view encompasses the Eiger, the Mönch, the Jungfrau, the Breithorn, and the Gspaltenhorn range (far right).

The **site**★★ of this village, completely free of car traffic, and its surrounding ski slopes, which bristle with every conceivable obstacle, account for the resort's popularity. The development of tourism in the area was largely due to the British, who came here at the turn of the last century to indulge in their favourite winter sports and succeeded in recreating a cosy, congenial atmosphere. It was here that the Kandahar Ski Club was founded in 1924 named after his founder, Earl Roberts of Kandahar. 1928 saw the start of the **Arlberg-Kandahar competition**, now regarded as the unofficial world championship of winter sports for the Alpine countries Mürren has only 350 inhabitants and is the highest-lying settlement in the canton of Bern, belonging politically to the municipality of Lauterbrunnen. .

Schilthorn★★★

Alt. 2 970m/9 744ft. About 1hr15min including 17min by cable car, leaving from Mürren. There is also a cable car leaving from Stechelberg down in the valley. www.schilthorn.ch. Round trip about 2hr including 1hr cable car via Stechelberg. Operates every 30 mins from 7.25am–4.25pm summer 7.55am–3.55pm winter Fare there and back from Mürren 74 CHF. For information on periods of closure, call (0)33 856 21 41. www.schilthorn.ch. From the top, in a desolate landscape of torrents and scree, is a **panoramic view**★★★ of the Jungfrau Massif with only the Lauterbrunnen cleft between that and the observer. Part of Lake Thun, and a total of 200 mountain peaks and 40 glaciers are visible. The panoramic restaurant features a popular revolving plateau; it makes a complete turn in 55min. This aluminum establishment with a futuristic look and exceptional location is famous and familiar for its role in the James Bond film *On Her Majesty's Secret Service*; several scenes

were shot on the premises (1967–68). Every year in January the locality hosts **Inferno**, an Alpine skiing competition in which contestants race from the Schilthorn summit down to Lauterbrunnen, a 16km/10mi circuit and a vertical drop of 2 134m/7 001ft in barely 20min! Seasoned skiers can follow the route on other days without racing.

ROUND TOUR OF THE JUNGFRAU BY RAILWAY★★★

This panoramic tour is magnificent. Reductions are available on the first train of the morning: ask for a Good Morning Ticket. Allow a whole day and choose one when the atmospheric conditions are the best possible in order to enjoy spectacular scenery; a veil of cloud on the summits is enough to spoil the excursion. Wear warm clothes, and if you want to go out into the open, take sunglasses and wear sturdy shoes.

The first part of the journey is to Kleine Scheidegg, where passengers change trains. The train then makes its way through tunnels cut into the Eiger, stopping occasionally to allow passengers to admire the glaciers, to reach the **Top of Europe** station (alt. 3 454m/11 329ft). Some of the slopes along this unforgettable route have gradients of 25%. .

Wengernalp

Alt. 1 873m/6 145ft.
A wild site at the foot of the rock and glacier slopes of the Jungfrau. The deep Trümmelbach Gorge in the foreground makes the height of this wall of rock even more impressive, and it is not unknown to witness an avalanche.

To the left of the Jungfrau you will recognize the snowy cleft of the Jungfraujoch—the terminus of the excursion (the Sphinx observatory is visible)—and then the Mönch, the Eigergletscher Glacier and the Eiger.

Kleine Scheidegg★★

Alt. 2 061m/6 762ft.
This mountain resort, isolated on the ledge linking the Lauterbrunnen Valley to the Grindelwald Valley, is a favourite with skiers, who find abundant snow

Conquest of the Eigerwand

One of the most dramatic climbs after the conquest of the Matterhorn was that of the north face of the Eiger (⟲ *see INTERLAKEN*). In 1858 the summit (3 970m/13 025ft) was reached by the Irishman Charles Barrington and Swiss guides Christian Almer and Peter Bohren. The south and southwest spurs were conquered in 1874 and 1876. From 1935 onwards there were many deadly attempts to climb the north face: that year, two Germans were killed; the next year, three roped teams of Germans and Austrians fell to their deaths.

These tragedies raised such a storm of protest that cantonal authorities in Bern forbade any further attempt. The ban was lifted in 1937, marked by the failure of the Austrian Rebitsch and the German Wiggerl Vörg. However, the follvowing year, Vörg and his companion, Anderl Heckmair, made secret preparations for an attempt. Though two Austrians, Kasparek and Harrer, started before them, they overtook them on the second day and decided to join forces with the rival team. Their slow and difficult progress, threatened at every step by the danger of storms and avalanches, was watched anxiously from the valley. Thanks to international press and radio, the whole world eagerly awaited details of their progress. When they surmounted the final crest, blinded by fatigue and storm, they were not even immediately aware of their victory. Their difficult descent by the west face, in the midst of a blizzard, sealed the success of their expedition.

here even late in the season. In summer it is frequented by tourists seeking tranquillity. Tourists who do not go up the Jungfraujoch may admire the Grindelwald Basin and pick out the Eiger-Mönch-Jungfrau group in excellent conditions by going up to the **belvedere**★★ on the north side of the pass (*1hr to 2hr on foot there and back.*)

Eigergletscher
Alt. 2 320m/7 612ft.

This stop near the snout of the Eiger Glacier, much broken and stained with morainic deposits, marks the beginning of the underground section, 7km/4mi long, which leads to the Jungfraujoch. In spring, great numbers of skiers come here.

Eigerwand★★
Alt. 2 865m/9 400ft.

The station is cut out of the rock. Ventilating bays giving on to the north face of the Eiger afford a bird's-eye view of the Grindelwald Basin and the Interlaken district. The situation is all the more impressive when you remember the dramatic efforts of mountaineers to conquer this rock wall, which was only climbed for the first time in 1938.

Jungfraujoch★★★
Alt. 3 475m/11 401ft.

This mountain resort, now marketing itself as Top of Europe, is the highest in Europe to be served by a **rack railway**. It presents a memorable and grandiose setting hemmed in by high mountains, with spectacular views of the surrounding mountain glaciers.

The site includes the famous summits of Mönch, the Eiger and the Jungfrau, as well as the Aletsch Glacier, and has been a UNESCO World Heritage Site since

Jungfraujoch

© Jungfrau Railways/Switzerland Tourism

Jungfrau Railway with a view of Jungfrau summit

© Jungfrau Railways/Switzerland Tourism

The Highest Railway Line in Europe

In 1893 the industrialist Adolf Guyer-Zeller, a member of the Alpine Club, had the idea of an "altitude metro". Extending the railway from the Wengernalp, a train would enter a tunnel and then climb the Eiger through to the heart of the Jungfrau. From there, a lift would lead tourists on the summit.

The construction lasted sixteen years because the conditions were difficult, with the wind and snow, avalanches and fog complicating the assault against the rock by teams of "mole workers" digging in three shifts a day. The summer pastures between the neck of the Kleine Scheidegg and the Eiger Glacier were invaded by hundreds of workers, with carts and mules. Provisions were transported and stored for the winter. Adolf Guyer-Zeller designed everything, even the panoramic windows carved into the rock for the tourists. The line was inaugurated on 1 August 1912, Swiss National Day, in dense fog.

2001. This was the first natural region in Switzerland—539sq km/208sq mi in the Bern and Valais cantons—to be declared a World Heritage Site.

Sphinx-Panoramaterrasse ★★★

Alt. 3 571m/8 435ft.
Access by the fastest lift in Switzerland (108m/355ft gained in 25 seconds with a maximum speed of 6.3m/20ft a second halfway up), then by 19 steps.
Breathtaking **panorama** of the Aletsch Glacier as it flows majestically like a wide river, sparkling among the rocky peaks. It is framed by the Mönch (4 099m/13 447ft), the Fiescherhorn (4 049m/13 282ft), the Aletschhorn (4 193m/13 755ft) and the Jungfrau (4 158m/13 641ft).
To the north, the steep Guggigletscher Glacier can be seen. The view includes

the Schilthorn, the Niesen, Interlaken and the Faulhorn.
A restaurant serving drinks and light meals is located at the summit of the Jungfraujoch. The Sphinx houses a research laboratory and an astronomical cupola. The pure quality of the air and easy access by railway are undeniable assets to carry out scientific experiments—you can actually observe some.

Aletschgletscher ★★★

Go back down by lift and follow directions for Aletschgletscher. You will reach the glacier itself, used as a piste for summer skiing (gentle slope, 100m/330ft).

Eispalast ★

10min access on foot and 15min visit.
The Ice Palace is a grotto carved out of the blue-tinged ice up to 8m/25ft in

depth, containing sculptures, particularly of animals.

Walk to the Mönchsjochhütte★★★

Alt. 3 629m/11 905ft.

This walk can be undertaken by any hiker wearing good mountain boots (⊘*do not stray from the beaten track—crampons are not necessary*).

A 1hr energetic walk up a steep slope will take you to a stunning **setting**★★★ and then to the small refuge at the foot of the Mönch. The pass (Obere Mönchsjoch) commands a pretty **view**★★ of the Schreckhorn.

◐ *Walk back along the same path.*

Wengwald

Alt. 1 182m/3 878ft.

Between this stopping-place and Wengen the route offers a splendid **view**★★★ of the Lauterbrunnen rift; the **Jungfrau** emerges in the distance. This is flanked on the right by the Silberhorn, a dazzling white, conical snow peak.

ADDRESSES

⌂STAY

INTERLAKEN

⌢⊜🏨 **Seehotel La Terasse** – *Seestrasse 22.* ✆*(0)33 822 07 70. Fax (0)33 822 07 40. www.seehotelterrasse.ch. 40 rooms.* Hotel with terrace situated on the shore of Brienz lake. Peace and quiet guaranteed.

⌢⊜🏨 **Beau Site** – *Seestrasse 16.* ✆*(0)33 826 75 75. www.beausite.ch. 50 rooms.* Superb views of the Jungfrau. Enjoy the pleasant garden after a hard day's trekking in the snow.

⌢⊜🏨🏨 **Goldey** – *Obere Goldey 85.* ✆*(0)33 826 44 45. www.goldey.ch. 41 rooms.* Lovely hotel at the water's edge. The starting-point for many excursions, it will provide a warm, cosy welcome when you return at the end of the day.

⌢⊜🏨🏨 **Hirschen** – *In Matten, Hauptstrasse 11.* ✆*(0)33 822 15 45. www.hirschen-interlaken.ch. 25 rooms.* Attractive wooden chalet typical of the region, dating from the 16C. Breathtaking panorama of the Jungfrau range from the terrace. Traditional cuisine and restful atmosphere.

THE JUNGFRAU

⌢⊜🏨🏨 **Belvedere** – *3818 Grindelwald.* ✆*(0)33 888 99 99. www.belvedere-grindelwald.ch. 54 rooms.* Stunning setting and panoramic views.

⌢⊜🏨🏨 **Bodmi** – *3818 Grindelwald.* ✆*(0)33 853 12 20. www.bodmi.ch. 23 rooms.* Idyllic setting with personal service.

⊻/EAT

INTERLAKEN

⌢⊜ **Restaurant Luegibrüggli** – *Kienbergstrasse 1, Unterseen-Interlaken* ✆*(0)33 822 88 22. www.luegibrueggli.ch.* Located halfway between Interlaken and Beatenburg, serving traditional Bernese cuisine with excellent views.

⌢⊜ **Restaurant Aarburg** – *Beatenbergstrasse 1, Unterseen.* ✆*(0)33 822 26 15. www.hotel-aarburg.ch. Closed Sun.* Small, 30-seat dining room on a terrace overlooking the town, serving local fare.

⌢⊜ **Chalet Oberland** – *Postgasse 1, Interlaken.* ✆*(0)33 827 87 87. www.chalet-oberland.ch.* Offers vegetarian meals, and a folklore night every Tuesday.

⌢⊜ **Gastro-Galerie** – *Schifffstation Interlaken Ost, Ländte Nr. 2, Interlaken.* ✆*(0)33 823 02 22.* Provides light fare and snacks.

THE JUNGFRAU

⌢⊜ **Hotel Alpenhof** – *3818 Grindelwald.* ✆*(0)33 853 52 70. www.alpenhof.ch.* This restaurant prides itself in using products from its own farm in most of its dishes.

⌢⊜ **Berghaus Bort** – *3818 Grindelwald.* ✆*(0)33 853 17 62. www.berghaus-bort.ch.* Located beside the first intermediate station of the Jungfraujoch cableway.

Grindelwald★★

On an unforgettable site, Grindelwald, the Eiger village, is the only great mountain resort in the Jungfrau area which can be reached by car. It therefore attracts not only holidaymakers—mountaineers or skiers depending on the season—but also crowds of day trippers from the Interlaken area. The bustling crowds which, on fine winter or summer days, surge exuberantly along the little town's main street, plunge the newcomer straight into the atmosphere of an Alpine capital. Events throughout the year include the famous **World Snow Festival**, held each January on the natural skating rink at the heart of the village: Several teams from different countries make ice and snow sculptures.

SIGHTS
The Skiing Area

The Grindelwald skiing area, linked to those of **Wengen** and **Mürren**, consists of about 200km/125mi of slopes suitable for downhill skiing, served by 49 ski lifts, and dominated by the hulking grandeur of the Eiger. Surprisingly, many of the pistes in this staggeringly steep terrain are mild enough for intermediate level skiers and snowboarders. The Bodmi area is for novices, where lifts rise to

▶ **Population:** 3 826.

Info: Postfach 124.
℘(0)33 854 12 12.
www.grindelwald.ch.

Location: Grindelwald is in the Bernese Oberland, central Switzerland.
Alt. 1 034m/3 392ft.

Don't Miss:
The Jungfraujoch—Top of Europe, from where you can see the longest glacier in the Alps. On the way to the top you pass Kleine Scheidegg with a spectacular view of the famous Eiger-Monch-Jungfrau triptych.

Kids: Children will love the ride up Jungfraujoch, as well as the cable car journey up the Männlichen.

Timing: Visitors should allow a minimum of two days to explore the top sights, but plan on at least three days to fully tour the area's numerous mountains.

First and Oberjoch (alt. 2 468m/8 097ft) before opening onto vast, sunny snowfields. The descent between Oberjoch and Grindelwald via piste 22 offers

Grindelwald with Wetterhorn In background

© Brian Lawrence Images/Travel Pictures

superb **views**★★ of the surrounding landscape and quaint villages. A carving piste and a snowpark have been laid out at the top. Kleine Scheidegg offers opportunities for splendid walks towards Grindelwald, especially at sunset. Seasoned skiers should choose the "Lauberhorn Rennstrecke" slope above Wengen, often used in official competitions for Alpine skiing. Steep and challenging slopes can be found on the Schilthorn Massif (including the Eiger Glacier), which is somewhat difficult to reach (train ride followed by a bus and four separate funiculars) but boasts the best pistes. For cross-country skiers, 35km/22mi of loops are available between Grindelwald and Burglauenen. Despite the low altitude, the snow coverage is usually satisfactory at the bottom of the valleys because there is little sunlight during the winter season.

The area also offers many opportunities for hikers, with 80km/50mi of marked out trails and 20km/12.4mi of pistes for sledges. One recommended route is to walk up to Faulhorn from First (2hr30min) and then to go back down to Grindelwald by sledge via Bussalp; this 12.5km/8mi itinerary is the longest sledge piste in Europe.

The area boasts an important Sports Centre (Centre Sportif) with facilities for a number of sports, a skating rink, indoor swimming pool, curling rink, gymnasium, etc.

The Town★★★

The site of Grindelwald combines a foreground full of country charm—fields planted with fruit trees or maples and containing pretty dwellings—with a grand rocky barrier stretching from the shoulder of the Wetterhorn to the pyramid of the Eiger. On one hand are the high mountains, a playground for mountaineers or skilled skiers; on the other, between the Grosse and Kleine Scheidegg Ridges, with the Faulhorn in between, is an immense amphitheatre-like shape of Alpine pastures and woods perfectly suited to cross-country skiing. Access is provided by the Wengernalp railway—much appreciated by skiers

in early spring—which serves the high altitude annex of the Kleine Scheidegg, and by the chain of chairlifts at First.

CABLE-CAR VIEWPOINTS
🧍🧍 Jungfraujoch★★★

Allow at least one day for this exceptional excursion. We recommend that you choose the round tour of the Jungfrau by railway (🕯️see p224).
🚞Circular ticket Interlaken-Jungfraujoch-Interlaken: 190.20CHF; when taking one of the two first morning trains (Nov–Apr) and the trains with direct interconnection: 130CHF. Ticket for departure from Lauterbrunnen: 169.80CHF; when taking the two first trains: 130CHF. Ticket for departure from Grindelwald Grund: 170CHF; when taking the first train and return before noon (May–Oct): 130CHF. Circular ticket Interlaken-Kleine Scheidegg-Interlaken (not going up to Jungfraujoch): 74.20CHF.

🧍🧍 Männlichen★★★

🚠 Access by the longest cable car ride in Europe (6.2km/4mi), 15min on foot from the centre of the resort. Allow 2hr there and back including 1hr by cable car.
🚶 The main attractions of this summit are the walks and hikes that it offers (🕯️see below).
The final platform (alt. 2 227m/7 306ft) commands a splendid view of Grindel-

Walking in Männlichen— Mönch in the background

© Grindelwald Tourismus/Switzerland Tourism

wald, at the foot of the Wetterhorn and the Schreckhorn. Go to the nearby viewpoint dominating the Lauterbrunnen Valley for a **panorama**★★★ of the legendary Eiger-Mönch-Jungfrau triptych, the sparkling Silberhorn, Breithorn and, down below, the village of Wengen, with Lake Thun lying to the north.

To enjoy a complete circular view of your surroundings, climb up to the top of the Männlichen (alt. 2 343m/7 687ft). The view is quite clear to the north.

First★★

Access by cable car. Allow 1hr30min including 1hr by cable car. The excursion can be combined with a walk.

Operates from 8am or 8.30am, times vary according to the season. Closed in Nov and Apr. Fare there and back 50CHF. (0)33 828 77 11.

When you reach the third section (alt. 2 168m/7 113ft), go to the restaurant's panoramic terrace (*viewing table*). Magnificent **view**★★ of the Grindelwald Basin in its wooded setting and the summits of the Wetterhorn, Grosser Fiescherhorn, Eiger, Jungfrau, Morgenhorn and Schreckhorn, hemmed in by the Upper and Lower Grindelwald Glaciers. The Titlis and the Sustenhörner can be glimpsed in the far distance. Lush pastures extend to the northwest, at the foot of the Faulhorn (note the hotel right on top).

🚶 HIKING TRAILS

Grindelwald is a great rambling and climbing centre, offering all types of excursions of varying degrees of difficulty (300km/187mi of paths at an altitude of 1 000–3 600m/3 280–11 810ft). Some of the more interesting circuits are listed below. There are also 100km/62mi of marked trails for mountain bikes.

Faulhorn★★★

Access to First by cable car. 2hr20min climb (500m/1 640ft difference in altitude). Inexperienced hikers can stop at Bachalpsee (50min easy walking).

Bachalpsee★★ is one of Switzerland's most beautiful lakes. It affords a spectacular **view**★★, enhanced by the twinkling reflections of the mountain cirque. From the verdant shores of the lake, you can admire the jagged crest of the Finsteraarhorn, framed between the Schreckhorn and the Fiescherhorn. The climb to Faulhorn is along a steep but even path. At the top (alt. 2 681m/8 796ft), you reach one of the highest mountain hotels in Europe, and certainly the oldest (opened in 1832) from where there is a sweeping **panorama**★★★ of the Bernese Oberland. To the south, you can see First, the Mönch, and the Breithorn. To the north, you overlook Lake Brienz and Lake Thun, lying at the foot of the Brienzerrothorn and the Niederhorn respectively. In the far distance, farther east, note the Pilatus and Rigi peaks.

Bachalpsee with the Schreckhorn and the Fiescherhorn

© Grindelwald Tourismus/Switzerland Tourism

From Faulhorn to Schynige Platte★★★

3hr15min walk with a 600m/1 968.5ft difference in altitude. 🏔 *This excursion is for experienced hikers only (sturdy mountain boots necessary) and can be undertaken after the walk to Grindelwald.* 🚫 *Do not attempt to go in wet weather. The return to Grindelwald is by train (enquire beforehand about times).*

The fascinating **path along the crest** offers a wonderful panorama at all times. After 1hr walking, heading towards the Mädlenen Restaurant, the rocky track becomes more tiring and more difficult to negotiate. It commands nearby **views**★ of Lake Sägistal and the formidable slopes of the Faulhorn. It then wends its way through mountain pastures before revealing a fantastic **panorama**★★★ of the Jungfrau Massif, extending from the Schreckhorn to the Morgenhorn. On reaching the Schynige Platte, those climbers who still have some energy left will discover an Alpine garden.

Hikers on Stieregg

© Walter Storto/Switzerland Tourism

⊙ *The climb down to Wilderswil is by rack railway. Then take the train back to Grindelwald.*

Mönchsjochhütte★★★

Alt. 3 629m/11 906ft. 1hr climb. Access from Jungfraujoch (⌚ see p225).

Stieregg and Bänisegg★★

🚠 *Access to Pfingstegg (alt. 1 391m/ 4 563.6ft) in 4min by cable car. Allow 1hr climb to reach the Baregg Restaurant (260m/853ft difference in altitude) and an extra 1hr to get to Bänisegg (160m/525ft difference in altitude).*

From Pfingstegg, look for an overall **view**★ of Grindelwald and the First area and an even path following the mountain slope. After 30min, you will admire a fantastic **view**★★ of the Lower Grindelwald Glacier and especially Fieschergletscher. Note the waterfalls gushing down the slopes of the Eiger. The path now becomes steeper and leads past local flora (orchids, rhododendrons, and forget-me-nots) and the occasional sheep. Allow 1hr30min to reach the Bar-

egg Restaurant (alt. 1 650m/5 413ft) commands an even more impressive **view**★★ of the majestic glacial cirque dominated by the Grossfiescherhorn (alt. 4 048m/13 280ft).

Experienced hikers who do not suffer from vertigo and who are equipped with proper mountain boots can continue toward Schreckhornhütte. Although it is still wild, the setting now features more and more species of regional flora and fauna. After a series of short ups and downs, the path follows a very steep course to reach Bänisegg (alt. 1 807m/5 927ft). From a bend to the left, you can discover the long ice tongue of the Ischmeer. It is a truly breathtaking **site**★★, with the Finsteraarhorn looming at a height of 4 274m/14 021ft.

⊙ *Go back down along the same path (1hr30min).*

From Pfingstegg, you can reach the **Milchbach Chalet** by a gently sloping track (*allow 1hr*). This route will take you past the mineral paradise of Breitlouwina (Gesteinparadies Breitlouwina), characterised by a remarkably wide range of sediments dating from several million years ago. View of the Upper Grindelwald Glacier, in which an **ice cave** has been set up. Visitors will be impressed by the blue ice walls of the cave, which is almost 30m/98.4ft deep.

Allow an extra 20min to climb down to the Hôtel Wetterhorn, where a bus will take you back to Grindelwald.

From Männlichen to Kleine Scheidegg★★

🚡 *Take the Männlichen cable car. 1hr 15min walk along an easy, pleasant path (170m/558ft difference in altitude).* All along the way, there are superb **views**★★ of the Eiger, Mönch, Jungfrau and Grindewald Basin.

▶ *From Kleine Scheidegg, continue with the walk to Eigerwand or return to Grindelwald by train.*

Eigerwand★★

Access to the Eigergletscher resort (alt. 2 320m/7 611ft) by train. Allow 2hr for the climb down to Alpiglen (700m/ 2 297ft difference in altitude). 😊*Good mountain boots essential. Do not stray from the beaten track, which cuts across a protected area for local fauna.*
Follow the railway tracks for 100m/328ft going downwards, then cross them and take the "Eiger-Trail" itinerary on the right. Walk a short distance up to the foot of the Eiger. The path goes through steep Alpine pastures and mounds of fallen rocks, following the imposing mountain face, offering pretty views of Grindelwald and the Wetterhorn. Reaching a steep slope, it leads to the Alpiglen pastures (alt. 1 615m/5 297ft). The climb down can be undertaken on foot or by train.

Gletscherschlucht★

2.5km/1.5mi on a very narrow road beginning at the far end of the village, on the right, after a church. Allow 30min sightseeing. 🕐*May and Oct, 10am–5pm; mid-Jun–Sept, 9am–6pm.* 🚫*Closed in winter.* 🎫*7CHF, children 3.5CHF.* 📞*(033) 853 24 88. www.rosenlauischlucht.ch.*
A rocky fissure, at the bottom of which the tail of the Lower Grindelwald Glacier (Unterer Grindelwaldgletscher) appears as a narrow strip of ice. This impressive geological formation was once described by Byron as a "frozen hurricane".

ADDRESSES

🛏STAY

Lehmann's Herberge – *3818 Grindelwald.* 📞*(0)33 853 31 41. www.lehmanns-herberge.ch.* 🅿 *12 rooms.* A nice young couple owns this B&B in the centre of Grindelwald, which will delight the budget-conscious. In the dormitory rooms, comfort is limited (toilets on the landing upstairs) but the view of the Eiger and Männlichen is beautiful from rooms 5 and 10.

Alpenhof – *3818 Grindelwald.* 📞*(0)33 853 52 70. www.alpenhof.ch. Closed November and several weeks after Easter.* 🅿 *12 rooms.* Guests will enjoy the view over the Alps and the quiet location at the foot of the ski slopes. Simple and comfortable modern rooms soberly arranged. The restaurant offers gourmet products from their own farm.

Gletschergarten – 📞*(0)33 853 17 21. www.hotel-gletschergarten.ch. Closed Apr–May and Oct–Christmas.* 🅿 *26 rooms.* If you are looking for an intimate or romantic atmosphere or if you dream of a warm fireside return after your hike or skiing, you will love this charming wooden cottage which will sooth and relax you.

🍽/EAT

Hilty-Stübli – *Marktgasse 57.* 📞*(0)33 854 40 80. www.kirchbuehl.ch. Closed Apr–mid-May, end Oct–beginning Dec.* The restaurant of hotel Kirchbühl offers good rustic fare.

Chalet Hotel alte Post – *Dorfstrasse.* 📞*(0)338 534 242. www.altepost-grindelwald.ch. Closed Wed and end Oct–end Dec.* In a cottage whose entry appears to be guarded by an old stagecoach, this restaurant serves delicious mountain cuisine. The tasty cheeses on the platter are produced in-house.

Brienz★

Brienz is one of the best preserved, old-fashioned summer resorts in the Bernese Oberland. The town is a great woodcarving centre and a technical school was founded here to keep up the tradition, as well as a music academy for stringed instruments. Most of the carvings of bears in all sizes and positions sold as souvenirs come from local workshops.

> ▶ **Population:** 2 996.
>
> **Info:** Hauptstrasse 143, Brienz 3855. ℘(0)33 952 80 80. www.alpenregion.ch.
>
> **Location:** Brienz lies along the shore of its lake, facing the Giessbach Falls. Alt. 570m/7 871ft.
>
> **Don't Miss:** The panoramic views from the Brienzer Rothhorn.

SIGHTS
Jobin Living Museum★

Hauptstrasse 111. ⏲Open May–Sept daily 9am–6pm; Oct, Mon–Sat 9am–noon, 1.30pm–5.30pm; Dec–Apr Tue–Sat 1.30pm–5.30pm. ⏲Closed Christmas, November, January. ☜5CHF. ♿ ℘(0)33 952 13 00. www.jobin.ch.

Founded in 1835, the workshop continues the tradition of local Jobin woodcarving. Visitors can freely attend to the work of craftsmen who work by hand or machine, in a bright and modern environment. Upstairs, a small museum features music boxes, wooden animals carved miniature cottages and utensils which have made the reputation of the workshop and the city. The boutique store sells some of the production line, also including some antiques.

EXCURSIONS
Brienzer See★

Shorter, narrower, perhaps less picturesque but nonetheless wilder than Lake Thun (☜see p214), Lake Brienz is linked to its "twin" by the River Aare. The main drive is along the **North shore**★—from Interlaken to Meiringen 30km/19mi—while the southern part of the lake can be visited more easily with a boat from Interlaken. The North shore is a beautiful 45-minute drive which can take longer depending on where you choose to spend your time.

From Interlaken the road runs through woods, climbing to the last slopes of the Harder and when you reach Ringgenberg, there are attractive views of the lake and the mountains from the lake shore, immediately overlooking Interlaken. A **church** was erected in 1670 on the ruins of a castle (Burg) whose keep was used again in the building of the belfry. Between Ringgenberg and Brienz, especially on the Oberried-Brienz section, the view opens out over **Brienzer See** and the south shore, enclosed by the Brienzer Rothorn Chain and the foothills of the Faulhorn. The best place to stop is 600m/656yds northeast of **Oberried-am-Brienzer-See**: Return to the lake shore, where, upstream, you begin to see the Sustenhörner Range, which reaches its highest point of 3 503m/11 493ft in the dome-shaped Sustenhorn, and Brienz in the distance.

Brienzer Rothorn★★★

Alt. 2 350m/7 710ft. Allow 3hr there and back (2hr 20min by rack railway). ⏲Open Jun–Oct, 7.30am–4.30pm. ☜Fare return to Brienz 80CHF. ℘(0)33 952 22 22. www.brienz-rothorn-bahn.ch.

Panoramic view of the Bernese Alps, Lake Brienz (*Brienzersee*) and Hasli. For an unforgettable experience, take the steam-powered Brienz Rothorn Bahn that takes you up the steep, 25% gradient to the top. The ride starts at the restored valley station, close to the Brienz railway terminal and the lake steamer landing.

Brienzer Rothorn overlooking Brienzersee and the Alps of Berner Oberland

Ballenberg Freilichtmuseum (Swiss Open-Air Museum)★★

2.5km/1.5mi. Leave Brienz E on the Hofstetten road which branches left off the main street (follow directions for Freilichtmuseum). ○*Open mid-Apr–end Oct, daily 10am–5pm.* ⊜*20CHF, concessions apply* ⑤*.* ℘*(0)33 952 10 30. www.ballenberg.ch.*

In a vast and superb wooded setting designed for pedestrians, this open-air museum, opened in 1978, is spread out over 80ha/200 acres. There is a free shuttle service bus between the west (nearest Brienz) and east entrances. Genuine examples of regional architecture from practically all the country's cantons were transported here and re-assembled piece by piece, along with ancient furniture. Within each building are daily demonstrations of crafts, from needlework to wood sculpture, and an Alpine cheese dairy, bakery, and blacksmith. Divided into 13 groups by geographical origin, the traditional rural houses are connected by paths complete with picnic spots, play areas and small enclosures with 250 domestic animals.

The most noteworthy buildings are: The Chaux-de-Fonds multi-purpose dwelling, typical of the Haut-Jura district; the Oberentfelden (Aargau) chalet (1609) crowned by a huge thatched roof; the half-timbered Old Bear Inn moved from Rapperswil; the chalet from Ostermundigen, with its *trompe-l'œil* windows beneath the gable; the imposing farmhouse from Lancy, originally a small outbuilding containing a winepress; the Richterswil house with pretty half-timbering, built in the Zürich area around 1780; the 17C dwelling from Erstfeld, a masterpiece of Late Renaissance "St Gotthard" style; and the Adelboden chalet (17C), notable for its lovely beams. Three inns serve traditional cuisine and shops sell local craftwork, usually made on the premises.

There's an impressive group of foaming waterfalls in a wooded setting at **Giessbachfälle**★★.

Starting from Brienz

○*Daily service during summer season.* ⊜*From Brienz, return fare 12CHF There is a regular bus from the railway station at Brienz to Ballenberg.*

Starting from Interlaken

About 3hr there and back, including 2hr by boat and funicular. ⊜*From Interlaken, return fare 64CHF by boat in 2nd class; Contact the Boat Company, BLS,* ℘*(0)58 327 48 11. www.bls.ch*

Separate Interlaken-Brienzersee or Bönigen embarkation stages.

ADDRESSES

☜ STAY

⊜⊜ **Lindenhof** – *Lindenhofweg 15. ℘(0)33 952 20 30. www.hotel-lindenhof. ch. Closed Jan–mid-Mar. 71 rooms. ⊡ Restaurant (⊜⊜) closed Mon & Tue March–April and Nov–Dec.* Lovely quiet hotel, consisting of six buildings overlooking the village. The rooms are individually decorated in various themes, and partly look at the lake. The restaurant has a mountain restaurant, conservatory and terrace are also with a view of the lake.

ⴹ EAT

⊜⊜ **The Red-Carpet** – *℘033 952 25 25. www.giessbach.ch. Closed mid-Oct–mid-Apr.* Cuisine in a classic and elegant atmosphere. On the terrace, you take your meals with superb views of the lake and waterfalls.

Meiringen★

Meiringen is an important tourist centre as the starting-point for excursions to the Aare Gorges and the Reichenbach Falls and also a convenient stop on the Grimsel and Susten roads. The generally accepted birthplace of meringue which are sold by weight in every shop, it has been overshadowed by its Sherlock Holmes connections: The great fictional detective supposedly fell to his death from the ledge of the Reichenbach Falls; today an "X" marks the spot and you can have a photo with a Holmes cut-out by the waterfall. This has led, unsurprisingly to a big Sherlock Holmes tourist market.

THE TOWN
Sherlock Holmes Museum

⏱*Open May–Sept, Tue–Sun 1.30pm–6pm; Oct, Wed–Sun 3pm–6pm.* ⊚*5CHF. ℘(0)33 971 42 21.*
This museum, based in an old church, has a collection of Holmes memorabilia and a reconstruction of the famous, fictitious London drawing room at number 221B Baker Street.

Kirche

The church (1684) is in a part of the village where wooden houses recall old Meiringen, ravaged by fire in 1879 and 1891. This is the fifth church built on this spot, succeeding others swept away by the flooding of the Alpbach, a waterfall located behind the building. For

▶ **Population:** 4 723.
🯄 **Info:** Bahnhofstrasse 22 – 3860. ℘(0)33 972 50 55. www.haslital.ch.
◑ **Location:** Meiringen is the chief town in the Hasli Valley, 13.5km/8.4mi east of Brienz. Alt. 595m/1 952ft.
🅿 **Parking:** Use the public car park and stroll to the sights, all nearby.
🙂 **Don't Miss:** Walk to Hochstollen via Planplatten. Also visit Reichenbachfälle (Reichenbach Waterfall), the site of the fictional disappearance of Sherlock Holmes and Moriarty.
🕐 **Timing:** Allow two hours for town sights; a day-and-a-half for all excursions.

this reason, its detached Romanesque tower has foundations over 7m/23ft deep. During restoration the remains of the original 11C structure, now the crypt, and a series of Romanesque frescoes in the upper church, representing scenes from the Old Testament, were discovered.

EXCURSIONS
Planplatten★★

Alt. 2 245m/7 365ft. 1hr by ski lift, then cable car (3 sections).
Stunning **route**★★ overlooking pretty pastures and forests. When you reach the top, bear right toward the viewing

Arthur Conan Doyle

On the square named after the Scottish novelist **Arthur Conan Doyle** (1859–1930), the creator of Sherlock Holmes, stands a bronze statue of the celebrated fictitious detective by the English sculptor John Doubleday. Conan Doyle, who loved Switzerland, was made an honorary citizen of Meiringen.

table. Superb **panorama**★★ presenting many different landscapes: To the east the summits and glaciers of Rhonestock, Sustenhorn, and Wendenstöcke; to the south the sparkling, snow-capped peaks of the Bernese Alps (Wetterhorn, Schreckhorn, Finsteraarhorn); to the west Lake Brienz; and to the north the Glogghüs dominating the Alpine gorges around Meiringen.

Planplatten is a popular departure point for microlite flying and hang-gliding and as a starting-point for hikes and walks 🏃. Less experienced hikers can stop after reaching the two lakes Tannensee and Melchsee (allow 5hr); those in excellent physical condition can continue on the route described below.

Walk to the Lakes and Hochstollen★★★

Leave Planplatten early in the morning to allow enough time to catch the last cable car back at the end of the day. Allow 5–6hr depending on your choice of route, not including stops.
It is essential to wear shoes with non-slip soles.

Walk to **Balmeregg** (alt. 2 255m/7 397ft) in 1hr by a track following the mountain slope. **View**★★ of the three lakes (Engstien, Tannen and Melch), the Titlis and Wendenstöcke. Pretty **mountain path**★★ heading towards **Tannensee**★, then a flat track until **Melchsee**★ (allow 1hr30min; to save 1hr, go directly from Balmeregg to Melchsee).

Bear left and walk round Melchsee: the lovely postcard view from the tip of the lake is enhanced by shimmering

reflections★★ on the Titlis. Climb up to small **Blausee**★. The route becomes very steep and after 1hr you will reach **Abgschütz Pass** (2 263m/7 424.5ft), which commands a sublime **view**★★. However, you will be able to get an even broader **panorama**★★★ of the surrounding landscape if you go up to **Hochstollen** (2 481m/8 140ft, marked out by a cross) along a strong, impressive incline. There are splendid views of the lakes and the Bernese Oberland, from the Eiger to Finsteraarhorn. Panoramic descent toward Käserstatt until you get to the track running down the slope before joining up with a path leading to **Mägisalp** (1 689m/5 541ft, allow 45min). Take the two cable cars to go back to the car park.

🚗 DRIVING TOURS

SUSTENPASS★★★
50km/31mi from Meiringen to Sustenpass. Allow 1hr30min.

Built from 1938 to 1945 from Wassen to Innertkirchen, the Susten road (from the French "Souste" meaning "goods warehouse"), this was the first of the major Swiss Alpine roads which has been subsequently studied extensively for its motor traffic. It is a masterpiece of civil engineering, which can be best appreciated in good weather.

▷ *From Meiringen, follow the road to Grimsel Innetkirchen, then head in the direction of the Sustenpass. The Gadmen valley begins 4km/2.5mi after Innetkirchen.*

A few kilometres before Nessental, at a bridge, turn left onto a small toll road. This detour is justified especially for hikers; Engstlenalp occupies a cul-de-sac at the bottom of the Gental valley. The road rises above the forest and runs through beautiful pastures with grazing cows. You then discover little by little, as you look behind, some remarkable **perspectives**★★ of the Bernese Oberland (Finsteraarhorn and Wetterhorn).

Sustenpass
© Christof Sonderegger/Switzerland Tourism

Engstlenalp★

A 13km/8mi detour intended mainly for seasoned ramblers.

A short distance below Nessental, level with a bridge, turn right into a narrow toll road *(at 4km)* that climbs up into the forest, passing through lovely pastures where cows are put out to graze. Behind you extend splendid **views**★★ of the Bernese Oberland (Finsteraarhorn, Wetterhorn). Several walks leave from the final car park: the stunning lake, the **Engstlensee**★★ *(10min)*, then proceed to **Joch Pass**★★ by chair-lift, to **Trübsee**★★ *(second chair-lift going down)* and finally **Titlis**★★★ (ⓒ *see ENGELBERG, allow a whole day)*. Alternatively, you may choose to visit lakes **Tannensee**★, **Melchsee**★ and **Blausee**★ *(2hr to get there, 1hr 45min to get back)*.

◖ *Between Innertkirchen and Meiringen you follow the road to the Grimsel.*

Gschletter Hairpin Bend★

🅿 *Park inside the bend.*

This loop forms a **belvedere**★ overlooking the lower Gadmental and the Gadmerflue and Wendenstöcke. Very high up, the massive walls of the Gadmerflue and the Wendenstöcke stand out. Between Gadmen and Innertkirchen is the Nessental shelf. At the last rise before arriving in the Innertkirchen Basin, the view opens out to the summits which enclose the Urbachtal, on the left of the crests of the Engelhörner.

Steingletscher★

1km/0.6mi before Himmelrank.

The enormous Steingletscher glacier seems almost overcome by a mass of reddish earth in places; a portion of the glacier reappears form the ground on the banks of a small nearby lake, in to which miniature floating icebergs often break off.

Ever since the hotel Steingletscher was built, the footpath to the glacier joins that of Steinalp and can be reached in 2hrs there and back. Motorists can also access it through a small toll road *(15 min walk from the car park upon arrival)*.

Himmelrank★★

🅿 *Park inside the bend.*

The road-builders named this Paradise Bend; it winds across a rocky slope formerly called Hell Upstairs by the people of Gadmental. Note the **view**★★ of the Gadmen and the Sustenhörner Summits (Sustenhorn, Gwächtenhorn).

Sustenpass★★

🅿 *Large car park at the west end of the tunnel (Bernese slope).*

The road reaches its highest point (2 224m/7 296ft) in the 325m/1 067ft long tunnel under the pass (alt. 2 259m/7 411ft—*which can be reached on foot)*. From this point on, the finest **scenery**★★★ is the 4km/2.5mi between

237

the western entrance and the Himmel-rank. In the foreground the flow of the **Steingletscher** dies away under a mass of reddish morainic deposits; the foot of the glacier reappears on the shores of a lake, where miniature icebergs float. View the Sustenhörner group summits at the Swiss Touring Club viewing table 2km/1.2mi below the pass.

GRIMSELSTRASSE★

33km/20.5mi from Meiringen to Grimselpass – Allow 1hr30min.

The Grimsel road, rising from the upper valley of the Aare (Haslital), runs through a setting of rounded rocks, polished by ancient glaciers. But at each level of the valley, dams and power plants are reminders of modern civilization.

Outside Meiringen, the valley is obstructed by the rocky mound of the Kirchet which cuts the Aare gorge (the Aareschlucht), invisible from the road. The basin is perfectly level at Innert-kirchen, dominated by great escarp-ments of Burg and the pyramid of Bän-zlauistock.

Aareschlucht★★

2km/1.2mi, plus 30min sightseeing.
[P] *The road to the gorges' car park branches off from the Grimsel road (number 6) on leaving Meiringen for Innertkirchen, 200m/219yds upstream from the bridge over the Aare.*

The gorge cut by the Aare through the Kirchet bolt between Meiringen and Innertkirchen, are among the most popular curiosities in the Bernese Oberland. The viewing galleries lead into the narrowest part of the gorge, the walls of which, sometimes sheer, sometimes polished and hollowed by erosion (traces of potholes and glaciated rocks), are very impressive. Stranger still is the dim light in the depths of the cleft where the jade-green stream of the Aare flows.

After about 1.5km/1mi within view of a tributary waterfall you arrive at the far end of the gorge (the last hairpin bend before Innertkirchen).

Guttannen

This is the only community in the Ober-hasli which can be called a village. Its **Kristallmuseum** (⊙ *open Jun–Sept, daily 8am–5pm; other times open by appointment;* ⊚*3CHF;* ℘*(0)33 973 12 47*) displays a wide variety of minerals and crystals.

The climb continues from level to level in a **setting**★★ of rounded greenish rocks, snowfields and waterfalls. In some places the road cuts through huge blocks of extraordinarily polished, light-coloured granite.

Handeggfall★

The River Arlenbach and River Aare min-gle their waters in a Y-shaped cascade which falls into a narrow gorge.

After the turquoise sheet of the reser-voir-lake of **Räterichsboden** comes the great artificial lake of Grimsel, whose muddy waters are held back by two dams anchored to the Nollen Rock—the site of a hotel which took the place of the Grimsel hostel, now submerged. In line with the drowned valley, the **view**★ reaches the crests of the Finster-aarhorn (alt. 4 274m/14 022ft, highest point of the Bernese Alps) in the dis-tance.

Gelmerbahn★★

Leaving from Handegg. ⊙*Open mid-Jun& Oct 9am–4pm, if the weather permits. Jul–Aug daily 8am–5pm in* ⊚*27CHF return (children 17CHF return, 2nd child free).*

Inaugurated in 1926 but open to the public only since 2001, the steepest funicular in the world (106%) climbs a 10min path to Lake Gelmer (Gelm-ersee), set in the mountains through untouched Nature. At the top, visitors have the choice between doing a tour of the lake (1h45mins) and continue to the Gelmer refuge (Gelmerhütte, 2hrs).

Grimselpass★★

Alt. 2 165m/7 103ft.

A "Lake of the Dead" recalls the fighting between the Austrians and the French in 1799. From the mound behind Hotel Grimselblick, the **view**★★ includes the

Gelmerbahn, the steepest funicular in the world

© Christof Sonderegger/Switzerland Tourism

desert region where the Rhône rises near the Rhône Glacier and, from left to right, the snowy Galenstock summit, the foot of the Rhône Glacier, the Furka Gap and its long, bare, monotonous crests stretching between the Upper Valais and the Piedmontese Toce Valley. Facing northwest you will see in the far distance the walls of the Lauteraarhorn (alt. 4 042m/13 261ft). The road then drops towards the **Gletschboden**, a desolate valley floor. The country loses its Arctic character and becomes more typically Alpine. The road develops hairpin bends on the Meienwand slopes and the terminal cataract of the Rhône Glacier, comes into sight, overlooked by the snowy dome of the Galenstock. You will also see Gletsch in the distance.

Rosenlauital★★

14km/8.7mi. About 1hr – by a narrow mountain path.

▷ *Leave Meiringen by the Grimsel road. After the bridge over the Aare at a crossroads, turn right and leave the car by the station of the Reichenbach funicular.*

Reichenbachfälle★

1km/0.6mi, 30min there and back, including 10min by funicular. Leave Meiringen by the road to Grimsel. After the bridge over the Aare, turn right and leave your car at the Reichenbach funicular station. ⏱ *Operates mid-May–*

mid-Oct, every 15min, 8.15am–11.45am, 1.15pm–5.45pm. 🚠*Fare there and back 10CHF.* ☏*(0)33 972 90 10.*

Crossing the lower falls on a viaduct, the funicular ends at a terrace from where you can view them from below, and there is a 10min steep walking path to a viewing platform at the top. At Willigen, turn right toward Rosenlaui which, after a series of sharp hairpin bends, enters the lonely Reichenbach Valley, dominated by the extraordinary rock formations of the Engelhörner. Soon you will see ahead, from left to right, the Rosenlaui Glacier, the Wellhorn and the Wetterhorn.

A bridge over the bed of the Reichenbach leads to the fields of Gschwandtenmad and a striking **view**★★★: The rocky shoulder of the Welhorn behind fir woods to the right of the Rosenlaui Glacier. This flanks the icy cone of the Wetterhorn, which stands above the Grosse Scheidegg Depression—a broad shelf over which you can walk from Rosenlaui to Grindelwald.

The mountaineering resort of **Rosenlaul** has given its name to a climbing school which has trained several guides for the conquest of the Himalayas. Here tourists may visit the (⦿ *see GLETSCHERSCHLUCHT*). The scenery now becomes quite rocky. On arriving at Schwarzwaldalp, at the end of the road suitable for cars, you will find a slope wholly planted with maple trees.

THE VALAIS

The Valais is one of the most isolated cantons of Switzerland, an area of the highest Alpine peaks and numerous glaciers. Almost completely cut off from the economic centres of German Switzerland, it has been kept busy for 2 000 years by intense international traffic through the Great St Bernard and Simplon Passes. It owes its distinctive regional character to the Mediterranean clarity of its sky, the deep Catholic beliefs of its people, and its impressive industrial development, which nevertheless does not prevent the survival in the high valleys of the most ancient ways of life.

Highlights

1. The **Roman Amphitheatre** at Martigny (p248)
2. The international panorama from **Mont Fort** (p258)
3. The **fortified hills** of Valère and Tourbillon at Sion (p262)
4. Visiting the **Barrage de la Grande Dixence** (p263)
5. View of the **Matterhorn** from Zermatt (p276)

Valaisans and Walser

All along the Rhône Valley, travellers might think they were in a purely Latin civilisation. Beyond Sierre, and especially near Brig, however, they will start to hear a Germanic dialect and the name Valais yields to Wallis.

The Upper Valais was invaded from the 6C onward by Germanic peoples who probably came down from the Grimsel and pushed on as far as Sierre. Later, these restless "Walser" infiltrated other southern Alpine valleys, forming centres of German culture in otherwise French-speaking districts, as at Davos. These hardy mountaineers, especially those of the Conches Valley, represented the most fiercely democratic element (Raron, Saillon), reducing the temporal rights of the prince-bishops of Sion and claims of local feudal lords by force.

Geography

Here you must not expect gentle pastoral scenes, but dramatic, high mountain landscapes like those of the **lateral valleys**★★★, dotted with chalets and *raccards* or *mazots* (small barns perched on piles and used as granaries or storehouses). In these wild, uninviting regions, it is common to find wayside wooden crosses, set up to protect travellers and local residents from the dark dangers of the mountain.

Raccards—old-fashioned Valais barns in Val d'Anniviers

The Canton is so named because it is effectively one big L-shaped valley, with several smaller valleys connected to it, through which the river Rhône flows on its journey from the Lepontine Alps in the east to Switzerland's largest body of water, Lake Geneva in the west. Flanked on both sides of the valley by massive mountain ranges, in the north lies the insurmountable (by road at least) Bernese Oberland which includes the Jungfrau, the Eiger and Mönch, while in the south lies the Valais or Pennine Alps, with the Matterhorn and Monte Rosa traversed only by the renowned Great St Bernard and Simplon Passes and Tunnels.

One fifth of the Canton is covered by glaciers but despite this the Valais is drier and sunnier than the rest of Switzerland. There are no large cities, the largest towns being the old roman town of Martigny and the capital of the canton, Sion, a bishopric founded in the 4C, both in the west. Sierre is the last French-speaking town before German-speaking Brig in the east. High up in the valleys the terrain is wild and desolate and resorts such as Zermatt and Crans-Montana are some of the only signs of human habitation.

History

Being surrounded by mountains, the Valais has always been difficult to access. But the indomitable Roman Army led by Julius Caesar invaded during the 1C BC by crossing the Alps via the Great St Bernard Pass. As he advanced east, the general was confronted by the fierce Aleman tribe and was effectively halted at Sierre, which helps to explain why even today this is the point where the French language, derived from Latin, stops and German, which derived from the language spoken by the Alemans, begins.

The Romans withdrew from the western Valais in the 5C, but Christianity, which was brought over Great St Bernard Pass by merchants and priests, had already established itself. Disputed by Franks and Burgundians, the latter eventually took control during the late 9C and their

King Rudolph III appointed the Bishop of Sion as Count of the Valais. Soon after, however, the Bishop was unable to prevent the Lower Valais being taken over by the Dukes of Savoy but by 1475 he managed to retake the territory with the help of the communes of the Upper Valais.

Due to its relative isolation, the Reformation passed the Valais by and it became a republic controlled by the Bishop until he was eventually removed by Napoleon in 1798. The Valais remained a semi-independent republic until 1810 when it was absorbed into France before finally becoming a canton of the Swiss Confederation in 1815. By the mid-19C many people in Switzerland were concerned about increasing centralisation of power and the Valais joined with six other Roman Catholic cantons to form the Sonderbund. The so-called Sonderbund War broke out in early November 1847 but by the end of the month it was all over with the Valaisians surrendering to the Confederate Army.

Today

The Valais is today heavily dependent on agriculture with dairy farming, cattle breeding and wine production the most important sectors. The climate is ideal for growing fruit and there are many orchards especially in lower Valais. Year-round tourism is also very important, with winter sports fans flocking to world-famous resorts such as Crans-Montana above Sion and Sierre, while during the summer months tourists are attracted by the excellent sunshine record of the canton.

The Chablais region, just south of Lake Geneva, is not only known for its fine wines it is also the home of much of the canton's industry, which consists of pharmaceuticals, agribusiness, oil-refining and other light industry. The region can also boast the world's highest gravity dam at Grande Dixence (285m/935ft), in the mountains south of Sion near Zermatt which collects the melt water of 35 glaciers.

THE VALAIS

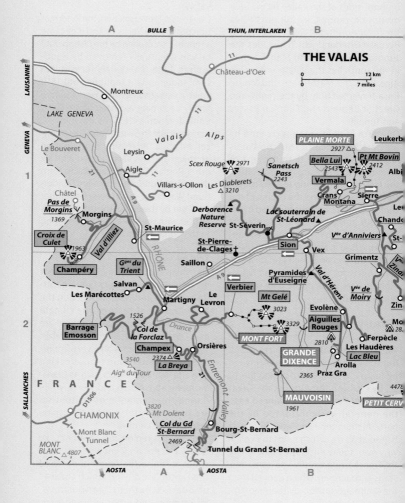

THE VALAIS

BULLE

THUN, INTERLAKEN

Château-d'Oex

LAUSANNE

GENEVA

Montreux

LAKE GENEVA

Le Bouveret

Leysin

Valais

Alps

Aigle

Villars-s-Ollon

Scex Rouge 2971

Sanetsch Pass 2243

Les Diablerets △ 3210

PLAINE MORTE

2927

Leukerb

Bella Lui 2543

Pt Mt Bovin 2412

Albi

Vermala

Derborence Nature Reserve

St-Séverin

Lac souterrain de St-Léonard

Crans Montana

Sierre

Le

Chando

Châtel

Pas de Morgins 1369

Morgins

St-Maurice

St-Pierre-de-Clages

Vée d'Anniviers

St-

Croix de Culet 1963

Val d'Illiez

Champéry

Gges du Trient

Saillon

Sion

Vex

Grimentz

Zina

Vée de Moiry

Zin

Pyramides d'Euseigne

Verbier

Mt Gelé 3023

Evolène

Aiguilles Rouges

Mo 28.

Ferpècle

Les Haudères

Lac Bleu

Arolla

Praz Gra

RHÔNE

Salvan

Les Marécottes

Martigny

Le Levron

Barrage Emosson

1526

Col de la Forclaz

Drance

Champex

3540

2374 △

La Breya

Aigte du Tour

Orsières

MONT FORT

2810

GRANDE DIXENCE

2365

MAUVOISIN

1961

PETIT CERV

4478

FRANCE

D1506

3820

Mt Dolent

Col du Gd St-Bernard 2469

Bourg-St-Bernard

CHAMONIX

Mont Blanc Tunnel

MONT BLANC △ 4807

Tunnel du Grand St-Bernard

SALLANCHES

AOSTA

AOSTA

A

A

B

B

Val d'Hérens

Entremont Valley

242

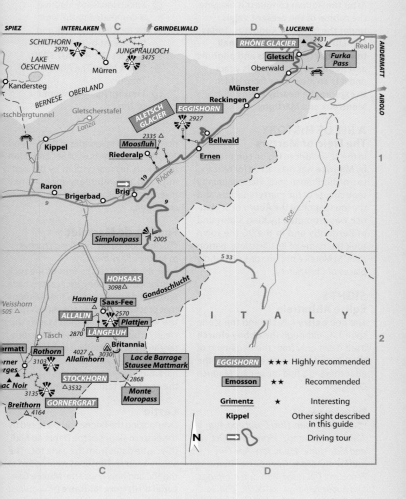

SPIEZ INTERLAKEN **C** GRINDELWALD **D** LUCERNE

ANDERMATT

AIROLO

SCHILTHORN
2970

LAKE
ÖESCHINEN

Mürren

Kandersteg

BERNESE OBERLAND

JUNGFRAUJOCH
3475

tschbergtunnel

Gletscherstafel

Lonza

ALETSCH GLACIER

EGGISHORN
2927

Kippel

2335 △

Moosfluh

Riederalp

Bellwald

Ernen

RHÔNE GLACIER 2431

Gletsch **Furka Pass**

Oberwald Realp

Münster

Reckingen

Raron

Brigerbad

19 Rhône

Brig

9

9 Simplonpass
2005

S 33

Toce

HOHSAAS
3098 △

Gondoschlucht

Weisshorn
505 △

Hannig

Saas-Fee

ALLALIN
2870

Plattjen
2570

LÄNGFLUH

3030

Britannia

I T A L Y

Täsch

rmatt

Rothorn
3103

rner
rges

ac Noir
3135

Breithorn
△ 4164

Allalinhorn
4027 △

STOCKHORN
△3532

GORNERGRAT

**Lac de Barrage
Stausee Mattmark**

2868

**Monte
Moropass**

EGGISHORN ★★★ Highly recommended

Emosson ★★ Recommended

Grimentz ★ Interesting

Kippel Other sight described
in this guide

➡ Driving tour

N

C **D**

St Maurice★

The little town of St Maurice occupies a picturesque **site**★. Agaune (from the Celtic name *acauno*, meaning a rock) was the chief village of the Nantuates tribe. After the Roman conquest it became the capital of the present Valais under the Emperor Augustus. Today St Maurice is a picturesque small town attracting tourists and pilgrims as it has done for hundreds years and it is an ideal base from which to explore the nearby towns of Montreux and Martigny.

> ▶ **Population:** 4 013.
> ⚙ **Michelin Map:** Michelin National Map 729: F7.
> 🛈 **Info:** 1 avenue des Terreaux. ℰ(0)24 485 40 40. www.saint-maurice.ch.
> ▶ **Location:** Saint-Maurice is dominated to the west by the Dents du Midi and to the east by the Dent de Morcles. Alt. 422m/1 384ft.
> 👁 **Don't Miss:** The Abbey Treasury.
> 🕐 **Timing:** Allow a minimum of 2hrs.

A BIT OF HISTORY
The Field of Martyrs
In the 3C an African legion commanded by **Maurice** was massacred for refusing to worship Roman gods. The community took charge of the martyrs' tombs, and the foundation of the Abbey of St Maurice was prompted by King Sigismund of Burgundy and in the 9C the town took the name of its illustrious patron saint. St Maurice became one of the holy places of Christianity.

SIGHTS
Église Abbatiale
The fine **belfry**★ is 11C and the stone spire 13C, although the **abbey church** itself dates only from the beginning of the 17C and has been restored. On the altar there is a fine mosaic by Maurice Denis.

Treasury★★
🎧Guided tours (1hr) 🕐Jul and Aug 10.30am, 2pm and 3.15pm; Sept–Oct and May–Jun 2.45pm; Jan–Apr, (Tue and Wed) 2.45pm. Open Easter Mon and Pentecost. 🕐Closed Mon, Sun mornings and public holidays. ⊛10CHF. ℰ(0)24 486 04 04. www.abbaye-stmaurice.ch.
This is one of the richest ecclesiastical treasuries in the Christian world. Pay special attention to a sardonyx vase, the Merovingian casket of Theodoric made of gold encrusted with pearls and cameos, the golden 9C ewer, said to be Charlemagne's, and the reliquary of St Maurice. Two other reliquaries of the 12C and 13C, the reliquary-bust of St Candid (on the plinth, his martyrdom by beheading) and the reliquary-monstrance given by St Louis, complete the priceless collection.

Fouilles de Martolet
🕐*Same admission times and charges as for the abbey treasury.*
Near the belfry, at the foot of the rock overlooking the abbey, excavations have uncovered foundations of the buildings that preceded the present church from the 4C onward; their plan stands out clearly. You may see traces of a baptistery and graceful modern cloisters in the Romanesque style. Visit the catacombs, narrow underground galleries leading to the crypt and tomb of St Maurice.

Castle
Overlooking the Rhône and sheltered by the eastern slopes of the Dents du Midi, this castle dates from the early 16C. The square keep and bastions were added in the 18C and now house the **Musée Cantonal d'Histoire Militaire** (🎧guided tours, Jun–Sept, 1p,m–6pm; ⊛12CHF, no charge the first Sun in the month; ℰ(0)24 485 24 58). On display are banners, medals, arms, and uniforms; another section includes models of the fortifications built along the Swiss borders during both World Wars. The dungeons house heavy artillery from the Second World

Valais Rhône

Rhône Glacier

From the Glacier to the Vines

Issuing from the famous cataract of the Rhône Glacier, the river is born at an altitude of 2 200m/7 218ft, crosses the Gletschboden Basin and enters the Conches Valley (also known as Goms). Its volume doubles at Brig where it receives waters of the Massa flowing from the Aletsch Glacier. It then ceases to be a mountain torrent and flows onto the floor of the alluvial plain between steep rocky banks at Visp (Viège) and Gampel.

The double obstacle created by the cone of debris of the Illgraben, cloaked in the Finges Forest (Pfynwald), and by the Sierre landslide, results in a wide break in the valley. This is where the boundary between German-speaking Upper Valais and French-speaking Valais developed (*see INTRODUCTION: Language and Religion*).

The Central Valais between Sierre and Martigny is sheltered from winds by mountain barriers and is the driest area in Switzerland. Favoured by this Mediterranean climate, the local vines (*see INTRODUCTION: Food and Wine*) flourish on rugged, sun-baked ridges of south-facing slope, opposite the wooded and pastoral slopes of the **mayens** (pastures where the herds wait in May for the snow to melt on the higher Alps).

At Martigny, the Rhône receives the Dranse and turns sharply north. Deflected toward the last foothills of the Bernese Alps by the cone of debris from the St Barthélemy Torrent, the river passes through St Maurice and opens out into the Lower Valais. This marshy plain, which spreads as it extends toward the shores of Lake Geneva, belongs politically to the Valais on the left shore of the lake.

The tumultuous natural phenomenon of the waters' meeting (*see Lake Geneva*) is the last sign of this 170km/106mi long mountainous Rhône.

The Rhône running through the Finges Forest

War and anti-aircraft guns occupy the courtyards. On the ground floor the elegantly furnished reception room is typical of the 18C.

Grotte aux Fées

Reached by path starting from the level of the castle and a bridge at the north entrance to the town. 🕐*Open mid-Mar –mid-Nov, daily 10am–5pm (until 6pm Jul & Aug); winter by reservation.* ✆*8CHF children 5CHF.* 📞*(0)24 485 10 45. www.grotteauxfees.ch.*

This grotto is formed by a natural gallery about 900m/990yds long leading to an underground lake and waterfall. From the terrace of the nearby restaurant there is a fine **view**★ of St Maurice and the Dent de Morcles.

🚗 DRIVING TOUR

VAL DE MORGINS★

34km/21mi – from Monthey to Châtel. Allow approx 2hrs. Swiss customs control near the pass, French customs at Vonne.

The Morgins Pass is the only international route in the pre-Alpine Chablais Massif joining the pastoral valleys of Dranse d'Abondance and Morgins, with their many large chalets. On the Valais side it is a modern road offering views of the Dents du Midi.

On leaving Monthey the road climbs quickly in hairpin bends above the Rhône Valley, overlooked (going upstream) by the summits of the Les Diablerets, Grand Muveran and Dent de Morcles. Ahead, in line with the Illiez Valley, are the snowy Dents Blanches and Dents du Midi. Fields planted with walnut trees succeed vineyards.

Champéry✳✳

Champéry lies on the mountainside at the beginning of the **Val d'Illiez**★★, in the shadow of the Dents du Midi Range. The resort clusters around its single narrow street and exudes a family atmosphere despite its international clientele. It is a favourite place for rock-climbers. A local feature is the church **belfry** roofed with a curious pierced stone crown. In winter the Panachaux Basin, served by several ski lifts, offers fine, sunny slopes to skiers.

Croix de Culet★★

From Champéry, about 45min, including 15min by cable-car and 1hr on foot. Jul–Aug, departure approximately every 30min, 9am–5.30pm; Jun, Sept and Oct, departures approximately every hr, 9am–5pm; Dec–mid-Apr, 9am–5pm. 🕐*Closed late-Oct–beginning of the skiing season.* ✆*15CHF there and back.* 📞*(0)24 479 20 20.*

From the upper station of the Planachaux cable-car, climb on foot, along the crest, to the cross (alt. 1 963m/6 440ft). There is an open view of the various peaks of the Dents du Midi, Mount Ruan, Dents Blanches and the Vaud Alps. The road continues to make hairpin bends, offering a widening **view**★ of the Rhône Valley, to the south of the Illiez Valley, the Dents du Midi Cliffs and, to the right of these, Mount Ruan. The road then becomes a corniche above the wooded ravine of the Vièze; it then reaches the floor of the softly shaped Alpine combe of the Morgins Valley. Here, chalets nestle under wide-eaved roofs covered with shingles; their two-storey balconies have a double overhang, forming a gallery.

▷ *Return towards Monthey and turn left at Troistorrents taking the Pass road.*

Pas de Morgins★

Alt. 1 369m/4 491ft.

The road, falling slightly, slips into this forest dell containing a small lake in which fir trees are reflected. Southeastward, in the middle distance, the Dents du Midi summits can be seen. The steeper descent into the Dranse d'Abondance Valley reveals the majestic **site**★ of Châtel. Ahead, the horizon is now barred by the slopes of Mount Chauffé (left) and the Cornettes de Bise (right).

Martigny

The town of Martigny, dominated by the Tour de la Bâtiaz and surrounded by vineyards, is an international road junction and a choice stopping-place for tourists. In this elbow of the Valais Rhône, where the Drance joins it, the flow of traffic from the Simplon and the Great St Bernard routes, and that from the Forclaz Pass all converge.

A BIT OF HISTORY

Martigny boasts several stone ruins dating to Roman times. Forum Claudii Augusti was a small town situated in the Forclaz Pass, linking Italy directly to France. Originally founded between AD41 and 47 under the Emperor Claudius, it was renamed Forum Claudii Vallensium (*guided tours: the tourist office organises archeological tours*).

WALKING TOURS
AROUND THE FONDATION PIERRE GIANADDA

Allow 3hrs to include visiting the museums at the cultural centre.

> *Begin at the Fondation Pierre Gianadda, S of the town centre.*

Fondation Pierre Gianadda★★

Open Jul–Nov, 9am–7pm; Dec–Jun, 10am–6pm. 18CHF. (0)27 722 39 78. www.gianadda.ch.
Léonard Gianadda opened this cultural centre named after his brother, who died in a tragic accident. It is built around the site of an ancient Celtic temple, the oldest of its kind in Switzerland. In addition to permanent collections, there are temporary exhibitions of works by such renowned artists as Goya, Renoir, Picasso, Klee, Braque, Degas, Manet, Dufy, Kandinsky, Van Gogh, Miró, and Modigliani.

The **Gallo-Roman Museum** displays statuettes, coins, jewellery, domestic utensils, and fragments of sculpted stones dating back to the 1C–4C. Do not miss the bronzes of Octodurum, including the tricorn head of a bull.

> ▶ **Population:** 15 635.
> **Michelin Map:** Michelin National Map 729: F7.
> **Info:** Ave de la Gare – 1920. (0)27 720 49 49. www.martigny.com.
> ▶ **Location:** On the Rhône in the lower Valais. Alt. 476m/1 562ft.
> **Don't Miss:** Fondation Pierre Gianadda or the Amphithéâtre Romain (Roman Amphitheatre).
> **Kids:** The St Bernard Dog Museum.
> **Timing:** Allow a minimum of one day for the highlights.

The **Automobile Museum** presents unique early vehicles, still in perfect working order, dating from 1897 to 1939. The oldest is an 1897 Benz with a maximum speed of 25kph/15.5mph. All the great names of the car industry are represented: Rolls-Royce, Bugatti, De Dion-Bouton, Delaunay-Belleville. The museum also displays cars made in Switzerland: Pic-Pic (1906 double-phaeton), Sigma (1910–11), Martini (1912 torpedo), Fischer (1913 six-seater torpedo), and Stella (1911).

The **Louis and Evelyn Franck Collection**, features Impressionists, including prominent works by Cézanne, Van Gogh, Ensor, Van Dongen, and Picasso. The **Garden** is an open-air sculpture museum, dotted with archeological ruins and more modern works by Henry Moore (*Reclining Figure*), Joán Miró (*Head*), Brancusi (*The Big Rooster*), Dubuffet (*Contortionist Element of Architecture V*), Segal (*Woman with Sunglasses on Park Bench*) and Rodin (*Meditation Scene with Arm*). Every year, from April to October, an exhibition dedicated to Leonardo da Vinci is held in the old arsenal of the foundation.

> *Turn left into chemin de Surfrête, then left again into route du Levant.*

Cow fights, Amphithéâtre Romain

Cow Fights

Popular cow fights take place in the Valais during spring and autumn when at least 100 contestants, usually of the Hérens breed, a sturdy, muscular race of cattle with curved horns and a lively, belligerent character bred primarily for their beef but also used for dairy production. They are grouped into categories according to age and weight and the fights take place before the cows are put out to grass or when they combine with another herd, these springtime contests deciding the Queen Cow who leads the herd to the summer pastures. Heads are lowered for the clash, horns are locked and the struggle begins with the weaker animal retreating, often chased by the winner. Organised fights determine regional and cantonal queens and a jury awards prizes to the first six in each category. The grand final is held in Martigny, where an overall champion emerges and is given the title "Queen of Queens".

Amphithéâtre Romain

The **Roman Amphitheatre** dates back to the 2C and bears witness to the prosperity of the Roman community that was here. Excavation work exposed ruins of residences, temples and public baths. The amphitheatre has been restored and is the site of open-air shows, concerts, and re-enactments of Roman gladiator fights and races.

⚫⚫ St Bernard Dog Museum

Route du Levant 34 in the old Arsenal building adjacent to the Roman Ampitheater; take the CFF bus to Pierre Gianadda Foundation. ⏱*Open daily 10am–6pm.* ⊜*12CHF.* ⚙ ☎*(0)27 720 49 20. www.musee-saint-bernard.ch.* This museum is dedicated to the history of the Great St Bernard hospice and pass and the history and role of the legend-

ary St Bernard dogs. There are special programs and exhibits for children, and a picnic area nearby.

▷ *Turn around; route du Levant leads back to Place du Bourg.*

Place and rue du Bourg

Pleasant small square with its turreted house (1609 heavily restored) and picturesque street. On the left note the old town hall (Maison de Commune du Quartier du Bourg—1645) with arcades supported by seven marble columns.

TOWN CENTRE
Tour de la Bâtiaz

20min on foot there and back by Chemin du Château.
Set in a strategic site, high on a rocky promontory, the circular keep and its

defensive wall are all that remain of a 13C fortress. From the tower there is a lovely **view**★ of the Martigny Basin and surrounding vineyards.

▷ *Just before the bridge, turn right along the west bank of the river.*

Chapelle Notre-Dame-de-Compassion

This 17C sanctuary contains an elegant Baroque gilt altarpiece and an unusual collection of ex-votos in the form of small paintings.

▷ *Cross the 19C wooden covered bridge (pont couvert) to avenue Marc-Morand.*

The 16C **Grand'Maison**, recognisable by its elegant spire-like shingle roof, was a hostel where a number of 18C and 19C European notables stayed.

On the right, at the beginning of Avenue du Grand-St-Bernard, is a powerful bronze bust by Courbet symbolising Liberty.

Return to Place Centrale and enter the 19C town hall to see the brilliant **stained-glass window**★ (55sq m/ 592sq ft) which illustrates the Rhône contemplating the Drance. There are also other fine stained-glass windows by **Edmond Bille** of Valais.

▷ *Continue to the Église Notre-Dame-des-Champs on Place du Midi.*

Église Notre-Dame-des-Champs

Rebuilt in the 17C in the Tuscan style and flanked in the 18C by a neo-Gothic bell tower (50m/164ft high), outstanding features are a monumental doorway with finely carved panels, a 17C baptismal font, a pulpit carved by local artisans, 18C statues of the Apostle, and a large Crucifix dating to 1495.

Go as far as rue des Alpes to see the restored **Maison Supersaxo**, an interesting example of 15C architecture. Take rue de la Délèze, rue Octodure, and rue du Forum, which passes in front of the Forum Claudii Vallensium, a Gallo-Roman site.

EXCURSIONS
Saillon

Alt. 522m/1 713ft. ▷*19km/12mi NE. Route du centre thermal.* ✆*(0)27 743 11 88. www.saillon.ch.*

The village of Saillon, a wine-making centre since Roman times, sits on the banks of the River Rhône surrounded by vineyards (200ha/494 acres) and market gardens. This wide, sunny valley has an ideal climate for the cultivation of grapes, strawberries, pears, apricots and asparagus.

Old Town

The old town, with its gray rooftops clustered around the ramparts, enjoyed a strategic position of vital importance before the Rhône changed its course in

The Bisses

In the middle section of the Valais (from Martigny to Brig) cultivation of tablelands overlooking the Rhône Valley caused irrigation problems. The lack of water in the gorges inspired the Valaisans to invent the *bisses,* narrow canals (207 at the turn of the last century; total length of 2 000km/1 243mi) that draw the glacier waters from the Rhône tributaries. They carry water along the mountainsides through wooden troughs, the upkeep of which requires dangerous acrobatics. The maintenance of the irrigating *bisse* and the distribution of its water among those who are entitled to it, hold an important place in the lives of these communities. The filling of the canals in early spring is still accompanied in some places by a religious ceremony. Technical progress in water supply has led to the abandonment of many of these rustic aqueducts, but some wooded sections offer tourists charming scenes for walks on level ground.

Farinet vineyards, Saillon

Joseph-Samuel Farinet

A Kind-hearted Crook

Born near the Grand-St-Bernard in 1845, Joseph-Samuel Farinet was a lively character who led an eventful life. A dedicated, self-proclaimed adventurer and forger, this Swiss Robin Hood would hand out the money he had forged to the poor and needy. Rebelling against the Establishment and forever on the run from the Swiss *gendarmes*, this kind-hearted, unorthodox figure was widely admired by the local population, who condoned his sense of justice and soon hailed him as a national hero. Hounded by the police, he was hit by a bullet and died in the Salentze Gorges, near Saillon, aged 35. He is buried in Saillon cemetery, at the foot of the church tower.

This outlaw is still seen by many as a benefactor who devoted his life to the poor. He remains a symbol embodying the values of freedom and mountain hospitality. His life story has inspired a ballad by the Vaud writer Charles-Ferdinand Ramuz and a film starring Jean-Louis Barrault, *Farinet et la Fausse Monnaie*. Barrault went on to create the Friends of Farinet Association which turned Saillon into a place of pilgrimage.

The Smallest Vineyard in the World

Planted by a group of admirers to mark the 100th anniversary of Farinet's death, this vineyard in the Colline Ardente consists of just three vines, covering an area of 1.67sq m/1.8sq yds. In 1999 the Dalai Lama, appointed by the "Amis de Farinet" took possession of these vines, following in the footsteps of the renowned Abbé Pierre, champion of the poor, and Jean-Louis Barrault. Other celebrities who have symbolically tended the vine include Gerard Depardieu, Maurice Béjart, Peter Ustinov, Danielle Mitterand, Roger Moore, Princess Caroline of Monaco, the Lord Mayor of London, Gina Lollobrigida, Paul-Émile Victor, Auxerre football coach Guy Roux, Zinedine Zidane and Michael Schumacher. Rocks carried from countries all round the world signifying that true friendship has no boundaries lie beneath the vines. Every year, wine produced by the three stocks is blended with the best Valais vintage. One thousand bottles are made, specially labelled and sold at an auction to benefit a charity fund in memory of Farinet.

this part of central Valais. The impressive ruins of the castle and the church, with its Romanesque belfry, are quite picturesque.

View★

From the village, a steep path soon leads to the foot of the great tower of the castle (a former keep), from where there is a lovely view of the terraced vineyards carpeting the slopes plain with its orchards. The Pennines can be seen like a massive wall in the distance.

Farinet's Path

45min walk.

Leaving from the foot of Saillon hill, this path is dotted with 21 stained-glass works depicting human experiences, such as childhood, love, suffering, and death. It wends its way through wine-growing fields to end up at the smallest registered vineyard in the world. **Farinet's Footbridge** was opened in 2001.

Spa

The spa complex (*Route de Centre Thermal, 1913, Saillon; check website for opening times and charges; ℘(0)27 743 11 70; www.bainsdesaillon.ch*) opened in 1983 carries on a tradition that dates back to Roman times. The hot springs of the Salentze provide four thermal baths ranging in temperature from 28°C/82°F to 34°C/93°F; the complex also has three steam baths, two saunas, swimming pools and foot baths.

🚗 DRIVING TOURS

ROUTE DE LA FORCLAZ★★

36km/22.5mi. About 55min – tour of the Emosson Dam and trek to the Trient Glacier not included. The road leading from the Le Châtelard to the Dam is narrow and winding with some steep climbs/descents.

The convenience of a direct link between the resort of Chamonix and the great Valais road junction of Martigny makes the Forclaz Pass Road one of the great international routes of the Alps.

▷ *24km/15m SW of Martigny. Take the Chamonix road from Martigny.*

Col de la Forclaz
Alt. 1 527m/5 010ft.

To the south the view is cut off by the detached crests of the Aiguille du Tour (visible on the extreme left, above the Grands Glacier). To the north the snowy peaks of the Bernese Alps seldom emerge from the bluish mist which rises from the great Valais Depression on fine summer days; the rocky Pierre-Avoi Peak, between the valleys of the Rhône and the Drance, is easier to distinguish. From the Forclaz Pass, many long signposted walks in the midst of the Valais mountains (*Information on trails: Marécottes, ℘ (0)27 761 31 01*) are available to visitors keen on wild nature. One of these walks, leading to the **Trient Glacier**★ (*allow 3hr there and back, ⬳inaccessible in winter because of snow*) follows an outflow channel (natural duct draining glacier waters toward the valley) along the mountainside and through a forest of larch, spruce and arolla pines. The path offers an open view of the Grands Glaciers and Dzornevattaz Valley, and the Pétoudes d'En Haut and Herbagères pastures below the Balme Pass. The ascent toward the Trient Glacier is breathtaking. The tongue of snow—a massive powdery stretch which appears to have frozen in mid-air like a lava flow—sparkles with bluish tints as one draws gradually nearer.

Halfway up the mountain, enjoy a well-deserved break at the Trient refreshments stall: This former refuge, rebuilt after an avalanche in 1978, was used in the late 19C as accommodation for workers farming the ice for commercial use. From the pass to Martigny the view of the Martigny Basin and the gap formed by the Valais Rhône really opens out only 2.5km/1.5mi below the ridge. The rocky snag-like Pierre-Avoi is still prominent in the foreground; soon you will pick out the narrow furrow of the Drance forming a way through to the Great St Bernard. The site of Martigny and La Bâtiaz Tower become visible where the road runs between vineyards.

☞ Glacier du Trient★

Access: from Col de la Forclaz.
Park in the car park and take the
waymarked footpath from the pass (alt.
1 526m/5 006ft). Follow signs to the
"Glacier du Trient et Fenêtre d'Arpette".

An easy walk (1hr) leads to a **snack bar** with views of the glacier, which is 5km/3mi long and 500m/547yds to 900m/984yds wide. The path continues to the tongue of the glacier along a more difficult route that follows the right bank of the river (1hr). From here, a **glacial hike** leads up the gentle slopes of the Trient, then up the steeper strips overlooking the river. Experience of glacial hiking is essential for this section of the walk, as are crampons and ice picks; beginners wishing to tackle the walk should contact a mountain guide.

▷ *Turn sharp right at Le Châtelard.*

A winding road (8km/5mi, closed in winter) leads from Le Châtelard, on the border between Switzerland and France, via Finhaut to the Emosson Dam. As the flower-and pine-tree lined road nears the dam, there are extensive views towards Mont Blanc in the distance.

Barrage d'Emosson★

Alt. 1 850m/6 068ft. ⊙Open May–Oct
(exterior). For further information,
contact the Parc d'attractions on
℘(0)27 769 11 11.

The dam of Emosson—the second largest in Switzerland after the Barrage de la Grande Dixence—was a joint Franco-Swiss project (1967–72). It rises to 180m/590ft, just below the Gueulaz Pass (alt. 1 970m/6 463ft) and harmonizes perfectly with its rocky, mountainous setting.

The reservoir has a capacity of 225 million cu m/7 946 million cu ft and a surface area of 327ha/808 acres. It replaced the old Barberine dam, which now lies 42m/138ft below the surface of the water when it was at its highest level. The water in the lake comes mostly from the Mont-Blanc Massif, on the other side of the valley. The sub-glacial water is collected at a higher altitude than the dam and is then transported here via underground tunnels and siphoned up to the lake.

The hydroelectric power station on the upper stage at Châtelard-Vallorcine is in French territory; the Swiss power station on the lower stage (la Bâtaz) lies on the floor of the Rhône Valley.

Annual production of some 850 million kWh is shared between the two national electricity companies EDF (France) and ATEL (Switzerland).

Access by funicular★★

From **Le Châtelard-Giétroz** take the funicular (one of the steepest in the world, with a gradient of 78%) which goes from the C.F.F. (Swiss Railway) power station to the water tower, and which offers lovely **views** of the Rhône Valley to one side and Mont Blanc to the other (☞*Access by funicular from Châtelard-Château d'Eau, Emosson train and Emosson mini-funicular;* ⊙*operates mid-May–mid-Oct, 9.40am–12.10pm, 1.10pm–4.10pm (5.10pm July–Aug);* ☞*Fare there and back 54CHF;* ℘*(0)27 769 11 11; www.chatelard.net*). A little train runs from here to the base of the dam. A second funicular, known as "Le Minifunic", then leads to the Gueulaz Pass (alt. 1 970m/6 461ft). Inaugurated on the occasion of the 700th anniversary of the Swiss Confederation in 1991, this ingenious piece of engineering can rise to a height of 260m/854ft in two minutes.

View★★

From the dam, there is a magnificent view of the Mont Blanc Massif (right to left) from Aiguilles Rouges to Mont Blanc, including Mont Maudit, Mont Blanc du Tacul, Aiguille du Midi, Aiguille du Dru, Aiguille Verte, the Aiguilles du Chardonnet and Argentière, Aiguille du Tour and Le Tour Glacier, and Grands Glaciers.

Above the café-restaurant stands the modern Chapelle Notre Dame des Neiges (Chapel of Our Lady of Snow), whose interior features pretty stained-glass windows depicting Alpine flowers and animals.

Climbing the Dam

In 1996, a climbing route was opened on the smooth side of the dam by climbers Marc Volorio, Paul Victor Amaudruz, Samuel Lugon Maulin, and Thierry Amaudruz from the Valais region. This is the highest artificial climbing wall in the world, with two sloping sections, a vertical section, and two final sections which curve back at 13m/42ft over a height of 60m/197ft. Around 600 synthetic resin footholds have been screwed into and stuck on to the concrete wall. This spectacular 150m/492ft route is very popular with experienced climbers.

Emosson Lakes★

3-4hr walk, there and back.

A wide paved path crosses the dam, leading to a route which follows the left bank of the **Lac d'Emosson**. The tranquil lake is almost Scandinavian in feel. The **Lac du Vieux Emosson** stands at the western end of the lake. The path climbs up to the Vieux Emosson Dam, where there is a snack bar. From here, there are fine views of the Cirque du Cheval Blanc (alt. 2 831m/9 285ft) and the Pointe de Finive (2 625m/8 610ft).

In the footsteps of the dinosaurs★★

5-6hr walk, there and back.

ⓘ *It is strictly forbidden to remove rocks or stones.*

Follow the left bank of the Lac d'Emosson. At the end of the lake, a footpath sign-posted to Col de la Terrasse climbs up to this protected site (alt. 2 400m/7 872ft) discovered on 23 August 1976 by the French geologist, Georges Bronner. The site contains more than 800 fossilised dinosaur footprints, left over 250 million years ago, before the Alps even existed. The dinosaurs stood at a height of 3–4m/10–13ft and weighed several tons. They have left prints 10–20cm/4–7.8in long and 5cm/2in deep.

The space between the prints shows that these animals had a stride of up to 2m/6.6ft.

VALLÉE DU TRIENT★

12km/7.2mi (excl Vallon de Van).

Allow 20-25 minutes driving time.

Beyond the covered bridge or the new bridge over the Drance in Martigny, a winding road heads toward Salvan (8km/5mi). The road, occasionally cut

Trient Gorge

© Thomas Andenmatten/Valais Tourism/Switzerland Tourism

into the rock, then climbs above the Rhône Valley and enters the wild scenery of the Trient Valley, a perfect destination for mountain walkers. The valley is particularly popular with cross-country and downhill skiers during the winter season.

Gorges du Trient★★

At Vernayaz.

Beginning in the Trient glacier, this stream gushes through a rocky fissure 200m/656ft high followed by a **way-marked footpath** and bridge across the gorge. Nearby, the old **Pont du Gueuroz** (1934) is now a listed monument. Cross the bridge on foot for a bird's-eye view of the gorge.

Vallon de Van

The narrow road overhanging the Rhône Valley at a height of 800m/2 625ft provides an exciting route to Van d'en Haut.

The drive back to Salvan offers views of the Vallon de Van and Martigny.

▶ *Return to Salvan, then follow the Trient Valley as far as Les Marécottes.*

Les Marécottes

Les Marécottes 1923. ℰ(0)27 761 31 01. www.marecottes.ch.
A mountain village with wooden chalets. A cable-car heads up to **La Creusaz** (alt. 1 777m/5 800ft), from where you can enjoy a panorama of Mont Blanc and the Valais Alps. Near the village, on the right as you come down the road, the ♠♦**Zoo des Marécottes** (⊙*open mid-May–mid-Sept, daily, 9am–nightfall; ⊙closed Mon & Tue in Sept and Oct; ▭10CHF; ℰ(0)27 761 15 62; www.zoo-alpin.ch*) is home to a wide variety of Alpine animals including chamois, reindeer, ibex, Valais goats and mouflons, llamas and bears.

GRAND-ST-BERNARD PASS★

From Martigny to the Great St Bernard Pass. 55km/34mi. Allow approx 3hr30min. Bourg-St-Pierre 1946. ℰ(0)27 783 32 48. www.saint-bernard.ch.
⊙*Once beyond the fork in Bourg-St-Bernard the road demands careful driving because of its numerous bends. When the road is blocked by snow, tourists should travel via the tunnel. Swiss and Italian customs control are at the top of the pass in summer. Those using the tunnel will find the customs control all the year round at Gare Nord in Switzerland and Gare Sud in Italy.*
The Great St Bernard Pass, connecting the valleys of the Drance and Dora Baltea, carries the most famous, historic transalpine route. The great tradition of hospitality has continued here since the 11C and such popular memories as that of Napoleon's crossing of the Alps in 1800 have drawn crowds. The opening of the tunnel beneath the pass has helped to separate the mass of hurried tourists crossing the frontier from the genuine pilgrims.
A short distance after Martigny, the road follows the deeply sunken Drance Valley as far as Les Valettes. The smallest valleys are still planted with vines and fruit trees (▭*see "VALAIS RHÔNE" box, p245*). The small road from Les Valettes to Champex is difficult. There are 22 hairpin bends, mostly sharp and awkward above the Durnant which flows through 1km/0.6mi of the impressive gorges (⊙*sightseeing facilities; inexperienced mountain drivers are advised to take the route via Orsières*).

Champex★★

Alt. 1 465m/4 806ft.
Champex stands high above the Orsières Basin at the mouth of a deep wooded valley containing a delightful lake. It is an elegant resort with views of a series of snowy summits; the Combin (Combin de Corbassière on the left, Grand Combin on the right). Those in search of views can see the range at their leisure while strolling along the Signal road connecting the hotel-belvederes of the resort. An alpine garden is open to visitors in summer.

La Breya★★

Alt. 2 374m/7 789ft. ✠1hr30min there and back, including 15min by chairlift. ⊙Operates mid-Jun–late Sept, 9.30am–11.30pm, 1pm; winter 9.15am–4.30pm. ▭Fare there and back 31–35CHF; 182CHF for a 6-day pass. ℰ(0)27 783 13 44.
A pleasant ascent by chairlift above Lake Champex; panorama of the Valais Alps.From Champex to Orsières, the winding, surfaced road (well laid out) within sight of the Combin Massif and the Valais foothills of the Mont Blanc sloping down to the Ferret Valley, lies between broad fields of strawberries. The scenery is wonderful.
The road passes **Bourg-St-Pierre** on its right, with its rust-coloured roofs nestling at the mouth of the Valsorey Valley and its waterfall. After crossing the Valsorey and its gorges, the road overlooks the Les Toules Dam of which there is a magnificent view (*a small section of the old pass road from Bourg-St-Pierre before you reach the dam is not surfaced*). Afterwards glaciated and striated rocks and rifts filled with landslides make the landscape more harsh.

Tunnel du Grand-St-Bernard

Entrance at Bourg-St-Bernard. ⊜*Cars: 29.20CHF one-way, 46.20CHF there and back; motorbikes: 17.20CHF one-way, 23.20CHF there and back.*

In view of the ever-increasing road traffic between the Rhône Valley and the Aosta Valley and to overcome the problem of snow blocking the road through the pass for over six months of the year, the Swiss and Italian governments combined to build a road tunnel, from 1959 to 1964, which would be open all year round and shorten the distance from Basel to Turin to 450km/279.6mi. Some sections of the road on the Italian side are not protected. Throughout the length of the road you can admire the daring construction of this freeway, with its viaducts high above the Artanavaz Gorges. Access roads on either side of the tunnel are generally covered and have a maximum gradient of 6%; they lead from below Bourg-St-Pierre on the Swiss side and above St Oyen on the Italian side.

After the Combe des Morts, it is a fast run to the Great St Bernard Pass (Col du Grand-St-Bernard).

Col du Grand-St-Bernard★

Alt. 2 469m/8 100ft.

The Great St Bernard hospice stands right at the top of the pass in a rocky gully, almost continually swept by an icy wind, on the edge of a lake which is frozen, on average, 265 days of the year and where the winter season lasts for more than eight months. It is open throughout the year to all travellers seeking a quiet haven.

The hospice was founded in 1050 as a refuge for those who had suffered at the hands of bandits or been victims of the mountain. Before the road, all supplies had to be carried by mules. The hospice continues to offer accommodation and meals to skiers, hikers, climbers, and all visitors.

The refuge exemplifies the survival of an admirable Christian tradition of assistance and hospitality. For nine centuries, the monks established here by St Bernard from Aosta—regular canons

belonging to the Augustinian Order— have taken in, comforted and rescued travellers in winter. A statue in honour of this "Hero of the Alps" has been erected at the summit of the pass, on Italian soil.

Church

This 17C Baroque church, fully incorporated into the hospice, was built on top of an early 13C sanctuary, presently serving as the crypt. The high altar is graced with statues of St Bernard and St Augustine. The carved walnut stalls and the painted vaulting in the chancel, wildly ornate with strong, bold colours, are characteristic of the Baroque period. The Holy Trinity is pictured surrounded by scenes taken from the New Testament: the Adoration of the Three Wise Men, the Annunciation and a Nativity scene. To the left, is the altar of St Bernard, bearing the gilt walnut casket containing the remains of the illustrious saint.

The **treasury** features a fine collection of sacred objects: a 13C polychrome bust-reliquary of St Bernard, sculpted in wood and ornamented with embossed gold and precious stones; a silver pilgrim's cross gilded and studded with gems (13–14C); a *Virgin and Child* dating from the 15C; and an illuminated 15C breviary.

ADDRESSES

⌂STAY

MARTIGNY

⊜⊜ **Alpes et Rhône** – *11 avenue du Grand-Saint-Bernard.* ℘*(0)27 722 17 17. www.alpes-rhone.ch. 50 rooms.* This hotel has a great restaurant serving international cuisine, using local and seasonal ingredients. There is also a bistro and a lovely terrace. Modern hotel conveniently located in the town centre.

⊜⊜ **Forclaz-Touring** – *15 rue de Leman. ℘(0)27 722 27 01. www.hotelforclaz touring.ch. 100 rooms.* Family-run hotel in the heart of Martigny. From the La Coupole restaurant on the 7th floor you can enjoy panoramic views over the Rhône Valley. During various themed

La Creusaz ski region in Les Marecottes

months Mexican, Indian, seafood or game dishes are served.

🍴🍴 **Mercure Hotel du Parc** – *19 rue Marconi.* ✆*(0)27 720 13 13. 90 rooms.* Modern hotel with distinctly contemporary architecture. 5 mins from the town centre museums of the world renowned Gianadda Foundation. Sophisticated cuisine and wine bar.

LES MARÉCOTTES

🍴🍴🍴 **Aux Mille Étoiles** – ✆*(0)27 761 16 66. www.mille-etoiles.ch. 24 rooms.* A cosy chalet near the skiing pistes will welcome you during the winter season. Splendid views. Covered pool. Peace and quiet guaranteed.

🍴EAT

BARRAGE D'EMOSSON

🍴 **Restaurant du Barrage d'Emosson** – *Rossens.* ✆*(0)27 768 12 74. www.emossonresto.com. Closed mid-Nov–Apr.* This secluded restaurant overlooking the dam is an ideal stop for a meal. Its exceptional location and breathtaking views of the surrounding mountains will strongly impress any visitor.

🍴🍴🍴🍴 **Alpes** – *1937 Orsières.* ✆*(0)27 783 11 01. Closed 13–27 Dec, 15–30 May, Mon lunchtime.* Traditional brasserie run for the past 30 years by the Joris family, who make the most of local Valais produce, and also specialise in excellent risotto.

MARTIGNY

🍴🍴 **Au Chapiteau Romain** – *51 rue du Bourg* ✆*(0)27 722 00 57. Closed Sun and 1–20 Aug.* À la carte menu only. Raclette and fondue served in the cellar.

🍴 **Les Trois Couronnes** – *8 place du Bourg 1.3km/0.8mi from Martigny.* ✆*(0)27 723 21 14. ad3c@net.plus. Closed 1–13 Feb, 9–14 Aug, Sun–Mon.* Located in a historic building dating from 1609 in a small square with a fountain. Serves traditional cuisine in a modern rustic atmosphere.

🍴🍴 **Le Virage** – *3km/1.8mi on the road leading to the Col de la Forclaz.* ✆*(0)27 722 11 53. www.surlescex.ch. Closed Sun eve, Mon.* This panoramic chalet-restaurant enjoys pretty views of Martigny and the Rhône Valley. Wide choice of traditional specialities.

🍴🍴 **Les Touristes** – *2 rue de l'Hôpital.* ✆*(0)27 722 95 98. Closed 24 Dec–12 Jan, 27 Jun–20 Jul, Sun & Mon.* Two brothers run this in the centre of town. There's a separate bar, recently refurbished dining room and sunny terrace. Fresh, tasty food with a Mediterranean twist.

🍴🍴🍴 **Le Belvédère** – *Chemin Dessous 1927 Chemin. 4.5km/2.8m S via Route de Chemin.* ✆ *(0)27 723 14 00. www. le belvedere.ch. Closed Sun eve, Mon– Tue.* This pretty pink chalet-gazebo above Martigny has a bright veranda in pale wood where you can admire the Rhône valley. Meticulous cuisine whichi s good value for money. Pleasant café.

Verbier ✱✱

Preceded by **Verbier-Village with its two churches,** the resort of Verbier is scattered over the sunny slope of the Bagnes Valley within view of the Grand Combin, the Dents du Midi and Mont-Blanc massifs, with luxurious hotels and traditional chalets in a glorious site✱. Its proximity to Geneva and good access to the Swiss motorway system makes it a popular weekend retreat year-round.

▸ **Population:** 2 163.
🕭 **Michelin Map:** Michelin National Map 729: F7.
▯ **Info:** Place Centrale – 1936. ℘*(0)27 775 38 88. www.verbier.ch.
◖ **Location:** Southwestern corner of the Valais region. Alt. 1 500m/4 921ft (resort).
🕭 **Don't Miss:** Mont Fort (international panorama), or Mont Gelé.
🕑 **Timing:** The resort is very crowded during holidays.

VISIT

The cirque of regular slopes converging here offers ideal topographical and climatic conditions for the great majority of present-day skiers, who find spacious and restful surroundings and considerable mechanical equipment suitable for downhill skiing. Verbier is also known to long-distance skiers as the starting-point of the High Road run, of which Zermatt or Saas-Fee is the terminus.

SKIING AREA

Verbier is the main attraction of **Les Quatre Vallées** (the Four Valleys), a huge skiing complex boasting a total of 410km/254.7mi of pistes and 100 chairlifts, one of the most interesting and varied Alpine ski resorts in Switzerland. A

150-person cable-car and an unusual lift combining a gondola and a six-passenger chair have enhanced uphill capacity significantly. The pistes around Verbier are fairly easy (Ruinettes and Savoleyres sector) but those on Mont Fort (highest summit of the complex), the Col des Gentianes, Mont Gelé, and the Plan-du-Fou Massif are recommended for experienced skiers (many steep slopes and bumpy sections). Some high-mountain itineraries are very impressive because of the austere landscape and the gradient of the slopes (Vallon d'Arbi from the Col des Mines, Mont Gelé, and Mont Fort toward Tortin and its legendary bumps). The long cruiser piste from Col des Gen-

Verbier-Village with view of the Grand Combin

tianes to La Chaux has fantastic views; this red piste and those from Savoleyres to La Tzoumaz and from Greppon Blanc to Siviez are ideal for intermediates.

The resorts connected to Verbier (La Tzoumaz, Nendaz, Siviez, Veysonnaz, Mayens-de-l'Ours, Thyon, and Les Collons) offer gentle slopes more attuned to beginners. The adventurous should take the opportunity to go paragliding in tandem with an experienced pilot-guide.

EXCURSIONS
Mont Fort★★★
Alt. 3 329m/10 922ft. *Access: by cable-car (allow 45min) from Verbier to Les Ruinettes; by shuttle (5min), or on foot (30min) up to La Chaux; by jumbo cable-car to Les Gentianes, then take another cable-car up to the top.* ○*Open daily 3 Jul–22 Aug, weekends late Aug & Sept, 8.45am–3.45pm; Dec–Apr, 9.15am–3.30pm.* *Fare there and back 34CHF, 49CHF for sunrise breakfast lift.* ℘*(0)27 775 25 11.*

A favourite with skiers and snowboarders for long-lasting snow and ice, including in summer, Mont Fort on a clear day offers a sweeping **international panorama**★★★ (*viewing tables*) of the Alps, covering Italy (Matterhorn), France (Mont Blanc), the Valais (Mont Fort, Grand Combin) and the Bernese Oberland (Eiger).

Mont Gelé★★
Alt. 3 023m/9 918ft.
Access (about 45min) via cable-car from Verbier to Les Ruinettes, then change and take another cable-car to Attelas I and change again for Attelas II (near the top). ○*Operates from mid-Dec–mid-Apr only, 9.40am–12.15pm, 1pm–3.30pm or 4pm.* ℘*(0)27 775 25 11.*

From the cross, which indicates that you are at the rocky summit of the Mont Gelé, admire the **circular view**★★: to the south Grand Combin Massif and its glaciers; to the east Mont Fort and its glaciers; to the north the peaks of Les Diablerets; to the west the Pierre d'Avoi Mountain and below, Verbier and the Entremont Valley.

Round tour of the passes★
Starting from Sembrancher, 14km/ 8.7mi from Verbier.
When the weather is fair this excursion is very pleasant. The road continues through Vollèges (elegant bell tower), **Le Levron** (terraced mountain village), the passes of Le Lein (a rocky larch-filled hollow), Le Tronc and Les Planches (restaurant) and the tiny village of Vens (*join the road to Mauvoisin*). It is a forest road at the beginning (*unsurfaced for 5km/3mi between Le Levron and Les Planches Pass*), becomes a corniche and then passes through woods of fir trees and larches. It affords splendid **views**★

Summit of Mont Fort

Christof Sonderegger/Switzerland Tourism

of the neighbouring valleys, the Pierre Avoi Mountain (northeast), the snowy summits of the French Alps (Mont Blanc) to the southwest and the Pennine Alps (Grand Combin) to the southeast.

Barrage de Mauvoisin★★★

Alt. 1 961m/6 433ft. 30km/18.5mi Se of Verbier.

The Mauvoisin Dam, which blocks a wild ravine in the Upper Bagnes Valley, is one of the highest arched-type dams in the world (237m/778ft). This huge wall has created a reservoir of 180 million cu m/40 000 milliongal of water to feed the turbines of the Fionnay and Riddes power stations.

▶ *At Mauvoisin, make for the visitors' car park* 🅿 *halfway between the hotel and the dam. After parking the car, take the path to the crown of the dam.*

🥾Walk to the Chanrion refuge★★

This strenuous walk (*6hr*) affords good views of the lake but requires hikers to be in excellent physical condition. It is possible to spend the night at the refuge to spread the outing over two days. Bear right and proceed down the long covered passageway (30min) then continue around the lake by a smooth path, walking for more than an hour. At the tip of the lake, you discover the Bec de Chardoney and the Bec de l'Épicourne. Go up to the refuge (1hr30min) by following the words "piétons" on rocks, then the "red and white" signposting. On reaching the top (alt. 2 462m/8 077ft), enjoy the **view**★★ of the Épicourne Glacier and, to the west, Mont Avril, Tour de Boussine, Combin de Tsessette (4 141m/13 586ft) and Tournelon Blanc, forming an imposing rocky barrier. The setting is enhanced by Lake Chanrion, where many plant and flower species thrive in this ideal location. Follow a charming path until the Col de Tsofeiret; the first part is relatively easy and offers **views**★ of the Brenay Glacier.

The pass (alt. 2 635m/8 645ft) affords a lovely **view**★ of Lake Tsofeiret. The expedition finishes by going down the

---

Milk on Tap

In difficult hilly terrain such as the Swiss Alps, there can be a problem transporting large quantities of milk from the milking stations to the dairies. The resourceful Swiss farmers above Verbier have come up with an ingenious way of transporting milk by pipelines. These milk ducts, which run between the Alpine pastures and the dairies, have a total length of about 220km/138mi. Problem solved!

---

gentle slope (2hr or more), glimpsing plunging **views**★★ of Lake Mauvoisin along the way.

ADDRESSES

🤸SPORT AND RECREATION

SUMMER ACTIVITIES

Summer is very popular for many sports and leisure activities. On Switzerland's largest state territory (296sq km/114sq mi), you can choose between **walks** covering altogether 400km/248.5mi: the most famous hike is the 🅇 **Sentier des Chamois**★★ between the Mont Fort refuge and Termin Pass. Moreover, 200km/124mi of lanes have been laid out for mountain bikes. Verbier also boasts facilities for hang-gliding and an 18-hole golf course. The **sports centre** *(rue de la Piscine;* 🕙*open daily 10am–9pm;* 🎫*8CHF;* 📞*(0)27 771 66 01)* features an indoor and an outdoor pool and a huge skating rink.

SIGHTSEEING

Tourists interested in traditional Swiss architecture can visit the picturesque villages of Bruson, Fionnay, and Sarreyer.

🎪EVENTS AND FESTIVALS

Verbier hosts one of the world's most prestigious classical music festivals to be held in a mountain setting *(last two weeks Jul, first week August, see www.verbierfestival.com for all times and charges. Some concerts free of charge).*

Sion★★

The attractive site★★ of the town of Sion has been inhabited for over 2 000 years: It can be fully appreciated when coming from Martigny or again when climbing to Savièze. The appearance of the two rocky Valère (Rhône side) and Tourbillon (mountainside) peaks, each crowned with episcopal fortresses, gives an immediate sense of history.

A BIT OF HISTORY
The Bishopric of Sion
The bishopric of Sion was founded in the 4C AD and played a key role in the religion and politics of the Middle Ages. In the early 11C the last King of Trans-Juran Burgundy, Rudolf III, made the bishop a temporal lord and a sovereign prince, enjoying full royal prerogatives: Dispensing justice, levying fines, minting coins. When the Communes were emancipated, these privileges disappeared one by one. However, until 1848 the Bishop of Sion was elected jointly by the canons and the Valais Diet, and subsequently by the Grand Council until 1918. Since then, the appointment has been the responsibility of the Vatican.

✿ WALKING TOUR
Allow half a day.

▷ *From Place de la Planta go along rue de Conthey before turning left onto rue St Théodule.*

Église St Théodule
Named after the first bishop of the Valais, the church was built under the episcopate of Matthäus Schiner at the beginning of the 16C. The vaults of the choir were decorated by the painter Hans Rinicher.

▷ *The Cathedral is adjacent.*

Notre-Dame du Glarier Cathedral
🕐 *Open only during services and celebrations.*

▶ **Population:** 29 304.
🚲 **Michelin Map:** Michelin National Map 729: G7.
ℹ **Info:** Place de la Planta 1950. ☎(0)27 327 77 27. www.siontourism.ch.
▷ **Location:** In the inner Valais plain. Alt. 512m/ 1 680ft.
🏛 **Don't Miss:** The church-fortress of Tourbillon surrounded by vineyards.
🕐 **Timing:** Allow a minimum of a day to take in the best of the sights; two days to fully enjoy the town.

The 11C and 13C Romanesque **belfry**★ is adorned with Lombard arcades and ends in a graceful octagonal steeple. The ogive-vaulted nave was completed at the beginning of the 16C. The chancel contains 17C stalls and is decorated behind the high altar with a gilded wood **triptych**★ depicting the Tree of Jesse. To the northwest stands the Sorcerers' Tower (Tour des Sorciers), originally part of the medieval fortifications.

▷ *Walk along rue de l'Église and cross the rue du Grand Pont.*

Town Hall
✿ *Guided tours of the town hall included in tour of the town.* 🕐 *Open Mon–Fri 8am–noon, 2pm–5.30pm.* 🕐 *Closed public holidays. For further information, contact the Tourist Office on ☎(0)27 327 77 27.*
The entrance of the 17C Hôtel de Ville is an elaborately carved wooden **door**. Roman inscriptions are exhibited in the entrance hall, one of which is Christian (377). The **Burgesses' Council Chamber**★ on the first floor has splendid woodwork and gorgeous furnishings.

▷ *Ascend the rue des Châteaux.*

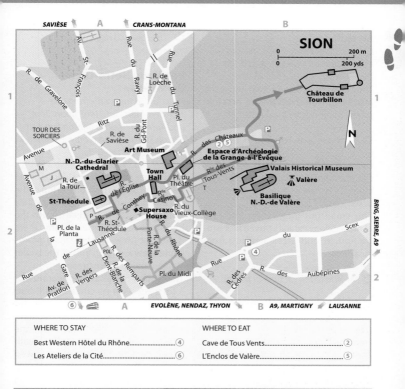

SION

SAVIÈSE   A   CRANS-MONTANA   B

0 200 m
0 200 yds

Château de Tourbillon

TOUR DES SORCIERS

Art Museum

N.-D.-du-Glarier Cathedral

Espace d'Archéologie de la Grange-à-l'Évêque

Valais Historical Museum

Town Hall

Pl. du Théâtre

Valère

Casino

St-Théodule

Basilique N.-D.-de Valère

Supersaxo House

R. du Vieux-Collège

Pl. de la Planta

Pl. du Midi

EVOLÈNE, NENDAZ, THYON   B   A9, MARTIGNY   LAUSANNE

BRIG, SIERRE, A9

WHERE TO STAY		WHERE TO EAT	
Best Western Hôtel du Rhône	④	Cave de Tous Vents	②
Les Ateliers de la Cité	⑥	L'Enclos de Valère	⑤

Vineyards of Sion with a view to the twin hills of Tourbillon and Valère

© Roland Gerth/Switzerland Tourism

Art Museum

🕐*Open daily 11am–6pm (5pm Oct–May).* 🕐*Closed Mon Oct–May 1 Jan, 25 Dec.* 🎫*8CHF.* 📞*(0)7 606 46 90.*
The Majorie and the Vidomat house the **Musée Cantonal des Beaux-Arts** (old prints, paintings by local artists).

▷ *Continue up the rue des Châteaux.*

Espace d'Archéologie

🕐*Same admission times as the History Museum.* 🎫 *Free with History Museum ticket.* 📞*(0)27 606 47 00.*
This small but interesting Museum of Archaeology exhibits carved prehistoric, Roman, and Greek artefacts from local digs.

▷ *Ascend to the car park at the top.*

Château de Tourbillon★

Allow 1hr. 🕐*Open daily 10am–6pm (11am–5pm Oct–May).*
From the car park, a path leads up to the imposing ruins of a former stronghold whose crenellated walls circle the hill. During the ascent (🚶rather steep), the **view** of Valère, its church-fortress and the surrounding hillsides planted with vines, is breathtaking.
The building and the chapel were erected in the late 13C by Bishop Boniface de Challant. Although originally defensive structure, the castle became a summer residence for bishops in times of peace. Repeatedly besieged and rebuilt in the 15C, it was razed to the ground by a terrible fire in 1788. After walking through a first doorway, pierced in a ring of ramparts, one enters the enclosure of the castle, dominated by its keep.

▷ *Return to the car park.*

History Museum★

🕐*Open daily 11am–6pm (5pm Oct–May).* 🕐*Closed Mon Oct–May 1 Jan, 25 Dec* 🎫*8CHF.* 📞*(0)27 606 47 15.*
Originally the canon's residence, this 12C castle, the interior of which was recently renovated, houses alternate exhibitions presenting the history of the Valais area.

▷ *The church is adjacent to the museum.*

Basilique Notre-Dame-de-Valère★

🔭*Guided tours only from mid-Jun–Sep, Mon–Sat 11am, noon, 2pm, and 4pm, afternoons only on Sun. Oct–Sep on Sun afternoons only.* 🕐*Closed 1 Jan and 25 Dec.* 🎫*4CHF.*
📞*(0)27 306 15 25.*
The church, the former residence of the Chapter of Sion, is built on the top of the hill of Valère and overlooks the valley from a height of 120m/394ft. Inside the fortified area at the end of a ramp there is a terrace *(viewing table)* which affords a fine **view**★ of Sion and of the Lower Valais, looking downstream.
The church has all the appearance of a fortress, with its curtain wall, battlemented tower and north wall and internal wall-walk. Building began in the early 12C and continued until the mid-13C. Magnificent 17C **stalls**★★ with panels depicting various scenes taken from the Passion adorn the chancel, which has historiated capitals dating from the Romanesque period and 16C frescoes. Note the organ-loft and organ, this is the world's oldest still-functioning organ (1390), and is played every year at the International Festival of the Old Organ.

▷ *Descend to the lower town via the roulles des Tout Vents and Casino, cross rue du Grand Pont to rue de Conthey.*

Supersaxo House

🕐*Open Mon–Fri 8am–noon, 1.30–6pm.* 🕐*Closed public holidays.*
📞*(0)27 323 85 50.*
This sumptuous dwelling was built in 1505 by Georges Supersaxo, who wished to dazzle his rival, Cardinal Matthäus Schiner, with its luxury.
The house has a very large, high **room**★ with a radially patterned woodwork ceiling with a huge rose-shaped pendant in the centre showing the Nativity of Christ. Around the room are 12 alcoves containing busts of the Magi and the Prophets.

EXCURSIONS
Barrage de la Grande ★★★

*400m/437.4yds downstream from the
original work, at an altitude of 2 365m/
7 759ft (crest of the dam).* ✆*(0)27 328
43 11. www.grande-dixence.ch.*

The new Grande Dixence Dam, the
greatest feat of civil engineering the
Swiss have ever undertaken, is of the
dead-weight type and 284m/932ft tall.
The first Dixence Dam, 87m/285ft, completed in 1935, had a storage capacity
of 50 million cu m/1 765 million cu ft
feeding the Chandoline power station on the floor of the Rhône Valley
opposite Sion with an average fall over
1 750m/5 700ft. This was already the
most powerful hydroelectric installation
in Switzerland and the biggest head of
water in the world.

The dam has been built up in stages is
now more than two and a half times the
height of St Paul's Cathedral in London.
About 6 million cu m/208 million cu ft
of concrete were required—enough to
build two Great Pyramids. A further part
of the project involved drilling about
100km/62mi of underground tunnels
to bring water from the foot of the Matterhorn Glacier. The water was then
distributed not only to the new power
station at Fionnay in the nearby Bagnes
Valley, but also to the Riddes-Nendaz
and Chandoline power stations in the
Rhône Valley. The hydroelectric output
of Switzerland has been increased by an
annual 1 600 million kWh.

Lac Souterrain de St-Léonard

*6km/3.5mi by on the road to Brig and
then left; from the car park. Allow 10min
on foot there and back.* ⊙*Open 15 Mar–
May 9am–5pm, Jun–Sept 9am–5.30pm,
Oct–1 Nov 9am–5pm.* ⊜*10CHF.* ✆*(0)27
203 22 66. www.lac-souterrain.com.*

The lake and cave were formed by water
infiltrating the gypsum bed and dissolving it little by little. The level of the lake
is maintained by pumping (its dimen-
sions are 300m/984ft long, 20m/65.5ft
wide and 15m/49ft). The electric lighting
enhances the site: The tormented relief
and contrasting shades of colour (whit-
ish gypsum, coal schist and gray marble)
of the vaulting and rocky surfaces reflect
onto the lake surface.

🚶 Alpe Bricola★★

Alt. 2 415m/7 923ft. 🅿*Park the car at
Salay/Ferplècle. 2hr15min up, 1hr30min
down. A comparatively easy ascent.*

This outing offers lovely **views**★★ over
the glaciers of Ferplècle, Mont-Mine and
La Dent Blanche. For a sweeping panorama of the landscape, continue to climb
a little higher toward the Dent Blanche
Hütte refuge.

🚶 Cabane des Aiguilles Rouges★★

*Alt. 2 810m/9 219ft. 3hr up, 2hr down.
Check timetables in advance to get
back to Arolla from La Gouille hamlet in
the evening.* 🅿*Park the car at the foot
of the Guitza ski lift. This lovely route*

Barrage de la Grande Dixence

© Dawn Cranie/fotoLibra

requires considerable stamina over a variety of landscapes.

Leaving behind the ski lift, proceed up a steep forest path commanding magnificent **views**★★ of Pointe de Tsa, Mont Collon and Pigne d'Arolla to a lovely path crossing an Alpine lawn (*avoid the winding lane*). After about 1hr, you reach the pretty perched village of **Remointse de Pra Gra** (2 479m/8 133ft), Start climbing towards the refuge, at the foot of the Aiguilles Rouges of Arolla (follow red signs when crossing the chasms).

The refuge affords a **sweeping panorama**★★ of the whole valley: the Aiguille de la Tsa, Pointe des Genevois, Dent de Perroc and La Grande Dent de Veisivi form a huge stone barrier.

The descent is steep leading down to the shores of **Lac Bleu**★★ (2 090m/6 857ft). Walk down to La Gouille hamlet and catch a bus back. *Avoid the path going from Lac Bleu to Arolla; it is both tiring and dangerous.*

🚶 Pas de Chèvres★★

Alt. 2 855m/9 367ft. 2hr up, 1h30min down, difference in height 850m/ 2 789ft.
🅿 *Park the car on leaving Arolla, just before you get to the highest chalet.*
Follow the lane for 50m/55yds, then take the steep path on the right, facing the slope, until you reach the broken-down hillocks (*40min*). Take the path opposite that winds its way through an open **landscape**, skirting the impressive Tsijiore Nouve Glacier and Pigne d'Arolla (3 796m/12 454ft). Around 30 min later, after crossing a track, the path becomes steeper. At the next fork, turn left. The pass offers beautiful **views**★★ of Mont Collon and the Aiguille de la Tsa. Go back down along the path on the right in the middle section, near the ski lift.

🚗 DRIVING TOURS

DERBORENCE ROAD★
24km/15mi.

▷ *Leave Sion by S and follow road number 9 as far as Pont-de-la-Morge.*

The road climbs through vineyards and crosses the villages of Conthey, Sensine and **St-Séverin** (church with stone bell tower) where you go left. After Erde, vineyards are replaced by shrubbery; in the bend before the Aven chalets is a good view of the Rhône Valley. After St Bernard's Church (last nice view of the valley), the road goes northward along the wild Triquent Valley, where the Lizerne runs. After the first tunnel, there is a view of the Les Diablerets blocking the combe to the north, The landscape is picturesque with snowfields here and there, pine trees, a torrent (the Lizerne, which the road crosses three times) surrounded by erratics, cascades.

The valley then opens into a **cirque**★★ of rocks, pine and larch. Bear left onto the rocky path, which ends in the Derborence Nature Reserve in a rock **corrie**★ created in the 18C, after an avalanche of the Les Diablerets.

SANETSCH PASS ROAD★★
33km/20.5mi.

▷ *Leave Sion by S and follow road 9 to Pont-de-la-Morge.*

After crossing the Morge, the narrow road through the vineyards climbs to Chandolin, offering views of neighbouring slopes covered with vineyards and the Rhône Plain. At the Pont du Diable the corniche descends, meets up with the torrent and then enters a landscape with fir trees and a lovely cascade.

At the junction of the road to Conthey (on the left), the rocky Crêta Besse summit stands straight ahead. A steep climb (15%—1 in 6.5) through woods ends at the chalets of Plan-Cernay.

2km/1mi farther, in front of the Zenfleuron Inn, the road crosses the Morge and in a corniche stretch passes the east slope, and after a tunnel, a **view**★ of the valley and at the opposite end onto the mountaintops (where three torrents tumble from melting glaciers). This is followed by a climb which opens, before the second tunnel, at the foot of the rocky face of the Sex Noir facing the snowy barrier of Les Diablerets.

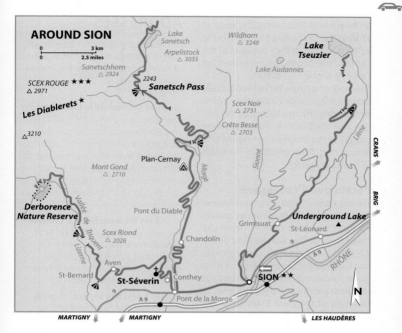

AROUND SION

0   3 km
0   2.5 miles

Lake Sanetsch
Wildhorn △ 3248
Arpelistock △ 3035
Lake Tseuzier
Lake Audannes
Sanetschhorn △ 2924
SCEX ROUGE ★★★ △ 2971
2243 Sanetsch Pass
Scex Noir △ 2731
Les Diablerets ★
Crêta Besse △ 2703
△ 3210
Mont Gond △ 2710
Plan-Cernay
Morge
Sionne
Lièvre
CRANS
BRIG
Derborence Nature Reserve
Vallée de Triquent
Pont du Diable
Grimisuat
Underground Lake
St-Léonard
Scex Riond △ 2026
Chandolin
Lizerne
Aven
St-Bernard
St-Séverin
Conthey
SION ★★
RHÔNE
A 9
9
Pont de la Morge
A 9
N
MARTIGNY   MARTIGNY   LES HAUDÈRES

After the last tunnel, the route continues its spectacular climb to the **Sanetsch Pass** (2 243m/7 359ft; lovely **view**★★ of Les Diablerets preceded by the Tsanfleuron Glacier), then descends to and halts at the dam's reservoir (Sanetsch Lake).

TSEUZIER ROAD★
23km/14mi.

▷ *Leave Sion on the road to Crans-Montana to the N.*

3km/1.8mi after Grimisuat bear left onto the road to Ayent and at St-Romain follow the narrow but easy road signposted Barrage de Tseuzier, which climbs amid fir trees above the Lième Valley and soon offers some lovely glimpses of the valley and the terraced resort of Crans-Montana beyond (a wide **view**★, especially at the entrance to the first tunnel). At the end of the road *(restaurant)* is the small lake of Tseuzier Dam in its rocky basin.

VAL D'HÉRENS★★
29km/18mi. About 2hr
(see THE VALAIS map).

The Hérens Valley is one of the most accessible of the lateral valleys in French-speaking Valais. The Évolène district, located in a very fine setting of high mountains, overlooked by the Dent Blanche (alt. 4 357m/14 290ft), has retained many traditional local customs. Sights like that of haymaking between Évolène and Les Haudères are among the most attractive in picturesque Switzerland. When you see the women working in the fields or driving herds of cows, you are often tempted to forget the rigours of their mountain life. The men seldom feature in these pastoral scenes. Most of them find work in local timber yards or factories.

Skiing Area
In winter, skiers can tackle 100km/62mi of downhill runs, two cross-country skiing tracks (33km/20.5mi) and two open-air ice rinks.

From Sion, crossing the Rhône and leaving on the right the Chandoline power station, fed by the Grande Dixence Dam, the road climbs in hairpin bends, affording good views of the site of Sion, marked by the fortified heights of Valère and Tourbillon. On arriving at **Vex**, the first village in the Hérens Valley, the superb rock pyramid of the Dent Blanche begins to emerge from the Ferpècle Corrie.

The road, which runs almost horizontally along a ledge, approaches the ravines overlooking the confluence of the Borgne and the Dixence. The eye will be caught by the astonishing ridge of broken country from which the Pyramids of Euseigne spring.

Pyramides d'Euseigne★

The road passes through a tunnel under the crowned columns cut out by erosion from masses of soft morainic debris and saved from destruction by their unstable, rocky crowns. The valley shrinks and the gradient grows steeper. Arrival in the Evolène Basin is marked by the reappearance of the Dent Blanche. To the right of the Dent Blanche, in the foreground, stand the twin sharp-edged pyramids of the Dents de Veisivi.

Évolène★

Alt. 1 400m/4 593ft.

The tall, flower-decked **wooden houses**★★ of this resort are among the finest in the Valais. Évolène is a popular mountaineering centre (Mount Collon and the Dent Blanche Massifs) with a climbing school in the village.

Les Haudères

The chalets stand in picturesque disorder. From here roads lead to **Ferpècle** (alt. 1 770m/5 807ft; 9km/5.6mi from Les Haudères), at the foot of the Dent Blanche, and Arolla (12km/7.4mi) at the foot of Mont Collon. The road passes through the hamlets of La Sage, Villa and La Forclaz, with their beautiful slate-roofed chalets, and offers clear views of the Upper Hérens Valley.

ADDRESSES

Despite the growth in tourism in Sion over the past few years, the choice of hotels in the town remains limited.

STAY

Les Ateliers de la Cité – *6 avenue de la Gare, Sion.* *(0)27 324 41 41. 13 rooms.* This accommodation offers a new type of hotel service which is primarily targeted at businessmen. However, its tasteful and well equipped studios are also convenient for holiday makers, plus the prices for two people are very competitive.

Best Western Hôtel du Rhône - *10 rue du Scex, Sion.* *(0)27 322 82 91. www.durhonesion.ch. 44 rooms.* A hotel in the middle of Sion with modern rooms. A comfortable option even if not the most charming.

Hôtel des Vignes – *9 rue du Pont, Uvrier 1958 (5km/3mi E of Sion).* *(0)27 203 16 71. www.hoteldesvignes.ch. 39 rooms. Closed Sun even and Mon.* A really charming hotel just a stone's throw from Sion, in its own grounds with vineyards closeby. Good size airy rooms.

EAT

SION

Cave de Tous Vents – *16 rue des Châteaux* *(0)27 322 46 84. www.cave-tous-vents.ch. Closed in Aug, Mon in May–Jun.* Dining in the lovely cellar which dates from the 13C, you can enjoy dishes from the Valais region.

L'Enclos de Valère – *18 rue des Châteaux.* *(0)27 323 32 30. www.enclosdevalere.ch. Open May–Sept, closed Sun eve and Mon, Oct–Apr, closed Sun and Mon.* Good quality French restaurant with one of the best terraces in Sion. During the summer guests will appreciate its calm and shade.

NEARBY

Relais du Mont d'Orge – *La Muraz (NW by route de Savièse).* *(0)27 395 33 46. www.ricou.ch. Closed hols, one wk end of Jun, Sun eve and Mon.* Modern cuisine with a good choice of Valais wines.

Sierre

Sierre is one of the sunniest cities in Switzerland. It lies in the Valais Rhône, below the vineyards of the Noble Country (Noble Contrée) and at the mouth of the Val d'Anniviers. A huge landslide in prehistoric times explains the unique site★ of the town, in a landscape like "a gravel pit dug and turned over with a spade." Sierre (Siders) marks the language boundary between French and German Switzerland (&see INTRODUCTION: Language and Religion).

A BIT OF HISTORY

Several strongholds such as the Castle of the Vidômes and the Goubin Tower, perched on its rock, recall the part played by Sierre at the time of episcopal and feudal Valais. Shortly before his death in 1926, the Austrian poet **Rainer Maria Rilke** stayed in the former Château de La Cour, which now houses the town hall.

SIGHTS
Hôtel de Ville

Formerly a manor house and a hotel, the town hall dates from the 17C and 19C. The **interior**★ is sumptuous in its decoration (elegant painted ceilings, frescoes, paintings and stained-glass windows) and yet it retains a certain intimacy. It houses a small museum: The **Musée des étains** (○open Mon–Fri, 9am–11am, 3pm–5pm; ○closed on public holidays in the Valais canton; ⇌no charge; ℘(0)27 452 01 11) Set up in the cellar, it displays approximately 180 pewter objects (tableware, utensils) from the 17C–19C.

Rue du Bourg

A small picturesque street with old houses. Note the unusual building with bartizans, known as the Château des Vidômes and the Catholic Church of St Catherine (17C–19C). Inside the church are a Baroque chancel, a carved pulpit and a lovely organ loft. At number 30, on the ground floor, the Maison Pancrace

> ▶ **Population:** 15 574.
> ⚙ **Michelin Map:** Michelin National Map 729: G7.
> 🛈 **Info:** Place de la Gare 10. ℘(0)27 455 85 35. www.sierre-salgesch.ch.
> ▶ **Location:** Valais region, southwestern Switzerland. Alt. 534m/1 752ft.
> ⊛ **Don't Miss:** Château de Villa.
> ◷ **Timing:** The city is crowded during the international festival in May and early June.

de Courten houses the **Fondation Rainer Maria Rilke** (○open Apr–Oct, Tue–Sun 2pm–6pm; ⇌6CHF; ℘(0)27 456 26 46; www.fondationrilke.ch), a tribute to the Austrian poet, who is spent a lot of time around Sierre and is buried near Visp (&see RARON, p283).

Château de Villa

The **Musée Valaisan de la Vigne et du Vin** (○open Mar–Nov, Tue–Sun 2pm–6pm; ○closed in winter; ⇌6CHF valid also for Salgesch wine museum. ℘(0)27 456 35 25; www.museevalaisanduvin.ch)

The International Comics and Graphic Art Festival

Every year, in late May and early June, the city of Sierre celebrates the joy of reading by staging a world festival devoted to comics and strip cartoons. Writers, illustrators, publishers and second-hand booksellers all gather in Sierre to attend Sismics. This popular festival also involves many exhibitions, street performances and concerts combining originality and humour. Children will be delighted since they, too, are included in the festivities, with a wide choice of games, quizzes, make-up workshops and drawing competitions.

has been set up in one of the château outbuildings. The visit to the Wine Museum begins with a video film about traditional techniques for pressing grapes. The two following rooms are devoted to wine presses. The second one explains the work of people employed in the cellars. The visit ends with a display of the different types of containers (bottles and labels, pewter pots, barrels) associated with the business of wine and the role it has played in society throughout the ages.

EXCURSIONS
Salgesch

From Sierre head E, take Gemmistrasse and then Unterdorfstrasse towards Salgesh.

A 6km/3.8mi-long **Wine Route** linking Sierre to Salgesch (**Salquenen** in French) enables you to discover part of the vineyard. The route is dotted with signposts which describe the different grape varieties (Chasselas, Pinot, Sylvaner, Malvoisie), the quality of the soil, the various pruning methods and the long-standing tradition of *vignolage* (a day's work in the vineyard in springtime, accompanied by fife and drum music). In this quiet village, the 16C **Maison Zumofen** (*open Mar–Nov, Tue–Sun, 2pm–6pm; closed in winter; free with ticket of Sierre Wine Museum*), easily recognisable by its double-gabled wooden roof, presents an exhibition which complements those of the **Musée Valaisan de la Vigne et du Vin** in Sierre. Several rooms enlighten visitors on the art of winemaking: Soil, grape varieties, techniques and tools used in wine making, and finally grape harvesting, conducted with the blessing of St Théodule, the patron saint of this noble profession.

Kippel★

Leaving Sierre take the E62 E and after 18km/11.2mi turn off to Gempeland head N to Kippel.
6 Rue Pré-Fleuri, Sion. (0)27 327 35 70. www.valaistourism.ch.
This is the most typical village in the the remote Alpine valley of Lötschentala and visitors not pressed for time may want to spend the whole day here. In the area around the church are numerous blackened **wooden houses**★★ with delicate friezes of dog-tooth and rosette patterns. The crowds which gather for High Mass make Sundays and feast days most spectacular events for lovers of folklore, but the Corpus Christi Procession (*see Calendar of Events*), with its procession of God's Grenadiers, is the most colourful spectacle. For this occasion flags are flown and the local men bring out their old-fashioned outifts, including plumes, bearskin caps and belts.

The valley remained cut off from the outside world until the Lötschberg railway tunnel was built between Kandersteg in the north and Goppenstein, in 1913. The River Lonza flows southwards through the valley to join the Rhône. In the past, when it was extremely difficult to maintain an open road in the lower sections of the valley, because of the frequent avalanches, the main access was by passes at an altitude of 2 500m/8 200ft. The people of this remote valley remain very attached to their traditional way of life.

Crans-Montana★★

Alt. 1 500m/4 921ft. 13km/8mi NW of Sierre. Avenue de la Gare, Montana – 3962. (0)27 485 04 04 and Crans-sur-Sierre – 3963. (027) 485 08 00. www.crans-montana.ch.

This resort, formed by the neighbouring towns of Crans and Montana, extends for 2km/1.2mi along a wooded plateau dotted with small lakes, facing the impressive backdrop of the Valais Alps. Seen from Montana, the Valais Alps give the impression of rising from the near background, whereas in fact the Rhône Valley lies between them and the observer. The road to Crans-Montana from Sierre is a succession of hairpin bends, climbing through vineyards and then pastures. On reaching Montana, motorists wishing to return to the floor of the Rhône Valley by a different road can find their way down along the by-road from Crans to road number 9—an interesting route which offers fine views of the Pennine Alps. Its splendid location, facing due south at an altitude of 1 500–1 700m/ 4 921–5 577ft, was initially responsible for the development of luxury hotels and sanatoria between the two wars. It was here that **Katherine Mansfield** stayed in 1921 and wrote some of her charming stories (*The Garden Party, The Doll's House*). Renowned for its skiing, Crans-Montana attracts visitors, who can spend their time away from the slopes playing golf or squash, or window-shopping in the many luxury boutiques. Despite its cosmopolitan attractions, the resort lacks the charm of a traditional Alpine village. However, in summer waymarked footpaths allow visitors to escape the modern buildings and busy roads in search of more typically Alpine scenes. *A map of footpaths (a total of 280km/174mi) is available from the Tourist Office.*

The skiing area – The skiing area of Crans-Montana, consisting of 160km/ 99.4mi of slopes served by 41 lifts, including four gondolas, is one of the most important in Switzerland. It is especially popular among beginners and intermediate skiers for its wide, groomed trails. Experts will find many off-piste opportunities, tree-skiing through the forest and some mogul sections around Bella Lui and La Toula. However, the most superb skiing slopes are on the Plaine Morte, which offers opportunities for skiing both in winter and summer, and where the vertical drop is considerable (1 500m/4 921ft to the resort). There are also opportunities for **cross-country skiing**, with 50km/31mi of loops extending over the lovely wooded plateau of Crans at Aminona and the Plaine Morte Glacier. A funicular (12min) connects Crans-Montana with Sierre.

Excursions and walks from Crans-Montana

Bella Lui★★

Alt. 2 543m/8 340ft. Access by cable-car. 1hr30min there and back. Service to Cry d'Er 8.30am–4.30pm, Jul–mid-Sept. Departure every 20min. (0)27 485 89 10.

Stop at Croix (or Cry) d'Er (alt. 2 263m/ 7 422ft with TCS viewing table) for a magnificent ascent by cable-car over the Rhône Valley, with a great panorama of the Valais Alps. To reach Bella Lui by foot, take the path from Vermala to Cry d'Er (2hr45min) around Mont Lachaux, then carry on to Bella Lui (45min).

Aminona

Alt. 1 515m/4 969ft.

This small modern resort, to the east of Montana, is the departure point for the **centenary walk**, designed in 1993 to commemorate the resort's centenary. This easy walk (*4hr30min there and back*) winds its way through parks and forest and crosses Crans-Montana by La Comba (1 428m/4 684ft) and Les Mélèzes (1 450m/4 756ft). Three orientation boards give information on the surrounding peaks of Brig and Martigny. *A bus service operates back to the resort.*

Petit Bonvin★★

Alt. 2 400m/7 873ft.

Access by cable-car from Aminona. **View**★★ of the Crans-Montana surrounded by spruce, the Bella Lui, the Grand Combin and the Dent Blanche.

Vermala★★

Alt. 1 670m/5 479ft. 1.5km/1mi.
P *Leave your car below the Café-Restaurant du Cervin and go to the viewpoint on the right, at the edge of a small escarpment.*

Enjoy a bird's-eye view of the Rhône Valley with a sweeping panorama of the high summits enclosing the Val d'Anniviers (especially the Weisshorn and the Zinalrothorn and, in the far distance, the Matterhorn).

Housed in an old Alpine chalet, the small **Colombire Museum** recalls life in the mountains in the 1930s, with information on cheesemaking and other rural activities. *Snacks available, guided walks at dawn, plus a typical mountain breakfast.* This chalet is the departure point for the **Bisse du Tsittoret**, an easy walk suitable for children across fields and through woodland (*4hr30min there and back*). Take the path toward the Marolires, Courtavey, Colombire caves and the Tièche (alt. 1 969m/6 460ft).

Plaine Morte★★★

9min by the Violettes Express cable-car reaching an altitude of 2 267m/7 437ft (Barzettes Station). Then take the Funitel to reach Plaine Morte. 5min on foot up a short but steep slope.

The summit (alt. 3 000m/9 843ft) affords an exceptional **panorama**★★★ of the Valais Alps. To the southwest loom the Grand Combin, Mont Blanc and, on the distant horizon, the Meije (on the frontier with the southern French Alps). To the north extends the gently sloping Plaine Morte Glacier, dominated by the Wildstrubel (3 243m/10 639ft).

Plans Mayens★★

Alt. 1 622m/5 322ft. 1.5km/1mi. It's possible to stop at the edge of the road, beside the terrace of the Restaurant du Mont-Blanc.

A wide panorama of the Valais Alps extends to the Mont-Blanc Massif in the distance. A picturesque walk (3hr 30min) can be followed from here along the old **Bisse du Ro** up to Er de Chermignon (1 733m/5 684ft). ⊙*The path is steep in parts and not suitable for children or those who suffer from vertigo.* Follow the path near the Hôtel de la Dent-Blanche. Return to Crans-Montana via Pra du Taillour and the Pas de l'Ours.

🚗 DRIVING TOURS

DALA VALLEY

28km/17mi. Allow 1 hour.

◐ *Leave Sierre on road number 9, heading E.*

Leuk

Alt. 750m/2 461ft. Bahnhof 5.
℘(0)27 473 10 94. www.leuk.ch.
Leuk sits above the Rhône Valley at the mouth of the Dala Gorges. The first stronghold encountered on entering the town is the Château des Vidommes: vidames were secular deputies appointed to command armies or to represent the interests of French abbots or bishops under the Ancien Régime. This building has become the town hall. From the castle's esplanade there is an astonishing view★ of the valley floor.

The great fluvial cone of rubble from the Illgraben, covered with a mixture of heath and forest vegetation (Forest of Finges or Pfynwald), stands below. This obstruction still forms the natural boundary between the French-speaking Central Valais and the Upper Valais with its German-Swiss culture.

Farther on, the 15C Château des Majors still features its square crenellated tower.

◐ *Continue towards Leukerbad and turn left in to a narrow road to reach Albinen.*

Albinen

This picturesque village is one of the most beautiful in the Valais. It contains a number of wooden houses that cling to the steep, sunny side of the Rhône valley.

◐ *Continue heading N.*

Leukerbad✼

Alt. 1 411m/4 628ft. Rathaus.
℘(0)27 472 71 71. www.leukerbad.ch.
This high-altitude spa was discovered by the Romans. It nestles in a grandiose **site**★, overlooked by the Gemmi Pass and approached from Leuk via a narrow, often vertiginous road. It was this austere landscape that inspired French author Guy de Maupassant to write his fantastic tale, *L'Auberge*. Bare rocky peaks overlook the valley, which is dotted with attractive chalets and pastureland.

The **Skiing Area** *(50km/31mi of downhill runs and 25km/15mi of cross-country tracks)* extends across the Gemmi and Torrent ranges, at an altitude between 1 400m/4 592ft and 2 800m/9 184ft. Leukerbad is particularly renowned for its **spa**, the largest in Europe, whose sulphurous, calcareous and gypsumrich waters are recommended for the treatment of rheumatism, circulatory diseases and skin problems. The resort is popular year-round with tourists, who come here to bathe in thermal waters (51°C/124°F at source and between 28°C/82°F and 44°C/111°F in the pools).

👥 Burgerbad

This spa complex houses an indoor thermal bath and a pool for children, a gym and a bar-restaurant. Outdoor facilities include a swimming pool, two thermal baths, a 70m/230ft water slide, Jacuzzis, a footbath, and a sauna in a grotto.

Lindner Alpentherme

Opened in 1993, this fitness centre has indoor and outdoor thermal baths, a swimming pool, plus a complex where visitors can choose between showers, hot-air baths, massage, steam baths, Jacuzzis, and cold-water baths.

Gemmi Pass

Alt. 2 314m/7 590ft.

Linked to Leukerbad by cable-car, this pass begins in Kandersteg in the Bernese Oberland and ends on the slopes of the Valais in a vertiginous road cut out of the rock, offering superb **views**★ of the Valais and Bernese Alps.

SIERRE TO ZINAL★

67km/42mi. Allow 2hrs.

▷ *Leave Sierre to the S, heading towards Vissoie.*

Val d'Anniviers★

Sierre-Anniviers Tourisme,
3960 Sierre. ℰ(0)84 884 80 27.
www.sierre-anniviers.ch.

Val d'Anniviers lies between the majestic Weisshorn, Zinalrothorn, Obergabelhorn and Dent Blanche mountains. The valley is known for the extraordinary nomadic habits of the people, continually on the move between the vineyards of the Rhône Valley, the main villages (Vissoie, for instance), mid-mountain pastures known as **mayens** and the Alps.

St Luc❋

Converted into a winter sports resort, the viewing platform at the village entrance offers an impressive **view**★★ of the valley and the mountain range dominated by Mount Marais (2 412m/7 915ft) on the left and Mount Boivin (2 995m/9 825ft) on the right.

Chandolin❋

Alt. 1 936m/6 348ft.

Chandolin is approached by the new village, a ski resort consisting of modern yet traditional chalets. Continue on foot to the old village, which is one of the highest permanently inhabited mountain villages in Europe. From here there is a splendid **panorama**★★ of the Valais Alps (from left to right: Zinalrothorn, Besso, Ober Gabelhorn, the Zinal Peak and the Dent Blanche).

Beyond Chandolin, the road climbs the west face of Roc d'Orzival, which at

View from Gemmi Pass onto Weisshorn, Matterhorn, and Dent Blanche

© Lucia Degonda/Switzerland Tourism

times becomes a breathtaking *corniche* overlooking the ravine. At the bottom flows the Navisence.

▷ *Return to Vissoie and drive S on the road to Grimentz.*

Grimentz✳
This resort faces the Corne de Sorebois, which separates the Zinal and Moiry valleys. It has preserved several *mazots* or *raccards* (♿ *see p240*), some of which date back to the 15C, and a beautiful **mansion** (1550). In summer, traditional festivals add to the atmosphere and In mid-August, Grimentz is the end of the longest **mountain bike race** in the world, the famous Grand Raid Cristalp. The resort has four waymarked Mountain biking trails, ranging in distance from 12km/7.4mi to 24km/15mi. The start of the **Bendolla** trail can be reached by cable-car, at 400m/1 312ft above the resort.

Grimentz

© Laura Frenkel/Dreamstime.com

Val de Moiry★
13km/8mi from Grimentz.
This valley is an extension of the Val d'Anniviers. After 2km/1.2mi there is a lovely waterfall on the left. At 4km/2.5mi there is a **view**★ of Grimentz and the Anniviers Valley. Less than 1km/.06mi further, the **Moiry Dam** is visible in front of the Dent Blanche; from the middle of

the dam (alt. 2 249m/7 379ft) there is a **view**★ of the reservoir, the Pennine Alps and their glaciers. Continue along the road (⊘*poor road surface—drive cautiously*), with its many small waterfalls. Overlooking the reservoir, at the end of the dam, there is a striking **view**★ onto the Moiry and **Zinal** glaciers. The road ends at a small lake facing the **Moiry Glacier**.

Walk to Cabane de Moiry★★★
Alt. 2 825m/9 269ft.
⌯*Allow 2hr45min on foot there and back from the end of the road (🅿 car park at 2 409m/7 904ft).*
The route first follows the left side of the Moiry Glacier at a reasonable gradient. It runs along a moraine, leading to a refuge after a steep climb. The Cabane de Moiry offers a magnificent **view**★★★ over the Pigne de la Lé (3 396m/11 143ft), Les Bouquetins (3 662m/12 015ft), Grand Cornier (3 962m/13 000ft), Dent des Rosses (3 613m/11 854ft) and the Pointe de Moiry (3 303m/10 837ft). The upper part of the Moiry Glacier sparkles under a thick layer of snow. Experienced hikers can continue (*an added 2hr15min—follow the cairns and yellow signposts*) to the edge of the glacier, for pretty views of the Col de Pigne. In dry, favourable weather (enquire at the refuge beforehand), seasoned climbers may continue to the top. The final section involves walking on *névés* (⊘*remember to bring an ice pick or a stick*). The pass (alt. 3 140m/10 303ft), dominated by the Pigne de la Lé, affords a superb sweeping **panorama**★★★ of the Zinal Valley (Weisshorn, Besso, Zinalrothorn).

▷ *Return to Grimentz and take the road to Zinal.*

Vallée de Zinal★★
The road offers a superb **view**: In the foreground lies the Zinal Valley with the town of Ayer high up on the east side, extended northward by the Val d'Anniviers and in the far distance the Wildstrubel. The valley then narrows and seems to shrink beside the overwhelming Weisshorn Mountain. After

crossing the Navisence, the road passes through **Zinal**, and ends 2km/1.2mi farther on at Tsoudounaz, in a small corrie at the foot of the Zinal Glacier.

Zinal✳
Alt. 1 670m/5 445ft.
Located high up in the mountains, Zinal is a multi-season resort including six villages: Ayer, Mission, Mottec, Curianey, La Combaz, and Les Morands. Zinal is circled by the Imperial Crown, formed by the summits of Weisshorn, Zinalrothorn, Besso, Obergabelhorn, Cervin, and Dent Blanche. Since the 19C it has enjoyed a good reputation as a mountaineering centre. It also offers wonderful opportunities for walking and hiking, with a total of 200km/125mi of signposted paths. The skiing area, virtually unknown outside Switzerland, is powder paradise dominated by the Weisshorn.

While there are slopes catering for all levels, Zinal has become a haven for free-riding. It is situated between 1 670m/5 479ft and 2 895m/6 835ft. A skiing pass also accesses the other facilities in the valley (Chandolin, St-Luc, Grimentz, Vercorin), including 46 ski lifts and around 200km/125mi of pistes. Cross-country skiers can enjoy a 12km/7.4mi circuit.

Soreboiss★★
Alt. 2 441m/8 008ft.
Access by cable-car from Zinal: 5min.
Lovely views of the Mont Durand, the Obergabelhorn, the rocky pyramid of Besso, the imposing Zinalrothorn and, farther to the left, the Weisshorn.

Walk to Petit Mountet★★★
4hrs30min from Soreboiss. Only attempt in dry weather. Take care at the start of summer, when damp terrain can be slippery. Turn left on disembarking the Zinal cable-car at Soreboiss.
The path hugs the side of the moutains and offers a continuous selection of stunning views. After about two hours walking and near the hut, take in a vista of the Col de la Dent Blanche and the peaks of Zinal and Cervin.

At 2 142m/7 000ft is another hut, and from here you pass waterfalls and ever thicker vegetation.

ADDRESSES

⌂STAY
SALGESCH
⊖⊜ **Hôtel Arkanum** – *1 Unterdorfstrasse- Salgesch. ℘(0)27 451 21 00. www.hotelarkanum.ch. 28 rooms.* ⊷. Seven of the rooms in this hotel are decorated with a wine theme—the beds (very comfortable they are too) are set into a barrel, a wine press and even a vat. The standard rooms are also pleasant. Very good value.

SIERRE
⊖⊜ **Hôtel Le Terminus** – *1 rue du Bourg. ℘(0)27 455 13 51. www.hotel-terminus.ch. 20 rooms. Closed 2 weeks end of Jun and during Christmas hols.* ⊷. This is really the only decent hotel in the town. The rooms are elegant and decorated with style. The hotel is particularly renowned for its gastronomic restaurant, and its chef Didier de Courten. The hotel's brasserie L'Atelier gourmand is excellent.

⌖EAT
⊖⊜ **Château de Villa** – *4 rue St Catherine. ℘(0)27 455 18 96. www.chateaudevilla.ch. Kitchen noon–2pm, 6pm–9.30pm. Closed 24, 25 and 31 Dec and 1 Jan.* Dishes from the Valais, seasonal menu, raclette. Nicely located in the grounds of a 16C château.

ⵜSPORTS AND LEISURE
ⵜHAPPYLAND THEME PARK
This theme park in **Granges** offers 13 rides over an area of 25 000 sq m/27 340 sq yd. Attractions include giant twisting waterslides, Splash River log ride, water jets for older children and a hot air balloon ride. Those who like thrills will want to ride the Low-G helicopter, and aspiring racers take a turn at the wheel of the Auto Moto Formula VS (*open daily 11am–6pm weather permitting; 25CHF (22CHF 3–12 years old); ℘(0)27 458 34 25; www.happylandnew.ch*).

Zermatt ✳✳

The hooked pyramid of the **Matterhorn** (alt. 4 478m/14 692ft) dominates the centre of Zermatt, situated in the Nikolaital Valley. The mountain has strongly influenced the development of this old mountain village, "discovered" a century ago by the British and launched as a resort in 1855 by the Seilers, a family of hotel-keepers.

A BIT OF HISTORY
Edward Whymper

In the 1860s, Edward Whymper, a young British illustrator thrilled by the mountain shapes had been wandering over the Alps of the Valais, Savoy, and Dauphiné, looking for unconquered peaks. He always came back to Zermatt or the Valtournanche, fascinated by the Matterhorn, which he had already vainly attempted eight times, starting from Breuil with the help of a well-known local guide, Jean-Antoine Carrel.

In 1865, changing his plan of action, Whymper decided to attack the peak along its northeast ridge. On 13 July three British climbers and a guide from Chamonix—Douglas, Hudson, Hadow and Michel Croz—joined Whymper and his two guides from Zermatt and set off for the mountain. Helped by ideal weather, the climbers set foot on the summit of the Matterhorn on 14 July. The climbers began their descent. Suddenly, young Hadow, the least experienced member of the party, slipped, dragging Croz, Hudson and Douglas with him in his fall. The life-line between Douglas and the elder Taugwalder snapped. Whymper and his guides watched the fall of their four companions, 1 200m/4 000ft below. An impressive celestial phenomenon, the appearance of two crosses shining in a great arc of clouds, is said to have appeared before they regained the valley.

RESORT

Zermatt is renowned as an important mountaineering centre, with a dozen peaks over 4 000m/13 120ft within easy

- ▶ **Population:** 5 775.
- **Michelin Map:** Michelin National Map 729: H7.
- **Info:** Bahnhofplatz – 3920. ✆(0)27 966 81 00. www.zermatt.ch.
- **Location:** The main street runs the length of the village from the train station at one end to the cablecar station at the other. Alt. 1 616m/5 302ft.
- **Parking:** This is a car-free village; you must park down the valley at Täsch and take the electric train the remaining 8km/5mi to the village.
- **Don't Miss:** The view of the iconic Matterhorn from the Stockhorn.
- **Kids:** Children under 9 travel free on all lifts and cable-cars.
- **Timing:** At least two days for skiing (winter) or rambling (other seasons).

access of the resort. It is popular with visitors of all nationalities. The resort is traffic-free, with the exception of small electric vehicles and horse-drawn carriages and sleighs. Zermatt can be reached only by rail either from Brig or Visp (Viège) where most visitors leave their cars, or from Täsch (5km/3.5mi from Zermatt), which has a car park.

SKIING AREA

Zermatt is one of Switzerland's most spectacular ski areas, in part for the view of the Matterhorn from several of the pistes and the opportunity to ski into Italy. It is defined by three high summits with a vertical drop of 2 300m/7 546ft on the Italian side (*a separate lift pass must be purchased for Cervinia, and it should be accessed only in fine weather to prevent being stranded there unable to return to Zermatt*) and 2 200m/7 218ft on the Swiss side. The 260km/161.5mi of gently sloping pistes combine high

Zermatt nestling at the foot of the Matterhorn

© Christof Sonderegger/Switzerland Tourism

and medium altitude slopes. **Telemark** skiing is now one of the resort's specialities. The highest summit is the **Klein Matterhorn** (3 820m/12 533ft), open for both winter and summer skiing along the Theodulgletscher (glacier); the slope here is groomed smooth and ideal for intermediates. Piste *20b* is especially recommended for its splendid views. The **Hörnli** is the starting-point for several excursions.

The **Gornergrat** Massif offers easy slopes near the railway tracks. Experienced skiers will be challenged on the **Rote Nase** (3 247m/10 653ft) and the Stockhorn (3 407m/11 178ft), featuring a difference in height of 1 200m/3 937ft. Finally, the **Rothorn** (3 103m/10 180ft) provides pistes suitable for intermediate skiers, in particular those numbered 22b and 23. There are also 90km/56mi of winter hiking and snowshoeing trails (6 sign-posted trails totalling 26km/16m) and 9k/5mi of prepared trails for cross-country skiing.

SIGHTS
Bahnhofstrasse
The main street, from the railway station to the parish church and the lower cable-car, is lined with fine hotels, shops, and restaurants. Note the medallion dedicated to Whymper on the façade of the Monte Rosa Hotel, opened in 1855 and a favourite with British high society. Beyond the main street, the quieter district of **Old Zermatt** is dotted with typical Valais chalets and toast-coloured *mazots*. Solar-powered buses and horse-drawn sleighs are the alternative to walking.

Matterhorn Museum
🕑*Open week after Easter–Jun, 2pm–6pm; Jul–Sept 11am–6pm; Oct 2pm–6pm; mid-Dec–week after Easter, daily 3pm–7pm (Fri to 8pm).* 🕑*Closed Nov–mid-Dec.* ⊜*10CHF, children 5CHF* ✆*(0)27 967 41 00.*
Recently re-opened in the former casino, entered through the garden of the Grand Hotel Zermatterhof, at the end of the Bahnhofstrasse, the museum incorporates the ongoing archaeological excavations of the old town.
In this experiential environment, the history and nature of the Matterhorn is explored from its geologic origins through the many explorations by climbers. Multi-lingual audio guides and lively video shows brings both the mountain and the town to life for all ages.

VIEWPOINTS ACCESSIBLE BY LIFT

A three-day summer pass for all destinations below is 187CHF.

Klein Matterhorn★★★

Alt. 3 886m/12 749ft. Access by three successive cable-cars. Allow half a day to discover the panoramas and a whole day if you combine the visit with an excursion. In winter, it can take 2hrs to get to the summit because of the queues. The departure station, accessible by shuttle service or on foot (15min), is at the far end of Zermatt. Departures from Zermatt every 20min, 8am to around 5pm. Fare there and back: 98CHF. (0)27 966 64 64.

The first section has a view straight ahead from the mid-station of **Furi** (alt. 1 865m/6 119ft) to Zermatt. This site has a number of *mazots* and inns, which are open in summer and winter. The second section is within view of the Cervin before ending at **Trockener Steg** (alt. 2 929m/9 610ft), where the **Theodulgletscher**★★ can be seen.

The last cable-car climbs over the glacier and stops at the highest altitude station in Europe. The actual summit (3 885m/12 746ft) can be reached by a lift and several flights of steps. The 360° **panorama**★★★ is truly breathtaking. To the west: Mont Blanc, Mont Maudit, Les Grandes Jorasses, Grand Combin, Dent d'Hérens, and the iconic Matterhorn; north: Zermatt, Dent Blanche, Obergabelhorn, Zinalrothorn, Dom and the Täschhorn. In the distance are the Jungfrau, Mönch, and Aletschhorn. The most spectacular sight is the long ice tongue of the Gorner (to the east) and the Breithorn (4 160m/13 648ft), Castor (4 226m/13 865ft) and Pollux (4 091m/13 422ft) summits.

Breithorn★

Alt. 4 164 m. 2hrs30min walk one way.
From the Matterhorn Glacier (*see below*) it is possible to reach the summit of the Breithorn, the easiest of the area's 4 000m peaks.

It is not necessary to be an experienced alpinist but hire a guide and be prepared to use crampons. You will need to be fit, to wear appropriate mountain gear and take sun screen.

Schwarzsee★ (Lac Noir)

Alt. 2 582m/8 461ft. Half a day's walk. Cable-car from Schwarzsee. Departures from Zermatt every 20min. Fare there and back: 48CHF. (0)27 966 64 64.

From Furi a cable-car goes up (*5min*) to the foot of the Matterhorn, which is mirrored in this small lake. A path goes around it. On its shore stands a chapel. The Black Lake is the starting-point for interesting walks toward Zermatt

---

Majestic Peaks

Some Swiss mountains over 4 000m/13 123ft:

◆	**Mount Rosa (Valais)**	4 634m/15 203ft
◆	**Dom (Mischabel; Valais)**	4 545m/14 911ft
◆	**Weisshorn (Valais)**	4 505m/14 780ft
◆	**Matterhorn (Valais)**	4 478m/14 692ft
◆	**Dent Blanche (Valais)**	4 357m/14 295ft
◆	**Grand Combin (Valais)**	4 314m/14 153ft
◆	**Finsteraarhorn (Valais)**	4 274m/14 022ft
◆	**Aletschhorn (Valais)**	4 195m/13 763ft
◆	**Breithorn (Valais)**	4 165m/13 665ft
◆	**Jungfrau (Bern-Valais)**	4 158m/13 642ft
◆	**Mönch (Bern-Valais)**	4 099m/13 448ft
◆	**Schreckhorn (Bern)**	4 078m/13 379ft
◆	**Piz Bernina (Graubünden)**	4 049m/13 284ft
◆	**Lauteraarhorn (Bern)**	4 042m/13 261ft

View from Gornergrat with
Monte Rosa on the left

© Marcus Gyger/Switzerland Tourism

(&see below). Return to Furi via Stafel
and Zmutt.

Gornergrat★★★

Alt. 3 135/10 272ft. 🚞*1hr40min by rack
railway there and back.* ⏱*Open all
year depending on weather conditions
7am–6pm, departures about every
30min.* 🎫*Fare there and back: 80CHF.*
📞*(027) 922 43 11/966 48 11.*
♿*Allow the whole day if you combine
this trip with a walk or the ascent of the
Stockhorn.*

The steep Gornergrat rack railway is
the highest open-air railway in Europe,
offering fantastic sweeping **views**★
of Zermatt. After the Riffelberg stop,
where there is a very good view of the
Matterhorn, you can see **Monte Rosa**
(crowning summit: Dufourspitze at
4 634m/15 203ft) and its glaciers.
Enjoy the breathtaking **panorama**★★★ of the numerous tongues
of ice and the Valais. The excursion
can be rounded off by the ascent first
to Hohtälli (3 286m/7 499ft), then to
Stockhorn★★★ (3 405m/11 129ft) If
you do not suffer from vertigo, walk
from Gornergrat to Hohtälli, following
a narrow **mountain path**★★★ for truly
breathtaking views.

Rothorn★★

Alt. 3 103m/10 180ft. 🚠 *From Zermatt
by funicular (access by a long corridor)
to Sunnegga, then by cable-car to
Blauherd and then again by cable-car
(20min including 5min by funicular).*
🎫*65CHF.*

The funicular climbs through a tunnel
(3min) to **Sunnegg**★ (alt. 2 285m/
7 497ft), on the edge of a plateau of
Alpine pastures enhanced by a small
lake. Here you get your first glimpse
of the Matterhorn (southwest). From
Blauherd (alt. 2 577m/8 459ft), the
second mid-station, in view of a lovely
fir forest (on the right), the cable-car
arrives on the flat, rocky summit of the
Rothorn. From here the spectacular
panorama★★, barred to the east by
the Oberrothorn, stretches southwest
to the Matterhorn, south to the Findelen
Glacier, west to Zermatt, and north to
the Nikolaital Valley.

🥾WALKING TOURS

There are around 400km/250mi of
footpaths crossing forests and Alpine
pastures, dotted with villages, lakes, and
glacial cirques.

From Schwarzsee (Lac Noir)
to Zermatt★★

🚶*There is a vertical drop of 900m/
2 952ft down to Zermatt or 700m/ 297ft
down to Furi. Remember to wear sturdy
mountain shoes. Allow at least half a
day. Access to Schwarzsee by cable-car
then 5min on foot.*

After walking for a few minutes, you
reach a second, smaller lake, a fantastic **setting**★★. Follow the path, which
continues to dip steadily: it affords
remarkable **views**★★ of the Matterhorn, the Zmutt and Arben glaciers, as
well as the Dom and Mont Rose. After
30min walking, keep to the left-hand

path then take the track on the right. This steep route brings you to Stafelalp (inn at 2 200m/7 217ft). Then there is a steep descent following the edge of the forest. Ramblers can either walk down to the pretty village of Zmutt or continue toward Furi and then the Gorner Gorges.

From Lac Vert (Grünsee) to Grindjisee and Leisee★★

Access to Riffelalp (alt. 2 200m/7 218ft) is via the Gornergrat cog train. An easy walk: a half day or full day with variants. Return by the funicular from Sunnegg★. From Riffelalp, a good path along the edge of the forest takes just 45 minutes to reach Lac Vert, from where there are fantastic views of the Matterhorn, the Dent Blanche, the Obergabelhorn, the Zinalrothorn and the Weisshorn. Another 45 minutes on is the Grindjisee (alt. 2 334m/7 658ft). Experienced walkers can complete the circuit of the lakes by taking a detour by the Stellisee—another 200m of ascent to 2 537m/8 324ft. Complete the day by exploring the traditional hamlet of Eggen, before tackling a short but steep ascent to the beautiful Leisee lake, (2 200m/7 218ft). From this lake climb another 10 minutes to **Sunnegg★** to catch the funicular railway down. (75 minutes to descend to Zermatt on foot).

Gorges du Gorner (Gornerschlucht)

A 2hr walk. From the S side of Zermatt, turn left by the bridge and then follow the signs. (0)27 966 81 00. www.zermatt.ch (Zermatt Tourist Office). This steep path overlooks superb gorges. It passes through forests of arolla pine and larch until it reaches the pretty village of Blatten. After Zumsee take the path which leads you back to Zermatt.

From Riffelberg to Zermatt★★

950m of descent which takes 2hr. Take the cog train from Gornergrat. The walk to Riffelalp boasts superb alpine scenery. Follow signs to Zermatt through larch and pine forest.

ADDRESSES

⌂STAY

⊜⊜ **Hotel Jaegerhof** – *Steinmatte 85. (0)27 966 38 00. www.hoteljaeger hofzermatt.ch. 45 rooms.* This charming chalet-style hotel is family-owned. Traditional rustic pine décor. Cosy, quiet, and attentive service.

⊜⊜⊜ **Seiler Hotel Schweizerhof** – *Bahnhofstrasse 5. (0)27 966 00 00. www.summithotels.com. 95 rooms and suites.* In the heart of the village, owned by the prominent Seiler family, this modern hotel is old-fashioned in style. Also noteworthy for its indoor pool.

⊜⊜⊜ **Christiania** – *Wiestistrasse 7, (0)27 966 80 00. www.christiania-zermatt.com. 72 rooms.* Located in the centre, but in a quiet setting, the hotel is good for families, with an indoor pool and play areas. The terrace, dining room, and many of the rooms have picture-perfect views of the Matterhorn.

⍩/EAT

⊜⊜ **Walliserstube** – *Gryfelblatte 2. (0)27 967 51 11.* Rustic décor, specialises in fondue: cheese, bourgignon (with meat), and chinoise (vegetables). Popular with families.

⊜⊜ **Le Gitan** – *Bahnhofstrasse 64. (0)27 968 19 40. www.legitan.ch.* Watch the chef grill racks of lamb, chicken, skewers of meat, and giant prawns in the open kitchen of this casual and centrally located family-run restaurant, which also has a cosy bar.

⊜⊜⊜ **Le Mazot** – *Hofmattstr 23. (0)27 966 06 06. www.lemazotzermatt.ch. Closed Mon and late-Apr to mid-June and late Oct.* Traditional grilled specialties and excellent service in a charming old farmhouse. Reservations recommended.

Saas Fee✷✷

Nicknamed the "Pearl of the Alps", Saas Fee enjoys a magnificent setting✷✷✷, where the mountains suddenly and dazzlingly soar to over 4 000m/13 123ft high. The view ranges from the icy dome of the Allalinhorn to the flattened, snow-capped summit of Alphubel and the rocky group of the Mischabel (highest point: Dom—alt. 4 545m/14 941ft, recognisable by its forked peak). Below, the huge Fee Glacier (Feegletscher) divides into two tongues around the rocky promontory of the Längfluh.

A BIT OF HISTORY

Saas Fee is a well-known mountaineering centre. For the sports enthusiast who likes ski touring it has become the terminal of the famous **Haute Route** (Chamonix—Saas Fee, or more often Verbier—Saas Fee). This quiet village became a fashionable resort in the 19C, thanks in part to the abbot Johann Josef Imseng (1806–69), whose statue is in the church square. In his spare time, he acted as a guide, taking tourists into the mountains. He was even heralded as the "best skier in Switzerland" in 1849, when he skied down the Saas Fee slopes

- ▶ **Population:** 1 675.
- **Michelin Map:** Michelin National Map 729: H7.
- **Info:** Postfach 3906 Saas Fee. ✆(0)27 958 18 58. www.saas-fee.ch.
- ▶ **Location:** Southern Valais region. Alt. 1 790m/5 873ft.
- **Parking:** Cars are not permitted in Saas Fee. Park on the outskirts and walk or use electric carts within the town.
- **Don't Miss:** Mittelallalin.
- **Timing:** Allow at least one full day to see the highlights of the area.

to Saas Grund on wooden skis of his own construction.

SKIING AREA

The Saas Valley covers 145km/92mi of pistes suitable for **downhill skiing**. Beginners will find easy slopes on the edge of the resort and along the Fee Glacier extending down to Längfluh. Do not miss a visit to **Egginerjoch**. In **winter**, the cable-cars of Plattjen and Längfluh serve the area; the Feldskinn cable-car works in **summer** and

Resort of Saas Fee surrounded by soaring mountains

© Tourist Office Saas-Fee/Switzerland Tourism

since 1984 an underground funicular has been operating to **Mittelalla-tin** (alt. 3 500m/11 483ft). There is an 11km/6.8mi toboggan run, plus air boarding and snow tubing, and ski-joring for experienced skiers (who are pulled by horses). Opportunities for **cross-country skiing** and winter hiking include more than 50km/31mi of prepared trails. The car-free village helps make Saas Fee a favourite for families.

SIGHTS
Saaser Museum
⏱Open Tue–Sun 10am–11.30am 2pm–5pm (1.30pm–5.30pm summer). 🎟4CHF. 📞(0)27 958 18 58.
This former vicarage (1732) houses a museum devoted to life in the Saas Valley. Local traditions are explored through reconstructed interiors, farming implements, local costume, liturgical objects, minerals, and photographs. Special attention is paid to the development of the spa: The growing expansion of tourism, accommodation, climbing, winter sports and the introduction of new equipment.

EXCURSIONS AND WALKS
Mittelallalin★★★
🚠Allow half a day.
👓Remember to dress warmly (trousers, jacket, sturdy mountain boots) and to bring sunglasses.
Take the Alpin Express cable-car, which affords sweeping views of the Saas Fee resort. Continue the climb up in the funicular (alt. 3 500m/11 482ft). Go to the upper station of the **revolving restaurant** (the highest in the world), where you can enjoy the **panorama**.
🚶 Follow the track marked out in the snow (in summer only) behind the restaurant. It dips over 100m/328ft and then climbs up to a rocky crag, dominating the glacier (20min on foot there and back). Be sure you use the handrail. To the south and west, the view encompasses the Allalinhorn (4 027m/13 211ft), the Feekopf, the Alphubel, and the Dom. To the north are Saas Fee and Saas Grund lying below at the foot of the Fletschhorn, and the Lagginhorn and

the Bernese Oberland (Jungfrau). To the east, the Hohlaub and the Allalin inch their way toward the Mattmark Dam.

🚶🚶Pavillon des Glaces★
🚠At Mittelallalin; 30min tour.
This 5 000sq m/5 975sq yd cave hollowed out of the Fee Glacier is the highest in Europe. It is a delightful walk in varied icy surroundings with many galleries and rooms embellished with sculptures, ice waterfalls, explanatory texts, and play areas for children.

Egginerjoch and Britanniahütte ★★★
🚶Allow 1hr20min.
From Felskinn (2 998m/9 840ft), the lower station of the cable-car, there are walks through the snow and along the glacier (it is essential to wear sturdy mountain boots and to bring a walking stick). After 20min, you will reach **Egginerjoch Pass**★★ (2 989m/9 813ft), lying at the foot of the red pyramid of the Egginer. Farther on, the route wends its way against a rocky and glacial backdrop, sometimes difficult to negotiate owing to poor or non-existent snow coverage, especially in late August and September (enquire beforehand at the Tourist Office). A 40min stroll will take you to **Britanniahütte** (3 029m/9 935ft), which commands a superb **view**★★ of Lake Mattmark, flanked on the right by the lovely tongues of ice of Hohlaub, Allalin and Schwarzberg, and on the left by Stellihorn. The most breathtaking **panorama**★★★, encompassing the whole landscape, can be seen from a promontory on your left.

Plattjen
Alt. 2 570 m/8 432ft. Access by telecabin.
Just five minutes walk from the arrival point there are **views**★★ across to the Saas glaciers and the man made Mattmark dam.

From Plattjen to Saas Fee★★
🚶Allow 1hr45min.
An easy walk near Berghaus Plattjen, with a beautiful descent through the woods and rhododendrons.

Längfluh★★★

Alt. 2 870m/9 416ft. *Access by the Gondelbahn Spielboden cable-car, then the Luftseilbahn Längfluh cable-car.* Längfluh offers wonderful **views** of the Fee Glacier. Note the lovely panorama of the Täschhorn. There is a restaurant at the site.

Hannig★

Alt. 2 350m/7 709ft.
Access by cable-car.
Lovely **view**★ of Saas Fee, Saas Grund, Saas Almagell and the Fee Glacier to the south, with the Fletschhorn to the northeast. There are many opportunities for interesting walks. In winter, you can return to the resort on foot or by the fine **sledge piste**. In summer, Hannig is the starting-point for fascinating hiking () toward **Mellig**★ and **Gebiden**★★ (alt. 2 763m/9 064ft, 1hr15min climb). Views of the Hohbalm Glacier dominated by the Nadelhorn (4 327m/14 194ft). Then 3hr30min climb down to Saas Fee via the Bärenfälle waterfalls.

Hohsaas★★★

Alt. 3 098m/10 164ft. Park the car in Saas Grund (alt. 1 560m/5 118ft), a small mountain resort located below Saas Fee. *Access by two cable-cars.* *Allow 1hr 45min there and back.*
As you walk, enjoy the pretty **views**★★ of the Saas Grund skiing area. The summit affords wonderful **views**★★ of Lagginhorn, the Hohlaub Glacier and Weissmies (4 023m/13 197ft). This peak is frequently used in competitions. Walk up toward Geissrück (15min) for a better view of the stunning séracs. Take in the **panorama**★★★ from Mont Rose to Dürrenhorn, featuring 18 summits above 4 000m/13 122ft.

From Kreuzboden to Saas Fee★★

3hr walk with a 850m/2 788ft drop in altitude as you proceed downwards.
From Kreuzboden (alt. 2 397m/7 863ft), the first cable-car section, take "Höhenweg" in the direction of Almagelleralp. This path, meandering its way across the slope, is bordered by a small alpine garden (edelweiss, astragalus, gentian, juniper berry). After about 1hr, you will discover broad **views**★★ of the Saas Fee glacial cirque and Lake Mattmark. Note the impressive avalanche barrier. A little farther on, you will come across a path, which you follow, heading downwards toward Saas Grund.

Leave it after 15min and choose a track on the left, marked out as "Alpenblumen-Promenade". This somewhat steep slope, dotted with edelweiss, ends in a forest of larch trees.

Lac de barrage Stausee Mattmark★★

Alt. 2 200m/7 218ft. Take the car or bus to Saas Grund.
A small road runs for some 12km/7.5mi in peaceful country side, through Alpine meadows and woods. There are lovely **views**★★ of the Saas-Fee glaciers. From the parking area at the end of the road, a five minute walk takes you to the left hand side of the dam wall which is 780m/853ft long.

From the lake there is **view**★★ of the four glaciers - Hohlaub, Allalin, Schwarzberg and Seewjinen, plus many waterfalls. Also note the Almagellhorn.

A path takes you around the **lake**— allow 2hr30min.

Monte Moropass★★

Alt. 2 868m/9 409tf. This is a 3hr15min ascent and a 2hr45min descent for good walkers.
Follow the Mattmark lake to its end, which takes about an hour. Then take the narrow path which has is a steady climb, up to the Monte Moro col. After about 45 minutes you will come out onto a flat section of ground from where you can see the mountain. Continue to the right. The access is steep and ends up in a boulder field so ensure you follow the red and white markers.

From the col, where a statue of the Virgin Mary has been erected there is a superb **view**★★ of Mont Rose and its glaciers.

Retrace your steps and upon reaching the lake, take the other bank to return.

ADDRESSES

STAY

⊜⊜ **Dom** – ℘*(0)27 958 50 00. www.uniquedom.com. 40 rooms.* Modern, well situated hotel with ample amenities and a "Popcorn Bar" that hosts live music. Kids will love the the in-room computer consoles 👥👤.

⊜⊜ **Rustica** – ℘*(0)27 957 21 75. www.hotelgletschergarten.ch. 11 rooms.* Family-run B&B-style lodgings in the heart of the resort; private baths for all rooms.

⊜⊜⊜ **Imseng** – ℘*(0)27 958 12 58. www.hotel-imseng.ch. 22 rooms.* Features indoor pool, on-site bar, and lounge with fireplace.

⟨/EAT

⊜⊜ **Drehrestaurant Allalin** – ℘*(0)27 957 17 71. www.drehrestaurant-allalin.ch.* Accessible via Alpin Express cable-car, the world's highest revolving restaurant serves a variety of Alpine specialties.

⊜⊜ **Hohnegg's Fondue-Hütte** – ℘*(0)27 957 22 68. www.hohnegg.ch. Closed until summer 2013.* Reached by 15min hike from town, serving cheese and meat fondue and Valaisian Raclette.

⊜⊜⊜⊜ **Waldhotel Fletschhorn** – ℘*(0)27 957 21 31. www.fletschhorn.ch.* Located a 30min hike from the town centre in a forest clearing. Award-winning food. Ideal for a relaxing meal with amazing views. Cooking courses.

Brig

Brig is located at the confluence of the rivers Rhône and Saltine. This charming town is a lively stopping-place at the junction of the Simplon road and the road to the Rhône Glacier and the Furka Pass. The railway station is important, as it stands on the frontier at the north end of the Simplon Tunnel, the longest rail tunnel in the world (19.8km/12.3mi). Brig is also on the route of the famous Glacier Express linking Zermatt and St Moritz.

A BIT OF HISTORY
The King of the Simplon
Brig owes its great attraction to the ideas and ambitions of **Kaspar Jodok von Stockalper** (1609–1691) who came from a Valais family, traditionally the guardians of the Simplon Defile. Through his enterprise Stockalper amassed great riches from the trade route over the Alps during the Salt Monopoly. He was courted by emperors and kings, but his wealth and success made him enemies and he fled to Italy, leaving his proud fortress unfinished. He returned to Brig to die a respected but ruined man.

▸ **Population:** 12 162.
⚭ **Michelin Map:** Michelin National Map 729: H7.
▤ **Info:** Bahnhofplatz 1 – 3900. ℘*(0)27 921 60 30.*
▷ **Location:** Brig is located at the confluence of the River Rhône and River Saltine. Alt. 681m/2 234ft.
⚭ **Don't Miss:** Take an hour or two to visit the open-air thermal baths at Brigerbad, 5km/3mi west of Brig, between Viège and Gamsen (www.brig-belalp.ch).

SIGHT
Stockalperschloss
⟡⟡*Guided tours (45min) May–Oct, Tue –Sun, hourly from 9.30am–10.30am, 1.30pm–4.30pm.* ⟡*No visit at 4.30pm in May and Oct.* ⟨8CHF. ℘*(0)27 921 60 30. www.brig-belalp.ch.*
Once the largest private residence in Switzerland, it can be recognised from afar by its three towers with bulbous domes, standing where the road to the Simplon begins. The first building you encounter as you come from the centre of Brig is the Stockalper family dwelling

(early 16C), flanked by a fine watchtower. The imposing main building (built over the original warehouse by the "Great Stockalper") features eight storeys, including cellars, linked to the smaller house by a picturesque gallery with two tiers of arcades.

The main **courtyard**✶ is surrounded by open galleries in two or three storeys. The three towers arranged around it, with their plain stonework, stand in sharp contrast to this elegant building.

EXCURSION
Raron
○ *Drive W from Brig on the E62. 18km/11.25mi. 20min.*

The hamlet of Raron or Rarogne (named after an influential feudal family from the Valais) spreads at the foot of a rocky spur. The village centre features a group of pretty 16C and 17C houses made with stone and wood. A steep path leads to the top of the hill.

Near the old tower, which is all that remains of the former castle, stands the 16C **Burgkirche**, clearly dominating the valley. Inside the church, a naïve fresco illustrates the Last Judgement. Note the demons, who have been portrayed in the costumes of Swiss mercenaries. The Austrian poet Rainer Maria Rilke is buried in the cemetery. At the foot of the hill, a small modern church has been carved out of the rock.

🚗 DRIVING TOURS

GOMS★★

54km/33.5mi. Allow approx 2hrs. The road that follows the Furka-Oberalp railway at a distance may be blocked by snow between Brig and Oberwald for short periods. Furkastrasse. ℘(0)27 970 10 70. www.goms.ch.

Conches Valley (**Val de Conches** in French or **Goms** in German) begins at Fiesch. The road, as it climbs up the Upper Rhône Valley, enters mountainous terrain; it serves the numerous resorts and ski lifts hanging on the side of the Aletschhorn Massif.

From Brig to the Grengiols fork, the road runs close to the foaming Rhône at the bottom of a narrow, winding cleft.

It passes by the large, isolated Baroque **Hohen Flühen Chapel** and serves the lower stations of the Riederalp-Greicheralp cable-car (starting from Mörel) and that of **Bettmeralp**. These lines serve a high Alpine plateau (alt. 2 000m/6 500ft) wonderfully situated within view of the Valais Alps and close to the Aletsch Glacier, the most extensive in the Alps (169sq km/65sq mi with its tributaries).

Riederalp✷, Moosfluh★★

🚠*Access to Riederalp by cable-car from Mörel; access to Moosfluh by chairlift from Riederalp.* ⏱*Operates summer, 8am–6pm; winter, 9am–4.30pm.* ✺*Fare there and back 16CHF.* ℘*(0)27 928 66 11.*

Located in a **site**✶ overlooking the Rhône Valley on the valley's north side, the **Riederalp**✷ chalets and hotels are terraced, beginning at 1 930m/6 332ft, and face the mountain range separating Switzerland from Italy. Above its westernmost point stands Villa Cassel, a Victorian-style mansion (1902), now the centre of the **Aletschwald Nature Reserve** with exhibitions on the nature reserve and its larch and arolla pine forests, which are among the highest in Europe. Visitors can also learn about the history of the Aletsch Glacier, which can be visited on excursions organised by the centre.

○ *From the cable-car's arrival station, walk (a few minutes) to the chairlift's departure station to go to Moosfluh.*

The chairlift passes by the mid-station of Blausee, before arriving at the upper station of **Moosfluh**★★ (alt. 2 335m/7 661ft), set amid a jumble of green rocks and dominating the spectacular curving form of the **Grosser Aletschgletscher**★★★, immediately to the north at the foot of the slopes and tributary glaciers of the Aletschhorn Massif, as well as the Rhône Valley to the south.

Lake Taelli on the Eggishorn—Aletsch Glacier with Jungfrau and Moench on the left and Strahlhorn and the Wannhoerner on the right

© Christof Sonderegger/Switzerland Tourism

The valley's second level stretches from Lax to Fiesch and is marked by the appearance—confirming a gain in height—of arolla pines and small barns on piles (*raccards*). This section marks the start of the Upper Rhône Valley, known as the Conches Valley. Below, in a gorge section, the Rhône is joined by the tributary River Binna. Farther up the valley, when Fiesch comes into view, it is possible to look up the Fieschertal Valley, on the left, and see in the far distance the snowy peak of the Finsteraar-Rothorn.

▷ *Return to the Valley via route 19. After Lax, take the small road on the right which goes to Ernen.*

Ernen★

With its sun bleached chalets, Ernen is one of the most typical villages of the Conches valley, and also one of the most charming. Several of its houses date from the 16C and 18C.

L'église St Georges is really worth a visit. It was rebuilt in the 16C on the foundations of a Roman basilica, and has a variety of works of art, including an important Baroque altar, a pietà from the 14C, a statue of St Georges, frescoes from the 16C and pews dating from the Renaissance.

▷ *Rejoin after Fiesch where you can take the cable-car to Eggishorn.*

Eggishorn★★★

Alt. 2 927m/9 603ft. ⛷ *Access by cable-car from Fiesch.* ⏱*Departures daily (30min) Jun–Oct, 9.15am–5.45pm, Dec–Mar (8am–6pm) restricted service Apr, May, Oct, Nov.* 🚠*Fare there and back* 🚠*42CHF summer, 53CHF winter.* 📞*(0)27 971 27 00.*

The first stage takes you up over a spruce forest and a scree of greenish-coloured, jagged rocks. From the upper station (alt. 2 869m/9 413ft) there is a superb **panorama**★★★; below in the immediate foreground the Aletsch Glacier, the Fiesch Glacier, a nearby cascade farther round to the right, and of all the other neighbouring mountain peaks. For an even wider view, climb to the top of one of the three mounds of scree which are quite close to the station. The Eggishorn summit is marked by a cross (🧗*difficult clamber*). After the next change in level beyond Fiesch, the view extends back downstream to the snow-covered slopes of the Weisshorn (alt. 4 505m/14 780ft).

After a few hairpin bends, notice the village of **Mühlebach**, the birthplace of Cardinal Schiner, on the opposite slope.

Getting the Guns Through

As early as the 17C the Great Stockalper (see p282), making the most of his monopolies and the position of Brig, adapted the Simplon road, used until then mainly by smugglers and mercenaries, to commercial traffic. He organised a mail service and built two hostels, which still stand at Gondo. But all this was for mule trains, not for wheeled traffic. The modern Simplon is a product of Napoleon. After a detachment sent by Italy via the Simplon had forced the passage only by perilous manoeuvres, the First Consul decided in 1800 that the road from Brig to Domodossola must be made accessible to artillery. The low altitude of the pass and its relatively scanty snowfall determined his choice, and the project received absolute priority. The undertaking was entrusted to Nicolas Céard, chief engineer of public works in the Léman *département*, who drew up plans for a road 7–8m/22–25ft wide with a maximum gradient of 10% (1 in 10). It was officially opened to traffic in 1805, but Napoleon never had occasion to use it.

Bellwald★

Access by a winding road 8km/5mi or by cable-car from Fürgangen.

A small summer and winter resort, Bellwald (alt. 1 600m/5 249ft), with its old larch wood chalets and hotels set on a curved terrace, presents a wide aerial **view**★ of the Conches Valley—from Fiesch to Brig—over the Eggishorn (identified by its cross), above and to the right of the Wannenhorn Massif and its glaciers and left onto the Alps of the Italian frontier. The valley opens out again beautifully. The third level is the longest in the Conches Valley. The Alpine combe now offers a bare, open landscape; the total lack of enclosures, the lone trees and scattered chalets make for striking views. The villages, with their blackish wooden houses adorned with geraniums, are grouped around slim white church towers. Upstream, to the right of the Galenstock summit, you will glimpse the Furka Gap, although the pass itself is out of sight.

 Rejoin route 19 and go as far as Reckingen.

Reckingen

Reckingen's **Baroque** church is one of the most beautiful in the Conches valley. It was built in the 18C, based on the plans of priest **Jean-Georges Ritz**. Ritz represented a group of artisans who had produced renowned sculpted altar pieces. The family gained worldwide renown thanks to **César Ritz** (born in Niederwald in 1850, died in 1918), who became a hotelier.

The **Seiler** family who made their fortune in Zermatt and built two hotels next to the Rhône Glacier (in Gletsch and in Belvédère) is also notable in the history of the Conche valley.

Münster

The **église** in the fine village has a bell tower adorned with a fine weather vane is worth a visit thanks to its flamboyant **alter shelf**, dedicated to the Virgin Mary, and created by an artist from Lucerne in 1509. Below **Oberwald**, the last village in the Conches valley, the road descends into decreasingly forested terrain where the Rhône tumbles downhill. You emerge onto the Gletsch lake from where you can see the Rhône glacier, source of this great river.

 Drive on to Gletsch.

Gletsch★★

Alt. 1 759m/5 771ft.

At the junction of roads from the Furka Pass, the Grimsel Pass and the Conches Valley (Upper Valais) lies Gletsch, on the floor of a desolate basin once covered by the tongue of the Rhône Glacier. Higher up, on the road to the Furka Pass (see FURKAPASS), the setting in which the Hôtel Belvédère stands draws many sightseers. This well-known stop offers a sweeping **panorama**★★ of the Bernese and Valais Alps.

After Gletsch, the Furka Col road climbs and passes in front of the Hôtel Belvédère. The **Rhône Glacier**★★★ (Rhonegletscher) starts at the same level from the other side of the road (parking). It is one of the most easily accessible European glaciers (200m/218yds from the road), but it is necessary to have the services of a professional guide.

Ice Grotto★

The access to the glacier and the grotto is via the Hotel Belvédère's souvenir shop.
🕐 *open Jun–Oct, 8am–6pm (7.30pm high season);* 🎫*7CHF;* 📞*(0)27 973 11 29) Jun–Oct 8am–7pm (weekend 7.30pm)* 🎫*7CHF.* 👕*Wear warm clothing.* 📞*(0)27 924 38 24.*

For over 120 years the tunnel underneath the ice has been redug every year. It allows the visitor the possibility to walk in a blue tinged world and to examine the different layers of ice.

▷ *Rejoin the route.*

The drive up to the col offers far reaching views of the Valais and Bearnais Alps. To get the best best possible **view** ★★★, stop at a fork 1500m before the col, where there is a military road (marked no entry) and walk a few metres into the meadow. Looking towards the Conches valley the snows of the Weisshorn and the Mischel glisten; closer at hand in the direction of the Grimsel col, are the 4 000m/13 123ft peaks of the Lauteraarhorn, Finsteraarhorn and Schreckhorn.

Furkapass★★

Alt. 2 431 m/7 976ft.
Stop at the Furkablick hotel to admire the majestic Galenstock. The Furka col, the highest access point to the snaking road which crosses the Swiss Alps from Martigny to Chur is a vital tourist link betwen French Switzerland, the Andermatt crossroads, and Graubünden. Since 1982 a railway tunnel, re-opened linking Realp to Gletsch. The journey takes

1hr35min to travel the 13.3km/8.3mi. The engine built for the line in 1913 was brought back from Vietnam and restored.

SIMPLONSTRASSE ★★

65km/40mi. Allow approx 3hrs.
🚧*The Simplon Pass is sometimes blocked by snow from December to May in spite of the galleries built to keep it clear year-round.*

The Simplon road is not the boldest in the Alps—the Splügen and the St Gotthard have more daring structures—but it is the noblest and most majestic. It is impossible not to succumb to the beauty of such a **site**★★★ as that which unfolds between the Simplon Pass (alt. 2 005m/6 578ft) and Brig, on the Rhône Valley slope. This gentle winding road along the mountain flank, without sharp hairpin bends, is a model of adaptation to topography.

The Alpine section begins at **Crevoladossola**, where you leave the warm inner plain of the Ossola, somewhat Mediterranean in character with its bushy, stony floor exposed to the meanderings of the River Toce.

From Crevoladossola to the border, the narrow Diveria Valley offers little interesting scenery. A few campaniles and the greenery of thickets of hazel, walnut and ash are not enough to make it attractive. A short distance from Crevoladossola, on the left, are the ruins of the little village of San Giovanni, razed by a landslide in 1958. The ruins increase still farther the bleakness of the valley.
🚧 *Italian and Swiss customs control are at Paglino and Gondo respectively.*

Simplonpass★★

Alt. 2 005m/6 578ft.
The road runs halfway up the side of this long, winding defile, with its uneven floor. It is overlooked from the south by the Böshorn, in the middle distance, by the snowy Fletschhorn and from the east by the greenish slabs of the Hübschhorn and the Chaltwassergletscher, coming from Mount Leone. Of the three main features of this scene, none is more

remarkable than the **Alter Spittel** (a former hostel built by Stockalper), which is high and flanked by a 17C tower and bell turret. The present hostel (Hospiz) was built at the same time as the road and is kept by the monks of the Great St Bernard. A stone eagle commemorates the watch kept on the frontier during the Second World War.

The **belvedere**★★ of the pass is at the highest point, that is, just before the hollow on the Valais side. Beside the Hotel Simplon-Kulm, it is possible to pick out the summits of the **Bernese Alps** which can be seen between the Schinhorn and the Finsteraarhorn (highest point of the Bernese Alps, alt. 4 274m/14 022ft).

On the Rhône side, the road between the pass and a tunnel clings to the upper precipices of a rocky cirque laced by the icy waters of the **Chaltwassergletscher** which can be seen above, protected by a series of concrete galleries and roofs. Approaching the Kapfloch Pass through a gap you see the Fletschhorn, flanked on its right by the Böshorn. From the Kapfloch to Rothwald a long stretch of corniche road under larch woods finally reveals, 1 000m/3 281ft below, the town of Brig framed in the opening of the **Saltine Gorges**. The mountains separating the Rhône Valley from the Lötschental now unfold on the horizon: From left to right, the Bietschhorn, Briethorn, Nesthorn and Schinhorn.

Between Rothwald and Schallberg, the road detours into the **Gantertal**. On the north slope of this beautiful valley are many crooked arolla pines (*see INTRODUCTION: Alpine Vegetation*). Between Schallberg and Brig the road at first overlooks the Saltine Gorges (Saltinaschlucht), the floor of which cannot be seen. It then leaves the forest and drops to the well-tilled slopes of the **Brigerberg**. The towers of the Stockalper Castle and of the churches of Brig stand out behind the shining ribbon of the Rhône, often shrouded by the factory smoke of Visp.

Gondoschlucht★

The wildest section of this long valley defile, hemmed in by granite walls, is the confluence of the **Alpienbach** and the **Diveria**, whose falls join at the foot of a spur pierced by a road tunnel. Between Gstein (Gabi) and the pass, the road, leaving the Lagintal in the southwest where it penetrates toward the higher levels of the Weissmies (4 023m/13 199ft), and climbs gradually among the Alpine pastures of the lower Simplon combe.

Above the village of **Simplon** the rugged appearance of the terrain still shows the devastating effects of the terrible avalanche of 1901 started by the collapse of a whole section of the **Rossboden Glacier**. Dominating this glacier, the **Fletschhorn** is the most attractive feature of the landscape.

ADDRESSES

STAY / EAT

Schlosshotel Art Furrer – *Schlosspark (near the château).* (0)27 922 95 95. www.schlosshotel.ch. *27 rooms.* Classic rooms of varying sizes, many with a balcony. Ask for a view of the château.

ON THE ROAD TO THE FURKA COL

Hôtel Belvédère – *A stone's throw from the Rhône glacier.* (0)27 924 38 24. www.gletscher.ch. *Open Jun–mid-Oct.* If you really want to stay at the glacier, enjoy the charms of this old-fashioned but delightful hotel. Built in 1900, it is perched above the road. The cheapest rooms are on the third floor with a communal shower. Splendid view over Gletsch and the mountains.

Commerce – *Sebastianplatz 2* (0)27 924 52 41. www.commerce-brig. ch/.Daily exc Mon. Well situated on the main square. Pizzas and fish dishes offer a pleasant change from the usual Valais fare.

Schlosskeller – *Alte Simplonstrasse 34* (0)27 923 33 52. *Closed Sun eve and Mon.* Located on the road that leads to the château, this restaurant for gourmets offers, among other treats, Mediterranean specialities. Pleasant interior courtyard.

TICINO

Ticino is located in the southeast of Switzerland and borders the Italian lakes of Maggiore and Lugano. This Italian-speaking canton, called Tessin by German- and French-speaking Swiss, and pronounced "*Tichino*" by the Italian speakers, is evidence of the cultural diversity typical of Switzerland: food, architecture, culture, climate and outlook on life here couldn't be more different from the cheese and chocolate Alpine cliché of the north and west. It covers 2 811 sq km/ 1 085 sq mi and is surrounded by the cantons of Valais and Uri in the northwest, by Graubünden in the north and east while the southern part of the canton abuts Italy.

Highlights

1 The panorama from **Monte San Salvatore** (p292)

2 The art museum of Villa Favorita at **Lugano** (p294)

3 The driving tour of the **Valle Maggia** (p303)

4 Attending one of **Ascona**'s cultural festivals (p308)

5 UNESCO World Heritage Site castles of **Bellinzona** (p310)

A Bit of History

Taking its name from the River Ticino which flows along the Levantina Valley from the St Gotthard Massif in the Lepontine Alps in the north to Lake Maggiore in the south, Ticino is for many the ideal blend of Swiss order and Italian flair. Territory to the north of the Monte Ceneri range is known as the Sopraceneri and to the south it is known as Sottoceneri. Lake Lugano (called Lago Ceresio by Italians) to the east of Maggiore and overlooked by Monte San Salvatore and Monte Generoso, has a wilder appearance than its larger neighbour but is no less beautiful. The city of Lugano, "the Queen of Ceresio", located at the end of a splendid bay, is ideally located for touring the area and Bellinzona, the capital of the canton, is also a fascinating town whose splendid castles constitute a UNESCO World Heritage site.

The region came under the control of the Romans during the reign of Augustus and remained part of Rome until the fall of the Western Empire in the 5C. Various invasions followed until eventu-

ally, during the Middle Ages the area, which was contested by both Milan and Como, finally came under the control of the powerful Dukes of Milan. During the 15C and 16C Ticino became part of the Swiss Confederation, the forerunner of the modern Swiss state, dominated by the Cantons of Uri, Scwhyz and Unterwalden, who had defeated the Milanese by securing Bellinzona in 1503. This situation lasted nearly 300 years until finally, following intervention by the French, Ticino became independent in 1798 before achieving canton status as a member of Napoleon's new Swiss Confederation in 1803. During the 19C Ticino suffered political unrest between the rival radical and conservative parties and, whilst things have been calmer since, tensions still remain.

Ticino Today

While the region used to be something of a rural backwater, it has now developed a strong tertiary sector which employs nearly 80% of the population and its banking industry is Switzerland's third largest after Zürich and Geneva. The establishment of a university at Lugano in 1996 further bolstered the region, as it meant that Italian-speaking students no longer have to study elsewhere in Switzerland in another language, or move to Italy.

It is economically closely linked to Italy with many *frontalieri*, Italian nationals who work in the region, contributing to the increasingly important tourist industry, a large number of whom are Swiss from the north and west.

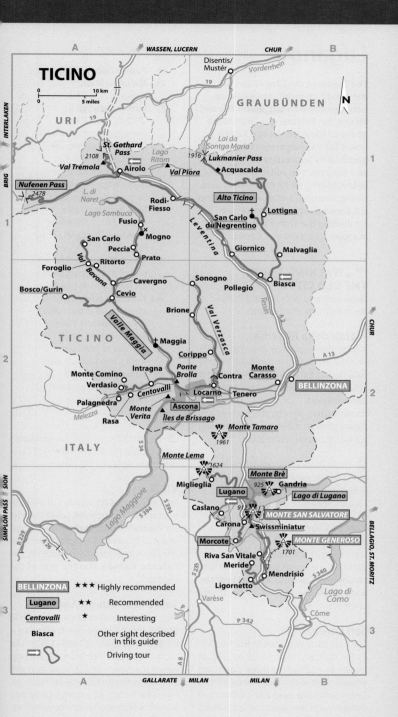

TICINO

0 ___ 10 km
0 ___ 5 miles

WASSEN, LUCERN   **CHUR**

GRAUBÜNDEN   N

Disentis/
Mustér

Vorderrhein

19

URI

19

*Lai da
Sontga Maria*

**St. Gothard
Pass**

2108

*Lago
Ritom*

1916   **Lukmanier Pass**

Val Tremola

Nufenen Pass

2478

Airolo

Val Piora   ◆ **Acqualcalda**

Alto Ticino

Lottigna

**San Carlo
du Negrentino** ●   †

*L. di
Naret*

Rodi-
Fiesso

Lago Sambuco

Fusio

Leventina

Giornico   **Malvaglia**

San Carlo

✕

Mogno

Peccia

Prato

Val Bavona

Ritorto

Sonogno

Pollegio

→ Biasca

Foroglio

Cavergno

Bosco/Gurin

Cevio

Brione

Val Verzasca

Tessin

A2

TICINO

Valle Maggia

† Maggia

Corippo

CHUR

A 13

Monte Comino

Intragna

*Ponte
Brolla*

Contra

**Monte
Carasso**

Verdasio

Centovalli ▲

Locarno   Tenero

→   **BELLINZONA**

Palagnedra

**Monte
Verità** ▲

Ascona ▲

Melezza

Rasa

Îles de Brissago

Monte Tamaro

✸
1961

ITALY

S 34

Monte Lema

✸ *1624*

Miglieglia

Monte Brè

Gandria

925 ✸

Lago Maggiore

S 394

Lugano
→

Lago di Lugano

912

Caslano

Carona

✸ **MONTE SAN SALVATORE**

▲ Swissminiatur

Morcote

MONTE GENEROSO

✸
1701

Riva San Vitale

Meride

Mendrisio

Ligornetto

S 340

*Lago di
Como*

Varèse

S 235

P 342

Côme

INTERLAKEN   **BRIG**   **SION**   **SIMPLON PASS**   *R 229*   *A 26*   *S 34*   *A 8*   **GALLARATE**   **MILAN**   **MILAN**   *A 9*   **BELLAGIO, ST. MORITZ**

289

Lugano★

The Queen of the Ceresio lies at the end of a beautiful bay framed between the wooded Mount Brè and Mount San Salvatore. It faces south and is an ideal tourist and health resort for its temperate climate, particularly appreciated in spring and autumn. You will find beaches, tennis courts, an 18-hole golf course, riding, boating, and a casino. Lugano is a convenient excursion centre for visiting the Ticino's three lakes: Maggiore, Lugano and Como.

> ▸ **Population:** 54 437.
> ⚲ **Michelin Map:** National 729: K7-8.
> ▯ **Info:** Palazzo Civico ℰ(0)91 913 32 32. www.lugano-tourism.ch.
> ◖ **Location:** Lugano lies about 29.6km/18.4mi southwest of Bellinzona, at the edge of Lake Lugano, between Lake Maggiore and Lake Como. Alt. 273ft/896m.
> ▣ **Parking:** The town centre is car-free.
> ⊛ **Don't Miss:** Villa Favorita, one of the largest private art museums in Europe.
> ≛ **Kids:** The adventure playground in the Parco Civico. Kids will also like Swissminiatur, small replicas of important sights, in a lakeside park.
> ◷ **Timing:** Allow two days for museums and lake excursions.

☜☜WALKING TOUR
THE OLD CITY★
Begin at Piazza della Riforma (behind the Tourist Office). Allow 2hrs.

Piazza della Riforma

A huge, lively square with outdoor cafés and the Municipio (town hall). In early July, during **Estival Jazz**, the square is swarming with jazz lovers enjoying live performances.
Its pedestrian streets, steep alleys and flights of steps make for an interesting walk or shopping expedition.

▷ *Head W out of Piazza della Riforma along the Via dei Pesci and turn right onto Via Pessina. On the left is the Piazza Cioccaro.*

Piazza Cioccaro

This Piazza, (funicular serving the train station), with the **Palazzo Riva**, a fine patrician villa with wrought-iron balconies gives onto to **Via Cattedrale**, a steep alleyway leading up to the cathedral.

San Lorenzo

The cathedral was built in the Romanesque style and it presents an elegant façade in addition to three doorways embellished with Renaissance motifs. See a splendid example of Baroque decoration in the Chapel of Santa Maria delle Grazie. The esplanade commands a lovely view of Lugano and its lake.

▷ *Return to Piazza Cioccaro and turn right into Via Pessina. At the end of the street turn right into Via Nassa.*

Via Nassa

This street and its arcades of elegant boutiques form the main axis of Lugano. On **Piazzetta San Carlo** note the Surrealist sculpture by **Salvador Dalí** called *The Dignity of Time*. At number 66, the **Palazzo Vanoni**, was the seat of the Bishop.

Santa Maria degli Angioli

This former convent church, begun in 1499, contains three fine **frescoes★★** by Bernardo Luini (c.1480–1532). The most impressive represents a *Passion*. Below it are pictured St Sebastian and St Roch. In the first chapel on the right, note the fresco *Virgin with Child and St John*, which was taken from the cloisters. The nave bears a representation of the Last Supper.

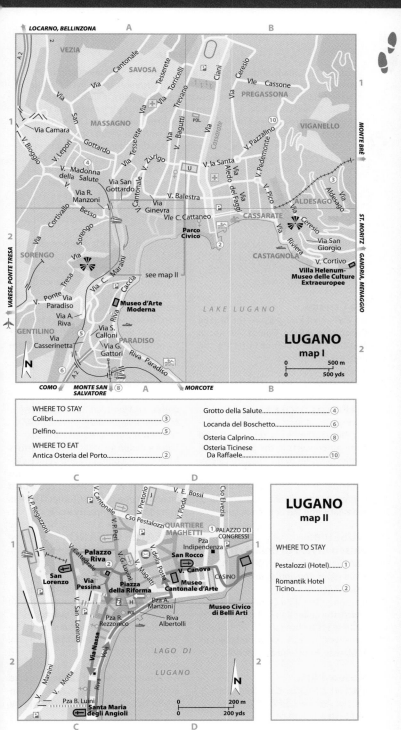

LOCARNO, BELLINZONA

VEZIA
SAVOSA
Cantonale
Via Tesserete
Via Torricelli
Ciani
Vle Cassone
PREGASSONA
VIGANELLO
Via Camara
Via San Gottardo
MASSAGNO
Via Tesserete
Via Bagutti
Via Trevano
POL.
Cassarate
V. Pazzalino
V. Pedemonte
MONTE BRÈ
V. Bioggio
V. Lepori
Gottardo
Via Z. Zurigo
V. la Santa
Aledo
Via del Faggi
Via Pico
V. Aldesago
Via Ceresio
ALDESAGO
ST. MORITZ
V. Madonna della Salute
Via San Gottardo
V. Balestra
U
V. la Santa Aledo
CASSARATE
Via Ceresio
Via Riviera
Via San Giorgio
GANDRIA, MENAGGIO
Via R. Manzoni
Via Ginevra
Vle C. Cattaneo
Parco Civico
CASTAGNOLA
V. Cortivo
Cortivallo
Via Besso
Sorengo
Via C. Maraini
Riva Caccia
see map II
Villa Helenum-Museo delle Culture Extraeuropee
SORENGO
V. Ponte Tresa
LAKE LUGANO
LUGANO
map I
GENTILINO
Via Paradiso
Via A. Riva
Via Casserinetta
Museo d'Arte Moderna
Via S. Calloni
PARADISO
Via G. Gattori
Riva Paradiso
0   500 m
0   500 yds
N
COMO   MONTE SAN SALVATORE   A   MORCOTE   B
VARESE, PONTE TRESA

WHERE TO STAY		Grotto della Salute...........................(4)
Colibri..................................(3)		Locanda del Boschetto...................(6)
Delfino.................................(5)		Osteria Calprino..............................(8)
WHERE TO EAT		Osteria Ticinese
Antica Osteria del Porto...........(2)		Da Raffaele..................................(10)

LUGANO
map II

WHERE TO STAY

Pestalozzi (Hotel)........(1)

Romantik Hotel
Ticino..............................(2)

V. P. Regazzoni
V. Cantonale
V. Pretorio
V. E. Bossi
V. Pioda
Cso Elvezia
Cso Pestalozzi
QUARTIERE MAGHETTI
PALAZZO DEI CONGRESSI
Pza Indipendenza
Palazzo Riva
V. Cattedrale
V. P. Peri
V. G. Luvini
V. della Posta
V. Magatti
San Rocco
V. Canova
San Lorenzo
Via Pessina
Piazza della Riforma
Museo Cantonale d'Arte
CASINO
V. San Lorenzo
Pza A. Manzoni
Riva Albertolli
Pza R. Rezzonico
Museo Civico di Belli Arti
V. Maraini
V. Motta
Via Nassa
LAGO DI LUGANO
Pza B. Luini
Santa Maria degli Angioli
N
0   200 m
0   200 yds

Mario Botta

Born in 1943, Mario Botta is unquestionably one of the most talented and renowned architects of his time. After studying technical design in Lugano, he attended the Institute of Architecture at Venice University. Influenced by Le Corbusier and Louis Kahn, with whom he had worked, he became one of the foremost representatives of the Ticino School. His work aims for a harmonious balance between landscape and architecture, with a curved perspective and compact shapes. His major accomplishments are the school at Morbio Inferiore (1972–77), the Arts Centre in Chambéry (1982–87), the Médiathèque in Villeurbanne (1984–88), the Museum of Modern Art of San Francisco (1990–94), Évry Cathedral (1995), the Tinguely Museum in Basel (1996), the Chiesa Santa Maria degli Angeli at Monte Tamaro (1996) and the Dürrenmatt Centre in Neuchâtel (2000).

◖ *Return to the centre along the Riva Bela bordering the Lake. After the Piazza Mazzoni turn left into Via degli Albrizzi then right into Via Canove.*

Via Canove

On Via Canove you will pass the **Musée Cantonale d'Arte**, Chiesa San Rocco and the Casino before entering the Piazza Indipendenza.

◖ *The Parco Civico is adjacent.*

♣♦ Parco Civico★★

During the summer season and providing the weather is fair, one can attend open-air concerts in the park. Several statues (*Socrates* by the Russian sculptor Antokolsky) and fountains lend charm to the delightful setting. Children will appreciate the adventure playground, the aviary, and the deer enclosure.

MUSEUMS
Museo Civico di Belli Arti

Villa Ciani, Parco Civico ◷Tue–Sun 10am–6pm, Thu until 9pm ◉12CHF. ℘(0)58 866 72 14.
Housed in the Villa Ciani in the Parco Civico, the collection includes work by Ticinese artists from the 15–20C as well some work by such renowned painters as Matisse, Rousseau and Monet.

Museo d'Arte

Riva Caccia 5 ◷Tue–Sun 10am–6pm, Thu until 9pm ◉12CHF. ℘(0)58 866 72 14. www.mdam.ch.

Set up in the Villa Malpensata, the Museum of Modern Art hosts temporary exhibitions of an exceptionally high standard. Painters such as Francis Bacon, Nolde, Soutine, Rouault, and Botero were revealed to the public during retrospective shows held here, which brought together works that had been lent by other museums or borrowed from private collections.

Museo Cantonale d'Arte

Via Canova 10. ◷Tue 2–5pm; Tue–Sun and Easter Mon 10am–5pm. ◷Closed Mon and 1 May. ◉8CHF. ℘(0)91 910 47 80. www.museo-cantonale-arte.ch.
The collection includes works by artists from Ticino, Lombardy and Venice dating from the Gothic period to the late 18C as well as some 19 and 20C works including one by JMW Turner. There is also some contempoary work.

GREATER LUGANO
Monte San Salvatore★★★

Alt. 912m/2 996ft.
⛰ *45min there and back, including 25min by funicular, starting from the Paradiso quarter. A five minute walk from the train station. ◷Operates 13 Mar– early Nov. Departures every 30min. ◉28CHF there and back. ℘(0)91 985 28 28. montesansalvatore.ch.*
An admirable view of Lugano, its lake and the Bernese and Valais Alps. You can return to Lugano from the summit by marked paths.

Monte Brè★★

Alt. 925m/3 051ft.
About 1hr there and back, including
30min by funicular, starting from
Cassarate. Access by funicular from
Cassarate via Suvigliana, 9.10am–
6.45pm. Departures after 9.45am every
30min. 23CHF there and back.
(0)91 971 31 71. www.montebre.ch.
You can also go by car, by taking the
road to Castagnola and then following
the directions. The summit has views of
the lake and the Alps (many hiking tours
in the area) from the terraces.

LAKE LUGANO★★

The greater part of Lake Lugano lies
within Switzerland. The Italians, who
call it Ceresio, have only the northeast
branch (Porlezza), part of the southwest shore (Porto Ceresio) and a small
enclave on the east shore (Campione
d'Italia). Lake Lugano looks wilder than
Lake Maggiore and Lake Como. It is
irregular in shape, with a total length
of 33km/21mi and a maximum depth
of 288m/947ft or 150 fathoms. From
the municipal park up to Paradiso, the
promenade following the lake shore is
an ideal place for a leisurely stroll.

Paradiso

This district is populated by luxury
hotels, restaurants, cafés, nightclubs,
and fashionable boutiques.

BY BOAT

The steamer services on Lake Lugano,
(1hr to half-day), are among the resort's
top attractions. **Società Navigazione
Lago di Lugano** *(Viale Castagnola;*
(0)91 971 52 23; www.lakelugano.ch).
A grand tour of the lake, called Grande
Giro del Lago, starts from Lugano.
If you wish to combine the tour of Gan-
dria with that of the Museum of Swiss
Customs, allow 3hr.

Gandria★

1hr there and back, if you do not go ashore.
Amid a maze of stepped streets this village, with terraces planted with geraniums, trellises, leafy bowers, arcaded
houses and a small Baroque church form
a charming picture appreciated by artists and tourists.
Museo Doganale Svizzero – Located
on the lake shore in a former Swiss
customs post *(at Cantine di Gandria*
on the south shore of the lake; access by
boat 1hr45min there and back, includ-
ing visit to the museum; accessible by
boat only; guided tours Easter–Oct,
1.30pm–5.30pm; no charge; (0)91
910 98 43), the museum explains the
role, past and present, of the customs
officer. Beneath the verandah is a car
illustrating the incredible number of
tiny hiding places that can be found
in an automobile. Other exhibits focus
on the perilous role they played dur-

View of Lake Lugano, Monte San Salvatore and the city from Mont Brè

© Christof Sonderegger/Switzerland Tourism

ing the Second World War, the most common devices (traps, weapons, trick objects) used by smugglers, drug dealers, and forgers (fake passports, fake garments). It also presents the highly sophisticated means used by customs officers to foil smugglers. Perhaps the museum's most unusual exhibit is the Zodiac submarine seized in 1946: its metal tubes were stuffed with salami! Under the eaves are temporary exhibitions on Swiss customs: recruitment and training techniques at the Liestal School near Basel and the role of women in this profession.

EXCURSIONS
Villa Favorita★★

Via Riviera 14. At Castagnola. ▶ *Take bus 1 leaving from Piazza Manzoni and get off at Villa Favorita.* ✍*It is advisable to take the bus since the car park can only accommodate a few cars.* ◷*Open Apr 15–Oct 31, Thu–Sun 10am–5pm.* ✍*12CHF.* ✆*(0)91 970 11 62.*

A garden park overlooking the lake planted with exotic trees and graced with statues leads to this late-17C mansion featuring three staggered storeys and crowned by a birdcage.

Although the greater part of the remarkable collection of paintings gathered since 1920 by Thyssen-Bornemisza, the famous German steel industrialists, has been transferred to the Thyssen-Bornemisza Museum in Madrid, the Villa Favorita regularly holds exhibitions of works taken from this collection, concentrating on a given theme or artistic style (e.g. 19C and 20C American artists Andrew Wyeth, Winslow Homer, and Edward Hopper).

Villa Heleneum – Museo delle Culture Extraeuropee

▶ *Take bus number 1 leaving from Piazza Manzoni. Get off at San Domenico, then continue on foot for 5min along Via Cortivo 24.* ◷*Open Tue–Sun, 10am–6pm.* ✍*12CHF.* ◷*closed 1 Jan and 24, 25 Dec* ✆*(0)58 866 69 60. www.mcl.lugano.ch.*

On the edge of the lake, a neo-Classical mansion houses the **Museum of Non-**

European Cultures. The collections are laid out on three levels. The ground floor is devoted to Oceania and Southeast Asia. The first floor focuses on New Guinea and the different regional cultures which make up its identity. The second floor is divided into themes, adopting a comparative approach on issues such as death, fertility, and power. Each display is amply illustrated with explanatory panels and objects, including finely carved wooden sculptures.

Caslano

▶ *5km/3mi SE. Leave Lugano on the airport road heading toward Ponte Tresa.* Switzerland is invariably associated with chocolate and for those who have a sweet tooth, the visit to a chocolate-making factory is a must. Near the Italian border, the firm **Alprose** welcomes visitors to its **Museo del Cioccolato** (◷ *open daily 9am–5.30pm (Sat–Sun 4.30pm);* ◷*closed 1 Jan and 24,25 Dec; film (20min); shop;* ✍*3CHF;* ✆*(0)91 611 88 56; www.alprose.ch).*

The museum unveils the world of chocolate before your eyes, starting with the cocoa plantations in Amazonia and ending with present-day manufacturing and marketing techniques. An upper passageway enables you to observe the methods of fabrication from above. All aspects of the industry are covered: milk, white, or bitter chocolate, small squares to have with coffee, and drinking chocolate, a warm nectar with an enticing aroma. The tour ends with a tasting session.

👤👤 Swissminiatur★

▶ *7km/4.5mi S.* ◷*Open 13 Mar–23 Oct, 9am–6pm.* ✍*19CHF.* ♿ ✆*(0)91 640 10 60. www.swissminiatur.ch.*

A joy to children and grown-ups alike. Spread over 1ha/2.5 acres of verdant and flowery land on the edge of the lake, the exhibit displays the country's main tourist attractions reproduced in miniature (monuments carved out of stone, mountains, bridges, sites, etc.) and evokes the country's main economic activities. The trains (3km/1.8mi network), boats and cable-cars all function.

🚗 DRIVING TOURS

ROAD TO MORCOTE★

Round trip of 26km/16mi. Allow about 3hrs – the route starts on a fairly hilly road. (Alternative access by boat from Lugano; ⏱operates Apr–Oct; tour lasts for approximately 1hr).

▶ Leave Lugano through Paradiso, then take the high road to Morcote via Carona.

This route via Pazzallo and Carona offers magnificent **bird's-eye views**★★ of the lake and the Monte Rosa Massif.

Carona

At the entrance to the village, lined at intervals with picturesque houses, the **Chiesa San Giorgio** (16C) is crowned by an octagonal dome and contains interesting 16C **frescoes**★. Adjoining the church is a portico with Tuscan columns, decorated with heraldic arms and *trompe-l'œil* paintings.

On leaving the locality, follow directions for **Madonna d'Ongero**. You can leave the car at a car park and continue on foot along a forest path. A wide path with Stations of the Cross leads to the church, which has a portico and an octagonal dome. The interior is heavily ornate, with abundant frescoes and stuccowork.

Return to the road to Morcote; after a short distance you can stop at a roadside belvedere to enjoy a view of the lake.

Morcote★★

The Lombardic arcaded houses of this village, dubbed the Pearl of the Ceresio, are reflected in Lake Lugano. By a staircase and alleys you will reach the **Church of Santa Maria del Sasso** containing splendid 16C frescoes and a fine organ case. Go through the church to see the Baroque baptistery (Battisteri da Sant Antoni). The whole ensemble forms a remarkable **picture**★★.

▶ Take the lake shore road back toward Lugano. After approx 4km/3mi turn right onto via Cantonale.

▶ Return to Lugano still taking the lake shore road, which is the most attractive.

MENDRISIOTTO REGION

40km/25mi.

▶ Leave Lugano S on the lakeside road and drive as far as Capolago. Leave the car and take the rack railway.

Morcote and its church Santa Maria del Sasso

© Lugano Turismo

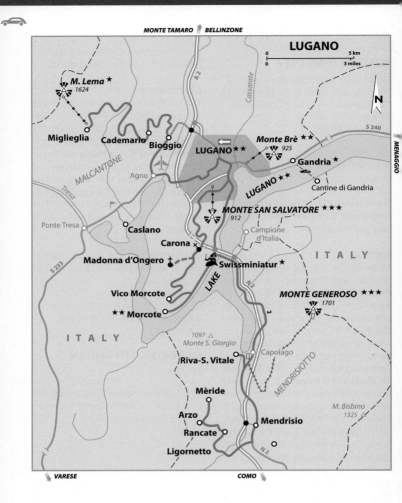

MONTE TAMARO | BELLINZONE

LUGANO

0 ____ 5 km
0 ____ 3 miles

M. Lema ★
1624

Miglieglia Cademario Bioggio

LUGANO ★★

Monte Brè ★★
925

Gandria ★

Cantine di Gandria

MALCANTONE

Agno

LUGANO ★★

MONTE SAN SALVATORE ★★★
912

Campione d'Italia

Ponte Tresa

Caslano

Carona ✕

ITALY

Madonna d'Ongero †

Swissminiatur ★

MONTE GENEROSO ★★★
1701

Vico Morcote

★★ Morcote

ITALY

LAKE

1097 △
Monte S. Giorgio

Capolago

MENDRISIOTTO

Riva-S. Vitale

M. Bisbino
1325

Mèride

Arzo

Rancate

Mendrisio

Ligornetto

VARESE   COMO

Monte Generoso★★★

Alt. 1 701m/5 581ft. Rack railway from Capolago. Departure every hour from mid-Mar–early Nov 9.20am –7.15pm. 42CHF there and back. 39CHF for 9.20am and after 1.35pm departures (0)91 648 11 05. www.montegeneroso.ch. Allow 2hrs. From the summit the splendid **panorama**★★★ extends over the Alps, Lugano, the lakes and the Lombardy Plain to the distant Apennines on a clear day.

◗ *Return to the main road and turn right to reach Riva San Vitale.*

Riva San Vitale

This village is worth a visit for its 5C baptistery *(battistero)*, in an octagonal room near the parish church. Remains of 11C frescoes adorn part of the walls.

At the opposite end of the village, the **Chiesa Santa Croce** (16C) can be recognised by its octagonal dome; note the sculpted wooden door with grotesque faces. The interior features fine mural paintings.

Mendrisio

This is the town where the famous Ticino architect **Mario Botta** was born. The old city is dominated by the Neoclassical Chiesa Santi Cosma e Damiano (19C) and its characteristic dome. It is reached by a monumental flight of steps; at the foot of these, a square tower is all that remains of the city's medieval ramparts. Note the fine Baroque palace nearby. Take the charming Via San Damiano, continued by Via Stella, which leads to the oratory of Madonna delle Grazie (13C). Behind the oratory, on Piazza dei Serviti, the former convent house contains the Museo d'Arte.

Ligornetto

Ligornetto is the birthplace of the Ticino sculptor **Vincenzo Vela** (1820–1891), a legendary figure in the region. His villa has been converted into a museum.

Rancate

This village is certainly worth a detour, if only to visit the **Pinacoteca Cantonale Giovanni Züst** (open Mar–Jun Tue–Sun 9am–noon, 2pm–5pm; Jul–Aug, Tue–Sun 2pm–6pm, Sept–1 Jan Tue–Fri 9am–noon, 2pm–6pm, Sat, Sun and Hols 10am–noon and 2pm–6pm; closed 24, 25 Dec, Jan, Feb and Mon; 7CHF; (0)91 646 45 65; www.ti.ch/zuest) which presents a fine selection of works by Ticino artists from the 17C to the 20C. The paintings of Antonio Rinaldi are in Room 3 on the ground floor (The Kitten, Portrait of Angiolino) and in Room 6 on the first floor (Sketch for a Portrait, The Shepherd, The Holy Virgin). Giuseppe Antonio Petrini (1677–1758) is represented with the intensely moving L'Addolorata, in room 7 on the first floor.

Arzo

Renowned for its marble quarry and the clocktower of the Baroque Church is covered with slabs of this material.

Meride

This village in the vines has some 18C houses with galleries and courtyards.

Return to Lugano.

MONTE LEMA★

22km/13mi NW via Bioggio.

> *From Bioggio the road winds through woods before entering Cademario.*

Cademario

From this terraced village there is a nice view of the plain below, part of Lake Lugano and the mountains. As you leave the village following directions to Lugano, the old **Chiesa di San Ambrogio** (for information, call (091) 605 68 30) stands alone with its campanile in the Lombardy style and its façade with partly-erased 15C frescoes. Inside are interesting 13C polychrome frescoes.

Miglieglia

At the foot of Monte Lema lies the village and its church, St Stefano (15C). The interior houses 16C–17C frescoes.

Monte Lema★

Alt. 1 624m/5 328ft.

Access by chairlift from Miglieglia. Departure every 30min Apr–Nov 9am–5pm. 24CHF there and back. (0)91 609 11 68. www.montelema.ch. The climb, above a landscape of fern and rocks, gives a bird's-eye view of Miglieglia and St Stefano church. From the restaurant of the upper station climb to the top (20min round trip along a steep path) between a television relay station and a large metal cross for a **panorama**★ which extends westwards to Lake Maggiore and the Monte Rosa and eastwards to Lake Lugano and Monte Generoso.

ADDRESSES

STAY

Owing to its ideal location, Lugano offers many opportunities for leisure activities and for boat trips on the lake or into the mountains, where spectacular panoramas can be had. As in many resorts with a prestigious reputation, prices are comparatively high and some visitors may prefer to stay outside the town.

⊜⊜⊜ Hôtel Pestalozzi – *Piazza Independenza 9. ℘ (0)91 92 146 46. www.pestalozzi-lugano.ch. ⌨. 51 rooms.* Very central and excellent value for money. Limited parking.

⊜⊜⊜ Colibri – *In Aldesago, 6km/3.7mi E – Via Bassone 7. ℘(0)91 971 42 42. www.hotelcolibri.ch. 30 rooms. Closed Jan and Feb.* A delightful setting atop the Monte Brè, commanding splendid views of the lake, the town, and the Alpine range, especially from the terrace near the swimming pool.

⊜⊜⊜ Delfino – *Via Casserinetta 6. ℘(0)91 985 99 99. www.delfinolugano.ch. 50 rooms. Open Mar–Dec. ⌨.* In the Paradiso quarter, away from the lake. Excellent service for a decent price. Terrace with solarium and pool, a definite asset for the summer season.

⊜⊜⊜ Romantik Hotel Ticino – *Piazza Cioccaro 1. ℘(0)91 922 77 72. www.romantikhotels.com. 18 rooms. Closed Jan.* This historic 14C residence nestles at the heart of the old quarter, among pedestrian streets dotted with fashionable boutiques. A touch of romanticism in a modern city.

⚑EAT

⊜ Locanda del Boschetto – *Via Boschetto 8 (Cassarina). ℘(0)91 994 24 93. Closed Mon and 1–15 Nov.* A rustic setting and lovely terrace. Good fish and seafood dishes are served.

⊜⊜ Osteria Ticinese Da Raffaele – *Via Pazzalino 19. ℘(0)91 971 66 14. Closed Sat lunchtime, Sun and end Jul– end Aug.* Serves German, Swiss, and Italian local specialties.

⊜⊜ Grotto della Salute – *In Massagno, 2km/1mi NW, Via del Sindicatori 4. ℘(0)91 966 04 76. Closed Sat, Sun, mid-Dec–mid-Jan and 4–19 Aug.* Reasonably priced menus offering regional specialities which vary by season.

⊜⊜⊜ Osteria Calprino – *Via Carona 18 in the Paradiso district. ℘(0)91 994 14 80. www.osteriacalprino.ch. Closed Wed.* Three small, cosy rooms, one of which has an open fireplace where polenta is cooked in the winter season. Reservations are recommended.

⊜⊜⊜ Antica Osteria del Porto – *Via Foce 9. ℘(0)91 971 42 00. www.osteriadelporto.ch. Open daily exc Tue.* Beside the port this relaxed restaurant offers excellent fish and tasty risotto.

🛒 SHOPPING

The town centre, cut by narrow streets, many of which are closed to traffic, is a great shopping area featuring attractive boutiques with eye-catching window displays (**Via Nassa, Via Pelissa, Piazza Cioccaro**). In the **Quartiere Maghetti** is a modern shopping complex laid out over several levels.

Christmas Market on Via Nassa

© Remy Steinegger/Ticino Turismo/Switzerland Tourism

🎭THEATRE AND MUSIC

The high season runs from May to October and many performances are held at the **Palais des Congrès** or on squares throughout the town (Piazza della Riforma, Piazza Maghetti, or Piazza della Chiesa Santa Marta).

☺NIGHTLIFE

The Paradiso area offers several fashionable and pleasant choices: the **Golfe** (Riva Paradiso 2), **Charlie's Pub** (Via Guisan 10) and the **Karisma Pub** (Via Geretta 6). In the town centre, sample delightful Ticino wines at the **Bottegone del Vino** (Via Magatti) or the **Trani** (Salira Mario e Antonio Chiattone).

Corso Pestalozzi becomes especially lively after 11pm, when crowds pour out of the **Corso Cinema** and settle down for a drink at the **Etnie** in the Maghetti district or for one of the tempting ice creams at the pavement café Vanini, on Piazza della Riforma. The **New Orleans** (Piazza Indipendenza) has a combination of live music and DJs.

Locarno★

Locarno lies in the hollow of a sunny bay which curves more sharply as the delta formed by the River Maggia juts into the waters of one of Italy's most famous lakes, **Lago Maggiore**★★★. Sheltered by the Alps, Locarno enjoys an exceptional climate in which hydrangeas, magnolias, and camellias blossom as early as March. This is a beautiful town with pleasant walks among the gardens, along the lakeshore, on the vine-covered slopes of Orselina, and in the Cardada Hills.

SIGHTS
Piazza Grande

This paved oblong square is frequented by locals who enjoy coming here for a stroll, as well as by tourists, attracted by the shopping arcades, cafés and restaurants. The old houses with balconies painted in pastel hues add charm to the whole scene. Each August, film buffs meet in Locarno to attend the **International Film Festival**, when Piazza Grande becomes a huge open-air cinema screen. To the east the square is extended by Largo Zorzi: it ends at the landing stage from which boat trips on the lake can be organised.

- ▶ **Population:** 15 123.
- **Michelin Map:** National 729: K7.
- **Info:** Largo Zorzi 1 – 6600. ℘(0)91 791 00 91. www.maggiore.ch.
- **Location:** Sits at the Northern tip of Lake Maggiore.
- **Parking:** Use a municipal car park and take public transport.
- **Don't Miss:** Boat tours on Lake Maggiore.
- **Timing:** Allow at least a full day to fully take in the sights and complete the driving tour.

Visconti Castle

Open mid-Apr–Oct, Tue–Sun 10am–noon, 2pm–5pm; Sat and Sun 10am–5pm ⊜7CHF. ℘(0)91 756 31 70 80.

The Museo Civico e Archeologico (Municipal and Archaeological Museum) housed within Visconti castle is devoted to the region's Iron and Bronze Age, Roman period, and Middle Ages. One room is devoted to the Pact of Locarno through photographs and press articles.

Piazza Grande during the International Film Festival

© Remy Steinegger/Ticino Turismo/Switzerland Tourism

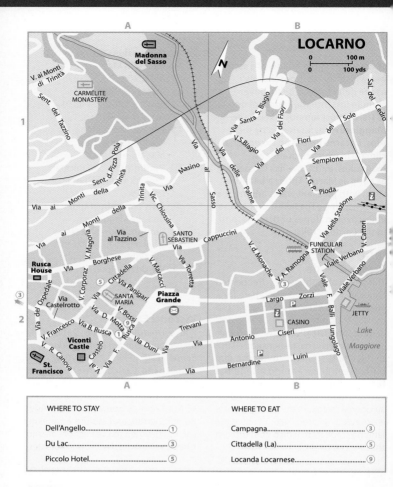

WHERE TO STAY		WHERE TO EAT	
Dell'Angello	①	Campagna	③
Du Lac	③	Cittadella (La)	⑤
Piccolo Hotel	⑤	Locanda Locarnese	⑨

Chiesa San Francesco

Consecrated in 1230 by Uberto di Monserrato, the Bishop of Como, the church attached to the former Franciscan convent was extensively restored in the 16C. The upper section of the chancel is decorated with a large fresco depicting the Annunciation of the Virgin.

Pinacoteca Casa Rusca

Piazza Sant'Antonio. ⏱*Open Tue–Sun 10am–noon, 2pm–5pm.* 👁*7CHF.* 📞*(0)91 756 31 85.*

Rusca house is a fine example of a 17C patrician residence. The exhibitions, renewed on a regular basis, are devoted to modern and contemporary art, focusing on the work of a specific artist. Traditionally, featured artists are expected to donate one of their works to the museum, continuously adding to the collections.

GREATER LOCARNO
Madonna del Sasso★★

At Orselina. Recommended access by funicular. Lower station at Via della Stazione.

This church stands on the summit (355m/1 165ft) of a wooded spur which can also be reached by car along the hairpin bends of the Via ai Monti della Trinità. At the upper level, stairs lead down to the basilica (excellent bird's-eye views). In 1480, the Virgin appeared before the brother of Bartolomeo of

The Pact of Locarno, or How to Maintain Peace in Europe

In October 1925, Locarno was at the centre of international politics. World attention was focused on the **Palais de Justice**, where delegations from France, Great Britain, Germany, Italy, Belgium, Poland and Czechoslovakia attended a conference led by their respective foreign ministers Aristide Briand, Austen Chamberlain, Gustav Stresemann, Vittorio Scialoja, Émile Vandervelde, Alexander Skrzynski and Edvard Benes. Seen as a sequel to the 1924 London Conference, which stipulated that the Ruhr area be evacuated within a year and that Germany join the League of Nations, the **Locarno Conference** led to the signing of a treaty on 16 October 1925. Germany recognised its borders with France and Belgium and the demilitarised zone included in the 1919 peace treaty concluded in Versailles. Germany also agreed not to alter her western borders through military action. For his key role in the negotiations and final peace agreement, the head of the British delegation, Austen Chamberlain, was awarded the Nobel Prize for Peace in 1925.

The **Pact of Locarno** was hailed as a resounding success by the international press. It introduced a new era of peaceful cohabitation and Lord d'Abernon, the British ambassador in Berlin, wrote: that it "marks a significant turning-point in the history of post-war Europe. It symbolises the abolition of the dividing line between the conquerors and the conquered." The treaty was ratified in London on **1 December 1925**. Briand, Chamberlain and Stresemann met regularly to supervise its implementation and to pave the way for economic cooperation between countries. Germany was accepted into the **League of Nations** in 1926, signifying reconciliation, it seemed that the future would be free from international tension. But in 1936 **Hitler** violated the treaty by occupying and remilitarising the Rhineland, plunging Europe, and, indeed, the world, into a bloody war three years later.

Ivrea, a monk from the San Francesco convent in Locarno, who had gone into retreat on the Sasso della Rocca. A chapel was erected to commemorate the vision. In the courtyard, follow directions for the "Chiesa". Before reaching the church, you can see several chapels containing groups of wooden sculptures (Chapel of the Pietà, Chapel of the Last Supper, Chapel of the Holy Spirit).

The **Church of the Annunciation** features an arcaded gallery embellished

Madonna del Sasso with a view to the Lake Maggiore

Walter Storto/Switzerland Tourism

with murals. The Baroque interior is particularly interesting for its frescoes and works of art, such as the *Flight into Egypt* painted by Bramantino (1522) and a *Descent from the Cross* (left side aisle) by Antonio Ciseri. The nearby loggia along the church commands a pretty **view**★ of Locarno and Lake Maggiore. Return to the courtyard to visit the **museum** set up in Casa del Padre. It presents 18C sculptures, liturgical objects, ex-votos, and other artefacts. Leaving the church, you can return either by funicular or on foot, following directions for Locarno via Crucis. This will take you along the path traditionally used by pilgrims. The steep climb down, dotted with Stations of the Cross, offers interesting views of the lake.

Cimetta★★

Chairlift leaving from Cardada.
Operates mid-Mar–Oct Mon–Thu 9.15am–6.15pm, Fri–Sun 8.15am–6.15pm; Jun–Aug daily 8.15am–6.15pm. 38CHF return.
(0)91 735 30 30. www.cardada.ch.
The funicular going to the Madonna del Sasso is continued by a cable-car which in 10 minutes climbs the **Alpe di Cardada** (alt. 1 350m/4 428ft) from where there is a very extensive **view**★★. From Cardada a chairlift goes to the top of the Cimetta (alt. 1 672m/5 482ft) and a fine **panorama**★★ of the Alps and Lake Maggiore.

Parco delle camelie

2km/1.25mi S, via Respini.
Open daily 9am–5pm.
Shaded by poplars and oaks, a unique collection of 520 varieties of camelias flourishes in the beneficial microclimate.

EXCURSION
Ronco Tour★★

17km/11mi. About 1hr30min – by a corniche road between Ronco and Porto Ronco on which it is difficult to pass.
The trip is very pleasant in the late afternoon. ▶ *Leave Locarno to the SW by the Ascona road.*
Soon after the bridge over the Maggia, turn right toward Losone. In this village, after the church, turn left (road to Ascona and Veritá Mountain) and right (road to Ronco) at the next crossroads. After running through a small valley, leave the Arcegno road on your right and follow directions for Monte Verita. At the next fork bear right.
The *corniche* byroad, emerging from chestnut woods, opens out above Lake Maggiore and immediately affords a series of beautiful **bird's-eye views**★★. Below, in succession, you will see Ascona,

View of the Lake Maggiore with Isole di Brissago and Monte Gambarogno from Porto Ronco

© Remy Steinegger/Ticino Turismo/Switzerland Tourism

the two wooded **Isole di Brissago** (📖 see ASCONA) and finally the lakeside town of Brissago. You come into sight of Ronco.

Ronco

The village clings to a slope in a typically Mediterranean **setting★★**. The church terrace offers a pretty view of Lake Maggiore, the Brissago Islands, and Monte Gambarogno. Take a winding road downward to rejoin the road along the lake at Porto Ronco.

🚗 DRIVING TOURS

VALLE MAGGIA★★

28km/17.5mi NW until you reach Bignasco.

▶ *First take the road to Ascona, then follow directions.*

This valley is one of the deepest on the southern slope of the Alps. It is wide at low altitude, with the steep cliff face jutting almost vertically, but narrows farther on, taking on Alpine features with pine and larch forests. Most of the vil-

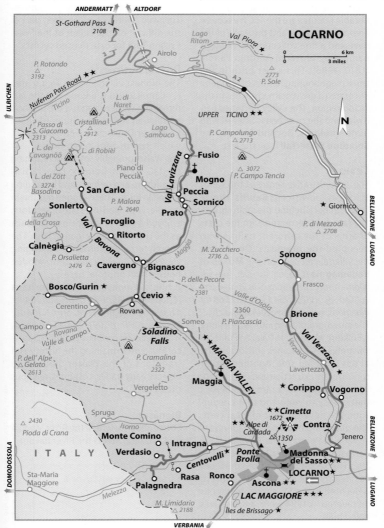

lages have rustic old houses with stone walls, roofs covered in gneiss. As in the Valais canton, you often come across chalets mounted on piles, known as *raccards* or *torbas*, which were used as lofts (*see THE VALAIS*).

◗ *Turn right into a narrow road which branches off the main road.*

Maggia

The village of Maggia has a lovely church, **Santa Maria delle Grazie**, which stands on the edge. Its most notable features are the 16C **frescoes**★ adorning the apse and the walls of the nave and a fine collection of ex-votos painted by Giovanni Antonio Vanoni (1810–1886). This artist born in the small neighbouring hamlet of Aurigeno decorated a great many churches in the Ticino region. The valley becomes narrower and the river bed is littered with huge boulders. Beyond Someo, the **Soladino Waterfall** is on the left.

Cevio

The administrative centre of the Valley Maggia is known for its **Bailiffs' House** (16C), set back behind the main square. The façade is decorated with the coats of arms of the different bailiffs who occupied the premises. On leaving the village, you can visit the **Museo di Vallemaggia** (Oopen Apr–Oct, Tue–Sat 10am–noon, 2pm–6pm, Sun 2pm–6pm; 6CHF; *(0)91 754 13 40/or 23 68 for directions; www.museovalmaggia.ch).
The museum is divided into two sections. A Folklore Museum in Palazzo Franzoni illustrates the costumes and local crafts of this secluded area. Another display concerns the extraction and use of granite and serpentine, a rare type of rock that is easy to work and that encouraged the development of local craft. The quarrying of serpentine (deposits at Valle di Peccia, Valle Rovana, Valle Verzasca and Centovalli) ended in the 19C. The second part of the museum lies nearby: the Casa Respini-Moretti is devoted to the Mogheno necropolis discovered in 1994 while a house was being built.

In the hamlet of Rovana (road to Busco/Gurin), near the bridge spanning the river, the church **Beata Vergine del Ponte** is a fine example of Baroque architecture. The interior is lavishly ornamented with stuccowork and frescoes.

◗ *16km/10mi W towards Cerentino.*

Follow the road and its hairpin bends through Alpine landscape to Linescio, then Cerentino. The countryside becomes more rugged and opens onto Bosco/Gurin, a cirque of Alpine pastures. This wild "world's end" is often part of the difficult official circuit of the Swiss Cycling Tour for experienced cyclists.

Bosco/Gurin★

The highest village in the Ticino area (1 503m/4 930ft) is unique: it is the last remaining Walser village where the local population still speaks Gurinerdeutsch or Walser Deutsch, a German dialect which incorporates Italian words.
The Walser probably settled here around the 13C, coming from the Upper Valais to cultivate and defend land belonging to Italian lords. These rugged mountain people, who lived in a state of serfdom, enjoyed certain privileges in return, such as the free hereditary loan of land. The church terrace commands a plunging view of the Lower Valley with wooden houses built on stone bases.
A fine old mansion, the **Walserhaus** (Oopen mid-April–Oct, Tue–Sun 10am–11.30am, 1.30pm–5pm, Sun 1.30pm–5pm; 3CHF; *(091) 754 24 23; www.walserhaus.ch*) contains an Ethnographical Museum explaining the history and traditions of the Walser (household objects, early trades, costumes, religious rites, etc.).

Bignasco

The confluence where the River Maggia (or Lavizzara) meets the River Bavona.

◗ *Choose between two itineraries: Val Lavizzara or Val Bavona.*

VAL LAVIZZARA
17km/10.5mi until Fusio.

Peccia
This village is renowned for its marble. The quarry is located near the small hamlet of Piano di Peccia. The marble is taken to Peccia, where it is worked. The shades go from white, as in the case of Carrara marble, to gray, with blue, brown, or even pink streaks. The road continues to climb, forming hairpin bends.

Mogno
Soon after the bridge, take a small road on the right to the chapel, designed by Ticino architect Mario Botta. The white and gray stone building, shaped as a truncated pyramid, replaces the former church, swept away by an avalanche in 1986.

Fusio
Perched at an altitude of 1 280m/4 199ft, at the foot of a rocky spur, Fusio is the highest village in Val Lavizzara, with many fine old houses. During the high season, you may continue beyond the dam lake (Lago Sambuco).
The road becomes steeper and narrower, with more bends (*caution is required here as there is no parapet and only room for one car to pass at a time*). The vegetation is scarce and the landscape appears barren. There are breathtaking views all the way up to the small mountain lakes.

▷ *Return to Bignasco.*

VAL BAVONA
12km/7.4mi until you reach San Carlo, where the road ends.
This wild area is characterised by high cliff faces and huge boulders which accumulated after a series of rockfalls, especially around **Cavergno**. All along the route, you will drive through villages with typical 16C architecture.

Foroglio
The most attractive feature of Foroglio is its waterfall. Leave the car near the bridge, cross the river and follow the green signpost "Punto Panoramico" near the restaurant. The path leads to the foot of the waterfall, whose gushing waters form an imposing sight.

Sonlerto
This little village is worth visiting with its church and its campanile, the fountain, the houses and the torba. The road winds its way upward along a sinuous course. As it crosses the river, it gets closer to the huge mass of rock looming on the horizon.

San Carlo
From the last village in Val Bavona, a cable-car will take you to Mont Robiei (1 894m/6 213ft). Experienced climbers may reach the summit on foot and proceed until they reach the three small mountain lakes: Zött, Robiei, and Bianco.

CENTOVALLI★
19km/11.8mi W.
The region of the Hundred Valleys is extremely popular with both hikers and nature lovers. The train linking Locarno to Domodossola (Italy) makes many stops and allows those who don't have a car to discover a highly attractive area.

▷ *Leave Locarno by the road to Ponte Tresa. At Ponte Brolla, turn left.*

Intragna
The village and its narrow streets are dominated by the campanile. The Baroque church features fine mural paintings in the chancel. To the right of the church, a small alley leads to the **Museo Regionale delle Centovalli e del Pedemonte** (*open Easter–Oct, Tue–Sun 2–6pm; 5CHF; (0)91 796 25 77; www.museo100valli.net*).
This little museum illustrates the history and life of the region through an exhibition of farming tools, everyday objects, costumes, sacred art, sculptures, and paintings.

Rasa

Access by cable-car (Funivia Verdasio-Rasa). Allow 10min there and back.

The village perched at an altitude of 900m/2 953ft presents many old stone houses. To the left of the church, a path leads to a fountain and some benches. From there you can enjoy a view of the Lower Valley, lake, and the villages nestling on the slopes. From right to left, you will see Verdasio, Borgnone, Lionza and, farther down, Comedo. Several paths for hikers start from Rasa, such as that of Pizzo Leone *(3hr)*, which affords pretty views of Lake Maggiore.

Monte Comino

Access by cable-car (Funivia Verdasio-Monte Comino) to the right of the road. Allow 15min there and back.

From the upper station (1 200m/3 936ft), a path winds its way down, toward a fork branching off into two directions. The right-hand path leads to Madonna della Segna, a small church fronted by a porch with three arcades dating back to 1700. The left-hand path will take you to an inn or *grotto* where hikers may stay the night. From the terrace (tables made with local granite), there is a sweeping panorama of the whole valley. The tiny village of Rasa can be glimpsed on the opposite slope.

Verdasio

Leave the car at the entrance to the village and continue on foot through a charming ensemble of narrow streets and vaulted passageways. The road climbs down toward a small reservoir, then snakes its way up in the direction of Palagnedra.

Palagnedra

The village architecture—one- or two-storey houses scattered over pastureland—provides a striking contrast with the other localities in the area. The road passes the rocky bank of Borgnone.

Camedo

This is the last Swiss village, separated from Italy by a bridge, the Ponte Ribellasca.

VAL VERZASCA★

25km/15.5mi NE.

After **Tenero**, a small village surrounded by vineyards, the road climbs toward the gigantic concrete mass of the Contra Dam.

Contra Dam

Leave the car by the roadside and walk up to the dam, which dominates the valley from a height of over 200m/656ft, built over a lake 5km/3.5mi long. In the centre of the dyke, a contraption has been set up with the inscription "007 Bungy Jumping," used in bungee jumping competitions and films (the famous scene in the James Bond movie *Goldeneye* was shot here). The best record to date is a 220m/722ft jump in 7.5 seconds!

The road skirts the dam, climbs upward and goes through several tunnels.

Vogorno

The houses are built on the mountain side. The church, entirely white with a stone campanile, presents a fine fresco in the Byzantine style. About 2km/1.2mi farther on, take a narrow road on the left which climbs up the opposite side of the valley.

Corippo★

This picturesque village is one of the most popular stopping-places for tourists. The setting is truly magnificent. Note the splendid panorama of the Lower Valley and the lake. Near the church stands the tiny *Sala Communale*.

Return to the main road, which crosses the river over a bridge with twin arches. The landscape becomes more barren and the river snakes through huge boulders.

Brione

Situated on a plateau where the Osola stream and the River Verzasca converge, this village is famous for its granite quarries. It is also a starting-point for many hiking excursions. The parish church boasts some beautiful 14C **frescoes★** attributed to one of Giotto's pupils from the Rimini School, centreing on religious themes *(The Last Supper, Presentation of the Virgin, etc.)*. The small castle with corner turrets (formerly the Trattoria del Castello) was once the private residence of the Marcacci barons of Locarno. Before reaching Frasco, you will see a waterfall on the right.

Sonogno

🅿 *Car park (fee) at the entrance to the village.*

The last village in Val Verzasca spreads its stone houses at the foot of a rocky barrier. The **Museo di Val Verzasca** (🕐 *open daily May–Oct, 1pm–5pm;* 👛 *5CHF;* 📞 *(0)91 746 17 77)* is a small Museum of Ethnography devoted to regional crafts, farming, costumes, and sacred art. Walk up the main street near the church you can see an early bread oven which is still used. The chancel in the church contains frescoes painted by Cherubino Pata, a pupil of Courbet who was born in Sonogno.

ADDRESSES

🛏STAY

☕🍽 **Hotel du Lac** – *Via Ramogna 3.* 📞 *(0)91 751 29 21. www.du-lac-locarno.ch. 31 rooms.* Located in the pedestrian area near Piazza Grande, barely 5min from the Madonna del Sasso funicular and near the landing for delightful boat trips on the lake. No restaurant.

☕🍽 **Hotel Garni Muralto** – *Via Sempione.* 📞 *(0)91 743 14 41. www.hotelmuralto.ch. 34 rooms. Closed 19 Dec–11 Jan.* A charming and quaint hotel, surrounded by a garden planted with palm trees. Most rooms have a balcony overlooking Lake Maggiore.

☕🍽 **Piccolo Hotel** – *Via Buetti 11.* 📞 *(0)91 743 02 12. www-piccolo-hotel.ch. 21 rooms. Closed mid-Nov–mid-Mar.* Good prices and service at this hotel away from the town centre. No restaurant.

☕🍽🍴 **Dell'Angelo** – *Piazza Grande.* 📞 *(0)91 751 81 75. www.hotel-dell-angelo.ch. 55 rooms.* Centrally located at the heart of the new town, this hotel is a good starting-point for discovering the old quarter. The top floor has a terrace offering nice views of the town and lake.

🍴EAT

☕🍽 **Campagna** – *In Minusio, 2km/ 1mi E – Via Rivapiana 46.* 📞 *(0)91 743 20 54. Closed Tue, and Wed evening.* This typical Ticino grotto has been converted into a restaurant with rustic decor. Eating at granite tables outdoors, in the shade of the trees, can be a charming experience.

☕🍽🍴 **La Cittadella** – *Via Cittadella 18.* 📞 *(0)91 751 58 85. www.cittadella.ch.* A trattoria on the ground floor and a dining room upstairs - in both the service and cuisine are impeccable.

☕🍽🍴 **Locanda Locarnese** – *Via Bossi 1/Piazza Grande.* 📞 *(0)91 756 87 56. www.locandalocarnese.ch. Closed Sun.* A young talented chef and inventive mediterranean cuisine.

🛒 SHOPPING

The main shopping streets are **Via della Stazione**, **Via della Ramogna**, **Via Sempione**, **Via Cattori**, **Via D. Recinto**, **Via F. Balli** and **Piazza Grande**.

🎭NIGHTLIFE

Enjoy an apéritif in a typical setting at **Alle Grotto** (in the Grand Albergo Locarno complex, access by Via della Stazione). On weekends, there is live music at **Cantina Canetti** (Piazza Grande 20), a well-known wine bar which has retained its old-fashioned charm. The **Kursaal** casino (Largo Zorzi) attracts the late-night crowd with its discotheque and slot machines.

In the Muralto district, along the lake shores, the **Al Pozz** (Viale Verbano 21) is a bar offering musical entertainment. A little farther on, the **Bussola** is for dedicated jazz enthusiasts.

🏃SPORT AND RECREATION

The Navigazione Lago Maggiore company (📞*(0)91 751 61 40; www.navigazionelaghi.it)* books a wide variety of boat tours on Lake Maggiore.

Ascona★★

Ascona's site on Lake Maggiore's shore resembles that of Locarno and its position at the mouth of the River Maggia. Like its larger neighbour, Ascona benefits from the river delta's flat lands, which provide a host of sporting facilities. This colourful fishing village, long a favourite with artists, has become an important venue for cultural events (New Orleans Jazz Festival in July, Classical Music Festival in September).

LAKE

Ente Turistico Lago Maggiore. Viale Papio 5. ℘(0)91 791 00 91. www.maggiore.ch.
The lake front, closed to cars, is a popular promenade area. During the high season, at night, strains of live music add to the festive atmosphere of the town. Regular boat trips leave for Locarno, Porte Ronco, the Brissago islands and destinations in Italy.

SIGHTS
Santa Maria della Misericordia
Via delle Cappelle.
Founded in 1399 and reconstructed in the 15C, the church is known for its 15C–16C polychrome **frescoes** in the nave and on the walls and vaulting of the chancel. The beautiful **altarpiece**, depicting the life of the Virgin, is attributed to Giovanni Antonio della Gaïa (1519).

Santi Pietro e Paolo
Piazza San Pietro.
At the heart of the town's narrow alleys, this parish church, dedicated to St Peter and St Paul, exhibits a fine altarpiece and splendid paintings by **Giovanni Serodine**, a pupil of Caravaggio.

Monte Verità
This wooded hillside which dominates Ascona could also be called "Utopian Hill". This present name was given by the community which established the village at the beginning of the 20C. They

▶ **Population:** 5 533.
Michelin Map: National 729: K7.
Info: The beautiful mansion on the square, whose windows are decorated with sculptures, houses the Tourist Information Centre. Ente Turistico Lago Maggiore Ascona, Via B. Luini 3. ℘(0)91 791 00 91. www.ascona-locarno.com. Alt. 210m/689ft.
Timing: Plan your visit around a boat tour on the Isole di Brissago.
Also See: The Botanical Park at San Pancrazio, created by Baroness Antonietta de Saint-Léger.

were looking for a new way of life, a classless society without money.

Casa Anatta
Monte Verita. Open Apr–Oct, Tue–Sun, 2.30pm–6pm.; Jul–Aug Tue–Sun 3pm –7 pm ℘(0)91 791 01 81. 6CHF. This house of 1904, constructed at the time of the community gives an idea of what life was like.

EXCURSION
Isole di Brissago★
Boat service is available from 28 Mar –19 Sept, daily 9am–6pm.
For information contact the Tourist Office in Ascona or Losone or ask at the offices of Navigazione Lago Maggiore d'Ascona, at Ascona harbour. Exotic park, art exhibition. 8CHF. ℘(0)91 791 00 91. www.isolebrissago.ch
The tiny Brissago islands enjoy an exceptional climate and the larger of the two, San Pancrazio, is the most popular holiday destination for tourists staying in Ascona. There is a tour of the Botanical Park which also affords pretty views of the lake. The mild climate permits cultivation of plant and flower species from all five continents. The small shady beach has a distinctly tropical feel.

Isole di Brissago

© Christof Sonderegger/Switzerland Tourism

ADDRESSES

🛏STAY

Al Faro– *Piazza G. Motta 27.*
(0)91 791 85 15. www.hotel-al-faro.ch.
Closed Nov–mid-Feb. 18 rooms. Located
in the centre of Ascona's famous Piazza.
Newly renovated, now offering Wi-Fi
service.

Castello – *Piazza G. Mottta.*
(0)91 791 01 61. www.castello-s-
eeschloss.ch. Closed early Nov–Feb.
46 rooms. This former medieval castle
near the lake and the centre of town is
extravagant with its cosy rooms with
period furniture. Outdoor pool.

Al Porto – *Piazza G. Motta.*
(0)91 785 85 85. www.alporto-hotel.ch.
36 rooms. Simple contemporary rooms
in pastel colours and rustic furniture.
On-site restaurant.

Tamaro – *Piazza G. Motta 35.*
(0)91 785 48 48. www.hotel-tamaro.ch.
Closed early Jan. 51 rooms. Situated on
the lakeside promenade wlth a pleasant
inner courtyard and garden where
meals are served.

LOSONE
Casa Berno – *(0)91 791 32 32*
www.casaberno.ch. Closed Nov–Mar.
65 rooms. Enchanting location near the
panoramic Ronco Tour. Beautiful views
of the mountains and lake. Peace and
quiet guaranteed.

🍽/EAT

Della Carrà – *Carrà dei Nasi.* *(0)91*
791 44 52. www.ristorantedellacarra.ch.
Closed Sun and Mon (except Sun evening
from Easter–Oct) and 1–20 Dec. Located in
the old town, offering regional cuisine.

LOSONE
Osteria Dell'Enoteca –
Contrada Maggiore 24. *(0)91 791 78 17.*
www.osteriaenoteca.ch. Closed Mon, Tue
and 1 Jan–7 Mar. Friendly osteria with
meals served in an enchanting garden.

PONTE BROLLA
Da Enzo – *6652 Tegna.* *(0)91 796*
14 75. www.ristorantedaenzo.ch. Closed
Wed all day, Thu at lunchtime and 15 Jan–
1 Mar. Located at the entrance to the
Valle Maggia and surrounded by palm
and bamboo this fine restaurant offers
Italian specialities in a lovely Ticino
house nestling amid the greenery.

BRISSAGO
Mirafiori – *Via Crodolo.* *(0)91*
793 12 34. Closed Nov–Feb. Enjoy a good
meal on the shaded terrace right on
the edge of the lake.

Osteria Grotto Borei –
At Piodina 3km/1.8mi SW of Brissago.
(0)91 793 01 95. Closed Thu, 15 Dec–18
Mar; week-days Nov–14 Dec (open Fri,
Sat and Sun only). Family business
serving typical Ticino dishes. Splendid
location in the mountains with pretty
views of the lake.

Bellinzona★★★

Bellinzona is an essential point of passage for traffic using the St Gotthard, Lukmanier or San Bernardino routes. It lies on the Italian side of the Alps and for 1 000 years has been a stronghold guarding the Ticino Valley. In 1803 it became the administrative centre of the canton, which took the name of the river.

HISTORICAL CENTRE
Collegiata dei Santi Pietro e Stefano

On Piazza della Collegiata, this church, dedicated to St Peter and St Stephen, stands out because of its imposing Renaissance façade carved out of Castione stone and adorned with a rose window. The interior is Baroque; fine frescoes decorate the side chapels, the most famous being the *Angel Musicians*, the work of Giuseppe Antonio Felice Orelli (c.1770). This arcaded square of **Piazza Nosetto** is the scene of a lively market held on Saturday mornings. The **Palazzo Civico** (town hall) is heavily influenced by the Italian Renaissance and has an elegant inner courtyard.

Teatro Sociale

Reopened in 1997 following extensive renovation, the Theatre of Bellinzona is the only existing Neoclassical theatre in Switzerland, and recalls Milan's famous La Scala.

CASTLES

The city fortifications rested on three castles, two of which (Castelgrande and Castello di Montebello) were connected by walls, a great part of which can still be seen, even from a distance. These castles are a UNESCO World Heritage Site.

Castelgrande★★

Recommended access by a lift situated on Piazzella Mario della Valle at the foot of the rock. ⓞ*Open Apr–Oct, 10am–7pm; Nov–Mar,10am–5pm.* ⛊*4CHF. (Three Castles ticket ⛊15CHF).* ⌕*(0)91 825 81 45.*

▸ **Population:** 17 286.
ⓒ **Michelin Map:** National 729: L7.
▯ **Info:** Palazzo Civico, via Camminata 2 – 6500. ⌕(0)91 825 21 31. www.bellinzonaturismo.ch.
◗ **Location:** Bellinzona is positioned at the southern entrance to the St. Gotthard, San Bernardino and Lukmanier passes. Alt. 223m/732ft.
◉ **Don't Miss:** UNESCO World Heritage Sites of Castelgrande, Castellos di Montebello, Sasso Corbaro
ⓞ **Timing:** Allow at least a half day to visit the three castles.

The oldest of the three castles is built on a rocky spur, its two quadrangular towers (Torre Bianca and Torre Nera) clearly visible from afar and from various vantage points in the town. Castelgrande endowed itself with additional fortifications between 1250 and 1500 following the wars that ravaged the area. The Torre Nera marked the centre of the castle; from there the crenelated ramparts formed three inner baileys. Substantial restoration work was carried out between 1982 and 1992 under the supervision of the Ticino architect Aurelio Galfetti. Buildings in the south courtyard now house a restaurant and a reception area. In the south wing the **Museo Storico Archeologico** (Museum of History and Archaeology) contains rooms explaining the history of castles and a gallery devoted to the gold and silver coins minted in Bellinzona during the 16C. In 1503 the Uri, Schwyz and Nidwalden cantons decided to found a minting factory in Basel, which became famous throughout the Confederation.

Castello di Montebello★★

Access by a ramp which starts from the railway station road (Viale Stazione). ▯*Car park.* ⓞ*Museum and Castle open*

Castello di Montebello

© Roland Gerth/Switzerland Tourism

Apr–Nov, daily 10am–6pm. ⌕*5CHF*
(Three Castles ticket ⌕*15CHF).*
℘(0)91 825 13 42.

This formidable citadel is typical of the Lombard military style in architecture. Built in the 13C by the influential Rusca family, the castle became the property of the Visconti in the late 14C. Under the reign of the Confederates in the 16C, it was renamed Castello di Svitto (Castle of Schwyz) and subsequently San Martino in the 18C. A drawbridge spanning the moat takes you to the defensive core of the stronghold, around which ramparts were erected in the 14C and 15C. The **Museo Civico** (Municipal Museum) presents ancient weapons and artefacts unearthed during digs carried out in the localities of Ticino, Gudo, Gorduno, Ascona, Giubiasco, Madrano, etc.

Castello di Sasso Corbaro

Access by car from the castle described above. Take the steep Via Artore, then Via Bebedetto Ferrini on the right and Via Sasso Corbaro. P *Car park.*
⊙*Open Apr–Oct, Mon–Sat 10am–6pm.*
⌕*5CHF (Three Castles ticket* ⌕*15CHF).*
℘(0)91 825 59 06.

This castle is the highest of the three, an isolated fortress standing among chest-

nut groves. Built to a square plan, it was commissioned in the 15C by the Duke of Milan to consolidate the defensive network of the city, deemed too vulnerable at that spot.

The terrace in the forecourt affords a beautiful **view**★ of the town and the Lower Ticino Valley as far as Lake Maggiore. Visit the **Museo dell'Arte e delle Tradizioni Popolari** (Museum of Popular Art and Tradition) installed in the keep. Room 3 (Sala Emma-Poglia) features a bedroom with fine wainscoting and a sculpted coffered ceiling taken from the residence belonging to the Poglia d'Olivone family. The following rooms display everyday objects which bring to life the Ticino region and its traditions.

GREATER BELLINZONA
Ravecchia

From Piazza Indipendenza, Via Lugano leads to the peaceful suburb of Ravecchia.

Santa Maria delle Grazie

Formerly attached to a 15C convent run by a minor order of monks, Santa Maria delle Grazie contains some interesting frescoes, including a poignant *Crucifixion*

Scene, surrounded by 15 paintings illustrating the Life of Christ.

San Biagio

This small medieval church with its square belltower and 14C frescoes, both inside and out, was known as the church of Bellinzona even though it was outside the walls.

Museo Villa dei Cedri

Piazza San Biagio 9. Tue–Fri 2pm–6pm, Sat–Sun and Hols 11am–6pm. ⊜*8CHF.* ℘*(0)91 821 85 20. www.villacedri.ch.*
Very close to the Chiesa San Biagio this museum is the town's art gallery. Situated in a pleasant park, it houses Suisse and Italian figurative art of the 19 and 20C. These works all donated carry the signatures of Chiesa, Franzoni, Rossi and Guide Tallone amongst many others.

EXCURSIONS
Monte Carasso★

❯ *2km/1.25mi W of Bellinzona.*
This village of 2300 inhabitants on the periphery of Bellinzona is a textbook case of an innovative urban project by the Ticino architect **Luigi Snozzi**. The most visible is the public area around the old convent which has become a community school. Some other buildings such as the Raiffeisen bank, the gymnasium and the new cemetery all contribute to the transformation of the village.

Monte Tamaro★

❯ *15km/9mi NW. Leave Lugano on the Como road and take the freeway towards Bellinzona. Turn off at Rivera.*
⏱*Open daily 27 Mar–7 Nov 8.30am–5pm. Reach Alpe Foppa by cable-car (20min).* ⊜*23CHF.* ℘*(0)91 946 23 03. www.montemaro.ch.*
Although it looks like a fort, it is the **Chiesa Santa Maria degli Angeli**, designed by the famous Ticino architect Mario Botta. A long upper passageway ends in a belvedere decorated with a metal cross supporting a bell. You can also reach the church via the lower passageway, whose ceilings are embellished with paintings by Enzo Cucchi (the same

artist decorated the interior). Notice the two hands symbolically united on a blue background, lit by a luminous source from above. The curved walls present two rows of 11 windows, which make for a light, radiant atmosphere.
Alpe Foppa (alt. 1 530m/4 018ft) is the departure point for many excursions. You can also hire cross-country bicycles or go paragliding from there. The Monte Tamaro summit (alt. 1 960m/6 397ft) commands a sweeping **view**★ of Lake Lugano, Lake Maggiore, the Monte Rosa and the Matterhorn.

ADDRESSES

⌂STAY

⊜⊜ Internazionale –
Piazza Stazione 35. ℘*(0)91 825 43 33. www.hotel-internazionale.ch. 90 rooms.*
Facing the station, the hotel offers modern, comfortable rooms, most with balconies.

⊜⊜⊜ Unione – *Via Generale Guisan 1.*
℘*(0)91 825 55 77. www.hotel-unione.ch. Closed 22 Dec–20 Jan. 40 rooms.*
Conveniently situated near the town centre, this hotel offers good service for highly affordable prices. Meals can be served in the garden.

⏲/EAT

⊜⊜ Osteria Sasso Corbaro –
In Castelo Sasso Corbaro. ℘*(0)91 825 55 32. www.osteriasassocorbaro.com. Closed Dec–mid-Mar.* A charming restaurant perched high up in a castle. Regional cuisine. Nice views of the town from the terrace.

⊜⊜⊜ Castelgrande – *Salita al Castello (access by lift). Closed Mon.* ℘*(0)91 814 87 81. www.ristorantecastelgrande.ch.*
The restaurant lies within the ramparts of the former medieval fortress of Castelgrande. Wines bottled on the estate.

Alto Ticino★★

The Alto or Upper Ticino consists of the valleys and mountains in the north of the Canton. The small town of Biasca, 24km/15m, north of Bellinzona is the gateway to the region and here the Val Levantina, leading northwest to Airolo, and the Val Blenio, leading north to Olivoni, head off to the Alpine passes of St Gotthard and Lukmanier respectively.

🚗 DRIVING TOURS

1 LUKMANIER PASS ROAD★
66km/40mi. About 45min.
The Lukmanier Pass is usually blocked by snow from November to May.

To the south, villages consist of groups of stone buildings around slender campaniles; to the north they feature wooden chalets and domed churches. The Lukmanier is the lowest of the Swiss transalpine routes, but due to its roundabout approaches on the north slope of the Alps, international traffic uses the St Gotthard. On the Rhine side, part of the high Alpine hollow is flooded by the waters of the Santa Maria Dam. Between the Santa Maria Dam and Disentis/Mustér, beyond a valley dotted with clumps of dwarf alders and rhododendrons, the road crosses the clear Cristallina Rhine and, as conifers begin to reappear, enters the central basin of the Medel Valley. Sloping pastures cut by zigzag ravines, dark chalets and the domed belfry of Curaglia make this little mountain retreat an attractive **scene**★. Notice the silos in which grain ripens, after being harvested early because of the harsh climate.

Biasca
This small town, at the intersection of the Ticino Valley and the Brenno Valley, is dominated by the 12C **Chiesa dei Santi Pietro e Paolo** (*Contact the Tourist Office for entry*), hollowed out of the rock and accessible by a long stairway.

🚗 **Michelin Map:** National 729.

ℹ️ **Info: Andermatt** – Verkehrsverein, Gotthardstrasse 2. ✆041 887 14 54. www.andermatt.ch. **Biasca** – Ente Turistico, Contrada Cavalier Pellanda 4 – 6710. ✆(0)91 862 33 27. www.biascaturismo.ch. **Faido** – Leventina Turismo. ✆091 966 16 16. www.leventinaturismo.ch.

▶ **Location:** Accessible via St Gotthard and Lukmanier Pass roads, and the Nufenenstrasse.

👁 **Don't Miss:** A cable-car ride up Gemsstock.

🕐 **Timing:** Allow a day to make the most of this area and complete the itineraries.

The Romanesque church, made of local granite, has a tall bell tower with arches, its façade, decorated with a fresco partly worn away; the chapel is in the Baroque style with remains of interesting polychrome **frescoes** (14C–15C).

Malvaglia
The Romanesque **campanile**★ of the church is in the Lombard fashion, with the number of arches increasing as they approach the summit.
The barrenness of the lower **Val Blenio**, accentuated by the destructive work of the tributaries of the Brenno, decreases beyond Dongio.
A verdant basin opens out with the bold pyramid of the Sosto looming ahead.

Lottigna★
This village stretches along the valley in terraces. The former Bailiffs' House (15C), decorated with the coat of arms of the first Swiss cantons, is now the **Museo della Valle di Blenio** (🕐*open Easter–31 Oct, Tue–Sun 2pm–5.30pm; ◓5CHF; ✆(0)91 871 19 77; museodiblenio. vallediblenio.ch*). The museum houses

St Gothard Pass at Val Tremola

© Roland Gerth/Switzerland Tourism

St Gotthard Massif

St Gotthard Road

One of the best-known Alpine passes in Switzerland, the St Gotthard provides a route from Airolo, in the Ticino, to Goschenen, in the canton of Uri, thus connecting the German and Italian-speaking regions. Despite being the shortest route between southern Germany and Milan, Italy, the pass was not heavily trafficked until after the 13C because the trip required fording the Schollen River at a steep gorge near Andermatt. Folktales surround the building of the bridges. Until the late 1700s the bridge carried only foot traffic, and was strengthened to accommodate carriages in 1775. The top of the pass is the continental divide; waters north of it flow into the Rhine and North Sea, and to the south flow to the Po and into the Mediterranean.

The old winding road over the top of the pass was replaced by a tunnel in 1980, but the old road remains and offers a far more scenic, though slower, alternative, especially for those heading south, where magnificent views open up as they descend along raised viaducts. To take the old road, leave the main road at the Goschenen exit, just before the tunnel entrance. At the top of the pass is a tourist centre with a restaurant, gift shop, and a small museum.

The St Gotthard Rail Tunnel

The trip through the pass by train is quite spectacular, not only for the steep cliffs and gorges of the Reuss Valley and the vertigo-inducing bridges of the south side, but for the tunnel itself. It climbs through the mountain in a series of spirals that allows the locomotive to reach the necessary height without making the gradient too steep. The highlight of the tunnel climb is the many sightings of the town of Wassen, with its pretty little church. This tunnel is being replaced by a new one that drills almost straight through the range, from Erstfeld, in Uri, to Bodio, in the Ticino (due to open in 2017).

A popular tourist pass, **The William Tell Express** combines a luncheon trip across the lake from Lucerne to Flüelen by vintage paddle steamer with the train ride through the pass. The programme is offered May to October, and operates in either direction. ⊕Reservations are compulsory: *www.raileurope. com/us/rail/specialty/william_tell.htm.*

historic tools, utensils and traditional regional costumes, religious art and a large arms collection (14C to today).

▷ *At Acquarossa bear left onto the small road that runs along the western side of Blenio Valley. Left of the church in Prugiasco, take the street that climbs, then narrows, and follow it for 2km/1.2mi. The sanctuary of Negrentino stands atop a grassy knoll.*

Chiesa Negrentino San Carlo★

30min on foot there and back. To visit, contact the Blenio Tourist Office in Acquarossa. ℘ *(0)91 871 14 87.*
The interior of this small 11C Romanesque church is painted with a series of polychrome **frescoes**★★ (11C–16C). After leaving Castro and Ponto-Valentino, you reach Aquila and the direct road to Lukmanier. From Olivone to Acquacalda the road has two series of hairpin bends separated by the Camperio shelf. Soon the **view**★ opens eastward to the snowy peaks of the Adula Massif.

Lukmanier Pass
(Passo del Lucomagno)
Alt. 1 916m/6 286ft.

2 THE ST GOTTHARD PASS ROAD★

🕰 *See the box opposite for the history of this road.*
Most of the present siting dates from 1830 but extensive resurfacing and widening has improved it considerably. On the Ticino side the road is much faster

than along the Reuss. 🚗*The St Gotthard road carries heavy traffic.*
🚗*The St Gotthard Pass is usually blocked by snow Nov–Jun. 65km/40mi – 2hr.*

Andermatt★
Alt. 1 436m/4 711ft.
Andermatt lies at the junction of the St Gotthard, Furka and Oberalp roads in a beautiful curve of the Urseren Valley, which is the heart of the St Gotthard Massif. The life of the town flows along its narrow main street, sections of which still show the typical Italian **binario** (road with granite paving stones). In winter, when snow covers the neighbouring slopes, punctuated with anti-avalanche barriers, Andermatt is crowded with skiers. The main ski resorts are in the Nätschen district (towards the Oberalp Pass), regularly served by local trains and chairlifts, as are the Gemsstock slopes, equipped with a cable-car.
The last climb to the St Gotthard begins at the foot of the ancient Hospental watchtower. The road climbs above the Urseren Valley, to the right of the Furka Pass, by the snowy Galenstock peaks, then into the Gams Valley.

Gemsstock★★

🚠*Allow at least 1hr there and back, including a 40min journey in a cable-car split up into two trips.*
🥾*Many opportunities for hiking.*
Proceed to the upper terrace with its viewing tables. The dramatic **panorama**★★ sweeps over 600 summits in the

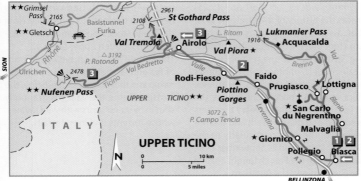

Panorama of the central Alps from Gemsstock

© Christof Sonderegger/Switzerland Tourism

distance. The Finsteraarhorn dominates the Bernese Oberland to the east.
In the foreground, the Göschen Valley is overshadowed by Dammastock. To the south lie the Mont Rose and the spectacular range of Italian Alps.

St Gotthard Pass
(Passo del San Gottardo)
Alt. 2 108m/6 919ft.

Set in a rugged but breathtaking landscape of rounded rocks and scattered lakes, the pass owes its name to a chapel erected about 1300 in honor of St Gotthard, Bishop of Hildesheim (near Hanover).
Situated at the top of the pass, the **Museo Nazionale del San Gottardo**★ (National St Gotthard Museum; ⊙open *Jun–Oct, daily 9am–6pm; slide show (25min)*; ⬤8CHF; ☏(0)91 869 15 25) traces the history of this strategic location, used by the Romans and which links together north and south, connecting Switzerland to the rest of Europe. Scale models, photographs, and other artefacts illustrate the road, the tunnel, flora and fauna, postal connections, the St Gotthard Inn (where weary travellers were fed and given a bed) and the relevance of the pass, particularly to the Battle of Tremola on 24 September 1799, during which the French fought against the Russians and the Austrians.

Val Tremola
Access in summer only. 13km/8mi from the St Gotthard Pass.

The road coils loop over loop within this steep corridor, which carries the alarming name of Trembling Valley. Seen from below (*stand on the disused bridge at the bottom of the ravine*), the road, with its interlaced sustaining walls, gives a good idea of the road-builders' audacity.
The modern road, an exceptionally bold piece of work, avoids the difficult crossing of the Tremola Valley by a change of route. It follows the mountainside with only three hairpin bends—one of which is built partly on a curved viaduct, another is a **viewpoint**★—and the third is a tunnel 700m/0.5mi long. The descent is very steep.
The Upper Leventina lies wide open between slopes dotted with villages nestling at the foot of a campanile. Note the Ticino stone houses and Alpine chalets with wooden upper storeys.
The Ambri-Piotta Basin, between woods of firs and larches, opens out between Airolo and the Piottino Defile. Below the Piottino Defile the valley is gradually shut in by steep spurs with wild ravines, whose torrents end in waterfalls.

Val Piora★

*Alt. 1 796m/5 900ft. 12min by
funicular from the Ritom power station.*
This is a pleasant walk along clearly laid-
out paths, bordered by charming Alpine
lakes: The walk affords an opportunity
to discover the local vegetation and the
many wild animal species inhabiting the
region.

Faido

Rich woodlands and gushing waters (La
Piumogna Cascades), makes this township a splendid summer resort. The
semicircular main square with shady
lime trees, a statue dedicated to local
glories, houses covered by curious conical stone roofs and dotted with outdoor
cafés, compose a lovely Italian scene.

Biasca – See Lukmanier Pass Road

③ NUFENEN PASS ROAD★★

*The Nufenen Pass is usually closed
November to May.*
Nufenpass is the highest elevation pass
to allow motor vehicles in Switzerland,
and is also home to many bicycle and
hiking trails. The bicycle tour, suitable
for experienced and very fit riders, spans
36.6 km/22.7mi over an altitude varia-
tion of 1 340m/4 396ft; this trip takes
the average cyclist four to six hours
to complete. The road offers many spectacular views.
From **Airolo** (alt. 1 142m/3 747ft) to
8km/5mi from Nufenen, the climb up
the Bedretto Valley (and from the River
Ticino to its source) begins between
slopes covered with fir trees. From
Airolo to Fontana there are audacious
examples (above and to the right) of the
engineers' ingenuity when constructing
the road. Then after Ossasco you can see
a series of villages halfway up the slope:
Bedretto is one of them. Beginning at
the hamlet of All'Acqua (*cable-car on
the left*) the foliage becomes scarcer,
the climb steeper and the hairpin bends
offer a succession of views behind onto
the valley's slopes. You then ascend the
barren right side of the Bedretto Valley.
The ascent stops abruptly at the
Nufenen Pass★★ (alt. 2 478m/8 130ft),

Mountain Roads

The highway code states that
on difficult mountain roads the
ascending vehicle has priority. On
"postal" roads, drivers must comply
with directions given by the drivers
of the yellow postal buses.

where you have climbed more than
1 300m/4 265ft since Airolo. This pass
offers an amazing landscape of incredible desolation. Higher up (*to the left
of the restaurant*) the **view**★★ encompasses the glacier and Gries Reservoir,
extending to the Upper Valais Range,
the Bernese Oberland (Finsteraarhorn
summit) and in the foreground the
black, vertically grooved face of the
Faulhorn. The downhill road on the
Valais side, after a close-up view of the
greyish-coloured Gries Glacier and its
meltwater lake, plunges dizzily into a
mineral landscape, brightened only by
patches of very short grass and thistles.
The glacier and the Faulhorn can still
be seen.

ADDRESSES

STAY

Albergo Ristorante Defanti – *6746
Lavorgo, Fiado. 2km/1.25m S. (0)91 865
14 34. www.defanti.ch. 26 rooms.* Quiet
hotel run by the Defanti family and
established for 100 years.

Albergo Ristorante Nazionale –
*Via Belinzona 24 CH-6710 Biasca. (0)91
862 13 31. www.albergonazionale.ch. 21
rooms.* Quiet, comfortable modern hotel
located in front of the railway station.
Excellent restaurant and pizzeria.

Zur Sonne – *Gotthardstrasse 76,
Andermatt. (0)41 887 12 26. www.hotel
sonneandermatt.ch. 21 rooms. Open
20 Dec–21 Apr and 2 Jun–27 Oct only.*
Comfortable hotel built in the chalet
style. Sauna. A few minutes from
the railway station. Two minutes to
Gemsstock (alt. 2 961m/9 714ft).

Badus – *Gotthardstrasse 25,
Andermatt. (0)41 887 12 86.
www.hotelbadus.ch. 23 rooms.*
Modern and comfortable.

CENTRAL SWITZERLAND

Central Switzerland is the core of the country, physically and psychologically: It contains the Rütli field where the founding 1291 oath was taken, the three cantons that participated, and is the where the William Tell legend originated. With Lake Lucerne as its epicenter, it is also a visitor's delight offering boat trips on glacial waters, magnificent unimpeded views over a stunning landscape, gilded Baroque churches, unforgettable railway journeys and splendid museums.

Highlights

1. The magnificent **Lucerne** (p322)
2. The view from the top of **Mount Rigi** (p340)
3. A **Lake Uri** boat trip (p342)
4. The ski resort of **Engelberg** (p347)
5. The **Einsiedeln** abbey (p352)

A Bit of History

Central Switzerland is where the current Swiss confederation started life as a small alliance between the three "early" cantons of Uri, Unterwalden and Schwyz whose oath was sworn in the field of **Rütli**. This is the region that gave Switzerland its **name** (from the canton of Schwyz), its **flag** (from an early version of the Schwyz arms) and its **National Day**. Though the written pact which is preserved in the **Bundesbriefmuseum** in Schwyz only mentions "the month of August" without a specific date, the national day is celebrated on 1 August by convention. Lucerne and Zug quickly joined these three cantons and have become (with Ticino) the Catholic conservative core of Switzerland.

William Tell

This is also the region where the **William Tell** legend takes place. Tell's deeds were first described in the **White Book of Sarnen**, a collection of medieval manuscripts found in the capital of Obwalden. He was allegedly born in **Bürglen** in the canton of Uri, a small village southeast of **Altdorf** where the Tell tourist industry now thrives. The newly appointed Austrian governor **Gessler** hung his hat in the middle of a field and demanded that all village folk bow in front of it in reverence and fealty. Tell refused and was punished by having to shoot an apple from the head of his young son with a crossbow. When Gessler asked him why he had two arrows in his quiver, Tell replied that the second was for Gessler in case he missed. Gessler had Tell arrested and carried him on his boat bound for

View from Pilatus—Lake Lucerne with Bürgenstock and Rigi

© Christian Perret/Luzern Tourismus/Switzerland Tourism

Mark Twain in Lucerne

Out of all of Mark Twain's celebrated travel memoirs, it is the sections on Switzerland in **A Tramp Abroad** that are among the most frequently quoted. His description of Lucerne in 1878 could still be valid today: "*Lucerne is a charming place. It begins at the water's edge, with a fringe of hotels, and scrambles up and spreads itself over two or three sharp hills in a crowded, disorderly, but picturesque way, offering to the eye a heaped-up confusion of red roofs, quaint gables, dormer windows, toothpick steeples, with here and there a bit of ancient embattled wall bending itself over the ridges, worm-fashion, and here and there an old square tower of heavy masonry.*" Though he woke up too late to see the sunset on the Rigi, he does write of the sunset: "*The great cloud-barred disk of the sun stood just above a limitless expanse of tossing white-caps—so to speak—a billowy chaos of massy mountain domes and peaks draped in imperishable snow, and flooded with an opaline glory of changing and dissolving splendors, while through rifts in a black cloud-bank above the sun, radiating lances of diamond dust shot to the zenith. The cloven valleys of the lower world swam in a tinted mist which veiled the ruggedness of their crags and ribs and ragged forests, and turned all the forbidding region into a soft and rich and sensuous paradise.*"

Gessler's castle in **Küssnacht** below the **Rigi** mountain, but a storm on **Lake Lucerne** helped Tell escape where the current **Tellkapelle** stands. He then made his way to Gessler's castle and killed him. Tell eventually drowned on the **Schächen** river by Bürglen, trying to save a boy.

All this would have been lost to the world, but **Antoine-Marin Lemierre** revived the legend with a play to inspire Revolutionary France; Napoleon's installed government in the **Helvetic Republic** depicted Tell in the new republic's official seal. **Johann Wolfgang von Goethe** was another admirer of the myth which had since become a symbol of the common man standing against tyranny, and passed it on to his friend **Friedrich von Schiller**. Schiller wrote an epic on William Tell, which **Gioachino Rossini** used in turn as the basis for his eponymous opera—this time as an allegory for the Austrian repression of early 19C Italian nationalist sentiment.

The St Gotthard Pass

There is a reason this was the heart of early Switzerland and even today it is impossible not to see why: the St Gotthard Pass. It has been called the Water Tower of Europe: westwards flows the Rhône through the Valais and Lake Geneva to end in the Mediterranean; southwards the Ticino that joins the Po; eastwards several small Rhines that join at Chur to make up the big Rhine which feeds lake Constance; and northwards the Reuss that flows into the Aare just before the latter joins the Rhine.

This Alpine route is the key trading route between Zürich and Milan, and, more widely, Southern Germany and Northern Italy. Much of the prosperity of the mountain cantons resulted from taxes on the movement of goods through the pass and the provision of guides. Many of the early wars and battles in the area have been fought around its control: the Swiss independence battles of Morgarten (1315) and Sempach (1386); the capture of Ticino to secure the pass during the wars between the Swiss and the Dukes of Milan in the early 15C; and Napoleon's capture of Switzerland in 1798 as a prelude to his campaigns against Italy and Austria. Finally, the threat of dynamiting the Gotthard tunnel was one of several factors that deterred Adolf Hitler from invading Switzerland.

The St Gotthard Pass offers visitors unrivalled access to some of central Switzerland's most dramatic scenery, as well as the opportunity to ride a marvel of engineering, the St Gotthard railway.

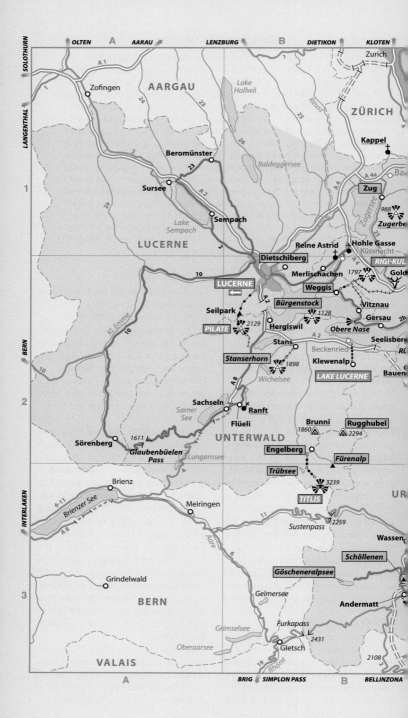

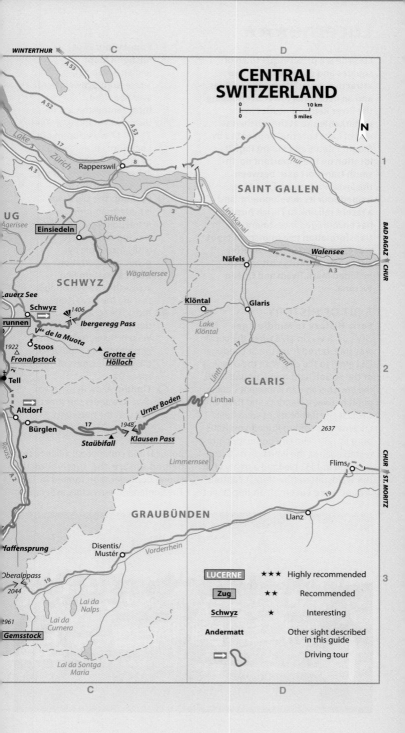

CENTRAL SWITZERLAND

0   10 km
0   5 miles

N

WINTERTHUR

SAINT GALLEN

Rapperswil

Einsiedeln

Näfels

Walensee

BAD RAGAZ
CHUR

Sihlsee

Wägitalersee

SCHWYZ

Lauerz See

Schwyz   *1406*

Ibergeregg Pass

Klöntal

Glaris

Lake
Klöntal

runnen

V¹⁹ de la Muota

1922

Stoos

Fronalpstock

Grotte de
Hölloch

GLARIS

Tell

Urner Boden

Linthal

Altdorf

Bürglen   17   *1948*

Staübifall   Klausen Pass

Limmernsee

2637

CHUR
ST. MORITZ

Flims

GRAUBÜNDEN

Vorderrhein

Llanz

Pfaffensprung

Disentis/
Mustér

Oberalppass

2044

2961

Gemsstock

Lai da
Nalps

Lai da
Curnera

Lai da Sontga
Maria

LUCERNE	★★★	Highly recommended
Zug	★★	Recommended
Schwyz	★	Interesting
Andermatt		Other sight described in this guide
⇨		Driving tour

Lucerne★★★

Lucerne is a picturesque town of squares and churches, with two attractive, covered wooden bridges and an octagonal tower overlooking the River Reuss. It nestles in a remarkable site at the northwest end of Lake Lucerne, dominated by Mount Pilatus and Mount Rigi. Its location on the important north-south transport axis, between the Swiss Plateau and the Alps, helped spur its development, and a recent rail link to Zürich Airport has encouraged investment. Its transformation to a tourism hotspot was established in the 19C after a string of celebrity visitors that included Mark Twain and Queen Victoria.

A BIT OF HISTORY

Early History to Middle Ages – The city's birth was in 1178 when the parish was transferred from the St Leodegar (St Leger) to the city. With the opening of the St Gotthard route around 1220, the town became an important staging-point between Flanders and Italy, and the first city fortifications were built. Lucerne was sold to Rudolf von Habsburg in 1291. The city population protested against the limits on its autonomy and in 1332 pledged a treaty with the Waldstätten (the "forest cantons" around Lake Lucerne), an important

▶ **Population:** 59 241.
◔ **Michelin Map:**
Regional Map 551,
Suisse Nord/Schweiz Nord/
Sviizzera Nord.
Info: Zentralstrasse 5 (in the railway station). ℘(0)41 227 17 17. www.luzern.org.
▶ **Location:** Lucerne is right by Vierwaldstättersee, 45km/28mi west of Schwyz. Alt. 436m/1 430ft.
Ⓟ **Parking:** The Old Town is pedestrian-only. Attractions beyond walking distance are easily accessible by public transportation.
⊛ **Don't Miss:** Strolling across the covered bridges that are the city's icons.
Kids: The sprawling transport museum, Verkehrshaus, includes the opportunity to experience the weightlessness of space travel.
ⓒ **Timing:** Allow at least two days to wander the streets and visit the museums.

political and commercial alliance that helped ensure the survival of the young Confederation formed in 1291. The Confederation victory at Sempach

Lucerne with Wasserturm and Kapellbruecke

© Lucia Degonda/Switzerland Tourism

(1386) permanently freed Lucerne from ties to Austria. When the Reformation began, Lucerne led the Catholic resistance. Because the city voted against the Federal Constitution in 1848, it was bypassed as the nation's capital for Bern. In the mid-19C, Lucerne gratefully seized upon opportunities offered by tourism to recapture some of its lost glory.

Development of Tourism – Lucerne remained a small town, with just 4 300 inhabitants at the end of the 18C; that changed with the arrival of tourists beginning in 1830. The Nationalquai and the esplanade by the Jesuit church were laid out during this period, fine hotels were built and the first steamboats began operating on the lake. Today, Lucerne welcomes over five million tourists every year, a quarter of whom are Swiss.

⚓WALKING TOURS

① ALTSTADT (OLD TOWN)★★
3hrs. Start from Schwanenplatz (Swan Square) and head towards Kapellplatz, fronted by the impressive 18C St Peterskapelle. See map p327.

The old town is built on the side of the mountain and is partially surrounded by vestiges of the old fortifications, of which seven large square towers remain. Note the ornate original covered wooden bridges spanning the river.

Kapellplatz
The centre of the square is adorned with the Fritschibrunnen (Fritschi Fountain), which represents carnival, spring, and joy. **Fritschi** is a legendary character in whose honour a carnival has been held since the 15C. The Kapellgasse, a lively street lined with shops, leads to **Kornmarkt** (Grain Market), a square built in the 16C. A market is held here on Tuesdays and Saturday mornings.

Old City Hall★
This handsome Renaissance Altes Rathaus was built from 1602 to 1606 and overlooks the Kornmarkt, once used as a grain storehouse. The Gasthaus zu Pfistern, to the right, has a fine painted façade. To the left, the Am-Rhyn town house is home to the **Picasso Museum** (*see Museums*).

▷ *Take Kornmarktgasse, and through an alleyway on the right, to Hirschenplatz.*

Hirschenplatz (Stag Square)
This square is lined with houses with painted façades, which are adorned with wrought-iron signs. The famous Johann Wolfgang von Goethe (1749–1832) stayed at the Hotel Goldener Adler in 1779.

Weinmarkt (Wine Market)★
The old houses in this pretty square, which are covered with paintings and decorated with many signs and flags, were once the seats of the various guilds. Note the Scales' Mansion, and the Wine Market Pharmacy (Weinmarktapotheke) built in 1530. The Gothic fountain represents warriors and St Maurice, patron saint of soldiers. The original is currently displayed in the Regierungsgebäude.

Follow Kramgasse to **Mühlenplatz** (Mills Square) which dates from the 16C. There is a fine view of the Spreuerbrücke, the old houses on the opposite bank of the Reuss and, in the distance, of Gütsch Hill.

Spreuerbrücke
This covered bridge, part of the fortifications of the old town, spans the River Reuss. It was built in 1408 and restored in the 19C. In German, *Spreu* means "chaff": The bridge was the only point where chaff and dead leaves could be thrown into the river. A small chapel (1568) stands in the middle of the bridge. The decoration of 67 painted panels representing a Dance of Death was executed in the 17C by Caspar Meglinger. From the bridge, there is a view of the quays of the old town and of the façade of the Jesuits' Church.

▷ *Beyond the bridge, follow Pfistergasse.*

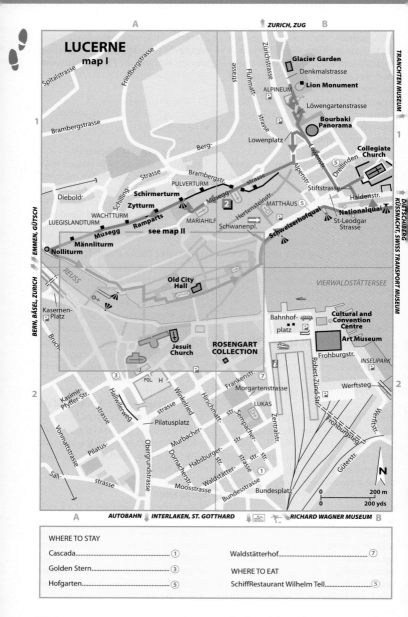

LUCERNE
map I

ZURICH, ZUG

Glacier Garden
Denkmalstrasse
Lion Monument
Löwengartenstrasse
Bourbaki Panorama
Lowenplatz
Collegiate Church
Stiftstrasse
Haldenstr.
Nationalquai
St-Leodgar Strasse
Schweizerhofquai
MATTHÄUS

ALPINEUM

TRANCHTEN MUSEUM

DIETSCHIBERG KÜSSNACHT, SWISS TRANSPORT MUSEUM

Spitalstrasse
Friedbergstrasse
Brambergstrasse
Diebold-
Schilling-
Strasse
Bramberg-
strasse
PULVERTURM
Schirmerturm
Zyttturm
Ramparts
see map II
Musegg
Männliturm
Nolliturm
WACHTTURM
LUEGISLANDTURM
REUSS
Kasernen-Platz
MARIAHILF
Schwanenpl.
Hertensteinstr.

Fluhmatt-
strasse
Zurichstrasse

EMMEN, GÜTSCH
BERN, BÄSEL, ZURICH
Bruch-

VIERWALDSTÄTTERSEE

Old City Hall

Jesuit Church

ROSENGART COLLECTION

Bahnhof-platz

Cultural and Convention Centre

Art Museum

Frohburgstr.

INSELIPARK

Werftsteg

Kasimir-Pfyffer-Str.
Hallwilerweg
Pilatusplatz
Winkelried strasse
Hirschmatt-str.
Frankenstr.
Morgartenstrasse
LUKAS
Sempacher-str.
Zentralstr.
Robert-Zünd-Str.
Frohburgsteg
Werftstr.
Werftsteg

Pilatus-strasse
Vonmattstrasse
Obergrundstrasse
Dornacher strasse
Murbacher-strasse
Habsburger-str.
Waldstätter-str.
Moosstrasse
Bundesstrasse
Bundesplatz
Güterstr.

N

0   200 m
0   200 yds

AUTOBAHN INTERLAKEN, ST. GOTTHARD   RICHARD WAGNER MUSEUM

WHERE TO STAY	
Cascada..①	Waldstätterhof..⑦
Golden Stern.......................................③	**WHERE TO EAT**
Hofgarten...⑤	SchiffRestaurant Wilhelm Tell...................⑤

Pfistergasse
Number 24, formerly the Arsenal, from 1567 to 1983, now houses the **Historisches Museum** (see Museums).
On the quay, (Reuss-Steg), houses with oriels, painted façades and flower-decked fountains; on the left are the towers from the old town fortifications.

Turn right at Münzgasse to reach Franziskanerplatz.

Franciscan Church★
Open Sun–Fri, 10.30am–6.30pm, Sun 12.30–6.30pm. (0)41 210 14 67.
The Gothic Franzisckankiche, built in the 13C and remodelled many times since,

is the oldest in Lucerne. It contains fine stalls, a 17C carved wooden pulpit and flags won by the city over the centuries. A Baroque chapel to the rear of the church is decorated with stucco in the Italian style.

Regierungsgebäude (Government Palace)

This building has ornate stonework in Florentine Renaissance style (1557–64) and since 1804 has housed the cantonal government. In the inner court stands the original Weinmarkt Fountain (*see above*) which dates back to 1481.

Jesuit Church

Built in 1666 by Pater Christoph Vogler, the Jesuitenkirche was the first Baroque church in Switzerland. The plain façade is framed between two tall towers surmounted by domed belfries, and the **interior**★ is nobly proportioned. The high altar is adorned with a huge pink marble stucco altarpiece. The central ceiling painting (1749) depicts the Apotheosis of St Francis Xavier, the patron saint of the church. The three chapels on the right house relics from **St Silvan**, **St Nicholas of Flüe** (*see LAKE LUCERNE*) and **St Karl Borromäus**.

▷ *Exit and continue to your right, past the Rathaus bridge.*

Kapellbrücke★

This covered wooden bridge, rebuilt after a fire in 1993, has been the symbol of Lucerne for more than 600 years. The 200m/656ft-long bridge was built in 1333 to protect the town on the lakeside. In the beginning of the 17C, it was adorned with 110 paintings on the wood triangles formed by the roof beams, depicting the history of Lucerne and Switzerland, as well as of St Leger and St Maurice. Only 47 paintings were salvaged from the fire but 30 have been restored and once again hang inside the walkway. The bridge has an octagonal tower, called the **Wasserturm**. Dating from around 1300, the tower was once part of the defensive fortifications of the town; in the past it has also been

an archives room, a prison and a torture chamber.

▷ *Cross the Reuss on the busy Seebrücke towards the station.*

Culture and Convention Centre

Built in 2000 by the French architect Jean Nouvel, the architecturally controversial Kultur-und Kongresszentrum consisting mainly of a glass structure (12 000sq m/129 120sq ft) and offers splendid views★ of Lucerne and the lake. It houses the Kunstmuseum (*see p328*), and a concert hall (acoustically one of the best in the world) where the Lucerne Festival is held. There is a café on the ground floor.

② TO THE RAMPARTS VIA LÖWENPLATZ★★

See map opposite.

▷ *Leave Schwanenplatz and follow the Schweizerhofquai.*

The **Schweizerhofquai** replaced the third covered bridge in Lucerne during the 19C. Both the Schweizerhofquai and the **Nationalquai** afford admirable **views**★★ of the town and Lake Lucerne, and beyond of the Alpine range stretching from the Rigi to the Pilatus (*viewing tables*). At the end of Carl-Spitteler-quai is the Lido beach.

▷ *Turn left before the Grand Hotel to join the narrow Stiftstraße.*

Abbey Court Church★

Open 7am–7pm. Guided tours available on request. Closed Nov–Feb, noon–2pm. (0)41 410 52 41.
The Hofkirche is dedicated to St Leodegar (St Leger), the patron saint of the town, which is said to derive its name from him, founded in 735. In 1633 all except the Gothic towers were destroyed by fire and it was rebuilt in the Renaissance style. It is a huge building, reached by a monumental stairway, and is surrounded by Italianate cloisters, containing tombs of the old families of Lucerne.

The **interior**★ is spacious and well proportioned, in the late Renaissance style. The high altar is black marble and statues of St Maurice and St Leodogar flank it. Two of the altars (*Pietà* in the south aisle; *Death of the Virgin* in the north aisle) are richly adorned and gilded. The organ (1650) is one of the best in Switzerland.

> *Take Löwenstrasse up to Löwenplatz, where the Bourbaki-Panorama (see Museums) is housed in a domed building. Take Denkmalstrasse up to the Lion's Monument.*

Lion's Monument

Known as Löwendenkmal, this statue was carved out of the sandstone cliff face in 1821. It portrays a dying lion with a spear embedded in its left flank and its right paw protecting a fleur de lys. The sculpture (9m/29.5ft long) commemorates the Swiss Guards, whose task it was to protect the royal palace in Paris during the French Revolution: about 850 mercenaries were either killed during the Storming of the Tuileries (Paris) in August 1792 or guillotined soon after. The monument was the brainchild of Karl Pfyffer von Altishofen, a Swiss officer who survived the massacre.

Gletschergarten★ (Glacier Garden)

Denkmalstrasse 4. Open Apr–Oct, 9am–6pm; Nov–Mar, 10am–5pm. Film (12min). 12CHF. (0)41 410 43 40. www.gletschergarten.ch.

In 1872, JW Amrein-Troller, a bank clerk, bought a meadow outside Lucerne with the intention of building a cellar. During construction work, 32 different cavities were discovered, hollowed out from the sandstone by the Reuss Glacier 20 000 years ago, when ice covered the entire plain as far as the Jura. Amrein-Troller built a park around this geological site, which is particularly popular with children.

In the **museum**, **glacier science** is explained in an easy and accessible way. Visitors can touch "cold" ice from Polar glaciers and the more "temperate" ice from Alpine glaciers. Displays document the life of glaciers and animal species, such as the glacial flea (2mm/0.08in long), The region's geological history, which was still subtropical 20 million years ago, is demonstrated by fossils marked with prints of palms and birds. Other exhibits include an old relief model of Central Switzerland made in 1786, a reconstruction of a peasant's bedroom, and lithographs, models and reconstructions of old Lucerne.

After the museum, enjoy a **panoramic walk** with views of Lucerne and Mont Pilatus in the beautiful gardens, planted with Alpine flowers. The gardens also house an unusual **Moorish-style hall of mirrors** built in 1896 for the Geneva National Exhibition. The **Alpineum** is situated opposite the glacier garden.

> *Return through Löwenplatz to Alpenstrasse, turn right into Hertenstreinstrasse.*

Museggmauer (Musegg Ramparts)

Open Easter–All Saints Day, 7.30am–7pm. No charge.

The remains of the fortified city walls (800m/875yds in length) include watch and defensive towers, dating from around 1400. Only one tower has undergone restoration work; three are open to the public: **Schirmerturm**, rebuilt after a fire in 1994; **Zytturm**, which has the oldest clock tower in Lucerne (1535); and **Männliturm**. The towers offer superb **views**★ of the town and the lake.

OLD TOWN MUSEUMS
Rosengart Collection★★

Pilatusstrasse 10. Open Apr–Oct, 10am–6pm; Nov–Mar, 11am–5pm. 18CHF incl. Plcasso museum. (0)41 220 16 60. www.rosengart.ch.

The Sammlung Rosengart art gallery was opened in 2002 by Angela Rosengart, daughter of the art dealer Siegfried Rosengart. There are more than 200 modern works of art dating from the 19C and 20C, including paintings by Picasso, Klee and Chagall. More than 100 **works**★★ by **Paul Klee** are displayed in

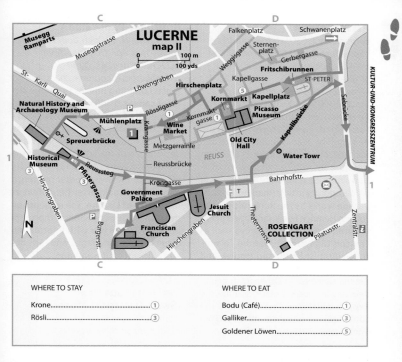

the basement. The collection includes *Belebte Strasse* (1910), *St Germain bei Tunis* (1914), and *Modebild*, 1922.

Among the many graphic works, *Bild mit Hahn* (1919) and *Bergdorf* (1934) are worthy of note.

On the ground floor, the stunning **Picasso collection**★★★ (over 80 works of art painted after 1938) includes many Cubist paintings, such as *Violin at the Café* (1913). Portraits of Nusch Éluard, Dora Maar and Marie-Thérèse Walter, painted in the 1930s and 1940s, are exhibited along with *Woman and Dog Playing*, a painting inspired by Françoise Gilot (1953). *The Studio* (1954) is that of the Villa Californie in Cannes.

Other interesting works include *Jacqueline's Profile* (1957) and *Women in Hats* (1961, 1963). In *Déjeuner sur l'herbe* (1961), inspired by Manet's famous painting, Picasso himself is depicted on the right.

The first floor is devoted to Impressionist works by artists such as Monet, Pissarro, Renoir, Bonnard and Cézanne (*L'Estaque, the village and the sea*, 1882).

Léger (*The Staircase*, 1914) and Matisse (*Lemons and Saxifrage*, 1943) are also well represented, as is Braque with his lyrical *Pot and Ivy* (1950). Thirteen works by Chagall are also displayed, ranging from *Evening at the Window* (1950) to *Red Sun* (1983). Other artists exhibited here include Seurat, Vuillard, Utrillo, Dufy, Rouault and Kandinsky.

Picasso Museum

Furrengasse 21. ○*Open Apr–Oct, 10am –6pm; Nov–Mar, 11am–5pm.* ∞*8CHF.* ℘*(0)41 410 35 33. www.rosengart.ch.* The **Am Rhyn-Haus** contains a small collection of lithographs, engravings and ceramics by Picasso, donated to the city in 1978 by the Rosengart family (*see Rosengart Collection opposite*). Most works date from the last 20 years of the artist's life. The museum also houses photographs taken during the same period (1956–73) by the American David Douglas Duncan, a close friend of the artist, and include portraits of Picasso and his last muse, Jacqueline Roque.

Art Museum★

Europaplatz 1. ○*Open Tue–Sun 10am –5pm (8pm Tue,Wed). Open on all public holidays, incl. Mon* ◒*10CHF.* ℘*(0)41 226 78 00. www.kunstmuseumluzern.ch.*

Since 2000, the **Kunstmuseum** has been housed on the fourth floor of the **Kultur- und Kongresszentrum** designed by Jean Nouvel. The permanent collection of mainly Swiss paintings from the 18C–20C is exhibited in rotation alongside temporary exhibitions of contemporary art. Permanent exhibits include works by the Romantic painter Johann Heinrich Füssli, landscape painters from the School of Geneva such as François Diday and Alexandre Calame, the Symbolist Ferdinand Hodler, and Félix Vallotton *(see INTRODUCTION: Art and Architecture).* Other artists exhibited here include Vlaminck, Soutine, the Expressionist Max Pechstein and the contemporary artists Joseph Beys, Paul Thek, Franz Gertsch, and Jeff Wall.

Historical Museum

Pfistergasse 24. ○*Open Tue–Sun 10am –5pm.* ○*Closed 1 Jan, 25 Dec.* ◒*10CHF.* ℘*(0)41 228 54 24. www.hmluzern.ch.*

The **Historisches Museum** displays 16C and 17C armour, traditional dress, and reconstructions of interiors.

Natural History Museum

Kasernenplatz 6 ○*Open Tue–Sun 10am –5pm.* ○*Closed 24, 25 Dec.* ◒*8CHF.* ℘*(0)41 228 54 11. www.naturmuseum.ch.*

Devoted mainly to the natural characteristics of central Switzerland, this museum presents an extensive collection of Alpine minerals and fossils and a remarkable **Gallery of Archeology** exhibiting objects such as weapons and pottery found in the area from the Neolithic lake dwellers, the Bronze Age and Celto-Roman period.

Also in this gallery, models and dioramas depict the life of the lake dweller. On the second floor are zoological and botanical collections as well as aquariums, terrariums, etc.

Bourbaki-Panorama★

Löwenplatz 11. ○*Open daily Nov–Apr, 10am–5pm; Apr–Oct, 9am–6pm* ◒*12CHF.* ℘*(0)41 412 30 30. www.bourbakipanorama.ch.*

A glass building houses this huge **circular canvas** (1 100sq m/1 315.5sq yds) painted by **Édouard Castres** (1881). The canvas hangs on the second floor, attached by hundreds of magnets, and depicts one of the last episodes of the Franco-Prussian war of 1870–71: the crossing of the Swiss border by French general Bourbaki after his defeat at the **Battle of Lisaine**. The museum on the ground floor provides a thorough portrayal of the war with information given in three languages, and includes an audio-visual presentation.

ADDITIONAL SIGHTS
Verkehrshaus★★★ (Swiss Transport Museum)

Lidostrasse 5 (near the lake) by Haldenstrasse. Buses 6 and 8; Verkehrshaus bus stop. ○*Open daily Apr–Nov, 10am–6pm; Dec–Mar, 10am– 5pm.* ℘*(08) 48 85 20 20. www.verkehrshaus.ch.*

This museum illustrates the **history of transport** in Switzerland. The different sections are housed in a dozen separate buildings dotted around a park, which is interspersed with play areas and snack bars. There is also an Imax cinema (*www. imax.ch*).

Rail transport – An 8 000sq m/ 9 568sq yds exhibition area featuring 1 000m/3 281ft of railway track presents the largest collection in the country. Exhibits include the Vitznau-Rigi locomotive, dating back to 1873, Switzerland's largest steam engine and the legendary Be 6/8 mountain locomotive, better known as the Crocodile. Exhibits also include tramcars from several Swiss cities and a collection of miniature trains. There is also a lively presentation of the building of the St Gotthard Tunnel: visitors are invited to settle in a carriage and be guided through the various stages of this exciting project, accompanied by typical sounds and smells.

Rail Transport Hall, Verkehrshaus

© PHOTOPRESS/Verkehrshaus der Schweiz

Road transport – The dramatic changes during the 19C and 20C are illustrated by the sledge used by the Simplon Post Office and the Grimsel horse-drawn carriage. The impressive Halle du Transport Routier contains more than 30 automobiles used by the Confederation in this thriving industry. The most remarkable exhibit is probably the 1905 racing car designed by Genevan manufacturers Charles and Frédéric Dufaux, presented alongside several Weber, Turicum, Pic-Pic and Martini models. Note the replica of an early Benz tricycle. From the dandy horse to the scooter, two-wheeled vehicles are represented by 50 or so bicycles, including a number of Swiss models.

Media Factory – This section devoted to the history of communication is equipped with radio, television and video-conference facilities as well as interactive systems that enable visitors to experiment with the latest technology.

Aviation and Space Travel Hall – Aviation through the ages: the first biplane—the Dufaux 4—in which Armand Dufaux flew over Lake Geneva in 1910, Swissair's DC 3, the supersonic carrier CV 990 Coronado, hot-air balloons, hang-gliders, microlites, and other aircraft. Exhibits include a Fokker F-VII, a collection of 200 miniature models and 30 engines and turbines. Visitors can try a flight simulator and take over the controls, or they can pose for a photograph on board the Blue Box. In the air traffic control tower, a radar console teaches the complexities of modern safety conditions at airports. On the second upper level, the **Cosmorama** boasts numerous special effects that plunge you into the fascinating world of asteroids and outer space, including experiencing weightlessness.

Planetarium ZEISS Longines – Beneath a huge cupola lies a replica of the firmament, where the life of the planets and their movements is explained.

Navigation, cable-cars, tourism – The ground floor exhibits the machinery of the paddle steamer *Pilatus* (1895), one of the legendary boats to glide on Lake Lucerne. The **Navigation Section** (*first floor*) presents a remarkable collection of reduced models and nautical instruments evoking the progress of navigation through the centuries. Note the shipowner's office, containing a wide range of miniature ships, marine books and seascapes donated to the museum by shipowner Philipp Keller in 1980. The multimedia show **Nautirama** retraces the history of navigation on Lake Lucerne. The cable-car section displays a cabin of the first public aerial cable-car (1908), which transported passengers to the Wetterhorn, and the ultra-modern

A National Hero

On 9 July 1386 a decisive battle took place near Sempach between the Swiss Confederates and Austrians commanded by Duke Leopold. **Arnold von Winkelried** spurred forward and grasped as many spears as he could hold in order to make a breach in the Austrian square, bristling with pikes. His heroic sacrifice secured the victory of the Confederates when Duke Leopold lost his life. A monument commemorates the events of that day, which heralded the decline of Habsburg rule in Switzerland.

cabin of the cable-car, built in 1984, linking Spielboden to Langfluh near Saas Fee. The tourism section displays the country's most typical products and activities and **Swissorama**, a multivision show, illustrates its most famous sites.

Richard Wagner-Museum

Access by boat from the landing-stage near Seebrücke. **By car:** *leave the town by Hirschmattstrasse; at the Bundersplatz take Tribschenstrasse and follow directions to Tribschen.* **Buses** *6, 7 or 8; bus stop Wartegg.* 🕐*Open mid-Mar–Nov, Tue–Sun 10am–noon, 2pm–5pm. Open Easter Mon.* 🎟*8CHF.* 📞*(0)41 360 23 70. www.richard-wagner-museum.ch.*
Wagner produced some of his major works here: *Die Meistersinger, Rheingold, Siegfried.* Here, too, he married Cosima, Franz Liszt's daughter, and received Nietzsche. The ground floor houses

Rack Railway

The Pilatus railway was opened in 1889 as a steam operated train and switched to electric in 1937. The descent, an average gradient of 38%, takes 10 minutes longer than ascent.

original scores, Wagner's death mask, a plaster of his right hand, photos, letters, and the **Érard piano** that accompanied him on his trips. On the first floor, there is a collection of musical instruments dating from the 17–19C.

EXCURSIONS
Dietschiberg★★
Alt. 629m/2 064ft.
At the station, take **bus** *14, alight at the Konservatorium stop, then walk for 20min, following signposts to Utenberg and Golfplatz.* **By funicular** *from Felsental, on the north bank: follow the lake shore as far as Carl-Spitteler-Quai, then take Gesegnetmattstrasse.*
Splendid **panorama**★★ of Lake Lucerne and Pilatus on the right, the Rigi on the left and the Bernese and Glarus Alps.

Glasi Hergiswil
At Seestrasse 12, Hergiswil, 8km/4.9mi S of Lucerne. Access by boat or train. 🕐*Mon–Sat 9am–6pm (4pm Sat).* 🎟*Free.* 📞*(0)41 632 32 32. www.glasi.ch.*
The oldest glassworks in the country, operating since 1817, opens its doors to admire the work of its glassblowing artisans. A small collection containing pieces from the 18 and 19C, a direct sales shop, games for children and a cafe on the lake nicely complement the visit.

Pilatus★★★
Pilatus-Bahnen, Schlossweg 1, 6010 Kriens/Lucerne. 📞*(0)41 329 11 13. www.pilatus.ch.*
The proud rock pyramid of Mount Pilatus (highest point: 2 132m/6 995ft at the Tomlishorn) dominates with its sharply defined ridges. The aerial cable-car, along a steep cliff to the top, is a marvel of modern engineering, and the view from the summit is astounding. Pilatus is both a useful landmark for the visitor to central Switzerland and a long time source of superstitious dread, as legend declared that the spirit of Pontius Pilate haunted a small lake near the summit and that anyone who approached that accursed spot would cause fearful storms.

Pilatus cog railway

© Philipp Giegel/Switzerland Tourism

A construction and renovation project of the Pilatus-Kulm and Bellevue Hotels and a panorama gallery aims to make the most of this stunning location.

Pilatus-Kulm railway★★★
The railway climb begins at Alpnachstad. Train time from Lucerne 2hr round trip, including 1hr by rack railway (Apr–Oct). ⊶*Return train fare 58CHF. Pilatus-Kulm can also be reached by cable-car from Kriens, in the suburbs of Lucerne. The Golden Tour (96CHF, recommended) combines a boat from Lucerne to Alpnachstadt, ascent by the cogwheel railway and descent by cable-car to Kriens forming a complete circuit. Bus number 1, outside Lucerne station takes 15 mins to Kriens, fare included.*
The red cogwheel railway, with a maximum gradient of 48°, is the steepest rack-and-pinion railway in the world, particularly impressive where it crosses the slopes of the Esel.
From the upper station, which has two mountain hotels (*Pilatus-Kulm and Belle-vue*), you will climb in a few minutes to the Esel summit (alt. 2 119m/6 952ft).

A walk through the gallery hollowed out of the side of the mountain showcasing Alpine plants is recommended.

🚗 DRIVING TOURS

Around Lake Sempach (Sempachsee)
68km/42mi NW of Lucerne.

▷ *Leave by Highway 2, direction Emmen, then Basel and Sursee, then bear right towards Sempach.*

Sempach
Alt. 518m/1 699ft.
Theaterstrasse 9. ℘*(0)41 920 44 44.*
www.sempachersee-tourismus.ch.
Founded by the Habsburgs, Sempach is built near the lake to which it gave its name. For a long time it owed its activity and prosperity to the considerable traffic on the St Gotthard route (Basel-Lucerne-Milan), which now follows the opposite shore. The main street has an old-fashioned air with its Witches' Tower, its town hall (Rathaus) with a

façade made cheerful by a red and white pattern, its flower-decked fountain, and its houses with brown tile roofs.

The **Swiss Ornithological Centre** (*Schweizerische Vogelwarte*) (🕐 *open Tue–Fri 8am–5pm (10am Sat–Sun and public holidays);* 🕐 *closed Mon and weekends Jan–Mar;* 🎫 *free* ♿*;* 🖉 *(0)41 462 97 00; www.vogelwarte.ch)* is devoted to local birds, as well as the survival of species and bird migration. It consists of several gardens, a number of large aviaries and a small museum presenting stuffed birds.

◯ *Take the little lakeside road.*

Sursee
Alt. 504m/1 654ft.

The small old town at the northwest corner of Lake Sempach has kept some of its old atmosphere in spite of the fires that ravaged it between the 14C and the 17C.

The **Old Town** boasts a fine town hall *(Rathaus)* from the Late Gothic period (mid-16C), flanked by two towers. One ends in a slender belfry, whereas the other is hexagonal and crowned by a dome. The façade with a stepped gable is pierced by many mullioned windows. The **Baseltor** or **Untertor**, the town gate, a vestige of the former ramparts, is flanked by a half-timbered house whose white façade is intersected by red beams.

Wallfahrtskirche Mariazell
On the eastern outskirts of town near the road to Beromünster .

Built in the 17C, this pilgrim's chapel is adorned with a ceiling decorated with naïve paintings representing Noah's Ark, the Tower of Babel and other Old Testament scenes. Near the gateway there is a **view**★ of the lake, the Alps and the Jura.

◯ *Head E on road 23.*

Beromünster
7.5km/4.6mi NE of Sursee.

This little town, near the transmitters of the Swiss National German-language Broadcasting Station, gets its name from the monastery (Münster) founded in 980 by Count Bero of Lenzburg and transformed in the 13C into a priory for lay canons.

Stiftskirche
🔹*Guided tours by appointment, Mon–Fri 10am–5pm.* 🎫*5CHF.* 🖉*(0)41 930 35 85.*

The collegiate church was built in the 11C and 12C but almost entirely remodelled in the Baroque style. The porch is adorned with many shields bearing the arms of former canons. The raised chancel is enclosed by a wrought-iron screen and furnished with remarkable **stalls**★ (1609). Their carved panels represent episodes in the Life of Christ. The treasury holds the reliquary of Warnebert (7C).

Schlossmuseum
🔹*Guided tours (1hr) May–Oct, Sun and public holidays 3pm–5pm.* 🎫*3CHF.* 🖉*(041) 930 36 17/14 82.*

The museum, housed in the castle's medieval tower, displays a collection of furniture, paintings, local costumes, tools and objects from Beromünster and its environs as well as a reconstruction of the Helyas Heyle print room where, in 1470, the very first book was printed in Switzerland.

Around Entlebuch and Lake Sarnen
105km/65mi W of Lucerne.

◯ *Leave by Highway 10, direction Wolhusen (19km/12mi), then Schüpfheim and Sörenberg (55km/34mi).*

Entlebuch
The region of Entlebuch, southwest of Lucerne, is Switzerland's only **Unesco Biosphere Reserve**: around the valley of the **Kleine Emme,** there is an outstanding protected area of upland moors and bogs, wild gorges and vast karst formations. **Sörenberg**, with its many hiking paths, is an ideal starting point. From Sörenberg one can con-

tinue to the **Glaubenbüelen Pass** to discover the snowy peak of the **Brienzer Rothorn**, and then descend down to **Giswil** by a winding road that provides beautiful views of Lake Sarnen and the surrounding countryside

From Giswil you can continue to **Lungern** and climb to the **Brünig Pass**. Between Giswil and Kaiserstuhl, you will get a good view of the Pilatus ridges rising above the shallow depression, dotted with farms and clumps of trees, partly submerged by Lake Sarnen. Upstream and in the far distance, the three snowy peaks of the Wetterhorn group appear through the Brünig Pass. Between the fir trees and maples, there are wonderful glimpses of **Lake Lungern** (Lungernsee), with its curving shores. Close by to Lungern lies the well known **Schönbühl** ski area in the Brünig Pass with 22km/13.6mi of trails.

▷ *Leave Entlebuch SE on Glaubenbergstrasse, or if coming directly from Lucerne, take the A2 towards Stans, then the A8.*

Sachseln

Sachseln is both the geographic centre of Switzerland and the land of **Nicolas of Flüe**, a saint whose role was crucial in the early formation of the Confederation. Swiss Catholics affirm their attachment to their faith and their patriotic fervor by coming to Sachseln to pray to St Nicholas of Flüe (*see LAKE LUCERNE*). The town, prettily situated on the shore of Lake Sarnen, is as much a moving place of pilgrimage as a trendsetter in environmental achievements. In 2004, Sachseln converted mountain spring-fed drinking water pipelines into hydro-electric power generators, fulfilling two essential requirements; the project was a national pilot, and is considered to be the first of its kind.

The great Baroque **church**, supported by columns of black Melchtal marble, enshrines the relics of **St Nicholas of Flüe** on a special altar at the entrance to the chancel. The remains are enclosed in a large, embossed recumbent figure (1934). Go around the building to reach the funeral chapel, where the faithful come to meditate before the tombstone, carved in 1518 with the effigy of the saint. Below is the worn step of the original sepulchre.

▷ *Leave Sachseln E on the hill road behind the church.*

Flüeli

Exit Sachseln E towards Flüeli (uphill behind the church). ▣*Leave the car in the car park on the village's central plaza.* The rustic character of this hamlet, where St Nicholas led the life of a mountain patriarch surrounded by his large family, has been preserved. The chapel (1618) can be seen on its mound from far off; it is reached by stairs and an esplanade. From the terrace there is a pleasant, open view of the Valley of Sarsen, Lake Sarnen, and Pilatus on one side and the deep cleft leading into the Melchtal on the other. Besides this sanctuary, pilgrims still visit the birthplace (the oldest wooden house in Switzerland—14C) and the family home of Nicholas.

Ranft★

Approaches are signposted on leaving Flüeli.

By a steep descent *(ramp or stairs)* toward the floor of the Melchtal Valley you will first reach the hermitage-chapel. The church (17C) is decorated with painted panels recalling the life of the recluse; outstanding is a fine Gothic **Christ**★ taken from the former Sachseln church. The cell nearby where the hermit could not stand upright—was built in 1468 by his fellow-citizens from Obwalden. Below, another chapel was built in the 16C on the spot where the Virgin appeared to St. Nicholas of Flüeli. On returning from Flüeli bound for Lucerne, take the fork to the right toward Kerns; then cross the River Melchaa (or simply Aa) on the **Hohe Brücke**★. This 30m-long bridge was built across the torrent at a height of 100m/329ft in 1943 by Swiss Army Engineers and is the highest covered wooden bridge in Europe.

ADDRESSES

🛏 STAY

Rösli – *Pfistergasse 12 . ☎(0)41 249 22 77. www.roesli.ch. 6 rooms.* A small pension very well located in a quiet street with great prices for Lucerne. The reception is opposite at the hotel Baslertor in the same street.

Goldener Stern – *Burgerstrasse 35. ☎(0)41 227 50 60. www.goldener-stern.ch. 16 rooms. Restaurant.* Ten minutes from the railway station, next to the Franciscan church, this simple, family-run hotel has well-maintained rooms at reasonable prices for Lucerne.

Hofgarten - *Stadthofstrasse 14. ☎(0)41 417 88 88. www.hofgarten.ch. 18 rooms. Restaurant.* Just steps from the Hofkirche, this timber-framed 15C house combining modernity and heritage is surrounded by a secluded garden. The vegetarian restaurant is a haven of peace.

Krone – *Weinmarkt 12. ☎(0)41 419 44 00. www.krone-luzern.ch. 25 rooms. Restaurant.* Situated in the heart of the old town, this modern hotel has spacious rooms. The restaurant overlooks the Weinmarkt, a pedestrian square with real medieval charm.

Cascada – *Bundesplatz 18. ☎(0)41 226 80 88. www.cascada.ch. 63 rooms. Restaurant.* Comfortable rooms, private car park ⓟ, Wi-Fi access, close to the station. The Boléro restaurant serves Spanish specialties.

Waldstätterhof – *Zentralstrasse 4. ☎(0)41 227 12 71. www.hotel-waldstaetterhof.ch. 75 rooms and 2 suites.* Ideally located opposite the station, the hotel has renovated some of the rooms, which are the most expensive. The proximity of bars makes it noisy on weekends. Alcohol-free restaurant.

NEARBY

Seeburg – *Seeburgstrasse 61 at Ost going towards Meggen (north shore of the lake). ☎(0)41 375 55 55. www.hotelseeburg.ch. 58 rooms. Restaurant.* A handsome, beautifully preserved residence with old-fashioned charm. The best rooms look over Lake Lucerne and Mount Pilatus. Lakeside garden with a charming creek for mooring boats, two restaurants and a lively lounge.

PILATUS

Bellevue – *Pilatus Kulm. ☎(0)41 329 12 12. www.pilatus.com. 28 rooms.* Circular structure with views of the sunrise.

Pilatus Kulm – *☎(0)41 670 12 55. www.pilatus.com. 20 rooms.* The Bellevue and the Pilatus Kulm both share a reception area located in the Hotel Bellevue and both offer dining.

🍴 EAT

Wilhelm Tell – *Schweizerhofquai. ☎(0)41 410 23 30. www.schiffrestaurant.ch. Closed Mondays.* Huge steamboat, many of which used to be seen gliding on Lake Lucerne. From the bar, you can glimpse the machinery which once operated the paddle wheels. The Art Nouveau dining hall adds a touch of refinement.

Galliker – *Schützenstrasse 1, near Kasernenplatz. ☎(0)41 240 10 02. Closed Sun and Mon.* Small, cosy and friendly establishment where you immediately feel at ease.

Goldener Löwen – *Eisengasse 1. ☎(0)41 410 11 33.* Tavern with ambiance to enjoy one of its innumerable Swiss fondues. Even the chocolate fondue is on the menu.

Café Bodu – *Kornmarkt 5. ☎(0)41 410 01 77.* French cuisine with a Mediterranean accent. Parisian brasserie atmosphere inside and a romantic evening terrace outside. Good service.

NEARBY

Schwendelberg – *Horw. ☎(0)41 340 35 40. www.schwendelberg.com. Closed May–Sept, Tue; Oct–Apr Tue & Wed.* Traditional guesthouse offering peace and quiet. Sweeping panorama of Lake Lucerne and the Swiss Alps.

Schlössli Utenberg – *Utenbergstrasse 643 (4km/2.5mi NE heading towards Dietschiberg). ☎(0)41 420 00 22. www.schlössli-utenberg.ch. Closed Mon, Tue.* An 18C mansion built in the Baroque style houses this ideal lunch-spot. Admire the 18C faience stove (1758) on the first floor. Pretty terrace views of the city and its lake.

NIGHTLIFE

Situated on the seventh floor of the Hôtel Astoria (*Pilatusstrasse 29*), the **Penthouse**, with its soft background music, is a favourite haunt among the young. In the same street, the **Hôtel Schiller** (*Pilatusstrasse 15*) offers two different bars: The **Bar Blue** in an old-fashioned setting and the **Pacifico**, a bar with a Mexican touch.

On the shores of the lake, both the **Hôtel National** and the **Hôtel Palace** feature a piano bar (*Haldenstrasse 4 and 10 respectively*), as does the **Casino**, which also has a large room where weekend shows are held.

In the old town, enjoy a good fondue to the strains of folk music at the **Stadtkeller** (*Sternenplatz 3*). The **Movie Bar** (*Weinmarkt*), whose décor will delight film buffs, attracts a casual crowd and offers a great variety of wines and beers. In the basement, you can order dishes bearing the name of a famous film: Try Al Capone, Jaws, or Love Story.

For dancers and nightclub-goers, the **Mad Wallstreet**, (*Industriestrasse 9, Kriens. www.madwallstreet.ch)* offers live music in Kriens, a few miles away from Lucerne. **Pravda Dance Club** (*Pilatusstrasse 29, www.pravda.ch*) is one of the hippest in the city. **The Loft** (*Haldenstrasse 21, www.theloft.ch*) is the destination for late clubbers and also offers a gay night on Fridays.

The alternative, indie and punk scene is centeed out of town, around the **Musikzentrum Sedel** (*www.sedel.ch*) which used to be a prison. There is a shuttle to the venue from Löwenplatz, Bundesplatz and Kasernenplatz every 30 mins until 2am during the weekends. A taxi from the station costs 15CHF.

For jazz enthusiasts, **Jazzkantine** (*Grabenstrasse 8, www.jsl.ch*) offers most days performances and jam sessions by the pupils of the Lucerne Jazz School.

SHOPPING

The main shopping area is the picturesque, pedestrian streets in the old town.

Department stores: Jelmoli (*Pilatusstrasse 4*), **Manor Warenhäuser** (*Weggisstrasse 5*), **Au Bon Marché** (*Kapellgasse 4*).

The **Emmen Center** (*EmmenBrücke 3, www.emmencenter.ch)* is a large shopping mall with over 80 stores, 13 min from the railway station on bus 53.

A well-stocked fruit and vegetable market is on the right bank of the Reuss River every Tue and Sat. A flea market operates on the Burgerstasse/ Reusssteg every Saturday May–Oct.

THEATRE/MUSIC/CINEMA

Stadttheater – *Theaterstrasse 2. ℘(0)41 228 14 14. www.luzerner-theater.ch.*

Boa cultural centre – *Geissensteinring 41. ℘(0)41 360 45 88. www.boaluzern.ch.*

EVENTS AND FESTIVALS
LUCERNE FESTIVAL

On 25 August 1938, Arturo Toscanini conducted *Siegfried* by Wagner in Tribschen Park. This performance marked the beginning of the **Lucerne Festival**, dedicated to classical and contemporary music, which now attracts over 110 000 people every year. The festival holds events at Easter, during the summer (around 30 concerts in August and September) and in November (piano recitals). For further information, contact *Hirschmattstrasse 13, 6002 Lucerne. ℘(0)41 226 44 00. www.lucernefestival.ch.*

SIGHTSEEING

Lake Lucerne Navigation Company offers trips on the lake, dinner cruises, and links with all the cable-cars and funiculars in the region. *℘(0)41 367 67 67. www.lakelucerne.ch.*

The **Tourist Office** inside the railway station (*www.luzern.com*)offers a 2hr city walk in English at 9.45am 25CHF. *Daily May–Oct, Wed & Sat Nov–Mar, Wed, Sat & Sun Apr.*

Lake Lucerne ★★★

Lake Lucerne is found on most maps under its German name, Vierwaldstätter See. The Lake Lucerne district offers picturesque old-fashioned villages and cities, and innumerable hills and majestic mountain summits. A total surface area of 114sq km/44sq mi makes Lake Lucerne the second largest lake within the country's boundaries after Lake Neuchâtel. It is comprised of three distinct sections from west to east: namely, the "lakes" of Vitznau, Gersau-Beckenried, and Uri, created by a narrowing of the lake shore. The River Reus joins the lake to the south and leaves it at Lucerne to the north.

A BIT OF HISTORY

The Cradle of Swiss Democracy – Long before the Confederation existed, the **Waldstätten** (forest cantons) on the lake shores had adapted without much difficulty to a symbolic fealty to the Holy Roman Empire. The attachment of the district of Uri to the Empire was formally guaranteed as early as 1231, special treatment due to its strategic location on the vital St Gotthard route. The relative autonomy of these cantons was threatened when the Austrian House of Habsburg, anxious to ensure profitable administration of its possessions, gave officials control over the revenues of estates without consulting with local authorities. These outsiders quickly became unpopular.

The situation became critical when Rudolf I, the first of the Hapsburgs, acceded to the Imperial throne in 1273. His death prompted representatives of Schwyz, Uri, and Unterwalden to form a permanent alliance. This mutual assistance pact is regarded by the Swiss as the founding pact of the Confederation. Its original text is carefully preserved at Schwyz, and the anniversary of its signature (1 August 1291) is celebrated as the national festival (⌖see Calendar of Events). The victory of Morgarten (1315) over the troops of Leopold of Austria

◔ Michelin Map:
Regional Map 551, Suisse Nord/Schweiz Nord/Svizzera Nord.

▯ Info: Bahnhofplatz 4. ℘(0)41 610 88 33. www.lakeluzern.ch.

▶ Location: The lake is overlooked by the summits of Mount Pilatus and Mount Rigi.

⊘ Don't Miss: A boat trip around the lake followed by a climb to one of the surrounding summits. Some of the lakeside sights, namely the historic Field of Rütli, can only be reached by boat.

◷ Timing: The boat trip from Lucerne to Flüelen takes 2h45min non-stop.

marked the definite liberation of the three original cantons.

Dawn of liberty – This story gained its fame as a result of one of the treasures of German literature: Schiller's **William Tell** (1804). His story involves a conspiracy long matured by the representatives of the three communities, represented as victims of Bailiff Gessler's despotism, and solemnly sworn on the Field of Rütli, opposite Brunnen, by 33 spokesmen for Schwyz, Uri, and Unterwalden. After having been subjected by Gessler to the famous ordeal of the apple, the archer William Tell became the arm of justice. He killed Gessler in the sunken road (Hohle Gasse) at Küssnacht, paving the way for an era of liberty.

"Protector of the Fatherland" – The district of Unterwalden (more exactly the half-canton of Obwalden) is proud to number among its sons the hermit **Nicholas of Flüe** (canonised in 1947), whose conciliatory intervention left an indelible mark on the Swiss patriotic temperament. Born in 1417 to prosper-

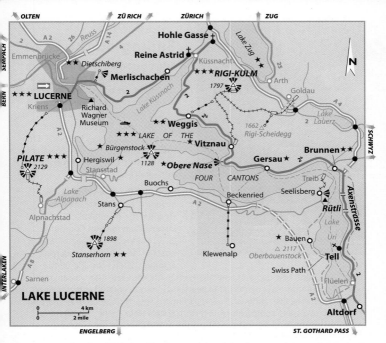

LAKE LUCERNE

Map labels: OLTEN, ZÜRICH, ZÜRICH, ZUG, Hohle Gasse, Reine Astrid, ★★ Dietschiberg, Küssnacht, ★★★ RIGI-KULM, Lake Zug, Emmenbrücke, ★★ Merlischachen, Reuss, 1797, Arth, Goldau, Lake Lauerz, ★★★ LUCERNE, Richard Wagner Museum, Lake Küssnach, ★★ Weggis, 1662 Rigi-Scheidegg, SCHWYZ, Kriens, ★★★ LAKE OF THE, Vitznau, Brunnen ★★, PILATE ★★★, ★ Bürgenstock, Hergiswil, 1128, ★ Obere Nase, Gersau ★, Treib, 2129, Stansstad, FOUR CANTONS, Seelisberg, Axenstrasse, Buochs, Beckenried, Rütli, Lake Alpnach, Stans, Lake Uri, Alpnachstad, 1898, ★ Bauen, 2117 Oberbauenstock, Tell, Sarnen, Stanserhorn ★★, Klewenalp, Swiss Path, Flüelen, ENGELBERG, ST. GOTHARD PASS, Altdorf, N, 4 km, 2 mile

ous peasants, Brother Nicholas (Bruder Klaus), as his fellow citizens called him, led a contemplative life. After decades of family and civic duties, at the age of 50, this father of 10 children separated from his family to live the life of an ascetic in Ranft. Meanwhile the confederates of the cantons (ⓒ see INTRODUCTION: History) faced serious internal difficulties. In 1477 the population around Lake Lucerne became agitated when they learned that Lucerne, in agreement with Zürich and Bern, had concluded a separate alliance with Fribourg and Solothurn. When Lucerne maintained the pact, in spite of the entreaties of its neighbours Uri, Schwyz, and Unterwalden, the conflict became acute. In despair the parish priest of Stans went to Ranft to consult Brother Nicholas. He returned with an admirable appeal for peace. A compromise was reached in 1481.

SIGHTS
THE SOUTH SHORE OF THE LAKE
The road round the south shore is far less picturesque than that of the north.

It is advised to travel these shores both by sea and land and take funiculars or lifts that provide access to breathtaking views.

Bürgenstock★★
Ascend the Bürgenstock by car from Stansstad (6km/3.7mi) or by funicular from the landing stage at Kehrsiten-Bürgenstock in 7min.

The name Bürgenstock is given to a massive rock ridge and also applies to a group of hotels perched 500m/1 640ft above the central basin (Chrüztrichter) of the lake. A favourite walk here is along the **Felsenweg**★★ (about 30min), a cliff road that completes a panoramic circuit around the Hammetschwand lookout. The summit (1 128m/3 701ft) can be reached by a lift up the mountainside which is the highest outdoor elevator in Europe (153m/501 ft).

A high-end hotel, spa and sports resort is set to be developed at Bürgenstock.

Stans
Bahnhofplatz 4. ℘(0)41 610 88 33.
Stans, the capital of canton Nidwalden, is an agreeable town, whose main sell-

Rütli field above the Lake Lucerne

© Christof Sonderegger/Switzerland Tourism

Sailing on the Lake

Before becoming solely the domain of tourist ferries, sailing on the lake used to be the only way to transport goods and passengers around the region and to the all-important St Gotthard Pass. From the 13C until the arrival of railways, boats used to roam on this vast expanse of water with the first steamboat brought into service in 1837.

Now, only five renovated vessels, including a paddle steamer and a steamboat, sail regularly. The **Lake Lucerne Navigation Company** (SGV) has the largest fleet of historic boats in the world. The steamship **Schiller** (1906) is considered the most elegant, boasting a Jugendstil (German Art Nouveau) first-class lounge with geometric inlays of mother of pearl and ebony decorated with panels of mermaids. The fleet connects Lucerne's famous resorts on the lake all year and offers cruises with commentary on historical sites (TellKapelle, Schillerstein), cruises at sunset, night cruises offering music and dance in the summer, gastronomic cruises (brunch or lunch) and connections or combinations with all funiculars and cable-cars in the area (Bürgenstock, Klewenalp, Seelisberg, Vitznau, Alpnachstadt). Some coastal sites—primarily the historic field of **Rütli**—are also only practically accessible via the lake.

From Lucerne, a complete circumnavigation of all lake branches requires about six hours. In season, boats from Lucerne to Flüelen via Brunnen and from Lucerne to Alpnachstadt leave approximately every hour. It is also possible to reach Locarno or Lugano in Ticino by combining a lake crossing on a steamer and a train ride aboard first-class panorama cars on the Gotthard line. This link, called **William Tell Express**, operates daily from May to October, in a north-south direction.

www.lakelucerne.ch. www.wilhelmtellexpress.ch.

Paddle wheel steamer "Schiller" on the Lake Lucerne

© SGV Luzern/Switzerland Tourism

ing point is its excursions, in particular the funicular/cable-car to the magnificent Stanserhorn belvedere. It is also a convenient place for a stopover when the hotels in the Lucerne district are full.

Pfarrkirche St Peter und Paul
The large Romanesque church **belfry**★, with four tiers of arcades, towers above the main square. The spire was added in the 16C. The spacious interior, in early Baroque style, is impressive: Statues adorning the nave stand out in dazzling white, whereas the chancel and aisles feature altarpieces carved in the local black marble. Below the church note the monument commemorating the sacrifice of Arnold von Winkelried at the Battle of Sempach.

Museum für Geschichte
◷*Open Apr–Oct, Mon-Sat, 2pm–5pm, Sun, 10am–noon, 2pm–5pm; Nov–Mar, Wed and Sat, 2pm–5pm, Sun, 10am–noon, 2pm–5pm .*⊜*5CHF.* ℘*(0)41 618 73 40.*
This small Museum of Local History situated in the heart of the town features a charming little chapel embellished with a 1604 altarpiece. One of the rooms evokes the Day of Horror—9 September 1798—when the French assault on the local mountain people caused bloodshed (⊙*audio-visual presentation in German only).*

Stanserhorn★★
Alt. 1 898m/6 227ft.
A pleasant ride in a funicular and cable-car (◷*operates Apr–Nov; departure every 30min (every 10min at busy periods) 8.15am–5.15pm;* ⊜*fare there and back 68CHF;* ℘*(0)41 618 80 40; www. stanserhorn.ch)* takes you to the upper station (the huge serrated wheels of the winch which hoisted the old funicular can be seen) from where a portion of the view *(viewing table)* seen from the top is offered.
Walk to the summit *(20min there and back)* from where there is a splendid **panorama**★★ of Lake Lucerne to the north, the peaks of the Swiss Alps to the south (Titlis Glacier) and to the south-

---

Switzerland's Largest Lakes
- ◆ Lake Geneva: 580sq km/224sq mi
- ◆ Lake Lucerne: 114sq km/44sq mi
- ◆ Lake Constance: 540sq km/208sq mi
- ◆ Lake Zürich: 88sq km/34 sq mi
- ◆ Lake Neuchâtel: 217sq km/84sq mi
- ◆ Lake Lugano: 48sq km/18.5 sq mi
- ◆ Lake Maggiore: 212sq km/ 82sq mi
- ◆ Lake Thun: 48sq km/18.5 sq mi

---

west, the summits of the Bernese Alps, including the Jungfrau Massif.
Enjoy a hot chocolate or fondue while taking in the views of ten lakes at the new revolving restaurant Rondorama.

Klewenalp
Reached via cable-car starting from Beckenried. Accessible by boat.
◷*May–Nov.* ⊜ *35CHF.* ℘*(0)41 227 17 17 25. www.klewenalp.ch.*
At 1 593m/5 226ft, Klewenalp offers a useful starting point for hiking and downhill mountain biking. There are also nice beaches lawn Beckenried, especially Freibad *(free)* with cabins, bar and swimming pool for children.

Seelisberg★
Alt. 845m/2 772ft. Bahnhof, 6377. ℘*(0)41 820 15 63. www.seelisberg.com. You can reach Seelisberg by car from Stans (22km/13.5mi; go under the motorway to Buochs on the south bank of the lake, continue along the shore via Niederdorf to the valley of Beckenried, then St Anna and Emmetten) or by funicular, from the Treib landing stage (services connecting with the steamers on Lake Lucerne; duration of the climb: 8min.* ◷*Operates all year round, times vary according to the season.* ⊜*17.20CHF return.* ℘*(0)41 820 15 63.*
Seelisberg stands on a wooded spur dipping into Lake Lucerne within view of the Bay of Brunnen and the Schwyz Basin. It is overlooked by the twin peaks of the Mythen. As one of the exclusive summer resorts in central Switzerland, this luxurious retreat is characterised by

its isolation, the majesty of its panorama and the quality of its tourist amenities. Visitors may indulge in fondue while on the last funicular ride of the day; the cars slow down and accordion music accompanies the ride.

The trip includes coffee and dessert at the Hotel Treib (summit) before descending at dusk, overlooking the valley lights. From the public belvedere-promenade there is a **view**★★ of the Fronalpstock and Lake Uri.

🚗 DRIVING TOURS

NORTH SHORE★★★

Lucerne to Altdorf. 54km/33.5mi. Approx 2hr30min.

Lucerne★★★ – ◐*See LUCERNE.*
Between Lucerne, Küssnacht and Weggis, the road skirts Lake Lucerne and Lake Küssnacht as it approaches the slopes of the Rigi. To the south, the foothills of the Nidwalden (Stans-Engelberg district) succeed one another.

Hohle Gasse
From Küssnacht, 3km/1.8mi there and back by the road to Arth (number 2), plus 15min on foot there and back.
Leaving your car at the Hohle Gasse Hotel, take the roughly paved Sunken Road (Hohle Gasse) uphill, where according to tradition William Tell lay in wait for Gessler. The road through the woods ends at the commemorative chapel.

Weggis★★
Weggis is a grand resort situated on the shores of Lake Lucerne within view of the Pilatus and Unterwalden mountains along a promenade quay which leads to the Hertenstein Promontory.

Vitznau★
Passing tourists may leave their cars for a few hours in this elegant resort, enclosed between the Rigi and the lake, to climb the Rigi-Kulm by rack railway. This was the first mountain railway built in Europe (1871).

Rigi-Kulm★★★
Tourist Information Rigi, Casa Margherita, Kaltbad. www.wvrt.ch.
Isolated on all sides by a depression largely covered by the waters of the Lucerne, Zug, and Lauerz lakes, this "island mountain," to quote the term used by German geographers, raises its heavy wooded shoulders, scarred by reddish escarpments, to an altitude of 1797m/5 896ft. It has been famous for a century for its highest point, the Rigi-Kulm, on the summit of which, traditionally, you should spend the night to see the sun rise over the Alps. Two of the first tourists were Queen Victoria (carried to the summit on a sedan chair) and Mark Twain who made it famous in his book *A Tramp Abroad*. Those who like easy walks through woods and Alpine pastures, or along mountain roads, which always offer interesting views, should stay in one of the hotels scattered high on the mountainside. One of the best-situated resorts is **Rigi-Kaltbad**.

For over 150 years the sunrise seen from the **Rigi-Kulm** has been the climax of a visit to Switzerland. "The splendor of the spectacle drove away memories of the harsh preliminaries, and the shivering, sleepy crowd reached a state of collective exaltation when the first rays of the sun lit up", according to Victor Hugo. However, the sun is often obscured by clouds, as Mark Twain famously found to his annoyance.

Vitznau-Rigi railway
From Arth-Goldau or Vitznau the climb by rack railway to the Rigi-Kulm takes 35min. Another way is to take the cable-car from Weggis to Rigi-Kaltbad and change there to the rack railway for the Rigi-Kulm. From Arth-Goldau, Vitznau or Weggis: ⊶Fare there and back 64CHF. For exact timetables, call ✆(0)41 399 87 42 (Vitznau Station), ✆(0)41 859 08 59 (Goldau Station) or ✆(0)41 390 18 44 (Weggis Station) or check www.rigi.ch.
A set of cog railways climbs to the top of Mount Rigi. Since the middle of the 19C steam trains have brought visitors to the top of Mount Rigi. Modern equipment has replaced the antique on most

Sunset on Rigi-Kulm with view of Mount Pilatus

© Max Schmid/Switzerland Tourism

runs, but from time to time fully restored antique engines and cars still bring visitors on the same breathtaking trip.
Cog railroads run from Vitznau and from Arth-Goldau up to the Rigi Kulm all year round. The railroad company also runs a modern cable-car from Weggis. The Rigi-Kaltbad lift rises some 274m/900ft and a 91.4m/300ft path at the top connects to the cog train station at Kaltbad. The top is famed for its views and for hiking and other outdoor activities, including winter sports.

Panorama★★★
Alt. 1 797m/5 896ft.
From the terminus station, near to a large hotel, 15min on foot there and back to the signpost and the cross at the summit.

Your eye may wander from end to end of the Alps' tremendous backcloth rising between Säntis and the Bernese Alps (Jungfrau), including the Glarus and Uri Alps and the Titlis Massif. The opposite half of the horizon is less dazzling, but is more attractive.
On this side the rounded hills of the Zürich countryside stretch into the distance, beyond the Lauerzer, Zug, and Lucerne lakes, to merge with the line of the Jura, the Vosges, and the Black Forest.

⚐ Walk from Rigi-Kaltbad to Hinterbergen★★★
A wonderful walk (*2hr–2hr30min*), easy to negotiate and clearly signposted, the perfect complement to a climb up Rigi. Get off the train at Kaltbad station (alt. 1 438m/4 718ft). Follow the path to First, flanked by explanatory panels about the geology of the area. The **view**★★ widens out over Lake Lucerne. The route continues toward Unterstetten, wending its way through spectacularly sheer cliffs. When you catch sight of the hotel, bear left and go up the lawn for 200m/220yds, then turn right in the direction of Gletti (a steep, short climb followed by a descent). From Gletti there is a sweeping **panorama**★★★ of the whole region. To end the tour, go down to Hinterbergen, either by the direct, steep route on the right, or by the gently sloping path on the left. At the heart of the village, look out for the white house with six small windows: It is the terminus of a cable-car that will take you back to Vitznau in 6min.

Horse-Drawn Carriage Rides
Contact the Tourist Office for reservations. 30min, 2hr and 4hr rides are available at Rigi-Kaltbad via three scenic routes.

▷ *From Vitznau, follow the lakeshore road towards Brunnen.*

Obere Nase★

The very pronounced bend in the road as it passes this cape is arranged as a **belvedere**★. This "Nose", thrown out by a spur of the Rigi, and the Untere Nase, an extreme outcrop of the Bürgenstock facing it, encloses a channel only 825m/2 707ft wide connecting two very different basins. Within a short distance you pass from Lake Vitznau, bounded on the south by the Bürgenstock, to Lake Gersau-Beckenried.

Gersau★

Lying in an open **site**★★ on the Alpine shores of the lake, this small municipality used to be the Independent Republic of Gersau in permanent alliance with the Swiss Confederation, but is now attached to canton Schwyz. You will now begin to skirt the Bay of Brunnen, followed by the Seelisberg.

Brunnen★★

Alt. 439m/1 440ft. Bahnhofstrasse 15.
℘(0)41 825 00 40.
www.brunnentourismus.ch.

Brunnen is one of the major resorts of Lake Lucerne; **Hans Christian Andersen**, the author of fairy tales, visited often on holiday. Until the opening of Axenstrasse, Brunnen was a key port for traffic between the Schwyz and Uri cantons and a major transit point on the St Gotthard route. It is busy today because tourists on the great transalpine road through Arth and those on the coastal route through Vitznau meet here. Brunnen deserves a stop for its **site**★★ at the head of the wild Lake Uri (Urnersee), in the heart of picturesque Switzerland. It was here after the victory at Morgarten in 1315, that the three cantons of Uri, Schwyz and Unterwalden renewed their pact of mutual assistance (🕮 *see INTRODUCTION: History*).

Quays★★

From the shaded quay, the extension of the Axenquai Promenade eastwards below Axenstrasse, there is a sweeping **panorama**★★ of Lake Uri, lying like a fjord between wild mountain spurs. The dominant feature is the Uri-Rotstock, whose bare twin peaks rise above a small glacier.

In the foreground, on the opposite shore, the tender green of the historic field of **Rütli** shows up against the wooded slopes of the Seelisburg spur. At the extreme point of this promontory you can see the natural obelisk known as the **Schillerstein** with an 1859 inscription by the first 3 cantons in memory of Friedrich von Schiller, whose epic "Wilhelm Tell" distilled Swiss nationalist sentiment. (🛥*A short trip in a motor boat will give a closer view.*)

From Brunnen to Flüelen the Axenstrasse corniche overhangs the romantic **Lake Uri** (Urnersee), with its deep blue waters. Its shores are marked by places of patriotic pilgrimage recalling the birth of the Confederation (Rütli, Tellskapelle).

> ◗ *This section of road, which is one of the best-known on the St Gotthard route, is also one of the busiest in the country.*

Tellskapelle

From the Hotel Tellsplatte, 30min on foot there and back by a steep path.

On the shore of **Lake Uri**★, this chapel commemorates an episode in the story of William Tell. As Gessler's prisoner after the ordeal of the apple, Tell was thrown into a boat which was assailed by a sudden storm; the bailiff and his minions had to appeal for their captive's help. He took advantage of this to steer the boat toward the shore, leapt out and kicked the boat back into the raging waves.

> ◗ *Continuing on the Axenstrasse we reach Flüelen and Altdorf (7km/4.3mi).*

FROM ALTDORF TO LINDTHAL

48km/30mi. Approx 2hrs.
🚗The Klausen road is closed to vehicles with a trailer. The Klausen Pass is usually blocked by snow Nov–May.

Altdorf

Alt. 462m/1 516ft.
Tellspielhaus Schützengasse 11.
℘(0)41 872 04 50. www.altdorf.ch.

The Escape from Gessler's Boat—*mural by Ernst Stueckelberg, Tellskapelle*

© Lucia Degonda/Switzerland Tourism

Altdorf stands between Lake Lucerne and the defile of the Upper Reuss Valley. The key to the St Gotthard Pass on the north side of the Alps, Altdorf preserves all the dignity of a small, old-fashioned capital town. Travellers will also notice the southern influences already apparent on restaurant menus, the presence of Ticino characteristics in the people, and traces of the **binario** *(road with granite paving stones)*, which will prepare them for a greater change of scene. It is no exaggeration to say that tourism today revolves rather obsessively about the William Tell myth and that most visitors are, indeed, Swiss.

Telldenkmal

The statue in honour of **William Tell**, the famous archer of Uri, stands in the main square of the town. The work dates from 1895 and is interesting chiefly for the fact that it created Tell's physical type, since made familiar all over the world by a postage stamp bearing his effigy. The statue of this national hero is appropriately erected in this canton, which was the first to throw off foreign control. There is a small **Tell-Museum** (○*open daily late May–mid-Oct, 10am–11.30am, 1.30pm–5pm; 10am–5pm Jul–Aug;* ○*5CHF;* ℘*(0)41 870 41 55; www.tellmuseum.ch*) at Bürglen on the Klausen Pass road (○*see KLAUSEN PASS*).

▷ *It is only a short distance from Altdorf to the next stopping-place.*

Bürglen

Bürglen is said to be the birthplace of **William Tell** and the village now has a **Tell Museum**. The exhibits include a host of documents, chronicles, sculptures, paintings, and other items relating to Switzerland's legendary hero over the past 600 years.

Between Bürglen and Unterschächen, the road, lined by chapels, runs at first along the verdant valley through which flows the river Schächen. This widens upstream and is then covered with birch, maple and fruit trees, but the south slope quickly becomes barren and gives a foretaste of harsher sections.

From Unterschächen to the pass, two big hairpin bends facing the mouth of the Brunnital, a tributary valley ending in a cirque at the foot of the Ruchen and the Windgällen precipices, lead to Urigen, the starting-point of a magnificent **corniche section**★★. From then on there is a bird's-eye view of the wild cul-de-sac of the Upper Schächental, enclosed by the gigantic **Chammliberg Cliffs.** The bend marked by a single rock on the side of the escarpment (600m/656yds above the first tunnel) forms a **viewpoint**★ overlooking the **Stäubi Waterfall** (Stäubifall) and the hamlet of **Aesch**,

343

400m/1 312ft below. The great snow-laden corniches of the Clariden can be seen behind the Chammliberg Cliffs.

Klausen Pass★
Alt. 1 948m/6 391ft.

The Klausen Pass road combines nearly all the physical and economic features of mountainous Switzerland. Within less than 50km/31mi the traveller passes from a high, wild primitive Alpine combe (Urner Boden) to one of the most industrial valleys in the range (Linth Valley). Motorists usually stop below the summit on the Schächental slope, at the Klausenpasshöhe Hotel.

From a spot near the hotel you can see the snowy crests of the Clariden, the Chammliberg Cliffs, the double Schärhorn peak, the rocky points of the Windgälen, and finally, in line with the Schächen Gap, the Uri-Rotstock Massif on the horizon. After passing the huts of Vorfrütt, where herdsmen shelter in the summer, you will be able to admire the north face of the Clariden and the Chlus, a corrie streaked by two cascades.

Urner Boden★
The run along the bottom of this very regular cleft offers motorists a long, level stretch, unexpected at this altitude (1 300–1 400m /4 250–4 600ft).

The belfry of the church in the main hamlet, standing in the middle of the hollow, behind fir trees, is an attractive feature of the run down from the Klausen Pass. There are hairpin bends as far as Linthal. The Linth Valley opens out below, abutting the walls of the Selbsanft (Tödi Massif) upstream.

SCHÖLLENENSTRASSE (Schöllenen Road)

From Altdorf to Andermatt. 56km/35mi – approx 1hr30min. Between Altdorf and Göschenen, the E 35 motorway runs parallel to road number 2 we recommend.

The itinerary, starting in the Lake Lucerne district and following the Reuss Valley, penetrates into the heart of the **St Gotthard Massif**. Its most unusual site, the Schöllenen Defile, lies at the end of the itinerary.

Altdorf (*see above*)
From Altdorf to Amsteg, as the valley narrows, the majestic conical Bristen Peak, rising steeply to 3 072m/10 079ft, catches the eye. The populous centre of **Erstfeld** marks the point where the line begins to climb the ramp to the north entrance of the **St Gotthard Tunnel**, 600m/1 968ft higher up.

Between Amsteg and Wassen, the floor of the **Reuss Valley**, where the mountain section of the road begins, contains pretty shaded nooks. Bends in the road—especially before reaching Wassen, whose church can be seen directly after leaving Gurtnellen—give glimpses of the shapely pyramid of the **Kleine Windgällen** lying below.

Pfaffensprung
From the car park, downstream from the bridge over the Reuss, cross the road to a belvedere overlooking the **Parson's Leap**. The overflow of the dam built nearby forms a spectacular cascade, with beautiful iridescent effects.

Wassen
Wassen became well-known when the builders of the St Gotthard railway

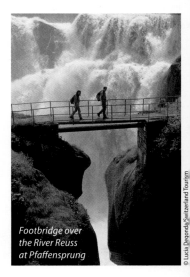

Footbridge over the River Reuss at Pfaffensprung

© Lucia Degonda/Switzerland Tourism

Suvorov's Retreat

During the Napoleonic Wars Switzerland became a battlefield between the French, Austrian and Russian Forces. In March 1799 **General Masséna** prepared an invasion of the Tyrol but he was repulsed and decamped in Zürich. He was further beaten in June by Austrian troops under the **Duke of Teschen** who subsequently left for the Netherlands and entrusted his position to a contingent of Russian troops under **General Korsakov**. He in turn, expected a large expeditionary force under **General Alexander Suvorov** from the south. Masséna sent sentries to harass Suvorov's force, while he attacked Korsakov whom he eventually routed. Suvorov had to make a strategic retreat through the snowy Alps in October and, although he lost many men, he regrouped in Austria undefeated. His crossing of the Alps through Airolo-Andermatt-Altdorf and retreat via the Muothatal, the Pragel pass to Glarus, the Panixer pass to Chur and eventually to Feldkirch and the Vorarlberg has been compared as second only to Hannibal's.

made two successive loops in the track, partly underground, on either side of the village. Uninitiated visitors struggling to keep their sense of direction after seeing three successive views of Wassen church from different angles are a constant source of amusement to regular travellers.

From Wassen to Göschenen the bottom of the corridor is partly obstructed by landslides; among them is an enormous single rock called the **Devil's Stone** (**Teufelsstein**). Impressive road construction has been achieved on this section.

Göschenen

Göschenen is best known for its railway station at the north end of the St Gotthard Tunnel (15km/9.3mi long, opened in 1882). It is a useful halt for tourists, who will find it pleasant to stand near the small central bridge and admire the ice field of the Upper Dammastock, which can be seen through the Göschenertal Gap.

Göscheneralpsee★★

The road that leads to this reservoir-lake offers close-up views of the **Dammastock Glaciers** (on the east side of the Rhône Glacier) which feed it. The road climbs the wild, narrow Göschenen Valley, with winding sections along the side of superb rock faces.

Leave the car in the car park near the restaurant (alt. 1 783m/5 850ft) and go to the centre of the dam's grassy crest. This gravity dam (capacity 9.3 million cum/204 600 million gal; 700m/2 297ft thick at base; 155m/508ft high; 540m/1 772ft length of crest) dams the reservoir-lake.

Ahead is a magnificent **landscape**★★ that includes the dam, cascades right and left and, separated by a rocky cone, gleaming glaciers below the Winterberg peak.

Schöllenen★★

Andermatt Gotthard Tourismus, Gotthardstrasse 2. ℘(0)41 887 14 54. www.andermatt.ch.

The remarkably smooth and polished granite walls of the Reus Valley form a bottleneck between Göschenen and Andermatt. This is the legendary **Schöllenen gorge**, which was the chief obstacle to the development of traffic on the St Gotthard route until about the 13C, when a road was boldly driven through it. The modern roads may be a bit of an anti-climax, so visitors are advised to walk the old road.

Teufelsbrücke

The bridge is 3km/1.8mi N of Andermatt.
In 1830, this bridge replaced one built, according to legend, at the instigation and the co-operation of the Devil. There

was one condition: the villagers had to pay for it with the soul of the first one to cross it—but the the wily people of Uri sent across a billy goat. Since motor traffic is no longer permitted, the bridge is an ideal viewing spot to admire the foaming **Reuss Falls** (*best seen in sunlight around noon*). Slightly downstream, take note of a cross hewn in the rocky wall of the east bank and an inscription in Cyrillic characters. It commemorates the hazardous venture of Russian **General Suvorov** (*see info box p345*).

Andermatt – *See ALTO TICINO.*
Andermatt is known worldwide for its grand pistes and challenging downhill ski slopes, but summer in the area has just as many outdoor adventures on offer.

There are several choices of **Mountain Bike** tours with incredible views along the way, from easy ones such as the 20km/12mi circuit Andermatt—Hospental—Zumdorf—Realp—Andermatt (1hr30min, 100m/0.6mi altitude difference) to the very difficult 31km/19mi Andermatt—Oberalp—Maighelspass—Andermatt (4hr, 1 200 m/3 937ft altitude difference). There is a famous **Mountain Climbing** route the **Via Ferrata Diavolo** (450m/1 476ft altitude difference) starting from the Suvorov monument and ending at **Tüfelstalboden**. For more info, *(0)41 888 83 21.*

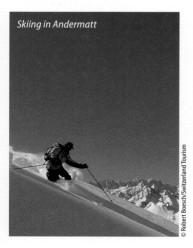

Skiing in Andermatt

© Robert Boesch/Switzerland Tourism

Rafting on the pristine glacial torrents is an experience unlike any other (*(0)43 888 53 00; www.rafters.ch*), or you can find a spot for **fishing** in these green-blue pools with an experienced guide (*Fischerpatente Oberalpsee; *081 949 12 13, or Fischerpatente übriges, Altdorf, *(0)41 875 20 17*). Avid **golfers** will not want to miss a round at Golfplatz Realp in Urserntal (*(0)41 887 01 62; www.golfgotthard.ch*).

Gemsstock★★ –
See ALTO TICINO.

ADDRESSES

STAY

RIGI-KULM

Bergsonne – *(0)41 399 80 10. www.bergsonne.ch. Restaurant .17 rooms.* Its ideal location above the village provides breathtaking views of the Alps and the nearby lake. Rooms are decorated with local furniture.

Edelweiss – *(0)41 399 88 00. www.edelweiss-rigi.ch. 27 rooms.* A blissfully quiet establishment with views of lake and mountains. The older part features rooms appointed with rustic-style furniture.

BRUNNEN

Weisses Rössli – *Bahnhofstrasse 8. *(0)41 820 11 22. www.weisses-roessli-brunnen.ch. 17 rooms.* Frescoes evoke the memory of Ludwig II of Bavaria, who once stayed at the hotel. The first-floor salon is decorated in blue and white, the official colours of Bavaria, and, naturally, the most prestigious room is the one which was occupied by the sovereign.

Schmid und Alfa – *On the lakeshore. *(0)41 820 18 82; www.schmidalfa.ch. 30 rooms. Closed Tue and Wed from 1 Mar to Easter.* The best rooms overlook the lake, from where, on a fine day, you can make out the Rütli and the memorial to Schiller on the opposite shore. Excellent service at this modern, comfortable hotel will make your stay even more special.

Engelberg ✱✱

Engelberg stands on a site which, although surrounded by heights, is nonetheless sunny. It is the great mountain resort of central Switzerland famous for both tourist and religious activities. A swimming pool, tea rooms, tennis courts, and a skating rink are found alongside one of the large, imposing Benedictine abbeys which lie concealed in the high valleys of Switzerland. Recently, it has become a resort of much renown in India, because it features regularly in Bollywood films whenever snowy peaks are required in the frame.

The mountaineer can choose between the glacier formation of the Titlis and the jagged crests of the Spannörter and Uri Rotstock, whereas the walker, using the high-tec ski lifts can easily reach attractive sites such as those of Trübsee and the Titlis.

SIGHTS
Benedictine Monastery

Guided tour of monastery (1hr) Wed–Sat, 10am, 4pm; monastery and exhibition hall (1hr30min) Sat at 4pm. Closed Nov & May. 8CHF (monastery), 10CHF (monastery and exhibition hall). (0)41 639 61 19. www.kloster-engelberg.ch.

▶ **Population:** 3 721.

Info: Klosterstrasse 3 – 6390. (0)41 639 77 77. www.engelberg.ch.

Location: Located in the very centre of Switzerland, home to Mt Titlis. Alt. 1 002m/3 287ft.

Don't Miss: Excursion to Titlis with the Rotair cable-car, and exploration of its glacial caves or the Engelberg-Titlis ski resort.

The monastery, founded in the 12C, ruled over the whole valley until the French invasion of 1798. Today most of the buildings are used as a religious college. One of the rooms displays an unusual collection of liturgical objects from the 11C to the 20C. The Baroque **parish church** features the arrangement and decoration characteristic of French Regency style (mid-18C) and was fully restored in 2005–2009. The organ is the largest in Switzerland.

EXCURSIONS
Titlis★★★

Alt. 3 239m/10 627ft. Allow 3hr there and back, preferably during the day, when you can combine the climb with a long walk. Remember to wear warm clothes, sturdy mountain shoes

Cable car to Titlis

© Christian Perret/Engelberg-Titlis Tourismus/Switzerland Tourism

and a pair of sunglasses. ○Operates 8.50am–5pm. ⊜Fare there and back 34CHF winter/65CHF summer. ℘(0)41 639 50 50. www.titlis.ch.

⚑A cable-car, the "Rotair", fitted with rotating cabins, operates on the upper section between Strand and Titlis. The journey takes 5min. The rotation of the cabins gives passengers a spectacular panoramic view; there is a restaurant at the top.

The cable-car service to **Trübsee**, split up into two journeys, commands a full **view**★ of Engelberg and its green pastures. Then take the cable-car to Stand (2 450m/8 038ft).

The splendid **views**★★ of **Trübsee** and the **Titlis Glacier** can be seen from above thanks to the **Rotair** cable-car (**views**★★ of Lake Engtsien). From the terrace (alt. 3 020m/9 909ft) enjoy the breathtaking **panorama**★★★ of Sustenhorn dominating a rough mountain range, the steep rocks of Wendenstöcke and Reissand Nollend and, farther west, the Valais Alps (Dom) and the Bernese Oberland (Jungfrau). A number of curious sights will delight visitors: An ice grotto and a panoramic window hollowed out of the south slope, 45m/145ft beneath the ice.

You are advised to climb up to the viewpoint and its viewing table (10min). A ski lift for children leads to a sledge piste. Experienced hikers who want a broader **bird's-eye view**★★★ should proceed to the summit (40min), taking care to observe the safety rules. From Stand, there is a panoramic route that takes you back down to Trübsee (1hr15min), offering lovely **views**★★ of the valley, interspersed with explanatory panels about the geology of the area.

Trübsee★★

Alt. 1 764m/5 786ft. ⚑Access in 5min after the second journey in cable-car.
Lying at the foot of the Titlis Glacier framed by rocky summits, this is one of Europe's most beautiful mountain lakes. Go on a **tour of the lake**★★, proceeding towards the right (allow 1hr10min) and appreciate the pretty path enhanced by clumps of spruce and rhododendron.

Fürenalp★★

Alt. 1 850m/6 069ft. ⚑Access by cable-car. 3.5km/2.2mi E of Engelberg.
The route leading to this rocky outcrop perched up high affords spectacular **views**★★ of the whole glacial cirque lining the valley, with its waterfalls, peaks and glaciers.

Walk to Stäfeli★★

1hr45min on foot and 5min by cable-car.
From Fürenalp, bear right onto a gently sloping path bordered by yellow gentian and herds of cows. Continue to walk straight on until you catch sight of Abnet village: Proceed towards it bearing right. For a hair-raising experience, jump into the small cable-car that will take you to Stäfeli, dropping by 300m/985ft amid sheer cliffs. You will eventually get back to your point of departure by a smooth path flanked by steep slopes, in an austere but lush green landscape cut across by a stream.

Brunnihütte★

Alt. 1 860m/6 102ft. www.brunnihuette.ch. ⚑Access by cable-car, then by chairlift. Allow 1hr there and back. ℘(0)41 637 37 32. www.brunnihutte.ch.
You will enjoy a **view**★ of the whole valley, particularly impressive at sunset. Accommodation and meals available.

Walk to Rugghubelhütte★★

Alt. 2 294m/7 526ft. www.rugghubel.ch.
Make your way down the right-hand path following the mountain slope, bordered with luxuriant alpine flora (30min). Proceed straight until the refuge (1hr15min). The early part of the climb offers fantastic **views**★★ of the Titlis, Grosser Spannort and the massive Hahnen barrier.

On reaching the top, enjoy views of Gemsispil, Reissend Nollen and the Bernese Alps in the distance. Continue for 100m/100yds beyond the refuge for a **sweeping panorama**★★ including the Griessenfirn Glacier and Wissigstock. Return the same way, then go towards Ristis (2hr altogether) by a good path in a charming bucolic **setting**★★. Finish the outing by cable-car.

Zug★★

This charming little town is built at the northeast end of **Zugersee** (Lake Zug)★★, a charming lake nestling among gardens and orchards at the foot of the first wooded foothills of the Zugerberg. Excavations reveal that the site of Zug has been inhabited by man without interruption since the Neolithic Era. In the Middle Ages it belonged successively to the Lenzburg, Kyburg, and Habsburg families before joining the Confederation in 1352. Its 13C castle has now been entirely restored.

▶ **Population:** 25 778.
▮ **Info:** Bahnhofplatz, ℘(0)41 723 68 00. www.zug-tourismus.ch.
◑ **Location:** Central Switzerland, just south of Zürich. Alt. 425m/1 394ft.
◉ **Don't Miss:** Zugersee, or guided tours of the old town.
◷ **Timing:** Allow a minimum of one day to see the principal sights.

GEOGRAPHY
Zugersee★★
The Zugersee, with a total area of 38sq km/15sq mi and a depth of almost 200m/656ft, is Switzerland's tenth largest lake. It runs in a north-south direction for 14km/9mi and is almost divided in two by a verdant peninsula. The lake, in an attractive hilly setting, is dominated by the Rigi-Kulm in the south and is very popular with visitors for its scenic beauty and many amenities.

SIGHTS
The Quays★
From Seestrasse to Alpenquai, a promenade beside the lake offers **views**★ of the summits of central Switzerland (Rigi, Pilatus, Bürgenstock, Stanserhorn) and, in the background, of the Bernese Alps (Finsteraarhorn, Jungfrau, Blümlisalp).

Old Town★
❧Guided tours of the town (1hr30min) daily by reservation. ⊜140CHF for groups of up to 25. Contact the Tourist Office.
℘(0)41 723 68 00.
Ruined fortifications—Powder Tower (Pulverturm), the Capuchin's Tower (Kapuzinerturm)—still mark the original nucleus of the town. The quarters known as Unter-Altstadt (Lower Old Town) and Ober-Altstadt (Upper Old Town), with their old step-gabled houses, strike a delightfully medieval note.

The **Fischmarkt** (Fish Market) has houses with painted weatherboards and overhanging balconies. The Clock Tower, **Zytturm**, features a tiled roof painted in the Zug colours (blue and white) and is crowned by a slim belfry. Under the clock face are the coats of arms of the first eight cantons of the Confederation, Zug having been the seventh canton to join the alliance.

Kolinplatz is surrounded by old houses, among them the Town House (Stadthaus), a 16C building adorned with a fine flower-decked fountain. This fountain bears the statue of the standard bearer **Wolfgang Kolin**, a local hero who performed brave feats to save his banner at the **Battle of Arbedo** (1422), when the Swiss Confederate forces, who were defending **Bellinzona**, were defeated by the Duke of Milan's army. Kolin's son, to whom the banner had been passed, was also killed.

St Oswald
◷Open 8am–6pm (5pm in winter).
❧For information on guided tours, call ℘(0)41 711 00 78.
This Late Gothic church (1478–1515) is dedicated to St Oswald of Northumbria. The interior, with ogive vaulting, is darkened by its massive pillars. The nave is separated from the chancel by a partition adorned with frescoes. The interior includes many statues of saints, painted and gilded wooden triptychs in the side chapels, and frescoes on the vaulting.

EXCURSIONS
Zugerberg★

Alt. 988m/3 241ft. ◯ *The easiest way to get to Zugerberg is to take bus number 11 leaving from Zug railway station (Bahnhof Metelli stop), then go to Schöneg and take the funicular.*

Operates all year. Departures every 30min Mon–Sun. *Fare there and back 10CHF.* *(0)41 728 58 30. www.zbb.ch.*
From the summit there is a almost circular **view**★ to the northwest, of Zug and the lake, to the southwest of the Pilatus, to the south of the Uri-Rotstock and the Uri Alps, and to the east—through a gap in the fir trees—of the village of Unter-Ägeri and its lake. To the north the hills of the Mittelland can be seen rising one behind the other toward Zürich.

Cistercian Abbey Church★
◯ *8km/5mi N by the road to Zürich.*
The imposing silhouette of the former Cistercian abbey church—buttresses, pointed roofs, and slim bell tower—can be seen in the distance with its village huddled against it. It is located not far from where Zwingli was killed. Built in 13C–14C, the abbey illustrates the Early Gothic style with pure lines and elegant lancet windows.

The vast nave is highlighted by stalls decorated with human or animal heads (note the bitch with her puppies). Note the remains of 14C frescoes decorating chancel walls (St Martin, Christ and Saints in medallions) and the **stained-glass windows**★.

Schwyz★

This quiet little town gave the Swiss Confederation both its name and its flag. It occupies a majestic **site**★ at the foot of the twin Mythen peaks, between the lakes of Lucerne and Lauerz. The resort of Stoos (alt. 1 295m/4 249ft), at the foot of the Fronalpstock moutain, is built on a sunny plateau with far-reaching views.

A BIT OF HISTORY
For the history of the original cantons, see LAKE LUCERNE: The Cradle of Swiss Democracy.

Soldiers of Fortune
When foreign princes recruited mercenaries for their service from the 16C onwards, the men of Schwyz enlisted in their armies, especially in the French regiments.

Their bravery and military qualities enabled many to return to their country, having made their fortunes, covered with honours and glory. They settled in their homeland and built the sumptuous homes that their descendants still own.

▶ **Population:** 14 183.
Info: Oberer Steisteg 14 – 6430. *(0)41 810 19 91. www.info-schwyz.ch.*
◯ **Location:** Central Switzerland, near Lake Lucerne. Alt. 517m/1 696ft.
Don't Miss: Bundesbriefmuseum, housing original Confederation documents.
Timing: The town's sights can be seen in under three hours.

SIGHTS
Forum der Schweizer Geschichte
Hofmatt/Zeughausstrasse 5. ◯*Open Tue–Sun, 10am–5pm* ◯*Closed 1 Jan, Good Fri, Easter Mon, 1 Nov and 25 Dec.* *10CHF.* *(0)41 819 60 11. www.forumschwyz.ch.*
Open to commemorate the 700th anniversary of the Swiss Confederation (1991), this thoroughly modern national museum is dedicated to the history and cultural life of Switzerland from the 14C to the 19C, including a history of the

Swiss knife. A relevant selection of over 800 items helps to understand better the Swiss people and their myths.

Bundesbriefmuseum★

🕐 *Open Tue–Fri, 9am–11.30am, 1.30pm–5pm, Sat–Sun 9am–5pm (1.30pm Nov–Apr).* 🕐 *Closed Good Fri and 25 Dec.* 👝*4CHF.* 📞*(0)41 819 20 64. www.bundesbriefmuseum.ch.*

A modern building, with a fresco by H Danioth on its façade, it was erected (1934–36) to house the most precious original documents of the Confederation. In the great hall adorned with a fresco, *The Oath* by W Clénin, and banners of the Schwyz canton are displayed. The Original Pact of 1291 (Bundesbrief), the Pact of Brunnen of 1315 (Morgartenbrief), charters of freedom and pacts of alliance concerning the "XIII Cantons" are also on show. Ask at the reception for a free brochure in English.

Hauptplatz

Rebuilt after a fire in the city in 1642 according to plans by a Venetian architect, the buildings define a beautiful Baroque square where five different roads converge. Unfortunately it has been lately turned into a roundabout and the constant traffic tends to dampen some of its charm.

Pfarrkirche St Martin

St Martin's Church (1769–74) has sumptuous 18C Baroque decorations. The nave is adorned with stucco and frescoes; the high altar, the altars in the side chapels, the marble **pulpit**★ and baptistry are all elaborately decorated. In the two transepts lie the reliquaries of St Polycarp (left) and St Lazarus (right).

Rathaus

🕐 *Open Mon–Fri, 10am–3pm.* 🕐 *Closed public holidays and when there are sittings.* 📞*(0)41 811 45 05.*

Burnt down and rebuilt in 1645, the town hall is ornamented on the two front sides with mural paintings (1891) recalling episodes in Swiss history. Inside are rooms with decorative woodwork and stained-glass windows.

EXCURSIONS

Lauerzer See

▶ *5 km/3mi from Schwyz. Take the exit direction Zürich. In Seewen, take Highway number 2 towards Lucerne.*

The lake shores, lined with reeds on the west side, form small coves for swimming or sunbathing on the eastern side. A tiny island houses a chapel and a restaurant.

Tierpark Goldau

▶ *11km/6.8mi NW of Schwyz.*

🕐 *Apr–Oct Mon–Fri 9am–6pm (Sat, Sun & holidays 7pm), Nov–Mar 9am–5pm.* 👝*18CHF (children 10CHF).* 📞*(0)41 859 06 06. www.tierpark.ch.*

Animals from temperate regions live freely in an enclosed forest created in the area where a terrible 1806 landslide buried alive 500 victims. The traces of the catastrophe are clearly visible on the flanks of Rossberg.

Muotathal valley

This valley, southeast of Schwyz, is part of a vast karst area which forks in the village of Muotathal. One branch goes towards Bisisthal and the cable-car to the Glattalp hiking area and a mountain restaurant. The other leads to the canton of Glarus via the Pragel pass and is covered by the largest primeval forest in Europe, 600 acres of spruces barely touched by man.

Höllochgrotte★

▶ *15km/9.3mi by the Muotatal road (SE of the plan) plus 1hr tour. Trekking-Team, 6652 Tegna.* 💬*Guided tours by appointment only, half-day, full-day, or two-day.* 👝*20CHF and up.* 📞*0848 808 007. www.trekkingteam.ch.* 🖐*Torches, hard hats and waterproof boots are strongly recommended.*

The Hölloch Cave is known for the size of its galleries, the number of its naturally formed chambers and the beauty of its concretions. It is the largest cave in Europe and, as a geological phenomenon, it enjoys a worldwide reputation. On the way out of Schwyz, take the Muotatal road which is narrow until Hinterthal, then cross the river and turn left into a steep uphill road going to Stalden *(signpost: Stalden-Hölloch)*. The cave must be visited with a guide. When doing this trip you can also go to **Stoos** in a funicular and then to the magnificent viewpoint of the **Fronalpstock**★ (alt. 1 922m/6 306ft).

🚗 DRIVING TOUR

Ibergeregg Road★
11km/7mi.

▶ *Leave Schwyz E via Rickenbachstrasse.*

Beginning at the hill's slope, after crossing Rickenbach, views open out on the left to the Mythen and on the right on part of Lake Lucerne and Lake Lauerz, separated by the Hochflue. After a magnificent stretch of corniche through woods above the deep Muotatal Valley and, in a bend in the road, there is a beautiful **view**★ behind this valley and the Lake Lucerne district. During the steep climb that follows, the snowy summits of the Glarus Alps can be seen. At the **Ibergeregg Pass** (alt. 1 406m/4 613ft) admire the remarkable **views**★ of the neighbouring valley. For Einsiedeln, drive down through Unteriberg to Sihlsee and then along the lakeshore road with the water on your right.

Einsiedeln★★
Alt. 881m/2 890ft. Hauptstrasse 85.
℘(0)55 418 44 88. www.einsiedeln.ch.
The small town of Einsiedeln, in a district of rugged hills and pinewoods, is the most famous and most frequented place of pilgrimage in the whole of Switzerland.
An original church was built on the site of the cell occupied by St Meinradthe hermit, killed by thieves in 861. A monastery was subsequently founded in 934 by Otto I and Duchess Reglinde of Swabia, and subsequently burnt down several times. The town's main street runs into the west side of the huge square on which the abbey church stands. The façade of the Benedictine abbey over-

looks a great semicircular courtyard, edged by arcades. in its centre stands a fountain in honour of the Virgin.
Abbey Church (Klosterkirche)★★ (🕐*open 5am–8.30pm)* The church was built (1719–35) in **Vorarlberg Baroque**, popular in regions around Lake Constance, and it is the most remarkable example of this style in Switzerland. Two tall towers flank the façade, which is slightly convex and very graceful. The length of the church, including the upper chancel, is 113m/370ft, the width of the nave 41m/131ft, and the height of the Dome of the Nativity up to the lantern 37m/118ft (Westminster Cathedral 93m/306ft x 47m/156ft x 85m/280ft). Above all, the decoration is extraordinarily ornate: The vaulting, domes and octagonal roof of the nave, the aisles and chancel are embellished with frescoes and stuccoes, largely the work of the Asam brothers from Bavaria. One was known as a painter, the other as an expert in stucco, but many other artists contributed to the construction. The altars were built and painted by the Carlone brothers from Sciara (near Como) and by Milanese artists and the chancel, built between 1674 and 1680, was remodelled later and painted by Kraus of Augsburg. The **Gnadenkapelle** built in neoclassical style at the entrance to the nave contains the statue of the **Black Madonna**, an object of special veneration for pilgrims.
🚶Arrive at 4.45pm to see the monks in procession chanting Salve Regina in front off the statue of the Black Madonna.

Grosser Saal
🕐*Open 1.30pm–6pm.* 🕐*Closed during concerts.* ⊜*3CHF.* ℘*(0)55 418 62 40.*
The Abbey Great Hall, on the second floor of the monastery buildings, is reached by skirting the church to the right. Enter the first door on the left, in the courtyard. It was built at the beginning of the 18C and is decorated with stuccowork and frescoes by Marsiglio Roncati of Lugano and Johannes Brandenberg of Zug. Exhibitions are held on a regular basis, displaying items from the monastery's different art collections.

Glarus

Glarus lies in a deeply ravined **site**★ at the foot of the Vorder Glärnisch Cliffs. Since its old quarters were destroyed by fire in 1861 it has had the appearance of a busy city, built on a regular grid plan. The great Zaunplatz holds the canton's open-air assemblies known as Landsgemeinde (◷see *INTRODUCTION*) every year on the first Sunday in May.

▶ **Population:** 5 892.
▯ **Info:** Gemeinde Glarus – Postfach 367. ✆ (0)55 610 21 25. www.stadt-glarus.ch.
◖ **Location:** Glarus is in central-eastern Switzerland, and is the capital city of Glarus canton. Alt. 472m/1 549ft.

A BIT OF HISTORY
A Hive of Industry

The row of factories, which gives a peculiar character to the Linth Valley as the main artery of the Glarus canton, recalls the valleys of the Vosges. In the 18C Pastor Andreas Heidegger introduced cotton spinning into the area.

The town enjoyed its golden age about 1860 when printing on cloth was introduced. Indian fabrics made in Glarus then flooded the market, as the town's weavers excelled in this technique. Today Glarus is still the only industrial mountain canton in Switzerland. This municipality is also a tourist area, however; a resort such as **Braunwald** keeps up the traditions of the canton, which was a pioneer of mountaineering (the very first shelter of the Swiss Alpine Club was built in the Tödi Massif in 1863) and skiing (the very first Swiss Ski Championship was held at Glarus in 1905). The Braunwald music weeks are extremely popular events and attract many music lovers every July.

EXCURSIONS
Klöntal★

13km/8mi. About 45min.
◖ *Leave Glarus by the road to Zürich, then make for Riedern. In this village follow the road straight on to the Klöntal, running up the Löntsch Valley.*
At the top of a steep climb under beech trees is Lake Klöntal (alt. 848m/2 781ft), which was enlarged when the dam was built. The Glärnisch's jagged steep slopes with inaccessible ravines, plunge from a height of 2 000m/6 500ft into the lake waters. The road climbs to follow the lake shore; after the second hairpin bend, stop at a bench: Facing you is a superb **view**★★ of the Klöntal.

Walensee★★

✆ (0)81 720 35 45.
www.walenseeschiff.ch.
Lake Walen forms a deep green-blue mirror beneath the gigantic rock bastions of the Churfisten, a memoravle sight to travellers from Zürich passing through the Wessen-Sargans Gap on their way to Austria, and Graubünden.

NÄFELS TO MURG

Between Näfels and Murg, the lakeside road, parallel with the railway, required large-scale engineering, including the construction of six tunnels and nine stretches of road cut into the mountainside.

It is still possible to go by the old, steep road which, as it climbs to the wooded terrace of the Kerenzerberg, affords many **bird's-eye views**★★ both westwards to the Linth valley and the low alluvial plain into which the torrent flows, and eastwards to the Walensee and the Churfirsten.

Schabzieger

One of the local specialities of the Glarus canton is *Schabzieger,* a green, cone-shaped cheese with no crust, made with skimmed cow's milk and crushed herbs. It owes its spicy flavour, name and colour to one of its ingredients, *ziegerklee* (blue fenugreek).

GRAUBÜNDEN

Graubünden is in the easternmost region of the country, bordering Austria and Italy. Three languages, two religions more or less equally represented, and a political evolution towards democracy similar to that of the original cantons, make Graubünden, the largest Swiss canton, a true model for the Confederation. This is undoubtedly the part of Switzerland where the traveller can enjoy the most complete change of scene: the Engadin, with the charm of its clear blue skies and open countryside, is the tourist lodestar of this little mountain state astride the Alps.

Highlights

1 An unforgettable trip on the **Glacier Express** or the **Bernina Express** (p355)

2 The incomparable view from the **Weisshorn** in Arosa (p365)

3 Snowboarding on the **Jacobshorn** in Davos (p368)

4 Skiing under a full moon in **Diavolezza** (p376)

5 An excursion in the **Swiss National Park** (p383)

A Bit of History

The territory of the canton corresponds with the most mountainous parts of ancient **Rhaetia**, whose "Welsch" tribes originally peopled the area between Lake Constance and Venetia. The Upper Valleys of the Rhine and the Inn, protected from Germanisation, remained Romansh-speaking districts whose language, derived from Latin, was officially recognised as the fourth Swiss national language in 1938.

A Transit Area – Under Roman rule and throughout the Middle Ages, Rhaetia, being crossed by the **High Road** (the Julier and especially the Septimer Pass) and the **Low Road** (the Splügen Pass) monopolised nearly all transalpine traffic through the present territory of the Confederation. The great advantage of the High Road is that there are few passes, so frequent along transalpine roads. The only comparable route was farther west along the Great St Bernard road. The present network of transalpine roads were jointly financed by Switzerland, Austria and Piedmont between 1818 and 1823 and the railways over

and around the Alps were built between 1885 and 1910 (The Bernina line). Already in 1892 posters were appearing in London and other European capitals advertising the Landquart-Klosters-Davos line.

Deeply Independent – The complex network of valleys enclosed by mountains and connected by easily defended alpine passes contributed to the isolation of communities that would speak mutually incomprehensible dialects and yet be only kilometres apart. Rhaetia, like Switzerland, was split into three loose confederations of smaller communities: the 1367 **League of God's House** (Gotteshausbund)—roughly today's Engandin—the **Grey League** in 1395—roughly the area between Dissentis and Flims—named after the colour of the garments worn by those early cantonal forefathers and the **League of Ten Jurisdictions** (Zehngerichtebund)—the area around the bishopric of Chur. All three signed a treaty of mutual assistance in 1471 and it was only in 1803 that the united leagues (Graubünden) joined the Swiss Confederation.

Geography

Graubünden (German), also referred to as Les Grisons (French), Grigioni (Italian) or Grischun (Romansh), contain the sources of the Rhine and Inn rivers. The Vorderrhein has its source in the Oberalp massif and runs from Disentis/Mustér along the Graubünden Oberland; the Hinterrhein comes down from the Adula Glaciers. They meet at the foot of Reichenau Castle near Chur. The Upper Inn Valley (the river joins the Danube at Passau on the borders of Germany and Austria), because of the Engadin, is also part of ancient Rhaetia.

Glacier Express over the Landwasser viaduct

UNESCO Railways

Graubünden has its fair share of Unesco cultural sites but, uniquely, one of them is the 122km/76mi of the railway line from Thusis to St Moritz (the Albula section) and from St Moritz to Tirano (the Bernina section). The first was finished in 1904 and astonished the civil engineering world in that the train climbed from 585m/1 919ft in Chur to 1 775m/5 823ft in St Moritz without using the rack-and-pinion method; it used wheel adhesion via a complex scheme of spiral tunnels over the Albula valley instead. These tunnels are the architectural highlights of the line in addition to the miracle of technology that is the Landwasser viaduct (1902). After St Moritz, the railway engineers went even further and utilised the new available power of the hydroelectric plant at Brusio to design an all-electric railway. The resulting Bernina line goes from the glaciers of the highest pass in Europe at an altitude of 2 253m/7 392ft (an all year operation since 1913) to reach the palms trees at Tirano that stands at only 429m/1 407.5ft above sea level.

Winter Wonderland

Here is where the ski and snowboard connoisseurs descend to: from glitzy St Moritz to youthful, exuberant Davos and elegant Arosa, tourism—and that means winter tourism—is the canton's main source of income. And with 937 mountains, 150 valleys, and 615 lakes reached by 500 cable-cars, chairlifts and mountain railways you can come here every year and never tire of the place. Yet, 100 years ago, the area would be better known by its sanatoriums: in the pre-antibiotic era, a six-month stay in the mountains was what was universally prescribed for lung diseases.

Thomas Mann visited Davos' Waldsanatorium in 1912 which was the inspiration for his famous novel *The Magic Mountain* (1924). It is now the slick Waldhotel, which welcomes visitors seeking a 21C approach to wellness, as well as delegates visiting Davos for the annual meeting of the World Economic Forum.

GRAUBÜNDEN

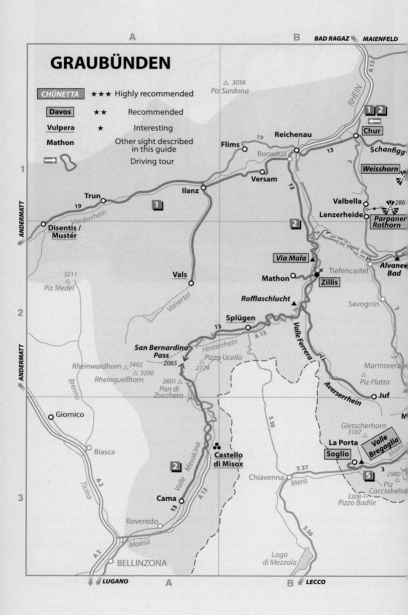

GRAUBÜNDEN

CHÜNETTA	★★★	Highly recommended
Davos	★★	Recommended
Vulpera	★	Interesting
Mathon		Other sight described in this guide
		Driving tour

BAD RAGAZ   MAIENFELD

△ 3056
Piz Sardona

Reichenau

Flims

Bonaduz

Schanfigg

Chur

19

1 2

RHEIN

A 13

13

Versam

Weisshorn

Ilanz

Trun

Valbella

286

19

Lenzerheide

Parpaner
Rothorn

Vorderrhein

2

Disentis /
Mustér

ANDERMATT

Via Mala

Alvaneu
Bad

Tiefencastel

Zillis

Mathon

3211
Piz Medel

Vals

Savognin

Rofflaschlucht

Valsertal

Valle Ferrera

Splügen

13

A 13

San Bernardino
Pass

Hinterrhein

Marmorera

Piz Platta

Rheinwaldhorn   3402

△ 3200

Pizzo Ucello
2724

2065

Rheinquellhorn

△

Averserrhein

Juf

Brenno

ANDERMATT

2601
Pan di
Zucchero

S 36

Gletscherhorn
3107

Giornico

Valle
Bregaglia

Biasca

La Porta

Soglio

Mesolcina

Castello
di Misox

Maira

Ticino

2

S 37

2980

Chiavenna

Mera

Piz
Cacciabella

Cama

5

A 13

13

3308
Pizzo Badile

A 2

Roveredo

Moesa

S 36

BELLINZONA

LUGANO   A

Lago
di Mezzola

B   LECCO

356

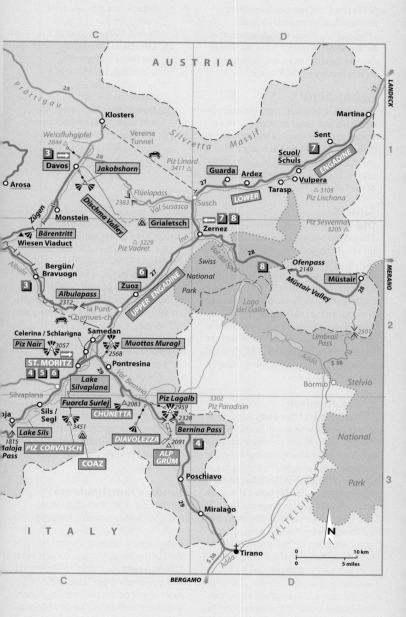

Chur★

Since the 16C Chur has been the historical, administrative and religious capital of Graubünden. It is built a short distance from the Rhine on a mound of rocky debris formed by a tributary of the Plessur.

GEOGRAPHY

To the east of Chur, the first hairpin bend on the road to Arosa (Arosastrasse) provides an ideal **viewpoint**★ of the whole town and its many belfries, set against a backdrop of steep rocky ridges, covered with the eternal snow of the Calanda.

SIGHTS
Old Town

The old town is grouped around St Martin's church below the cathedral and the bishop's palace, reached by climbing a stairway and passing under an old gateway known as Hoftor. Chur remains a cathedral city with narrow streets with fine houses, occasionally flanked by towers, pretty squares with fountains adorned with flowers and the arms of Graubünden canton, and finally the 15C town hall (Rathaus), all of which make for a picturesque scene.

Chur Cathedral

The **Cathedral of Our Lady** was built in a mixed Romanesque and Gothic style in the 12C and 13C and is unique because the choir lies at an angle to the nave. The exterior was remodelled after a fire in 1811, and restored in 2007. The tower is crowned with a domed belfry, the porch adorned with painted recessed arches. The nave, which is roofed with ribbed vaulting, is very dark, lit only by clerestory windows on the south side. The interior, restored in the 1920s, features massive piers, surmounted by fine, if somewhat unusual, capitals. The chancel contains a 15C **triptych**★ in carved and gilded wood at the high altar; it is dedicated to Our Lady and is the largest Gothic triptych in Switzerland. Four 13C statues depicting the Apostles are arranged on either side of the altar.

▶ **Population:** 32 957.

▪ **Info:** Grabenstrasse 5 – 7000. ✆(0)81 252 18 18. www.churtourismus.ch.

◗ **Location:** Chur lies in the Rhine Valley at the crossroads of Latin and German influences. Alt. 585m/1 919ft.

◉ **Don't Miss:** The Cathedral and the Bishop's Palace Hof.

◷ **Timing:** It's best to overnight in the town.

Domschatz

◷*Mon–Sat 6am–7pm. Sun 7am–7pm* ◷*Closed during mass, Good Fri and Corpus Christi and religious holidays.* ●*Guided tours Sun 2.30pm.* ◈*6 CHF.* ✆*(0)81 252 92 50/19 70.*

The treasury includes reliquaries from the Carolingian period and the Middle Ages and valuable reliquary-busts. The Bishop's Palace **Hof** is an elegant 18C edifice.

Rätisches Museum

Hofstrasse 1 ◷*Open Tue–Sun 10am– 5pm.* ◷*Closed most public holidays.* ◈*6CHF.* ✆*(0)81 254 48 40.* *www.raetischesmuseum.gr.ch.*

This museum is housed in the late 17C Buol Mansion. It contains interesting displays of folklore relating to the canton, a prehistory collection and historical specimens.

Bündner Kunstmuseum

◷*Open Tue–Sun 10am–5pm (8pm Thu)* ◷*Closed most public holidays.* ◈*12CHF.* ✆*(0)81 257 28 68.* *www.buendner-kunstmuseum.ch.*

Most of the works displayed in the **Fine Arts Museum** are by 18C to 20C artists and sculptors from Graubünden by birth or adoption: Barthelemy Menn, Angelica Kauffmann, Giovanni Segantini—and contemporaries, namely Giovanni, Augusto and Alberto Giacometti, and E-L Kirchner.

© Swiss Cities/Phillip Giegel/Switzerland Tourism

Chur

EXCURSIONS
Lenzerheide-Valbella✷✷
www.lenzerheide.com.

The twin resorts of Lenzerheide and Valbella are located in Lenzerheide Valley, their modern buildings are set in a hollow (at an altitude of 1 500m/4 900ft; the hollow forms the top of the first ridge crossed by the road from Chur) enhanced by two lakes. It owes its popularity to the charming **parklike country**✷ which the motorist will appreciate between Valbella and Lenzerheide-Centre. In winter the smooth slopes encourage downhill skiing, especially on the Piz Scalottas and the Stätzerhorn. A long chain of chairlifts reaches up the 2 861m/9 382ft of the Parpaner Rothorn.

Parpaner Rothorn★★

Access by cable-car in 15min from Lenzerheide-Valbella. *Departures every 20min, 8.10am–12.10pm, 1.10pm –5.10pm.* *Closed mid-Apr–late May.* *Fare there and back 30CHF.* *(0)81 385 03 85.*

The climb above the fir trees as far as Scharmoin (alt. 1 900m/6 234ft) gives way to barren slopes before reaching the rocky peak of the Parpaner Rothorn (alt. 2 861m/9 382ft). The superb **view**★★, which to the west reveals the Valbella hollow, its resort and clear lake, is blocked to the east by the snowy summits of the Weisshorn, Tschirpen, and Aroser Rothorn. For a more open view, walk (*15min return*) to a nearby

mountain top such as the Ostgipfel (alt. 2 899m/9 511ft). From Lenzerheide to Lenz, approaching the chapel of San-Cassian, the view opens out toward the depression of the Oberhalbstein, its entrance narrowed between the wooded foothills of the Piz Mitgel and the more pasture-like slopes of the Piz Curvèr. The first Romansh houses, giving a foretaste of the Engadin style, (*see INTRODUCTION: Rural Architecture*) can be seen at **Lenz**.

Flims✷✷

20km/12.5mi W of Chur, on the road towards Disentis. Via Nova 62. *(0)81 927 77 77. www.flims.com.*

Flims is divided into **Flims-Dorf**, the traditional residential section and **Flims-Waldhaus**, where the hotels are scattered over a forested area of conifers. Thickly wooded slopes all the way to the Vorderrhein Gorge have hardly changed since prehistoric times. This is when an enormous landslide along the axis of the present Flem Valley blocked the Rhine Valley and forced the river to find a new course. The southern facing site of Flims, and its woods that are a joy for walks, make it a much sought-after family resort, with many marked trails for hiking and bike enthusiasts. Swimming is another popular activity because of the proximity of Lake Cresta and Lake Cauma, whose shimmering waters remain beautifully warm all summer. Still, high season here is undoubtedly winter, characterised by a lively, festive atmosphere and a majority of young visitors.

The skiing area

Commonly known as **Alpenarena**, it incorporates three resorts, Flims, Laax and Falera, and is among the largest in Switzerland (220km/137mi of pistes and around 30 ski lifts). Spread out over 4 summits,including the Vorab Glacier, it features altitudes ranging from 1 100m/3 608ft to 3 000m/9 843ft. It is possible to move around by skiing along the many narrow tracks linking together the massifs. These pistes are particularly suitable for intermediate skiers (Crest da Tiarus and Crappa Spessa on Crap Masegn, Curtgani on Crap Sogn Gion and Naraus). Experienced skiers can tackle the few steep slopes such as Fatschas, Sattel, Alp Ruschein and Stretg (**views**★ from the forest). The area is has several snowparks and has become extremely popular with snowboarders; the towns of Flims and Laax host some of the most prestigious snowboard events in November and April.

⚤**Maienfeld**

▶ 17km/11mi. Head NW on Nikolaigasse towardS Grabenstrasse to Route 13/Route 3.

This small town surrounded by vineyards attracts tourists from around the world because of a girl: the famous Heidi. The heroine of Johanna Spyri's (1827–1901) eponymous novel has inspired a "village", Heididorf, with its Heidi house museum, its bucolic hiking trail and gift shop. This appropriation of the myth of a small mountain girl for commercial purposes can cause some gnashing of teeth to those craving old values (Heididorf, Maienfeld (A13, exit 3); ⏱open Mar–Nov 10am–5pm; 25min walk from Maienfeld; ✆5 CHF, children 2 CHF; ✆(0)81 330 19 12. www.heididorf.ch).

Bad Ragaz★

▶ 22km/14mi. As per Maienfeld but follow the signs to Bad Ragaz.

Bad Ragaz is a leading Swiss spa located in one of the Alpine Rhine

Valley's finest settings and facing the rugged crests of the Falknis. Since the 11C the resort has been known for its mineral waters, which rise to a temperature of 37ºC/98ºF in the Tamina Gorges below the village of Pfäfers. The waters are particularly recommended for circulatory troubles, rheumatism, paralysis and the aftereffects of accidents. Bad Ragaz has been a mid-winter ski resort since a cable-car and ski lifts linked the town with the great snowfields in the Pizol district.

Taminaschlucht★★

2hr there and back on foot by the road branching off the road to Valens on the left, SW of Bad Ragaz. ⏱Open May–Oct, 10am–5.15pm (4.15pm in May and Oct). ✆5CHF. ✆(0)81 302 71 61.

These gorges are truly breathtaking. To take the waters, before they were piped, patients were lowered down on ropes to the bottom of this tremendous fissure.

🚗 DRIVING TOURS

① VALLEY OF THE VORDERRHEIN

Total distance from Chur to Medel gorge 105 km/65mi. Allow half a day.

▶ Exit Chur to the west by Highway 13.

Reichenau

With its three bridges forming a triangle enclosing the confluence of the Vorderrhein and the Hinterrhein, this little settlement owes its existence to a site exceptionally convenient for collecting tolls. It is still an important road junction at the fork of the main roads to the Domleschg (Thusis) and the Graubünden Oberland (Disentis/Mustér). During the French Revolution, buildings here were occupied by an Institute of Education.

Versam Road★

From Bonaduz to Ilanz 21km/13mi.

The road offers vistas of the Rhine Gorges and the Bifertenstock (Tödi Massif) Crests, to the left of the Vorab. The clearing just before the village of Versam is a good place to stop for a **view**★ of the Vorab group, with its great plateau glacier, on the left, and the Ringelspitz on the right. In the foreground stands the Flimserstein promontory, girdled with imposing cliffs.

The narrow road is soon suspended on a ledge along the flank of white precipices formed by the Rhine and its tributary, the Rabiusa, and runs through debris brought down by the Flims landslide.

▷ *Drive W on road number 19.*

Ilanz

Ilanz is the only place in the Graubünden Oberland which bears the official title of "town". It was the former capital of the Grey League, founded here in 1395 (*see p354*), Disentis being considered more of a religious capital.

The most picturesque quarter, reached by crossing the bridge over the Rhine and following the exit route towards Vals or Vrin, has retained its 17C mansions with Baroque ornamentation, especially the Casa Gronda (black and yellow shutters) with its corner turret, window grilles and finely decorated door frames.

▷ *Leave Ilanz S on Valserstrasse.*

Vals★
20km/12.4mi from Ilanz.

A detour along a charming, winding road in the Valsertal Valley leads to this spa resort (alt. 1 248m/4 093ft), which nestles among a grandiose cirque of mountains. **Felsen-Therme**★ was the first spa to be built in natural stone. Opened in 1996, it was designed by the famous Swiss architect Peter Zumthor. The walls of this cube construction are made of quartzite, extracted from within the valley.

The spa's sophisticated facilities include an indoor pool (32°C/89°F), an open-air pool (36°C/96°F), saunas, a cold plunge pool and a "musical" grotto which plays "mineral" music composed by Fritz Hauser.

▷ *Return to Ilanz by the same route and take the direction to Disentis/Mustér.*

Trun

The imposing mass of the **Cuort Ligia Grischa** (black and white shutters) (🕐*open mid-Apr–Nov, Mon, Wed, Sat and the second and last Sun of the month 2pm–5pm. ▰Guided tours available (1hr) at 2pm, 3pm and 4pm. ⊙7CHF. ℘(0)81 943 23 09/33 88)*, a former residence of the abbots of Disentis built in 1674, once housed the Parliament and Law Court of the League.

Inside, the apartments open to visitors include the Abbot's Bedchamber, with 17C panelling, and the Law Court decorated in the Baroque style. It was in the shade of The maple tree planted from the Maple of Trun that the Pact of the Grey League was solemnly confirmed in 1424.

▷ *After Somvix and its elegant onion dome, beyond the railway bridge and the modern road bridge that crosses the Russeinbach ravine you will arrive at an old covered bridge.*

Disentis/Mustér✤
Via Alpsu 62. ℘(081) 920 40 30. www.disentis-sedrun.ch.

Disentis, the centre of Romansh culture and a health resort, was colonised in the Middle Ages by the monks of St Benedict. From its terrace it overlooks the junction of the Tavetsch Rhine, flowing down from the Oberalp Pass to the west and the Medel Rhine from Lukmanier Pass to the south. In winter, skiers are offered a network of ski lifts which take them up to the runs at an altitude of 3 000m/9 240ft.

Abbey and Abbey Church

This is one of the oldest Benedictine institutions in Switzerland, dating from the 8C. The present buildings date from the 17C, 19C and 20C. The **abbey**, from which the town derives its Romansh name of Mustér, forms a massive quadrilateral ensemble of buildings lying on a long, rugged Alpine slope. The

Abbey Church★ (1695–1712) is flanked by two domed towers. The two tiers of windows are invisible from the nave in accordance with the Baroque rules of indirect lighting.

② SAN BERNADINO PASS ROAD ★★

170km/106mi from Chur to Cama. Allow one day.

The San Bernardino Pass is usually blocked by snow from November to May. The itinerary outlined below follows the old road (blue signposts). Note that Route A 13 goes through the pass via a tunnel.

The San Bernardino Pass is a historic transalpine road linking Bellinzona (near Lake Maggiore) in the sunny Lower Ticino Valley to Chur, the historical capital of Graubünden, located downstream from the confluence of the Vorderrhein and Hinterrhein.

The road goes up the Rhine Valley towards Reichenau, the Rhine and later, Thusis at the entrance of the gorges of the Via Mala.

Via Mala★★

15min, not including the walk through the galleries.

This famous stretch of road, which for centuries has been the main obstacle to the development of traffic along the **Untere Strasse**, is divided into two gorges separated by the small, verdant Rongellen Basin. The **upstream defile**★★ —the Via Mala proper— plunges between formidable schist escarpments connected by four successive bridges. Leave the car by the pavilion at the entrance to the galleries and go to the second bridge (upstream), spanning the gorge under which flows the Rhine, 68m/223ft below.

Visit the **galleries**★ (◷*open May–Aug, 8am–7pm; Mar, Apr and Nov, 9am–6pm;* ◎*5CHF; ♗(0)81 651 11 34; ⊕341 steps— 30min there and back).* The road avoids the floor of the ravine downstream and the section called the Verlorenes Loch (Lost Hole).

Zillis★★

Before arriving at Zillis take the road to right marked "zur Kirche" to go to church. ◷*Apr–Oct 9am–6pm, Nov– Mar 10am–4pm.* ◎ *4CHF. Booklet description panels* ◎*4CHF.* ♗*(0)81 661 10 21. Information and Exhibition Centre (slideshow) in the village centre.* ◷*Apr– Oct 8am–8pm, rest of the year Sat–Sun 10am–4pm.* ♗*(0)81 661 22 55.*

The **ceiling**★★ of the church at Zillis (Kirche St Martin) is a unique example of its kind in Western Europe. Dating from the second half of the 12C, the quality and style of decoration evokes the exquisite work of illuminated manuscripts. 153 square panels are arranged in two cycles.

Those in the perimeter symbolise the Primitive Ocean and the Sea of the Apocalypse, its waters inhabited by mythical creatures, and four angels of the Last Judgement in the corners. The inner panel (follow the scenes with your back to the choir, from left to right) relate to the life of Christ and scenes from the life of St Martin.

▷ *Upon exiting Zillis, a steep and winding road (7 km) leads to the village of Mathon.*

Mathon

Situated in a **site**★ on the slopes of the Piz Beverin, this mountain village (alt. 1 521m/4 990ft) overlooks the Schons Basin in view of the peaks of the basin's east side. Below the church are the ruins of a former church (1528, parts of which date from the 9C).

▷ *Make a U-turn on the main road. After Andeer, leave the road for the Val Ferrera, then for the valley of Avers up to Juf (50km/31mi round trip).*

Averserrhein Valley★★ (Ferrera Valley, Avers Valley)

The Averserrhein route moves through the Piz Grisch and Piz Platta massifs. Following the torrent, the road climbs through the **Ferrera Valley** within view of Piz Miez, and crosses the village of **Ausserferrera** (waterfalls).

After **Innerferrera**, the road deviates southeasterly. It follows a hilly landscape and opens out onto the Avers Valley and its first village, **Campsut**.

Starting at Cröt, a sudden rise in the road reveals a view of **Avers-Cresta** (charming white church). The road ends at **Juf** (alt. 2 126m/6 975ft). Continuing down the Hinterrhein, the road enters the Schons Basin.

Rofflaschlucht

May–Oct daily 9am–7pm; Apr Thu–Mon 9am–6pm; Closed rest of the year. 3 CHF. (0)81 661 11 97.
The 300m/985ft-long tunnels, built between 1907 and 1914, allow you to cross the Rhine underground, and lead to a waterfall.

Splügen★

Upon exiting the gorge, past the cliffs and spruces growing along the stream, the road comes to the vast reservoir of Sufers and to the back upper Rhine valley (Rheinwald) around Splügen. The village features fascinating traditional houses and barns as if clothed in green velvet. From edge of Hinterrhein the **view**★ extends upstream, taking in the large Zaportgletscher and the what remains of the cone of Rheinquellhorn.

San Bernardino Pass

Alt. 2 065/6 775ft.
The **San Bernardino Pass** is littered with rounded rocks left behind by Quaternary glaciers. Open between the Zapporthorn and the Pizzo Uccello, the pass marks the dividing line between the Moesa, southward, a tributary of the Ticino and thus of the Pô and the Hinterrhein, northward.

On the north side, the **Upper Inner Rhine Valley** (**Hinterrhein**) presents as far as Splügen a landscape which is open and pastoral but still harsh.

From the approach to the Hinterrhein, the **view**★ opens out upstream toward the massif containing the sources of the Rhine. The range is also remarkable for the size of its glaciers: The great Zapportgletscher overlooked by the Rheinquellhorn is particularly impressive.

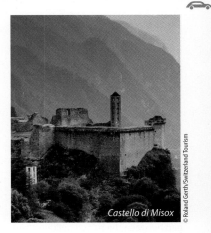
Castello di Misox
© Roland Gerth/Switzerland Tourism

Between **Splügen** and **Andeer** the road runs through woods of Norway spruce, skirts the vast Sufers Reservoir and crosses the deepest section of the Rheinwald, the Roffla Defile.

The galleries, 300m/984ft long, cut out of the rock (1907–14) in this **gorge** (*open May–Oct, 9am–5pm (otherwise enquire in advance), Thu–Mon 9am–6pm; closed Nov–Easter; 3CHF; (0)81 661 11 97*) through which the Rhine flows, end under an impressive waterfall, which passes just above the spectator's head. As you leave, notice the **Bärenburg Reservoir**.

▷ *After the pass, along the beautiful lake Moesola in the beginning of Mesolcina, one of the four valleys of the Italian canton of Grabünden. The descent is performed in stages with views of the highway. It passes quickly from a zone of pine forest to one of spruce, followed by beech and fir.*

Castello di Misox★

The feudal ruins of Misox Castle, the most impressive in Graubünden, sits on a high rocky peak. This massive fortified group once belonged to the counts of Sax-Mesocco.

The castle was sold in 1483 to the Trivulce of Milan and dismantled by the Graubünden Leagues in 1526 (*see INTRODUCTION*). It was saved from complete destruction by the intervention of Swiss students in 1924.

Santa Maria del Castello

The key is available at the cancelleria comunale in Mesocco.
℘(0)91 822 91 40.

This chapel contains an interesting series of 15C **frescoes**★ including images of St George slaying the Dragon, St Bernardino of Siena (patron saint of the valley), and rural life in the Alps.

Castle

Access by the footpath from behind the chapel to the entrance drawbridge.

To enjoy a superb **bird's-eye view**★ of the Mesolcina Valley and the village of Soazza, turn left as soon as you find a gap between the ruined buildings and make for an uncrowned wall on the edge of the escarpment, the top of which can be reached by a staircase without a balustrade.

▷ *From Soazza onwards, note the appearance of chestnut trees and Mediterranean crops: palm trees, plane trees, fig trees and vineyards.*

Cama

The 46 grottos, situated behind the village, is the largest ensemble of its kind in Graubünden and a characteristic example of one style of traditional architecture in Italian Switzerland. A current of cold air coming from below maintains the caves at a constant temperature of 3C to 12C throughout the year. The small stone houses where natives come to spend a cool summer are side by side with restaurants on whose tables iced red wine is served.

THE AROSA CLIMB

29km/18mi. Allow one hour.

The Arosa Express reaches Arosa from Chur in an hour. The train wanders quaintly like a streetcar in the city, along the Plessur river, the Powder Tower and the Obertor before becoming a true mountain railway.

▷ *Leave Chur from the SE in the direction of Arosa.*

The **Arosa road**★, a high, winding, picturesque corniche along the Schanfigg valley, passes through flower-decked villages with quaint churches. During the last part, the road cuts through unusual sharp limestone ridges, which are convex and wooded on the north side and concave and barren on the south side. Note the railway viaduct spanning the chasm on the outskirts of Langwies.

Arosa★★

Alt. 1 742m/5 715ft.
Poststrasse – 7050. ℘(0)81 378 70 20.

The elegant resort of Arosa spreads its hotels in the Upper Schanfig Basin of the Plessur Valley. It charms the visitor at once with its setting of gently sloping woodlands, reflected in three small lakes. In the summer the section from Arosa to Langwies is free, as are all cable-cars, with every hotel night spent in the resort.

Arosa station was inaugurated in 1880 with the opening of the sanatoriums and hotels as well as the arrival of the first skiers. It remained a minor health resort until the 1950s when it experienced a boom with the construction of many hotels and apartments.

Today, tiny Arosa with only 2 267 permanent inhabitants has become one of the country's major mountain resorts. Its superb setting of gently inclined wooded slopes with shimmering small lakes, which become skating rings in winter, remains undiminished.

Its golf course is one of the main attractions in the summer, as it is the highest in Europe. Other summer attractions include some excellent hikes and mountain biking, while pedalo and boat hire on the lake is free.

The Chur road passes through **Ausser-Arosa**, the chief centre of activity and location of the railway station and the lakes. The road emerges from the forest and ends at **Inner-Arosa**, where the upper depression of the Plessur (Aroser Alp) begins.

The nearby centre of **Maran** is more isolated; visitors to Arosa walk to it along delightful, gently sloping paths through the woods (*Eichhörnliweg*: squirrel path). The settlement spreads over the open Alpine pastures. The Weisshorn cable-car is the ski area's backbone in winter, Arosa's real season. Long, wide runs, some of which drop over 1 000m/3 280ft, make this resort ideal for the beginner or intermediate; the descent from the top of the Weisshorn is only for accomplished skiers and snowboarders. The first week of January every year is **Gay Ski Week** and prices rise accordingly.

Weisshorn★★

Alt. 2 653m/8 704ft. 🚡 *Access in 15min by cable-car.* 🕐 *Departure every 10min, 9am–5pm.* 🕐 *Closed mid-Apr–late Apr.* ✆ *Free with a hotel stay, otherwise 13CHF.* ✆ *(0)81 378 84 84.*
The climb up to the mid-station, Law Mittel (alt. 2 013m/6 640ft), offers wide vistas of Arosa, its lakes, verdant basin and mountains. From the top (*viewing table*) there is a magnificent **panorama**★★ of the Graubünden Alps' neighbouring heights and snowy ridges, blocked to the south by the Piz Kesch, Piz Ela and Erzhorn; Arosa is visible on one side and Chur can be glimpsed on the other, to the northwest at the foot of Calanda Mountain. The Bernina range is also visible towards the south.

ADDRESSES

🏠 STAY

🛏 **Hotel Drei Könige** – *Reichgasse 18, Chur.* ✆ *(0)81 354 90 90. www.dreikoenige.ch. 38 rooms.* At the heart of Old Town, this is a simple hotel with some cheaper rooms with shared facilities. Restaurant in house with traditional Graubünden cuisine.

🛏🛏 **Hotel Alte Herberge Weiss Kreuz** – *Splügen.* ✆ *(0)81 630 91 30. www.weisskreuz.ch. Closed Nov and May. 4 rooms.* A hotel out of place and out of time set in a 18C inn which blends historic and contemporary architecture. Magnificent view of the village.

🛏🛏 **Romantik Hotel Stern** – *Reichsgasse 11, Chur.* ✆ *(0)81 258 57 57. www.stern-chur.ch. 65 rooms.* This quiet house at the entrance of the Old City is home to a hotel for three centuries. Rooms have been renovated in traditional but comfortable style. Tavern with tasty local specialties.

🛏🛏🛏 **Waldhotel National** – *Arosa.* ✆ *(0)81 378 55 55. www.waldhotel.ch. 83 rooms.* A historic ex-sanatorium, renovated in pine decor. A must if staying in Arosa, since the half board it offers includes a gourmet five-course dinner, itself worth the price of the room.

🍴 EAT

🍽 **Muntsulej** – *Mathon.* ✆ *(0)81 661 20 40. Closed Wed–Thu.* Without doubt one of the most beautiful terraces in Graubünden. Inventive kitchen uses local produce from nearby farms and offers curtginatsch (local cheese) or Rotel (spicy cherry liqueur).

🍽🍽 **Süsswinkel** – *Süsswinkelgasse 1.* ✆ *(0)81 252 28 56. Closed Sun–Mon.* A bistro with tasty food in an atmosphere of yesteryear.

🍽 **Romantik Hotel Stern** – *Reichsgasse 11.* ✆ *(0)81 258 57 57. www.stern-chur.ch.* Traditional fare served in an historic regional house. Beautiful terrace.

🍽🍽 **Basil** – *Susenbülhstr, 43, on the Malix / Lenzerheide road.* ✆ *(0)81 253 00 22. Closed Mon, Sun noon.* A very creative gourmet restaurant overlooking the city of Chur.

Davos✱✱

Davos is Europe's highest altitude resort, situated in the heart of one of the most famous skiing areas in Switzerland. This is a go-getting, dynamic place that seems more in tune with its twin town Denver, Colorado, than with the genteel, almost Tyrolean old-fashioned village of Klosters just over the Wolfgang Pass. Davos has reinvented itself three times in its history: it first established itself as a sanatorium town during the Belle Époque period when it became very popular with the British. (It was here that Robert Louis Stevenson wrote *Treasure Island* in 1881). From the 1930s onwards it became a sports and holiday resort that at the beginning of the 21C accepts more than 700 000 hotel bookings in the winter. And finally from 1971 onwards, it acquired worldwide fame for staging the World Economic Forum, which put it on the map as a Congress destination.

SIGHTS
The Village
The village of Davos developed in the 13C on the floor of the mountain valley in which the Landwasser flows. To

▶ **Population:** 11 142.

Info: Talstrasse 41. ℘(081) 415 21 21. www.davos.ch.

Location: The two main stations, Platz and Dorf, are like bookends to the city. Alt. 1 560m/5 120ft.

Parking: There is ample parking in garages throughout the city.

Don't Miss: The nightlife, with its clubs, casinos and all-night parties in the winter.

the northeast, beyond Lake Davos, the gentle, wooded slope towards Wolfgang offers easy access to the Prättigau (towards Klosters). The site is dominated by the Flüela Schwarzhorn (3 146m/10 318ft) and the Alpihorn (3 006m/9 859ft).

The resort
The resort extends between Davos-Dorf and **Davos-Platz**, the chief administrative centre. Around the central square stand the **Church of St John** (St Johann) and the **town hall**. Davos has the largest **natural skating rink** in Europe and is renowned for its giant **sledge runs**: Rinerhorn and Wiesen (2 505m/8 216ft

Davos by night

© Christof Sonderegger/Switzerland Tourism

GETTING AROUND

Train – Rhaetian railways – Talstrasse 4, Davos Platz. ℰ *(0)81 288 32 50*. *www.rhb.ch*. Connections to Lanquart and Zürich possible from 8am–9pm and every hour to St Moritz via Filisur by train. Frequent service to Klosters.
Bus – VBD. *www.vbd.ch*. Connection with the Engandin via Susch every two hours by bus via the Flüelapass (summer only). Frequent service between Platz and Dorf as well as in the Sertig and Dischma valleys. Good connections with start and end of hiking paths. All town and cable-car transport is free in the summer when you are staying overnight.

and 3 500m/11 480ft long respectively), and Schatzalp (2 500m/8 200ft in winter and 600m/1 968ft in summer). During the winter, 80km/49.7mi of footpaths remain open to walkers. In summer, visitors can choose from 450km/279.6mi of marked **paths** and superb **mountain bike trails**, including the route (14km/8.7mi) from Weissfluhjoch to Klosters, with an altitude difference of 1 463m/2 340ft.

The skiing area – 44 ski lifts serve 320km/198.8mi of pistes, which run over a difference in altitude of 1 600m/5 249ft as far as Klosters (ℰ *see KLOSTERS*). The area extends over seven massifs, most of which are linked by train or bus, rather than by ski lifts. The main section is **Parsenn**✳✳✳ (120km/74.5mi of pistes), accessible by funicular from Davos-Dorf. Skiers leaving from Weissfluhgipfel or Weissfluhjoch will discover splendid, beautifully maintained snowfields of surprising variety suitable for all levels of expertise. From the top (2 844m/9 331ft) you go down to 810m/2 657ft in Küblis (train journey back) or even 190m/623ft in Klosters. Most slopes offer hiking paths with lovely views in the lower sections; the longest run (12km/7.4mi) is from the top of Parsenn to Kublis.

Jacobshorn offers 45km/28mi of pistes characterised by a difference in height of 1 000m/3 281ft, some of which should only be tackled by experienced skiers. This massif is particularly popular with snowboarders.

The remaining massifs are smaller and farther away from Davos: **Pischa** (1 800m/5 905ft to 2 483m/8 146ft) on the Flüelapass road, **Rinerhorn** (1 450m/4 757ft to 2 490m/8 169ft) at Glaris and **Madrisa** (1 120m/3 674ft to 2 600m/8 530ft) at Klosters-Dorf. Davos is also famous for its 75km/46.6mi of pistes for **cross-country skiing** between Wolfgang and Glaris, which follow the lake shores before reaching the lateral valleys of Flüela.

Kirchnermuseum

Ernst Ludwig Kurchner Platz.
🕑*Christmas–Easter and Jul–Sept Tue–Sun 10am–6pm; rest of year 2pm–6pm.* 🎫*12CHF/children 5CHF.* ℰ *(0)81 410 63 00*. *www.kirchnermuseum.ch*.

Ernst-Ludwig Kirchner (1880–1938), a leading German Expressionist painter, left Berlin in 1917 to settle in Davos. In 1936, his intense artistic style was declared "degenerate" by the Nazis. Kirchner was badly affected by this condemnation of his art and committed suicide in Davos two years later. This museum *(number 67 on the Promenade)* houses the world's largest collection of works by Kirchner, including *Davos in Summer*. It also hosts annual special exhibitions.

Hohe Promenade★

1hr on foot there and back.
The promenade is a perfectly planned road, level and sometimes under trees, kept clear of snow in winter. This walk begins in Davos-Dorf by the road behind the Arabella Sheraton Hotel (near the Parsenn funicular station) or from Davos-Platz by a steep path which continues the lane to the church.
It is high above the town, so it is like a walk on the countryside, while overlooking the city and the Jacobshorn opposite.

The Capital of the World Economy

The **World Economic Forum** is held in January every year in Davos, bringing together heads of state, politicians, economists and business people from around the world. The original idea was launched by Klaus Schwab, a lecturer on corporate strategy, who decided to bring together leading company managers in an informal manner in 1970. The first meeting was held in Davos in January 1971, the year in which Klaus Schwab founded what would eventually become the World Economic Forum. In 2001, the town was the scene of violent clashes between police and pressure groups opposed to globalisation; as a result, and because of 9/11, the Forum was held in New York the following year. Since then, the policing of Davos has been such and restrictions on movement so draconian, that any protest demonstrations have only been held in the capital, Bern.

EXCURSIONS

Walk from Weissfluhjoch to Davos★★

Allow 3hr30min without breaks (difference in height 1 000m/3 280ft).
Walk to the Parsennhütte refuge (*45min*) along a steep, stony path, passing pretty Lake Totalpsee half-way down. Inexperienced hikers may take the cable-car. On reaching the lower station (300m/300yds ahead), bear right and take **Panoramaweg★★**, a smooth path flanked by benches following the mountain slope and offering superb **views★★** of Lake Davos, Dürrboden Valley, Pischa, and Silvretta. After walking for about 1hr15min, turn left and proceed toward the intermediate platform of the funicular. Continue in the direction of Büschalp 1850, with its dreamlike setting, then go back down to Davos-Dorf or Davos-Platz (*allow 1hr30min*).

Jacobshorn★★

Alt. 2 590m/8 497ft. Allow at least 1hr round trip. Access is by two funiculars, then 5min on foot up a steep incline.
Daily services leaving every 15min, 8.30am–5pm. Combined fare 37CHF return. (0)81 415 21 21.
There is a **panorama★★** over the whole Davos and Klosters area as well as Sertig Valley.

Dischma Valley★★

12km/7.4mi SE of Davos.
Allow 20min. Bus line 13 from Dorf.
This narrow road running along the peaceful waters of the Dischmabach wends through a heavenly setting: Lovely pastures dotted with woods, cottages, and hillocks, with the Scaletta Glacier in the far distance. To fully enjoy these natural beauties, make good use of the hiking and biking trails that have been marked out for visitors.

Walk to Grialetschhütte★★

Alt. 2 542m/8 340ft.
Park the car at the end of the road to Dürrboden (2 007m/6 584ft).
Walk up the gentle slope (*allow 1hr45min*) facing the Scaletta Glacier until you get to **Fuorcia da Grialetsch Pass★★**. From there it is easy to reach the refuge, surrounded by a cluster of lakes. This is a typical bare mountain **setting★★** that contrasts sharply with the luxuriant vegetation thriving down in the valley. The Scaletta and Grialetsch Glaciers are overlooked by Flüela Schwarzhorn and Piz Vadret. To get a **bird's-eye view★★** of the whole area, continue the ascent toward the glacier for 20min and take in the sweeping panorama of the valley and lakes. Go back down along the same route.

Klosters★★

11km/7mi N. Alte Bahnhofstrasse 6.
(0)81 410 20 20. www.klosters.ch.
Klosters (alt. 1 194m/3 917ft) nestles in a valley below Davos, but unlike its neighbour, has remained a traditional Alpine village. In the setting, still quite rural, of the Prättigau, the resort is ideal for both summer and winter holidays. In summer the Silvretta summits, jutting up on the

horizon, are enjoyable expeditions for mountaineers.

In winter, skiers using the cable-cars from Gotschnagrat and Madrisa or the railway shuttle service between Klosters and Davos can reach the famous Parsenn snowfields; skiers in search of more challenging terrain should proceed to the Weisspfluhgipfel (alt. 2 844m/9 328ft). In March and April, spring skiing weeks are organised as excursions led by guides in the Silvretta and Vereina Massifs. Klosters has been fashionable with the rich and famous since the 1950s. Celebrities who have spent time here include Gene Kelly, Vivien Leigh, and Audrey Hepburn. The Prince of Wales is also a regular visitor to the resort.

🚗 DRIVING TOUR

③ THE ZÜGEN AND ALBULA PASS ROADS★★

85km/53mi from Davos to St Moritz.

▷ *Leave Davos SE by the Tiefencastel Road. After the village of Glarus, take a left up the hill.*

Monstein★

Its chalets made with heavy timbers are typical of the architecture of this village where Walser settled the highest brewery in Europe. Visits Tues

2.30pm–5.45pm Jul–Oct. 📞*(0)81 420 30 60. www.biervision-monstein.ch.*

▷ *Return to the main road.*

Since the opening of the Landwasser tunnel in 1974, the road now avoids the most dramatic area, the "Zügen", so-called due to frequent avalanches (which sound like trains—zügen). Take time to walk towards Bärentritt following the course of the river Landwasser.

Bärentritt★★

2hr on foot there and back by the old road to the Zügen taking the exit E of the tunnel (on the Davos side). 🅿 *Park the car at Schmelzbaden.*

From this point, a projecting parapet forms a belvedere that marks the beginning of the Zügen defile. There is an impressive downward view of the confluence 80m/262ft below, of the Landwasser and of the torrent forming the Sägetobel Cascade on the right. Coming out of the deep Tieftobel Ravine, you will see below you the **Wiesen Viaduct**★ (length 210m/689ft, central span 55m/180ft, height 88m/288ft), one of the largest structures of the Rhaetic railways.

▷ *After Schmitten the view plunges to the left onto the Albula and the Landwasser river. After Alvaneu, instead*

Monstein

🚗

of going to Tiefencastel, turn left towards Alvaneu Bad and Filisur.

Alvaneu Bad

🕐*Baths open daily 9am–10pm.*
🕐*Closed Nov.* 🛁*28CHF (sulphur baths and steam, sauna, solarium).* ✆*(0)81 420 44 00. www.bad-alvaneu.ch.*
These sulfur springs, perhaps already exploited in Roman times, enjoyed some popularity in the second half of the 19C Closed in 1962, today they have been resurrected in full spa mode around a golf course and a pleasant outdoor pond.

▷ *Follow the road to the Albula Pass towards Filisur.*

Coming from Chur or Davos the most impressive way to St Moritz and the Upper Engadin is via the Julier Pass. Past Filisur the Albula valley, more and more wooded and wild, gradually forces the road to carve a passage through the rock at the Berguener Steina.

Bergün

This village has several Engadin-style houses with oriel windows and window grilles, far more rustic than those of the Inn Valley.
From Bergün to Preda, while the road climbs steeply through mossy woods and fields, you will see the extraordinary contortions (loops and spiral tunnels) imposed upon the railway to gain height. Arrival at Preda is marked by an opening-out of the mountainous horizon. Between Preda and the pass are pleasant pastures as far as the little green **Lake Palpuogna**. Higher up, beyond the Crap Alv, the road rises among rocky ledges as it skirts a marshy plateau, where numerous small cascades indicate one of the sources of the Albula. You then reach the grassy coomb marking the pass.

Albulapass

Alt. 2 312m/7 585ft.
⛄*The pass is usually blocked by snow Nov–Jun. Served by the Tiefencastel–Samedan rail-car service.*

The pass divides the Albula Basin to the north, a tributary of the Rhine from the Val d'Alvra, and to the south, a tributary of the Inn. From La Punt to Samedan follow the flat floor of the Inn Valley until the peaks of the Bernina Massif appear through the Pontresina Gap.

ADDRESSES

🛏STAY

Many hotels in the summer offer half board included the room price. Check whether your hotel is part of the Dine Around scheme whereby you can use your half-board option to dine in any of the participating hotels.

🍴🍴 **Hotel Alpina** – *Richtstattweg 1.* ✆*(0)81 416 47 67. www.alpina-davos.ch. Closed Nov and May. 19 rooms.* A nice pension with good service, good value on the higher slopes of Davos. Ask for a southern-facing room with balcony.

🍴🍴 **Hotel National** – *Obere Strasse 31.* ✆*(0)81 415 10 10. www.national-davos.ch. 65 rooms.* 🕐*Closed in the shoulder season.* Very central (near Platz) and yet quiet, plus parking. Large rooms, helpful staff. Member of Dine Around.

🍴🍴🍴 **Hotel Bahnhof Terminus** – *Talstrasse 3.* ✆*(0)81 414 97 97. www.bestwestern.ch/bahnhofterminus. 53 rooms.* This place in front of the railway station is very convenient. Superb sauna and three restaurants to choose from.

🍴EAT

🍴 **Flüela Stübli** – *Bahnhofstrasse 5.* ✆*(0)81 410 17 17. www.fluela.ch. Closed Apr-Nov.* The restaurant of the eponymous 5-star hotel, this is as sophisticated a gourmet experience as you can have in Davos.

🍴🍴🍴 **Morosani Posthotel** – *Promenade 42.* ✆*(0)81 415 20 60. www.posthotel.morosani.ch.* Try to eat at least once in this restaurant when in Davos if only to experience the immaculate service and the superb wine list. Member of Dine around.

St Moritz ✳✳✳

In St Moritz (San Murezzan in Romansh), the sun shines an average of 322 days a year, more than anywhere else in Switzerland; unsurprisingly, the town's symbol is a sun. Switzerland's most famous ski resort promotes itself as the "Top of the World," its popularity with tourists lasting year-round due to the reliably clear blue sky, stunning scenery, and sport and leisure activities. Local sports include bobsleigh competitions, horse racing, and golf on the frozen lake, while a wide array of elegant boutiques, gourmet dining, and world-class hotels cater for weary bones at the end of the day.

> ▶ **Population:** 5 175.
> 🕭 **Michelin Map:** Town plan in the Michelin RED Guide Switzerland.
> 🗊 **Info:** via Maistra 12 – 7500. ✆(0)81 837 33 33. www.stmoritz.ch.
> ◗ **Location:** The heart of the village is the Plaza da Scoula (pedestrians only). Alt. 1 865m/6 089ft.
> ⊛ **Don't Miss:** Take the funicular up to Piz Nair for a memorable view over the Engadin Valley.
> 🕔 **Timing:** Allow at least two days, summer or winter, for exploring, events and excursions.

SKI AREA
Twin Resorts

St Moritz-Dorf has the world's oldest skiing school (1927) and is grouped halfway up a slope at the foot of a campanile. This is where you will find remnants of traditional Engadin architecture, which is also a feature of the typical villages of Silvaplana, Sils, and Pontresina. In contrast, the mostly modern urban sprawl of **St Moritz-Bad** at the lake's southwest corner, is where many of the spa installations are found, offering waters rich in iron. Frequent buses connect the two halves of St Moritz.

The Skiing Area

This resort has hosted the Winter Olympics twice, in 1928 and 1948. The ski area, which extends over the **Piz Nair Massif** (alt. 3 087m/10 128ft), offers slopes for all levels, with more than 80km/50mi of downhill pistes and 23 chairlifts. The Corviglia and Piz Nair peaks offer mostly intermediate terrain on groomed runs. The Ski Engadin pass allows you to enjoy facilities at **Piz Corvatsch** (3 303m/10 837ft, 65km/40mi of pistes), **Diavolezza** (alt. 2 978m/9 755ft, 49km/30mi of pistes

Bar on the Corviglia ski slopes above St Moritz with a view of the Upper Engadine Alps with Piz Corvatsch on the right

Christof Sonderegger/Switzerland Tourism

for more experienced skiers), **Piz Lagalb** (alt. 2 959m/9 708ft, 29km/18mi of pistes), and **Muottas Muragl** (alt. 2 453m/8 048ft, 8km/5mi of pistes), which together form a vast ski area (230km/143mi of pistes). Snowboarders can enjoy numerous "half-pipes" and a "boardercross" at Corviglia (Piz Nair). Cross-country skiers can explore about 150km/93mi of loops throughout the area. Silvaplana and Pontresina are the two most popular resorts for cross-country skiing. St Moritz has been the sight of the Women's Alpine World Cup downhill race and the Engadin Cross-Country Marathon, held annually since 1969, in which thousands of skiers race 42km/26mi from Maloja to Zuos, running through Sils, Silvapana, St Moritz, and Pontresina. Once a month during the full moon, ski lifts remain open until 10pm in Diavolezza for a **moonlight ski experience★★**. Corvatsch offers similar night skiing every Friday, but it is Diavolezza that has become legendary.

🚶 In **summer**, St Moritz becomes an ideal setting for hiking excursions through the Engadin Valley. Itineraries go past the nearby villages of Silvaplana-Surlej (☝ see ENGADIN) and Pontresina (☝ see MUOTTAS MURAGL).

SIGHTS

Engadiner Museum★

Via del Bagn 39. 🕐*Open Sun–Fri, 10am–noon, 2pm–5pm.* 🕐*Closed Sat, Easter, and Christmas, May and November.* ⊜*CHF.* ✆*(0)81 833 43 33.* www.engadiner-museum.ch.
This visit is a useful preliminary to an excursion through the villages of the Engadin. The following rooms are particularly worthy of note: The **Engadin Room no II** (Zuoz house), with its elegant beamed ceiling; the luxurious **State Room no IX** (the Visconti-Venosta house at Grosio); and **State Room no VII** (a nobleman's house at Marca de Mesocco).

Segantini-Museum

Via Somplaz 30. 🕐*Open Tue–Sun 10am –noon, 2pm–6pm.* 🕐*Closed May & Nov and public holidays.* ⊜*10CHF.* ✆*(0)81 833 44 54.* www.segantini-museum.ch.
This rotunda contains several works by the painter Giovanni-Segantini (1858–99), who enjoys widespread popularity in Switzerland.
Note especially the symbolic **trilogy**★ *To Be—To Pass—To Become*, where details of the upper mountain landscape are illustrated.

Berry-Museum

Via Arona 32. 🕐*Wed–Mon 10am–1pm, 4pm–7pm.* ⊜*15 CHF.* ✆*(0)81 833 30 18.* www.berrymuseum.com.
Situated in the spacious Villa Arona, this museum has brought together many works by Peter Robert Berry, a local doctor and painter (1864–1942) who studied in Paris and was influenced by the greatest fin-de-siècle French masters.

HIKING

Piz Nair★★

Alt. 3 057m/10 029ft. About 45min, including 20min by funicular to Corviglia, then by cable-car, and 15min on foot round trip. Cable-car: Departure every 30min Jun–mid-Oct and Dec–Apr,

Alpine Palaces

It was at St Moritz in 1896, that the word Hotel and the word Palace were first spoken next to each other after the inauguration of the eponymous Palace by Johannes Bradrutt. The edifice was a neo-Gothic castle which the critics marked as a success. Today called Badrutt's Palace Hotel, it is still the place where glamorous resort celebs like to parade. Above it, the Kulm Hotel, J. Badrutt's first property, is the oldest of the current five-star hotels (1856). Still higher, the Carlton, built for Tsar Nicolas II, is the smallest. In St Moritz Bad, the Kempinski Grand Hotel des Bains looks like a fairytale castle, as does the Suvretta House, in a forest clearance on the road to Champfèr.

8am–5.30pm. 🚠Fare there and back
48CHF/35CHF. ✆(0)81 836 50 50.
From the terrace of the upper cable-
car station look down on the Upper
Engadin and its lakes. Then walk to
the highest point to enjoy the circular **panorama**★★ embracing the
Bernina Summits.

Val Suvretta da S Murezzan★★

*From the upper station of the gondola to
Piz Nair – 3hr30mins walk. 🏔1 200m/
3 937ft change in altitude during the
decent.*

You start with a descent for about 50
minutes, in a rough rocky peak devoid
of vegetation, to Pass Suvretta. From the
pass (alt. 2 615m/8 580ft), the **view**★★
of Val Suvretta da Samedan dominated
by the Piz Bever and Piz Julier and its
glacier in the south. Turn left and within
10 minutes you reach **lake Suvretta**★★
which provides a superb view south to
the Bernina Massif (Piz Roseg Scerscen
and Bernina).

From there the descent, is more agreeable as it continues along the river,
through alpine meadows with grazing cattle. After 1 hour of walking, the
stream rushes into a cascade. Just after,
turn left onto a path uphill. The steepness is short and the path then continues without a perceptible difference in
altitude on the mountainside, offering
quick **views** ★★ of the village of Surlej,
Piz Corvatsch and Lake Silvaplana. Finish
by following the directions to St Moritz-
Dorf (nice views over the village).

Piz Corvatsch★★★

*🚡Access by cable-car in 16min; leave
from Surlej (to the left of Lake Silvaplana
which is reached by the causeway).
🕐Departure every 20min 8.10am–5pm
Jul–mid-Oct, Dec–Apr 8.20am–5pm.
🚠Return fare 73CHF/46CHF. ✆(0)81
838 73 73.*

The ride up to the mid-station of Murtel
(alt. 2 702m/8 865ft) offers views onto
Lake Silvaplana and Lake Sils. The upper
station is situated below the superb ski
jump formed by the Piz Corvatsch (alt.
3 451m/11 319ft). Go to the panoramic

*Hiker on Piz Corvatsch with view
of Lake Silvaplana and Lake Sils*

© Christof Sonderegger/Switzerland Tourism

terrace, which commands a splendid
overall view★★★ of the surrounding landscape. To the east you can
see the glaciers of the Piz Tschierva,
Morteratsch, Palü, Bernina, Scerscen
and Roseg. To the northwest, one overlooks the Engadin Valley and its lakes,
dominated by the Piz Lagrev, Julier,
Bever and Ot. And in the background,
one can make out the Säntis and, farther east, the Jungfraugruppe and the
Sustenhorn.

Fuorcia Surlej★★

Alt. 2 755m/9 038ft.

This is an easy, gentle walk, leaving from
the intermediate station of Murtel. From
the pass, where a refuge has been set
up, there is a lovely **view**★★ of the
Bernina Massif. You can return to Surlej
on foot (*2hr30min*) via Hahnensee. This
will take you along a rocky path affording a beautiful **panorama**★★★ of four
lakes: Sils, Silvaplana, Champfer, and St
Moritz.

Chamanna Coaz refuge★★★

Alt. 2 610m/8 562ft.

*👟Remember to bring sturdy shoes and
a hiking stick. Allow 5hr not including
stops. The walk is challenging, especially
on the way down. Enquire beforehand
about times of buses and carriages to
get back to Surlej in the late afternoon.
This is one of the most popular walks
in the area, after you have climbed Piz*

View of St. Moritz and the Upper Engadin lakes from Muottas Muragl, easily reached by funicular

© Christof Sonderegger/Switzerland Tourism

Corvatsch and reached Fuorcia Surlej early in the morning.

Starting from the pass, the clearly signposted path follows the mountain slope, gradually offering an increasingly stunning **view**★★★ of the glacial corrie coating the valley, dominated by Piz Roseg. After following the path for 2hr, enhanced by burbling streams and waterfalls, you will see the refuge, nestled in a secluded **setting**★★ amid mountain tops. The Roseg and Sella Glaciers plunge down towards a vast white lake.

Retrace your steps and after about 15min bear right towards Pontresina (Puntraschigna). The 40min descent along a stony path towards Lake Vadret is very steep and trying. The impressive glacier (see INTRODUCTION: Nature) ending in the lake, dotted with ice floes, is a truly breathtaking sight. Continue following the stream and notice that the flora gradually becomes more lush: alpine meadows, mountain flowers, larch and pine trees.

After 1hr30min, you reach a hotel (alt. 2 000m/6 561ft) that marks the end of this wonderful outing.

Do not miss the striking **panorama**★★★ of glaciers standing out against bursts of vegetation, basking in the glowing sunset. At the hotel, treat yourself to a

carriage ride to Pontresina, then catch a bus back to Surlej.

Muottas Muragl★★

From the lower station at Punt Muragl, about 1hr there and back, including 30min by funicular.

 Operates June–mid-Oct and Dec–Mar. Departure every 30min, 8am–11pm. Summit trail pass 33CHF (more in high season); children up to 12yrs 11CHF; young persons up to 17yrs 22CHF (all tickets more in high season; euros welcome). (0)81 842 83 08. www.muottasmuragl.ch.

The grassy ridges of Muottas Muragl, easily reached by funicular from the Samedan Basin, form the classic belvedere of the Upper Engadin.

From the upper station (hotel), at an altitude of 2 453m/8 048ft there is a **view**★★ of the Upper Engadin Gap, framed by the small Piz Rosatsch and Piz Julier ranges. The string of lakes between St Moritz and the Maloja are also clearly visible. Farther left are the Roseg corrie and the shining peaks of the Bernina Massif: Piz Morteratsch, Piz Bernina and Piz Palü. Many tourists will enjoy walking on this high ground, famous for its flora and fauna, along broad, gently sloping paths superbly sited on the mountainside, such as the Hochweg.

Walk to Pontresina★★

Allow one day to ascend by funicular to Muottas Muragl, walk to, and then tour Pontresina village. From Muottas Muragl, allow at least 2hr30min on foot. The classic route is through peaceful pastureland to Alp Languard (*3hr on foot*), offering superb **views**★★ of the Roseg and Morteratsch glaciers and the Pontresina Valley. The climb down from to Pontresina can be done on foot or by chairlift. You may, however, decide to stop at the Unterer Schafberg Restaurant perched at a height of 2 231m/7 319.5ft (*1hr on foot before reaching Alp Languard*) before heading directly for Pontresina through the forest (*45min*). From Pontresina, a path following the bed of the valley will take you to the foot of the funicular (*45min*), wending its way through many houses whose architecture is typical of the area. While on this trail, note the 15 informational displays set up by Climate Trail, a project of the SESN (Natural Science Society of the Engadin) and WWF Switzerland. These displays explain the phenomenon of global warming and its effects on the Alpine environment. Also discussed are ways that everyone can help stop and reverse the process on a local and global level.

🚗 DRIVING TOUR

4 THE BERNINA ROAD★★★

56km/34mi from St Moritz to Tirano. Allow 2hr.

This magnificent mountain road climbs up the Bernina Valley as far as the pass and then descends along the Poschiavo Valley to Tirano.

It is inadvisable to start across the Engadin slope late in the afternoon; it will be difficult to see the Morteratsch. The Bernina Pass is usually blocked by snow from October to May. The pass road is not cleared at night. The railway—the highest in Europe without racks—runs all year round. The Swiss customs control is at Campocologno and the Italian control at Piattamala.

▷ *Leave St Moritz in the direction of Pontresina.*

Pontresina ✵✵

Alt. 1 777m/5 863ft.
Kongresszentrum Rondo – 7504.
℘(0)81) 838 83 00. www.pontresina.ch.
Pontresina, in the heart of the Engadin, is still tied to Romansch traditions. The town is situated in the highest region of the Upper Engadin, at the mouth of the Bernina Valley, within view of the Roseg corrie and the snowy ridges of the Piz Palü. Pushing up the Roseg or the Morteratsch valleys, mountaineers set out from here for magnificent glacier climbs in the Bernina Massif, especially the famous Diavolezza tour. Walkers can continue along the woodland paths of the forest of Tais (Taiswald) or climb the last foothills of the Piz Languard, via a corniche from Muottas Muragl (*7km/4.3mi*).

Old Town

The names of the streets and houses, some dating to the 16C, are in Romansch, which is still spoken here; the façades of many of the buildings are painted with intricate, ancient designs. There are also modern, well-appointed hotels which are more affordable than in St Moritz 4km/2.5mi away. The little Romanesque chapel of Santa Maria, near the pentagonal 13C Spaniola Tower, contains a series of mural paintings, created in the 13C and in the 15C. The series devoted to the story of Mary Magdalene will interest tourists familiar with the Golden Legend and the great Provençal traditions.

Skiing Area

The winter season at Pontresina lasts until April. It offers long-distance excursions for skiers and sunny ski runs served by the ski lifts of Alp Languard and the Muottas Muragl funicular. The resort is also popular for **cross-country skiing**. The famous Engadin marathon, which covers a distance of 40km/25mi, is held here every year (*for further information, contact Engadin Skimarathon, CH 7504 Pontresina*).

Between Pontresina and the Chünetta road fork, the valley quickly becomes wilder. The three glittering peaks of the Piz Palü appear to the right of the Munt Pers, and farther to the right, the snowy summits of the Bellavista.

Chünetta Belvedere★★★

Alt. 2 083m/6 832ft. From the Bernina road 2km/1.2mi there and back – plus 1hr on foot there and back.

After branching off on the road to the Morteratsch Glacier, leave your car before the wooden bridge leading to Morteratsch station. Cross this bridge and the railway track and after passing a bed of stones brought down by the torrent, take a path going uphill to the right, under the larches. After 20min, at the second fork, when the view opens out, turn right to climb to the viewpoint. From there you will see the grand picture formed by the **Morteratsch Corrie**, overlooked from left to right by the Piz Palü, the Piz Bellavista, the cloven summit of the Piz Bernina (highest point: 4 049m/13 284ft), the Piz Morteratsch with its heavy snowcap and the Piz Boval. The lower end of the glacier dies away in the foreground; it is framed by terminal moraines and divided longitudinally by a central moraine. The **view**★★ is splendid after two hairpin bends. To the right of Bellavista the

glorious twin peaks of the Bernina Massif—Piz Bernina and Piz Morteratsch—appear. From the latter the Morteratsch Glacier descends—a truly breathtaking sight. After this the road emerges into the Upper Bernina Depression.

Diavolezza★★★

Alt. 2 973m/9 754ft. About 1hr there and back from the Bernina road, including 9min by cable-car. Operates in summer only 8.30am–5pm. Fare 33CHF return. (0)81 842 64 19.

For generations of mountaineers and skiers the Diavolezza refuge (now a restaurant) has been the starting-point of one of the most famous glacier runs in Europe. Thanks to a cable-car, tourists can now reach this high mountain pass and admire its spectacular glacier landscape. Take in the splendid **view**★★★ encompassing the Piz Palü, Piz Bellavista, Piz Zupó, Crast Agüzza (easily identifiable because of its white peak), Piz Bernina, Piz Morteratsch, and the Boval refuge.

The Bernina Pass★★

Alt. 2 328m/7 638ft. After leaving the valley, followed throughout its length by the railway and in which the Lago Bianco lies, the road climbs to the Bernina Pass from which there are clear **views**★★★ of the Piz Cambrena and its glacier.

Diavolezza with Piz Palue and Piz Bernina

© Christof Sonderegger/Pontresina Tourismus/Switzerland Tourism

Alp Grüm★★★

Alt. 2 091m/6 860ft. From the "Ospizio Bernina" station (🚗 accessible by car along a downhill road starting from the Bernina Pass), about 1hr there and back, including 10min by rail. 🚃4.40CHF for a one-way ticket.

A famous viewpoint overlooking the Palü Glacier and the Poschiavo Valley. From the Bernina Pass to the Rösa Plateau the road dips into the Agone Valley, framed between the warmly coloured slopes of the Piz Campasc and Cima di Cardan. It then follows a winding course, taking advantage of every natural feature to maintain a practicable gradient. Looking back, the Cambrena group offers glimpses of its glaciers. Forest vegetation is once more reduced to a few stunted larch. You will make your entry to La Rösa facing the majestic, rocky Teo cirque.

From La Rösa to Poschiavo the wooded slopes, clothed with spruce, grow darker. 1km/0.6mi after two hairpin bends, in a section where the road winds above a green valley, a widely sweeping stretch of corniche reveals, lying below, the villages of San Carlo and Poschiavo, overshadowed by the icy shoulder of the Pizzo Scalino.

Poschiavo★

Tall, uniform buildings with regularly spaced windows quite unlike those in the Engadin, is typically transalpine in style. The early 16C church of San Vittore on the main square shows the peculiar position of Graubünden as a transitional area for men and goods and for artistic influences. Although the low-pitched roof and slim campanile with five storeys of arches is Lombard style, the intricate star vaulting, most remarkable in the chancel, derives from a typically Germanic style belonging to the last Flamboyant Gothic period (👆*see INTRODUCTION*). **Lago di Poschiavo** (a hydroelectric reservoir) is the best feature of the Poschiavo-Miralago section. Very high on the steep and wooded eastern slope stands the steeple of San Romerio.

Miralago

From this hamlet, whose name ("look at the lake") refers to the **view**★, upstream is your last glimpse of a mountain skyline.

ADDRESSES

🛏️STAY

🍽️🍽️🍽️ **Hotel Hauser** – *Via Traunter Plazzas 7.* 📞*(0)81 837 50 50. www.hotel hauser.ch. 51 rooms. Restaurant* 🍽️🍽️. Downtown, in a modern building, the Hotel Hauser has very spacious rooms. Brasserie, tearoom and sweet shop on the ground floor.

🍽️🍽️🍽️🍽️ **Igloo Village** – *Muottas Muragl.* 📞*(0)41 612 27 28. www.iglu-dorf. com. Open Christmas to April. Offers half board.* A unique experience of sleeping in an igloo in the mountains. Igloos for six or two, with fondue, hiking and breakfast for all, sauna and Jacuzzi for the more expensively priced rooms.

🍽️🍽️🍽️🍽️ **Hotel Soldanella** – *Via Somplatz 17.* 📞*(0)81 830 85 00. www.hotel-soldanella.ch. Closed mid-Nov–mid-Dec, late March–late May. 36 rooms.* The hotel offers the allure of a small palace of yesteryear (built 1905). The rooms overlooking the lake are worth the extra cost.

🍴EAT

🍽️🍽️ **Grischuna** – *Via Maistra 17.* 📞*(0)81 837 04 04. www.monopol.ch. Closed Apr–May, Oct–Nov.* This elegant restaurant offers Italian-influenced cuisine with a contemporary twist, known as 🍽️*Cucina Casalinga.*

🍽️🍽️ **Engiadina** – *Plazza da Scuol.* 📞*(0)81 833 32 65. www.restaurant-engiadina.ch. Closed Mon and May.* A friendly family restaurant, far from the luxurious palaces. Graubünden specialties.

🍽️🍽️🍽️🍽️ **Cascade** – *Via Somplaz 6.* 📞*(0) 81 833 33 44. www.cascade-stmoritz.ch. Open evenings only. Closed late Apr-Jun, mid Oct–Nov.* International cuisine with Italian influences in an elegant bistro with Belle Epoque atmosphere.

Engadin★★★

Engadin, the valley of the river Inn, traditionally approached by the High Road, presents a different landscape from that of the great, deep valleys of the Alps, where basins and gorges often alternate in a somewhat monotonous manner. Since the altitude averages 1 500m/4 900ft (1 800m/5 900ft in Upper Engadin) motorists travelling from the north through the Julier or Albula Pass will experience only a modest fall. As for motorists coming from Italy through the Maloja Pass, they drive into the cradle of the Upper Inn without any change in altitude.

A BIT OF GEOGRAPHY

The Engadin Mountains reach 4 000m/ 13 000ft (Piz Bernina: 4 049m/13 284ft). They are sought after mainly for the splendour of their glaciers and the continental mountain climate, almost entirely protected against disturbances from the sea.

Romansh in the Engadin

Both Italian and German are spoken in the Engadin Valley, in addition to **Romansh**, which was declared the fourth official language of the Swiss Confederation in 1938. Romansh, a Rheto-Romance language, is distantly related to French and Italian, and is spoken by 40 000 people in Graubünden. Here, the word for bread is *pan*, and child is *uffant*. Romansh developed as a result of the conquest of Rhaetia 2 500 years ago by the Roman legions of Tiberius and Drusus. Latin was mixed with the local languages, evolving into the Romansh dialects spoken today. There are two main dialects: *Putèr* is spoken in the Upper Engadin Valley and *vallader* in the lower valley.

Info: Via San Gian 30. ℘(0)81 830 08 00. www.engadin.stmoritz.ch.

Location: Located in the Grabünden region.

Don't Miss: Views from Pix Coratsch or the Piz Corvatsch ski area (2 800m/9 185ft).

St Moritz/Muotas Muragl and Pontresina also part of the Upper Engandin but have been considered separately in this guide.

🚗 DRIVING TOURS

5 VAL BREGAGLIA★★

39km/24mi from St-Moritz to Soglio. Allow 1hr30mins.

Leave St Moritz by the S via route 27, which joins route 3 at Silvaplana.

On leaving St Moritz, the road goes up the slopes of the upper valley of the Inn along the lakes of **Silvaplana**★★ and Sils, made more vivid by a wooded peninsula.

Sils★

This quiet, elegant resort in the Upper Engadin includes the two townships of Sils-Baselgia and **Sils-Maria**✳, situated at the beginning of the Inn Valley in thickly wooded countryside. The two lakes and the soft lines of the landscape, both in the main valley and in the tributary **Fex Valley**, which is very wide, contribute to the restful atmosphere of the resort. In spite of the large hotels of Sils-Maria, which stand out between the trees, across the way at the foot of the slope, visitors can take in a view to the south of the very wide glacier gap at the beginning of the Fex Valley from between the lakes. The German philosopher **Friedrich Nietzsche** (1844–1900) spent seven summers here (1881–88) and found inspiration for many of his most famous works during his walks along the lake shore. Photos, letters, and other mementoes can be found in the house where he stayed, which has been converted into a museum and which stands near the Church of Sils-Maria.

Passo del Maloja
Alt. 1 815m/5 955ft.

The Maloja Pass, the lowest one between Switzerland and Italy, establishes the actual boundary of the Engadin and is the watershed between the Danube and the Italian sides of Graubünden. Downhill from the pass the **Val Bregaglia**★★ (Bergell) is the continuation of the Inn Valley. A series of hairpin bends leads you to Casaccia, which marks the junction with the old Septimer road from Bivio. Beyond rises the Piz Cacciabella, distinguished by its small rounded snowcap.

Downhill from Löbbia, the **view**★ opens towards Stampa and Vicosoprano framed on the slope facing north by magnificent fir woods interspersed by pale green clumps of larches. The villages between Vicosoprano and Promontogno—including Stampa, Giacometti's native village—show the waning influence of the Engadin style (tall houses with deep, sunken windows, narrow, cobbled streets, and groups of little barns with rows of open gables). Even the Alpine flora gives way to chestnut groves, vineyards, and orchards.

La Porta

This narrow valley, fortified in Roman times, marks naturally the boundary between the Alpine and Southern Val Bregaglia. The Castelmur tower appears on a spur contrasting with the Romanesque Campanile of the church of Nossa Donna, while the remains of the old castle floor and perimeter wall can still be seen. Castelmur was the key position of the High Road on the Italian side.

Soglio★★
Access by a narrow and very steep by road.

The **site**★★ of this village is one of the most picturesque in the Bergell. It stands on a terrace surrounded by chestnut groves facing the rocky cirque that closes off the Bondasca Valley. The smooth slopes of the Pizzo Badile are among the most amazing in the Alps. Standing out against the houses which cluster around the church and its Italian-style campanile, the noble façades of several Salis palaces (one is now the Hotel Palazzo Salis) conjure memories of a Graubünden family best known over-

Village of Soglio

seas, since many of its members made their career in the diplomatic service.

6 UPPER ENGADIN

34km/21mi from St Moritz to Zernez. Allow 1hr30mins.

▷ *Leave St Moritz N by route number 3, and then take route 27 on the left.*

After the wooded slope separating St Moritz from Celerina, the road goes along the lower plateau of the Upper Engadin.

Celerina

6km/3.7mi NE of St Moritz. Plazza da la Staziun 8. ℘(0)81 830 00 11. www.celerina.ch.
Celerina (Schlarigna in Romansh) lies at the foot of the larch-clad ridge separating the Samedan Basin from the upper levels of the High Engadin lakes. It is rather like an annex of St Moritz in regard to sports opportunities: In the Cresta quarter, where the great hotels of the resort are found, the famous bobsleigh and "skeleton" runs end. Nearer the banks of the Inn, an attractive group of typical **Engadin houses** make up old Celerina.

San Gian

🕐*Open summer, Mon 2pm–4pm, Wed 4pm–5.30pm, Fri 10.30am–noon; winter, Mon and Wed 2pm–4pm, Fri*

Celerina New Orleans Jazz Festival

During one weekend towards the end of August the mountains are alive with the sound of jazz. Big bands parade through the streets, an open air concert is held in the main square and by Lake Staz, an open-ended late-night Jam *really* goes into the early hours and there' a jazz church service on the Sunday. Details at www.celerina-sounds-good.ch.

10.30am–noon. 🚶Guided tours in summer only: mid-Jul–mid-Sept, Wed 4pm–4.30pm. ℘(0)81 830 00 11.
Standing alone on a mound to the east of Celerina, the uncrowned tower of **St John's Church** is a familiar landmark of the Inn Valley, dating back to Romanesque times, with a 15C painted ceiling and frescoes.

Samedan

Plazzet 21. ℘(0)81 851 00 60. www.engadin.stmoritz.ch/samedan.
At the entrance to the little triangular plain where the great resorts of the Upper Engadin have found room for a golf course, aerodrome and glider field, Samedan's horizons are bounded by the high summits of the Bernina to the south: Piz Morteratsch and Piz Palü. This old-fashioned village is dotted with houses in traditional Engadin style. Notice, in the heart of the village, the imposing double Planta House (Chesa Planta, from the name of one of the oldest families in Graubünden), which contains the **Romansch Library**, dedicated to the preservation of local language and traditions. Also don't miss the Old St Peter Parish Church and the 1771 Parish Church (in the square).

Zuoz★★

Alt. 1 716m/5 561ft.
Zuoz is a high-altitude resort, well equipped for a stay in summer.
It has preserved a group of **Engadin houses** ★★, mostly built by members of the Planta family, who played an important part in the history of Graubünden. The town is small and everything can be reached on foot.

Hauptplatz★★

Its fountain is surmounted by the heraldic bear of the Plantas. The square is bounded on the north by the Planta House, designed in the Engadin style but its unusual size and its outdoor staircase with a Rococo balustrade give it a lordly air.
On the main street the Crusch Alva Inn (1570) has a gable decorated with a series of coats of arms.

Hauptplatz, Zuoz

© Christof Sonderegger/Switzerland Tourism

Between Punt Ota (the traditional boundary between Upper and Lower Engadin) and Zernez, the valley narrows and near Zernez the Piz Linard looms into sight.

Zernez

Alt. 1 474m/4 836ft.
Chasa Fuschina, ℘(0)81 856 13 00.
www.zernez.ch.
This large, picturesque village overlooks the confluence of the Rivers Spöl and Inn dividing the valley into Upper and Lower Engandin. It is the gateway of the Swiss National Park (&see p383). The park centre and museum is situated here.

7 LOWER ENGADIN

44km/27mi from Zernez to Martina.
Allow 3hrs.

▷ *Leave Zernerz from the N via route numbers 27 and 28.*

From Zernez to Susch, the road, going alongside the Inn river, plunges into the ravine of the Clüs. Piz Linard can be gradually discerned in the axis of this landscape, its rock faces veined with snow. Beyond Susch the valley, guarded from its terraced site by the village of Guarda, grows narrower, which makes the road feel more claustrophobic as it runs next to the blue-green waters of the river Inn.

Leave the main road and drive up from the valley floor to Guarda (2.5 km). To make the most of the sunlight on the slopes, try to drive this route in the direction Guarda–Scuol in the afternoon or Scuol–Guarda in the morning.

Guarda★

With its fountains, houses decorated with sgraffiti and family coats of arms over the doors, and its steep, narrow streets paved with cobblestones, Guarda is regarded as a typical village of the Lower Engadin. Notice the **Steinsberg Tower** standing upstream on a rocky hill, against which the white village of Ardez is built.

Ardez

This village at the foot of the Steinsberg is worth a stop for its painted houses with charming flower-decked oriel windows. The theme of original sin has enabled the decorator of the "Adam and Eve House" to paint a study of luxuriant foliage.

Between Ardez and Schuls the corniche road overlooks a third wooded defile, sinking finally towards its floor. From the start it offers a first glimpse of the proud **Schloss Tarasp** (castle). The many mountain crests of the Lower Engadin Dolomites (Piz Lischana and Piz St Chalambert Mountains) follow one another in the distance as far as

Schloss Tarasp

© Roland Gerth/Switzerland Tourism

the Swiss, Italian and Austrian frontier ridges.

Scuol/Schuls✳

Stradun – 7550. ℘(0)81 861 22 22. www.scuol.ch.

This spa town and its surrounding area on the eastern tip of the Grabünden region are popular for their dramatic setting of scattered forests and rocky slopes, here in the widest basin of the Lower Engadin. The Lower Engadin Dolomites stand above the town, which enjoys a dry, sheltered climate, and bright sunshine.

The village on the tilled slope of the valley has become a tourist and business centre sustained by traffic using the international Engadin-Austria route (St Moritz-Landeck). At the same time, below the through road, Lower Scuol, the former nucleus of the community still stands around two paved squares built in pure Engadin style.

The most imposing building is the **Cha Gronda House and Museum** (🕐*open mid-May–end Jun and in Oct, Tue–Thu 4pm–6pm; Jul and Sept, Fri–Wed 3pm–6pm; ▰▰guided tours in winter, Tue–Thu at 5pm; ✎5CHF; ℘(0)81 861 22 22*), which can be recognised thanks to its two superimposed galleries. It houses the Lower Engadin Museum.

Downhill from Scuol, the valley narrows between the crest line marking the Italian side on the right and the slopes

streaked with torrents descending from the Silvretta Massif on the left.

Munt la Crusch★

Alt. 1 474m/4 835ft.

From this impressive viewpoint east of Scuol, and beyond Sent, you can admire the pretty **site**★★ of the castle and a **panorama**★ embracing the whole of the Lower Engadin with its Dolomites (Piz Lischana and Piz Pisoc) and its perched villages (Ftan and Sent).

Tarasp

This is the collective name of the communities facing Scuol opposite the Inn. A bus leaves Scuol station every hour.

Vulpera★

Beautiful scenery and houses as well as some four star hotels. The main attraction is the 9-hole golf course, which is bisected by the road to Tarasp castle. Check out the traffic signs warning the drivers against flying golfballs.

Schloss Tarasp ★★

▰▰*Guided tours daily (1hr), late May to early Jul, at 2.30 & 3.30pm; Jul to late Aug at 11am, 2.30pm, 3.30pm and 4.30pm; late Aug to late Oct at 2.30pm and 3.30pm; Christmas to Easter, Tue and Thu 4.30pm. ✎12CHF. ℘(0)81 864 93 68. www.schloss-tarasp.ch.*

This castle remained an Austrian enclave until 1803. It was restored (1907–16) but

Schweizerischer National Park (Swiss National Park)

🕐*Open Jun–Oct, 8.30am–6pm (10pm Tue).*
No charge. 📞*(0)81 856 12 82.*
www.nationalpark.ch.

Switzerland's only national park was also one of the first to be created in Europe. Founded in 1914 by the Nature Protection League, it covers an area of 172sq km/66sq mi between the Müstair Valley, the Inn Valley and the Ofen Pass, ranging in altitude from 1 400m/4 592ft to 3 200m/10 496ft.

© Hans Lozza/Tourismus Engadin St. Moritz/Switzerland Tourism

Larch trees in Swiss National Park

The aim of the park is to protect local flora and fauna and to this end visitors are required to leave their car in one of the designated car parks. Walkers must stay on marked trails. Camping, cycling, lighting of fires and picking flowers are forbidden.

Guided Tours – The national park and local Tourist Offices provide advice on walks and organise guided tours of the park. Some of the tours follow particular themes, such as deer-watching in the Trupchun Valley, which is especially rich in game. **Special excursions** include a visit to the park during the deer-rutting season in autumn. For further information, contact Tourismus Organization Engadin Plaiv/Engadin, 7524 Zuoz, 📞*(0)81 20 20,* plaiv@spin.ch, www.engadin.ch.

Nationalparkhaus

At Zernez (see ZERNEZ), along route 28. 🕐*Open May–Oct, 8.30am–6pm (10pm Tue); else timetables vary by month.* *No charge.* 📞*(0)81 856 13 78.* *www.nationalpark.ch.* The National Park Centre provides information on the history of the park, as well as hosting temporary exhibitions, illustrated by films, which introduce visitors to the protected species within its boundaries. Guides and a 1:45 000 scale map of the park are also available from the centre.

Walks

Access: continue along route 28, which winds its way through the Spöl Valley. Car parks at the entrance to the park. Contact the Tourist Office in Zernez, 📞*(0)81 856 13 00* or the Maison du Parc National in Zernez, 📞*(0)81 856 13 78.*

The park is dotted with information panels in five languages, some of which are designed specifically for children, and has 80km/50mi of marked paths of varying lengths and difficulty (walking trails are marked with yellow signs; mountain trails that can require crossing steep or slippery sections are marked with a red stripe on a white background; alpine trails that require climbing or glacier traverse are marked by a blue stripe on a white background). One of these starts at Ofen Pass, crosses Stabelchod Valley as far as the Margunet Pass (alt. 2 328m/7 635ft) and then rejoins the Botsch Valley.

The walks cross some magnificent scenery, especially striking from June to August, when the last snow is melting and the woods and meadows are full of flowers, such as edelweiss and gentian. Lucky visitors may even catch a glimpse of a marmot, deer, chamois, ibex or the bearded vulture, reintroduced to the park in 1991.

Gradients in Percentages

Gradients are usually represented as percentages in Switzerland. These figures will give the motorist some idea of slopes ahead.

10% 1:10, 14% 1:7, 18% 1:5.5
20% 1:5, 25% 1:4, 30% 1:3.3

has been hardly used and it now provides a snapshot of what was the apex of comfort 100 years ago.

Sent

To reach Sent drive along a little road shaded by maples, traced along the flank of the ridge, within view of the Lower Engadin Dolomites and Tarasp Castle. Sent is a fine village with perfectly kept houses with Baroque gables, known as Sent gables.

8 OFENPASS ROAD★★

Müstair Valley: 38km/23.5mi from Zernez to Müstair. Allow 2hrs.

The road links the Engadin with the Val Venosta in Italy and winds its way in the Val dal Spöl before entering the Swiss National Park at the Ova Spin stream. Once in the park you can only park at certain designated areas only.

Pass dal Fuorn (Ofenpass)
Alt. 2 149m/7 051ft.

The pass separates the Val dal Spöl, to the north, from the Val Müstair, to the south, whose torrent, the Rom, is a tributary of the Adige.

From the pass to Tschierv several sections of corniche afford pretty glimpses downstream, especially of the snow-capped Mount Ortler. After Tschierv the road runs pleasantly between stretches of turf and larch woods. It owes some of its character to the Tyrolean note introduced by the domed belfries of Valchava and Fuldera.

Müstair★

7532 Tschierv. ℘(0)81 858 58 58. www.val-muestair.ch.

Chief town of the **Val Müstair**, Müstair is the only part of Swiss territory in the Adige Basin. **The Abbey of St John the Baptist** is one of the most ancient buildings in Switzerland, founded according to tradition by Charlemagne. The wood used for its construction has been dated

Frescoes depicting the story of Saint Stephanus, Church of St John

© Heinz Schwab/Switzerland Tourism

to AD 775, so it stems from that period. Originally a Benedictine monastery for men, in 1163 it became a nuns' convent to this day. You can hear the nuns sing at 11am and 5pm during the summer.

Church of St John★★

Guided tours in English available for groups of more than six. Open 7am-8pm. (0)81 851 62 28. www.muestair.ch.
The nave, originally built in the style of a basilica (8C) was transformed in the 15C by an Abbess of the Planta family (*see ZUOZ*) into a vaulted late Gothic structure with two aisles. The tower stems from c.960 and the bell tower stems from 16C. The Reformation stopped at Müstair and the grateful nuns donated the church to the village which has remained until today. The **frescoes**★★★ on the walls are listed as a **UNESCO World Heritage Site** and are the most imposing cycle of Carolingian frescoes in Europe. The originals (early 9C) are partially overpainted by Romanesque frescoes (1150–70) which are in excellent condition. The series over the north apse show the martyrdom of St Peter and Paul, over central apse the martyrdom of St John the Baptist, and on the right that of St Stephen. Among the other works of art is a 12C statue of Charlemagne.

Convent Museum★ (Planta Tower)

The museum (*open May–Oct Mon–Sat 9am–noon, 1.30pm–5pm, Sun 1.30pm–5pm, Nov–Apr Mon–Sat 10am–noon, 1.30pm–5pm, Sun 1.30pm–4.30pm; 12 CHF*) covers three floors of the 10C Planta tower containing objects of religious art from the baroque era in rooms of the original refectory, dormitory and kitchen; the nuns' 17C cells and the abbess' own (the remarkable 18C Hohenbalken room) can also be visited.

ADDRESSES

STAY

Alpine Astrovillage – *Lü. (0)76 547 11 33. www.alpineastrovillage.com. 5 rooms.* Relax during the day and look at the stars at night through three high-powered telescopes in this superbly located B&B, in Val Mustair.

Hotel Baer & Post – *Zernez. (0)81 851 55 00. www.baer-post.ch. 54 rooms. Hostel accommodation available in an annex with 64 beds (2x4, 7x8). Gourmet restaurant.* In the same family for more than 100 years, this fine hotel has helpful staff who will arrange guides and packed lunches for your National Park hiking. Sauna for guests.

Hotel Il Fuorn – *Between Zernez and the Pass dal Fuorn. (0)81 856 12 26. www.ilfuorn.ch. 22 rooms. Restaurant.* The only hotel inside the National Park is easily reached by an hourly bus from Zernez to Mustair.

Hotel Liun – *Müstair. (0)81 858 51 54. www.hotel-liun.ch. 20 rooms. Restaurant.* Rooms with valley views and a vast spa centre.

Hotel Piz Buin – *Guarda. (0)81 861 30 00. www.pizbuin.ch. Closed 10–20 Jan, 15 Mar–15 Jun, 30 Oct–end Dec. 22 rooms. Restaurant.* One of those peaceful hotels for writers you read about in novels set in Switzerland. All rooms are comfortable rooms; those facing south have magnificent views.

Badehotel Belvair – *Scuol. (0)81 861 25 00. www.belvair.ch. 33 rooms.* Modern rooms with direct free access to the main Scuol thermal spa below. Excellent restaurant.

EAT

Crusch Alba – *Scuol. (0)81 864 11 55. www.crusch-alba.ch.* Specialities from the Engandin at reasonable prices.

Mürtaröl – *Plaun da Lej, next to Maloja. (0)81 826 53 50. Closed Mon and Tue.* Restaurant specialising in fish freshly caught from the surrounding rivers and lakes.

Stüa Granda – *Soglio. (0)81 822 19 88. www.stuagranda.ch. Closed Jan–Mar, mid-Nov–20 Dec, Mon and Tue in Apr and Nov.* Local cuisine with Southern flavours (try the chestnut tagliatelle). Offers a sublime panorama towards Piz Badile.

THE NORTH

People in Austria—in perpetual competition with Switzerland, from the Winter Olympics to the quality of the ski pistes—have a rather unkind saying about their neighbour: "it's a fantastic place to be born and a nice place to die—but what do you do in between?" Maybe this was true in the past, but anyone who has been to Basel and Zürich—the twin pillars of German culture in Switzerland—can only shake their head in disbelief. Basel plays the cultured older brother to Zürich's brash, petulant teenager and their cultural lives complement each other perfectly.

Highlights

Cultural Giants

With German-speaking cities from Cologne to Berlin and Vienna lying in ruins after WWII, Zürich, and to a secondary degree Basel, were catapulted to the centre of German cultural life in the postwar era. With the reputation of their northern neighbour (the great canton up north, as the Swiss refer to Germany) in tatters, it was left to writers and dramatists such as **Friedrich Dürrenmatt** and **Max Frisch** to continue the tradition of Goethe and Schiller. As centres for modern architecture, fine arts and as providers for gallery space for artists, both Basel and Zürich stood up to the challenge and became the hives of activity we see today. Already financially rich—Basel with its pharmaceutical industries and Zürich with its banks—the cities enriched themselves further as cultural centres that now rank them next to Vienna and Berlin in the German-speaking world. One only has to visit the **Kunsthaus** in Zürich or the **Kunstmuseum** in Basel to be immediately impressed with some of the best collections of 20C art in Europe. In addition, generous sponsorship ensures that Zürich's **Opernhaus** offers a varied opera and ballet repertoire every day, something that many cities with more famous opera houses would envy.

Abbey Library at St Gallen

© Stephan Engler/Switzerland Tourism

LSD and Other Swiss Inventions

Basel's contribution to counter-culture was accidental, but nonetheless as important as they come. One Friday in April 1943, Dr Albert Hoffmann who was working for the company Sandoz Laboratories, was researching the chemistry of a fungal growth on rye when he started having hallucinations. He had accidentally discovered the mind-altering properties of lysergic acid diethylamide, commonly known as **LSD**, which kickstarted the 1960s counter-culture movement a quarter of a century later. This was only one of many Swiss inventions that have changed Western life, including: **the penknife** (or Swiss army knife)—Karl Elsener started the Victorinox company in Ibach, Schwyz in 1884; **Velcro**—Georges de Mestral from canton Vaud patented his invention in 1955; **stock cubes**—first unveiled to the world by Maggi (now part of the giant Nestlé conglomerate) in 1908; **cellophane**—invented by Jacques E Brandenberger, a textile engineer in 1908 who had the idea of a clear, waterproof film when a waiter spilled wine on his tablecloth at a restaurant. One invention that is frequently and erroneously believed to be Swiss, is the **cuckoo clock**, which actually comes from southern Germany.

Counter-culture and Nightlife

Yet there is also an aspect of life, particularly in Zürich, that is often overlooked. Maybe it was the presence of the banks that spawned a counter culture movement whose traces can be seen today in the **Rote Fabrik** (see p394) and the graffiti that adorns Züri-West. The down side of tolerating the drift to the anti-establishment was the city's descent into heavy drug use in the early 1990s. This is when the triangular park behind the Landesmuseum became known as the **Needle Park**, where the city's heroin addicts injected themselves openly. As the park became more and more crime-ridden, for a time it became the unthinkable: a no-go area in a Swiss city. (Even today, since the area has been cleaned up, there is still saturation policing from the station to the park's end where the Sihl meets the Limmat.) Instead of criminalising addiction and driving the users underground, the city pioneered a programme whereby registered addicts would obtain their drug doses free from designated distribution points. This policy saw the addicts as sick people who need medical treatment rather than criminals who must go to jail. At the same time, a huge rehabilitation and education initiative was established to stop any new addicts and help the existing ones. The success was astonishing. Not only did crime fall as there was no reason to resort to stealing or mugging to fund addiction, but also the number of users actually fell despite the original fears that giving drugs out for free would encourage further use. Fifteen years later, in 2008, the Swiss voted in a national referendum to employ the Zürich experiment countrywide.

The relaxation of the licensing and opening hours in Zürich during the 1990s—a move not followed by Basel—has also resulted in a no-holds-barred nightlife which draws people from miles around, including from Konstanz across the border in Germany. The focus of the nightlife is **Niederdorf**, the area around **Langstrasse** and industrial **Züri-West** with its abandoned warehouses. Indeed, swish **Kaufleuten**, housed in a large building a stone's throw from the Paradeplatz, was voted as one of the top clubs in the world by the *New York Times*. Away from the cities of northern Switzerland, picture-book pretty green fields surround picturesque Medieval settlements such as Stein am Rhein, castles line the shores of the region's lakes and rivers, and time seems to stand still in the gentle valleys of the Appenzellerland. Take time to visit the tiny Principality of Liechtenstein to take in the museums of Vaduz, its small capital, and walk to breathtaking Tamina Gorge.

THE NORTH

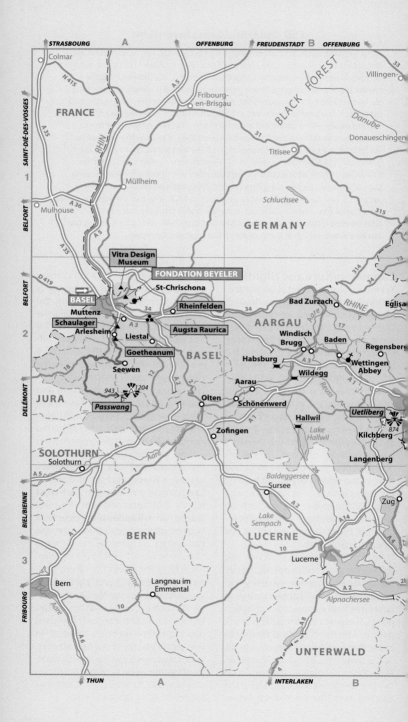

Zürich★★★

Zürich is built between the wooded slopes of the Uetliberg and the Zürichberg at the point where the river Limmat, emerging from Lake Zürich, merges with the Sihl. It is the most important financial, industrial and commercial centre in Switzerland and its canton has a population of over one million, the largest in Switzerland. It has a reputation for being particularly receptive to contemporary trends and youth culture, and the city is much more lively at night than any other Swiss town, offering a wide choice of restaurants, cinemas, nightclubs and concert halls.

A BIT OF HISTORY

Zwingli and the Reformation – When **Ulrich Zwingli** was made parish priest of Glarus in 1506 at the age of 22, he lost no time denouncing social institutions from his pulpit, attacking the corruption of the magistracy and the practice of mercenary soldiering abroad, which he felt was weakening the nation. After two years at Einsiedeln, he was given the pastorate of the Grossmünster (cathedral) of Zürich and began to institute his most controversial religious reforms, namely that the Bible not the Church is the sole Christian authority. In 1523, after a public debate at the Zürich town

▶ **Population:** 365 132. Alt. 408m/1 339ft.

Michelin Map: Town plan in The Michelin red Guide Switzerland.

Info: In the train station, ℰ(0)44 215 40 00. www.zuerich.com.

Location: Bahnhofstrasse, the city's main street, is lined by elegant shops and considered one of the world's most exclusive shopping areas.

🅿 **Parking:** Leave the car and use the Zürich Card (ℰsee Getting Around), which provides unlimited transportation on trains, buses, trams, boats and cable-cars.

Don't Miss: The Swiss National Museum (Landesmuseum) behind the main railway station, or a stroll on the banks of the Limmat in the Old Town.

Kids: The Zoo, the lake, the circus when in town.

🕐 **Timing:** At least three days for museums, shopping, and lake excursions. Try to fit in a weekend for its famed nightlife.

View of the river Limmat and Old Town towards Lake Zurich and the Central Swiss Alps

© Christof Sonderegger/Switzerland Tourism

hall between Zwingli supporters and opponents, the Council declared itself in favour of his new ideas. Within three years Zürich had become a stronghold of the Reformation in German-speaking Switzerland. Zwingli closed monasteries, destroyed religious paintings and sculptures, abolished pilgrimages, processions and certain sacraments, and advocated the marriage of priests, setting the example himself in 1524. His authority alarmed the Catholic cantons. Lucerne, Uri, Schwyz, Unterwalden, and Zug allied against Zürich and gradually excluded it from federal affairs. However, another great religious debate took place at Bern in 1528 after which Bern, Basel and St Gallen adopted what we now called Reform Protestantism. War was narrowly avoided in 1529, but broke out in 1531. His death that year at Kappel did not diminish the influence of his religious theories, which spread throughout German Switzerland.

Tremendous growth – Zürich still had only 17 000 inhabitants in 1800. It had to cede the title of federal capital to Bern in 1848, but six years later it became the official seat of the Federal Polytechnic School—the famous Polytechnikum. The democratic constitution it gave itself in 1869 became the model for other cantons and even, in part, for the Federal Constitution of 1874. At the beginning of the 19C the town already extended beyond its fortifications and new buildings were mushrooming in the surrounding country. Industrial suburbs subsequently developed along the lines of communication and today Zürich is the economic capital of the Confederation.

🐾 WALKING TOURS

1 WEST BANK OF THE LIMMAT

Bahnhofstrasse★
This avenue (1.4km/0.8mi) is the busiest street in the city. It was built along the former site of the Fröschengraben (Frogs' Moat) and leads from the central station (Hauptbahnhof) to the shore of the lake. With its banks and insurance offices, department stores and luxury boutiques, this is the most important business centre in Switzerland.

▷ Turn left at Werdmühlestrasse and descend to the Limmat just below Rudolf-Brun-brücke.

Schipfe
This is the heart of the old town, with narrow, medieval streets running down to the Limmat. Some houses here have roof gardens. Take a detour into Augustinerstrasse, where some of the houses are adorned with oriel windows —a rare sight in Zürich.

Lindenhof
This esplanade, shaded by 90 lime trees and adorned with a fountain, marks the summit of a hill. This strategic location guarded the crossing of the Limmat and

GETTING AROUND
PUBLIC TRANSPORT
It is both difficult and expensive to park in the city centre. However, there is an excellent public transport network of trams, buses, trains (the S-Bahn), boats, and trains, which operates downtown and to the suburbs. Unlimited day passes can be bought from the Tourist Office, railway station, and from automatic ticket machines. Other passes combine public transport with museum entry or excursions.

ZÜRICH CARD
The Zürich Card (*20CHF for 24 hours, 40 CHF for 72 hours*) includes free admission to more than 40 attractions, public transport, and shopping discounts.
BICYCLES
The city is well equipped with cycle lanes. In summer, bicycles can be borrowed free of charge (deposit and passport required) from Bahnhofstrasse near the station, Marktplatz, Oerlikon, and Altstetten.

The Advent of the Dada Movement

The **Cabaret Voltaire** (Spiegelgasse 1—note the commemorative plaque) was inaugurated in 1916 by poet/director Hugo Ball and wife Emmy Jennings, with friends and artists including Tristan Tzara, Marcel Janco, Jean Arp, Richard Huelsenbeck and Sophie Taeuber, to create an avant-garde movement as a reaction to established art. They decided to disrupt conventional rules by staging dance performances, reciting poems, and exhibiting their paintings, an unprecedented approach to cultural life that was a resounding success. The term Dada was coined quite by accident when Ball and Huelsenbeck were trying to find a name for the cabaret singer. The word *Dada* appeared in the first issue of *Cabaret Voltaire,* a magazine published in German, English, and French: it expressed the first quiverings of a moral and intellectual rebellion against the complacency of contemporary society. Although the Cabaret Voltaire had to close down after only six months of existence, the Dadaist magazine managed to survive longer.

was the site of the Celtic and Roman settlements from which Zürich sprang. Note the old Roman stone on the way down with the inscription **Turicum**, the Latin name that became Zürich. From the edge of the terrace you will see the old quarters of the town rising in tiers on the east bank.

▷ *Walk down Pfalzgasse and S on Schlüsselgasse - on your right rises the Peterkirche.*

St Peterkirche

The origins of this church, the oldest in Zürich, date back to the 7C. The largest clock face in Europe (8.70m/28ft in diameter), built in 1534, adorns the 13C bell tower.

Weinplatz

South of the square you will find fine houses with Flemish roofs, the town hall (Rathaus)—a neo-Gothic building dating from 1900—and the Wasserkirche, a recently restored 15C chapel. The cathedral (Grossmünster) dominates the whole with its two tall towers.

Fraumünster

🕐 *Open Apr–Oct, Mon–Sat 10am–6pm; Nov–Mar until 4pm daily.* ✆ *(0)44 211 41 00. www.fraumuenster.ch.*
This church replaced a convent founded in 853 by Ludwig the German and his daughters Hildegard and Bertha. Construction began in 1250; the façade was restored in 1911 in neo-Gothic style. The chancel is Romanesque and the nave has pointed vaulting. Note the remarkable **stained-glass windows**★; those in the north transept are by Giacometti (*The Celestial Paradise*, 1947).
The five windows in the chancel (1970) and south transept (1980) are by Marc Chagall and illustrate biblical scenes. On the south side of the church, remains of the Romanesque **cloisters**★ (Kreuzgang) are ornamented with frescoes by Paul Bodmer (1920–41).

▷ *Turn right to Paradeplatz and down the Bleicherweg to reach the old moat.*

Schanzengraben

A detour via the Bleicherweg leads to this old moat, one of the last remains of city's old fortifications, which runs from the railway station to the lake. Panels along the moat provide information on its history.

2 EAST BANK OF THE LIMMAT

▷ *Start at the Rathaus, go up the Marktgasse and turn left.*

Niederdorfstrasse

This partially pedestrianised street crossing the Niederdorf district is particularly lively at night, with a good choice of cafés and restaurants. The street is

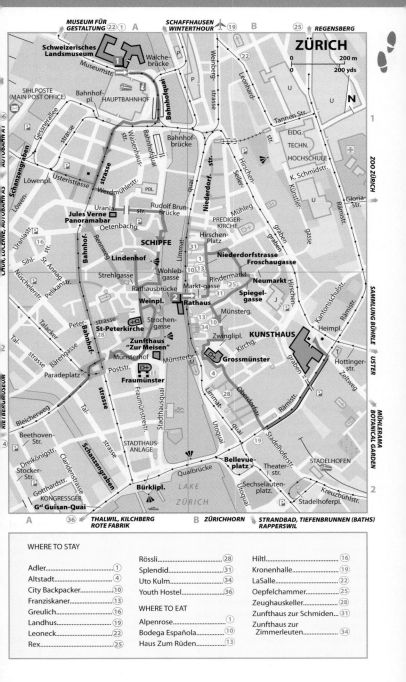

lined with beautiful old houses that bear witness to the past wealth of Zürich's old corporations.

▶ *From Hirschenplatz, turn right into the Brunngasse, then the charming old Froschaugasse.*

Neumarkt

This small street is home to a beautiful baroque facade of the 18C, seat of the ancient guild of shoemakers at number 5. The building now houses a municipal theatre. At number 4 next to the restaurant Kanterei, push the door of the house "Zum Rech", to admire the model representing Zürich in 1800 (note the presence of vines). Free admission.

◐ *Walk down Spiegelgasse.*

Spiegelgasse

A small lane which is full of history! At number 14, Lenin prepared the Russian Revolution of 1916-1917. Political exiles, refugees of war, communists and artists occupied the area in the early 20C. At number 1, the Cabaret Voltaire was the birthplace of Dadaism (◐ *see info box p392*). It is now a trendy cafe, which perpetuates the movement of Tristan Tzara in programming exhibitions, readings and various artistic events.

◐ *Take the Münstergasse to the cathedral.*

Grossmünster★

◐*Tower open Mar–Oct, Mon–Sat 10am–6pm; Nov–Feb, 10am–5pm.* ◐*Guided tours every second Sunday of the month ◐8CHF. Cathedral mid-Mar–Oct, Mon–Sat, 10am–6pm; Nov–mid-Mar, Mon–Sat 10am–5pm. ℘(0)44 252 59 49. www.grossmuenster.ch.*

This impressive cathedral, erected between the 11C and the 13C, replaced a collegiate church said to have been founded by Charlemagne, and is a symbol of the Reformation for German-speaking Swiss. Zwingli preached here from 1519 until he died. Its façade is flanked by three-storey towers surmounted by wooden domes faced with metal plates.

The south tower is crowned by a colossal statue (the original is in the crypt) of Charlemagne seated with a sword across his knees. The bronze doors were sculpted by Otto Münch between 1935 and 1950. The nave has pointed vaulting; the raised chancel ends in a flat chevet, and a gallery runs above the aisles. Traces of frescoes may be seen in the chancel and the crypt with its characteristic triple nave. The modern stained-glass windows are by Augusto Giacometti (1932).

The Romanesque **cloisters** are decorated with groin vaulting. Groups of three arcades, their rounded arches are supported by finely sculpted capitals, open onto a courtyard.

Oberdorf

South of the cathedral unfolds this quaint little neighbourhood. Above Oberdorfstrasse, a handful of steep, cobbled streets contain beautiful old houses and some great art galleries. In this oasis of calm and romance, the bustle of the city seems far away.

RIVERSIDE AND LAKESIDE WALKS★★

This walk starts along the banks of the Limmat, near Quaibrücke which links Bürkliplatz and Bellevueplatz and marks the beginning of Lake Zürich (Zürichsee). Continue the walk along the quays, along which beautifully maintained gardens are dotted with flower beds and several species of trees.

WEST BANK FROM BÜRKLIPLATZ

The landing-stages in Bürkliplatz are always busy with sailing and motor boats, some of which offer boat trips on the lake (◐*see Boat trips*).

Heading farther along the **Mythenquai** the **views**★ of the lake and the Alps (with the Oberland Massif in the far distance) become more open. (*About 1hr.*)

Rote Fabrik

Seestrasse 395. Bus 161 or 165 from Bürkliplatz. ℘(0)44 481 91 43. www.rotefabrik.ch.

This old brick factory is now a popular student haunt, housing artists' studios, the Shedhalle gallery and a large concert hall.

EAST BANK FROM BELLEVUEPLATZ

▷ *Take Utoquai, then Seefeldquai.*
Trams number 2 or 4, Fröhlisstrasse.

Zürichhorn Gardens
By Utoquai.
There is an excellent **view**★ of the town from the Zürichhorn Gardens, where a sculpture (*Heureka*, 1964) by the Swiss sculptor Jean Tinguely (🕯*see box p73*) is on permanent display.

Centre Le Corbusier (Heidi Weber museum)
Höschgasse 8.
⊷Free. ♿. ☎(0)44 383 64 70.
To the left of the Tinguely sculpture and slightly obscured by trees is Le Corbusier's last building, erected in 1967, which now serves as a permanent exhibition to the architect himself.

Chinese Garden
🕐*Open late Mar to late Oct daily 11am–6pm. ⊷4CHF (children 1CHF). ♿.*
This park, opened in 1993, was given to Zürich by its twin town, Kunming. Hidden behind the heavy red gates—in central China red is the colour of the emperor—is a perfectly kept garden, where the theme "three friends in winter" is illustrated by pines, bamboo, and winter cherry trees. Canals criss-crossed by small bridges run through the gardens, which are dotted with gingko trees and bamboo.

Mühlerama
Access by Kreuzbühlstrasse, E of the town plan. 🕐Open Tue–Sat, 2pm–5pm; Sun, 10am–5pm. ⊷9CHF. ☎(0)44 422 76 60. www.muehlerama.ch.
This Belle Époque-style flour mill, built in 1913, was in operation until 1983 and now houses a museum with functioning milling machines, allowing visitors to learn about the production of flour. The exhibition covers the development of milling techniques; the role of the miller in history; bread in popular culture; and the themes of abundance and famine.

Zoo Zürich★
Access by Gloriastrasse. Tram 6.
🕐*Open 9am–6pm (5pm Nov–Feb).*
⊷*22CHF, (6–16 years, ⊷11CHF). ♿.*
☎*(0)44 254 25 05/25 31; www.zoo.ch.*
Nicely laid out at Zürichberg, in a very pretty, leafy setting, this zoo houses more than 2 000 animals. Giant tortoises, an otter, and a beaver can be seen playing in the water and on land. Just as fascinating are the monkeys and the elephants' bath (*around 10am*).

Fluntern Cemetery
About 5 minutes in the opposite direction to the Zoo entrance from the final stop of Tram number 6 is the **Fluntern Cemetery** notable for the grave and statue of **James Joyce**★.

Botanical Gardens
Access by Kreuzbühlstrasse, E of the town plan.
The botanical gardens comprise three huge plexiglass domes and are planted with tropical forest vegetation, as well as species from the Alps and the Mediterranean.

MUSEUMS
WEST BANK OF THE LIMMAT
Swiss National Museum★★★
Behind the main railway station.
🕐*Open Tue–Sun 10am–5pm (Thu 7pm)*
⊷*10CHF. ☎(0)44 218 65 11.*
www.landesmuseen.ch.
This French chateau-like building (1898) houses the magnificent collections of the **Swiss National Museum**, with exhibits on all aspects of Switzerland's artistic and cultural heritage. Whole rooms have been dismantled from the regions and painstakingly reassembled in here, such as that of a typical **Schwyz chapel** (1518) with stained-glass windows and ribbed vaulting, the **Mellingen council room** (1467), and **three rooms from the Fraumünster** in Zürich decorated in wood from top to bottom and adorned with friezes and rich metal fittings, as well as a **Gothic corridor** from the same abbey that looks exactly as it would in the Middle Ages.

History of Switzerland exhibition,
Schweizerisches Landesmuseum

© The Swiss National Museums

Ground floor – One wing houses exhibits from the Middle Ages and the modern era: Romanesque era religious objets d'art, such as the unusual **Christ with Palms** on a donkey with wheels, and ivory tablets that once adorned Carolingian bindings. The late-Gothic period is represented by stained-glass, paintings on panels (view of Zürich, 1500) and polychrome sculptures, such as the king made from walnut wood (c.1320) with slanting eyes and wavy hair, similar in style to images found in illuminated manuscripts. Note also the ceramic stove decorated with a bearded man dressed in animal skins, representing the forest (1440). Other interesting exhibits include a parchment decorated with 559 coats of arms and 18 banners from (1340).

First floor, west wing – A huge gilded celestial globe with four images of Hermes symbolises the ages of man, made by the Swiss astronomer Jost Bürgi (1594), and the fine reconstructions of **interiors from 1600** are not to be missed. The 16C and 17C stained-glass window cabinets are decorated with coats of arms and biblical scenes. Dating from the same period, a profusion of silverware (cups, goblets with lids, etc.) demonstrates the wealth of the city's corporations. Among the 17C

and 18C furniture, note the wardrobe decorated with Mannerist low reliefs. The Baroque room from the **Zum langen Stadelhof** house, with its gallery of famous men, commemorates Swiss soldiers who fought for foreign armies (c.1660).

First floor, south wing – It is dedicated to the History of Switzerland using multimedia reconstructions and findings from the **Bronze Age** including the remarkable 910g/2lbs golden **Beaker of Altstetten** decorated with animals, the sun and the moon. The **Celtic** and **Roman** eras follow with busts, statues and gold treasure troves as they run into the **Middle Ages** and the invasion of Germanic tribes. A special section on **Huguenot immigration** is followed by rooms on the **Reformation** and **Enlightenment**. The final section 17C–20C shows how the Swiss became a rich nation from the export of watches and clocks to tourism and finance. Don't miss an old set of safe deposit boxes from a bank.

Second and Third Floors – The collection continues with an array of clothes and toys from the late 18C and early 19C. The headdress made of black silk ribbons is typical of the Zürich area around 1770. The **rural costumes** on display are particularly varied: the best known is the shepherd's costume from the Appenzell, which is red and yellow and decorated with cow motifs. Also exhibited here are reconstructions of 19C artisan workshops and the detailed **model of the battle of Murten**, won by the Confederates against Charles the Bold in 1476. Finally on the third floor is the museum's armoury.

Museum für Gestaltung Zürich
Access by Sihlquai. ○*Open Tue–Sun 10am–5pm, Thu 10am–8pm, .* ◎*12CHF.* ✆*(0)44 446 67 67.* *www.museum-gestaltung.ch.*
Exhibits at the **Museum of Design** include applied arts, architecture, graphic art, and industrial design from 1900 onwards. The museum also houses a collection of posters and graphic designs.

Zunfthaus "Zur Meisen"
Opposite the Fraumünster.
○*Open Thu–Sun 11am–4pm.* ◎*3CHF.*
This building dates from 1757 and is adorned with a fine wrought-iron balcony from where Winston Churchill gave his famous 1946 speech on a United Europe. It contains the collections of 18C ceramics (faience and porcelain) belonging to the Schweizerisches Landesmuseum. The ceramics are displayed in two Rococo-style rooms on the first floor.

Museum Bärengasse
From Sep 2012 entrance Limmatstrasse 270, Tram 4, 13, 17 stop Dammweg ○*Open Tue–Fri noon–6pm (Thu 8pm) Sat–Sun 11pm–5pm* ◎*5CHF; Free Thursdays from 5pm.* ✆*(0)44 272 15 15.*
The museum occupies two adjoining houses of the late 17C, now restored. The permanent exhibition, spread over three floors, offers a glimpse of the daily life and mentality of Zürich between 1750 and 1800. Furniture, ovens and objects of common use or ornaments dating from the mid-17C to the mid-19C are highlighted in the context of their time. On the ground floor, there is a collection of dolls created in the 1920s by a local artist, Sasha Morgenthaler (1893–1975).

Rietbergmuseum★★
Gablerstasse 15. Access by Bleicherweg (off the town plan). Tram 7. ○*Open Tue –Sat 10am–5pm (until 8pm Wed & Thu).* ○*Closed most public holidays.* ◎*16CHF.* ♿ ✆*(0)44 206 31 31.* *www.rietberg.ch.*
This museum contains the collections of Baron von der Heydt: statues from India, Cambodia, Java, China, Africa, and the South Sea Islands. The collections of Japanese prints by Willy Boller and Julius Mueller, works of art from the Near East, Tibet and pre-Columbian America, paintings from the Far East, a collection of Swiss masks and some Flemish and Armenian carpets complete the exhibition.

EAST BANK OF THE LIMMAT
Kunsthaus★★★
○*Open Sat, Sun & Tue 10am–6pm, Wed–Fri 10am–8pm.* ○*Closed some public holidays.* ◎*20CHF (permanent collections).* ✆*(0)44 253 84 84.* *www.kunsthaus.ch.*
The **Fine Arts Museum** displays paintings, as well as sculpture from the early French, Swiss and German Middle Ages. On the first floor are canvases of Ferdinand Hodler, considered to be the leading Swiss painter of the early 20C, and pictures by Vallotton, Böcklin, Anker, Auberjonois, and Barraud. The French School is represented by works by Delacroix, Toulouse-Lautrec,

Kunsthaus

© Gian Marco Castelberg & Maurice Haas/Switzerland Tourism

Cézanne, Renoir, Degas, Matisse, Utrillo, Léger, Braque, and Picasso. One room contains 14 works by Marc Chagall. The museum also houses the largest collection outside Scandinavia of the work of Edvard Munch, as well as Dada works by Man Ray and Hans Arp. Finally the Alberto Giacometti Foundation has on view a considerable collection of the artist's works.

Sammlung Bührle★★

Access by Zeltweg. *Guided tours by appointment* *25CHF.* *Individual visitors first Sunday of the month.* *(0)44 422 00 86.*

This villa houses one of the most important private art collections in Switzerland: works of art collected by Emil Bührle between 1934 and 1956. A fervent admirer of Claude Monet, Bührle succeeded in barely 20 years in bringing together a superb collection of some 300 paintings, mainly 19C French works. As the result of a major heist in the winter of 2008, the museum was closed to heighten security. To date two of the four paintings stolen have been recovered, but the museum's most famous, Cézanne's, *The Boy in the Red Waistcoat*, is still missing.

Ground floor – Four rooms are devoted to works from the 16C to the 19C: the landing and the Dutch Gallery present Hals *(Portrait of a Man)*, Rembrandt, Van Ruysdael *(View of Rhenen)* and Teniers; works on display in the Louis XVI Salon include paintings by Boucher, Degas *(Portrait of Mme Camus,* with two sketches), Fragonard and Ingres *(Portrait of M. Devillers)*; the Venetian Salon exhibits works by Canaletto, Goya *(Procession in Valencia)*, El Greco and Tiepolo *(Diane Bathing)*.

The Pink Salon and the Music Chamber contain important Impressionist works: *Sunflowers on an Armchair* by Gauguin, *The Road to Versailles at Louveciennes* by Pissarro or Manet's *The Swallows*. The portrait *Little Irène* was painted by Renoir just before he broke loose from the Impressionist movement. *The Poppies near Vétheuil* is a landscape by

Monet. *Messalina* by Toulouse-Lautrec was to influence the Fauves by its luminous colour. Finally, the dazzling *Chestnut Tree in Blossom*, reflects influences from Japanese on van Gogh.

Staircase and First Floor – Seven Delacroix paintings *(Self-Portrait)* and canvases by Courbet and Dufy laid out along the first flight of steps are followed by another series by Chagall, Picasso, Rouault, and a *Recumbent Nude* by Modigliani. The landing is devoted to the 20C with Cubist works by Braque *(The Violinist)*, Picasso and Gris, and several Fauvist pictures by Derain, Marquet, Matisse (note the change in technique between *The Pont St-Michel in Paris* and *Still Life*, executed five years later) and Vlaminck *(Barges on the Seine near Le Pecq)*. The Courbet Gallery shows Realist works such as *Free Performance* by Daumier and *Portrait of A Sisley* by Renoir. An adjoining room set aside for Renoir also features the splendid *Garden at Giverny* by Monet and *Sailing Boats* by Boudin. In the Manet Gallery are *La Sultane, Pond with Water-Lilies* and *Waterloo Bridge* by Monet, alongside one of the 22 original bronzes of *The Dancer* by Degas. The last three rooms concentrate on Vincent van Gogh *(Self-Portrait* and *The Sower)*, Sisley *(Summer in Bougival)* and Bonnard *(Portrait of Ambroise Vollard*, clearly a tribute to Cézanne).

Also of interest are *The Offering* by Gauguin (painted on the Marquise Islands shortly before he died), *The Milliners* by Paul Signac and *Salon Natanson* (the meeting-place of the Nabis) signed by E Vuillard. The Gothic Gallery (note two landscapes by Patenier) and the second floor house a set of fine religious sculptures (12C–16C).

Felix-und-Regulakirche★

Access by Talacker, W of the plan. Open 8.30am–5.30pm. *(0)44 405 29 79.*

This modern church is dedicated to St Felix and St Regula, siblings who, according to tradition, were martyred in Zürich, beheaded on the orders of Decius. The tall bell tower is detached from the rest of the building. The interior is unusual: the oblong church is roofed with a barely curving vault supported by sloping pillars. Stained-glass windows near the vault are modern.

Migros Museum für Gegenwartskunst and Kunsthalle★

Limmatstrasse 270. ⏰*Open Tue, Wed and Fri 12pm–6pm, Thu 12pm–8pm, Sat–Sun 11am–5pm.* 🎫*8 CHF (reduced 4CHF); combination ticket: 12CHF (discounted 6CHF).* ✆*(0)44 277 20 50 (Migros Museum).* ✆*(0)44 272 15 15 (Kunsthalle). www.migrosmuseum.ch. www.kunsthallezurich.ch.*

These two museums of contemporary art that will delight fans of the genre, occupy the former Löwenbräu brewery. They welcome temporary exhibitions throughout the year that are usually dedicated to young promising artists. The cutting-edge facilities and daring works resonate especially in the vast halls of pure white. The brick building also houses several art galleries and a good bookstore on the ground floor.

EXCURSIONS

Uetliberg and Felsenegg ★★

Access by train: 20min on line number 10 from Zürich station, platform 2; departures every 30min. 🎫*Ask for Albis Day Pass 16.40CHF.* 🗺*A map is available from the Tourist Office.*

The **Uetliberg** (alt. 871m/2 856ft) is a favourite day trip for locals. The railway journey is mainly through woods. From the arrival station (no cars), there is a fine view of the summits of the Alps. Take the steep path to the nearby terrace of the Gmüetliberg restaurant (*viewing table*).

You can go to the top of the belvedere tower (*167 steps*) for a sweeping **panorama**★★ of the whole Zürich district, the Limmat Valley, Lake Zürich, and the Alpine range—from Säntis in the east to the Jungfrau and Les Diablerets in the southwest. From here, it is possible to follow the ridge to Felsenegg (alt. 804m/2 637ft; a walk of approximately 1hr45min). A "planet path" (Planetenweg) features models of the planets on a scale of 1:1 billion. At Felsenegg,

Sunrise on the Uetliberg

© Christof Sonderegger/Switzerland Tourism

a cable-car climbs to Adliswil (*return to Zürich by train, line number 4*).

Kilchberg

▷ *7km/4mi. Leave Zürich by General Guisan-Quai.*

Highway 3 runs along the west shore of the lake to Kilchberg, a suburb of Zürich. Swiss poet Conrad Ferdinand Meyer (1825–1898) and German writer Thomas Mann (1875–1955) spent their last days in this area and are buried in its small cemetery.

Wildpark Langenberg

This wildlife park extends on either side of the road (mostly on the left side) north of Langnau am Albis on a couple of acres of forest and rocky hillocks: deer, chamois, marmots, ibex and wild boar can sometimes be seen. The road climbs to the Albis Pass (alt. 791m/2 596ft) from where magnificent views extend over the countryside, then descends between Lake Turler and the Albis Mountain before turning left toward Hausen at the foot of the Albishorn. Some time after Hütten, there is a stretch of corniche (*2km/1mi*) that overlooks the widest part of Lake Zürich. The road then rises as far as Feusisberg in the countryside with glimpses of the lake. After a winding section of road through woods, there is a plunging **view**★, which reveals both sections of the lake (Obersee on the right) which the Rapperswil causeway divides.

© Circus Knie/Manuela Matt-Merk

Knie—The Swiss National Circus

In 1803 Friedrich Knie, son of Empress Maria-Theresa's personal physician, was studying medicine at Innsbruck when a chance encounter with a horsewoman from a troupe of travelling artistes changed his life. He joined them, becoming an acrobat. Later, he founded his own troupe and performed throughout Germany, Austria, Switzerland and France, gaining fame as a tightrope walker. His children and grandchildren kept up the tradition. The Knie family became Swiss citizens in 1900; in 1919 Friedrich's cherished dream came true when the Knie Circus was founded. Today the Knies are one of the great circus families; their one-ring circus remains a family affair with the sixth generation now active. It is Switzerland's national circus, although it remains financially independent. The circus and its itinerant zoo tour March to November, giving 375 shows under the big top to capacity audiences of 3 000 in some 60 towns. Their winter quarters are in Rapperswil.

Rapperswil★

Alt. 409m/1 342ft. Hintergasse 16.
℘(0)848 811 500.
Sitting on a short peninsula on the north shore of Lake Zürich, the little town of Rapperswil has kept its medieval appearance, emphasised by the imposing mass of its castle. Rapperswil is a pleasant place to stay in summer, with plenty of walks and drives around the lake and in the neighbourhood. Below the town, a wooden crossing, stretching for 841m/0.5mi, bridges the narrowest part of the lake. It has been part of the pilgrims' way to the abbey of Einsiedeln opposite (&see p352) for centuries.

Castle

A massive structure flanked by three grim-looking towers, the castle was built by the counts of the district in the 13C. From the outer terrace there is a fine **view** of the town below, Lake Zürich

and, beyond it, the Glarus Alps and St Gallen. On the opposite side, above the former ramparts and overlooking the lake, a deer park has been there since the castle was built.

Ritterhaus

◷ *Open Apr–Oct, Tue–Thu, 1pm–5pm, Fri 1pm–8pm; Sat – Sun and public holidays, 10am–5pm.* ◷ *Closed Good Fri, Easter Sun and Whitsun.* ⊗*8CHF.* ℘ *(0)55 243 39 74. www.ritterhaus.ch.*
Founded in 1192 and rebuilt in the 15C and 16C, the Bubikon Commandery of the Order of the Hospital of St John of Jerusalem, is now used as a museum. It recounts the history of the Hospitalliers' Order with the aid of documents, arms, paintings. Also visit the chapel, 16C kitchen, library and large common rooms with their *trompe-l'œil* ceilings and panelling, fireplaces, and Gothic-Renaissance furnishings.

ADDRESSES

🛏 STAY

Affectionately nicknamed the "little big city", Zürich is expensive. During the high season, allow at least 160CHF for a double room, including breakfast. For the younger traveller, there is a **youth hostel** at Mutschellenstrasse 114, ℘(0)43 399 78 00. The **Seebucht campsite** is at Seestrasse 559, on the west bank of the lake; ℘(0)44 482 16 12.

🛏 **City Backpacker** – Niederdorfstrasse 5. ℘(0)44 251 90 15. www.city-backpacker.ch. 65 beds. An address for backpackers that proves that Zürich is not just for wealthy tourists. The rooms and dorms provide basic comfort, but you will not find anything cheaper or more central (in the middle of Niederdorf). Bathrooms on the landing. Friendly international atmosphere, and a beautiful roof terrace.

🛏 **Splendid** – Rosengasse 5. ℘(0)44 252 58 50. Fax 0(0)44 262 61 40. www.hotelsplendid.ch. 24 rooms. Splendid might be overdoing it, but this one-star, simple and rather dated hotel is in a decent location (close to the Limmat) for the price. Toilets and showers on the landing.

🛏 **Youth Hostel** - Mutschellenstrasse 114 ℘(0)43 399 78 00. www.youthhostel.ch. 76 rooms. Globetrotters keen to save money can drop their backpack in this clean, comfortable and well equipped building .The hostel is, alas, away from the centre: the lake is only 10 min walk, but the station is 6.5km/4mi away so downtown is a tram ride away. Reception 24/7, self-service restaurant, bar, washing machines.

🛏 **Altstadt** – Kirchgasse 4. ℘(0)44 250 53 53. Fax (0)44 250 53 54. www.hotel-altstadt.ch. 23 rooms. Pictorial compositions and poems signed by contemporary artists adorn the walls of regularly renovated rooms, at this hotel in the charming district of Oberdorf. Nice bar downstairs.

🛏 **Franziskaner** – Niederdorfstrasse 1. ℘(0)44 250 53 00. Fax (0)44 250 53 01. www.hotel-franziskaner.ch. 19 rooms. A three-star hotel recently refurbished with care and taste. Excellent value for the bustling neighbourhood of Niederdorf. Special rates on weekends (on request). Bar and restaurant.

🛏 **Landhus** – Katzenbachstrasse 10. Zürich-Seebach. ℘(0)44 308 34 00. www.landhus-zuerich.ch. 28 rooms. This hotel has English-style décor and comfortable rooms.

🛏 **Leoneck** – Leonhardstrasse 1. ℘(0)44 254 22 22. www.leoneck.ch. 78 rooms. This hotel features an unusual interior which revolves around the world of cows. The whole decoration, including frescoes, depict these large, friendly creatures. Conveniently located on a hill, a few minutes from the old town. No parking facilities.

🛏 **Rex** – Weinbergstrasse 92. ℘(0)44 360 25 25. www.hotelrex.ch. 41 rooms. Restaurant 🛏. Modern, recently renovated comfortable hotel near the town centre. On-site parking for guests.

🛏 **Uto Kulm** – Giusep Fry, in Ütliberg ℘(0)44 457 66 66. www.utokulm.ch. 55 rooms. Perched above Zürich, this hotel has a superb view of the city below. Perfect for a restful break in the countryside.

🛏 **Adler** – Rosengasse 10, am Hirschplatz. ℘(0)44 266 96 96. www.hotel-adler.ch. 52 rooms. Situated in the lively district of Niederdorf (soundproof windows keep out the noise), this old-fashioned hotel, with a charming bohemian touch, displays works of Basel artist Heintz Hum, along with frescoes illustrating the city's main sights. Restaurant serves traditional cuisine (fondues, raclettes).

🛏 **Sorell Hotel Zürichberg** – Orellistrasse 21. ℘(0)44 268 35 35. www.zuerichberg.ch. 66 rooms. Nestling in the forest not far from the lake, a few minutes from Zürich by tramway, this hotel has a terrace offering lovely city views. The combination of modern and traditional styles creates an unusual atmosphere.

🛏 **Greulich** – Herman Greulich-Strasse 56. ℘(0)43 243 42 43. www.greulich.ch. 18 rooms. 🍽18 CHF. Fans of contemporary design and architecture will love this stylish hotel which celebrates the marriage of wood, glass and concrete. Arranged around a quiet courtyard, it combines minimalist decor in the rooms with modern comforts. The hotel has a "slow food" restaurant with Mediterranean cuisine and a trendy lounge bar. The hotel is a good 20-minute walk from the Bahnhofstrasse.

Rössli – *Rössligasse 7. ℘(0)44 256 70 50. www.hotelroessli.ch. 27 rooms.* This very central hotel, is nestled in an alley in the district of Oberdorf. It occupies a historic building which has been completely refurbished. The decor and the elegant rooms, the impeccable comfort and the professional service is second to none in Zürich. Prices are, of course, high, but you will not find a better example in this category in the city centre. The hotel has no garage (parking close but expensive). Free Internet.

⸮/EAT

Zeughauskeller – *Bahnhofstrasse 28A. ℘(0)44 211 26 90. www.zeughauskeller.ch. Closed public holidays.* Generous portions of regional cuisine served in a former 15C arms depot. Art Nouveau décor and shaded terrace in summer.

Öpfelchammere – *Rindermarkt 12. ℘(0)44 251 23 36. Closed Sun, Mon 24 Dec –8 Jan and mid-Jul–mid-Aug.* This is Zürich's oldest tavern, dating back to the 13C. The old-fashioned setting, medieval rafters, and traditional furniture make for a delightful dining experience.

Zum Kropf – *In Gassen 16. ℘(0)44 221 18 05. www.zumkropf.ch Closed Sun and public holidays.* A stone's throw from the Fraumünster, this large tavern dating from 1888 has three Art Nouveau beer halls, whose ceilings are decorated with frescoes. Generous portions.

Zunfthaus zur Schmiden – *Marktgasse 20. ℘(0)44 250 58 48. www.zunfthausschmiden.ch.* This renovated blacksmiths' guildhall in the old quarter presents a fine 15C Gothic dining hall and an attractive coffered ceiling. Call for opening times.

Kronenhalle – *Rämistrasse 4. ℘(0)44 262 99 00. www.kronenhalle.com.* Typical brasserie with an artistic ambience, displaying works by contemporary painters. Charming bar and restaurant serving local fare and wide selection of wines and beers.

Haus zum Rüden – *Limmatquai 42 (1st floor). ℘(0)44 261 95 66. www.hauszumrueden.ch. Closed Sat and Sun except for group reservations.* This former guildhall from the 13C features a remarkable dining room with groined vaulting, which adds charm and atmosphere to the restaurant.

Zunfthaus zur Zimmerleuten – *Limmatquai 40 (1st floor). ℘(0)44 250 53 63. www.zimmerleuten.ch. Closed public holidays and mid-Jul–mid-Aug.* Charming 18C guild-house. Choose from a rustic, cosy setting with wooden beams, a charming, light room for romantic dinners, and a scenic restaurant overlooking the Limmat.

Bodega Española – *Münstergasse 15. ℘(0)44 251 23 10. Closed 25 & 26 Dec.* For over 100 years, this authentic wine cellar has been serving excellent Spanish paella and tapas in an old Zürich café. Iberian atmosphere with hams hanging from the rafters, garlands of garlic and waiters speaking in Spanish. Very busy every night.

Hiltl – *Sihlstrasse 28. ℘(0)44 227 70 00. www.hiltl.ch.* Founded in 1898, the oldest vegetarian restaurant in Zürich serves excellent dishes from around the world: curries, paella, tagines, etc. A wide choice which, combined with a cozy and chic environment, has seduced the city. Eat à la carte or, more economically, use the buffet where you pay by weight. Also serves as a takeaway.

Alpenrose – *Fabrikstrasse 12. ℘(0)44 271 39 19. Open daily except Mon (Sat, Sun and Tues nights only). Closed mid-Jul–mid-Aug and Christmas/ New Year period.* Draws a clientele of regulars—quite understandably so, as feasting under the high ceiling and panelling define this restaurant as a warm and pretty mountain chalet. The traditional Swiss dishes always manage to surprise. Top recommendations are "Bündner Pizokel", a specialty of the Engadin, and fresh fish from Lake Zürich. Friendly and attentive. A good choice and excellent value for money.

Roi International – *Seestrasse 457. (0)44 487 14 14.* Breathtaking view of Lake Zürich and the lights from the windows of this recently revamped (and renamed—it was previously called Blu) restaurant located near the Rote Fabrik. The kitchen uses regional ingredients in Mediterranean-style dishes. Depending on the day, up to the full cost of your meal is given as credit to spend in the adjacent lifestyle (homeware, fashion, gifts) shop.

LaSalle – *Schiffbaustrasse 4 (tram 4 / 13 Escher-Wyss-Platz). (0)44 258 70 71. www.lasalle-restaurant.ch. Open Mon–Fri for lunch and Mon–Sun for dinner until very late.* Located in the renovated Schiffbau factory in Züri-West, this restaurant offers a sophisticated decor and trendy design, which combines raw concrete, metal, and glass (note the Murano chandelier). The menu is varied and daring. Finish the evening in the third floor bar to admire the city lights.

SIGHTSEEING

BOAT TRIPS ON LAKE ZÜRICH

Information from the Tourist Office or at the main landing-stage at Bürkliplatz, near Bellevue. Tram numbers 2, 5, 8, 9 and 11 run to the landing stage. Boat trips Mar–Oct. Trips last from 1hr to 5hr; meals are served on board from Apr–Oct. To reserve, call (0)44 487 13 13. www.zsg.ch Boat trips run along the Limmat *(1hr30min),* from the Schweizerisches Landesmuseum as far as the Zürichhorn. Large boats operate trips on the lake, including a short trip *(1hr30min),* stopping at Erlenbach and Thalwil, and a longer half-day excursion on a steamboat, stopping at Rapperswil *(see RAPPERSWIL)* and Schmerikon, at the other end of the lake. If you opt for the longer trip to Rapperswil you can return by rail using the same ticket.

SHOPPING

Bahnhofstrasse is Zürich's main shopping street. It is lined by smart boutiques with attractive window displays and is home to several **department stores**, such as Globus, Jelmoli and Coop. The street becomes more and more expensive the further you move from the station. Interesting shops selling designer items, wooden toys and confectionery can be found in the **old city**, along the narrow streets surrounding Weinplatz on the left bank and in the district around Niederdorfstrasse on the right bank.

Flea market – *On Bürkliplatz, open every Sat from May–Oct, 6am–4pm.*

SOUVENIRS

The long-established confectioner's **Sprüngli** (Bahnhofstrasse 21) sells all kinds of truffles and chocolates, including Luxemburgerli, a local speciality. **Schweizer Heimatwerk** (Rudolf Brun-Brücke) is part of a chain of shops selling typical Swiss souvenirs, including designer items, toys, and children's clothes inspired by traditional costumes. The **Pastorini** toy shop (Weinplatz 3) in the old town specializes in wooden toys.

THEATRE AND MUSIC

Opernhaus – *Falkenstrasse 1. (0)44 268 66 66. www.opernhaus.ch.* Richard Wagner once conducted in this neo-Baroque opera house (1891).

Tonhalle – *Gotthardstrasse 5 and Claridenstrasse 7. (0)44 206 34 34. www.tonhalle.ch.* Built in 1895, this large hall was inaugurated by Johannes Brahms.

Schauspielhaus – *Rämistrasse 34. (0) 44 258 77 77. www.schauspielhaus.ch.* This theatre (1884) is renowned for excellent music and drama programmes.

Bernhard-Theater – *Theaterplatz. (0) 44 268 66 66. www.bernhardtheater.ch.*

Theater Stok – *Hirschengraben 42. (0)44 251 22 80. www.theater-stok.ch.*

NIGHTLIFE

Niederdorf is buzzing every night—not just on weekends—and a walk down the street is recommended. Before 10–11pm you can sit outside while afterwards you congregate indoors because of noise regulations.

For a more quiet night out try the **Jules Verne bar** at the Brasserie Lipp (*Uraniastrasse 9*) that offers a fine selection of cocktails and affords a lovely view of the city, or enjoy the cosy, intimate atmosphere of the **Hôtel Central Plaza**, not far from Bahnhofbrücke. Sample a *"déci"* (*short for décilitre*) of Swiss wine in the pleasant setting of the **La Barrique** (*Marktgasse 17. www.barrique-wineandbar.ch*) The famous **Café Odéon** (*Limmatquai 2*) with Art Nouveau décor was once frequented by writers and famous personalities such as Thomas Mann and Lenin, but its clientele is now mostly gay. Many of the trendier dance clubs are to be found in industrial Zürich-West. The chic clientele gravitates to **Bling** (*Neufrenkengasse 22, www.bling-zuerich.ch*), electro and hip-hop fans flock to **Besame Mucho** (*Pfingstweidstrasse 6, www.besamemucho.ch*) while **Loop38** attracts an alternative crowd (*Albulastrasse 38, www.loop38.ch*). To watch live bands almost every night check out the **Hive Club** (*Geroldstrasse 5, www.hiveclub.ch*) and if you like eighties music the **Labor Bar** which is gay on Sundays (*Schiffbaustrasse 3, www.laborbar.ch*). Jazz, blues or soul fans should not miss visiting club **Moods** (*Schiffbaustrasse 6. www.moods.ch*) next door. Finally the **Rote Fabrik** (*see Riverside Walks*) houses the **Ziegel oh Lac bistro** (*www.ziegelohlac.ch*) and a huge **concert hall**, popular with Zürich's rock fans. Dance club and concerts are on several times a week.

For a British ambience and a wide selection of beers go to the **Lion Pub** (*Ötenbachgasse, left bank*) or further up to the **Nelson** (*Beatengasse 11*)

BATHS ALONG THE LIMMAT

These traditional, old-fashioned baths are situated along the banks of the Limmat and are open June–August.

Stadthausquai *(0)44 211 95 92. www.barfussbar.ch*. These baths, located close to Zürich's city hall, are for women only and include a solarium. Concerts and DJ-hosted events open to all are held here in the evening at the **Barfussbar** (where you enter barefoot).

Schanzengraben (off the town plan) *(0)44 211 95 94*. Also in the city centre, near the Stauffacherbrücke and the stock exchange, this swimming pool is for men only.

Flussbad Oberer Letten – *Pier West, Lettensteg 10. (0)44 362 92 00*. Take Limmatstrasse behind the railway station, then turn right toward Sihlquai. These baths, situated in the Letten district, are the oldest in the city. Open to men, women, and children.

EVENTS

The Tourist Office inside the train station offers a weekly guide to what is happening in Zürich.

During the **Sechseläuten** spring festival, usually held on the third Monday in April, the various corporations of Zürich march through the city centre in traditional costume. The city's symbol of winter, the **Böögg**, a snowman made from cotton wool and filled with fireworks, is burned at 6pm on Sechseläutenplatz, at Bellevue.

The **Knabenschiessen**, a shooting competition for children aged between 12 and 16, is one of the oldest festivals in Zürich. It is held on the Albisgütli fields (last stop on tram number 13) on the second weekend in September.

The **Züri-Fäscht**, a large fair held along the banks of the River Limmat in the old town, takes place every three years, over three days in early July and includes firework displays along the lake. The next Züri-Fäscht will take place between 5 and 7 July 2013.

Basel★★★

Situated on the northwest border of Switzerland, facing Alsace and the Baden region, Basel town is washed by the River Rhine at the point when it becomes navigable. The Old Town is part of Grossbasel (Greater Basel) and is separated from Kleinbasel (Lesser Basel) by the wide river which opens up opportunities for maritime trade. The third largest city in the country, Basel is a vibrant cultural centre with over 30 museums: at present, new museums are opening at a rate of one every year. The city's prosperity is derived from banking, insurance, sea traffic and a number of important chemical and pharmaceutical companies based here. Some 30 000 workers commute to Basel each day; approximately a third come from Germany and two-thirds from France, mostly from the Alsace region.

A BIT OF HISTORY

Origins – The city's origins date back to pre-Roman times, as testified by ruins of a fortified Celtic settlement dating from around 100 BC, in the St Johann district. The Roman city of Augusta Raurica (see AUGST/AUGUSTA RAURICA) was later founded here in 44 BC. In 1032 Basel became part of the Germanic Empire but later came under the rule of a prince-bishop, vassal of the Emperor; these events are recalled in the town's coat of arms, which bears an Episcopal cross.

From the Council of Basel to the Reformation – From 1431–48, the Council of Basel tried to reform the clergy and bring heretics back to the Church. However, its existence was threatened by serious disagreements dividing the Pope and his bishops. The Council offered the papal tiara to Amadeus VIII, Duke of Savoy, who took the title of Pope Felix V. It was only in 1501 that the city joined the Helvetic Confederation.

▶ **Population:** 164 937.
Info: SBB Railway station. ☎(0)61 268 68 68. www.basel.com.
Parking: Parking may be difficult to find in Old Town. See the map for outlying parking areas. A day-pass for public transport within the city is available from the Tourist Office.
Don't Miss: The Kunstmuseum: The country's largest art museum.
Kids: Basel's large zoo, situated southwest of Old Town and the Museum of Caricature and Comic Strip.
Timing: Allow at least 4 hours for a walking tour of Old Town and the Kunstmuseum. To visit the majority of attractions, reserve 4 days plus an additional day for the excursions.

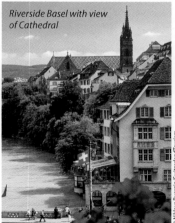
Riverside Basel with view of Cathedral

© Nikolaus Buergin/SwitzerlandTourism

The industrial age – Basel welcomed many French Huguenots who had fled following the Revocation of the Edict of Nantes when Protestantism in France was outlawed. They introduced silk weaving into Basel, paving the way for

GETTING AROUND

BY FERRY – Four Fähri routes cross the River Rhine (5min). These passenger-only ferries are propelled solely by the river flow holding on to a cable across the Rhine. *The ferries run daily in summer from 9am–7pm. In winter, the two middle routes run from 11am–5pm.*

BY BICYCLE – A map of cycle routes is available from the Tourist Office. Bikes can be borrowed free of charge in summer from 8am–10pm from the railway station, Theaterplatz, Claraplatz and Schifflände; a deposit is charged. Visitors must show a passport or identity card.

PUBLIC TRANSPORT – Tickets for public transport are available from automatic ticket vendors; a pass valid for one or several days (from 8.5CHF) can be bought at the Tourist Office. Anyone spending the night in a hotel in Basel Town is given a Mobility Ticket, which provides unlimited access to all forms of local transport.

---

industrial expansion. The town started to manufacture ribbons, an activity in which it came to specialise. The industry of dyeing was introduced and began to expand; the creation of the Geigy factory in 1785 signaled the beginning of the chemicals industry in Basel. The golden age of the 18C has left its mark in the handsome Classical hotels. During the 19C, the town expanded into the surrounding countryside. After a violent civil conflict, two half-cantons were created in 1883: Basel-Stadt (Basel Town, represented by a black crosier) and Basel-Land (Basel District, represented by a red crosier).

Basler dialect – Compared with other German-speaking areas, this dialect has slightly muffled vowels and is softer on the ear. Situated on the border of three countries, Basel borrows words from French, such as *Baareblyy* (*parapluie*—umbrella), *Boorpmenee* (*portemonnaie*—wallet) and *Exgyysi* (*Excusez-moi*—Excuse me). Unusually, locals say *Aadie* derived from the French *adieu*, meaning goodbye, to say "hello".

⤜⤜WALKING TOUR

OLD TOWN★★★

Allow approx 3hrs. Leave from Marktplatz (the market place).

Surrounded by corbelled houses the Marktplatz is animated Monday to Saturday by the market stands in front of the arcades of City Hall next to the Coopers' Guildhouse (1578).

Rathaus (H)

⤜⤜*Guided tours available. ⤜No charge. Call for info.* ✆ *(0)61 268 68 68.* The town hall was erected between 1508 and 1514 in the Late Gothic style and restored between 1898 and 1902. The façade is decorated with frescoes and flanked by a modern belfry adorned with pinnacles. In the inner courtyard, note the fresco on the theme of justice by Hans Bock (1610) and a statue of Munatius Plancus, the founder of Augusta Raurica that developed into Basel.

▷ *Take the Eisengasse to the Rhine and walk right on the Rheinsprung.*

Cathedral★★

🕐*Open mid-Apr–mid-Oct, mid-Apr–mid-Oct, 10am(11.30am Sun)–5pm (4pm Sat); mid-Oct–mid-Apr, 11am (11.30am Sun) to 4pm.* ✆ *(0)61 272 91 57.* ⤜*4CHF (Tower).* ✆ *(0)61 272 91 57. www.baslermuenster.ch.*
The great 12C münster was partly rebuilt in the 14C and 15C and restored in the 19C. It is built with red sandstone and surmounted by two Gothic towers (good view of the city). Between the towers is a porch dating from the mid-13C. The recessed arches of the main doorway are decorated with small statues depicting prophets, angels and garlands of foliage and flowers.

The Carnival

The Basel Carnival dates back to the Middle Ages, the only Catholic celebration to have survived the Reformation in a Protestant city. Created to mark the beginning of Lent, the carnival interrupts the daily life of the population with three days of processions and masquerades meticulously governed by coded rituals.

On the first Monday after Ash Wednesday, at 4 o'clock in the morning, all the lights are switched off and the "**Morgestraich**," a custom dating back to the 18C, heralds the start of the festivities. During "**die drei scheenschte Dääg**"—the three most beautiful days—the revellers rule the city.

Participants (whose number can reach 15–18 000) sporting masks and costumes are divided into "groups" (called **cliques,** because you have to be invited to join one) of 20 to 200 people each and line up. Each clique dresses around a subject such as Harlequins, Centurions or American Presidents. They never take their masks off and it is impolite to ask someone to identify himself. The procession marches through the streets to the strains of fifes and drums and under showers of confetti (supposedly invented here) ending up in the local restaurants at 6 o'clock, where they are served onion pie and soup made with flour.

These colourful displays of masks and musical performances—both highly organised and individually celebrated—continue to enliven the town until Wednesday. Tuesday afternoon is reserved for the children's parade; do not miss their procession.

Skirting the building to the left you reach the **portal** of St Gallen (12C) showing *Christ the Judge* on the tympanum, *The Wise and Foolish Virgins* on the lintel and the *Resurrection of the Dead* over the main vault. There is a pretty **view**★ of the Rhine, the town, the Black Forest and the Vosges from the Pfalz terrace. A narrow, dark passage leads into 15C Gothic **cloisters**, extended by other cloisters dating from the same period.

The cathedral houses the **tomb of Erasmus**, the writer who made Basel a centre of Humanist learning, and who died here in 1536. Steps lead to the crypt, which houses tombs of the bishops of Basel from the 10C–13C.

▷ *Walk down the Münster hill until Barfüsserplatz.*

Barfüsserplatz

Criss-crossed constantly by the comings and goings of trams, the busiest place in Basel is dominated by the steeple of the church of St Leonard. It houses the Historical Museum (M1. Note at number 10 the beautifully painted façade of the restaurant-brewery Zum Braunnen Mutz.

▷ *Turn left to Steinenberg.*

Fassnachtsbrunnen

The Carnival Fountain designed by **Jean Tinguely** (1925–91) is the center of attraction on the esplanade in front of the municipal theatre. Nine cleverly articulated metallic structures in perpetual motion provide a telling example of Tinguely's wit and ingenuity.

▷ *Rejoin Barfüsserplatz and take Gerbergasse, the main street of the Old City. Walk to the Marktplatz, which extends the Marktgasse (Market Street) to Fischmarktplatz.*

Fischmarktplatz

This lively sector of Basel's shopping district, Fish Market Square, is ornamented with the Fish Market fountain (**Fischmarktbrunnen**), one of the most beautiful Gothic fountains in Switzerland. The fountain (11m/36ft high) is decorated with angels, saints and prophets. The

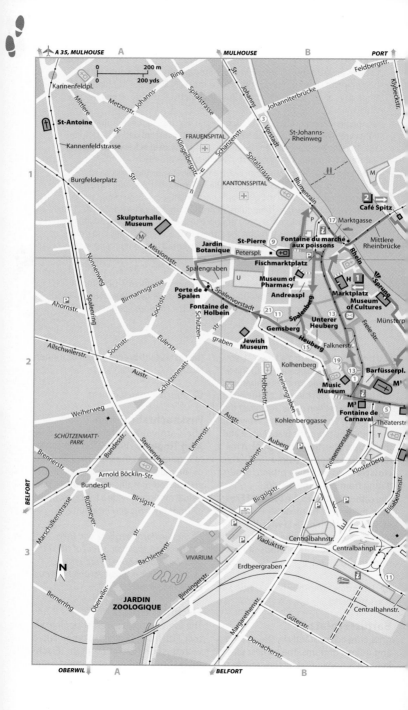

A 35, MULHOUSE   A   MULHOUSE   B   PORT

0   200 m
0   200 yds

Kannenfeldpl.

Feldbergstr.

Klybeckstr.

Mittlere   Metzerstr.   Johanns-   Ring   Spitalstrasse

St-Antoine

Kannenfeldstrasse

FRAUENSPITAL

St-Johanns-Rheinweg

Johanniterbrücke

Blumenrain

Café Spitz

Burgfelderplatz

KANTONSSPITAL

Klingelbergstr.   Schanzenstr.   Spitalstrasse   Vorstadt   St-Johanns

1

Skulpturhalle Museum

Missionsstr.

P   Marktgasse

Mittlere Rheinbrücke

Jardin Botanique   **St-Pierre**   **Fontaine du marché aux poissons**

Peterspl.   **Fischmarktplatz**

Spalengraben

Nonnenweg   Spalenring   Birmannsgrasse   Socinstr.   Eulerstr.   Schützenmatt   **Museum of Pharmacy**   Andreaspl   Spalenberg   **Marktplatz Museum of Cultures**   Münsterp.

Porte de Spalen   Spalenvorstadt   **Fontaine de Holbein**   **Gemsberg**   Unterer Heuberg   Falknerstr.

Ahornstr.   P

Ailschwilerstr.

Austr.   Schützen   graben   **Jewish Museum**   Heuberg

2

Weiherweg   Bundesstr.   Steinenring   Austr.   Leimenstr.   Holbeinstr.   Steinengraben   Kolhenberg   Kohlenberggasse   Auberg   Steinenvorstadt   Kolhenberg   **Music Museum**   **Barfüsserpl.**   **Fontaine de Carnaval**   Theaterstr.

SCHÜTZENMATT-PARK

Brennerstr.   Marschalkenstrasse   Rütimeyer   str.   Arnold Böcklin-Str.   Bundespl.   Birsigstr.   Bachletten   str.   Binningerstr.   Holbein   str.   Birsigstr.   Viaduktstr.   Centralbahnstr.   Centralbahnpl.   Klosterberg   Elisabethenstr.

BELFORT

N

VIVARIUM

JARDIN ZOOLOGIQUE

Bernerring   Oberwiler   str.

3

Erdbeergraben   Margarethenstr.   Dornacherstr.   Güterstr.   Centralbahnstr.

OBERWIL   A   BELFORT   B

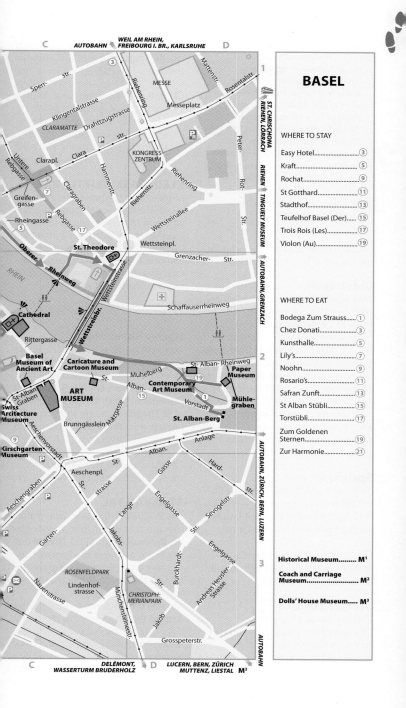

BASEL

WHERE TO STAY

Easy Hotel.............................③
Kraft.......................................⑤
Rochat...................................⑨
St Gotthard...........................⑪
Stadthof.................................⑬
Teufelhof Basel (Der)...........⑮
Trois Rois (Les)....................⑰
Violon (Au)............................⑲

WHERE TO EAT

Bodega Zum Strauss......①
Chez Donati....................③
Kunsthalle......................⑤
Lily's...............................⑦
Noohn.............................⑨
Rosario's........................⑪
Safran Zunft...................⑬
St Alban Stübli...............⑮
Torstübli........................⑰
Zum Goldenen
Sternen.........................⑲
Zur Harmonie.................㉑

Historical Museum.......... M¹

Coach and Carriage
Museum........................... M²

Dolls' House Museum..... M³

Cakes and biscuits

The *Leckerli*, a speciality of Basel since the Middle Ages, is a small, rich biscuit made from honey, flour, almonds, walnuts, orange and lemon concentrate, spices and eau-de-vie. It is sold in pastry shops all over town, including the **Läckerlihaus** (Gergerstrasse 57), which specialises in this particular biscuit. Local specialties served at Carnival time include the Fastnachtskiechli, a fried pastry sprinkled with sugar, and the Fastenwähe, a butter brioche flavoured with cumin.

original (1390), sculpted by Jacob Sarbach, is in the Historical Museum.

Old streets★

Take Stadthausgasse on the left and continue along Schneidergasse. This leads to **Spalenberg**, a steep picturesque street lined with art galleries and antique shops. Turn left into **Gemsberg** to a charming square lined with 13C and 14C houses and a flower-decked Chamois fountain. Turn into Untere Heuberg, a side street with attractive houses, then right into **Heuberg** where you see 13C and 14C residences; numbers 24, 20 and 6 have retained the pulley systems once used to lift objects to the attic.

Spalentor

This fine monumental gate was built in 1398 and restored at the end of the 19C. The summit of the west façade is adorned with Basel's coat of arms.

◐ *Go through the Botanical Gardens to the Petersplatz, shaded by trees and bordered by the University.*

St Peter's Church

🕐*Open Tue–Sun, 9am–5pm.*
👥*Guided tours available; for further details, contact the Tourist Office on ✆(0)61 268 68 68 or the presbytery on ✆(0)61 261 87 24.*
A Late Gothic church, Peterskirche was built in pink sandstone. In the south

aisle and in the chapel to the left of the chancel 14C–15C frescoes can be seen. On the left of the east end of the church, take **Petersgasse**, graced with medieval charm.

◐ *Walk away from the church down the stairs to the Spiegelgasse, which leads to Mittlere Rheinbrücke (Middle Rhine Bridge). This bridge joins the left bank to the Little Basel on the right bank of the Rhine.*

KLEIN BASEL (LITTLE BASEL)

At the end of the bridge on the right, stands the famous Café Spitz. This was where in 1833 the guild of the three main Kleinbasel fraternities (symbolised by the wild, the lion and the griffin) was founded. The terrace of this famous seafood restaurant offers spectacular views over the Rhine.

◐ *Descend a few steps to the right.*

Oberer Rheinweg

This esplanade set along the Rhine affords a panoramic **view**★ of the area, especially from the **Wettsteinbrücke**. Narrow alleyways link the esplanade to Rheingasse, which leads to the church of **St Theodore,** where you find some fine late-4C stained-glass windows and a bell tower dating from 1277.

◐ *With the old church on your right, cross the Wettsteinbrücke.*

ST ALBAN TAL

The St Alban district was named after the oldest convent in town, founded by the Bishop of Basel in 1083. Now all that remains is a wing of the Romanesque cloisters, visible from the old graveyard of St Alban's Church (Gothic chancel and tower, 19C nave).
It was in this residence that the painter **Arnold Böcklin** spent his childhood days. The traditional paper industry, dating back to the creation of a canal by monks in the 12C, is evidenced by a number of mills; there is a view over the canal and several mills at the beginning of the street, St Alban-Tal.

Mühlegraben

Next to the Museum of Paper, this wooden walkway, which has been renovated, is one of the remains of walls of Basel, built in the 14C. The medieval fortifications of the city were destroyed, mostly after 1860, a period of population growth due to the industrialisation of the 19C.

▷ *Follow the canal after the Paper Museum.*

St Alban-Berg

Cross the canal, from where you see the foundations of the town's former fortifications; continue along the path up St Alban hill. At the top, St Alban gateway and its portcullis (St Alban-Tor) built in the 13C, are surrounded by a pretty garden.

OUTSIDE THE OLD TOWN
👫🏻 Zoologischer Garten★★★

🕐*Open 8am–5.30pm; extended hours Mar–Oct.* ♿*18CHF (7CHF ages 6–16).* ♿ ℘*(0)61 295 35 35. www.zoobasel.ch.*
This **zoological garden** was founded in 1874 and, with Bern, is one of the largest in Switzerland (13ha/32 acres). It includes more than 6 000 animals from each of the five continents. The zoo specialises in the reproduction and rearing of endangered species such as rhinoceroses, gorillas and spectacled bears. Its park, with ponds where swans, ducks, flamingoes and other exotic birds splash about, is equipped with restaurants, picnic spots, and children's play areas.
The children's zoo has young or newborn animals which children can pet, and ponies or elephants on which they can ride. Several buildings are entirely devoted to one species, such as the Monkey Pavilion, the Aviary, the Elephant House, and the Wild Animal House.
The **vivarium** houses 250 varieties of fish (sea and freshwater), 250 reptile species, and 40 amphibian species, some of which are exceedingly rare. Before leaving, don't miss the zoo's star attractions, the several dozen or so penguins and king penguins.

St Antonius Kirche

Lovers of contemporary architecture will admire the church made out of reinforced concrete, which was erected in 1925–1931, according to the plans of the architect Werner Moser. The nave is set as a system of barrel-vaulted chambers and the aisles are covered with coffered ceilings, while the stained-glass windows of Hans Stocker and Otto Staiger illuminate the immense interior.

Hafen (Port)
Via Klybeckstrasse.
Since the Middle Ages, the town has played a part in trade between the North Sea and the Mediterranean, Swabia and Burgundy. River navigation ceased following the building of the great Alpine roads and railway lines and it was not until 1906 that traffic resumed as far as Antwerp and Rotterdam.
The city's main docks extend downstream as far as Kleinhünigen, where an obelisk in the shape of an unfolding needle—the **Dreiländereck** memorial—and a viewing platform mark the junction of the French, German, and Swiss frontiers.
The ports of Basel Town and Basel District (Basel-Stadt and Basel-Land) are equipped to handle the larger motor vessels and barges. Coal, hydrocarbons, grain, metallurgical products, and industrial raw materials make up most of this traffic, which is mainly concerned with imported goods.

Boat trips
Tours of the harbour passing through the locks, May–Oct. Contact Basler Personenschiffahrts-Gesellschaft AG, Hochberstrasse 160, Postfach 4019. ℘(0)61 639 95 00/08. www.bpg.ch.
In summer, there are tours of the port along the Rhine and the Kembs Canal. 🕐*For details of embarkation points see the town plan.*

GROSSBASEL MUSEUMS
Art Museum★★★
🕐*Open Tue–Sun 10am–6pm.* ♿*15CHF.* ♿ ℘*(0)61 206 62 62. www.kunstmuseumbasel.ch.*

PRACTICAL INFORMATION
MUSEUMS

The **BaselCard**, valid for one, two or three days allows tourists free entry to 25 museums, free ferry rides, city tours, and entry to shows and other cultural events. See *www.basel.com* for prices.

The **Oberrheinischer Museums-Pass** allows free entry to the museums in Basel and the surrounding area for one year and can be purchased at the Tourist Office or participating museums.

In this sprawling Kunstmuseum, which has a large collection of masterpieces, particular emphasis is laid on 15C–17C paintings and drawings from the Upper Rhine and the Netherlands. The museum boasts the world's largest collection of works by the Holbein family. Donated to the city in 1661, they served as a starting-point for the creation of the museum.

Entrance courtyard, gallery, ground floor – Here stand sculptures by Rodin (*The Burghers of Calais*), Alexander Calder (*Die Grosse Spinne*) and Edouardo Chillida, and an extensive collection of works by **Arnold Böcklin**, a Basel native who produced many symbolic and mythological paintings.

The **First floor** covers 15C–17C art in the Upper Rhine, including a series of altarpiece panels, *The Mirror of the Holy Salvation*, by the Basel master **Konrad Witz** (c. 1440–45). The Alsatian painter Martin Schongauer (c.1430–91), drawing on the experience of Witz and his followers, depicts moving family scenes, notably in *Mary and Child in Their Room*. Next is Grünewald (1460–1528) and his *Christ on the Cross*, and his contemporary from Strasbourg, **Hans Baldung Grien** with his *Death and the Maiden* (1517).

Hans Holbein the Younger (1497–1543), one of the greatest painters of all time, marked the peak of the Renaissance. Among some 20 paintings are the admirable *Portrait of the Artist's Wife*

with her Children and Portrait of Erasmus as an Old Man with his shrewd gaze. Lucas Cranach the Elder (1472–1553) is present with *Virgin with Child Holding a Piece of Bread* and *Judgement of Paris*. Other rooms contain 17C Dutch paintings, including an outstanding work by the young Rembrandt (1606–69), *David before Saul*.

Portrait of Bonifacius Amerbach (1519) by Hans Holbein the Younger

© Kunstmuseum Basel

Another section contains artists such as Rubens, Goltzius, Ruysdael, Brouwer, and Stoskopff, and by masters of Romanticism (Delacroix, Géricault, Daumier) and Realism (Courbet, Manet). These rooms also display a fine collection of Impressionist and Post-Impressionist art, with works by Monet (*Snow Scenes*), Pissarro (*The Harvesters*) and Sisley (*The Banks of the Loing at Moret*); *The Racetrack* by Degas; *Young Girl Lying in the Grass* by Renoir; *Montagne Sainte-Victoire* by Cézanne; landscapes and portraits by Van Gogh; and several works by Gauguin, including *Nafea Faa ipoipo ("When Will You Marry?")*, an important painting dating from his Tahitian period, and major works by Caspar Wolf and Johann Heinrich Füssli. The Nazarene movement is represented with pictures by Josef Anton Koch and Johann Friedrich Overbeck.

Second floor – A painting by Georg Baselitz (*Animals*) in the foyer marks the beginning of the remarkable 20C collection. Cubism is particularly well represented with canvases by Braque (*Landscape, Pitcher and Violin*), Picasso (*Bread Loaves and Fruit Bowl on Table*),

Juan Gris (*The Violin*), and Fernand Léger (*The Woman in Blue*). Fauvism can be admired in compositions by Matisse. German Expressionism is present with Franz Marc (*Tierschicksale*), Emil Nolde (*Vorabend: Marschlandschaft*), Oskar Kokoschka (*Die Windsbraut*) and Lovis Corinth (*Ecce Homo*); Surrealism with Giorgio de Chirico, Dalí, Miró, Max Ernst and Yves Tanguy. Some rooms contain Abstract art by Arp, Mondrian (*Composition in Blue, Yellow and White*), Van Doesburg (*Composition in Black and White*), Vantongerloo (*Enigmatic L2 = S*), Kandinsky and Schwitters, and works of Henri Rousseau, Chagall, and Paul Klee. The museum also pays tribute to American art after the year 1945.

Abstract Expressionism, also known as the New York School, is represented with works by Franz Kline (*Andes*) and Clyfford Still (*Painting*); Colour Field by Barnett Newman (*Day Before One, White Fire II*) and Mark Rothko (*No 1*); Minimal Art heralded by Frank Stella. Body Art saw a flourishing era with Sam Francis (*Deep Orange and Black*), Cy Twombly (*Nini's Painting*) and Bruce Nauman. Pop Art is represented with pieces by Jasper Johns, Andy Warhol and Claes Oldenburg.

Museum of Cultures★★
Open Tue–Sun, 10am–5pm.
Closed 1 Jan, 1 Aug, 24, 25 and 31 Dec.
11CHF. (0)61 266 56 00.
www.mkb.ch.
The **Museum der Kulturen** houses the largest collection of its kind in Switzerland, with around 140 000 masks, arms, carvings, along with Oceanian and Pre-Columbian works of art. Of particular note is the Melanesian section (ground floor): a Papuan temple hut, masks, totem poles, etc. Other galleries display objects from Ancient Egypt, such as mummies and sarcophagi. Another section is devoted to European and Swiss customs and traditions, including popular religious art, rural life, and the carnival.
There are also extensive **collections devoted to natural sciences** as well as a prehistory section. Exhibits include information on animals from the region, exotic species and dinosaurs, as well as live animals.

Contemporary Art Museum
Open Tue–Sun, 11am–5pm. 12CHF.
(0)61 206 62 62.
A modern, bright building next to a 19C factory provides a pleasant setting for the **Museum für Gegenwartskunst**, part of the Fine Art Museum. It houses temporary exhibitions on prominent contemporary art movements since 1960: Minimal Art, Conceptual Art, Arte Povera and Free Figurative Art, and permanent works by such artists as Frank Stella, Bruce Nauman, Cindy Sherman and Joseph Beuys.

Antikenmuseum Basel und Sammlung Ludwig★★
Open Tue–Sun, 10am–5pm.
Closed 1 Jan, 1, 9 May, and 24, 25 Dec.
10CHF. (0)61 201 12 12.
www.antikenmuseumbasel.ch.
This is the only museum in Switzerland dedicated exclusively to the Ancient art of the Mediterranean. Its exhibits cover five millennia, from 4000 BC to the 7C AD, and include artefacts from Greece, Rome, Egypt and other civilisations in the Middle and Near East.

The Middle East, Cyprus and beginnings of Ancient Greece★★
(Basement)
Some 350 works illustrate the close ties between the island of Cyprus and the civilisations of the Near and Middle East (Iran, Mesopotamia, Syria, Urartu and Anatolia) with the Aegean.
Noteworthy are Syrian cups decorated with lions (8C BC), bronze caldrons from Urartu adorned with a bull's head, and votive statuettes from Cyprus, whose style is influenced by many countries, including Anatolia and Egypt (7C BC). The civilisations of the Near and Middle East also influenced Greek art, as shown by the containers with animal motifs (c.600 BC).

Ancient Egypt★★
(Basement)

This is the most important collection of Egyptian artefacts in Switzerland. The section is arranged in chronological order, with more than 600 exhibits on display. The Predynastic Period is represented by a simple but skillfully sculpted brown ceramic hippopotamus (c.3500 BC). A remarkable head in red jasper and a rare faïence statue of Ramses II with a falcon's head date from the Ramesside Era (c.1250 BC). An almost complete version of a Book of the Dead dating from the Ptolemaic Period (305–30 BC) is on one of the walls. The basement features works from **Roman and Hellenic times**: clay statuettes, small bronzes, funerary stelae from Phrygia, a scene representing Achilles and Penthesilea, and Roman tombs, including a fine marble sarcophagus.

Archaic and Classical eras
(Ground, first and second floors).

Exhibits include marble sculptures and bronze statuettes (600–300 BC). Note the funerary stela (480 BC), locally known as the "relief of the Basel doctor." A superb collection of vases (520–350 BC) includes works by an artist known as the "Berlin painter," as well as a huge amphora complete with lid, bearing the twin figures of Athena and Hercules, plus exhibits of jewellery and coins (from Sicily and southern Italy).

Historisches Museum Basel: Barfüsserkirche★ (M1)

🕐*Open Tue–Sun 10am–5pm.* 🕐*Closed 1 Jan, Good Fri, 1 May, Ascension, 24 and 31 Dec.* ✆*12CHF (*☎*(0)61 205 86 00. www.hmb.ch.*

This original Franciscan church belonged to the mendicant monks of the Order (barfüsser means barefoot) who occupied this old triple-aisle church (1231) until the Reformation in 1529. Near the steps leading downstairs stands a 17C painted bronze head of the *Lällenkönig* (King Lälli) whose significance is still debated and which used to adorn the old Rhine gate. Downstairs, exhibits retrace the town's

history since the days of the Celts, with a strong emphasis on the 13C, when Basel became a truly independent city. Besides this historical exhibition, reconstructed rooms present some fine period furniture. Also in the basement are precious, non-religious objects (such as Erasmus' beaker, 1531, and a provost's crown, 1671) and the cathedral treasury (with a bust-reliquary of St Ursula in partly gilded repoussé silver and copper, 14C; monstrance of the Innocents or the Apostles in gilded silver, 1335–40).

In the chancel, note the large altarpiece with panels from the Church of Santa Maria in Calanca (Graubünden). This polychrome retable made in Ivo Strigel's workshop was carved out of limewood. The rood screen corridor is decorated with fragments of Konrad Witz's *Dance of Death* (15C), a famous fresco painted in the days of the Council of Basel. The north side aisle is devoted to the Basel Corporations.

During the 18C, they played a major role in the city's political, administrative, religious, social and economic life. The south aisle presents objects from the Upper Rhine region: tapestries woven in Basel workshops, sculpted or painted wooden chests with romantic motifs, bowls, and faience work for the ornamentation of stoves.

In the nave, note the magistrates' stalls from Basel Cathedral (solid oak, 16C) and the 16C Holbein Fountain in painted sandstone, known as the Bagpiper's Fountain.

Music Museum

🕐*Open Wed–Sat 2pm–6pm, Sun 11am–5pm.* 🕐*Closed most public holidays.* ✆*7HF.* ☎*(0)61 205 86 00.*

The Musikmuseum, the largest of its kind in Switzerland, is part of the Historisches Museum. Its collection of 650 musical instruments is displayed in the Lohnhof, an old monastery, part of which dates from the 11C. The building, for a long time used as a prison, was restored in 2000. The "Music in Basel" section presents musical instruments in their social context, with rooms dedicated to themes such as public concerts.

Another section, "Concerto, Chorale and Dance," displays instruments played in different musical genres, including chamber music and religious music. "Parade, Celebration and Signals" exhibits instruments played during particular events, such as hunts or at royal courts. Visitors can listen to 200 extracts of music selected via an interactive display, which also provides information in a number of languages.

Karikatur & Cartoon Museum

Open Tue–Fri 2pm–6pm, Sat Sun and public holidays, 11am–6pm. Closed during Carnival, 24 –26 Dec, 1,2 Jan. 9CHF (-10 years, free). (0)61 226 33 60. www.cartoonmuseum.ch.

Set up in a superbly renovated old house, the Museum of Caricature and Cartoons stands out because of its highly original and refreshing approach. Adults and children will enjoy leafing through original albums, drawn by some of the leading names in this field: Tomi Ungerer, EK Waechter, Claire Bretécher, etc. Children can even try their hand at drawing in a special room set aside for this purpose.

Basel Paper Museum★★

Open Tue–Sun 11am (Sat 1pm)–5pm. Closed 1 Jan, Carnival, Good Fri, Easter Sun and Whitsun, Ascension, 1 May, 1 Aug, 24,25 and 31 Dec. 14CHF. (0)61 225 90 90. www.papiermuseum.ch.

In 1980, this former flour mill attached to Klingental Convent, later converted into a paper mill (1453), was turned into a museum devoted to the many aspects of the paper industry. It provides a lively presentation of the history of paper and paper-related activities, laid out on four levels. As in former times, the mill is still operated by its paddle wheel. Each floor is devoted to a particular theme.

Visitors can take part in the demonstrations and keep the objects they have made to remind them of their visit. They can choose between papermaking, fonts, typography and binding.

Museum of Pharmacy

Totengässlein 3. Tue–Fri 10am–6pm; Sat 5pm. Closed Sun, Mon, public holidays. 5CHF (-12 years, free). (0)61 264 91 11. www.pharmaziemuseum.ch.

Endowed with one of the richest collections on the history of pharmacy, the museum houses ancient instruments and drugs used in the past. A chemistry lab and a pharmacy with woodwork from the 18C and 19C has been restored. Note the curious Japanese medicine chest of the 18C, a sort of wooden box fitted with small drawers, and the exhibition on African and its remedies.

Schweizerisches Architekturmuseum

Steinberger 7. Mon–Wed 11am–6pm, Thu 11am–8.30pm, Sat/Sun 11am–5pm (hours change during public holidays). Closed during Carnival. 10 CHF (-12 years, free). (0)61 261 14 13. www.sam-basel.org.

The museum hosts temporary exhibitions of Swiss and international modern architecture. The emphasis is on Swiss architects (Le Corbusier, Baur, Bernoulli, Meyer, Wittwer), whose contribution to modern architecture was fundamental. It also offers guided tours of key monuments of the city (4hrs, in German, English, Italian and French). Individual tours available on request.

Jewish Museum

Kornhausgasse 8. Open Mon and Wed 2pm–5pm, Sun 11am–5pm. No charge. (0)61 261 95 14. www.juedisches-museum.ch.

The Jüdisches Museum der Schweiz is the only Jewish Museum in Switzerland. At the encouragement of Theodor Herzl, Jews from throughout Europe and America gathered in Basel to attend the first Zionist Congress, held in the Casino concert hall in August 1897. This momentous event marked a turning point in the long history of the Jewish community of Basel (the earliest Jewish settlements date back to the 12C and Hebrew books were printed here as early as the 16C). Exhibits include

Jewish law, the Jewish year and Jewish life. Artefacts from Jewish communities around the world include tombstones from the Middle Ages, Persian amulets studded with precious stones and sumptuous 19C silver menorahs from Vienna, plus embroidered prayer shawls, inscribed and painted Torah scrolls (*Book of Law*), and passports from World War II with the telltale "J" stamped on them.

Haus zum Kirschgarten

Open Tue–Sun, 10am–5pm, Sat 1pm –5pm. Closed most public holidays. 7CHF. (0)61 205 86 78.
The museum is housed in a beautiful 18C town house owned by the silk ribbon manufacturer JR Burckhardt. There is a fine collection of clocks, balance-cocks and watches from the 16C to the 19C, porcelain stoves and a large collection of porcelain figurines on the ground floor. Upstairs are drawing rooms adorned with Aubusson tapestries, pictures and French furniture; boudoirs and 18C and 19C costumes. The third floor offers a collection of antique toys: dolls' houses, miniature carriages, rocking horses, boats and vintage cars. The basement contains porcelain and ceramics from Switzerland, Germany, France and China; and carved casks, one of which dates from 1723 and holds 10 000l/2 200gal.

Skulpturhalle

Mittlere Strasse 17. Open Tue–Fri 10am–5pm, Sat–Sun 11am–5pm. Closed first Sun of every month 10 CHF (children 5 CHF). (061) 261 52 45 www.skulpturhalle.ch.
Part of the Museum of Ancient Art, it exhibits many Greek and Roman sculptures—including a large collection of sculptures from the Parthenon.

Puppenhausmuseum (M3)

Steinenvorstadt 1. Open daily 10am– 6pm. Closed 25 Dec and Carnival. 7 CHF (-16 years, free). (0)61 225 95 95. www.puppenhausmuseum.ch.
The largest doll museum in Europe on four floors with over 6 000 teddy bears (the largest collection in the world) and dolls in their original doll houses,

assembled by a collector, Ms. Oeri. As for teddy bears, there are yellow, green, blue, mechanical, musical—you name it, there's a bear in that style. The oldest teddy is displayed on the 4th floor and dates from 1904.

Schaulager★★

Ruchfeldstrasse 19 Münchenstein. Open summer depending on exhibitions. Closed Oct–May. Tours Thu 11am, Sun 5.30pm. 14 CHF (children, students 8CHF). (0)61 335 32 32. www.schaulager.org.
This huge cube lost in the suburbs of Basel certainly deserves a visit, if only for its futuristic architecture, by Herzog & de Meuron. Neither museum nor warehouse, the Schaulager houses works by the Emmanuel Hoffmann Foundation. It opens its doors only to temporary exhibitions, so it is advisable to inquire before going there. Avant-garde installations are seen at their best in the vast halls of the immaculate ground floor and basement, while the upper floors, lit by neon in a dizzying effect of symmetry, remain closed to the public. End your visit to the library and bar, which seem straight out of Moloko Bar in *A Clockwork Orange*.

Museum Jean Tinguely

Paul Sacher-Anlage 2. At the SBB train station, take tram number 2 to Wettsteinplatz, then bus number 31 in the direction of Habermatten/Hörnli and get off at the Museum Tinguely stop. Open Tue–Sun, 11am–6pm. Closed 1 Jan, Good Fri and 24,25 Dec. 15CHF. (0)61 681 93 20. www.tinguely.ch.
The renowned Ticino architect Mario Botta designed this museum, located along the banks of the Rhine in Solitude Park, which features a long glassed-in ramp adjoining a construction in pink sandstone. The museum pays tribute to the great metal sculptor **Jean Tinguely**, a dominant post-war artist who conceived the famous "strange machines" (*see FRIBOURG*). Each gallery is devoted to a specific period in the sculptor's life. The 1950s are represented

by reliefs driven by engines (*Méta-Mécanique, 1955*). In the 1960s, Tinguely created objects from scrap metal, followed by machine-sculptures painted black. The 1980s are marked by large compositions such as *Lola T 180—Memorial to Joachim B.* The machines can be operated by visitors however they choose. The upper floor displays letters and drawings as well as other sculptures like *Lotus and the Widows of Eva Aeppli, Hannibal II*, an impressive work reflecting Tinguely's obsession with death, and an unusual collection of philosophers' busts: *Friedrich Engels, Jean-Jacques Rousseau, Martin Heidegger,* and *Henri Bergson*. The tour finishes where the most striking item in the huge room is unquestionably *Grosse Méta Maxi-Maxi Utopia* (1987), of which the artist himself said: "I would like to make something gay, something for children, who can climb and jump; I would like it to turn into something good, impressive, merry, wild, something suggesting a funfair."

RIEHEN

Although a separate administrative division, Riehen is a suburb of the city.

▷ *Access by car via Wettsteinbrücke and Riehenstrasse. To avoid traffic and parking problems, visitors are advised to take tram number 6 from Marktplatz.*

Fondation Beyeler★★★
Tram no 6, Fondation Beyeler stop. 🕐*Open daily, 10am–6pm, Wed until 8pm.* 🕐*Closed 24, 25 Dec.* 💷*25CHF; reduced admission fees every Mon (except holidays).* *Guided tours available on request, contact* ℰ*(0)61 645 97 00. www.fondationbeyeler.ch.*
For half a century, Basel art enthusiasts **Hildy and Ernst Beyeler** collected paintings and sculptures from celebrated 20C artists; they commissioned Italian architect **Renzo Piano** and Richard Rogers to design a museum to display this collection. This simple building (2 700sq m/29 052sq ft) was constructed in 1997; three large bays open onto the lovely Berower Park, where a sculpture by Calder (*The Tree*, 1966) can be

admired. A water garden evokes *Pond with Waterlilies* by Monet, a 9m/29ft triptych on display in the museum. A long glass roof supported by red porphyry walls provides excellent lighting.

Around 200 paintings and sculptures trace the development of modern art from Impressionism to Cubism. Famous works include *Seven Bathers* by Cézanne, *Wheatfield with Cornflower* by Vincent van Gogh, *Rouen Cathedral* by Monet, *Woman Reading* by Braque, *Hungry Lion Attacking Antelope* by Douanier Rousseau, *Woman in Green* by Picasso, and *Interior with Black Fern* by Matisse. Abstract Art is represented here by *Fugue* by Kandinsky, and *Painting* no 1 by Mondrian.

Tribute is paid to Switzerland in the works of Klee (*Diana, Ein Tor*) and Alberto Giacometti (*Seated Woman, Caroline, The Street*). Post-war Abstract Art is represented by works of Mark Rothko, Robert Rauschenberg (*Windward*) and Roy Lichtenstein (*Girl with Tear III*). One room is devoted to British artist Francis Bacon (1909–92), whose compositions are characterised by distorted perspective and hallucinatory themes *(Portrait of George Dyer Riding a Bicycle)*. Paintings by Jean Dubuffet, Georg Baselitz, and Anselm Kiefer are also on display. Tribal art from Alaska, Oceania and Africa are interspersed with the paintings and sculptures.

Spielzeugmuseum★
Access by tram number 6, Riehen Dorf stop. 🕐*Open Mon, Wed–Sun 11am–5pm, Sun 10am–5pm.* 🕐*Closed 1 Jan, Good Fri, 1 May, 1 Aug, 24–26 and 31 Dec.* 💷*7CHF.* ℰ*(0)61 641 28 29.*
The **Toy Museum** occupies a large section of Wettsteinhaus, a magnificently restored former mansion which belonged to Johan Rudolf Wettstein, mayor of Basel (1645–1666). The collections include an astounding variety of toys and games. Exhibits illustrate the evolution of toy making and reflect the changes in trends and fashions throughout history. The mansion also houses the **Dorfmuseum**, devoted to daily life in Riehen, and the **Rebbaumuseum**,

which explains winemaking techniques and the art of winemaking.

EXCURSIONS
Vitra Design Museum★★
In Weil am Rhein, Germany.
▶ *Take bus number 55 from Claraplatz or Badischer Bahnhof in Basel to Vitra. By car, follow the Riehenstrasse and the Riehenring toward Freiburg.*
🕐*Open Mon–Sun 10am–6pm.* 💰*8CHF.* 🅿 *(free of charge).* 🚶*2hr guided architectural tours daily 11am. 1pm, 3pm.* 📞*+49 (0)7621 702 32 00. www.design-museum.de.*
This startling white **building**★ at the Vitra Campus is the work of Californian architect Frank Gehry, the first example of his "deconstructivist" style in Europe. The museum has a vast permanent collection of modern furniture design and hosts temporary exhibitions.
The VitraHaus (Herzog & de Meuron) opened in 2010 to showcase a variety of furniture products in different contexts, which you can purchase or order here.

AUGUSTA RAURICA★★
District of Basel. ▶ *11km/6.8mi SE of Basel.* 📞*(0)61 816 22 22. www.augusta-raurica.ch.* 🚶*Guided tour (30min–1hr depending on the route). The ruins are signposted in French and German.*
A series of plans explains how buildings were laid out originally. 🕐*Open Mar–Oct,10am(Mon 1pm)–5pm; Nov–Feb, 11am (Mon 1pm)–5pm.* 💰*No charge.* 📞*(0)61 816 22 22. www.baselland.ch.*
It is to the Roman general Munatius Plancus, a friend of Julius Caesar, that

Switzerland owes the existence of the "Colonia Raurica" ruins, the oldest Roman settlement situated alongside the Rhine, founded in 44–43 BC. It is believed that the actual colonization of the Augst site dates back to the year 10 BC.

An important ancient city – By the year AD 200, Augst had grown to a city of 20 000 people and had become a prosperous centre for both trade and craft. Owing to its privileged location on the northern border of the Roman Empire, artistic activity thrived, as shown by the many imposing public buildings. Towards the end of the 3C, characterised by severe political unrest, most of the city was destroyed when the Alemanni assaulted the defensive system, or *limes*. In order to keep control over this strategic passage of the Rhine, the army built the powerful Kaiseraugst stronghold slightly north of Augst soon after the year AD 300. Most of these fortifications remained standing after the fall of the Roman Empire and served to protect the local population during the early Middle Ages.

Excavation work – During the 16C, influenced by the doctrines of the great Basel humanists, the famous jurist **Amerbach** was the first to carry out scientific research, making use of the excavation work formerly conducted by the tradesman Andreas Ryff. In 1839, the Historical and Archaeological Society of Basel commissioned research on the Roman city. From 1878 onwards, this site has been the subject of in-depth investigations.

Ancient ruins – Restored monuments include the **Theatre**, the largest Roman ruin in Switzerland, with a seating capacity of 8 000. Today it is used as a venue for outdoor concerts and live performances. The administrative, political and religious core of the city was the **forum**, consisting of the basilica, the Temple of Jupiter, and the **curia** (display of mosaics in the cellar). Markets and various local festivities were held at the forum. The

sewers were designed to evacuate the waters from the central baths to the Violental Valley; visitors may enter this huge cylindrical pipe (*diameter 70cm/28in*), with limestone walls and a sandstone paved floor. The amphitheatre was the scene of many games, races and fights between gladiators and wild beasts.

🧑‍🦽 Römermuseum★

🕐*Open same hours as the site .* 👜*7CHF (children 5CHF).* ♿ 𝄞*(0)61 816 22 22.*
Adjoining the Roman House, the Roman Museum presents some of the 700 000 objects unearthed during the excavations. The **silver hoard**★★ discovered at the foot of the Kaiseraugst fortifications in 1962 features many precious objects, including 68 items of sumptuous tableware: dishes decorated with mythological scenes, tumblers, spoons, candelabra and platters. This treasure also contained three silver ingots which experts traced back to the year AD 350. It is thought that the treasure might have been buried during the Germanic invasion in AD 352–353. There is also a small **animal park** (*Haustierpark*) 🧑‍🦽 of old breeds, some threatened by extinction, including wooly-haired pigs, Alpine sheep and small cattle.

Römisches Wohnhaus★

🕐*Same admission times and charges as the Römermuseum.*
This Roman House was a private residence and is considered to be a faithful reconstruction of the type common in Augst under the Roman Empire. The kitchen, dining room, bedroom, bathroom, workshop and shop contain authentic artefacts and utensils found on the site. The floor of the steamroom carries a diagram of an ingenious heating system devised by the Romans in which hot air circulated under the floor and between double walls. The right wall bears a fragment of the famous **Gladiators' mosaic**, thought to be the largest and finest in the Roman city. It used to adorn the dining-room floor of a patrician villa nearby.

Rheinfelden★

▷ *15km/8.5mi E of Basel on Highway 3. Marktgasse 16.* 𝄞*(0)61 835 52 00. www.tourismus-rheinfelden.ch.*
Rheinfelden is separated from its German namesake by the Rheinbrücke, an arched stone bridge. Founded in 1130 by the Zähringen, the town is thought to be the oldest in the Aargau. It was given to the Habsburgs in 1330 by Duke Ludwig I of Bavaria and remained in their possession until 1802.

This small town is the last stopping-place for **cruises along the Rhine**, and it has an attractive old centre with narrow streets, as well as a shaded riverside park with thermal baths. For a good **view** of the town, cross the bridge to the German side of the river. The discovery of salt deposits in 1844 allowed the town to develop its renowned spa. The old **no. 6 drilling tower** of Riburg saltworks—now a museum—can be seen in the thermal park (*follow signs to the Kurzentrum*).

The main street is **Marktgasse**, which runs from near the customs post by the bridge. Attractive houses with painted façades and attractive signs line the street; starting from the Tourist Office, numbers 36, 16 and 10 are particularly interesting. Also noteworthy are the painted murals in the courtyard of the **town hall** (Rathaus), recognisable by its medieval tower.

The **Fricktaler Museum** (number 12) (🕐*open May–Dec, Tue and Sat–Sun 2pm–5pm;* 🕐*closed Whitsun and the third Sun in Sept (Bettag);* 👜*4CHF;* 𝄞*(0)61 831 14 50; www.fricktaler-museum.ch*) is dedicated to local history and to the Saint Sebastian Brotherhood. This unique organisation has 12 members, one of whom carries a lantern. The members dress in black and wear long coats and tall hats. On 24 and 31 December, the Brotherhood maintains the tradition of singing canticles (short Biblical songs) in front of the town's fountains in memory of the epidemic of 1541 that killed a large percentage of the population. The nearby **Albrechtsplatz** is adorned with the Banneret Fountain. Johannmittergasse, a little farther up on the left, leads to the St Johann chapel, which once belonged to the Knights of Malta (note the frescoes). A small road to the left of the chapel leads to a terrace overlooking the Rhine.

Marktgasse leads into Kupfergasse, which runs up to the Storchennestturm and a section of the ramparts. Other streets and squares with attractive façades or fountains include Geissgasse, Obertorplatz, Kapuzinergasse, and Bahnhofstrasse. The Gothic-style church on Kirchplatz, **St Martinskirche**, was heavily restored at the end of the 18C, as shown by its Baroque interior.

Bräuerei Feldschlösschen

Guided tours (1hr30min) Mon–Fri 9.15am, 9.45am, 1.45p, 2.30pm and mornings first Sat of the month. Closed public holidays of the Aargau canton. 12CHF. (0)848 125 000.
Switzerland's largest **brewery** is housed in an imposing red and yellow brick building adorned with towers and ramparts. Founded in 1876, it still delivers beer to its nearest customers by horse-drawn cart. Guided tours provide insight into the production of beer; the huge copper stills and Art Deco interior of the **brewing room** are definitely worth a visit. The tour finishes with a tasting of the brewery's six different beers.

St Chrischona Kapelle★

8km/5mi – allow 15min. Leave Basel by the road to Riehen. At the post office at Riehen turn right toward Bettingen.
The road runs through residential suburbs of Basel and Bettingen before climbing to St Chrischona Chapel. From a terrace nearby there is a **panorama**★ from Säntis in the east to the Jura mountain ranges in the west. Basel can be seen nestling in the Rhine plain.

Wasserturm Bruderholz★

3.5km/2mi. Leave Basel to the S. Bear right in Jacobsbergstrasse to Bruderholz.
A water tower stands on the great Esplanade of the Battery, in memory of the redoubts built by the Confederates in

1815 during the last campaign of the Allies against Napoleon I. A stairway (*164 steps*) leads to the top of the tower, which commands a lovely **panorama**★ of Basel, the Birse Valley, the Jura, and the Black Forest.

Muttenz

5km/3mi SE of Basel.
In the town centre stands **Pfarrkirche**, a strange fortified church surrounded by crenellated circular walls; originally Romanesque, it was remodelled in the 15C and 16C. The small single nave, with its carved wooden ceiling, presents some superb fragments (restored) of early Renaissance religious frescoes.

Liestal★

16km/10mi SE of Basel.
This charming locality, on a promontory between the Ergolz Valley and the Orisbach, is the capital of the canton of Basel-Land. Its main street (**Rathausstrasse**) lined with painted 19C houses, leads from the city's medieval gate to its red sandstone town hall, built in 1586 and extended in 1938. The town hall is decorated with Renaissance frescoes which were restored in 1900.

The **Kantonsmuseum Baselland** (*Zeughausplatz;* open Tue–Sun, 10am–5pm closed 1 Jan, 1 May, Pentecost, 1 Aug 24,25 Dec &31 Dec; 7CHF, children 5CHF; (0)61 925 59 86) focuses on the natural environment and especially the ribbon-making industry—an important regional activity for over four centuries. The stages of fabrication, ranging from design to the marketing, are illustrated with display cabinets and equipment. On the heights of Schleifenberg, the Aussichtsturm belvedere affords a lovely **view** of the Rhine and, in fine weather, the landscape stretching to the Alps. The surrounding forests offer many pleasant walks. On summer Sundays, a little **steam train** (Waldenburger Dampfzug) links Liestal to Waldenburger, located 14km/8.7mi to the south.

🚗 DRIVING TOUR

PASSWANGSTRASSE★

56km/35mi. The harsh Lüssel Valley, along with the welcoming Birse Valley, make up the major part of this itinerary along the Passwing Road. Leave Basel on road 18 in the direction of Münchenstein, then Reinach and Arlesheim.

Arlesheim

The **collegiate church**★ of Arlesheim is one of the most charming examples of Baroque art in Switzerland. Built in 1680 for the episcopal principality of Basel, it was later transformed in the Rococo style (1769–71). It stands in a quiet, shaded little square bordered by the former canons' houses. The church interior, whose harmony is untarnished by any detail, is adorned with stucco discreetly picked out in pink or pale yellow, while the low vaulting bears large, misty compositions in pale colours by Joseph Appiani (1760).

▷ *Drive to Dornach to the S.*

Goetheanum★★

Rüttiweg 45, Dornach. 🕐*Open daily 8am–10pm.* 🎫*15CHF (-14 years, free).* 📞*(0)61 706 42 49. www.goetheanum.org.* The seat of the School of Spiritual Science and centre of the worldwide Anthroposophical Society (founded in 1912 by Rudolf Steiner, proponent of "free schooling") is an immense concrete edifice hugging the slopes above Dornach and Arlesheim, made entirely of concrete and without one right angle. Don't miss the incredible boiler house or other buildings on the campus.

▷ *At Dornach church, head towards Hochwald and Seewen.*

Seewen

On the outskirts of this charming village, huddled in a wooded basin at the foot of its white church, stands the **Musik-automaten-Museum** *(Tue–Sun 11am–6pm;* 🎧*guided tours (1hr) 12.20pm &*

2.40pm 🕐*closed 1 Jan, Good Fri and 25 Dec;* 🎫*10CHF;* ♿ 📞*(0)61 915 98 80).* Its galleries house a total of 800 musical mechanisms dating from the 18C to the early 20C and all in perfect working order: mechanical pianos, barrel organs, street organs, music boxes, orchestrions (imitating orchestra instruments) and especially amusing automata designed to resemble a bird, a painter and a magician.

▷ *Join road 18 and follow the signs to Laufen and Zwingen. Between Büsserach and Erschwll are the ruins of Thierstein tower.*

Passwanggipfel★★

Alt. 1 204m/3 950ft. From the N exit of the Passwang Tunnel, 2km/1.2m along a narrow road with sharp gradients (close the gates behind you), plus 45min on foot there and back.
Leaving the car at the Wirtschaft Ober-Passwang café-restaurant, continue the climb on foot. Upon coming out of a wood, after passing through a gate, leave the road and climb, to the right, to the summit. From this point a varied **panorama**★★ extends, to the north, over the last undulations of the Basel Jura, the Plain of Alsace (note the double ribbon of the Rhine and the Kembs Canal, part of the great Alsace Canal) framed between the Vosges and the Black Forest, and to the south, to the Solothurn Jura and part of the Bernese Alps.

Between the pass and Laufen, the Lüssel Valley shrinks to a narrow wooded cleft. Between Erschwill and Büsserach, the ruins of Thierstein, a massive tower flanked by a turret, stand like a sentinel. You come out in the Laufen Basin where the tilled, undulating floor lies spread before the forest ridges of the Blauen. Between **Laufen**, a little town with fortified gates, and Aesch, the **Birstal** continues green in spite of increasing industrialisation. The keep of the Angenstein Burg, a former residence of the bishops of Basel, seems to block the last defile.

ADDRESSES

🛌STAY

🛏 **Hostel** – *St Alban, Kirchrain 10.* ☎*(0)61 272 05 72. www.youthhostel.ch/ basel. Closed Dec 24–Jan 2. 39 rooms (197 beds).* A whiff of the countryside lingers here.

🛏 **Easy Hotel** – *Riehenring 109.* ☎*900 327 927 (1.50 CHF/min). www.easyhotel.com. 24 rooms.* Minimalist and clean. The less expensive rooms are no bigger than cupboards.

🛏 **Hotel Stadthof** – *Gerbergasse 84.* ☎*(0)61 261 87 11. www.stadthof.ch. 9 rooms.* On Barfüsserplatz, one of the cheapest hotels in Basel. Tiled and white rooms are monastic but clean. Shared bathroom facilities.

🛏🛏 **Rochat** – *Petersgraben 23.* ☎*(0)61 261 81 40. www.hotelrochat.ch. 50 rooms.* Dating from 1899, this listed building with a bright red façade is a stone's throw from the town centre. Light, quiet rooms at reasonable prices.

🛏🛏 **Hotel Brasserie Au Violon** – *Im Lohnhof 4.* ☎*(0)61 269 87 11. www.au-violon.com. 20 rooms. Brasserie open Tue–Sat.* Hard to believe that in 1995 this elegant hotel perched on the heights of the Old City was a prison. For comfort, opt for rooms with views of the Barfüsserplatz and the cathedral.

🛏🛏🛏 **Hotel Kraft** – *Rheingasse 12.* ☎*(0)61 690 91 30. www.hotelkraft.ch. 45 rooms.* 🅿. A recommended hotel in Kleinbasel. The rooms are spacious, bright and elegant. The restaurant serves Mediterranean cuisine.

🛏🛏🛏 **Der Teufelhof Basel** – *Leonhardsgraben 47-49.* ☎*(0)61 261 10 10. www.teufelhof.com. 33 rooms.* 🅿. The term "art hotel" could have been coined for this small group housed in four buildings in the old city: two hotels, a restaurant, café, wine cellar and theatre.

🛏🛏🛏 **Les Trois Rois** – *Blumenrain 8.* ☎*(0)61 260 50 50. Fax (0)61 260 50 60. www.lestroisrois.com. 101 rooms.* With an 1844 decor, the interior recalls "old Europe". The institution has received royalty and celebrities from Napoleon to Picasso. Three restaurants, a brewery and Belle Epoque ballroom.

🛏🛏🛏🛏 **St Gotthard** – *Central-bahnstrasse 13.* ☎*(0)61 225 13 13. www.gotthard.ch. 104 rooms.* Well-located just opposite the railway station and close to a tram stop. Easy access to the town centre. Delicious buffet breakfast.

🍴EAT

🛏 **Rosario's** – *Spalenberg 53.* ☎*(0)61 261 03 76. Open Mon–Sat.* Beautiful Art Nouveau décor in this old wine bistro. The Sicilian boss ensures the quality of Italian wines and Mediterranean dishes.

🛏 **Lily's** – *Rebgasse 1.* ☎*(0)61 683 11 11. www.lilys.ch.* Fans of wok cooking, curry and spicy noodles will delight in this elegant Asian place in Little Basel. Service is unfussy and smiling.

🛏🛏 **Bodega zum Strauss** – *Barfüsserplatz 16.* ☎*(0)61 261 22 72. Daily except Sunday lunchtime.* Cosy little downtown pub. Delicious, mostly Italian cuisine.

🛏🛏 **Harmonie** – *Petersgraben 71.* ☎*(0)61 261 07 18. www.harmonie-basel.ch.* This small, friendly restaurant, situated on Spalenberg Hill, is popular with locals. The restaurant serves generous portions of simple cuisine, featuring dishes such as Zürich-style veal, liver with *Rösti* and a giant-sized *im Schlüsseli* salad.

🛏🛏 **Noohn** – *Henric Petri-Strasse 12.* ☎*(0)61 281 14 14. www.noohn.ch. Daily except Sat lunchtime and Sun.* The Noohn houses a sushi bar, a self-service restaurant (fusion kitchen) and a bar. Something for every taste and budget.

🛏🛏 **Torstübli** – *Riehentorstrasse 27.* ☎*(0)61 692 01 10. www.torstuebli.ch. Closed Sat–Sun.* Kleinbasel restaurant with good reputation for the quality of its dishes.

🛏🛏 **Restaurant Kunsthalle** – *Steinenberg 7.* ☎*(0)61 272 42 33.* Conveniently located near the Tinguely Fountain, it houses both a fancy restaurant and a cheaper bistro with old woodwork and frescoes painted in 1878. Good wine list.

🛏🛏🛏 **St Alban-Stübli** – *St Alban-Vorstadt 74.* ☎*(0)61 272 54 15. www.st-alban-stuebli.ch. Closed 23 Dec–9 Jan, Sun, Sat lunchtime and public holidays.*

This building is tucked away in a quaint, picturesque street. Affordable meals.

⊜⊜⊜ **Zum Goldenen Sternen** – *St Alban-Rheinweg 70. ℰ(0)61 272 16 66. Fax (0)61 272 16 67. Closed Sun evening, Mon and 23 Dec–3 Jan.* On the banks of the Rhine, under the chestnut trees, this is the oldest restaurant in Basel, opened in 1412. Fish specialities and seasonal cuisine are served beneath the dining hall's splendid coffered ceiling.

⊜⊜⊜ **Chez Donati** – *St Johanns-Vorstadt 48. ℰ(0)61 322 09 19. www.lestroisrois.com. Closed Sun, Mon, mid-Jul–mid-Aug, 24–30 Dec..* A fashionable restaurant, decorated with lovely Murano glass lamps, serving fine Italian food and wine.

⊜⊜⊜ **Saffron Zunft** – *Gerbergasse 11. ℰ(0)61 269 94 94. www.safran-zunft.ch. Closed Sun.* This old guildhall restaurant offers the amazing "Out of South Africa" menu: crusty antelope, medallions of springbok and kudu steaks.

SIGHTSEEING
BOAT TRIPS

The city offers a number of boat trips, including dinner cruises, excursions through the locks between Basel and Rheinfelden, and night trips. Tickets can be purchased from Basel Personenschiffahrt, Schifflände, next to the Tourist Office, ℰ(0)61 639 95 00.

⊕THEATRE AND MUSIC

Theater Basel – *Theaterstrasse 7. ℰ(0)61 295 11 33. www.theaterbasel.ch.* This theatre has an excellent reputation for opera, theatre, and dance. **Junges Theater Basel** – *Wettsteinallee 40. ℰ(0)61 681 27 80. www.jungestheaterbasel.ch.* **Stadtmusik** – *Steinenberg 14. ℰ(0)61 225 93 93. www.casinobasel.ch.* **Musical Theater** – *Feldbergstrasse 151. ℰ(0)61 699 88 99.*

⊕ SHOPS AND MARKETS

Basel's shopping district is centred around the Marktplatz. The Globus department store and smaller shops selling clothes, designer goods, crystal and souvenirs are on the Freie Strasse and Gebergasse, as far as Barfüsserplatz. The Manor department store is on Greifengasse, in the St Alban district.

SOUVENIRS

The local emblem is the Basilisk, a type of dragon with a cockerel's head, which is often depicted on brooches.

MARKETS

General stalls: Barfüsserplatz, Thu, Jan–mid-Oct, 7am–6.30pm.; **Food, flower and organic market:** Marktplatz, daily every afternoon; Mon, Wed, Fri, until 7pm. NB: prices are often based on pounds and not kilos. **Flea market:** Peterplatz, Sat. **Christmas market:** Dec, on Barfüsserplatz and Claraplatz.

≈ PUBLIC BATHING IN THE RHINE

Rheinbad Breite – *St Alban-Rheinweg 195. ℰ(0)61 311 25 75.* View of the cathedral.

Rheinbad St Johann – *St Johanns-Rheinweg. ℰ(0)61 322 04 42.*

⊕NIGHTLIFE

The bar of the **Drei Könige** (*Kleinhüningeranlage 39; ℰ(0)41 61 631 15 10*) is pleasant, especially in summer with its covered terrace overlooking the Rhine. The **Schiesser** tea-rooms (*Marktplatz 19; ℰ(0)41 61 261 60 77*) on the nearby Marktplatz have been serving delicious confectionery since 1870. Beyond the right bank of the river lies **Kleinbasel**, a district where nightlife is particularly active. In Clarastrasse, a lively shopping street, there are several popular places including **le Plaza Club** and its theme evenings (karaoke, concerts, shows) and the **Grischuna Bar** in the Hôtel Alexander (concerts every evening).

Near the railway station, you can have a cocktail in a discreet, refined ambience at the bar of the **Hotel Euler** (*Centralbahnplatz 14*). Those who like soft music and piano bars should visit the **Old City Bar** in the Hotel Hilton (*Aeschengraben 31*).

Le Caveau (*Grünpfahlgasse 4, near the post office*) offers a wide range of Swiss, French, Italian, Californian and other wines. In the heart of the old city, the **Atlantis** (*Klosterberg 9*) is reputed for its rock , hiphop, electronica and punk concerts.

Aarau

The capital of the Aargau canton, Aarau is one of the richest towns in Switzerland, thanks to the textile and machine industries. Formerly the capital of the short-lived Helvetic Republic, it became a separate canton in 1803. The best view of the old town is from the bridge spanning the River Aare.

▶ **Population:** 15 753.

Info: Aarau info Verkehrsbüro, Graben 42, 5001 Aarau. ℘(0)62 824 76 24. www.aarauinfo.ch.

▶ **Location:** Aarau is 46km/ 28.5mi west of Zürich. Alt. 383m/1 273ft.

Don't Miss: Lenzburg Castle—housing the History Museum of the canton of Aargau as well as offering a spectacular panoramic view.

OLD TOWN

The narrow streets are lined with fine old houses, some adorned with oriel windows and wrought-iron emblems from the long-standing Bernese domination; other façades are covered with frescoes, and roofs have stepped gables and eaves. The **Stadtkirche** (parish church) is surmounted by an elegant late-17C belfry. The fine **Fountain of Justice** (1643) stands in a small adjacent square. Throughout the city, the painted roofs (Dachhimmel) date from the 16C.

EXCURSIONS

Schönenwerd★

▶4.5km/2.8mi SW towards Olten.
Away from the old town, dominated by a collegiate church dating from the 12C, a modern area has developed, which owes its existence to the Bally shoe brand. The **Bally Schuhmuseum**★★ (Bally Shoe Museum) (Felsgarten House, Oltnerstrasse 6; ⟋guided tours 2pm Fri, Sat; open Jan–mid-Jul and mid-Aug–mid-Dec; no charge; ℘(0)62 849 99 45) traces the history of footwear throughout the centuries and across cultures.

Schloss Hallwyl★

▶18km/11mi SE towards Suhr. Apr–Oct Tue–Fri 10am–5pm. 12CHF (children 6CHF). ℘(0)62 767 60 10. www.schlosshallwyl.ch.
An enchanting castle, with round towers and sharp, high crenellated walls expanded from the 11C to 16C (and now restored) built on two islets of a tributary of Lake Hallwil. Its entrance is via a drawbridge and a courtyard from where you walk to the second island to visit the main building, a museum of art

and popular traditions. In the tower of the main building of the first island you can examine a first floor apartment with 17C furniture and on the second floor a 19C bourgeois apartment.

Olten

▶ 12 km/7.5mi SW of Aarau on Route 5. Klosterplatz 21, 4600. ℘(0)62 212 30 88.
Olten is situated at the boundary of the Jura, on the banks of the River Aare.
A wooden covered bridge (Alte Brücke), reserved for pedestrians, leads to the old town. However, since the beginning of the last century, the appearance of the town, which continues to spread on both sides of the Aare, has been altered by its great industrial activity: Soap and cement works, food processing, and the workshops of the Federal Railways.
The **Kuntsmuseum** (Fine Arts Museum) (open Tue–Sun 2pm–5pm (Thu 7pm), Sat–Sun 10am–5pm; closed most public holidays and between exhibitions 7CHF; ℘(0)62 212 86 76; www.kunstmuseumolten.ch) possesses a fine collection of 19C and 20C paintings and sculpture, including excellent caricatures, studies and drawings by **Martin Disteli** (1802–44). This talented painter and caricaturist interpreted scenes from Swiss military history and political life, as well as fables.

Zofingen

▶ 16km/10mi; Head S on Route 24 then along Highway 1 until Zofingen exit.

The old part of the town is contained within the quadrilateral formed by the alleys which have taken the place of its ramparts. The Pulvertum, a square 12C tower, is all that remains of the old fortifications. The Niklaus-Thut-Platz (town square) has numerous 17C and 18C houses. The Church of St Maurice, has a 17C Renaissance bell tower. Two large mosaics from the Roman period (*under shelter*) can be seen as you leave the town from the south.

Schloss Habsburg

▶ *17km/10.6mi. From Aarau head NE to route 24 and then route 5 to Habsburg village.* ◷*Open 9am–midnight* ◷*Closed Mon–Tue Oct–Apr; Mon May–Sept.* ✆*(0)84 887 12 00. www.schlosshabsburg.ch.*

A narrow country lane wends its way to the castle, which has been converted into a **restaurant** (⊜⊜⊜). In former days, it was the cradle of the Habsburg dynasty: Several members of this illustrious family were to influence the course of European history for many centuries.

Note the family tree and map illustrating the possessions they acquired. Climb the wooden staircase: The **view** at the top encompasses the surrounding countryside, cut across by the pretty meanderings of the River Aare.

Schloss Wildegg★

▶ *11km/6.8mi. From Aarau take Route 5 E.* ◷*Open mid-Mar–end Oct, Tue–Fri 9am–noon 1.30pm – 5pm.* ◷*Closed Good Fri.* ☞*12CHF.* ✆*(0)62 887 12 30.*

The impressive mass of Wildegg Castle, looming above the Aare Valley, was built in the 12C by a Habsburg Count and enlarged and altered several times since (particularly by the Effinger family who were the owners for four centuries).

The castle contains fine **furniture**★ dating from the 17C–19C. The Blue Room, the Armory and the Library deserve special attention for the beauty of their ceilings and furnishings. From the upper storeys there is a wide view of a gently undulating landscape of fields and forests.

Baden★

The spa and the industrial quarters extend below the old town, built on a promontory overlooking the river, dominated by the ruins of Stein Castle (Ruine Stein). This imposing fortress served as an arsenal and a refuge for the Austrians during their unsuccessful campaigns against the Swiss, which ended in the victories for Swiss independence at Morgarten (1315) and Sempach (1386). In 1415 the Confederates seized the city and burnt it. It was rebuilt in the 17C and destroyed again in 1712 by the people of Bern and Zürich.

A BIT OF HISTORY

Known in Roman times as Aquae Helveticae and famous for its 19 sulphur hot springs (47°C/116°F), Baden became one of Switzerland's most important spas

▶ **Population:** 17 446.
Info: Bahnhofplatz 1 – 5400. ✆(0)56 210 91 91.
▶ **Location:** Baden lies at the foot of the last spurs of the Jura at a picturesque site on the banks of the Limmat. Alt. 385m/1 273ft.
◷ **Timing:** Allow an hour or two to wander the town and visit the museum. Allow a full day if you plan to do the excursions as well.

towards the end of the Middle Ages. Famous personalities who have taken the waters here include the writers Goethe, Thomas Mann and Hermann Hesse, and the conductor Karl Böhm. Today, Baden is also a centre of electromechanical engineering.

SIGHTS
Old town★

From the modern road bridge *(Hochbrücke)* there is a fine **view**★ of the old town. Its houses, with their stepped gables and fine brown roofs, pierced by many dormer windows, come down to the Limmat, which is crossed by an old covered wooden bridge *(Holzbrücke)*. The parish church *(Stadtkirche)* and the city tower *(Stadtturm)*, with a belfry and corner turrets with glazed tiles, dominate the whole scene.

Historiches Museum Baden★

ⓒ*Open Tue–Sun, 1pm–5pm, Sat–Sun, 10am–5pm.* ⌘*7CHF.* ✆*(0)56 222 75 74. www.museum.baden.ch.*

The museum stands near the covered bridge (Holzbrücke) on the right bank of the Limmat. It occupies the central tower of a 15C castle and, since 1992, a modern extension building by Basel architects pair Wilfrid and Katharina Steib as well. The permanent exhibition in the extension is on the industrial history of the city and that of the baths (from 1790–1960), illustrated by an inventive and elegant set design. It also hosts temporary exhibitions. The bay window offers a fine view of the covered bridge and old town with its gables and sawtooth roofs with dormer windows. The tower contains a collection of conventional weapons, antique furniture, paintings and sculptures, pottery, bronzes and coins of Roman origin found in the area and costumes of the Canton of Aargau. A 1930s interior has been restored on the top floor.

Baden in winter

© Christof Sonderegger/Switzerland Tourism

Stiftung Langmatt Sidney und Jenny Brown★

Römerstrasse 30. Temporary exhibitions on the first floor. ⓒ*Open Apr–Oct, Tue–Sun 2pm–5pm, Sat–Sun 11am–5pm.* ⌘*12CHF.* ✆*(0)56 200 86 70. www.langmatt.ch.*

The house formerly belonging to the industrialist **Sidney Brown**, whose name is perpetuated by the company ABB (Asea Brown Boveri), contains mostly Impressionist paintings, including two series by Renoir and Cézanne. There are also superb canvases by other famous artists: *Study of a Nude* by Degas, *Return of the Fishing Boats in Trouville* by E Boudin, *Chestnut Trees in Louveciennes* by Pissarro, *The Torments of the Seine* by Monet, sketches attributed to Henri Matisse, and noteworthy pictures by Corot, Courbet, Fantin-Latour, Gauguin, Sisley, and Vincent van Gogh. A small salon presents 18C French works (Fragonard, Greuze and Watteau) and landscapes by a native of Zürich, S Gessner.

EXCURSIONS
Old Cistercian Abbey at Wettingen★

▶ *3km/1.8mi S of Baden, between the railway and the Limmat.* ⓒ*The cloisters can be visited Mar–Oct, Mon–Sat 10am–5pm, Sun and public holidays noon–5pm. Church:* ↝*guided tours daily Mar–Oct, 2pm.* ⌘*12CHF.* ✆*(0)56 437 24 10.*

This former Cistercian abbey, founded by Count Heinrich von Rapperswil in the 13C, presently houses a school. The Gothic **cloisters** have been glazed and now display a collection of stained glass. The **interior**★ is richly decorated in Baroque style with frescoes, paintings, stucco and marble. Note the splendidly carved 17C **choir stalls**★★.

Brugg

▶ *10km/6 mi W of Baden on Route 3.*
Founded by the Habsburgs in the early 12C, the "city of the bridges", which stands at the confluence of the River Aare and the River Reuss, Brugg has preserved many of its old buildings. An important industrial town that

plays a central role in the country's road and railway network. Among the monuments still standing in the **old city** (*leave your car in one of the car parks (fee) located outside this area*) are the Archive Tower, the Storks' Tower (Storchentum) and the imposing 12C and 16C Black Tower, **Schwarzer Turm**, which overlooks the bridge spanning the Aare. This vantage point affords a good view of its wooded banks and old houses. Note the 16C former town hall and the Late Gothic Protestant church with its 18C interior. On the pretty **Hofstatt**, a paved square embellished with a white fountain, you will find the former 17C arsenal and the old storeroom, dating from the 18C.

Vindonissa-Museum

Open Tue–Sat 1pm–5pm, Sun 10am–5pm. 5CHF. (0)56 441 21 84. www.ag.ch/vindonissa.

Housed in the newly renovated museum are the finds from the Roman site of Vindonissa: jewellery, arms, coins, statues, pottery, glasswork, plus articles made from wood and leather. Note the 4C skeleton of a Roman woman in a sarcophagus and the model of the Vindonissa military camp. Outside is a lapidary museum (stelae, votive inscriptions).

Kloster Königsfelden (Abbey of Königsfelden)

9.2km/5.7mi W of Baden.

The Franciscan abbey of Königsfelden was founded in 1308 by Queen Elizabeth and the Habsburg family on the spot where King Albrecht I was assassinated by Duke Johann of Swabia. The monastic buildings presently house a psychiatric hospital.

Klosterkirche

By the side of the abbey.

Open Apr–Oct, Tue–Sun 10am–5pm. Other times by appointment 5CHF. (0)56 441 88 33.

A pretty park is the setting for this large Gothic church. The nave, lit by clerestory windows, has a flat wooden ceiling, and the aisles are decorated with painted wooden panels representing portraits

of knights and coats of arms. A memorial in the nave recalls that Königsfelden became the burial place of the Habsburgs.

The long **chancel**★ is lit by 11 windows of which the **stained glass**★, made between 1325 and 1330, forms an interesting series. You will recognize the Childhood of Christ, the Passion, scenes from Lives of the Saints and Death of the Virgin. The colours, in which a silvery-yellow predominates, are iridescent.

Vindonissa: Roman Amphitheatre

At Windisch 1km/0.6mi from Brugg via the Zürich road, then to the right of Königsfelden Church take Hauserstrasse.

This is the most important find of the Vindonissa site, a military camp which, in the 1C AD, was the Roman headquarters for the whole of Switzerland, on the present-day site of Windisch. The huge oval amphitheatre with its double wall of ashlar stone (average height 2m/6.5ft) sat approximately 10 000 people.

Zurzach

19km/1.5mi N of Baden on Route 17.

Near the Rhine on the site of the Roman town, Tenedo, Zurzach is now a spa centre (cures for rheumatic disorders). On its main street are some 17C and 18C monuments and houses and beside the river stands a 19C château.

August Deusser Museum

Open daily 1pm–6pm. Closed 1 Jan, Easter Thu, Fri and Sat, 24 Dec and in Jan and Jul. 6CHF, no charge on preview days. (0)56 249 20 50.

The château houses this museum, which contains the personal collection of the German painter **August Deusser** (1870–1942) as well as his own works of art. On the first floor are furnishings, works of art, an 18C Chinese low relief and a carved gilt bed made for Ludwig II of Bavaria. The second floor presents works bequeathed by Deusser. The park contains trees, pond and many modern sculptures by Johann Ulrich Steiger.

Winterthur★

A town named Vitudurum was established here during the Roman era. At the end of the Middle Ages, Winterthur was the manufacturing centre for large porcelain stoves, which can still be admired in some Swiss houses. The industrial development of the town has not interfered with its artistic reputation: the city boasts several museums with fine collections that show a complete record of 19C European painting. Concerts given by the Collegium Musicum, founded in 1629, always draw a large audience. The city is also a lively centre for comedy and cabaret, has a charming old quarter with street cafés and interesting shops, and graceful parks and gardens.

SIGHTS

Oskar Reinhart Collection

Oskar Reinhart (1885–1965) a merchant who made his fortune in textiles, bequeathed his famous private collection, one of the most important of the 20C, to the Swiss Confederation, provided it remains in his hometown.
The collection includes nearly 200 works of European art from Late Gothic to the modern avant-garde, dominated by French painting of the 19C. It is divided into two separate museums.

Museum Oskar Reinhart am Stadtgarten★

Stadthausstrasse 6. ◷Open Tue–Sun 10am–5pm (8pm Tue). ✆12CHF. ℘(0)52 267 51 72.
www.museumoskarreinhart.ch.
Works by Swiss, German, and Austrian painters from the 18C, 19C, and 20C are displayed. Excellent drawings by Rudolf Wasmann, portraits of children by Anker, works by Böcklin and Koller, paintings by the German Romantics and by artists of the Munich School as well as animal studies by Jacques Laurent Agasse may be seen. The many canvases by Ferdinand Hodler (1853–1918) show the

importance attached to this leader of pre-1914 Swiss painting.

Collection Oskar Reinhart "Am Römerholz"★★★

Haldenstrasse 95. ◷Open Tue–Sun, 10am–5pm, 8pm Wed. ◷Closed 1 Jan, Good Fri, Easter Sun and 25 Dec. ✆12CHF. ℘(0)52 269 27 40.
www.roemerholz.ch.
The artwork bequeathed by Reinhart is presented in this house set in large grounds overlooking the town. Works span five centuries including paintings by Brueghel and El Greco and drawings by Rembrandt, French works from the late 17C to the 19C with Poussin, Claude Lorraine, Watteau, Chardin and Fragonard, and sketches by Daumier.
The 19C is represented by artists whose works reflect the main contemporary trends in pictorial art, such as Corot, Delacroix, Courbet, Manet, Renoir, and Cézanne, as well as Van Gogh and, closer to the present, Picasso, with drawings from his Blue period.

▸ **Population:** 98 238.

Michelin Map: Town plan in The Michelin Red Guide to Switzerland.

Info: In the main railway station. ℘(0)52 267 67 00. www.winterthur-tourismus.ch.

Location: Zürich region, northern Switzerland. Alt. 439m/1 440ft.

P Parking: There are several public car parks; it is easiest to use one and take public transport.

Don't Miss: Villa Flora (art museum) or Schloss Kyburg.

Kids: Technorama, the interactive science centre.

Timing: Allow at least half a day to see the starred sights; a full day to see everything.

Kunstmuseum★★

🕐*Open 10am–8pm Tue, Wed–Sun 10am–5pm.* 🕐*Closed 1 Jan, Good Fri, Easter Sun, Whitsun, Ascension, 1 May, St Alban's Sunday, 1 Aug and 25 Dec.* ✏*15CHF.* ✆*(0)52 267 51 62. www.kmw.ch.*

The **Fine Arts Museum** contains works from the 16C (Cranach), 17C and 18C regional art (Graff, Mayer, Füssli), and Swiss and German painters from the 19C and 20C (Hodler, Vallotton, Giacometti, Auberjonois, Corinth, and Hofer). The French Schools are represented by artists such as Renoir, Bonnard, Vuillard, and Van Gogh. Part of the building is devoted to sculpture by Rodin, Maillol, Haller, Marini, and Alberto Giacometti. The museum also houses the town's library and a natural history section.

Villa Flora★

Tösstalstrasse 44. 🕐*Open Tue–Sat 2pm–5pm, Sun 11am–3pm.* 🕐*Closed 1 Jan, Good Friday and 25 Dec.* ✏*12.50CHF.* ✆*(0)52 212 99 60. www.villaflora.ch.*

The post-Impressionist works accumulated between 1907 and 1930 by Arthur and Hedy Hahnloser-Bühler are interesting in that they were acquired not through art dealers, but through their personal friends and relatives of the artists themselves. Visitors will be impressed by the high quality of the works, and the prophetic nature of the paintings, laid out in the house once occupied by these dedicated art lovers. The largest part of the collection is works by the Nabis—artists born between 1860 and 1870, who chose to rebel against academic conventions, including the Swiss Félix Vallotton (*The Barrow*), E Vuillard (*The Game of Draughts*, with its incredible plunging perspective)—and to Pierre Bonnard (*The Fauns*, combining many different viewpoints). Fauvism—the term was first coined by art critic Louis Vauxcelles during the Salon d'Automne in 1905—is represented by H Manguin, a close friend of the Hahnloser-Bühlers, and by Matisse. Besides the Fauves and the Nabis, of particular note is the rare series of nine paintings (*Andromède*) by Odilon

Redon, dubbed "the artist of the Irrational", of which Hedy Hahnloser-Bühler had already said in 1919: "All the main components characteristic of contemporary artistic inspiration are already present in his work". Finally, note the outstanding *Portrait of the Artist* by Paul Cézanne, *The Sower* and *Night Café* by Vincent van Gogh, and many sculptures (bronzes by Bonnard, C Despiau, A Maillol, Henri Matisse, M Marini, PA Renoir, A Rodin, and F Vallotton). The garden (two sculptures by Aristede Maillol) sadly is open only to groups.

👥Technorama★★

Technoramastrasse 1. Leave the motorway at the Oberwinterthur exit and then follow directions. You can also take bus number 12 from the main station. 🕐*Open Tue–Sun, 10am–5pm public holiday Mondays.* 🕐*Closed 25 Dec.* ✏*25CHF.* ✆*(0)52 244 08 44. www.technorama.ch.*

This attractive and amusing museum is a perfect tool to introduce young people to the world of science and technology. The permanent exhibitions of the Swiss **Science Centre** include physics, trains and toys, energy, water, nature and chaos, mechanical music, materials, textiles, and automatic technology. The purpose of the visit is to operate the various machines and watch demonstrations, of which the most impressive is no doubt that of high-voltage, one of many interactive opportunities. The "laboratory", supervised by a team of trained instructors, enables visitors to acquire scientific knowledge while having fun. The park can be used to experiment with flying machines (🕐*open Sat–Sun only*).

Fotomuseum Winterthur★★

Grüzenstrasse 44. 🕐*Open Tue–Sun 11am–6pm (8pm Wed.).* ✏*9CHF.* ✆*(0)52 234 10 60. www.fotomuseum.ch.*

The collections comprise 30 000 works of 19C and 20C master photographers, as well as works of contemporary photographers. Part of its collections document cultural history and sociology with applied photography from industry, architecture, fashion, and other areas of life and work, in line with its mission of representing photography both as an art form and as a means of documenting all facets of life in each era. Each year the exhibits change to display different parts of the vast collection.

EXCURSIONS
Schloss Kyburg
▶ *6km/4mi S. Leave Winterthur by the Seen road. At Sennhof take the small road to the right and follow it along the Töss; after 1km/0.6mi turn left to go to Kyburg village.* ⏲*Open Apr–Oct Tue–Sun 10.30am–5.30pm; Nov–Mar Sat–Sun 10.30am–4.30pm.* ⏲*Closed 25, 26 Dec, 1 Jan.* ⬚*8CHF.* ✆*(0)52 232 46 64. www.schlosskyburg.ch.*

This feudal castle was built in the 10C and 11C and passed successively from the line of the Counts of Kyburg to that of the Habsburgs. In 1424 it came within the bailiwick of the town of Zürich and remained so until 1798; since 1917 the castle has belonged to the canton. Inside are remarkable collections of furniture and arms that will interest visitors with a knowledge of history and antiques. There is a good view of the surrounding countryside.

Kartause Ittingen★ (Ittingen Charterhouse)
▶ *The old charterhouse is situated in the small village of Warth, about 20min N of Winterthur (toll).* ⏲*Open Oct–Mar Mon–Fri 2pm–5pm, Sat,Sun 11am–5pm; May–Sep daily 11am–6pm.* ⬚*10CHF.* ✆*(0)52 748 41 41. www.ittingermuseum.tg.ch.*

The Ittingen Charterhouse stands on a hill overlooking the Thur Valley, surrounded by vineyards, it was founded in 1152 as an Augustinian priory dedicated to St Lawrence and became affiliated to the Carthusian Order in 1461. The monastery was almost entirely rebuilt between the 16C and 18C. A foundation (Stiftung Kartause Ittingen) was established in 1977 to administer the old monastery, which has been carefully restored and now houses two museums run by the canton of Thurgau.

The building is also occupied by a hotel, restaurant, and pottery and furniture workshops. Surrounded by its own agricultural land, including 8ha/20 acres of vines, the monastery enjoys a peaceful location, with magnificent views extending as far as the Alps. The foundation, which also administers a nature reserve (14ha/34.6 acres), has details on walks in the area: Ask for a map at reception.

Ittinger Museum
⏲*Closed mid-Dec –mid-Jan.*
A small cloistered gallery surrounds the garden where the monks were buried. The history of the charterhouse, from the pillages of the 15C to 18C prosperity, is explained in the old cellar. The museum collections—paintings, models and furniture—provide an insight into the austere life led by the monks, who renounced all worldly pleasures. In the refectory where the monks met for meals on Sundays, without breaking their vow of silence, the decoration is decidedly religious in tone. One of the cells is dedicated to St Bruno, who founded the Carthusian Order in the 11C. Note also the carved **stalls** dating from around 1700 in the chapter house, as well as the religious works of art from Ittingen in the sacristy. A small chapel on the first floor contains a Baroque display cabinet of relics. The guestrooms within the charterhouse have beautiful painted ceilings, 18C four-poster beds and **faience stoves** decorated with emblems and landscape scenes.

Church★
This Baroque church is striking for its exuberant décor: the interior is covered with frescoes recounting the life of St Brun, red-veined green and white stuccowork, statues, and cherubs. Farm workers sat slightly apart from the rest of the church; the gallery was reserved for guests. The superb **choir stalls★** were sculpted in the 18C. The main altar is adorned with Rococo-style ornamentation. There is no organ in the church as the Carthusian monks sang unaccompanied chants.

Kunstmuseum des Kantons Thurgau

This art gallery houses a collection of 20C paintings, most of which are Swiss in origin. Artists exhibited include Adolf Dietrich, with work inspired by the landscapes of Thurgau, Carl Roesch, Ernst Kreidolf and Hans Brühlmann. Of particular interest is the *Self-portrait* by Helen Dahm. Temporary exhibitions of contemporary art are held in the basement.

Kreuzlingen

▶ *48.5km/30mi on Route 1 NE of Wintherthur and then Route 7* Sonnenstrasse 4. ℘ *(0)71 672 38 40. www.kreuzlingen.to.*

The Swiss town of Kreuzlingen is built on a former moraine of the Rhine Glacier. It forms a single town with the German city of Constance, divided only by the frontier. The town owes its name to a relic of the Holy Cross (Kreuz), which was brought back from the Holy Land in the 10C and deposited in the basilica. It is locally revered as "the first town of Switzerland."

Old Klosterkirche St Ulrich

This basilica was built in the 17C and the Baroque interior decoration completed in the following century. The building was damaged by fire in 1963 and restored in 1967. The Olive Grove Chapel (Ölbergkapelle) contains an extraordinary group of 250 carved wooden figurines set in curious rock work, representing scenes taken from the Passion. The top floor of the sacristy houses a **museum** displaying paintings and documents from the long history of the monastery. (◷*open during services or upon request;* ℘*(0)71 672 22 18*).

Gottlieben

▶ *45km/28m NE of Winterthur via A 7 (toll).*

Gottlieben lies at the western end of the arm of the Rhine joining the Untersee, or lower lake, to the main basin of Lake Constance. It has a 13C castle, remodelled in the 19C. In the 15C the building was used as a prison for the deposed

Pope John III and for the Czech reformer **Jan Hus**. Prince Louis-Napoleon Bonaparte, the future Napoleon III, lived here from 1837 to 1838.

Schloss Arenenberg

▶ *6km/4mi W of Gottlieben along the Untersee shore road.* Thurgau Tourismus, Egelmoosstrasse 1. ℘ *(0)71 414 11 44. www.thurgau-tourismus.ch.*

The little Arenenberg Castle, stands on a terrace overlooking the western basin of Lake Constance, Untersee. Built in the 16C, it became, in 1817, the property of Queen Hortense, daughter of Louis Bonaparte, after which the family lived here for generations. In 1906 it became a museum devoted to Napoleon.

Napoleonmuseum★

◷*Open year-round Tue–Sun 10am–5pm; mid-Apr–mid-Oct, daily10am–5pm.* ◷*Closed Good Friday.* ☜*12CHF.* ℘*(0)71 663 32 60. www.napoleonmuseum.tg.ch.*

Works of art and furniture collected by the Bonapartes have remained in the castle. Note Queen Hortense's drawing room, furnished in the style of the period, and the library, bedrooms and boudoirs, which contain many mementos of the imperial family. Queen Hortense's bedroom affords a sweeping **view** over Lake Constance and Reichenau Island.

ADDRESSES

🛏STAY / 🍴EAT

▭▭ **Gästehaus** – *Kartause Ittingen.* ℘*(0)52 748 44 11. www.kartause.ch.* The hotel run by the foundation has 48 rooms (33 double, 15 single). It is situated in a warm, modern building, attractively decorated.

▭▭ **Zur Mühle** – *Kartause Ittingen. In the courtyard, on the right.* This restaurant, housed in one of the buildings belonging to the foundation (1870), offers a reasonably priced menu.

Schaffhausen★

The old city of Schaffhausen is home to a host of wonderful Renaissance and classical buildings, making it one of the most attractive towns in Switzerland. The city is also the starting-point for a visit to the Rhine Falls (Rheinfall), traditionally an important attraction of romantic Switzerland.

A BIT OF HISTORY

As the Rhine Falls compelled boatmen to unload their cargoes here, merchants settled in the town and set up a depot. Schaffhausen entered the Swiss Confederation in 1501.

Nowadays, it depends largely on its situation as a communications junction and bridgehead. It has also become an industrial centre, drawing electric power from the river, including, machine and electrical goods factories, spinning mills and steel works.

SIGHTS

Old Town★

Dominated by the remains of the ramparts crowned by the **Munot**, a massive 16C keep (*accessible via stairs and a footbridge across the moat, now a deer park*), the old town forms a **belvedere★** (🕐*open May–Oct, 8am–7pm, Nov–Apr, 9am–5pm;* ➡️*5CHF;* 𝄢*(0)52 632 40 20*) overlooking the town and the Rhine Valley. The lower town has fine houses with painted façades, often embellished with oriel windows. The **Vordergasse★** is one of the most typical streets, its houses adorned with stucco and carvings, its roofs with numerous dormer windows.

The **Haus zum Ritter** (Knight's House) deserves special mention: the paintings adorning the façade were restored in 1938–39 by Care Roesch, signed by the famous Schaffhausen artist, **Tobias Stimmer**. Some of these murals (1570) can be seen in the Museum zu Allerheiligen. You also should see the pretty fountains in Fronwagplatz and the Regierungsgebäude (Government

▶ **Population:** 34 076.

📋 **Info:** Fronwagplatz 4 – 8200. 𝄢(0)52 632 40 20. www.schaffhausen-tourismus.ch.

🔵 **Location:** Schaffhausen is on the north bank of the Rhine at the foot of the Munot Keep, 51km/32mi north of Zürich. Alt. 403m/1 322ft.

👁 **Don't Miss:** Rheinfall, or the old town's belvedere.

🕐 **Timing:** Allow a minimum of one day to enjoy the sights.

GETTING AROUND

BOAT SERVICES

www.urh.ch, daily July–mid-Sep, May–June and mid-Sept–Oct Sat and Sun only. 22CHF to Stein am Rhein one way. ➡️*43CHF to Konstanz. Day ticket 37CHF.* Excursion steamers sail between Schaffhausen and Kreuzlingen on the Rhine and the Lower Lake (Untersee), offering glimpses of the river banks, overlooked by ruined castles, and of charming little towns like Diessenhofen and Stein am Rhein.

House), a 17C building with a fine sculptured façade and a stepped gable.

Museum zu Allerheiligen★★

🕐*Open Tue–Sun 11am–5pm.* 🕐*Closed 1 Jan, Good Fri and 25 Dec.* ➡️*9CHF.* 👣*Guided tour by appointment.* ♿ 𝄢*(0)52 633 07 77. www.allerheiligen.ch.* The museum is housed in the former **All Saints Abbey**. It contains prehistoric artefacts from excavations in the region, manuscripts and early printed books, mostly 15C, which belonged to the monastery library, and works of Swiss artists from the 15C–20C.

The most remarkable exhibit is an early-13C onyx, mounted on gold and inlaid with precious stones.

SCHAFFHAUSEN

A 4 ▲ SINGEN, DONAUESCHINGEN, STUTTGART

13 BASEL A4, ZÜRICH,

CONSTANCE, FRAUENFELD

RHINE FALLS 13

15 BENKEN ⚓ WINTERTHUR

Münster zu Allerheiligen (All Saints Abbey)

🕐 *Open 9am–5pm (8am–8pm summer).* ☎*(0)52 624 39 71. www.muenster-schaffhausen.ch.*
This Romanesque abbey basilica was built in the 11C with yellow ochre-coloured stone. The cloister, abutting the south aisle of the church, has a gallery with Gothic bays and contains numerous tombstones. A bell known as Schiller's Bell, which inspired the poet's famous *Lied von der Glocke*, or *Ballad of the Bell*, is kept in a small courtyard nearby.

Museum of Contemporary Art★

🕐 *Open Sat 3pm–5pm, Sun 11am–5pm.*
🕐 *Closed 25 Dec.* 💶*14CHF.* ☎*(0)52 625 25 15. www.modern-art.ch.*
Situated along the banks of the Rhine, this former textile factory pays tribute to the Conceptual and Minimalist movements of the 1960s–1980s. The Hallen

für Neue Kunst is laid out over an area of 5 500sq m/59 200sq ft comprising four different levels; the first is set aside for temporary exhibitions.
The permanent collections feature works by Mario Merz, Dan Flavin, Joseph Beuys (*Das Kapital 1970–77*), Richard Long (*Lightning Fire Wood Circle*), Lawrence Weiner, Bruce Nauman (*Floating Room*), Jannis Kounellis representing Arte Povera, Carl Andre (*Cuts*), Sol Lewitt, and Robert Ryman.

EXCURSIONS
Rheinfall★★

The **Rhine Falls** are the most powerful in Europe. The river plunges from a height of 21m/70ft and its flow sometimes reaches 1 070cu m/37 500cu ft per second (average flow, 700cu m/ 25 000cu ft per second). The spectacle, which Goethe described as "the Source of the Ocean," is best seen in July when the waters are swollen.

Rheinfall by Schloss Laufen

© Christof Sonderegger/Switzerland Tourism

The Rhine

The Rhine's source is in the canton of Graubünden, from whence it flows north to Germany, France and the Netherlands. It flows through Switzerland for barely a quarter of its course, reaching Basel after 388km/242mi. Over this relatively short distance it falls from 2 200m to 250m/7 218ft to 820ft, making it a wild and fast-flowing river.

The Rhine Basin is by far the largest river basin in Swiss territory. The Rhine is a typical **Alpine River**, with low levels in winter and flash-flooding in summer. It rises in Graubünden; its two main arms, the Vorderrhein and the Hinterrhein, meet at Reichenau, above Chur, and provide the power for the large-scale hydroelectric works. The courses are followed respectively by the San Bernardino and the Oberalp roads.

The river is swollen at Chur by the Plessur and farther on by the Landquart and the Tamina. It follows the **Rheinthal** cleft, which resembles Alsace by its north-south orientation, its size and its varying vegetation (maize, vines, etc.). It then flows into the immense **Lake Constance** (12km/8mi wide and 64km/40mi long), which acts as a regulator for it, as Lake Geneva does for the Rhône. At Constance, the Rhine leaves the main basin for the Lower Lake (Untersee), from which it escapes at Stein am Rhein.

Between Schaffhausen and Basel the character of the river changes. Hemmed in between the slopes of the Black Forest and the Jura foothills, it forces its way among slabs of hard rock. Below Schaffhausen, where the valley narrows, the flow becomes faster and the river plunges between the rocks, forming impressive falls (see Rheinfall). Farther on, other rocky slabs produce rapids (*Laufen*), whose presence accounts for place names like Laufen and Laufenburg. These breaks in level make navigation impossible, but have enabled hydroelectric power from power stations on the river banks, the most recent of which is the power-dam at Rheinau.

Observing the River

Between Lake Constance and Basel, driving along the Rhine Valley is complicated by the meandering border of the canton of Schaffhausen. Therefore do not try to follow the course of the Rhine very closely in Swiss territory. It is better to choose a few characteristic observation points for excursions:

- The castle, **Burg Hohenklingen**, near Stein am Rhein;
- The **Munot Terrace**, at Schaffhausen;
- The **Laufener Schloss**, at the Rhine Falls (see Rheinfall);
- At **Laufenburg** (Swiss shore), the terrace laid out below an old tower.

Scene from the north bank (Rheinfallquai)

▶ *4km/3mi via Neuhausen, where you will leave the Basel road and follow signs to Rheinfallstrasse.*

Close views from the south bank

▶ *5km/3mi – plus 30min on foot there and back. Leave Schaffhausen on the road to Zürich, which you will then leave to turn right toward Laufen.*
Park the car at the entrance to Laufener Schlosses, which is now a restaurant.

Belvederes

Enter the courtyard of the castle. You will go down a staircase to the level of the falls. View also from a little kiosk the top of the staircase. There are numerous viewpoints along the way. Boats take you to the rock in the middle of the falls and ferry you from one bank to the other.

Rheinau

▶ *Take Route 4 SW from Shaffhausen and then take the Postrasse W at Marthalen Station. Schulstrasse 11.*
℘ *(0)52 305 40 80. www.rheinau.ch.*
Rheinau was the seat of a Benedictine abbey (now converted into a psychiatric hospital) on an island in the river. Its abbey church is an outstanding example of Baroque art. In 1956 a large hydroelectric power station and dam were completed across the Rhine downstream of Rheinau; its reservoir stretches for 6.5km/4mi up to the Rhine Falls.

Klosterkirche

🕐 *Open Apr, May and Oct, Tue–Sat 2pm–5pm, Sun and public holidays 1.30pm–5pm; Jun–Sep, Tue–Sat 10am–noon, 1pm–5pm, Sun and public holidays 10.30am–noon, 1pm–6pm.*
🕐 *Closed Nov–Mar.* 🎫 *3CHF.*
℘ *(0)52 319 31 00.*
The abbey church was rebuilt at the beginning of the 18C. The **interior**★ is striking for its Baroque-style decoration. The nave, whose vaulting is covered with frescoes, is flanked by four chapels adorned with a profusion of marble and gilding. A balustrade runs under the

Rhine-Danube Canal

Ever since Roman times, emperors, kings, engineers and visionaries dreamed of linking the Rhine and Danube rivers. Charlemagne began the great enterprise, hence the name Charlemagne's Ditch (Fossa Carolina). Bavaria's Ludwig I made another attempt, building the Ludwig Canal. However, it took until 1992—12 centuries after it was begun—that the waterway linking Europe from the north Sea to the Black Sea became a reality. The 177km/110mi canal with its hundreds of locks takes the barges up and down the 245m/800ft climb. It is truly a marvel of modern engineering. Charlemagne and Ludwig would be proud.

clerestory. The chancel, enclosed by an elaborate grille, has beautiful stalls. The organ dates back to 1715.

Stein am Rhein★★

Best reached by boat from Schaffhausen Oberstadt 3. ℘ *(0)52 742 20 90. www.steinamrhein.ch.*
The unbelievably picturesque medieval town of Stein am Rhein is built on the north bank of the Rhine, close by the outflow of the Untersee, the western basin of Lake Constance.

Old Town★★

The old town's character is apparent as you approach the bridge spanning the Rhine; on the right are half-timbered houses, whose foundations dip into the river.
The Town Hall Square (Rathausplatz) and the main street (Hauptstrasse) form an exceptional picture with flower-decked fountains and oriel-windowed houses, whose fully painted façades develop the theme of each house sign: The House of the Pelican, Inn of the Sun, House of the Red Ox and the House of the White Eagle—each has its own motif.

Stein am Rhein with Hohenklingen Castle in background

Lucia Degonda / Switzerland Tourism

Historische Sammlung

Housed on the second floor of the town hall (Rathaus). 🗣 *Guided tours (45min) 10am–11.30am, 2pm–5pm.* 🕐*Closed Sat–Sun and public holidays.* 🎫*3CHF.* 📞*(0)52 742 20 40.*

A historical collection of weapons, Delft porcelain and historiated stained-glass windows from the 16C and 17C recall the town's past.

Kloster St Georgen

🕐*Open Apr–Oct Tue–Sun, 10am–5pm.* 🕐*Closed Good Fri.* 🎫*3CHF.* 📞*(0)52 741 21 42.*

This former Benedictine monastery, set up at Stein in the 11C by the German Emperor Heinrich II, has kept its medieval character but has been converted into a **museum**★ (history, local art). Rooms are adorned with carved ceilings, panelling and inlaid furniture and are sometimes decorated with 16C monochrome paintings (*grisaille*).

You will notice the monks' cells, with their fine stone paving, the bailiff's room, the cloisters and the chapterhouse. The Romanesque church, a 12C basilica with a flat ceiling and no transept, has been restored.

Burg Hohenklingen★

▶ *2.5km/1.2mi N of Stein am Rhein.*

A steep uphill road running partly among vineyards, partly through woods, leads to Hohenklingen Castle. From the tower you will see a **panorama**★ of Stein am Rhein, the Rhine, the surrounding hills and beyond them the Alps, from which the Säntis emerges.

ADDRESSES

🛏STAY

SCHAFFHAUSEN

🍽🍽 **Sorell Hotel Rüden & Zunfthaus** - *Oberstadt 20.* 📞*(0)52 632 36 36.* *www.rueden.ch. Closed Dec. 24–Jan 3.* 🛏 *30 rooms.* The contemporary decor blends perfectly with the old stones and wooden beams of this historic house, where the guilds of the city once sat. It would be wrong to leave the enjoyment of this very central hotel (in the heart of Old Town) to businessmen, who are the main clients. Hearty breakfast and a reduction of 25CHF per person during weekends.

St Gallen★★

The economic and cultural capital of eastern Switzerland, St Gallen owes its fortune to an abbey, founded on the spot where **Gallus** died in 650. It's Baroque cathedral and magnificent abbey library, both UNESCO World Heritage Sites since 1983, are situated in the old town, surrounded by typical corbelled houses with oriel (Erker) windows.

ABBEY BUILDINGS★★★

The Catholic Abbey was largely destroyed during the Reformation, introduced in 1524 by Joachim von Watt (known as Vadian) a physician and mayor of St Gallen. It was not until the mid 18C that the prince-abbots resumed their secular power with the creation of the church and the library; it soon became the seat of the largest ecclesiastical state in Switzerland. In 1805, the prince-abbots lost their power and the abbey was "secularised". In 1846 it became a separate See.

From the Klosterhof (monastery court-yard) there is a fine view of the former Benedictine abbey. The abbey buildings are attached to the cathedral; they now house the bishop's residence, the famous abbey library, the Cantonal Government and several schools. Along with that of Einsiedeln it is the most important Baroque structure in Switzerland.

Cathedral★★

The cathedral was built from 1755 to 1767 on the site of a 14C Gothic edifice. In the centre of the immense structure, the **dome**★★ is richly decorated. The **chancel**★★★, enclosed by admirable grilles, is adorned with a high altar executed in the Empire style in 1810.

Stiftsbibliothek★★★

○Open 10am–5pm (4pm Sun); some public holidays, 10am–4pm. ○Closed mid-Nov–early Dec & major holidays. ☜10CHF. ℰ(0)71 227 34 16. www.stiftsbibliothek.ch.

A UNESCO World Heritage Site, the **Abbey Library** is considered to have

▶ **Population:** 72 040.
⚙ **Michelin Map:** Town plan in the Michelin Red Guide Switzerland.
▤ **Info:** Bahnhofplatz 1. ℰ(0)71 227 37 37. www.st.gallen-bodensee.ch.
◖ **Location:** St Gallen, the highest town in Switzerland, nestles in the narrow Steinach Valley in the east of the country, 10km/6.2mi southeast of Lake Constance (Bodensee). Alt. 668m/2 201ft.
☺ **Don't Miss:** The Abbey Library, the finest secular baroque room in Central Europe.
👥 **Kids:** Peter and Paul Zoo.
◷ **Timing:** Allow at least two days for museums and excursions. While here, take the 2hr guided city tour from the Tourist Office (May–Oct Mon–Sat 2pm; Jul & Aug also Sun 2pm; Jan–Apr 1st and 3rd Sat of the month 11am). ☜20CHF).

Abbey buildings

© Daniel Ammann/St.Gallen-Bodensee Tourismus/Switzerland Tourism

the finest non-religious Rococo interior in Switzerland, built during the same period as the cathedral (1758–67). Architectural features include a parquet floor, monochrome *(grisaille)* paintings, and ceiling frescoes by the Gigi brothers.

The collections include around 100 000 volumes, including over 2 000 parchments from the 8C–12C, early printed books (prior to 1500), and illuminated manuscripts from the Renaissance period. A mummy from Upper Egypt (700 BC), donated in 1824, can be seen in a double sarcophagus made from sycamore at the back of the library.

OLD TOWN★★

Around the cathedral are many 16C and 18C houses, some with painted façades, often adorned with wrought-iron signs and carved and painted wooden **oriel windows**★, typical of the region. Many houses in this district are noteworthy for their elaborate sculpture and ornamentation; a stroll down the various streets (**Gallusplatz, Gallusstrasse, Marktgasse, etc.**) will afford fine views.

MUSEUMS
Art Museum★

🕐*Open Tue–Sun 10am–5pm (8pm Wed).* 🎟️*10CHF.* ✆*(0)71 242 06 71. www.kunstmuseumsg.ch.*

The **Kunstmuseum** includes German, Austrian and Swiss art from the 15C-18C, as well as several 19C and 20C paintings. One of the highlights of the museum is its collection of 17C Dutch art. Of particular interest are *Odalisque* by Corot, *Adoration of the Virgin* by Delacroix, *Garden* by Sisley, *Lake Geneva* by Courbet, *Hermitage* by Pissarro and *Palazzo Contarini* by Monet.

The museum also boasts a collection of modern and contemporary art, with works by Sophie Taeuber-Arp, Klee, Picasso, Tapiès, Richard Serra, Donald Judd and Nam June Paik. Temporary exhibitions are also hosted here.

Natural History Museum

🕐*Same opening times as Art Museum.* 🎟️*Same ticket as Art Museum.* ✆*(0)71 242 06 70. www.naturmuseumsg.ch.*

Housed in the same building as the Fine Arts Museum, the **Naturmuseum** has nature exhibits, including displays on birds and mammals of the region. Note the skeletons of a *Plateosaurus*, a *Pterosaurus* and an *Anatosaurus* (around 80 million years old).

Historical Museum

🕐*same opening times as Art Museum.* 🎟️*Same ticket as Art Museum.* ✆*(0)071 242 06 42. www.hmsg.ch.*

This **Historisches und Völkerkunde Museum** exhibits the history and traditions of the St Gallen region from the Prehistoric period to the 18C. Also exhibited are artefacts from Africa, the Pacific and Asia, Japan, Inuit articles, and antique Greek and Etruscan sculptures.

Textile Museum

🕐*Open daily 10am–5pm; Thu 7pm.* 🕐*Closed 1 Jan, Good Fri, 23–25 Dec.* 🎟️*12CHF.* ✆*(0)71 222 17 44. www.textilmuseum.ch.*

The modern **Textile Museum** pays tribute to a traditional industry that brought prosperity to St Gallen and eastern Switzerland for over seven centuries.

Botanischer Garten

In Neudorf; via Rorschacher Strasse then bear left onto Stephanshornstrasse (off map). 🕐*Open 8am–5pm. Greenhouses 9.30am–noon, 2pm–5pm.* 🕐*Closed 1 Jan and 25 Dec.* 🎟️*No charge.* ♿ ✆*(0)71 288 15 30.*

These gardens (1.5ha/3.5 acres) are home to 8 000 species from the five continents. A gazebo stands in front of a pond where rushes and reeds grow, while nearby two tropical greenhouses are teeming with cacti, palm trees, euphorbias, orchids and water lilies .

EXCURSIONS
Dreilinden Hill★

Alt. 738m/2 420ft.

▸ *Take the Mühleggweiher automatic railway (1893). Mühleggbahn station is situated in Moosbruggstrasse. Turn right out of the station.*

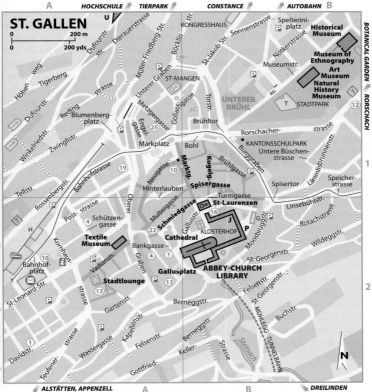

The three pools (**Weiher**) on this hill are 200m/220yd long and were created by the monastery to supply the mills, textile workshops and canals of the town; the monks also used to fish in them. At around the turn of the 20C, the pools were made suitable for **swimming**. A Baroque-style house (1677) can be admired near the central pool.

From the pools, a path (**Höhenweg**) winds its way through pine forests and meadows up the Dreilinden Hill, heading as far as **Freudenberg**★ peak (alt. 884m/2 899ft), from where there is a **view**★ of the old town of St Gallen.

🚶🚶 Tierpark Peter und Paul

Alt. 793m/2 601ft. 3.5km/2mi N of St Gallen. ◗ *Leave St Gallen by Müller-Friedbergstrasse.*

This zoological park (deer, chamois, mouflons) is situated in an open setting. Ibex from the Gran Paradiso Massif in Italy were brought here in 1911.

Trogen

▶ *10km/6mi SE of St Gallen.*
Speicherstrasse 11. ℘(0)71 344 13 16.
www.trogen.ch or www.appenzell.ch.
Trogen is in the district of Appenzell within view of Lake Constance. Built on a hill, it boasts many bourgeois houses, some of which are real palaces built by rich merchants of former days. Its central square, the Landsgemeinde-platz is where the traditional meeting (ⓛ*see INTRODUCTION: Government*) of the half-canton of Appenzell–Ausser-rhoden takes place in even years; in odd years, the ceremony is held at Hundwil. Among the fine houses surrounding it you will notice the Zur Krone, an inn with its overhanging roof and two superim-posed gables. Just outside Trogen, 1km south on the road to Bühler there is the Pestalozzi Children's village. Here, the houses are reserved for war orphans from different countries. Johann Heinrich Pestalozzi, a citizen of Zürich (1746–1827), is honoured throughout Switzerland and abroad for his educa-tional work and innovative teaching methods.

🚗 DRIVING TOUR

1 SITTER VALLEY

21km/13mi from St Gallen to Appenzell.

▶ *Leave St Gallen to the S towards Altstätten.After 6km/4mi turn right towards Hundwill.*

This recommended route from St Gallen affords pleasant views all along the Sitter Valley. This is at first a deep ravine, but turns into a depression dotted with traditional farms. Look especially for a group of buildings 1km/0.6mi southeast of the Hundwil junction.

Stein

As you cross this village, located on a plateau (alt. 823m/2 700ft) above its neighbours, there are sweeping views of the surrounding countryside. The **Appenzeller Volkskunde Museum** (ⓛ*open Tue–Sun 10am–5pm, Sun 10am–5pm;* ⓛ*closed 25, 26 Dec;* ✆*7CHF;* ℘(0)71 368 50 56; www.avm-stein.ch*) presents a reconstruction of a typical Alpine cheesemaking dairy (*production starts at 1.30pm*), surrounded by traditional objects such as bells, saddles, and casks. In the basement, two craftsmen dem-onstrate the functioning of a weaving loom and an embroidery hoop (superb jacquard fabrics). On the first floor, note the three 16C wooden panels, illustrated with naive drawings, which were found in the nearby district of Gais.

Appenzell – ⓛ*See APPENZELL.*

ADDRESSES

🛏️ STAY

◠◠ **Vadian Garni** – *Gallusstrasse 36.*
℘*(0)71 228 18 78. www.hotel-vadian.com.*
16 rooms. Bright, well-maintained rooms. Homemade jam for breakfast.

◠◠ **DOM** – *Webergasse 22.*
℘*(0)71 227 71 71 www.hoteldom.ch.*
Closed Christmas–New Year. 🅿 *31 rooms.*
Conveniently located next to the cathedral, this hotel offers no-frills, comfortable and very well kept rooms.

◠◠ **City Weissenstein** –
Davidstrasse 22. ℘(0)71 228 06 28.
www.cityweissenstein.ch. 🅿 *6 rooms (suites).* Located in a quiet neighbour-hood away from the old city, offering all the comforts of a modern hotel.

◠◠ **Radisson Blu** – *St Jakob-Strasse 55.*
℘*(0)71 242 12 12. www.radissonblu.com/ hotel-stgallen.ch.* 🖵 *27 CHF. 123 rooms.*
Comfortable, modern and technically well-equipped rooms. Casino and restaurant on site.

◠◠◠◠ **Metropol** – *Bahnhofplatz 3.*
℘ *(0)71 228 32 32. www.hotel-metropol.ch.*
🖵 🅿 *32 rooms.* The dull façade of the building does not do justice to this hotel, located just opposite the station. Excellent, very well rated restaurant.

🍴 EAT

◠ **Marktplatz** – *Neugasse 2. ℘(0)71 222 36 41.* This modern brasserie, with its bright walls, brickwork and TV screens offers a variety of dishes at moderate prices: flammeküeche, burgers, salads, fries, Spätzle, grilled meats. Every dish can come in half portions for smaller appetites. It is also open on Sundays, which is quite rare in St Gallen.

◷ **Atrium** – *Schützengasse 8.* ✆*(0)71 223 37 17. Closed Sun.* Cream walls, paintings of artists, Art Deco chandeliers: it's enjoyable just to sit in this elegant Italian restaurant. The chef excels in preparing manicotti and risotto. Wide variety of pasta and Mediterranean wines. Impeccable service and reasonable prices.

◷◷ **Zum Goldenen Leuen** – *Schmiedgasse 30.* ✆*(0)71 222 0262. Closed Sun (and Sat after 6pm).* A cosy and popular address rightly so given the warm décor of this perfectly preserved 17C brasserie. At noon you can watch the locals having a soup, salad or a cheese pie, reading the newspapers. The restaurant has been brewing its own beer since 2002.

◷◷ **Zum Goldenen Schäfli** – *Metzgergasse 5.* ✆*(0)71 223 37 37. www.zumgoldenenschaefli.ch. Closed Sun.* This traditional restaurant is in the oldest remaining guildhall dating from the 17C. The sloping ceiling and floor add to the rustic charm.

◷◷ **Maximilian** – *Schreinerstrasse 6.* ✆*(0)71 230 21 21. www.maximilian restaurant.ch. Closed Sun.* This bar-restaurant has a tasteful 70s décor and a small but varied menu.

◷◷ **Seeger** – *Oberer Graben 2.* ✆*(0)71 222 97 90. www.seeger-restaurants.ch.* Businessmen, travellers and regulars like to gather in this pleasant restaurant. Affordable daily specials for lunch just a few steps from the train station and old town.

◷◷ **Schlössli** – *Zeughausgasse 17, adjacent to the Spisertor railway station.* ✆*(0)71 222 12 56. www.schloessli-sg.ch. Closed Sat–Sun and mid-Jul–mid-Aug.* This small 16C château is worth a visit for its frescoes, furniture, salons with vaulted ceilings, and its excellent local food.

◷◷ **David 38** – *Davidstrasse 38.* ✆*(0)71 230 28 38. www.david38.ch. Closed Sun.* This elegant restaurant attracts the local gourmets of the region by its cuisine, which takes

pleasure in mixing styles and flavours. The curry soup and the veal escalope with lemon are worth a taste.

◷◷◷ **Am Gallusplatz** – *Gallustrasse 24.* ✆*(0)71 223 33 30. www.gallusplatz.ch. Closed Mon, Sat lunch, mid-Jul–early-Aug and 12–18 Oct.* Situated in the medieval district of half-timbered houses around the cathedral. Specialising in hearty roasts, good regional cuisine and a wide choice of wines. Pleasant terrace.

🛒 SHOPPING

The main shopping streets are **Multergasse**, **Spisergasse**, **Neugasse**, and **Marktgasse**. Find genuine St Gallen embroidery at **Boutique La Bambola** (*Brühlgasse 35*).

🎭 THEATRE AND MUSIC

Stadttheater – *Museumstrasse 24.* ✆*(0)71 242 06 06. www.theatersg.ch.*

Sinfonieorchester – *Museumstrasse 25.* ✆*(0)71 242 05 05. www.sinfonie orchestersg.ch.* Classical symphony orchestra concerts in an early-20C building, a reminder of the prosperity brought to the town by the textile industry.

Kellerbühne – *St Georgenstrasse 3.* ✆*(0)71 223 39 59. www.kellerbuehne.ch.*

Figurentheater (Puppet Theatre) – *Lämmlisbrunnenstrasse 34.* ✆*(0)71 222 60 60. www.figurentheater-sg.ch.*

🎭 NIGHTLIFE

The **Einstein Bar**, the piano bar of the Hôtel Einstein (*Berneggstrasse*) offers a cosy atmosphere, where you can enjoy a cocktail or a local beer.

🎟 EVENTS

In-line one-eleven is the longest rollerblade race in Europe (Aug). It starts in St Gallen and runs for 111km/69mi, through 20 villages and two cantons, before finishing back in the town.

Appenzell★

Appenzell is an old-fashioned town which succeeds in reconciling rural and city life, a trait common to many Germanic countries. It is a *flecken*, a word denoting communities that are neither towns nor villages, whose buildings boast highly-decorated façades and undulating gables typical of the region.

▶ **Population:** 5 787.

Info: Appenzellerland Tourismus, Hauptgasse 4. ℘071 788 96 41. www.appenzell.ch.

Location: Appenzell lies at the foot of the lush Alpstein hills, 18km/11mi south of St Gallen. Alt. 789m/2 589ft.

Don't Miss: The Appenzell Museum with its collections of local crafts and folklore.

Kids: Appenzell Museum.

A BIT OF HISTORY

The name of Appenzell (*Abbatis cella*, the Abbot's cell) dates from the early settlement of the country by the monks of St Gallen. The **Hauptgasse**★, the main street crossing the village, offers various temptations (embroidery shops; Appenzell cakes decorated with portraits of cowmen in yellow breeches and scarlet waistcoats). It lies between the church, with its astonishing Baroque embellishments, and the Löwendrogerie, whose curved gable bears a series of paintings of medicinal plants with this mournful comment: "Many plants against illness, none against death".

SIGHTS

▲▲ Museum Appenzell

◔*Open Apr–1 Nov, daily, 10am–noon, 2pm–5pm; 2 Nov–Mar, Tue–Sun, 2pm–5pm.* ⌖*Guided tours on request; free guided tour every Fri.* ◔*Closed 25 Dec, 1 Jan.* ◉*7CHF.* ℘*(0)71 788 96 31. www.museum.ai.ch.*

Set up in the town hall and the adjoining house (1560), this museum focuses on regional lore, including a collection of coins which the Inner-Rhoden people were able to mint for only five years (1737–42), a prison cell dating back

to 1570, typical Appenzell costumes (featuring the sophisticated black tulle headdress), banners, a 16C triptych attributed to Jacob Girtanner and coffin-shaped hatchments (a bygone practice, they were once used to drive away evil spirits). The museum also boasts an Egyptian sarcophagus (c.1000 BC), found in a temple at Thebes.

Museum Liner

◔*Open Apr–Nov Tue–Fri, 10am–noon, 2pm–5pm Sat–Sun 11am–5pm; Nov–Mar, Tue–Sat 2pm–5pm, Sun 11am–5pm.* ◉*9CHF.* ℘*(0)71 788 18 00. www.museumliner.ch.*

This museum, housed in a postmodern building (1998) by the architects Annette Gigon and Mike Guyer, presents temporary exhibitions dedicated to work by local artists, such as the landscape painter Carl-August Liner (1871–1946) and Carl-Walter Liner (1914–1997), an early exponent of Abstract art. A collection of modern art by painters such as Arp, Kirchner and Tapiès can also be admired in the museum.

Appenzellerland

The soft, undulating landscape of green hills is dotted with farms and rich townships with their pretty, curvilinear gabled houses which still hold meetings of the traditional Landsgemeinden (⌖*see INTRODUCTION: Government*). Traditions are still very much alive here: special dishes such as Appenzell fat cheese (one of the strongest Swiss cheeses) and small, dry sausages called *Alpenklübler*. Another long-standing custom to have survived is that of fine old-fashioned embroidery, which continues to flourish as a cottage industry in Inner-Rhoden.

EXCURSIONS
Hoher Kasten★★
Alt. 1 795m/5 890ft. ◗ *7km/4.3mi SE on the road to Weissbad and Brülisau.* ⛰ *Cable-car leaves from Brülisau (alt. 924m/3 030ft) every 30min.* ◠*38CHF return fare. Information on operating periods* ✆ *(0)71 799 13 22. www.hoherkasten.ch.*

The ride up in the cable-car (8min) offers a view below of spruce trees, mountain pastures and shepherds' huts and ahead to the massive limestone spur of the Hoher Kasten. The belvedere, with its attractive Alpine garden, is higher than the restaurant but easily accessible. It offers a magnificent **panorama**★★: west and northwest, the town of Appenzell and surrounding hills; eastward, the view plunges down to the Rheinthal and its river, winding from Lake Constance (north) to the

Liechtenstein mountains (south), with the Austrian Alps in the background. The Alpstein Massif and its highest peak, Säntis, are clearly visible to the southeast. There is a marked path to Staubern and on to the lakes of Fälensee and Sämtisersee, as far as Brülisau.

Ebenalp★★
Alt. 1 640m/5 380ft. ◗ *7km/4.3mi – about 1hr30min following the Weissbad-Wasserauen road to its terminus, plus 8min by cable-car.* ⛰ *Cable-car – Departures every 15min Jun–Aug, 7.30am–6pm; May and Oct, 7.30am–5.30pm, Nov–Apr, 8.30am–5pm.* ◠*27CHF return.* ✆ *(0)71 799 12 12. www.ebenalp.ch.*

This Alpine promontory is edged with cliffs jutting out over the Appenzell country. From Ebenalp you can return on foot (*about 1hr30min*) to Wasserauen

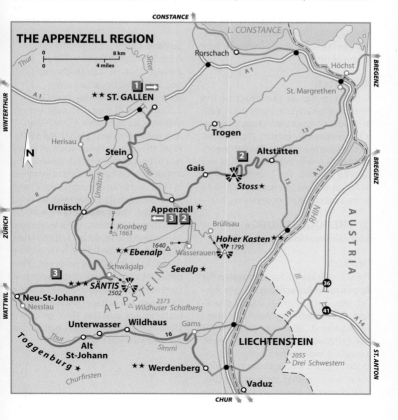

THE APPENZELL REGION

via the **tunnel-grotto of Wildkirchli** (80m/262ft long), where excavations have exposed traces of the oldest prehistoric settlement in Switzerland. The path passes the **Seealpsee**★, whose dark waters lie at the foot of the Rossmad.

🚗 DRIVING TOURS

1 **SITTER VALLEY** *see p440.*

2 **STOSS ROAD**★
16km/10mi. Allow 1hr.

▶ *Leave Appenzell to the W.*

Stoss★

In 1405 this plateau was the scene of a battle which secured the liberation of Appenzell from Austrian rule. To enjoy the distant **panorama**★★ of the Rheinthal and the Vorarlberg Alps, proceed towards the commemorative chapel and, 100m/110yd to its right, the obelisk marked out from afar by a clump of trees.

Altstätten

Altstätten lies at the heart of the Rheinthal on a warm inner plain with orchards, vineyards and crops of maize. It has a markedly medieval character: picturesque Marktgasse (Market Street), lined with pointed-gabled houses and pillared arcades. The Engelplatz, with its flower-decked fountain and crooked houses makes another pretty picture.

3 **THE TOGGENBURG**★
62km/38.5mi. Allow approx 2hr30min.

Urnäsch

The village is known for its **Museum für Appenzeller Brauchtum** (*open Apr–Oct, Mon–Sat 9.30am–11.30am 1.30pm–5pm, Sun 1.30pm–5pm, Nov–Mar Mon–Sat 9.30am–11.30am; 6CHF; (0)71 364 23 22; www.museum-urnaesch.ch*), a small folklore museum located in a 19C chalet. There is a sumptuous collection of carnival costumes and hats plus daily local costumes, jewels, pipes, paintings

and painted figurines, cowbells, as well as a carpenter's workshop. The second floor displays an Appenzell interior with painted furniture, complete with its box bed and the bedroom occupied by the cowherd, a music room, dairy, and a collection of old wooden toys. A short distance past Appenzell, between Urnäsch and Schwägalp, the road emerges from the bottom of a dell dotted with fir and ash trees, at the foot of the cliffs of the north face of Säntis.

Säntis★★★

(0)71 365 65 65. www.saentisbahn.ch. (Also for Nature Discovery Park.)
Säntis, at an altitude of 2 502m/ 8 207ft, is the highest peak in the Alpstein Massif between Toggenburg, the Rhine Valley, Lake Constance and the chief belvedere of eastern Switzerland. The summit's calcareous shoulders, sometimes gently folded, sometimes sharply ridged (Wildhuser Schafberg), make this the most easily identified peak in the range.

Summit Climb

From Schwägalp, the terminus of the roads coming from Urnäsch or Neu St Johann: Departure every 30min. Open mid-May–mid-Oct, 7.30am–6pm (6.30pm Sat–Sun); Nov–mid-May, 8.30am–5pm. mid–late Jan. 45CHF return. (0)71 365 65 65.
From the upper station you can easily reach the summit, which is crowned by a telecommunications centre installed in 1956, and whose two restaurants and panoramic terraces have recently been renovated. The **panorama**★★★ of the Vorarlberg Mountains, the Graubünden, Glarus and Bernese Alps and the lakes of Zürich and Constance is incredibly grand. Its immensity is, however, often difficult to appreciate in the height of summer, especially in the middle of the day, when a heat haze obscures distant features. For a better view, go down steps to the Hôtel du Säntis, built above the wild valley of the Seealpsee .

Nature Discovery Park
www.naturerlebnispark.ch.
This interactive park covers topics from plants and wildlife to geology and culture, not to mention guided trails, a working dairy and a technology park. The section from Schwälgalp to Nesslau leads along the southwest barrier of the Alpstein (Silberplatten, Lütispitz), where Alpine formations succeed the parklands. The spa of Rietbad is framed in a valley dotted with green knolls. Between Nesslau and Wildhaus, uphill from two wooded clefts, the High Toggenburg Valley spreads harmoniously, with dwellings whose walls are protected by weatherboarding. On the climb from Unterwasser to Wildhaus, admire the deeply folded escarpments of the Wildhuser-Schafberg and the serrated crests of the Churfirsten.

Wildhaus★
This pleasant resort lies on the plateau separating the Toggenburg from the Rheinthal, within sight of the Wildhuser-Schafberg, the Churfirsten and the Drei Schwestern. Wildhaus is the birthplace of the great reformer **Ulrich Zwingli**, whose home may still be seen, but not visited (⊶ *closed to the public*). From Wildhaus to Gams, the road dips towards the Rheinthal. From the hairpin bends immediately before Gams you will appreciate the size of this trough, dominated on its eastern side by the mountains of the Vorarlberg and of Liechtenstein, separated by the Feldkirch Gap, negotiated by the road and railway to the Arlberg region of Austria.

Werdenberg★★
At the north end of the settlement of Buchs, the old village of Werdenberg is a particularly welcome little **scene**★. You enter the tiny hamlet by a narrow alley flanked by a row of well-restored wooden arcaded houses. The atmosphere is typical of small 17C–18C towns from the Rhine Valley. Between numbers 8 and 9, a passageway leads to a path circling the pond. There you face the houses of Werdenberg, closely grouped at the foot of the Castle of Counts.

Schloss
⊙*Open Apr–Oct, Tue–Sun 9.30am–5pm;* ⊜*4CHF;* ℘*(0)81 771 29 50; www.schlosswerdenberg.sg.ch).*
The section under the eaves is devoted to the Rhine, and the tower commands a lovely **view** of the Rheinthal.

ADDRESSES

STAY
⊜⊜ **Schwägalp** – *Säntis.* ℘*(0)71 365 65 65. www.saentisbahn.ch. 30 rooms.* Quaint wooden chalet nestling in a peaceful setting with pretty views overlooking the terrace.

⊜⊜ **Kaubad** – ℘*(0)71 787 48 44. www.hotel-kaubad.ch.* ⇆ *15 rooms.* This chalet is a haven of peace in a secluded spot surrounded by nature. Heated pool and reasonably priced restaurant.

⊜⊜⊜ **Appenzell** – *Hauptgasse 37.* ℘*(0)71 788 15 15. www.hotel-appenzell.ch.* ⇆ *16 rooms.* A cosy, welcoming establishment at the heart of Appenzell. A good base to rest after an excursion.

⊜⊜⊜ **Säntis** – *Landsgemeindeplatz.* ℘*(0)71 788 11 11. www.saentis-appenzell.ch.* 🅿⇆ *37 rooms.* Comfortable hotel with a romantic atmosphere and a wooden façade typical of the Appenzell region. Sauna and solarium.

EAT
⊜ **Rössli** – *Postplatz.* ℘*(0)71 787 12 56. Closed Mon, Tue and mid-Jan–mid-Feb.* Typical old-fashioned café.

⊜ **Bären** – *Schlatt, 5km/3mi from Appenzell.* ℘*(0)71 787 14 13. Closed Tue, Wed, 11 Feb–1 Mar and 15–31 Jul.* Lovely views of the Alps and the valley from the terrace.

⊜⊜ **Bären** – *Gonten, 6km/3.7mi from Appenzell.* ℘*(0)71 795 40 10. Closed Sun evenings and for 3 weeks from end of Mar.* Delicious regional specialities from the Appenzell area, served in a peaceful, rustic setting.

⊜⊜⊜ **Schäfli** – *In Störgel Nord, 3km/1.8mi from Teufen.* ℘*(0)71 367 11 90. www.schaefli-stein.ch.* This beautiful house, built in the Appenzell tradition, offers regional cuisine.

Liechtenstein

The Principality of Liechtenstein is a fragment of the former Germanic Confederation, whose territory extended from the east bank of the Rhine to the Vorarlberg Mountains. The little state was made a sovereign principality by Emperor Charles VI in 1719 to benefit Prince Jean Adam of Liechtenstein; it owes the preservation of its statute largely to the wise policy followed by Prince Johann II (the Good), whose reign (1858–1929) was the longest of any Western European sovereign except Louis XIV (1638–1715). Today, numerous multinational companies based here benefit from a favourable tax regime.

▶ **Population:** 34 247.
🛈 **Info:** Städtle 37, Postfach 139 – 9490. ℘(00423) 239 63 00. www.welcome.li.
▶ **Location:** Liechtenstein is 24km/15mi from north to south. Situated in the Upper Rhein valley of the Alps, its western border is formed by a river.
🅿 **Parking:** Ample parking in major areas.
☺ **Don't Miss:** Post Office; philatelists collect stamps issued by this small state.
🕑 **Timing:** Allow one day to tour the country by car.

A BIT OF HISTORY

After 1919 Liechtenstein loosened its last bonds with Austria and concluded monetary, postal, customs and diplomatic conventions with the Swiss Confederation; today it is to all intents a part of the Swiss economic sphere. The dividing line between the Germanic and Rhaetic civilisations is, however, clearly marked by the southern boundary; large villages scattered among the orchards at the foot of a castle or around churches with pointed spires make a contrast with the Graubünden cities closely gathered among their vines.

VADUZ

Liechtenstein's small capital lies on the Rhine river valley, with a beautiful view of the Swiss mountains of Faulfirst, Wissifrauen and Alvier opposite.

Lying at the foot of the imposing **castle**, Schloss Vaduz, the residence of the royal family *(⚷ closed to the public)*, and seat of the present government, has become a busy international tourist attraction. You can drive (or climb up a very steep hill) to the castle gate (and even ring the bell), but the royal family will not receive you.

Schloss Vaduz

© Christof Sonderegger/Switzerland Tourism

Liechtenstein Fine Arts Museum

Open Tue–Sun, 10am–5pm (8pm Thu). Closed 1 Jan, 24, 25 and 31 Dec. 8CHF. (00423) 235 03 00. www.kunstmuseum.li.

This Fine Arts Museum is devoted primarily to paintings and 20C graphic artwork. It houses some of the works taken from collections belonging to the Prince of Liechtenstein. There is also a fine outdoor sculpture park dotted with modern works.

Liechtensteinisches Landesmuseum

Städle 43, Vaduz. Open Tue–Sun 10am –5pm (8pm Wed). Closed 24, 25, 31 Dec and 1 Jan. 8CHF. (00423) 239 68 20. www.landesmuseum.li.

In the restored buildings of an old inn, this museum covers the important periods of the principality's history. There is a relief model of the country, a mineralogy collection, and a display of art from the prehistoric age, the Bronze Age, the Roman era (coins, objects), and the Alemanic period (jewellery, arms). Also exhibited are arms (medieval cutting and thrusting weapons, 16C–18C firearms), utensils, local folk art, works of art and cult objects.

Philatelic museum

Open daily 10am–noon 1pm–5pm. Closed 1 Jan and 25 Dec. No charge. (00423) 236 61 05.

Located in a small gallery of the Fine Arts Museum, this museum highlights the principality's philatelic art and the history of the country's postal system (stamp collections). Temporary exhibitions are regularly organised.

EXCURSIONS

Tamina Gorge★★

2hr there and back on foot by the road branching off the road to Valens on the left, SW of Bad Ragaz.

Museum open May–Oct, 10am–6pm (5pm in May and Oct). 5CHF. (0)81 302 71 61. www.altes-bad-pfaefers.ch.

This gorge is breathtaking. To take the waters, before they were pumped up, patients were lowered down on ropes to the bottom of this tremendous fissure.

Malbuntal (Malbun Valley)

30km/19mi to Malbun. Take the route towards Vaduz castle, follow the signs to Triesen and then enter the valley towards Malbun.

In the heart of the country, this road passes through numerous pretty hamlets of Triesenberg and climbs to the corrie at the foot of the Sareiser Joch (alt. 2 000m/6 562ft), part of the Vorarlberg foothills and which can be reached on foot or by cable-car from Malbun.

INDEX

INDEX

INDEX

INDEX

INDEX

INDEX

S

INDEX

INDEX

🛏 STAY

INDEX

♀/EAT

INDEX

MAPS AND PLANS

MAP LEGEND

	Sight	Seaside Resort	Winter Sports Resort	Spa
Highly recommended	★★★	🏖🏖🏖	❄❄❄	♨♨♨
Recommended	★★	🏖🏖	❄❄	♨♨
Interesting	★	🏖	❄	♨

Tourism

◉⟹	Sightseeing route with departure point indicated	AZ B	Map co-ordinates locating sights
🏛 ⛪ 🏛 ⛪	Ecclesiastical building	🛈	Tourist information
✡ 🕌	Synagogue – Mosque	⌂ ⁘	Historic house, castle – Ruins
▭	Building (with main entrance)	⌣ ✿	Dam – Factory or power station
■	Statue, small building	☆ ⌓	Fort – Cave
✝	Wayside cross	⛏	Prehistoric site
◎	Fountain	▼ ϓ	Viewing table – View
●━━■	Fortified walls – Tower – Gate	▲	Miscellaneous sight

Recreation

🏇	Racecourse	🏃	Waymarked footpath
⛸	Skating rink	♦	Outdoor leisure park/centre
🏊 🏊	Outdoor, indoor swimming pool	🎿	Theme/Amusement park
⚓	Marina, moorings	🦌	Wildlife/Safari park, zoo
⛺	Mountain refuge hut	✿	Gardens, park, arboretum
□┅┅□	Overhead cable-car	🐦	Aviary, bird sanctuary
🚂	Tourist or steam railway		

Additional symbols

══ ══	Motorway (unclassified)	✉ ☏	Post office – Telephone centre
❶ ❶	Junction: complete, limited	⊠	Covered market
⊏⊐ ══	Pedestrian street	⋅⋅✕⋅⋅	Barracks
⊤═══⊤	Unsuitable for traffic, street subject to restrictions	△	Swing bridge
⊞⊞⊞ ⋯⋯	Steps – Footpath	⌣ ✕	Quarry – Mine
🚆 🚌	Railway – Coach station	🅱 🅵	Ferry (river and lake crossings)
□┼┼┼┼┼□	Funicular – Rack-railway	⛴	Ferry services: Passengers and cars
━⋅━ ◉	Tram – Metro, underground	⟿	Foot passengers only
Bert (R.)...	Main shopping street	③	Access route number common to MICHELIN maps and town plans

Abbreviations and special symbols

Ⓒ	Capital of a "Canton" (Kantonshauptort)	**P**	Offices of cantonal authorities (Kantonale Verwaltung)
G	Local police station (Kantonspolizei)	**POL.**	Police (Stadtpolizei)
H	Town hall (Rathaus)	**T**	Theatre (Theater)
J	Law courts (Justizpalast)	**U**	University (Universität)
M	Museum (Museum)	🅿	Park and Ride

COMPANION PUBLICATIONS

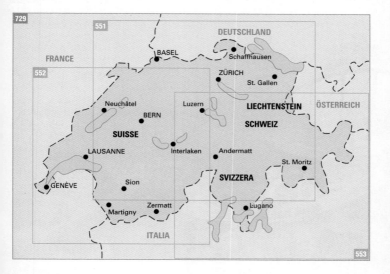

MICHELIN MAP 729 SUISSE

◆ a practical map on a scale of 1:400 000 which includes an index of towns and shows the major roads subject to snow cover.

MICHELIN ATLAS EUROPE

◆ Main road atlas with a full index. 1:1 000 000 scale map of Western Europe and 1:1 000 000 scale map of Eastern Europe. 74 town and city plans.

◆ 1136 Small Spiral
◆ 1129 Large Spiral
◆ 1135 Paperback
◆ 1133 Hardback

INTERNET

Michelin is also pleased to offer an online route-planning service: **www.viamichelin.com and www.travel.viamichelin.com**

The Michelin Adventure

It all started with rubber balls! This was the product made by a small company based in Clermont-Ferrand that André and Edouard Michelin inherited, back in 1880. The brothers quickly saw the potential for a new means of transport and their first success was the invention of detachable pneumatic tires for bicycles. However, the automobile was to provide the greatest scope for their creative talents. Throughout the 20th century, Michelin never ceased developing and creating ever more reliable and high-performance tires, not only for vehicles ranging from trucks to F1 but also for underground transit systems and airplanes.

From early on, Michelin provided its customers with tools and services to facilitate mobility and make traveling a more pleasurable and more frequent experience. As early as 1900, the Michelin Guide supplied motorists with a host of useful information related to vehicle maintenance, accommodation and restaurants, and was to become a benchmark for good food. At the same time, the Travel Information Bureau offered travelers personalised tips and itineraries.

The publication of the first collection of roadmaps, in 1910, was an instant hit! In 1926, the first regional guide to France was published, devoted to the principal sites of Brittany, and before long each region of France had its own Green Guide. The collection was later extended to more far-flung destinations, including New York in 1968 and Taiwan in 2011.

In the 21st century, with the growth of digital technology, the challenge for Michelin maps and guides is to continue to develop alongside the company's tire activities. Now, as before, Michelin is committed to improving the mobility of travelers.

MICHELIN TODAY

WORLD NUMBER ONE TIRE MANUFACTURER
- 70 production sites in 18 countries
- 111,000 employees from all cultures and on every continent
- 6,000 people employed in research and development

Moving
for a world

Moving forward means developing tires with better road grip and shorter braking distances, whatever the state of the road.

CORRECT TIRE PRESSURE

RIGHT PRESSURE

- Safety
- Longevity
- Optimum fuel consumption

-0,5 bar

- Durability reduced by 20% (- 8,000 km)

-1 bar

- Risk of blowouts
- Increased fuel consumption
- Longer braking distances on wet surfaces

forward together
where mobility is safer

It also involves helping motorists take care of their safety and their tires. To do so, Michelin organises "Fill Up With Air" campaigns all over the world to remind us that correct tire pressure is vital.

WEAR

DETECTING TIRE WEAR

The legal minimum depth of tire tread is 1.6mm. Tire manufacturers equip their tires with tread wear indicators, which are small blocks of rubber moulded into the base of the main grooves at a depth of 1.6mm.

Tires are the only point of contact between the vehicle and road.

The photo below shows the actual contact zone.

NEW TIRE

WORN TIRE
(1,6 mm tread)

If the tread depth is less than 1.6mm, tires are considered to be worn and dangerous on wet surfaces.

Moving forward
means sustainable mobility

By 2050, Michelin aims to cut the quantity of raw materials used in its tire manufacturing process by half and to have developed renewable energy in its facilities. The design of MICHELIN tires has already saved billions of litres of fuel and, by extension, billions of tons of CO_2.

Similarly, Michelin prints its maps and guides on paper produced from sustainably managed forests and is diversifying its publishing media by offering digital solutions to make traveling easier, more fuel efficient and more enjoyable!

The group's whole-hearted commitment to eco-design on a daily basis is demonstrated by ISO 14001 certification.

Like you, Michelin is committed to preserving our planet.

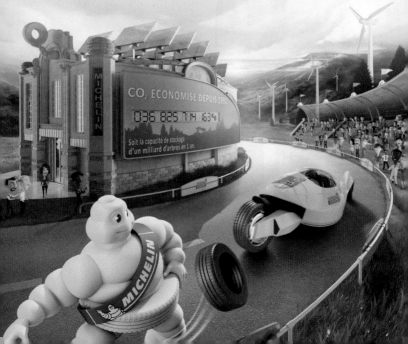

Chat with Bibendum

Go to
www.michelin.com/corporate/en
Find out more about
Michelin's history and the
latest news.

QUIZ

Michelin develops tires for all types of vehicles.
See if you can match the right tire with the right vehicle...

A
B
C
D
E
F
G

1
2
3
4
5
6
7

Solution : A-6 / B-4 / C-2 / D-1 / E-3 / F-7 / G-5

DATE DUE

PRINTED IN U.S.A.

Prir

...LIN

...tner

...90 EUR
(...rance)
...77 721

...y form
...lisher.

...artner

...9-78-3
...2012
...7.0386